MAN OF PEACE

Tibet House US—Select Publications

Tibetan Art and Culture Series

My Appeal to the World • H. H. DALAI LAMA AND SOFIA STRIL-REVER • 2015
Worlds of Transformation • MARYLIN RHIE AND ROBERT THURMAN • 1999
A Shrine for Tibet • MARYLIN RHIE AND ROBERT THURMAN • 2009
The Dalai Lama and the King Demon • RAIMONDO BULTRINI • 2013
A Drop from the Marvelous Ocean of History • LELUNG TULKU • 2013
Dolgyal Shugden: A History • THE DOLGYAL SHUGDEN RESEARCH SOCIETY • 2014

Treasuries of the Buddhist Sciences and the Indic Sciences

(with the American Institute of Buddhist Studies and the Columbia University Center for Buddhist Studies)

Universal Vehicle Discourse Literature (Mahāyānasūtrālaṁkāra) •
MAITREYA / ASAṄGA & VASUBANDHU (TRANS. L. JAMSPAL) • 2004
The Kālacakra Tantra and the Vimalaprabhā Commentary, II and IV •
VAJRADHARA & PUṆḌARĪKA (TRANS. V. WALLACE) • 2004, 2010
Nāgārjuna's Reason Sixty with Chandrakīrti's Commentary •
(TRANS. J. LOIZZO) • 2007
Āryadeva's Lamp that Integrates the Practices • (TRANS. C. WEDEMEYER)
• 2007
The Cakrasamvara Tantra: The Discourse of Śrī Heruka • VAJRADHARA
(TRANS. D. GRAY) • 2007
Scholastic Sanskrit: A Manual for Students • G. TUBB & E. BOOSE • 2007
Brilliant Illumination of the Lamp of the Five Stages • TSONG KHAPA
(TRANS. R. THURMAN) • 2010
Consciousness, Knowledge, and Ignorance • PRAKĀŚĀTMAN (TRANS. B. GUPTA)
• 2011
Great Treatise on the Stages of Mantra (The Creation Stage) • TSONG KHAPA
(TRANS. T. YARNALL) • 2013
The Adamantine Songs (Vajragīti) • SARAHA (TRANS. L. BRAITSTEIN) • 2014
Illumination of the Hidden Meaning, vol. I • TSONG KHAPA (TRANS. D. GRAY)
• 2017
The Kālacakra Tantra and the Vimalaprabhā Commentary, III and V •
VAJRADHARA & PUṆḌARĪKA (TRANS. J. ANDRESEN; J. HARTZELL) • 2017
The Esoteric Community Tantra & Illuminating Lamp Commentary, I–XII •
VAJRADHARA & CHANDRAKĪRTI (TRANS. AIBS TEAM) • 2017

MAN OF PEACE

THE ILLUSTRATED LIFE STORY OF THE DALAI LAMA OF TIBET

by
William Meyers, Robert Thurman,
& Michael G. Burbank

Art by
Steve Buccellato, Donald Hudson,
Kinsun Loh, Miranda Meeks,
& Andrey Pervukhin

Tibet House US • New York City

Published by:

Tibet House US
22 West 15th Street
New York, NY 10011
http://www.tibethouse.us

Distributed by:

Hay House, Inc.
www.hayhouse.com

Library of Congress Cataloging-in-Publication Data

Names: Meyers, William, 1942– , author. | Thurman, Robert A. F., 1941– , author.
| Burbank, Michael G., 1978– , author.

Title: *Man of peace : the illustrated life story of the Dalai Lama of Tibet* /

by William Meyers, Robert A. F. Thurman, and Michael G. Burbank.

Description: New York, NY : Tibet House US, 2016. | Includes bibliographical references.

Identifiers: LCCN 2016042433 (print) | LCCN 2016045563 (ebook)
| ISBN 9781941312032 (hardcover : alk. paper) | ISBN 9781941312049 (pbk. : alk. paper) | ISBN 9781941312056 (E-book)

Subjects: LCSH: Bstan-'dzin-rgya-mtsho, Dalai Lama XIV, 1935– —Comic books, strips, etc.
| Dalai lamas—Biography—Comic books, strips, etc. | Tibet Autonomous Region (China)—History
Comic books, strips, etc. | Graphic novels.

Classification: LCC BQ7935.B777 M49 2016 (print) | LCC BQ7935.B777 (ebook) |
DDC 294.3/923092 [B]   dc23

LC record available at https://lccn.loc.gov/2016042433

Book Production
Publishing • Robert Thurman
Interior Design • William Meyers
Lettering Design • Michael G. Burbank
Cover Design • Milenda Nan Ok Lee

Art Direction
Storytelling Thumbnails • Steve Buccellato

Illustration
Pencil Art • Donald Hudson

Digital Painting
Parts One, Four, Five, Seven, and Ten • Kinsun Loh
Parts Two and Nine • Miranda Meeks
*Parts Three, Six, Eight, Epilogue / Pages 120–121 /
Final Gloss* • Andrey Pervukhin

Cover Painting
Dalai Lama • Alex Grey

Iconography
Line Drawings • Robert Beer

Cartography
Maps • Tsering Wangyal Shawa

With heartfelt thanks to:
Rabkar Wangchuk, Tom Yarnall, Leslie Kriesel, John Van Fleet, Angelica Sibrian, and Comicraft's John Roshell

Printed in Canada on acid-free paper

25 24 23 22 21 20 19 18 17 16   5 4 3 2 1

CONTENTS

FOREWORD

This work is a graphic novel, not an autobiography or an authorized biography. It is a story of a dramatic ongoing struggle between one man and a ruthless empire. The Dalai Lama has written two autobiographies, from which we have drawn many events. But the Dalai Lama is a spiritual practitioner and is too humble to recite the depth and vastness of his own acccomplishments. He means it when he says his default disposition is that of a "simple Buddhist monk."

Since it is a novel, we imagine, in scenes that we know happened from ample sources, what was said, and we show what was going on around the scene. The main point of this portrait of the Dalai Lama in action is to show how he holds fast all his life to the Buddhist path of nonviolence, and how that path is leading inevitably to its goal. He was inspired spiritually and politically by Mahatma Gandhi and by the thousands of years of Buddhist and Tibetan experience in dealing with conquerors and emperors. To this day, he draws on the supreme power of truth, manifest from Emperor Ashoka's *dharmavijaya* (truth-conquest) to Gandhi's *satyagraha* (truth-reliance), to triumph against overwhelming odds. It is all too hard to predict the outcome—the suspense is still enormous.

It has not been easy since sovereign Tibet suffered a brutal invasion starting in 1950, and the Dalai Lama's six million Tibetan people have been treated as worse than an inconvenience ever since. The Chinese insist on pretending to the world that there never was any "Tibet," never were any Tibetans, only a variety of high-altitude Chinese with a funny dialect. This pretense is stubbornly maintained in order to support their conquerors' claim to the land and resources of the vast high plateau, where Chinese people had never even set foot in any significant numbers until the 1950s. This puts them in the awkward position of denying the obvious facts of Tibet's distinct culture, distinct language, unique form of Buddhism inherited from Buddhist India, Tibetan individuals' distinct sense of identity, and even distinct physiology from living at three miles of altitude for a thousand generations. Indeed, the Chinese are embarrassed by the existence of Tibet and the Tibetan people—which inclines them toward ethnicide, even genocide.

The Dalai Lama does not blame the Chinese exclusively for this dreadful treatment of his people and their land. The Chinese themselves are the hapless tools of the modern way of materialism and industrial colonialism, which they learned from the Europeans, only a century or so later than the European genocide of the First Americans and the ruthless pollution of the American environment. The Chinese are merely driven by confusion and insatiable greed to expand the global industrial destruction of planet Earth, the modern self-destruction of the human race. After all, no other nation on earth, including the "land of the free and home of the brave," has shown the honesty and courage to effectively call the Chinese leadership to account for what everyone knows they are doing. The whole global nation system runs on confusion, greed, and aggression, so: "Why shouldn't the Chinese have their turn at colonialism? Oh, and by the way, they will become a huge market for the technology and tools needed to emulate our own Euro-American colonialism."

So, since we all live in such glass houses, we are sorry that we have had to recount the numerous shocking atrocities committed by Chinese communist leaders, officials, soldiers, and settlers, and abetted by some other leaders around the world. The true story has to show these things because the Dalai Lama never forgets for an instant about the sufferings of his people, and we must pay homage to how he still maintains a compassionate attitude toward their tormentors. The picture would not have been complete if we had merely dwelt on the sweetness and light of the Dalai Lama's own presence and his positive vision for the future of his people—and all peoples, including the Chinese people. His nature is to love them all—"to love" meaning to a Buddhist "to will the happiness of the beloved."

The amazing thing about the Dalai Lama is that he continues to appeal to the Chinese to turn away from the genocidal oppression of the Tibetans, for their own sake as much as for Tibet's. As a Nobel Peace Prize Laureate, he has worked whenever possible to intervene in other situations of conflict—between white and black in apartheid South Africa, Catholic and Protestant in Northern Ireland, Jew and Arab in Israel and Palestine, and between Americans and their foes in the struggles in the Middle East from Turkey to Pakistan. At the same time, while agonizingly aware of the extreme suffering of three generations of his people in Tibet, he has never risen up in righteous anger and called for bloodshed or revenge. He tried to turn his own brothers and the fierce Khampa warriors away from their armed resistance, in spite of his admiration for their personal bravery. He has spoken to Tibetans still living in or escaped from Tibet and entreated them to hold on and take up the real fight within themselves against the urge to retaliate, to hate the Chinese, to want to kill them in revenge for the loved ones they have lost, for the bitter hurts they have suffered. Acknowledging the pain they feel, he has wept as he shared it with them, but through

his tears he has urged them to focus within—not to let themselves be destroyed by nursing hate and resentment, but to practice the Buddhist universal-compassion precept of exchange-of-self-and-other, turning their anger and hatred against the only real enemy, which is none other than hatred itself. He constantly challenges his people in exile by insisting upon his "Middle Way" approach of accepting union with China, provided the Chinese rulers change their policy of suppression to one of restoring and preserving Tibet and its people and their culture.

This graphic novel strives honestly to display how the Dalai Lama himself truly adheres to the path of peace, without turning away and glossing over the horrors of what actually goes on, and continues to go on.

With only a temporary let-up in the early '80s, Tibet has been unrelentingly exploited as a source of timber, minerals, herbal medicine, and water, with the urban Tibetans smothered by "wild West" frontier settlers, the country farmers and nomads stripped of their lands and herds and corralled into tightly controlled roadside reservations without jobs or amenities. Their children are forced to learn Chinese, if they are educated at all. They are prisoners in their own homeland, which has been turned into a gulag under militarized lockdown, and are forced to watch their land be clear-cut, strip-mined, dammed, and polluted, its natural wealth hauled down to China. Adding insult to injury, their own precious Universal Vehicle Buddhism, with its savior-bodhisattva teachers, exalted contemplatives, healing doctors, and consoling rituals, continues to be suppressed and denied them.

Unfortunately, we can only recount in a sequel to this graphic novel how some Chinese leaders in the near or far future will experience an awakening in their hearts and will decide that enough is enough and their Tibet policy is a totally unsustainable failure. They will realize the self-destructive effect of destroying "others" and come to see how Tibetans will always be Tibetans, and how China itself could hugely benefit from the contributions its Tibetan citizens would make as free Tibetans, voluntarily staying within a truly supportive China.

So we conclude this novel with an epilogue that presents the Dalai Lama's hinted vision for the soon-to-be-free Tibet, released and elevated by China as its crown jewel of an offering to a sustainable world: all of the Tibetan people released from military suppression, Tibet's

damaged environment repaired, its sustainable economy back in Tibetan hands, since they know best from experience how to live at high altitude, and its society once again enlivened by the powerful spirituality and exquisite pageantry of its religious traditions.

We take full responsibility for any inaccuracies or misrepresentations, and we apologize to those who may be shocked to see some of the harsh realities we also wish had never happened. This is a novel of the struggle between a truly enlightened leader—the kind the Ch'an Buddhist tradition calls "a true man of no rank," a man barred from his homeland, without an economy, in exile, a stateless wanderer on our troubled planet—and his six million Tibetan people, against the authoritarian leadership of a giant nation of one billion, three hundred million—an empire with colonies, with a vast economy, a huge military, and a nationalistic self-identity of being the central civilization of the earth. Our Man of Peace returns patient friendliness for ruthless violence, positive vision for zero-sum exploitation, forgiveness for frustration, and the offer of freedom for the master of the Chinese-Tibetan master-slave bondage condition. The suspense of this titanic struggle is ongoing, as it is not yet concluded, though we hope and pray that it will be soon, and our hero, this living exemplar of the nonviolent life, this Man of Peace, will see, in his many further years of joyful lifetime, the "Final Reunion" he and his people so ardently and faithfully await.

—The Coauthors

For the Shakya Monk,
Jambel Ngawang Lobsang Tenzin Gyatso Pelzangpo,
His Holiness the Great Fourteenth Dalai Lama of Tibet . . .

. . . and for the late
Mary Allen Meyers, M.D.,
who got us started

PART ONE

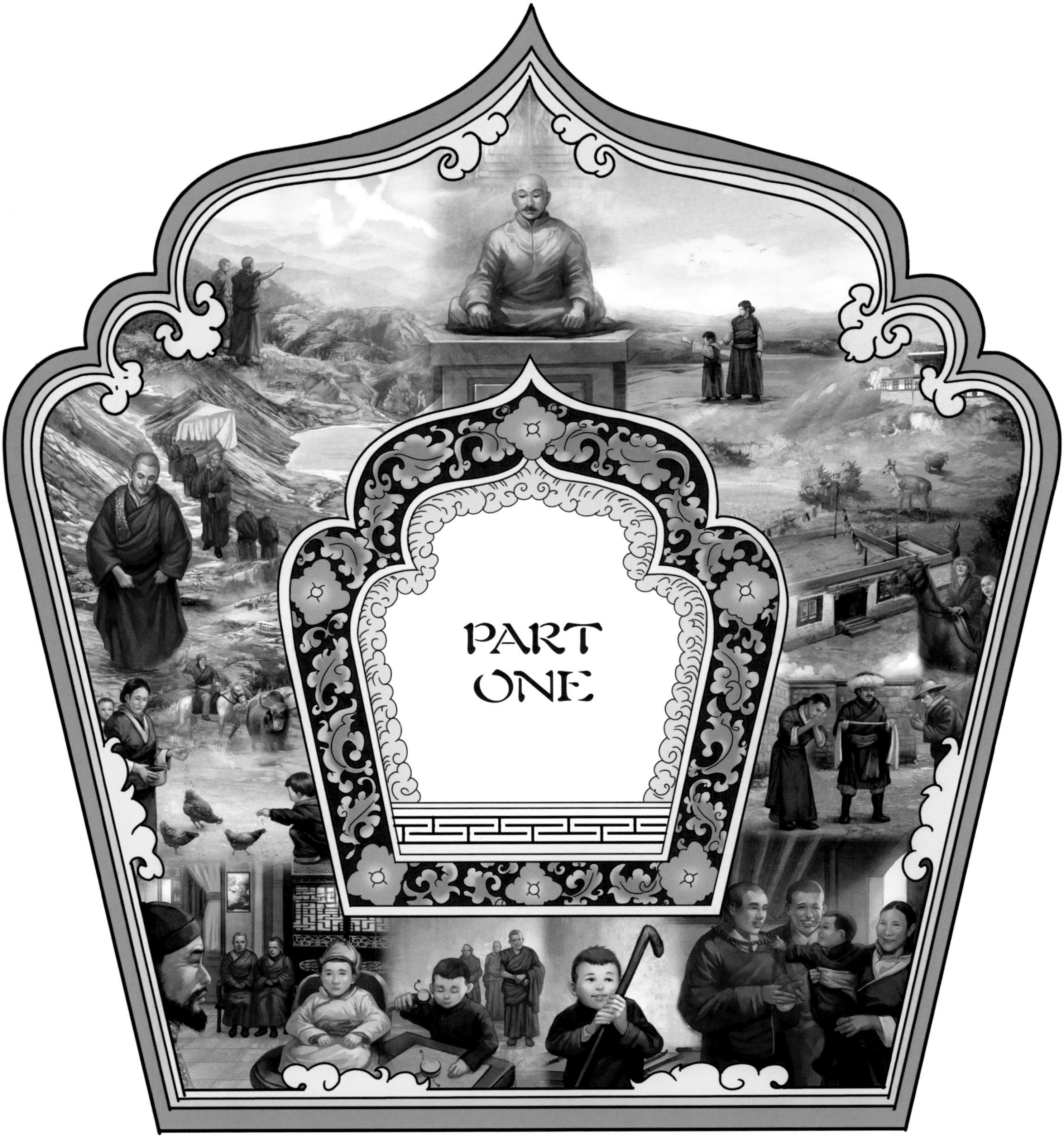

AS THE SOLAR SYSTEM HURTLES THROUGH THE GALAXY
AT TENS OF THOUSANDS OF MILES PER SECOND, THE **EARTH**—A
FERTILE BLUE AND GREEN PLANET—REVOLVES AT JUST THE RIGHT DISTANCE
FROM THE SUN TO SUSTAIN LIFE. ITS EXQUISITELY DELICATE SURFACE OF LAND
AND OCEAN TEEMS WITH COUNTLESS CREATURES. BUT HUMANITY, ALIENATED
FROM LIFE-SUSTAINING NATURE, HAS BEGUN TO THREATEN THIS COSMIC
HOME OF LIVING BEINGS WITH INDUSTRIALIZED GREED AND VIOLENCE.

ON THE HIGH PLATEAU OF **TIBET**, THE ROOF OF THE WORLD,
ENLIGHTENED LAMAS FACE A DEVASTATING CRISIS AT HOME AND LOOK
WITH LOVING CONCERN AT ALL THE WARRING NATIONS AROUND THE
WORLD, PRAYING THAT THEIR LEADERS AND PEOPLES WILL AWAKEN
TO REALITY IN TIME TO AVERT PLANETARY DISASTER...

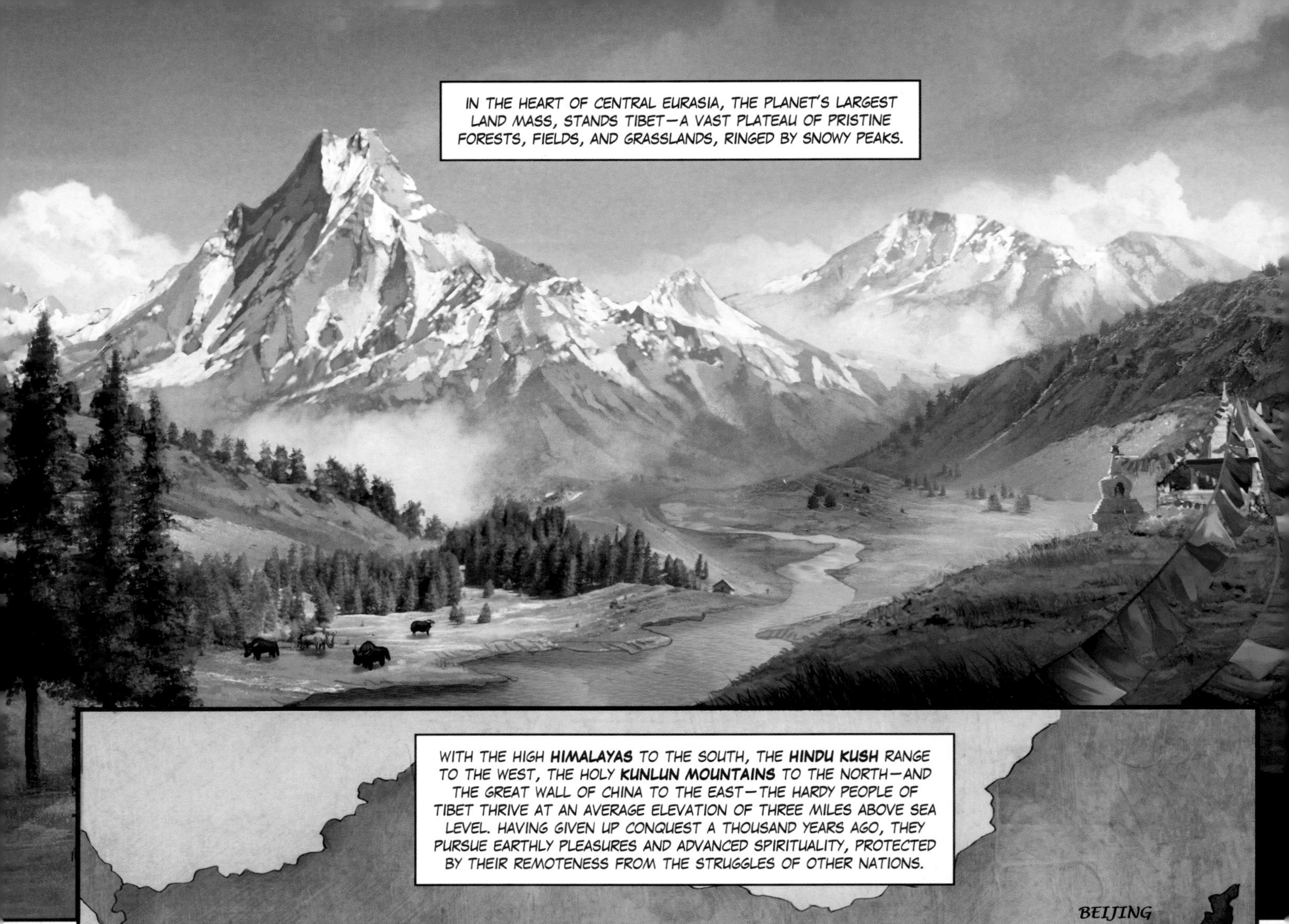
IN THE HEART OF CENTRAL EURASIA, THE PLANET'S LARGEST LAND MASS, STANDS TIBET—A VAST PLATEAU OF PRISTINE FORESTS, FIELDS, AND GRASSLANDS, RINGED BY SNOWY PEAKS.

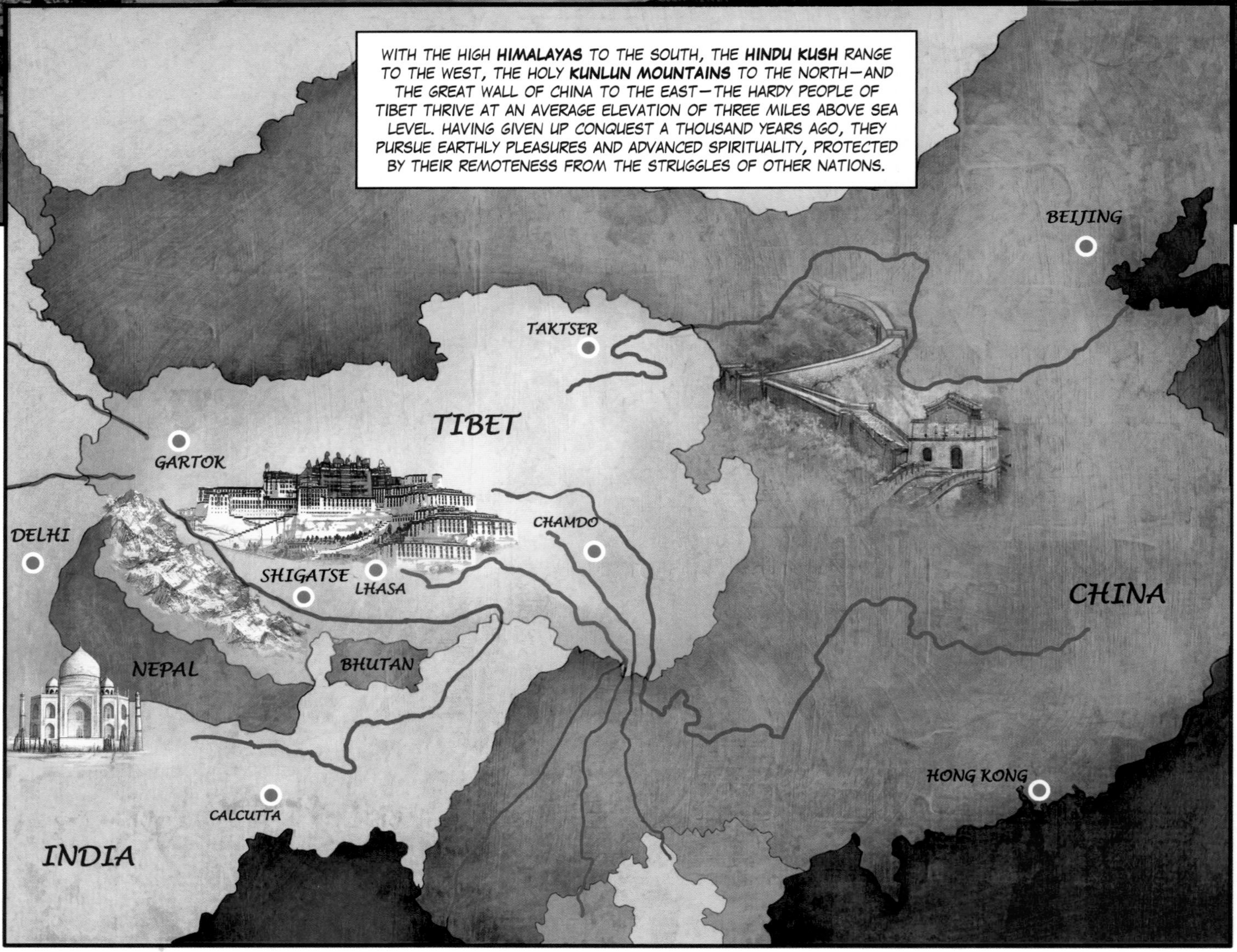
WITH THE HIGH **HIMALAYAS** TO THE SOUTH, THE **HINDU KUSH** RANGE TO THE WEST, THE HOLY **KUNLUN MOUNTAINS** TO THE NORTH—AND THE GREAT WALL OF CHINA TO THE EAST—THE HARDY PEOPLE OF TIBET THRIVE AT AN AVERAGE ELEVATION OF THREE MILES ABOVE SEA LEVEL. HAVING GIVEN UP CONQUEST A THOUSAND YEARS AGO, THEY PURSUE EARTHLY PLEASURES AND ADVANCED SPIRITUALITY, PROTECTED BY THEIR REMOTENESS FROM THE STRUGGLES OF OTHER NATIONS.
BEIJING
TAKTSER
TIBET
GARTOK
DELHI
CHAMDO
SHIGATSE
LHASA
CHINA
NEPAL
BHUTAN
HONG KONG
CALCUTTA
INDIA

THE **DALAI LAMA** REINCARNATIONS, BELOVED AS HUMAN EMANATIONS OF THE BUDDHIST ARCHANGEL OF COMPASSION, **AVALOKITESHVARA**, HAVE REIGNED AS SPIRITUAL AND POLITICAL RULERS OF TIBET, KEEPING A RELATIVE PEACE SINCE THE 17TH CENTURY.

IN 1642 THE GREAT FIFTH DALAI LAMA—THE FIRST OF HIS INCARNATIONS ENTRUSTED TO RULE—ORDERED THE CONSTRUCTION OF THE **POTALA PALACE** IN THE CAPITAL CITY OF **LHASA**. THE LARGEST PALACE IN THE WORLD, IT IS A COMBINATION OF GOVERNMENT SEAT, MONASTERY, AND MYSTIC MANDALA OF UNIVERSAL COMPASSION.

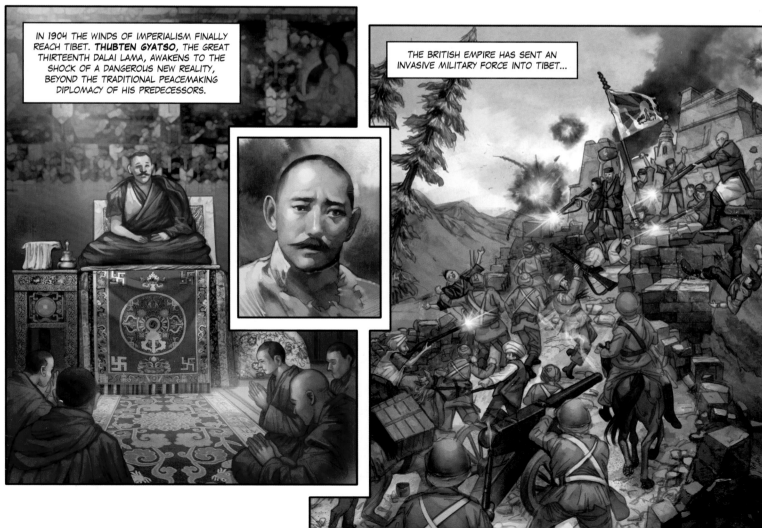

IN 1904 THE WINDS OF IMPERIALISM FINALLY REACH TIBET. **THUBTEN GYATSO**, THE GREAT THIRTEENTH DALAI LAMA, AWAKENS TO THE SHOCK OF A DANGEROUS NEW REALITY, BEYOND THE TRADITIONAL PEACEMAKING DIPLOMACY OF HIS PREDECESSORS.

THE BRITISH EMPIRE HAS SENT AN INVASIVE MILITARY FORCE INTO TIBET...

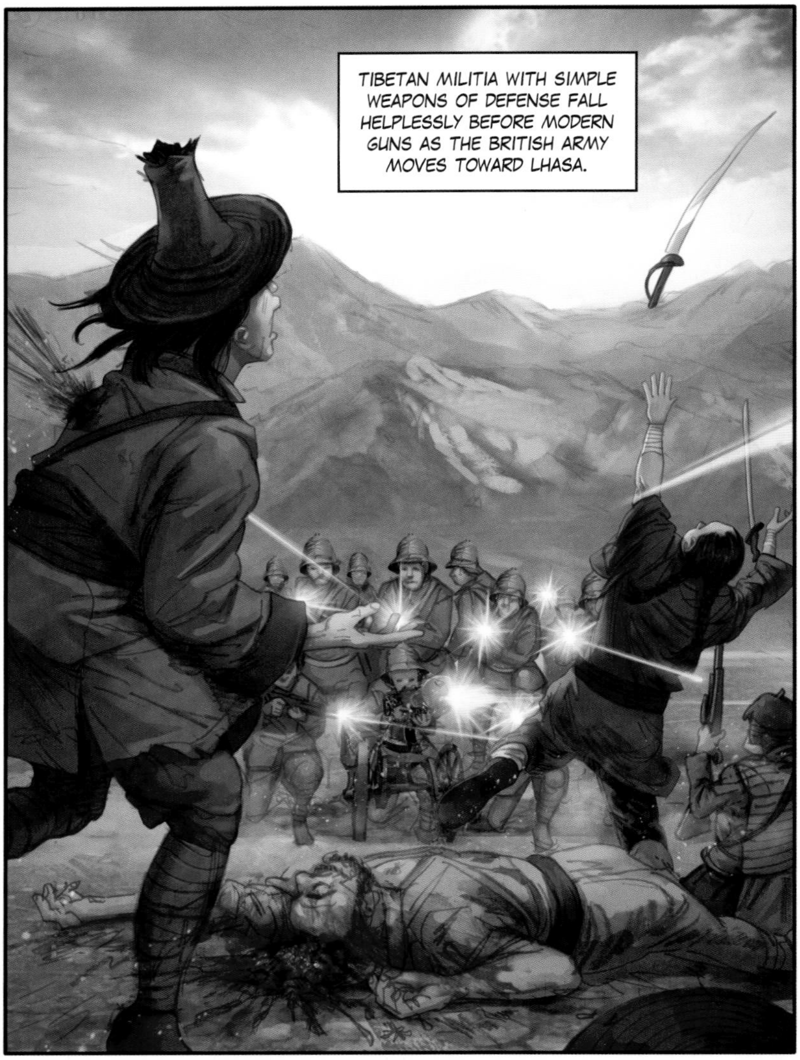
TIBETAN MILITIA WITH SIMPLE WEAPONS OF DEFENSE FALL HELPLESSLY BEFORE MODERN GUNS AS THE BRITISH ARMY MOVES TOWARD LHASA.

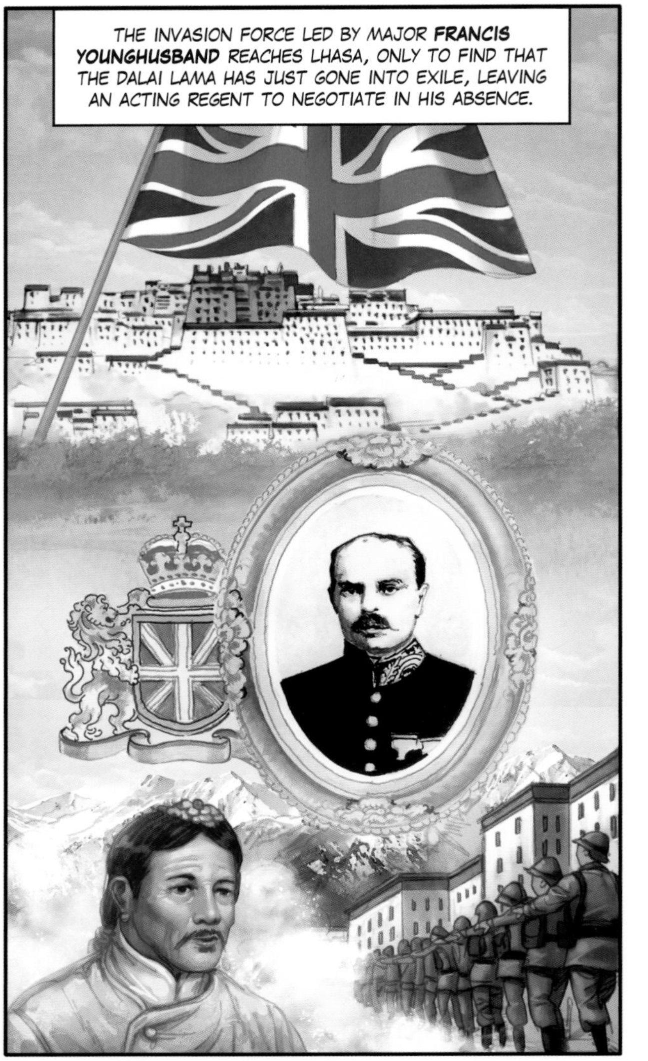
THE INVASION FORCE LED BY MAJOR **FRANCIS YOUNGHUSBAND** REACHES LHASA, ONLY TO FIND THAT THE DALAI LAMA HAS JUST GONE INTO EXILE, LEAVING AN ACTING REGENT TO NEGOTIATE IN HIS ABSENCE.

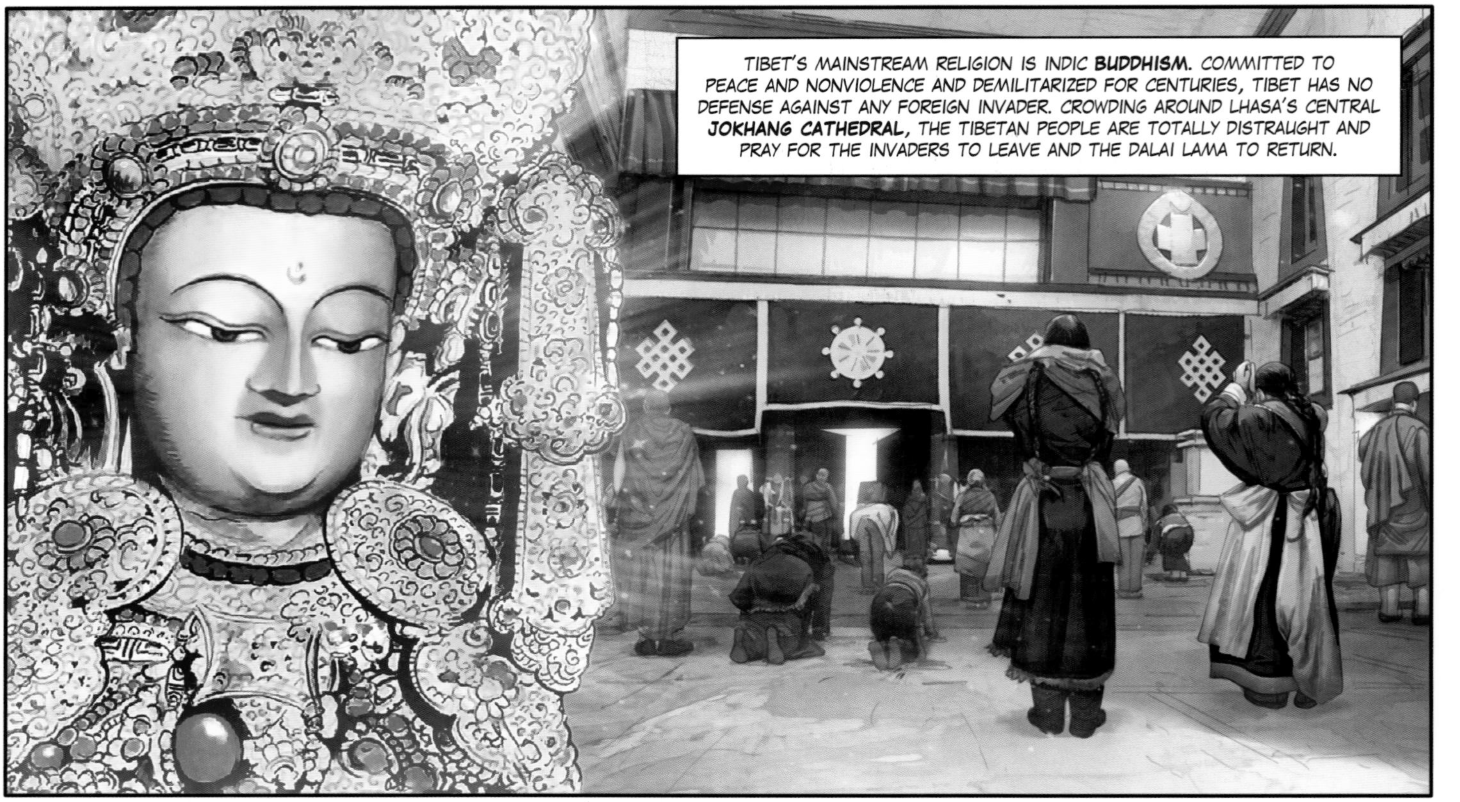
TIBET'S MAINSTREAM RELIGION IS INDIC **BUDDHISM.** COMMITTED TO PEACE AND NONVIOLENCE AND DEMILITARIZED FOR CENTURIES, TIBET HAS NO DEFENSE AGAINST ANY FOREIGN INVADER. CROWDING AROUND LHASA'S CENTRAL **JOKHANG CATHEDRAL,** THE TIBETAN PEOPLE ARE TOTALLY DISTRAUGHT AND PRAY FOR THE INVADERS TO LEAVE AND THE DALAI LAMA TO RETURN.

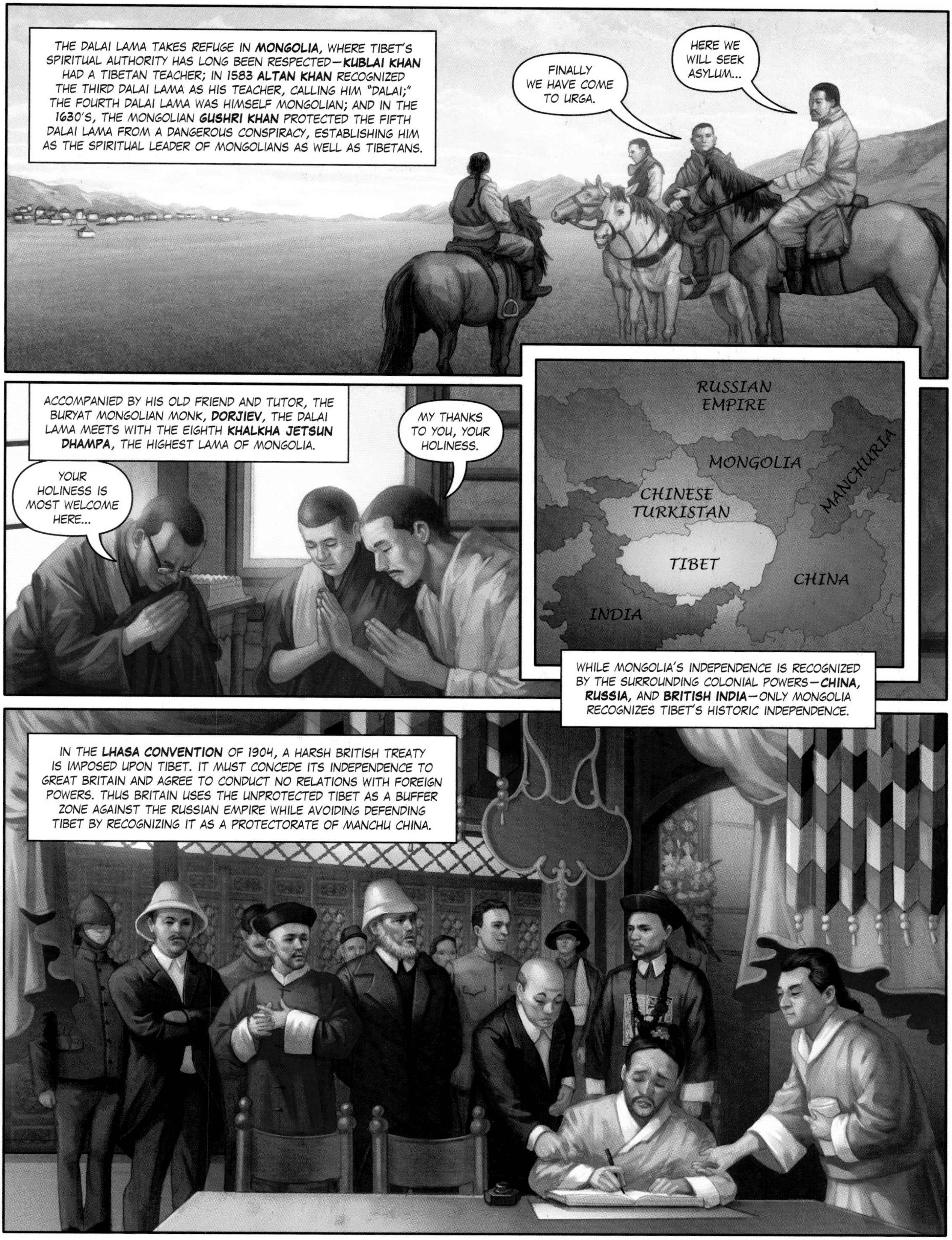
THE DALAI LAMA TAKES REFUGE IN MONGOLIA, WHERE TIBET'S SPIRITUAL AUTHORITY HAS LONG BEEN RESPECTED—KUBLAI KHAN HAD A TIBETAN TEACHER; IN 1583 ALTAN KHAN RECOGNIZED THE THIRD DALAI LAMA AS HIS TEACHER, CALLING HIM "DALAI;" THE FOURTH DALAI LAMA WAS HIMSELF MONGOLIAN; AND IN THE 1630'S, THE MONGOLIAN GUSHRI KHAN PROTECTED THE FIFTH DALAI LAMA FROM A DANGEROUS CONSPIRACY, ESTABLISHING HIM AS THE SPIRITUAL LEADER OF MONGOLIANS AS WELL AS TIBETANS.
FINALLY WE HAVE COME TO URGA.
HERE WE WILL SEEK ASYLUM...
ACCOMPANIED BY HIS OLD FRIEND AND TUTOR, THE BURYAT MONGOLIAN MONK, DORJIEV, THE DALAI LAMA MEETS WITH THE EIGHTH KHALKHA JETSUN DHAMPA, THE HIGHEST LAMA OF MONGOLIA.
MY THANKS TO YOU, YOUR HOLINESS.
YOUR HOLINESS IS MOST WELCOME HERE...
RUSSIAN EMPIRE
MONGOLIA
MANCHURIA
CHINESE TURKISTAN
TIBET
CHINA
INDIA
WHILE MONGOLIA'S INDEPENDENCE IS RECOGNIZED BY THE SURROUNDING COLONIAL POWERS—CHINA, RUSSIA, AND BRITISH INDIA—ONLY MONGOLIA RECOGNIZES TIBET'S HISTORIC INDEPENDENCE.
IN THE LHASA CONVENTION OF 1904, A HARSH BRITISH TREATY IS IMPOSED UPON TIBET. IT MUST CONCEDE ITS INDEPENDENCE TO GREAT BRITAIN AND AGREE TO CONDUCT NO RELATIONS WITH FOREIGN POWERS. THUS BRITAIN USES THE UNPROTECTED TIBET AS A BUFFER ZONE AGAINST THE RUSSIAN EMPIRE WHILE AVOIDING DEFENDING TIBET BY RECOGNIZING IT AS A PROTECTORATE OF MANCHU CHINA.

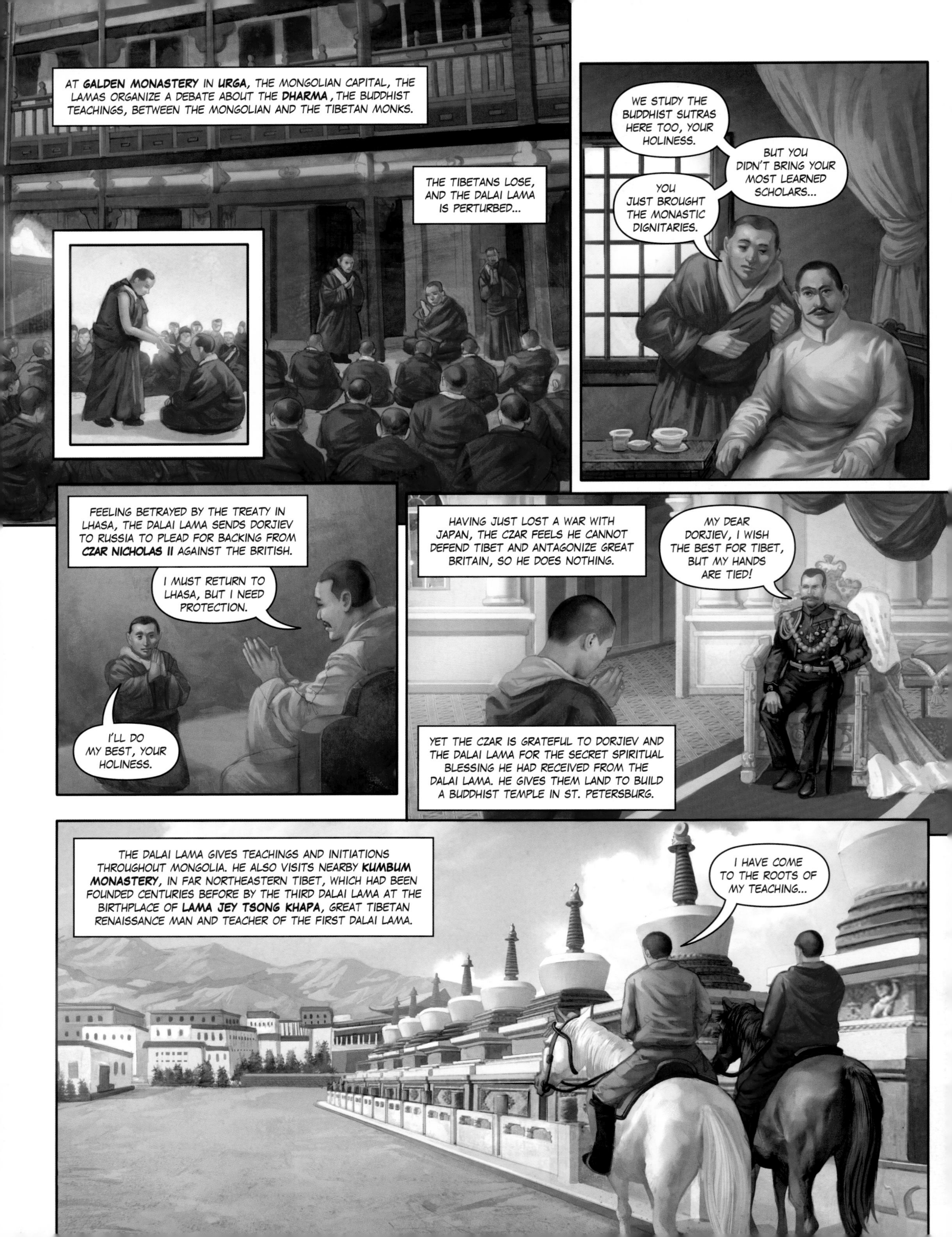
AT GALDEN MONASTERY IN URGA, THE MONGOLIAN CAPITAL, THE LAMAS ORGANIZE A DEBATE ABOUT THE DHARMA, THE BUDDHIST TEACHINGS, BETWEEN THE MONGOLIAN AND THE TIBETAN MONKS.
THE TIBETANS LOSE, AND THE DALAI LAMA IS PERTURBED...
WE STUDY THE BUDDHIST SUTRAS HERE TOO, YOUR HOLINESS.
YOU JUST BROUGHT THE MONASTIC DIGNITARIES.
BUT YOU DIDN'T BRING YOUR MOST LEARNED SCHOLARS...
FEELING BETRAYED BY THE TREATY IN LHASA, THE DALAI LAMA SENDS DORJIEV TO RUSSIA TO PLEAD FOR BACKING FROM CZAR NICHOLAS II AGAINST THE BRITISH.
I MUST RETURN TO LHASA, BUT I NEED PROTECTION.
I'LL DO MY BEST, YOUR HOLINESS.
HAVING JUST LOST A WAR WITH JAPAN, THE CZAR FEELS HE CANNOT DEFEND TIBET AND ANTAGONIZE GREAT BRITAIN, SO HE DOES NOTHING.
MY DEAR DORJIEV, I WISH THE BEST FOR TIBET, BUT MY HANDS ARE TIED!
YET THE CZAR IS GRATEFUL TO DORJIEV AND THE DALAI LAMA FOR THE SECRET SPIRITUAL BLESSING HE HAD RECEIVED FROM THE DALAI LAMA. HE GIVES THEM LAND TO BUILD A BUDDHIST TEMPLE IN ST. PETERSBURG.
THE DALAI LAMA GIVES TEACHINGS AND INITIATIONS THROUGHOUT MONGOLIA. HE ALSO VISITS NEARBY KUMBUM MONASTERY, IN FAR NORTHEASTERN TIBET, WHICH HAD BEEN FOUNDED CENTURIES BEFORE BY THE THIRD DALAI LAMA AT THE BIRTHPLACE OF LAMA JEY TSONG KHAPA, GREAT TIBETAN RENAISSANCE MAN AND TEACHER OF THE FIRST DALAI LAMA.
I HAVE COME TO THE ROOTS OF MY TEACHING...

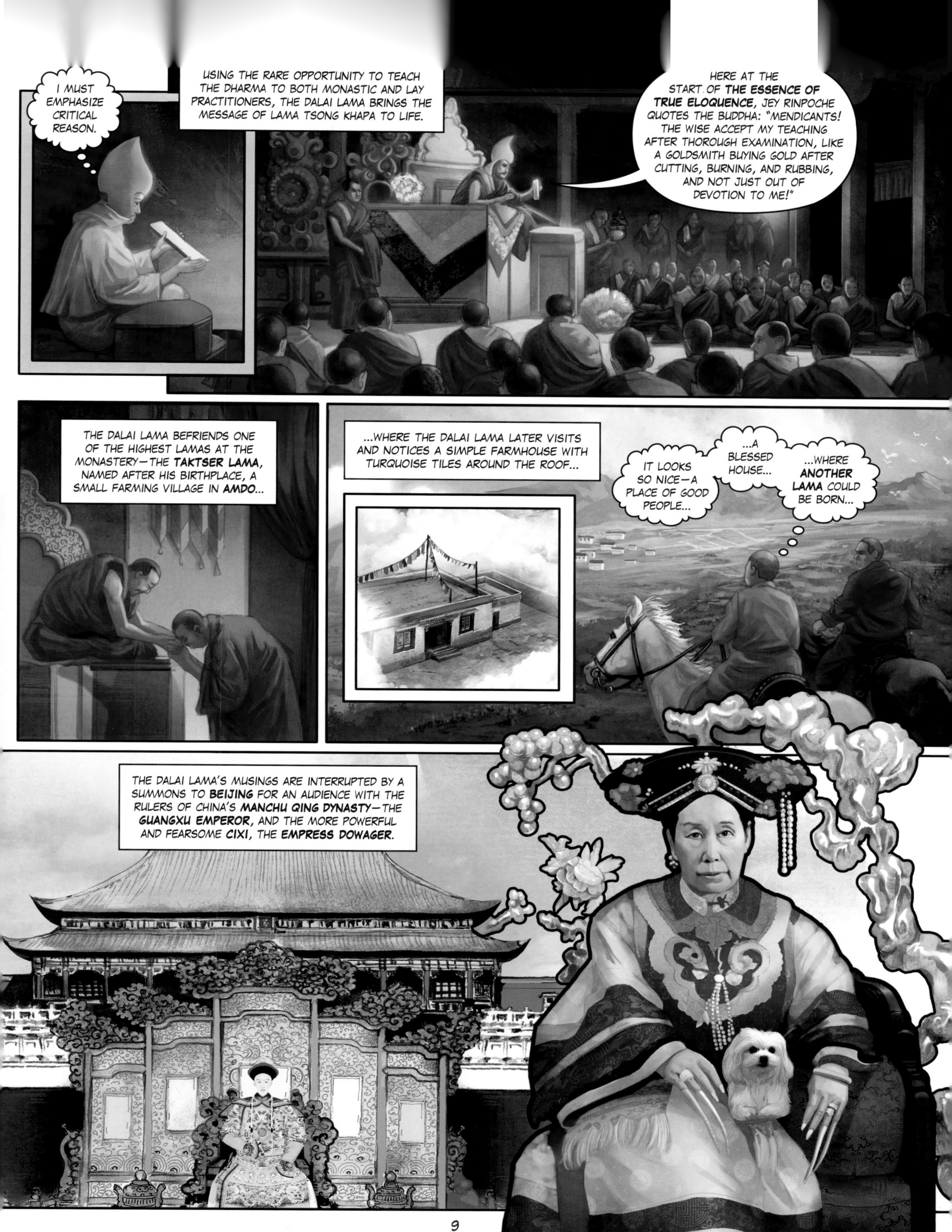
I MUST EMPHASIZE CRITICAL REASON.
USING THE RARE OPPORTUNITY TO TEACH THE DHARMA TO BOTH MONASTIC AND LAY PRACTITIONERS, THE DALAI LAMA BRINGS THE MESSAGE OF LAMA TSONG KHAPA TO LIFE.
HERE AT THE START OF THE ESSENCE OF TRUE ELOQUENCE, JEY RINPOCHE QUOTES THE BUDDHA: "MENDICANTS! THE WISE ACCEPT MY TEACHING AFTER THOROUGH EXAMINATION, LIKE A GOLDSMITH BUYING GOLD AFTER CUTTING, BURNING, AND RUBBING, AND NOT JUST OUT OF DEVOTION TO ME!"
THE DALAI LAMA BEFRIENDS ONE OF THE HIGHEST LAMAS AT THE MONASTERY—THE TAKTSER LAMA, NAMED AFTER HIS BIRTHPLACE, A SMALL FARMING VILLAGE IN AMDO...
...WHERE THE DALAI LAMA LATER VISITS AND NOTICES A SIMPLE FARMHOUSE WITH TURQUOISE TILES AROUND THE ROOF...
IT LOOKS SO NICE—A PLACE OF GOOD PEOPLE...
...A BLESSED HOUSE...
...WHERE ANOTHER LAMA COULD BE BORN...
THE DALAI LAMA'S MUSINGS ARE INTERRUPTED BY A SUMMONS TO BEIJING FOR AN AUDIENCE WITH THE RULERS OF CHINA'S MANCHU QING DYNASTY—THE GUANGXU EMPEROR, AND THE MORE POWERFUL AND FEARSOME CIXI, THE EMPRESS DOWAGER.

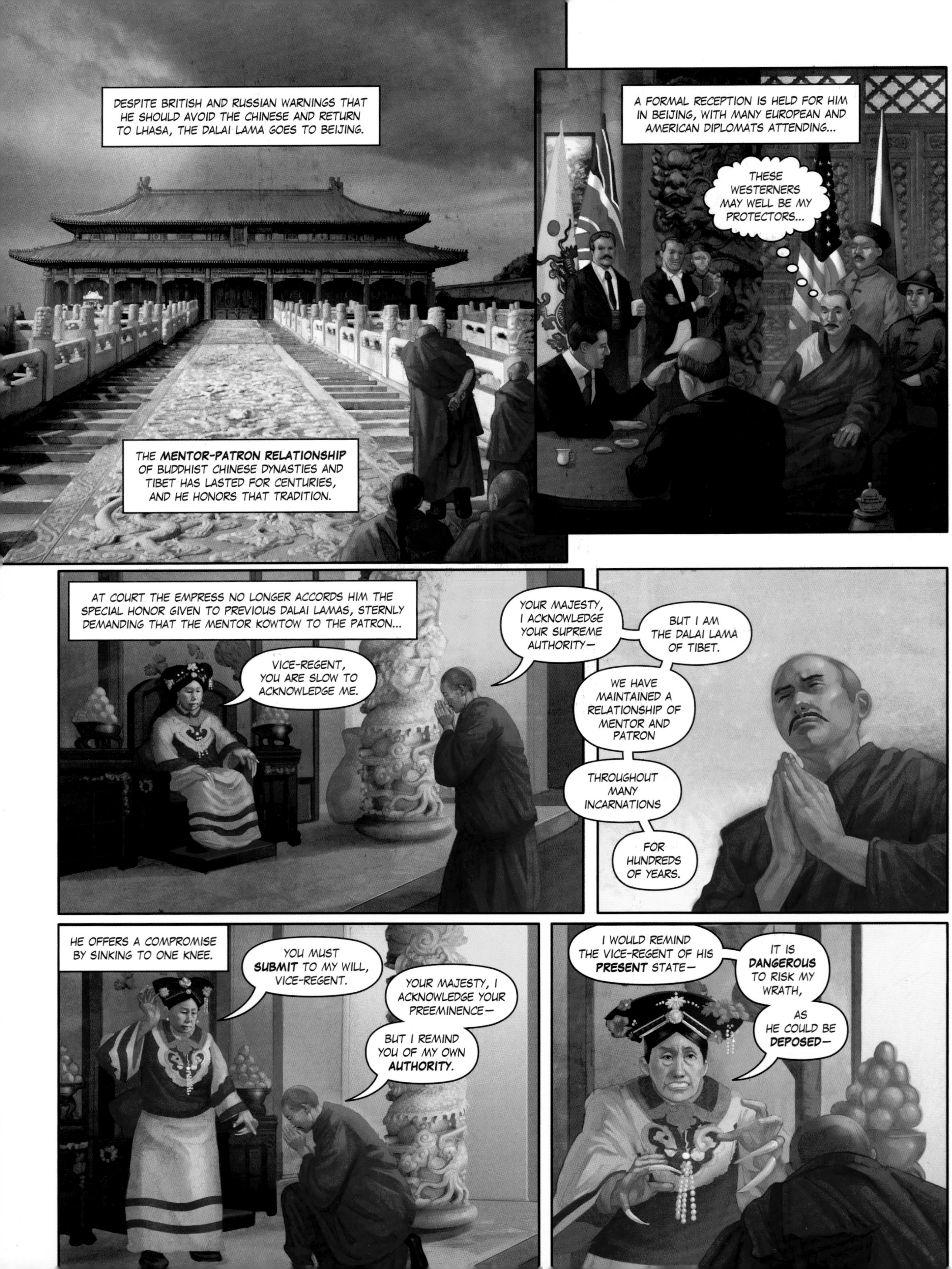
DESPITE BRITISH AND RUSSIAN WARNINGS THAT HE SHOULD AVOID THE CHINESE AND RETURN TO LHASA, THE DALAI LAMA GOES TO BEIJING.
THE **MENTOR-PATRON RELATIONSHIP** OF BUDDHIST CHINESE DYNASTIES AND TIBET HAS LASTED FOR CENTURIES, AND HE HONORS THAT TRADITION.
A FORMAL RECEPTION IS HELD FOR HIM IN BEIJING, WITH MANY EUROPEAN AND AMERICAN DIPLOMATS ATTENDING...
THESE WESTERNERS MAY WELL BE MY PROTECTORS...
AT COURT THE EMPRESS NO LONGER ACCORDS HIM THE SPECIAL HONOR GIVEN TO PREVIOUS DALAI LAMAS, STERNLY DEMANDING THAT THE MENTOR KOWTOW TO THE PATRON...
VICE-REGENT, YOU ARE SLOW TO ACKNOWLEDGE ME.
YOUR MAJESTY, I ACKNOWLEDGE YOUR SUPREME AUTHORITY—
BUT I AM THE DALAI LAMA OF TIBET.
WE HAVE MAINTAINED A RELATIONSHIP OF MENTOR AND PATRON
THROUGHOUT MANY INCARNATIONS
FOR HUNDREDS OF YEARS.
HE OFFERS A COMPROMISE BY SINKING TO ONE KNEE.
YOU MUST **SUBMIT** TO MY WILL, VICE-REGENT.
YOUR MAJESTY, I ACKNOWLEDGE YOUR PREEMINENCE—
BUT I REMIND YOU OF MY OWN **AUTHORITY**.
I WOULD REMIND THE VICE-REGENT OF HIS **PRESENT** STATE—
IT IS **DANGEROUS** TO RISK MY WRATH,
AS HE COULD BE **DEPOSED**—

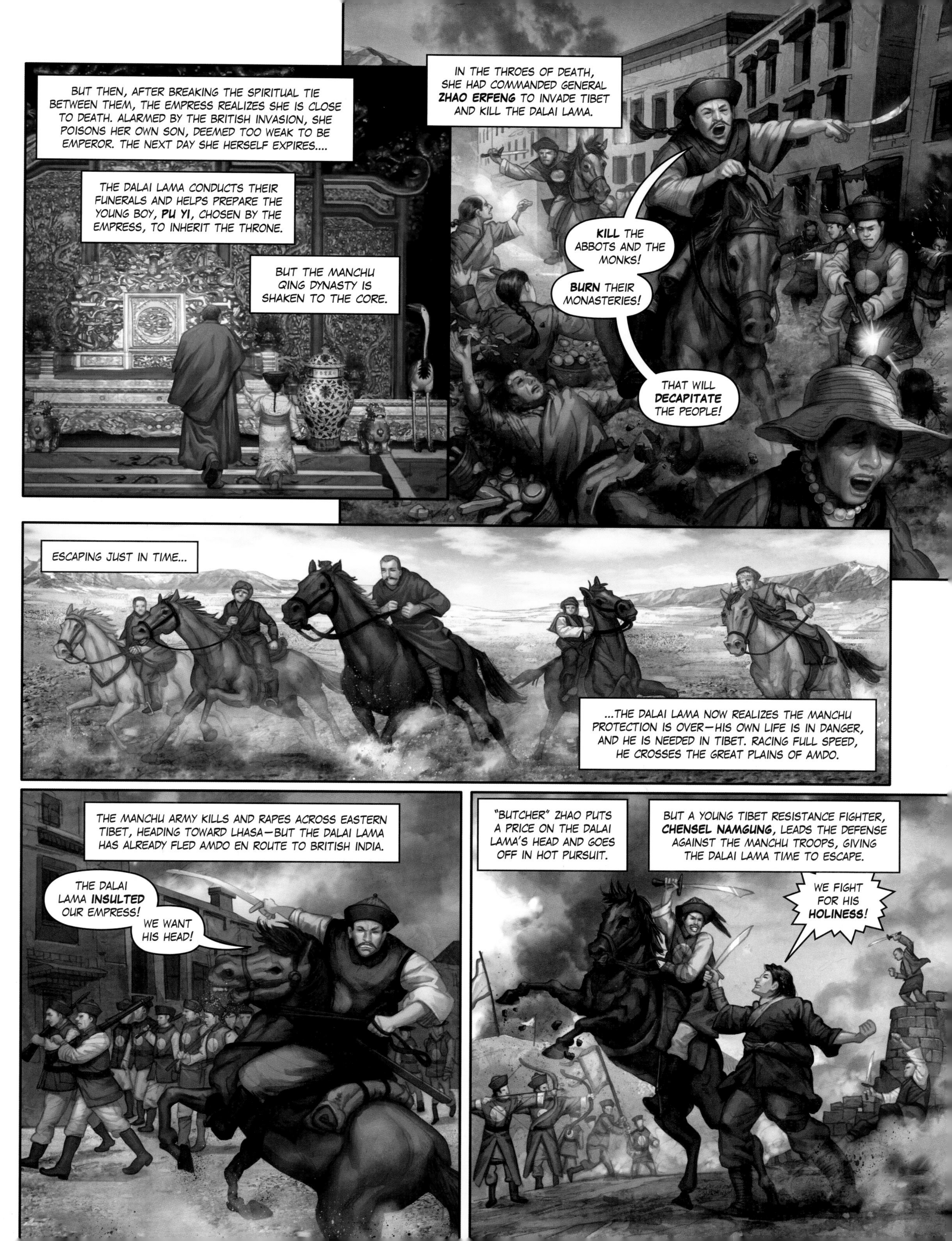
BUT THEN, AFTER BREAKING THE SPIRITUAL TIE BETWEEN THEM, THE EMPRESS REALIZES SHE IS CLOSE TO DEATH. ALARMED BY THE BRITISH INVASION, SHE POISONS HER OWN SON, DEEMED TOO WEAK TO BE EMPEROR. THE NEXT DAY SHE HERSELF EXPIRES....
THE DALAI LAMA CONDUCTS THEIR FUNERALS AND HELPS PREPARE THE YOUNG BOY, PU YI, CHOSEN BY THE EMPRESS, TO INHERIT THE THRONE.
BUT THE MANCHU QING DYNASTY IS SHAKEN TO THE CORE.
IN THE THROES OF DEATH, SHE HAD COMMANDED GENERAL ZHAO ERFENG TO INVADE TIBET AND KILL THE DALAI LAMA.
KILL THE ABBOTS AND THE MONKS!
BURN THEIR MONASTERIES!
THAT WILL DECAPITATE THE PEOPLE!
ESCAPING JUST IN TIME...
...THE DALAI LAMA NOW REALIZES THE MANCHU PROTECTION IS OVER—HIS OWN LIFE IS IN DANGER, AND HE IS NEEDED IN TIBET. RACING FULL SPEED, HE CROSSES THE GREAT PLAINS OF AMDO.
THE MANCHU ARMY KILLS AND RAPES ACROSS EASTERN TIBET, HEADING TOWARD LHASA—BUT THE DALAI LAMA HAS ALREADY FLED AMDO EN ROUTE TO BRITISH INDIA.
THE DALAI LAMA INSULTED OUR EMPRESS!
WE WANT HIS HEAD!
"BUTCHER" ZHAO PUTS A PRICE ON THE DALAI LAMA'S HEAD AND GOES OFF IN HOT PURSUIT.
BUT A YOUNG TIBET RESISTANCE FIGHTER, CHENSEL NAMGUNG, LEADS THE DEFENSE AGAINST THE MANCHU TROOPS, GIVING THE DALAI LAMA TIME TO ESCAPE.
WE FIGHT FOR HIS HOLINESS!

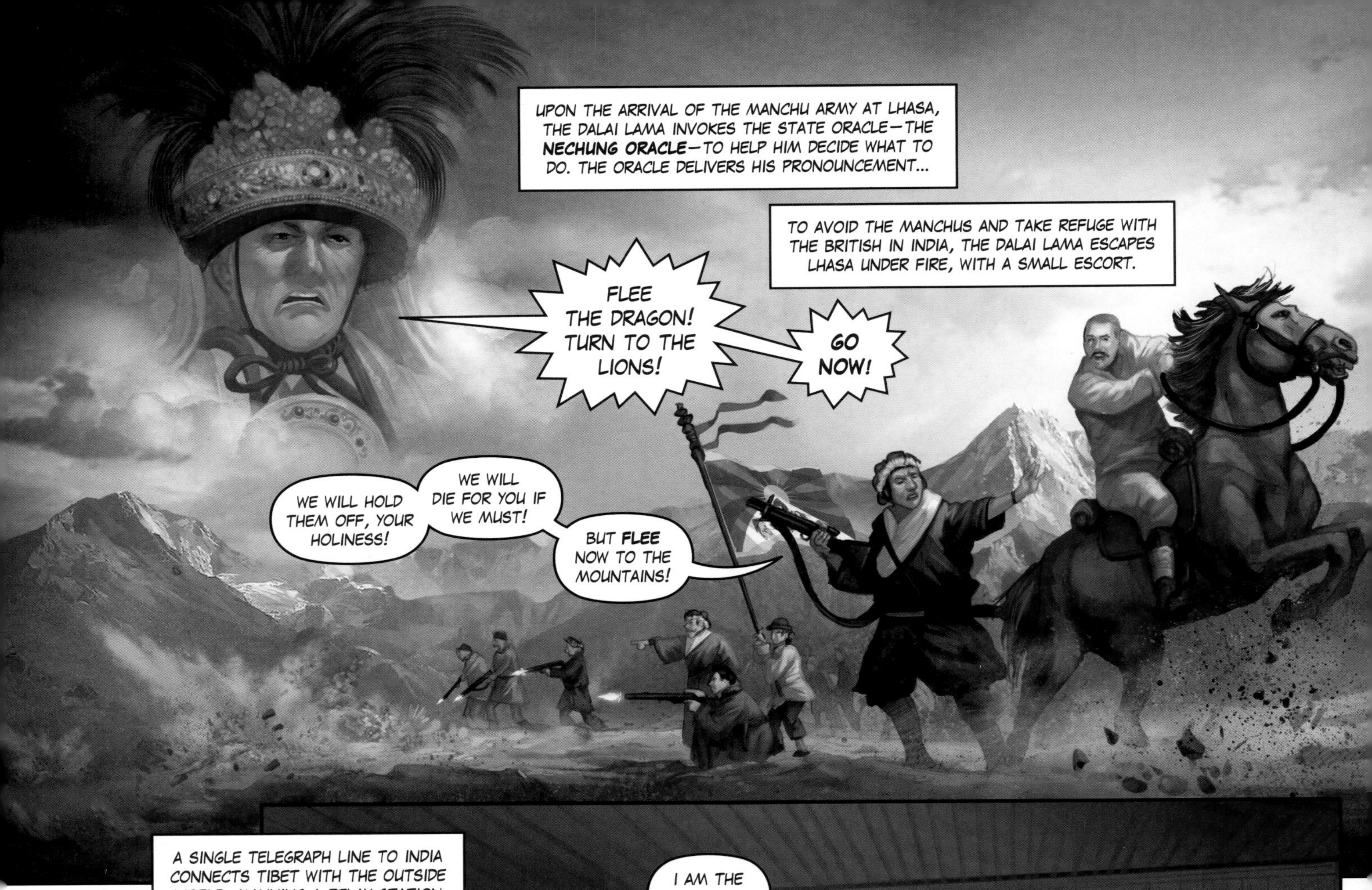
UPON THE ARRIVAL OF THE MANCHU ARMY AT LHASA, THE DALAI LAMA INVOKES THE STATE ORACLE—THE **NECHUNG ORACLE**—TO HELP HIM DECIDE WHAT TO DO. THE ORACLE DELIVERS HIS PRONOUNCEMENT...
FLEE THE DRAGON! TURN TO THE LIONS!
GO NOW!
TO AVOID THE MANCHUS AND TAKE REFUGE WITH THE BRITISH IN INDIA, THE DALAI LAMA ESCAPES LHASA UNDER FIRE, WITH A SMALL ESCORT.
WE WILL HOLD THEM OFF, YOUR HOLINESS!
WE WILL DIE FOR YOU IF WE MUST!
BUT **FLEE** NOW TO THE MOUNTAINS!

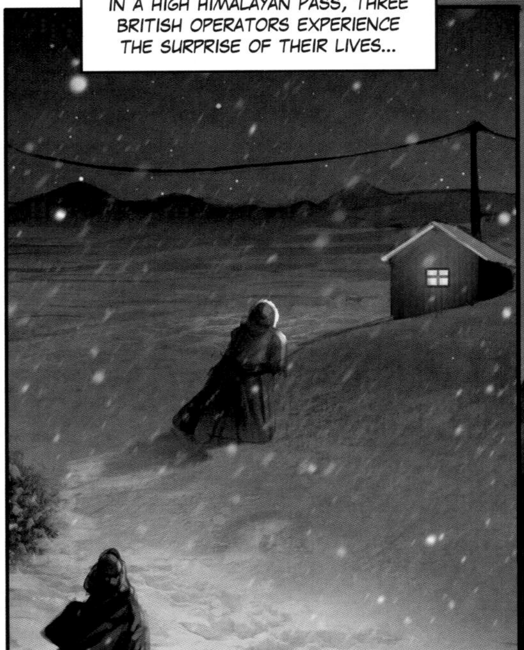
A SINGLE TELEGRAPH LINE TO INDIA CONNECTS TIBET WITH THE OUTSIDE WORLD. MANNING A RELAY STATION IN A HIGH HIMALAYAN PASS, THREE BRITISH OPERATORS EXPERIENCE THE SURPRISE OF THEIR LIVES...

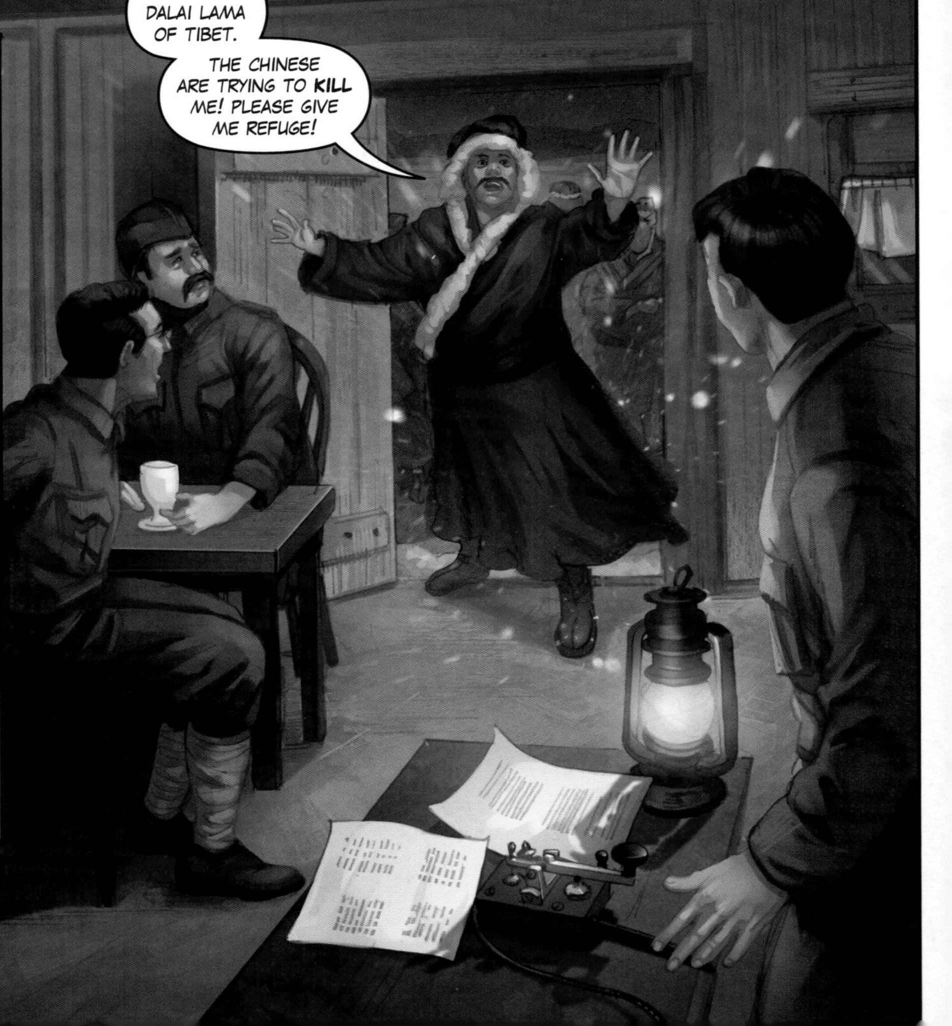
I AM THE DALAI LAMA OF TIBET.
THE CHINESE ARE TRYING TO **KILL** ME! PLEASE GIVE ME REFUGE!

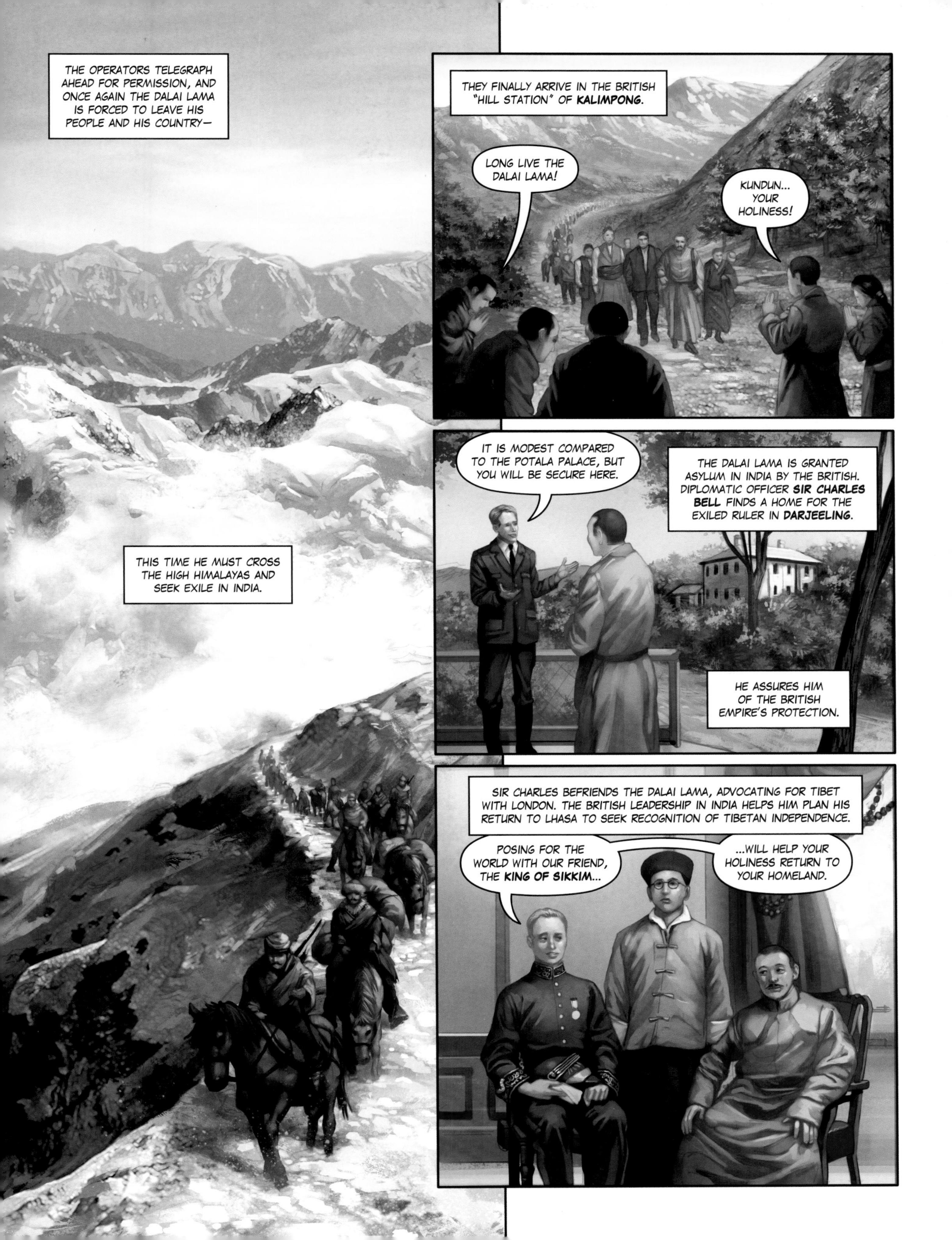
THE OPERATORS TELEGRAPH AHEAD FOR PERMISSION, AND ONCE AGAIN THE DALAI LAMA IS FORCED TO LEAVE HIS PEOPLE AND HIS COUNTRY—
THIS TIME HE MUST CROSS THE HIGH HIMALAYAS AND SEEK EXILE IN INDIA.
THEY FINALLY ARRIVE IN THE BRITISH "HILL STATION" OF **KALIMPONG**.
LONG LIVE THE DALAI LAMA!
KUNDUN... YOUR HOLINESS!
IT IS MODEST COMPARED TO THE POTALA PALACE, BUT YOU WILL BE SECURE HERE.
THE DALAI LAMA IS GRANTED ASYLUM IN INDIA BY THE BRITISH. DIPLOMATIC OFFICER **SIR CHARLES BELL** FINDS A HOME FOR THE EXILED RULER IN **DARJEELING**.
HE ASSURES HIM OF THE BRITISH EMPIRE'S PROTECTION.
SIR CHARLES BEFRIENDS THE DALAI LAMA, ADVOCATING FOR TIBET WITH LONDON. THE BRITISH LEADERSHIP IN INDIA HELPS HIM PLAN HIS RETURN TO LHASA TO SEEK RECOGNITION OF TIBETAN INDEPENDENCE.
POSING FOR THE WORLD WITH OUR FRIEND, THE **KING OF SIKKIM**...
...WILL HELP YOUR HOLINESS RETURN TO YOUR HOMELAND.

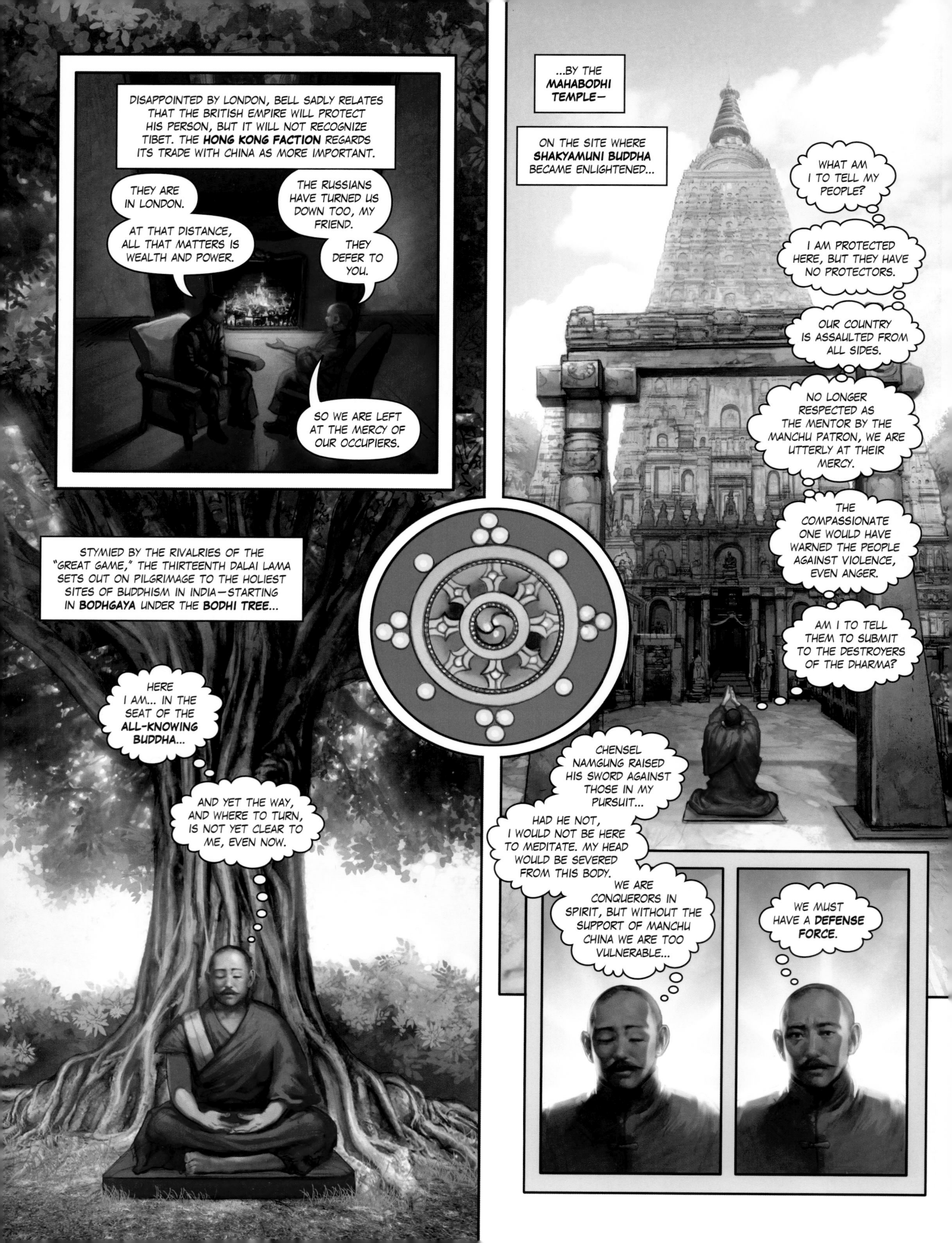

DISAPPOINTED BY LONDON, BELL SADLY RELATES THAT THE BRITISH EMPIRE WILL PROTECT HIS PERSON, BUT IT WILL NOT RECOGNIZE TIBET. THE HONG KONG FACTION REGARDS ITS TRADE WITH CHINA AS MORE IMPORTANT.
THEY ARE IN LONDON.
AT THAT DISTANCE, ALL THAT MATTERS IS WEALTH AND POWER.
THE RUSSIANS HAVE TURNED US DOWN TOO, MY FRIEND.
THEY DEFER TO YOU.
SO WE ARE LEFT AT THE MERCY OF OUR OCCUPIERS.
STYMIED BY THE RIVALRIES OF THE "GREAT GAME," THE THIRTEENTH DALAI LAMA SETS OUT ON PILGRIMAGE TO THE HOLIEST SITES OF BUDDHISM IN INDIA—STARTING IN BODHGAYA UNDER THE BODHI TREE...
HERE I AM... IN THE SEAT OF THE ALL-KNOWING BUDDHA...
AND YET THE WAY, AND WHERE TO TURN, IS NOT YET CLEAR TO ME, EVEN NOW.
...BY THE MAHABODHI TEMPLE—
ON THE SITE WHERE SHAKYAMUNI BUDDHA BECAME ENLIGHTENED...
WHAT AM I TO TELL MY PEOPLE?
I AM PROTECTED HERE, BUT THEY HAVE NO PROTECTORS.
OUR COUNTRY IS ASSAULTED FROM ALL SIDES.
NO LONGER RESPECTED AS THE MENTOR BY THE MANCHU PATRON, WE ARE UTTERLY AT THEIR MERCY.
THE COMPASSIONATE ONE WOULD HAVE WARNED THE PEOPLE AGAINST VIOLENCE, EVEN ANGER.
AM I TO TELL THEM TO SUBMIT TO THE DESTROYERS OF THE DHARMA?
CHENSEL NAMGUNG RAISED HIS SWORD AGAINST THOSE IN MY PURSUIT...
HAD HE NOT, I WOULD NOT BE HERE TO MEDITATE. MY HEAD WOULD BE SEVERED FROM THIS BODY.
WE ARE CONQUERORS IN SPIRIT, BUT WITHOUT THE SUPPORT OF MANCHU CHINA WE ARE TOO VULNERABLE...
WE MUST HAVE A DEFENSE FORCE.

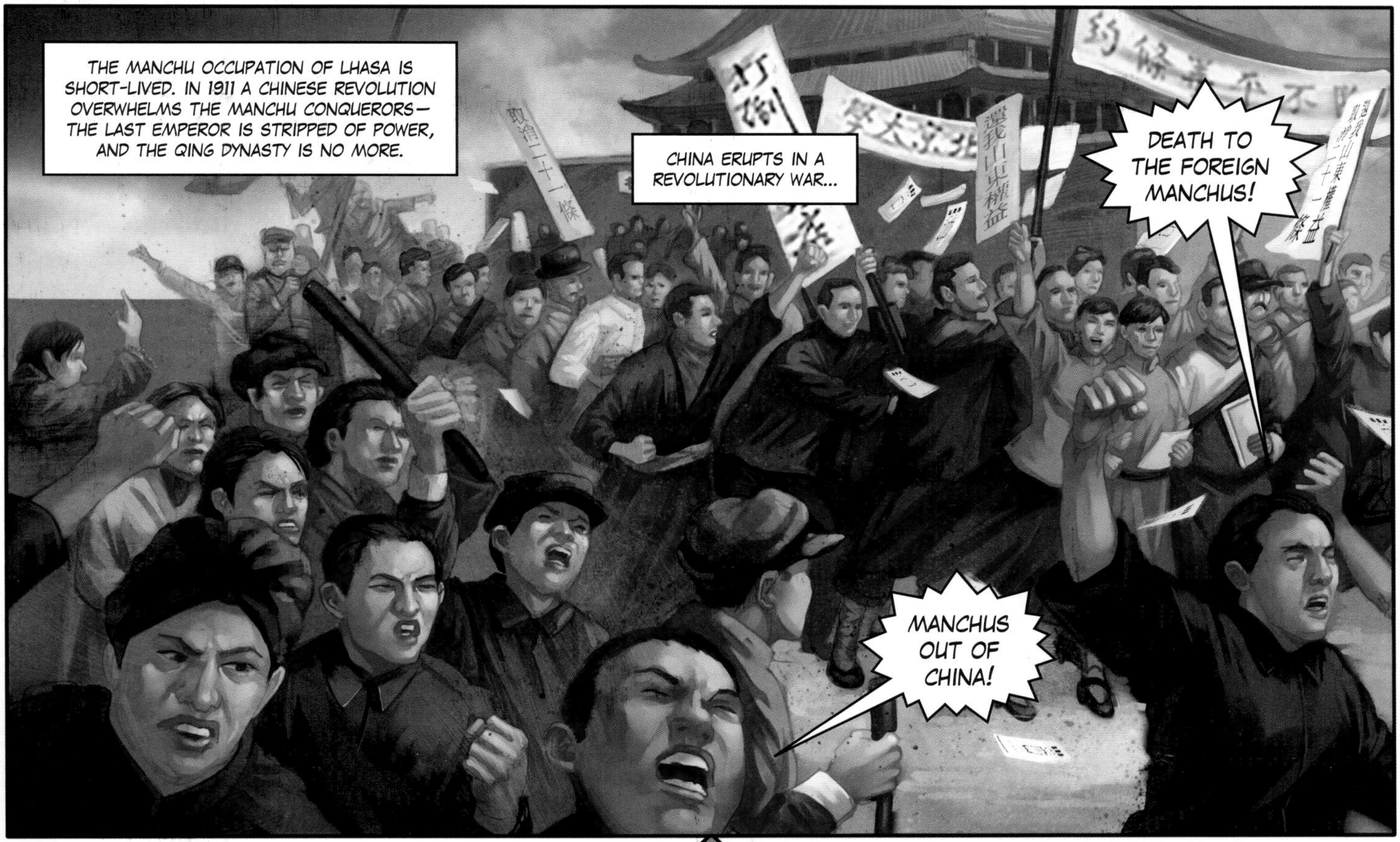
THE MANCHU OCCUPATION OF LHASA IS SHORT-LIVED. IN 1911 A CHINESE REVOLUTION OVERWHELMS THE MANCHU CONQUERORS— THE LAST EMPEROR IS STRIPPED OF POWER, AND THE QING DYNASTY IS NO MORE.
CHINA ERUPTS IN A REVOLUTIONARY WAR...
DEATH TO THE FOREIGN MANCHUS!
MANCHUS OUT OF CHINA!

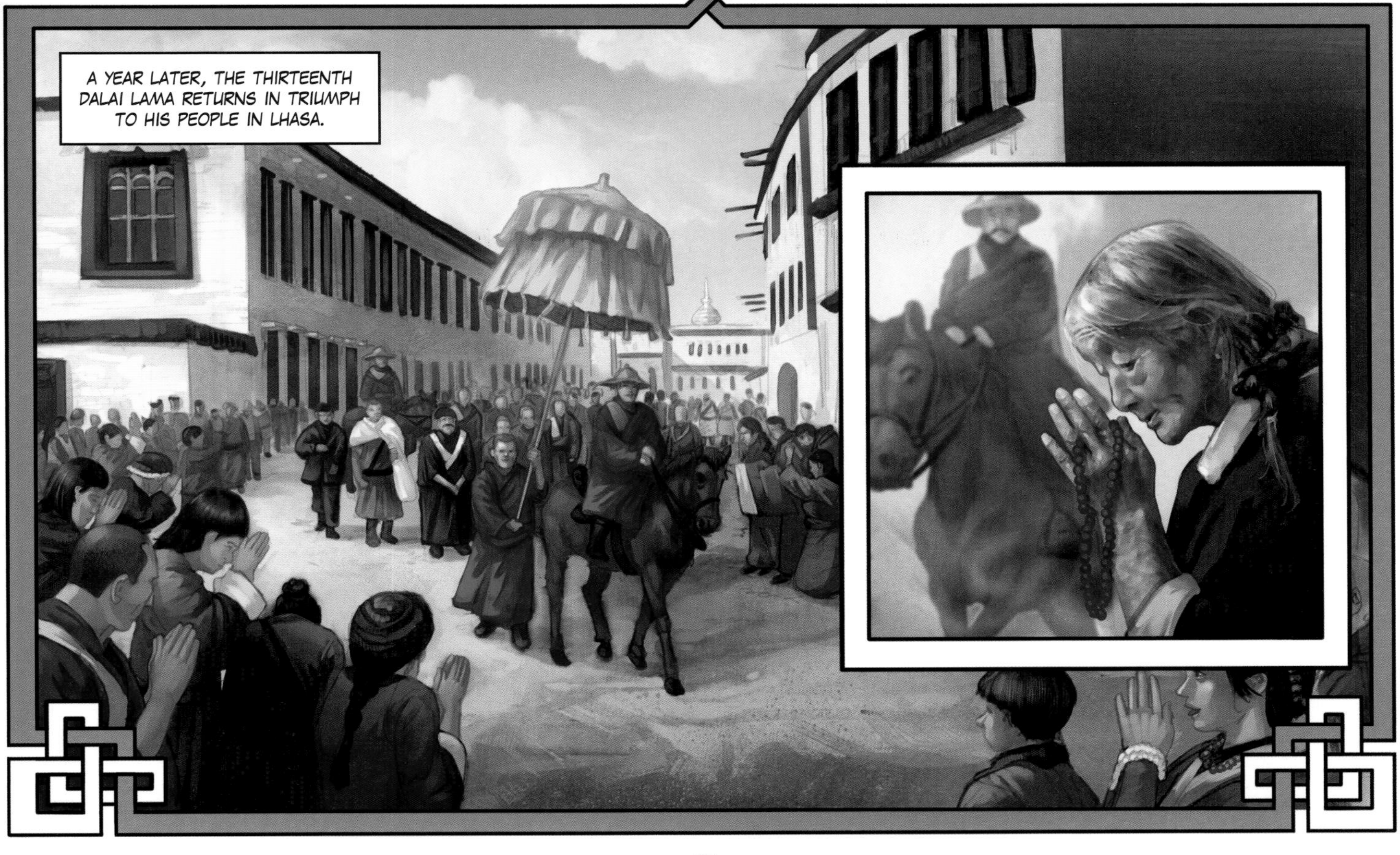
A YEAR LATER, THE THIRTEENTH DALAI LAMA RETURNS IN TRIUMPH TO HIS PEOPLE IN LHASA.

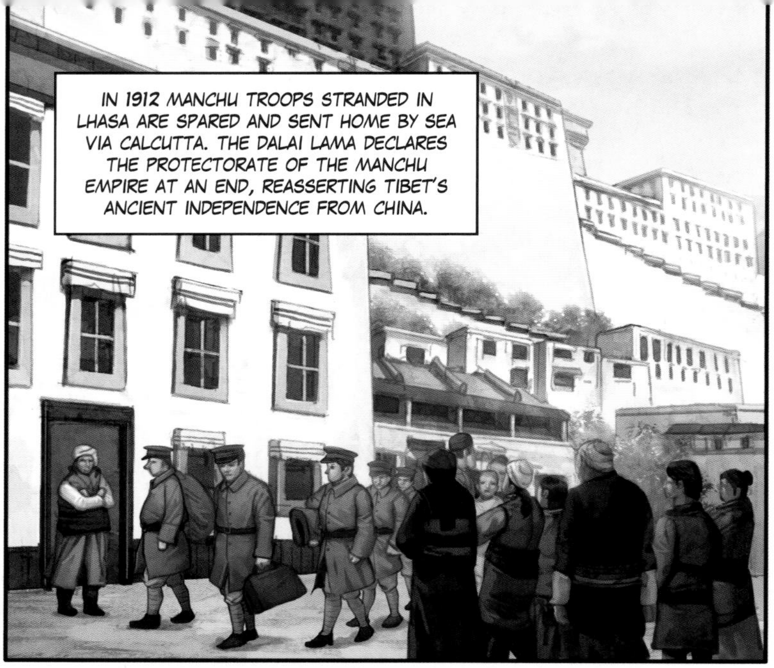
IN 1912 MANCHU TROOPS STRANDED IN LHASA ARE SPARED AND SENT HOME BY SEA VIA CALCUTTA. THE DALAI LAMA DECLARES THE PROTECTORATE OF THE MANCHU EMPIRE AT AN END, REASSERTING TIBET'S ANCIENT INDEPENDENCE FROM CHINA.

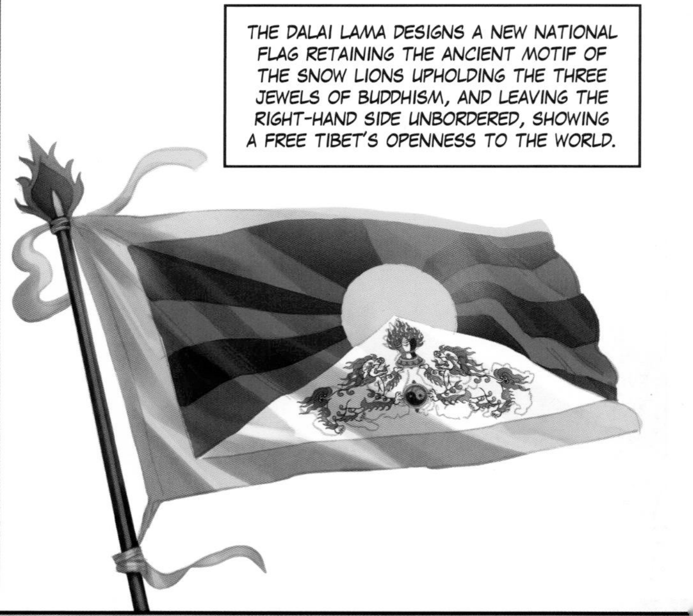
THE DALAI LAMA DESIGNS A NEW NATIONAL FLAG RETAINING THE ANCIENT MOTIF OF THE SNOW LIONS UPHOLDING THE THREE JEWELS OF BUDDHISM, AND LEAVING THE RIGHT-HAND SIDE UNBORDERED, SHOWING A FREE TIBET'S OPENNESS TO THE WORLD.

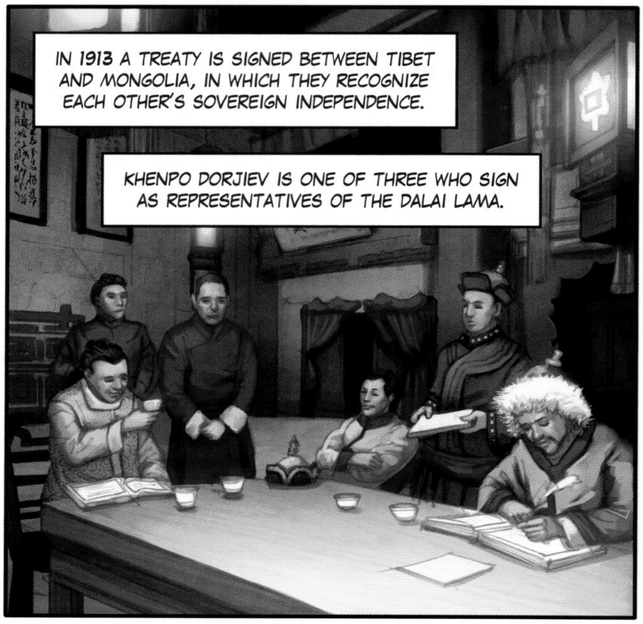
IN 1913 A TREATY IS SIGNED BETWEEN TIBET AND MONGOLIA, IN WHICH THEY RECOGNIZE EACH OTHER'S SOVEREIGN INDEPENDENCE.
KHENPO DORJIEV IS ONE OF THREE WHO SIGN AS REPRESENTATIVES OF THE DALAI LAMA.

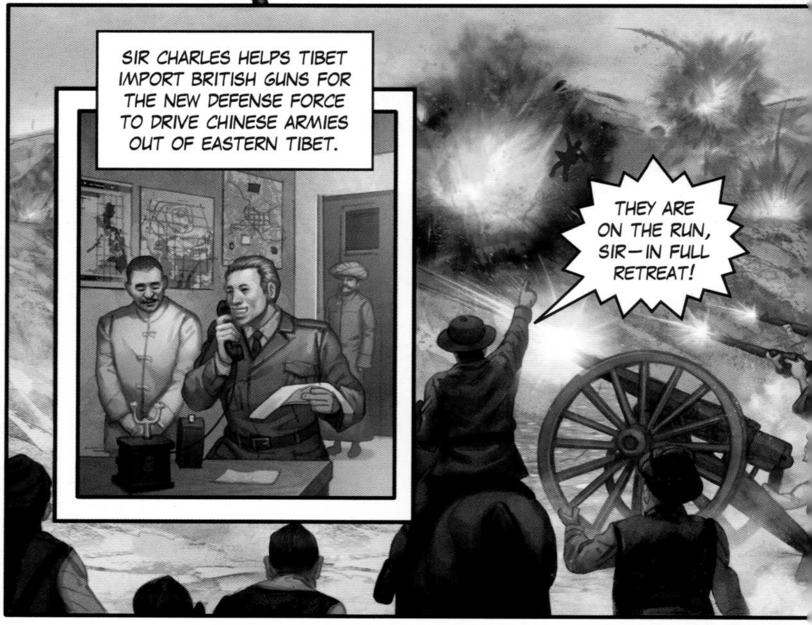
SIR CHARLES HELPS TIBET IMPORT BRITISH GUNS FOR THE NEW DEFENSE FORCE TO DRIVE CHINESE ARMIES OUT OF EASTERN TIBET.
THEY ARE ON THE RUN, SIR—IN FULL RETREAT!

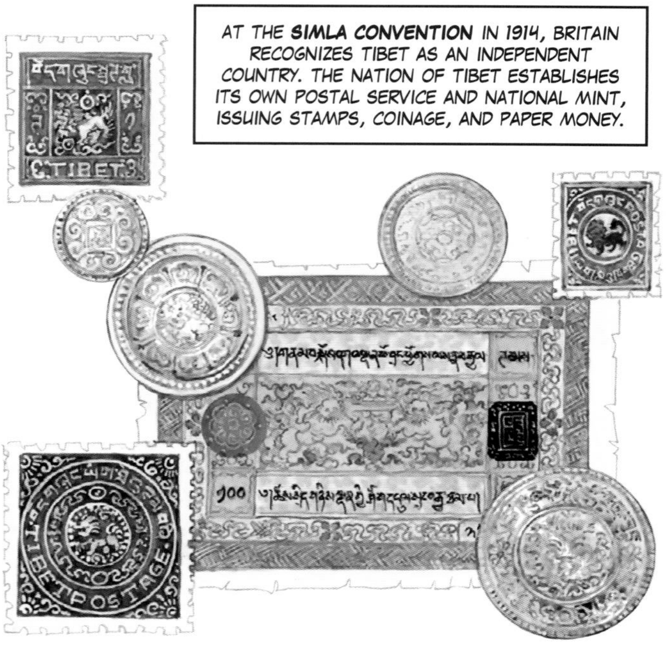
AT THE **SIMLA CONVENTION** IN 1914, BRITAIN RECOGNIZES TIBET AS AN INDEPENDENT COUNTRY. THE NATION OF TIBET ESTABLISHES ITS OWN POSTAL SERVICE AND NATIONAL MINT, ISSUING STAMPS, COINAGE, AND PAPER MONEY.
TIBET
TIBET POSTAGE

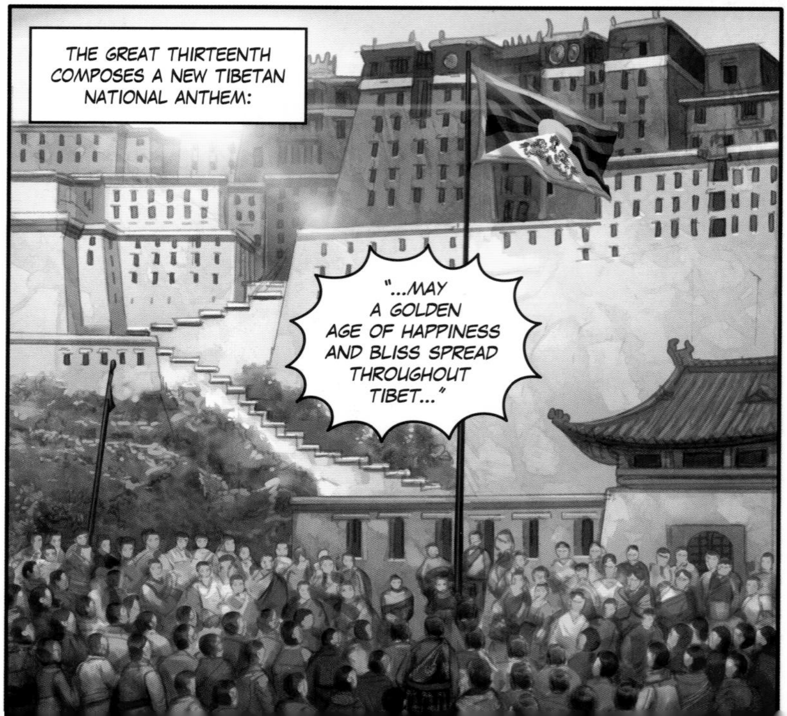
THE GREAT THIRTEENTH COMPOSES A NEW TIBETAN NATIONAL ANTHEM:
"...MAY A GOLDEN AGE OF HAPPINESS AND BLISS SPREAD THROUGHOUT TIBET..."

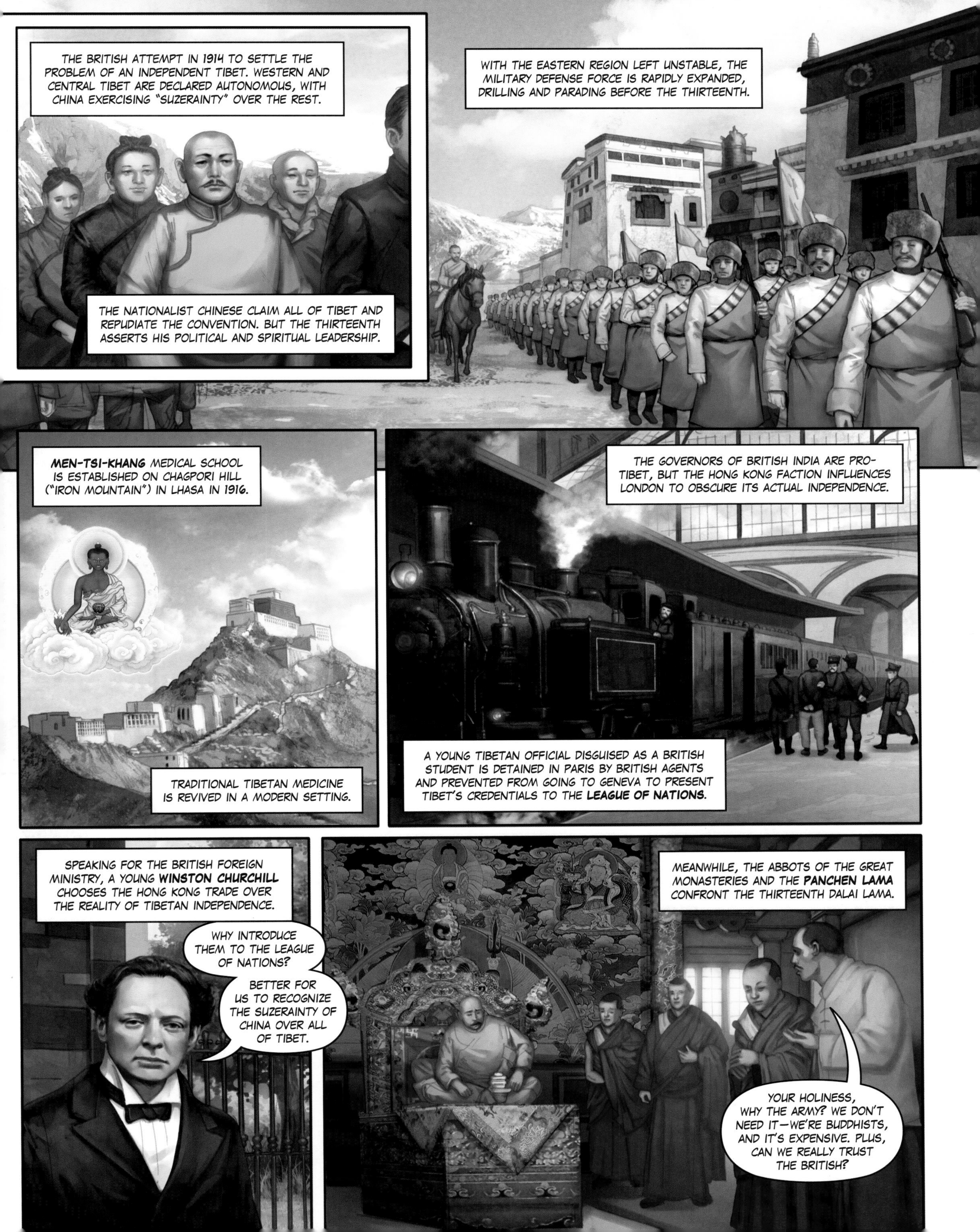
THE BRITISH ATTEMPT IN 1914 TO SETTLE THE PROBLEM OF AN INDEPENDENT TIBET. WESTERN AND CENTRAL TIBET ARE DECLARED AUTONOMOUS, WITH CHINA EXERCISING "SUZERAINTY" OVER THE REST.
THE NATIONALIST CHINESE CLAIM ALL OF TIBET AND REPUDIATE THE CONVENTION. BUT THE THIRTEENTH ASSERTS HIS POLITICAL AND SPIRITUAL LEADERSHIP.
WITH THE EASTERN REGION LEFT UNSTABLE, THE MILITARY DEFENSE FORCE IS RAPIDLY EXPANDED, DRILLING AND PARADING BEFORE THE THIRTEENTH.
MEN-TSI-KHANG MEDICAL SCHOOL IS ESTABLISHED ON CHAGPORI HILL ("IRON MOUNTAIN") IN LHASA IN 1916.
TRADITIONAL TIBETAN MEDICINE IS REVIVED IN A MODERN SETTING.
THE GOVERNORS OF BRITISH INDIA ARE PRO-TIBET, BUT THE HONG KONG FACTION INFLUENCES LONDON TO OBSCURE ITS ACTUAL INDEPENDENCE.
A YOUNG TIBETAN OFFICIAL DISGUISED AS A BRITISH STUDENT IS DETAINED IN PARIS BY BRITISH AGENTS AND PREVENTED FROM GOING TO GENEVA TO PRESENT TIBET'S CREDENTIALS TO THE **LEAGUE OF NATIONS**.
SPEAKING FOR THE BRITISH FOREIGN MINISTRY, A YOUNG **WINSTON CHURCHILL** CHOOSES THE HONG KONG TRADE OVER THE REALITY OF TIBETAN INDEPENDENCE.
WHY INTRODUCE THEM TO THE LEAGUE OF NATIONS?
BETTER FOR US TO RECOGNIZE THE SUZERAINTY OF CHINA OVER ALL OF TIBET.
MEANWHILE, THE ABBOTS OF THE GREAT MONASTERIES AND THE **PANCHEN LAMA** CONFRONT THE THIRTEENTH DALAI LAMA.
YOUR HOLINESS, WHY THE ARMY? WE DON'T NEED IT—WE'RE BUDDHISTS, AND IT'S EXPENSIVE. PLUS, CAN WE REALLY TRUST THE BRITISH?

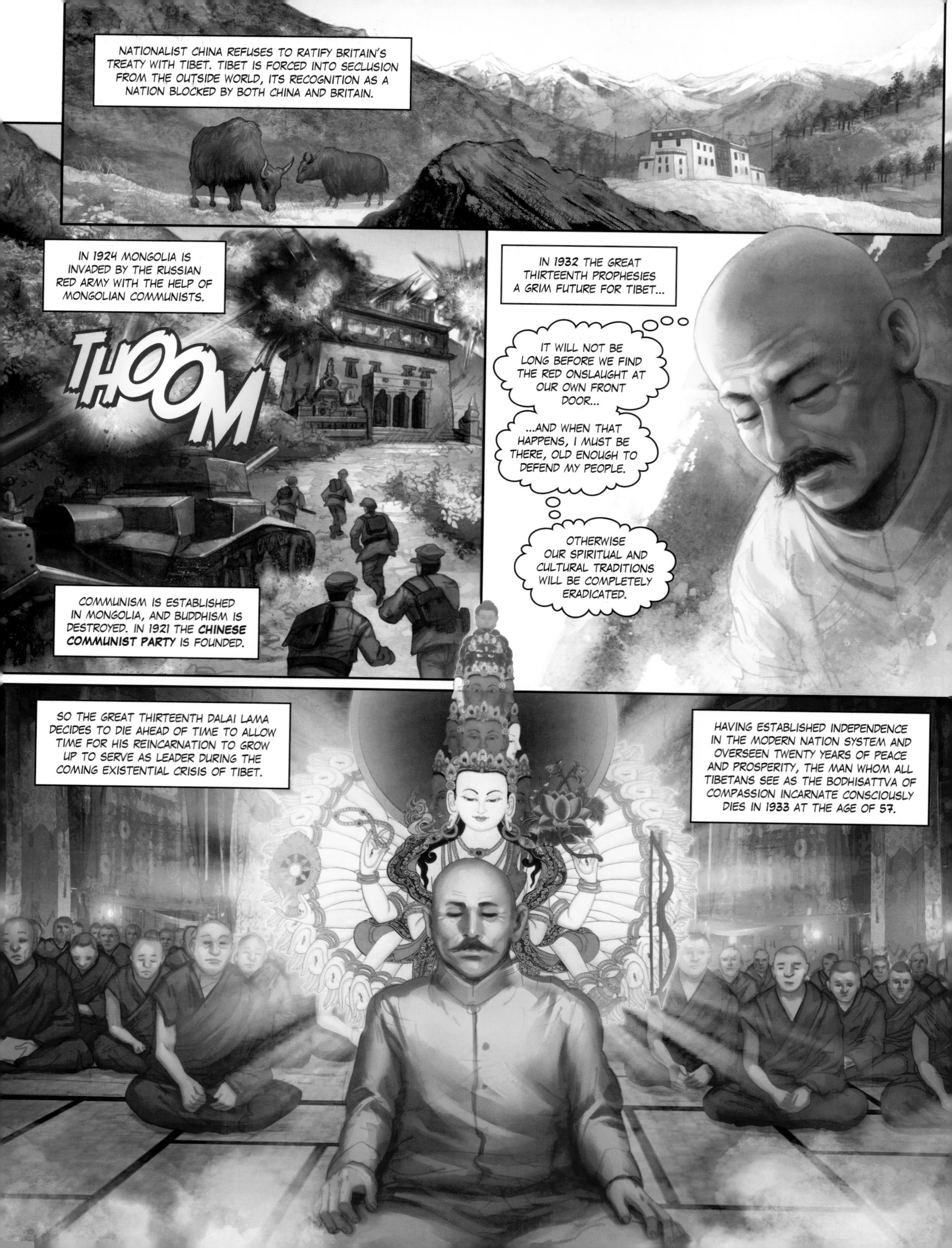
NATIONALIST CHINA REFUSES TO RATIFY BRITAIN'S TREATY WITH TIBET. TIBET IS FORCED INTO SECLUSION FROM THE OUTSIDE WORLD, ITS RECOGNITION AS A NATION BLOCKED BY BOTH CHINA AND BRITAIN.
IN 1924 MONGOLIA IS INVADED BY THE RUSSIAN RED ARMY WITH THE HELP OF MONGOLIAN COMMUNISTS.
THOOM
COMMUNISM IS ESTABLISHED IN MONGOLIA, AND BUDDHISM IS DESTROYED. IN 1921 THE **CHINESE COMMUNIST PARTY** IS FOUNDED.
IN 1932 THE GREAT THIRTEENTH PROPHESIES A GRIM FUTURE FOR TIBET...
IT WILL NOT BE LONG BEFORE WE FIND THE RED ONSLAUGHT AT OUR OWN FRONT DOOR...
...AND WHEN THAT HAPPENS, I MUST BE THERE, OLD ENOUGH TO DEFEND MY PEOPLE.
OTHERWISE OUR SPIRITUAL AND CULTURAL TRADITIONS WILL BE COMPLETELY ERADICATED.
SO THE GREAT THIRTEENTH DALAI LAMA DECIDES TO DIE AHEAD OF TIME TO ALLOW TIME FOR HIS REINCARNATION TO GROW UP TO SERVE AS LEADER DURING THE COMING EXISTENTIAL CRISIS OF TIBET.
HAVING ESTABLISHED INDEPENDENCE IN THE MODERN NATION SYSTEM AND OVERSEEN TWENTY YEARS OF PEACE AND PROSPERITY, THE MAN WHOM ALL TIBETANS SEE AS THE BODHISATTVA OF COMPASSION INCARNATE CONSCIOUSLY DIES IN 1933 AT THE AGE OF 57.

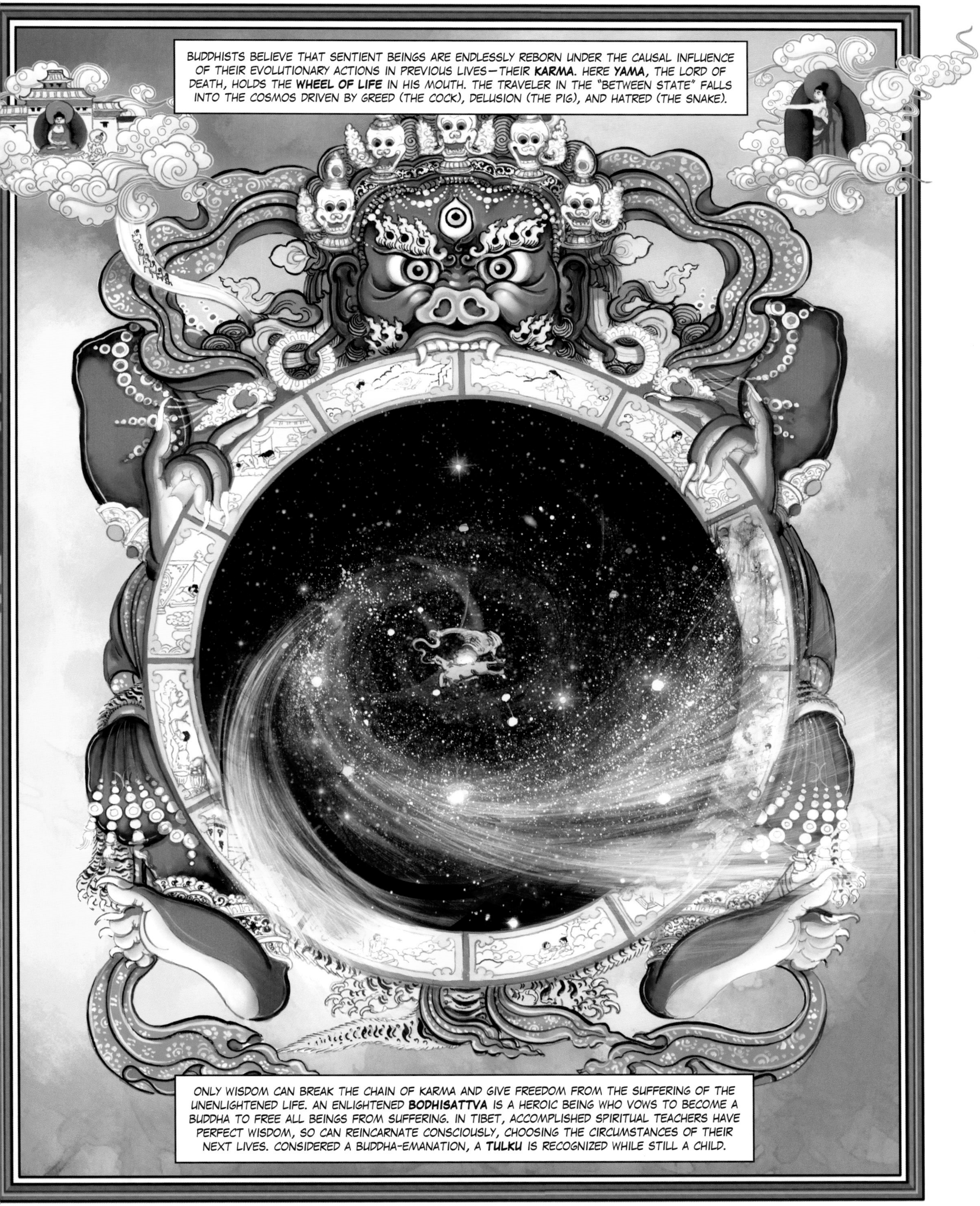
BUDDHISTS BELIEVE THAT SENTIENT BEINGS ARE ENDLESSLY REBORN UNDER THE CAUSAL INFLUENCE OF THEIR EVOLUTIONARY ACTIONS IN PREVIOUS LIVES—THEIR **KARMA**. HERE **YAMA**, THE LORD OF DEATH, HOLDS THE **WHEEL OF LIFE** IN HIS MOUTH. THE TRAVELER IN THE "BETWEEN STATE" FALLS INTO THE COSMOS DRIVEN BY GREED (THE COCK), DELUSION (THE PIG), AND HATRED (THE SNAKE).
ONLY WISDOM CAN BREAK THE CHAIN OF KARMA AND GIVE FREEDOM FROM THE SUFFERING OF THE UNENLIGHTENED LIFE. AN ENLIGHTENED **BODHISATTVA** IS A HEROIC BEING WHO VOWS TO BECOME A BUDDHA TO FREE ALL BEINGS FROM SUFFERING. IN TIBET, ACCOMPLISHED SPIRITUAL TEACHERS HAVE PERFECT WISDOM, SO CAN REINCARNATE CONSCIOUSLY, CHOOSING THE CIRCUMSTANCES OF THEIR NEXT LIVES. CONSIDERED A BUDDHA-EMANATION, A **TULKU** IS RECOGNIZED WHILE STILL A CHILD.

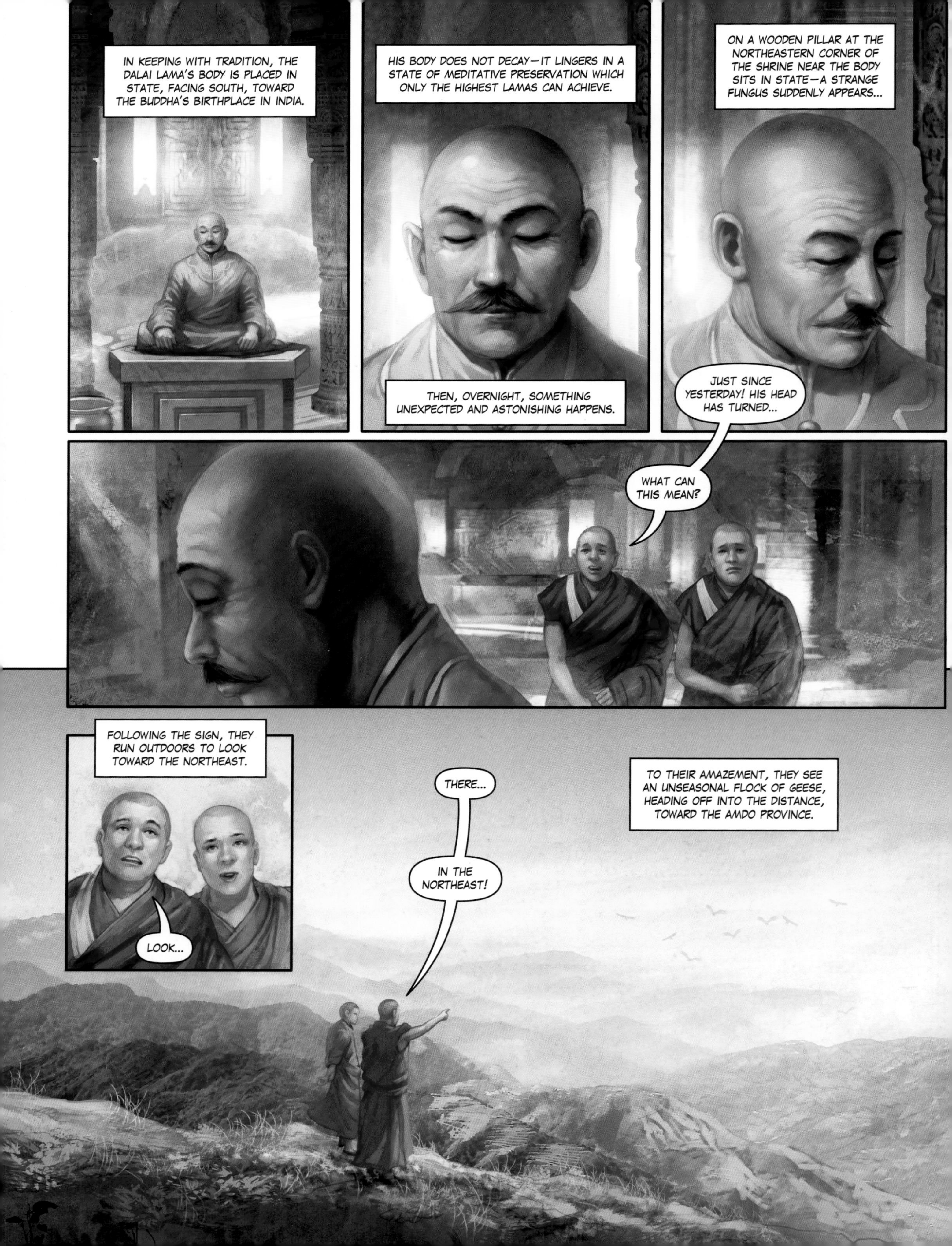
IN KEEPING WITH TRADITION, THE DALAI LAMA'S BODY IS PLACED IN STATE, FACING SOUTH, TOWARD THE BUDDHA'S BIRTHPLACE IN INDIA.
HIS BODY DOES NOT DECAY—IT LINGERS IN A STATE OF MEDITATIVE PRESERVATION WHICH ONLY THE HIGHEST LAMAS CAN ACHIEVE.
THEN, OVERNIGHT, SOMETHING UNEXPECTED AND ASTONISHING HAPPENS.
ON A WOODEN PILLAR AT THE NORTHEASTERN CORNER OF THE SHRINE NEAR THE BODY SITS IN STATE—A STRANGE FUNGUS SUDDENLY APPEARS...
JUST SINCE YESTERDAY! HIS HEAD HAS TURNED...
WHAT CAN THIS MEAN?
FOLLOWING THE SIGN, THEY RUN OUTDOORS TO LOOK TOWARD THE NORTHEAST.
LOOK...
THERE...
IN THE NORTHEAST!
TO THEIR AMAZEMENT, THEY SEE AN UNSEASONAL FLOCK OF GEESE, HEADING OFF INTO THE DISTANCE, TOWARD THE AMDO PROVINCE.

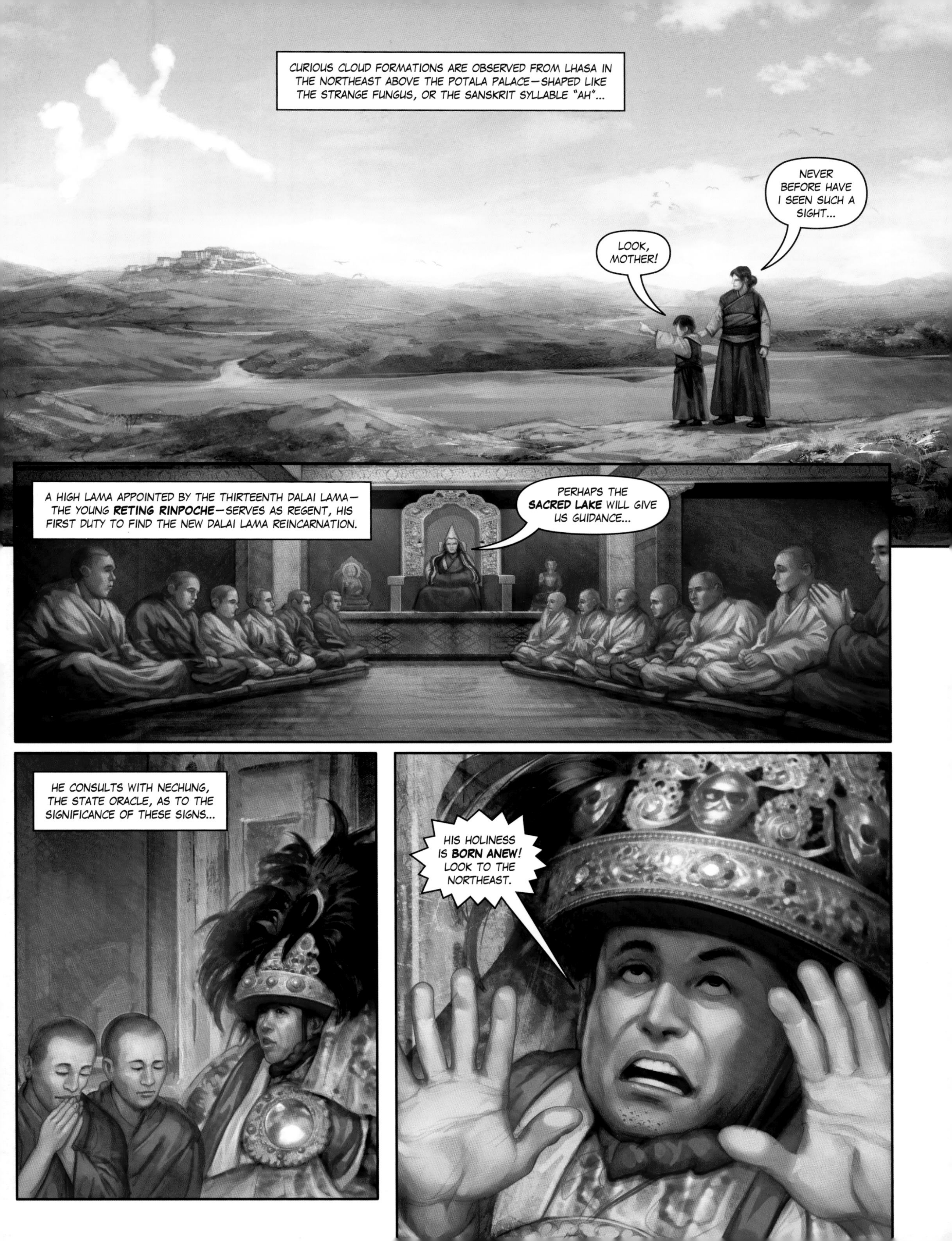
CURIOUS CLOUD FORMATIONS ARE OBSERVED FROM LHASA IN THE NORTHEAST ABOVE THE POTALA PALACE—SHAPED LIKE THE STRANGE FUNGUS, OR THE SANSKRIT SYLLABLE "AH"...
LOOK, MOTHER!
NEVER BEFORE HAVE I SEEN SUCH A SIGHT...
A HIGH LAMA APPOINTED BY THE THIRTEENTH DALAI LAMA—THE YOUNG **RETING RINPOCHE**—SERVES AS REGENT, HIS FIRST DUTY TO FIND THE NEW DALAI LAMA REINCARNATION.
PERHAPS THE **SACRED LAKE** WILL GIVE US GUIDANCE...
HE CONSULTS WITH NECHUNG, THE STATE ORACLE, AS TO THE SIGNIFICANCE OF THESE SIGNS...
HIS HOLINESS IS **BORN ANEW**! LOOK TO THE NORTHEAST.

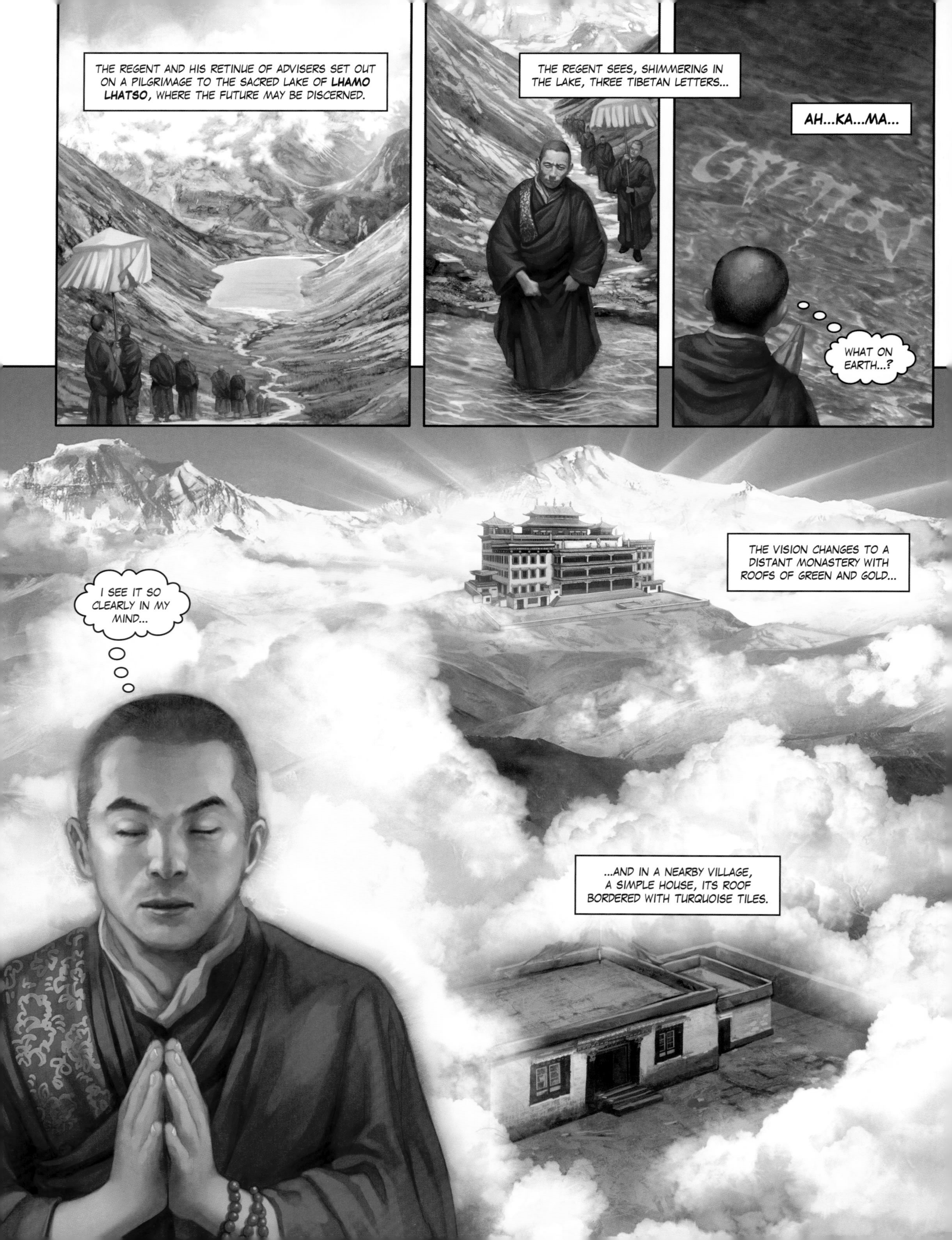

THE REGENT AND HIS RETINUE OF ADVISERS SET OUT ON A PILGRIMAGE TO THE SACRED LAKE OF **LHAMO LHATSO**, WHERE THE FUTURE MAY BE DISCERNED.
THE REGENT SEES, SHIMMERING IN THE LAKE, THREE TIBETAN LETTERS...
AH...KA...MA...
WHAT ON EARTH...?
THE VISION CHANGES TO A DISTANT MONASTERY WITH ROOFS OF GREEN AND GOLD...
I SEE IT SO CLEARLY IN MY MIND...
...AND IN A NEARBY VILLAGE, A SIMPLE HOUSE, ITS ROOF BORDERED WITH TURQUOISE TILES.

1936—TIBET'S NORTHEASTERN PROVINCE OF AMDO...

SINCE THE BREAKUP OF THE MANCHU EMPIRE, LOCAL CHINESE WARLORDS HAVE ASSERTED CONTROL, BUT IN SMALL FARMING COMMUNITIES SUCH AS THE VILLAGE OF **TAKTSER**...

...THE CHINESE HAVE LITTLE INFLUENCE.

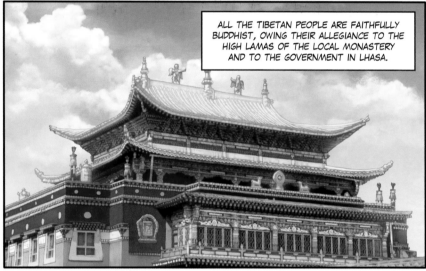

ALL THE TIBETAN PEOPLE ARE FAITHFULLY BUDDHIST, OWING THEIR ALLEGIANCE TO THE HIGH LAMAS OF THE LOCAL MONASTERY AND TO THE GOVERNMENT IN LHASA.

THE PEOPLE TURN THEIR PRAYER WHEELS, PRAYING FOR THE BIRTH OF THE NEW DALAI LAMA.

23

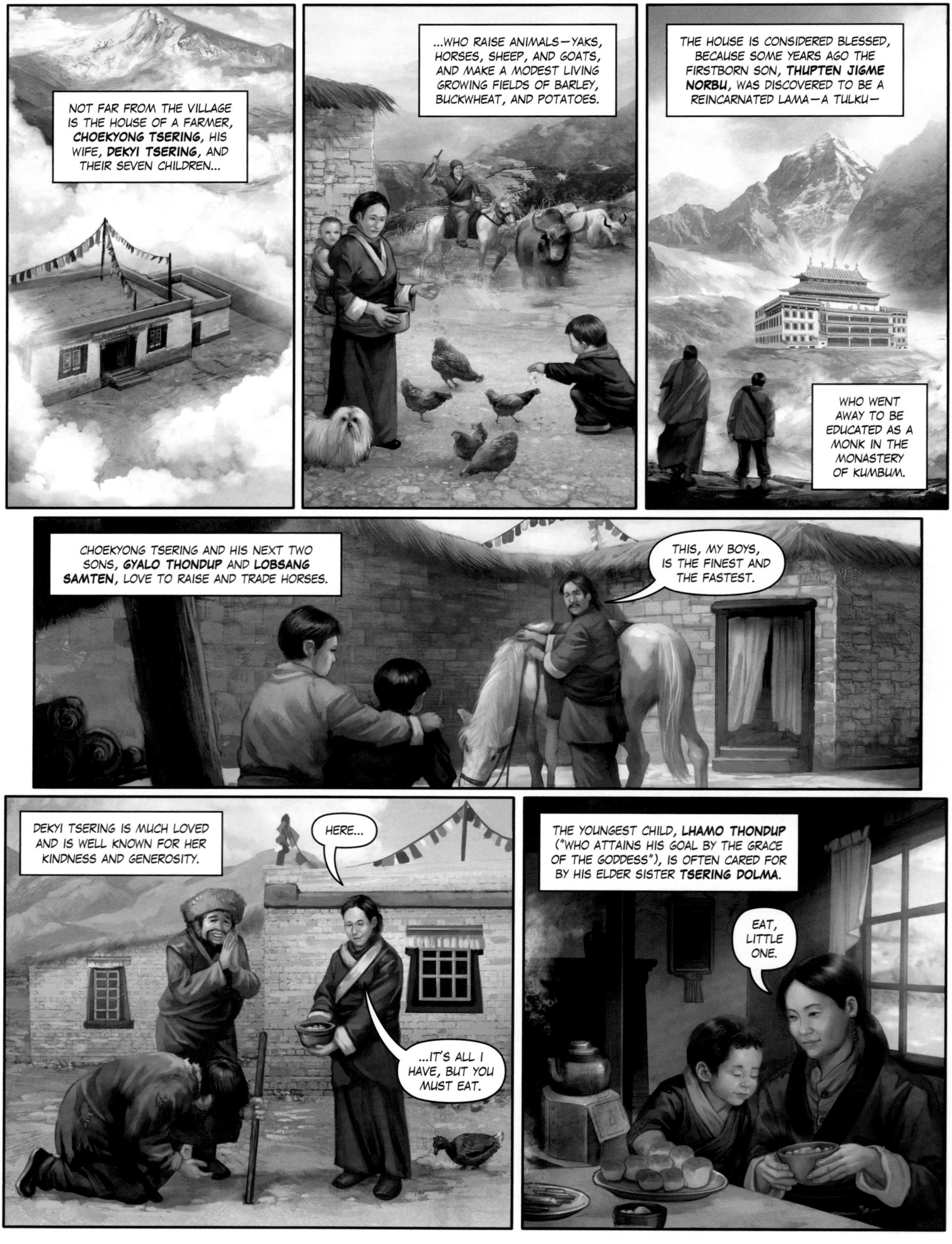
NOT FAR FROM THE VILLAGE IS THE HOUSE OF A FARMER, **CHOEKYONG TSERING**, HIS WIFE, **DEKYI TSERING**, AND THEIR SEVEN CHILDREN...
...WHO RAISE ANIMALS—YAKS, HORSES, SHEEP, AND GOATS, AND MAKE A MODEST LIVING GROWING FIELDS OF BARLEY, BUCKWHEAT, AND POTATOES.
THE HOUSE IS CONSIDERED BLESSED, BECAUSE SOME YEARS AGO THE FIRSTBORN SON, **THUPTEN JIGME NORBU**, WAS DISCOVERED TO BE A REINCARNATED LAMA—A TULKU—
WHO WENT AWAY TO BE EDUCATED AS A MONK IN THE MONASTERY OF KUMBUM.
CHOEKYONG TSERING AND HIS NEXT TWO SONS, **GYALO THONDUP** AND **LOBSANG SAMTEN**, LOVE TO RAISE AND TRADE HORSES.
THIS, MY BOYS, IS THE FINEST AND THE FASTEST.
DEKYI TSERING IS MUCH LOVED AND IS WELL KNOWN FOR HER KINDNESS AND GENEROSITY.
HERE...
...IT'S ALL I HAVE, BUT YOU MUST EAT.
THE YOUNGEST CHILD, **LHAMO THONDUP** ("WHO ATTAINS HIS GOAL BY THE GRACE OF THE GODDESS"), IS OFTEN CARED FOR BY HIS ELDER SISTER **TSERING DOLMA**.
EAT, LITTLE ONE.

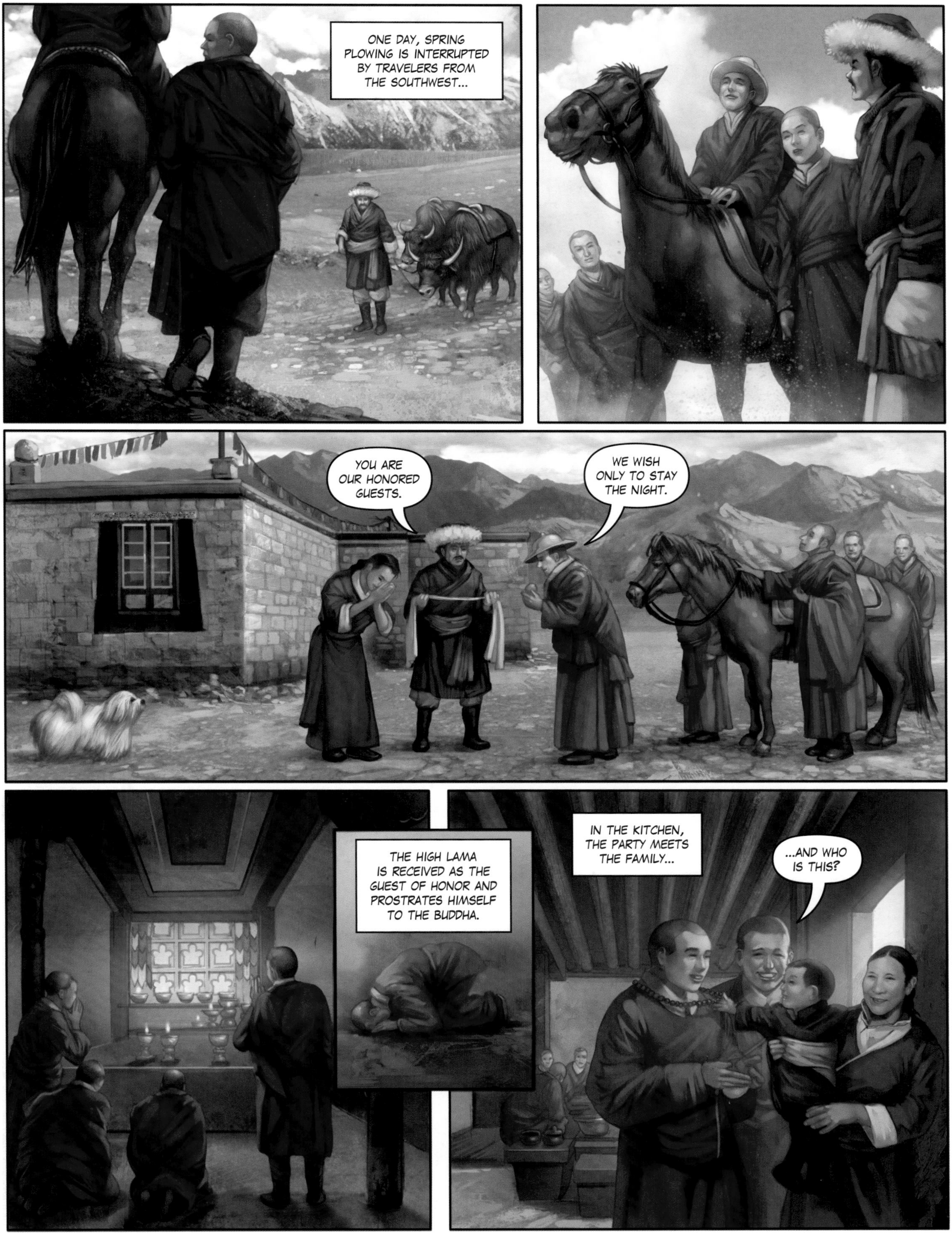
ONE DAY, SPRING PLOWING IS INTERRUPTED BY TRAVELERS FROM THE SOUTHWEST...
YOU ARE OUR HONORED GUESTS.
WE WISH ONLY TO STAY THE NIGHT.
THE HIGH LAMA IS RECEIVED AS THE GUEST OF HONOR AND PROSTRATES HIMSELF TO THE BUDDHA.
IN THE KITCHEN, THE PARTY MEETS THE FAMILY...
...AND WHO IS THIS?

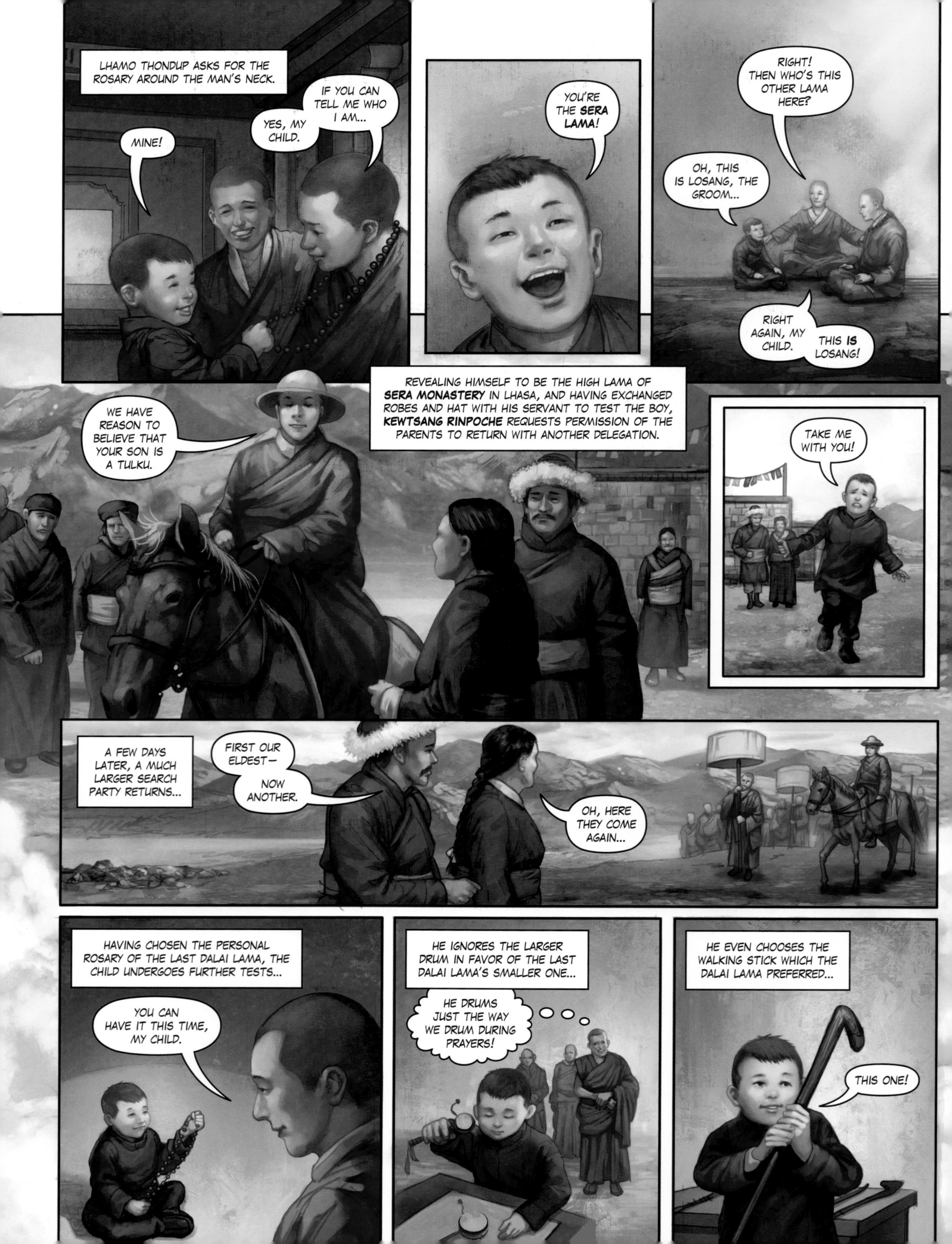

LHAMO THONDUP ASKS FOR THE ROSARY AROUND THE MAN'S NECK.
MINE!
YES, MY CHILD.
IF YOU CAN TELL ME WHO I AM...
YOU'RE THE **SERA LAMA**!
RIGHT! THEN WHO'S THIS OTHER LAMA HERE?
OH, THIS IS LOSANG, THE GROOM...
RIGHT AGAIN, MY CHILD.
THIS **IS** LOSANG!
REVEALING HIMSELF TO BE THE HIGH LAMA OF **SERA MONASTERY** IN LHASA, AND HAVING EXCHANGED ROBES AND HAT WITH HIS SERVANT TO TEST THE BOY, **KEWTSANG RINPOCHE** REQUESTS PERMISSION OF THE PARENTS TO RETURN WITH ANOTHER DELEGATION.
WE HAVE REASON TO BELIEVE THAT YOUR SON IS A TULKU.
TAKE ME WITH YOU!
A FEW DAYS LATER, A MUCH LARGER SEARCH PARTY RETURNS...
FIRST OUR ELDEST—
NOW ANOTHER.
OH, HERE THEY COME AGAIN...
HAVING CHOSEN THE PERSONAL ROSARY OF THE LAST DALAI LAMA, THE CHILD UNDERGOES FURTHER TESTS...
YOU CAN HAVE IT THIS TIME, MY CHILD.
HE IGNORES THE LARGER DRUM IN FAVOR OF THE LAST DALAI LAMA'S SMALLER ONE...
HE DRUMS JUST THE WAY WE DRUM DURING PRAYERS!
HE EVEN CHOOSES THE WALKING STICK WHICH THE DALAI LAMA PREFERRED...
THIS ONE!

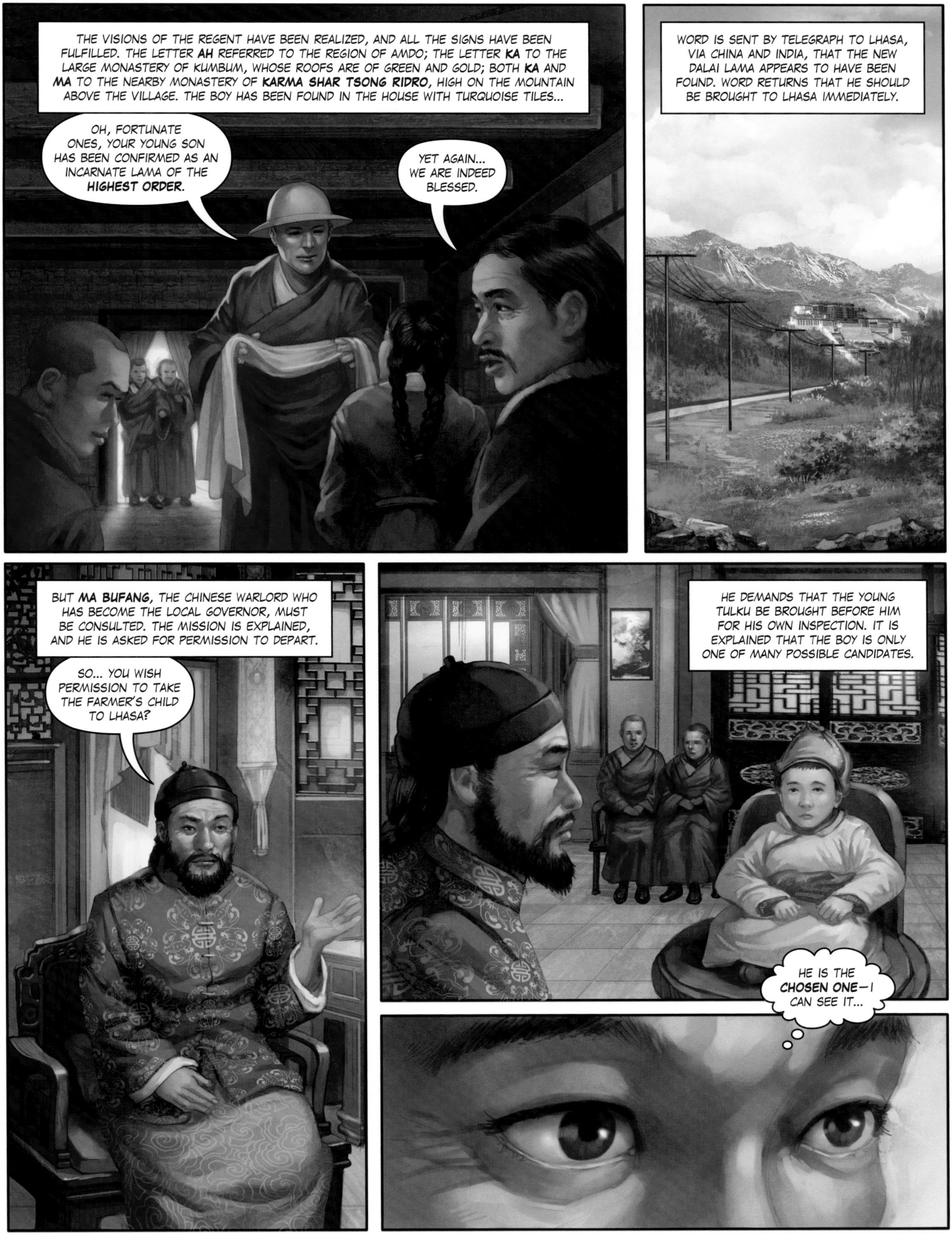

THE VISIONS OF THE REGENT HAVE BEEN REALIZED, AND ALL THE SIGNS HAVE BEEN FULFILLED. THE LETTER AH REFERRED TO THE REGION OF AMDO; THE LETTER KA TO THE LARGE MONASTERY OF KUMBUM, WHOSE ROOFS ARE OF GREEN AND GOLD; BOTH KA AND MA TO THE NEARBY MONASTERY OF KARMA SHAR TSONG RIDRO, HIGH ON THE MOUNTAIN ABOVE THE VILLAGE. THE BOY HAS BEEN FOUND IN THE HOUSE WITH TURQUOISE TILES...
OH, FORTUNATE ONES, YOUR YOUNG SON HAS BEEN CONFIRMED AS AN INCARNATE LAMA OF THE HIGHEST ORDER.
YET AGAIN... WE ARE INDEED BLESSED.
WORD IS SENT BY TELEGRAPH TO LHASA, VIA CHINA AND INDIA, THAT THE NEW DALAI LAMA APPEARS TO HAVE BEEN FOUND. WORD RETURNS THAT HE SHOULD BE BROUGHT TO LHASA IMMEDIATELY.
BUT MA BUFANG, THE CHINESE WARLORD WHO HAS BECOME THE LOCAL GOVERNOR, MUST BE CONSULTED. THE MISSION IS EXPLAINED, AND HE IS ASKED FOR PERMISSION TO DEPART.
SO... YOU WISH PERMISSION TO TAKE THE FARMER'S CHILD TO LHASA?
HE DEMANDS THAT THE YOUNG TULKU BE BROUGHT BEFORE HIM FOR HIS OWN INSPECTION. IT IS EXPLAINED THAT THE BOY IS ONLY ONE OF MANY POSSIBLE CANDIDATES.
HE IS THE CHOSEN ONE—I CAN SEE IT...

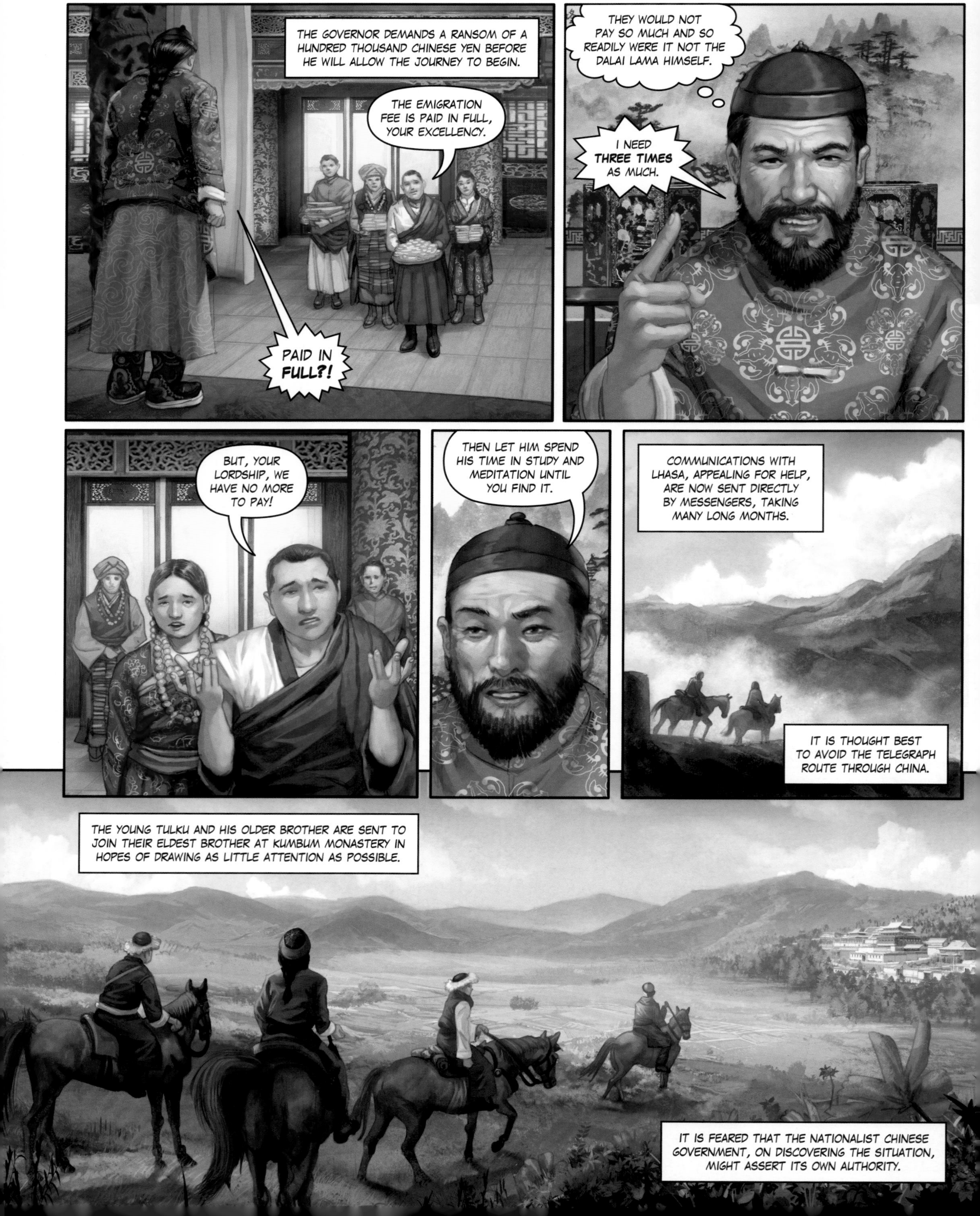

THE GOVERNOR DEMANDS A RANSOM OF A HUNDRED THOUSAND CHINESE YEN BEFORE HE WILL ALLOW THE JOURNEY TO BEGIN.
THE EMIGRATION FEE IS PAID IN FULL, YOUR EXCELLENCY.
PAID IN FULL?!
THEY WOULD NOT PAY SO MUCH AND SO READILY WERE IT NOT THE DALAI LAMA HIMSELF.
I NEED THREE TIMES AS MUCH.
BUT, YOUR LORDSHIP, WE HAVE NO MORE TO PAY!
THEN LET HIM SPEND HIS TIME IN STUDY AND MEDITATION UNTIL YOU FIND IT.
COMMUNICATIONS WITH LHASA, APPEALING FOR HELP, ARE NOW SENT DIRECTLY BY MESSENGERS, TAKING MANY LONG MONTHS.
IT IS THOUGHT BEST TO AVOID THE TELEGRAPH ROUTE THROUGH CHINA.
THE YOUNG TULKU AND HIS OLDER BROTHER ARE SENT TO JOIN THEIR ELDEST BROTHER AT KUMBUM MONASTERY IN HOPES OF DRAWING AS LITTLE ATTENTION AS POSSIBLE.
IT IS FEARED THAT THE NATIONALIST CHINESE GOVERNMENT, ON DISCOVERING THE SITUATION, MIGHT ASSERT ITS OWN AUTHORITY.

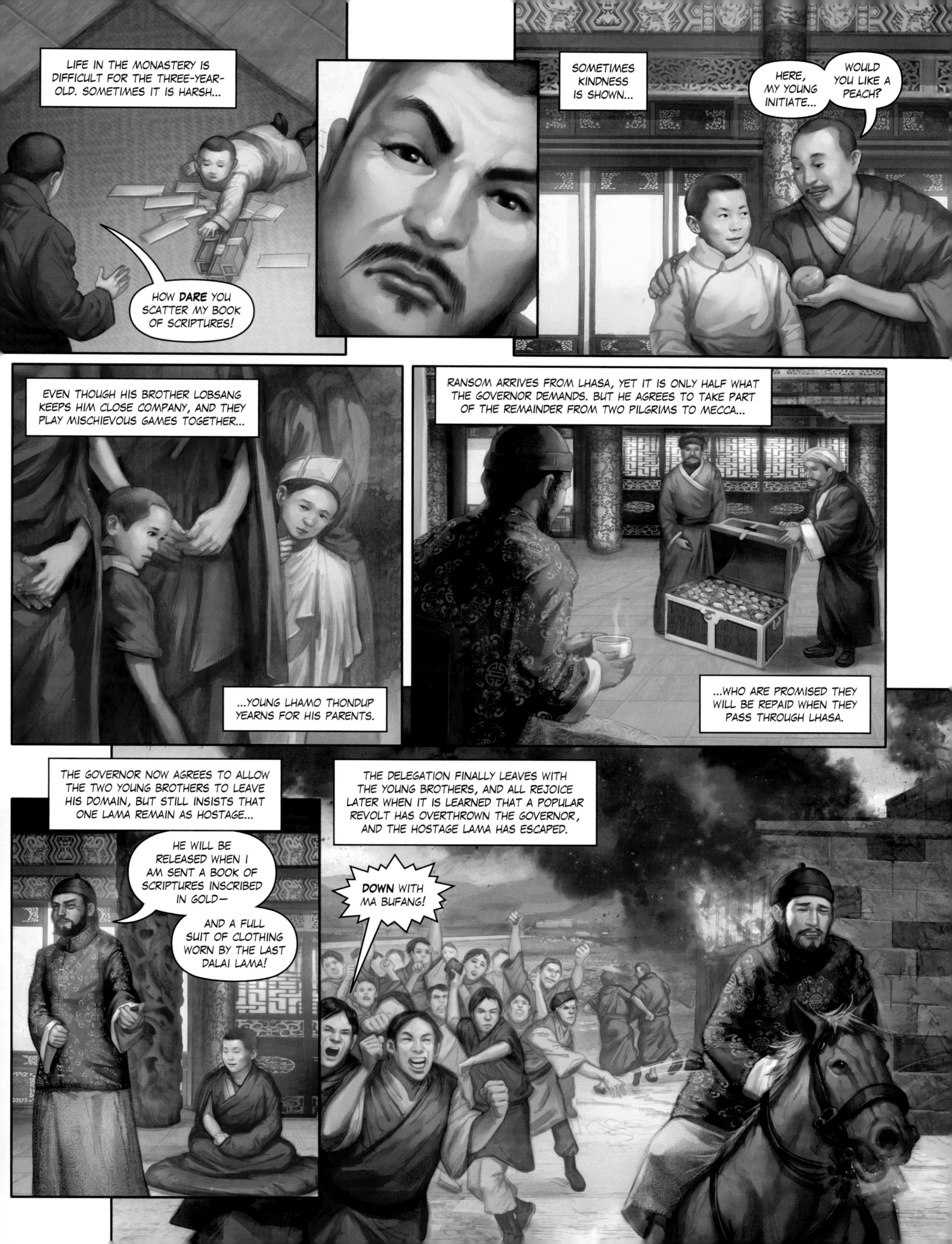
LIFE IN THE MONASTERY IS DIFFICULT FOR THE THREE-YEAR-OLD. SOMETIMES IT IS HARSH...
HOW **DARE** YOU SCATTER MY BOOK OF SCRIPTURES!
SOMETIMES KINDNESS IS SHOWN...
HERE, MY YOUNG INITIATE...
WOULD YOU LIKE A PEACH?
EVEN THOUGH HIS BROTHER LOBSANG KEEPS HIM CLOSE COMPANY, AND THEY PLAY MISCHIEVOUS GAMES TOGETHER...
...YOUNG LHAMO THONDUP YEARNS FOR HIS PARENTS.
RANSOM ARRIVES FROM LHASA, YET IT IS ONLY HALF WHAT THE GOVERNOR DEMANDS. BUT HE AGREES TO TAKE PART OF THE REMAINDER FROM TWO PILGRIMS TO MECCA...
...WHO ARE PROMISED THEY WILL BE REPAID WHEN THEY PASS THROUGH LHASA.
THE GOVERNOR NOW AGREES TO ALLOW THE TWO YOUNG BROTHERS TO LEAVE HIS DOMAIN, BUT STILL INSISTS THAT ONE LAMA REMAIN AS HOSTAGE...
HE WILL BE RELEASED WHEN I AM SENT A BOOK OF SCRIPTURES INSCRIBED IN GOLD—
AND A FULL SUIT OF CLOTHING WORN BY THE LAST DALAI LAMA!
THE DELEGATION FINALLY LEAVES WITH THE YOUNG BROTHERS, AND ALL REJOICE LATER WHEN IT IS LEARNED THAT A POPULAR REVOLT HAS OVERTHROWN THE GOVERNOR, AND THE HOSTAGE LAMA HAS ESCAPED.
DOWN WITH MA BUFANG!

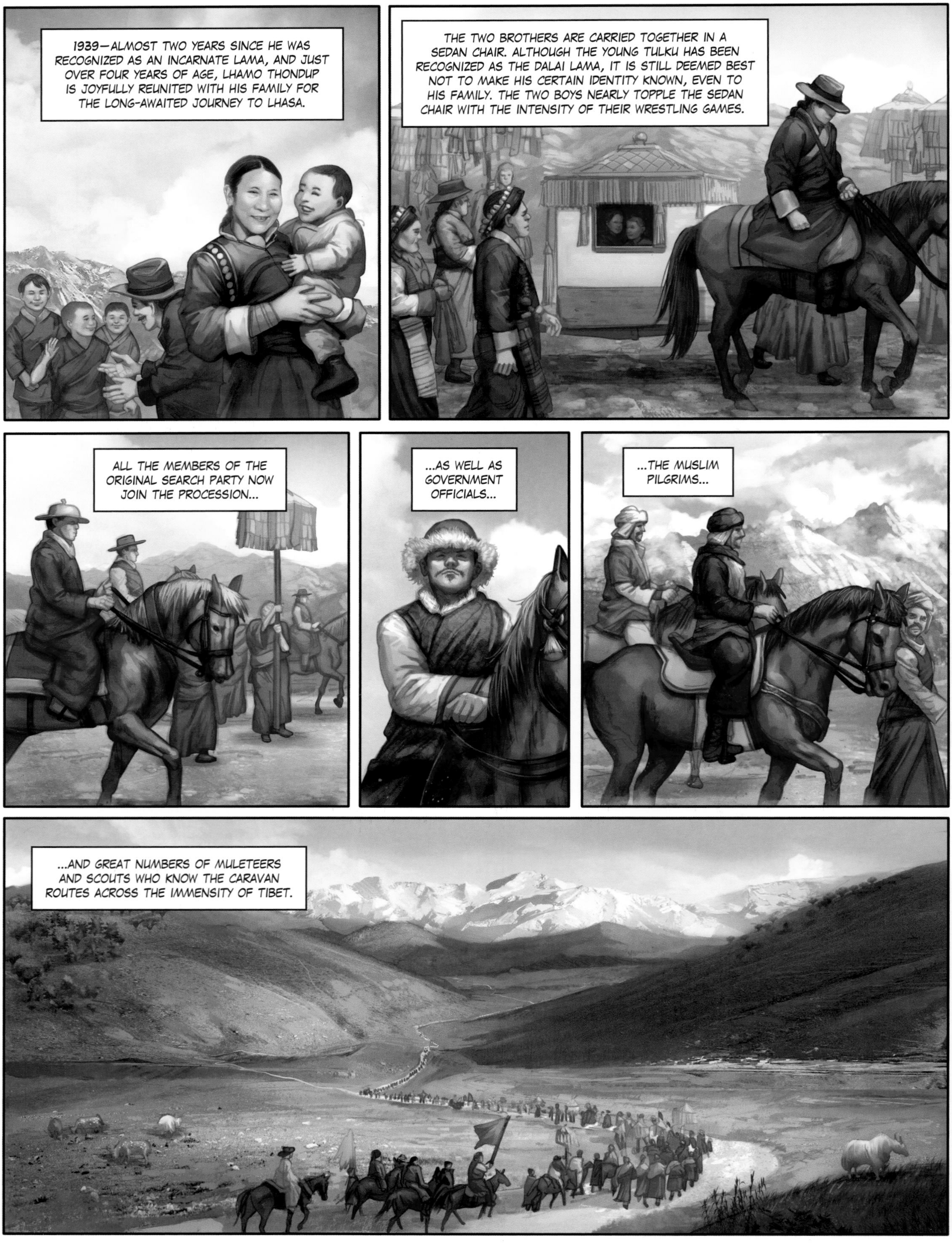
1939—ALMOST TWO YEARS SINCE HE WAS RECOGNIZED AS AN INCARNATE LAMA, AND JUST OVER FOUR YEARS OF AGE, LHAMO THONDUP IS JOYFULLY REUNITED WITH HIS FAMILY FOR THE LONG-AWAITED JOURNEY TO LHASA.
THE TWO BROTHERS ARE CARRIED TOGETHER IN A SEDAN CHAIR. ALTHOUGH THE YOUNG TULKU HAS BEEN RECOGNIZED AS THE DALAI LAMA, IT IS STILL DEEMED BEST NOT TO MAKE HIS CERTAIN IDENTITY KNOWN, EVEN TO HIS FAMILY. THE TWO BOYS NEARLY TOPPLE THE SEDAN CHAIR WITH THE INTENSITY OF THEIR WRESTLING GAMES.
ALL THE MEMBERS OF THE ORIGINAL SEARCH PARTY NOW JOIN THE PROCESSION...
...AS WELL AS GOVERNMENT OFFICIALS...
...THE MUSLIM PILGRIMS...
...AND GREAT NUMBERS OF MULETEERS AND SCOUTS WHO KNOW THE CARAVAN ROUTES ACROSS THE IMMENSITY OF TIBET.

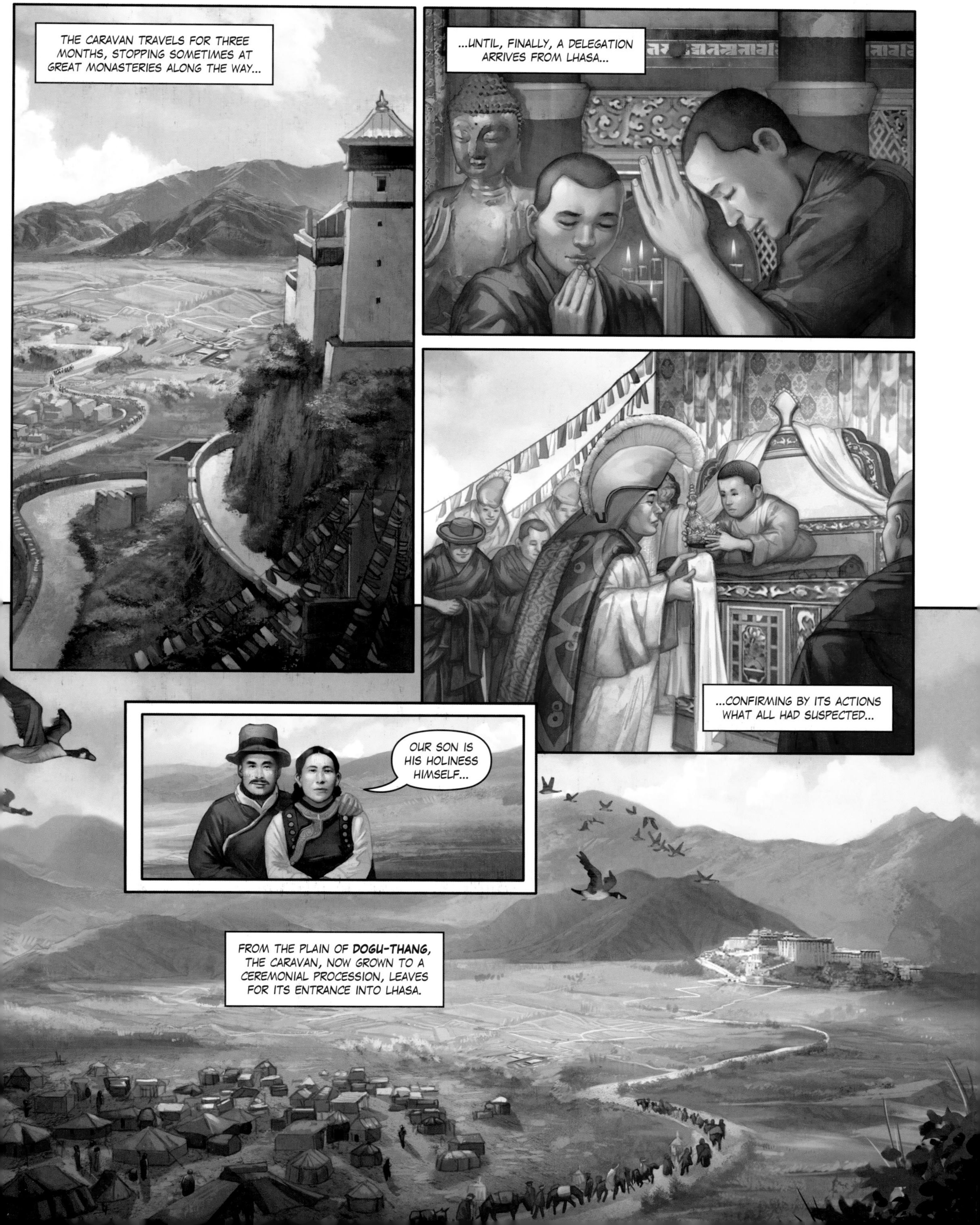
THE CARAVAN TRAVELS FOR THREE MONTHS, STOPPING SOMETIMES AT GREAT MONASTERIES ALONG THE WAY...
...UNTIL, FINALLY, A DELEGATION ARRIVES FROM LHASA...
...CONFIRMING BY ITS ACTIONS WHAT ALL HAD SUSPECTED...
OUR SON IS HIS HOLINESS HIMSELF...
FROM THE PLAIN OF **DOGU-THANG**, THE CARAVAN, NOW GROWN TO A CEREMONIAL PROCESSION, LEAVES FOR ITS ENTRANCE INTO LHASA.

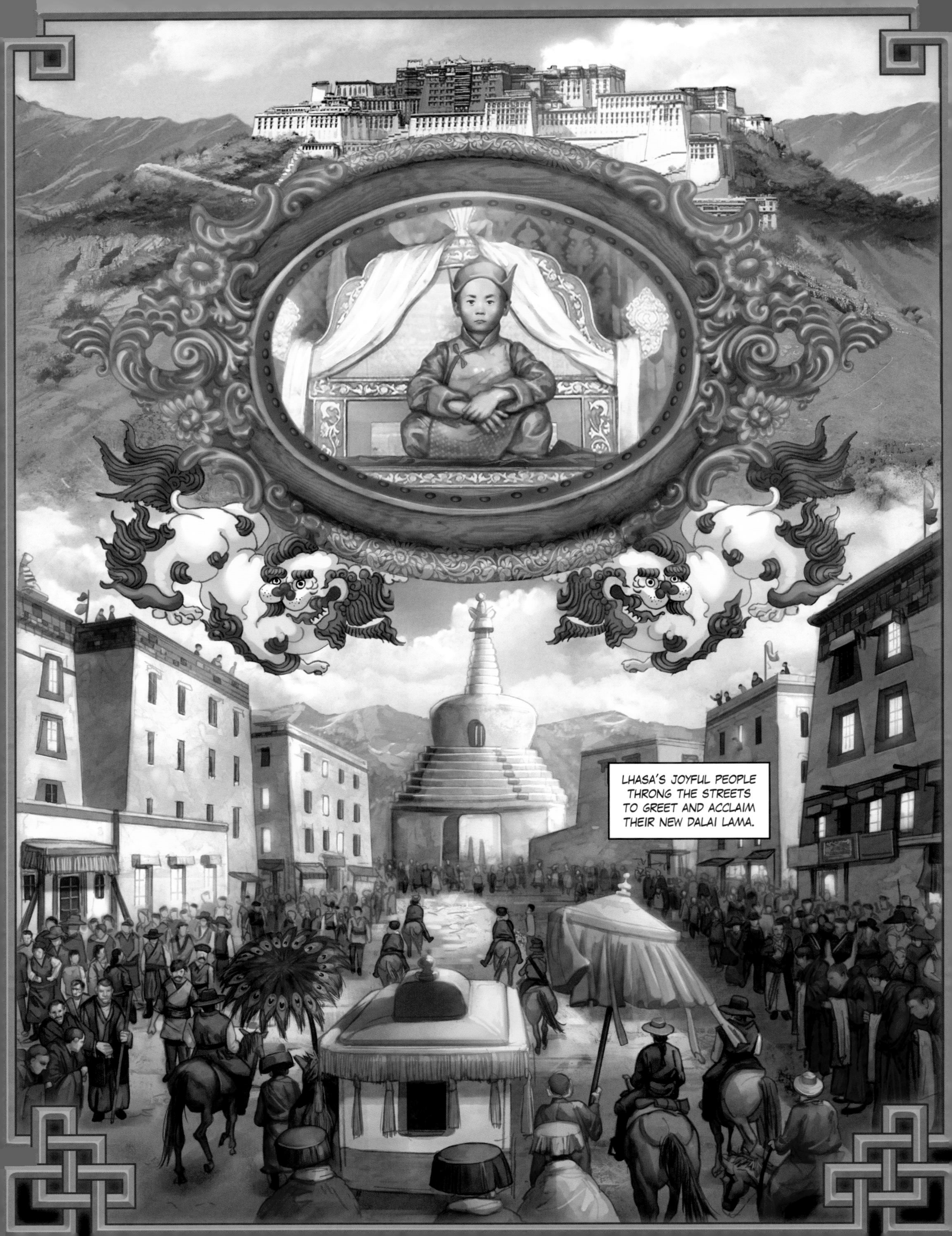
LHASA'S JOYFUL PEOPLE THRONG THE STREETS TO GREET AND ACCLAIM THEIR NEW DALAI LAMA.

PART
TWO

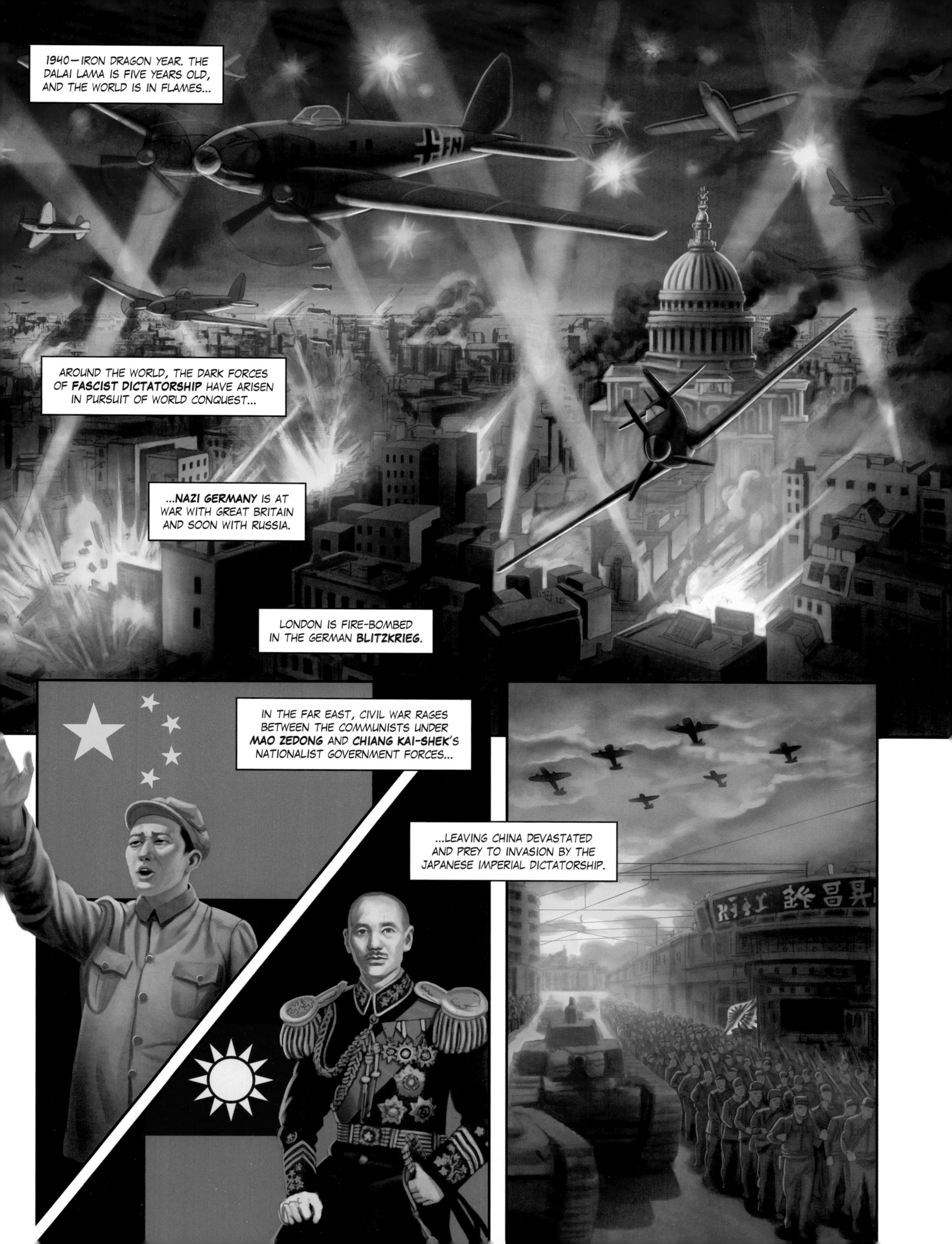
1940—IRON DRAGON YEAR. THE DALAI LAMA IS FIVE YEARS OLD, AND THE WORLD IS IN FLAMES...
AROUND THE WORLD, THE DARK FORCES OF **FASCIST DICTATORSHIP** HAVE ARISEN IN PURSUIT OF WORLD CONQUEST...
...**NAZI GERMANY** IS AT WAR WITH GREAT BRITAIN AND SOON WITH RUSSIA.
LONDON IS FIRE-BOMBED IN THE GERMAN **BLITZKRIEG**.
IN THE FAR EAST, CIVIL WAR RAGES BETWEEN THE COMMUNISTS UNDER **MAO ZEDONG** AND **CHIANG KAI-SHEK**'S NATIONALIST GOVERNMENT FORCES...
...LEAVING CHINA DEVASTATED AND PREY TO INVASION BY THE JAPANESE IMPERIAL DICTATORSHIP.

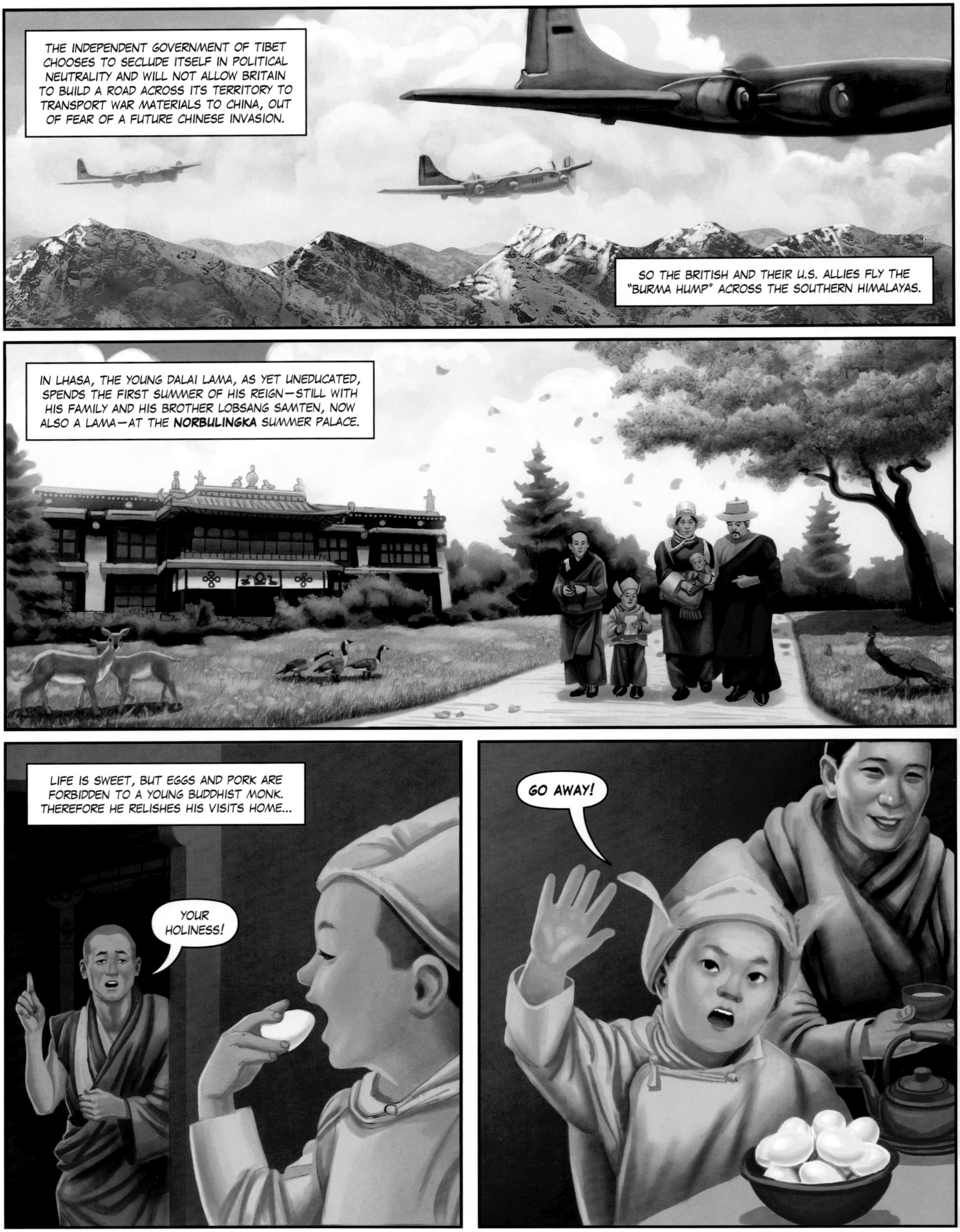

THE INDEPENDENT GOVERNMENT OF TIBET CHOOSES TO SECLUDE ITSELF IN POLITICAL NEUTRALITY AND WILL NOT ALLOW BRITAIN TO BUILD A ROAD ACROSS ITS TERRITORY TO TRANSPORT WAR MATERIALS TO CHINA, OUT OF FEAR OF A FUTURE CHINESE INVASION.
SO THE BRITISH AND THEIR U.S. ALLIES FLY THE "BURMA HUMP" ACROSS THE SOUTHERN HIMALAYAS.
IN LHASA, THE YOUNG DALAI LAMA, AS YET UNEDUCATED, SPENDS THE FIRST SUMMER OF HIS REIGN—STILL WITH HIS FAMILY AND HIS BROTHER LOBSANG SAMTEN, NOW ALSO A LAMA—AT THE NORBULINGKA SUMMER PALACE.
LIFE IS SWEET, BUT EGGS AND PORK ARE FORBIDDEN TO A YOUNG BUDDHIST MONK. THEREFORE HE RELISHES HIS VISITS HOME...
YOUR HOLINESS!
GO AWAY!

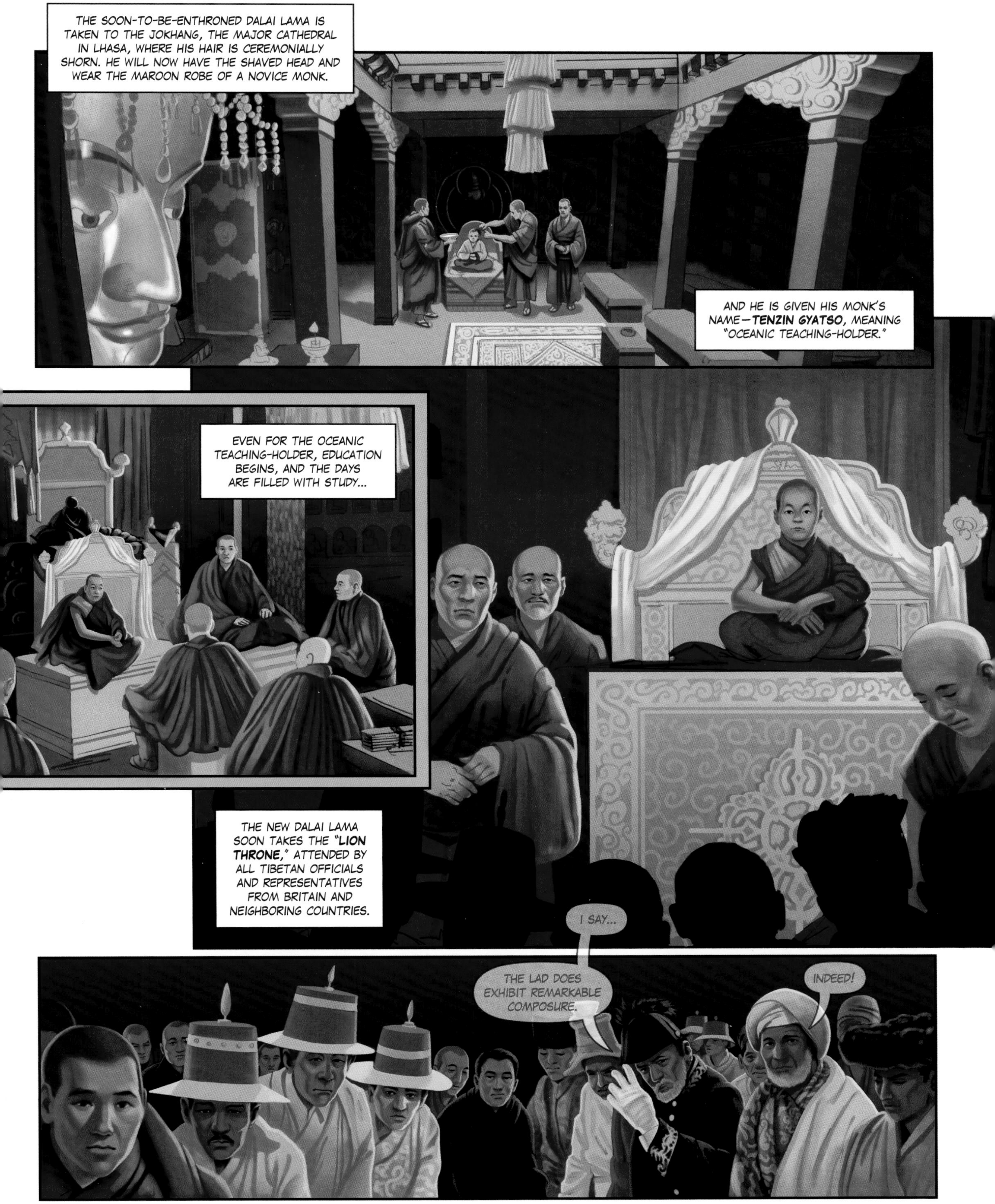
THE SOON-TO-BE-ENTHRONED DALAI LAMA IS TAKEN TO THE JOKHANG, THE MAJOR CATHEDRAL IN LHASA, WHERE HIS HAIR IS CEREMONIALLY SHORN. HE WILL NOW HAVE THE SHAVED HEAD AND WEAR THE MAROON ROBE OF A NOVICE MONK.
AND HE IS GIVEN HIS MONK'S NAME—**TENZIN GYATSO**, MEANING "OCEANIC TEACHING-HOLDER."
EVEN FOR THE OCEANIC TEACHING-HOLDER, EDUCATION BEGINS, AND THE DAYS ARE FILLED WITH STUDY...
THE NEW DALAI LAMA SOON TAKES THE **"LION THRONE,"** ATTENDED BY ALL TIBETAN OFFICIALS AND REPRESENTATIVES FROM BRITAIN AND NEIGHBORING COUNTRIES.
I SAY...
THE LAD DOES EXHIBIT REMARKABLE COMPOSURE.
INDEED!

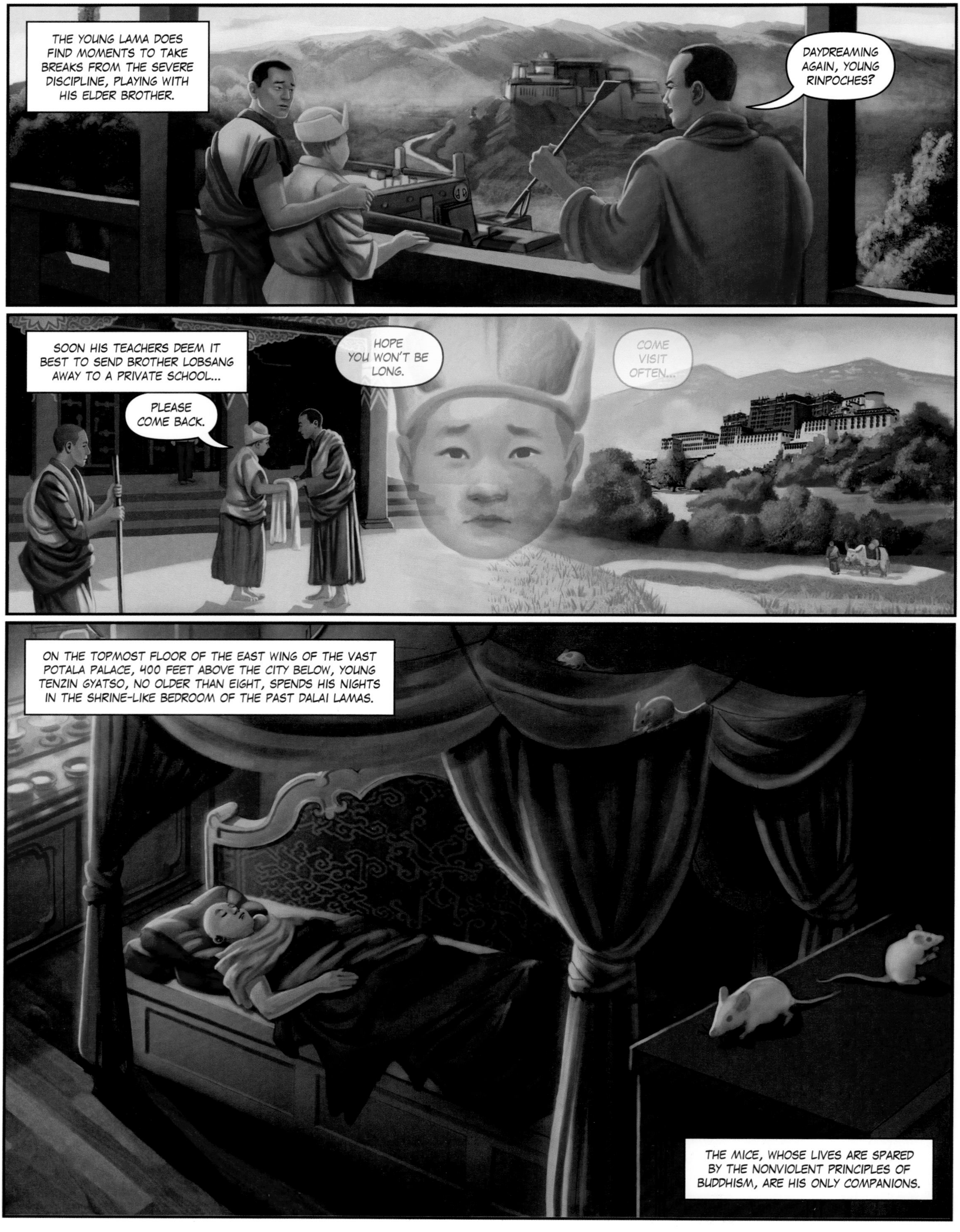
THE YOUNG LAMA DOES FIND MOMENTS TO TAKE BREAKS FROM THE SEVERE DISCIPLINE, PLAYING WITH HIS ELDER BROTHER.
DAYDREAMING AGAIN, YOUNG RINPOCHES?
SOON HIS TEACHERS DEEM IT BEST TO SEND BROTHER LOBSANG AWAY TO A PRIVATE SCHOOL...
PLEASE COME BACK.
HOPE YOU WON'T BE LONG.
COME VISIT OFTEN...
ON THE TOPMOST FLOOR OF THE EAST WING OF THE VAST POTALA PALACE, 400 FEET ABOVE THE CITY BELOW, YOUNG TENZIN GYATSO, NO OLDER THAN EIGHT, SPENDS HIS NIGHTS IN THE SHRINE-LIKE BEDROOM OF THE PAST DALAI LAMAS.
THE MICE, WHOSE LIVES ARE SPARED BY THE NONVIOLENT PRINCIPLES OF BUDDHISM, ARE HIS ONLY COMPANIONS.

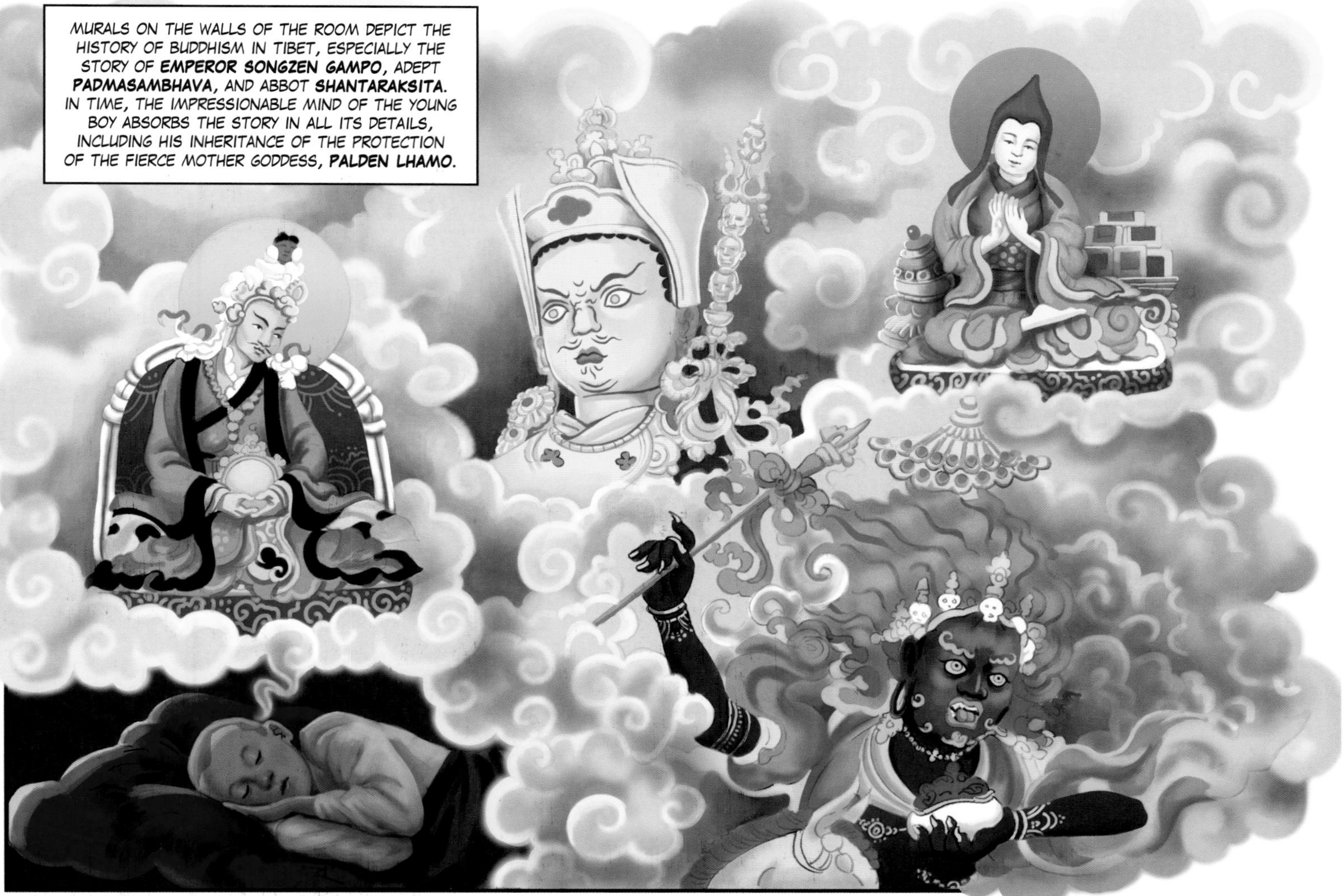
MURALS ON THE WALLS OF THE ROOM DEPICT THE HISTORY OF BUDDHISM IN TIBET, ESPECIALLY THE STORY OF **EMPEROR SONGZEN GAMPO**, ADEPT **PADMASAMBHAVA**, AND ABBOT **SHANTARAKSITA**. IN TIME, THE IMPRESSIONABLE MIND OF THE YOUNG BOY ABSORBS THE STORY IN ALL ITS DETAILS, INCLUDING HIS INHERITANCE OF THE PROTECTION OF THE FIERCE MOTHER GODDESS, **PALDEN LHAMO**.

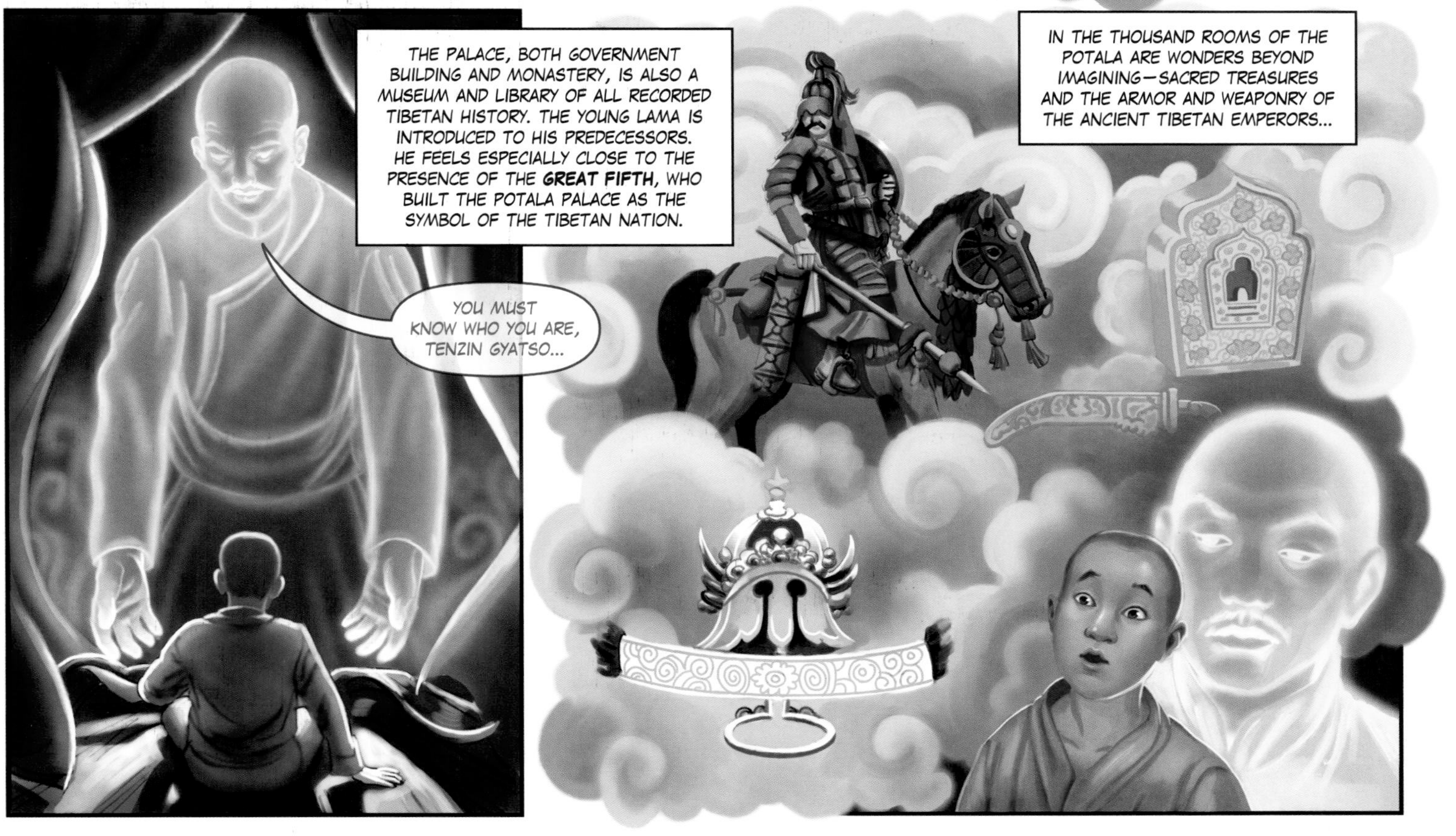
THE PALACE, BOTH GOVERNMENT BUILDING AND MONASTERY, IS ALSO A MUSEUM AND LIBRARY OF ALL RECORDED TIBETAN HISTORY. THE YOUNG LAMA IS INTRODUCED TO HIS PREDECESSORS. HE FEELS ESPECIALLY CLOSE TO THE PRESENCE OF THE **GREAT FIFTH**, WHO BUILT THE POTALA PALACE AS THE SYMBOL OF THE TIBETAN NATION.
YOU MUST KNOW WHO YOU ARE, TENZIN GYATSO...
IN THE THOUSAND ROOMS OF THE POTALA ARE WONDERS BEYOND IMAGINING—SACRED TREASURES AND THE ARMOR AND WEAPONRY OF THE ANCIENT TIBETAN EMPERORS...

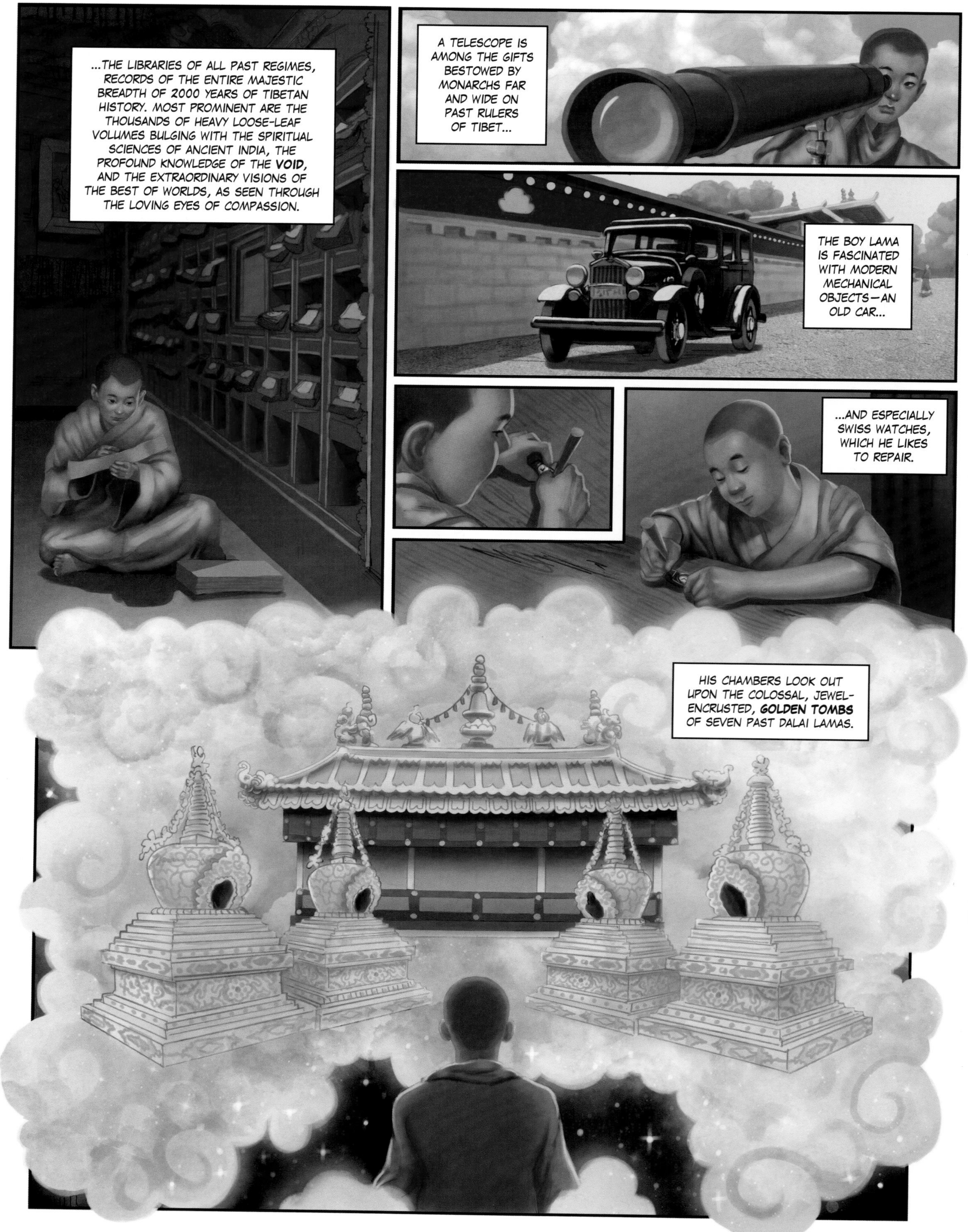
...THE LIBRARIES OF ALL PAST REGIMES, RECORDS OF THE ENTIRE MAJESTIC BREADTH OF 2000 YEARS OF TIBETAN HISTORY. MOST PROMINENT ARE THE THOUSANDS OF HEAVY LOOSE-LEAF VOLUMES BULGING WITH THE SPIRITUAL SCIENCES OF ANCIENT INDIA, THE PROFOUND KNOWLEDGE OF THE **VOID**, AND THE EXTRAORDINARY VISIONS OF THE BEST OF WORLDS, AS SEEN THROUGH THE LOVING EYES OF COMPASSION.
A TELESCOPE IS AMONG THE GIFTS BESTOWED BY MONARCHS FAR AND WIDE ON PAST RULERS OF TIBET...
THE BOY LAMA IS FASCINATED WITH MODERN MECHANICAL OBJECTS—AN OLD CAR...
...AND ESPECIALLY SWISS WATCHES, WHICH HE LIKES TO REPAIR.
HIS CHAMBERS LOOK OUT UPON THE COLOSSAL, JEWEL-ENCRUSTED, **GOLDEN TOMBS** OF SEVEN PAST DALAI LAMAS.

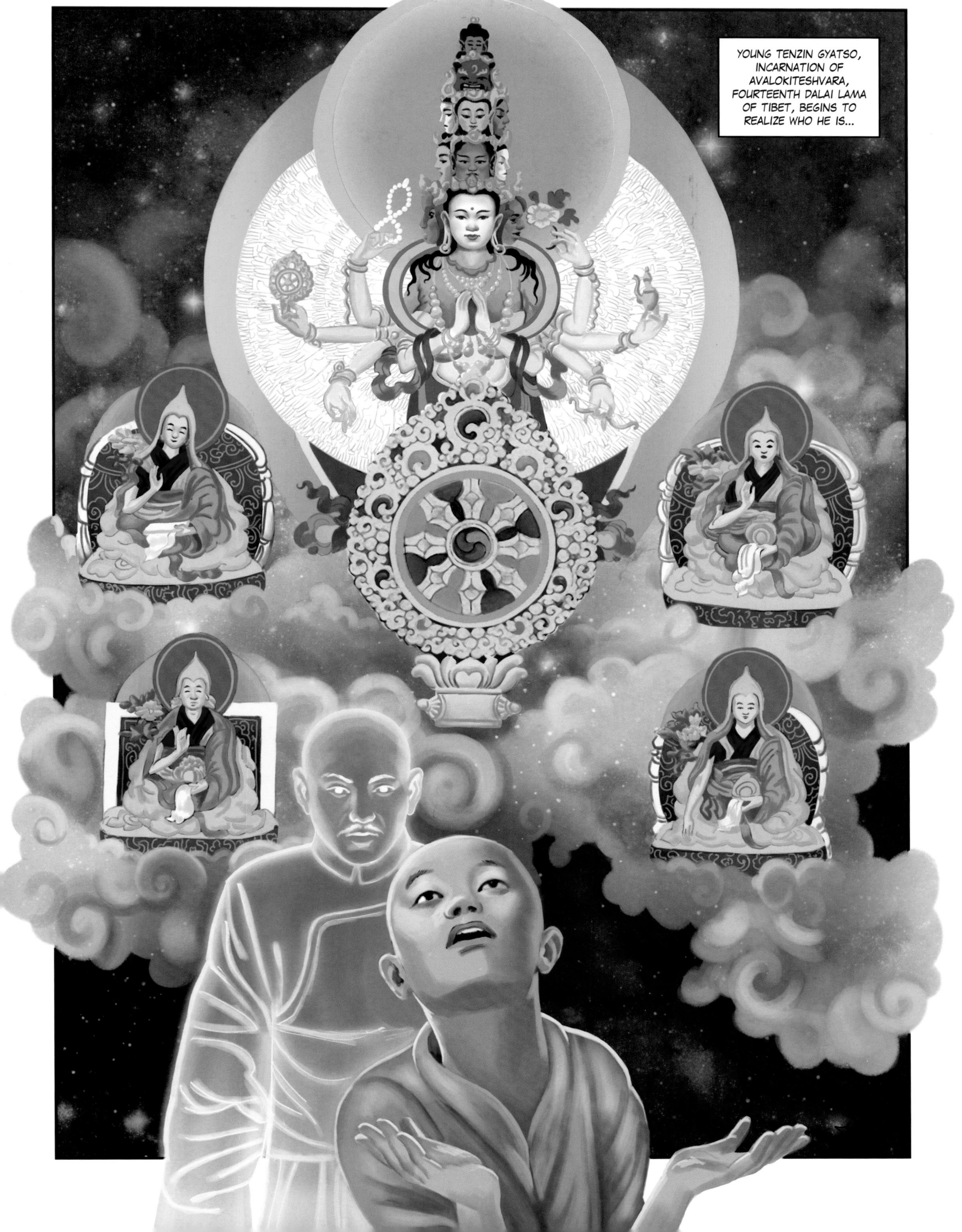
YOUNG TENZIN GYATSO, INCARNATION OF AVALOKITESHVARA, FOURTEENTH DALAI LAMA OF TIBET, BEGINS TO REALIZE WHO HE IS...

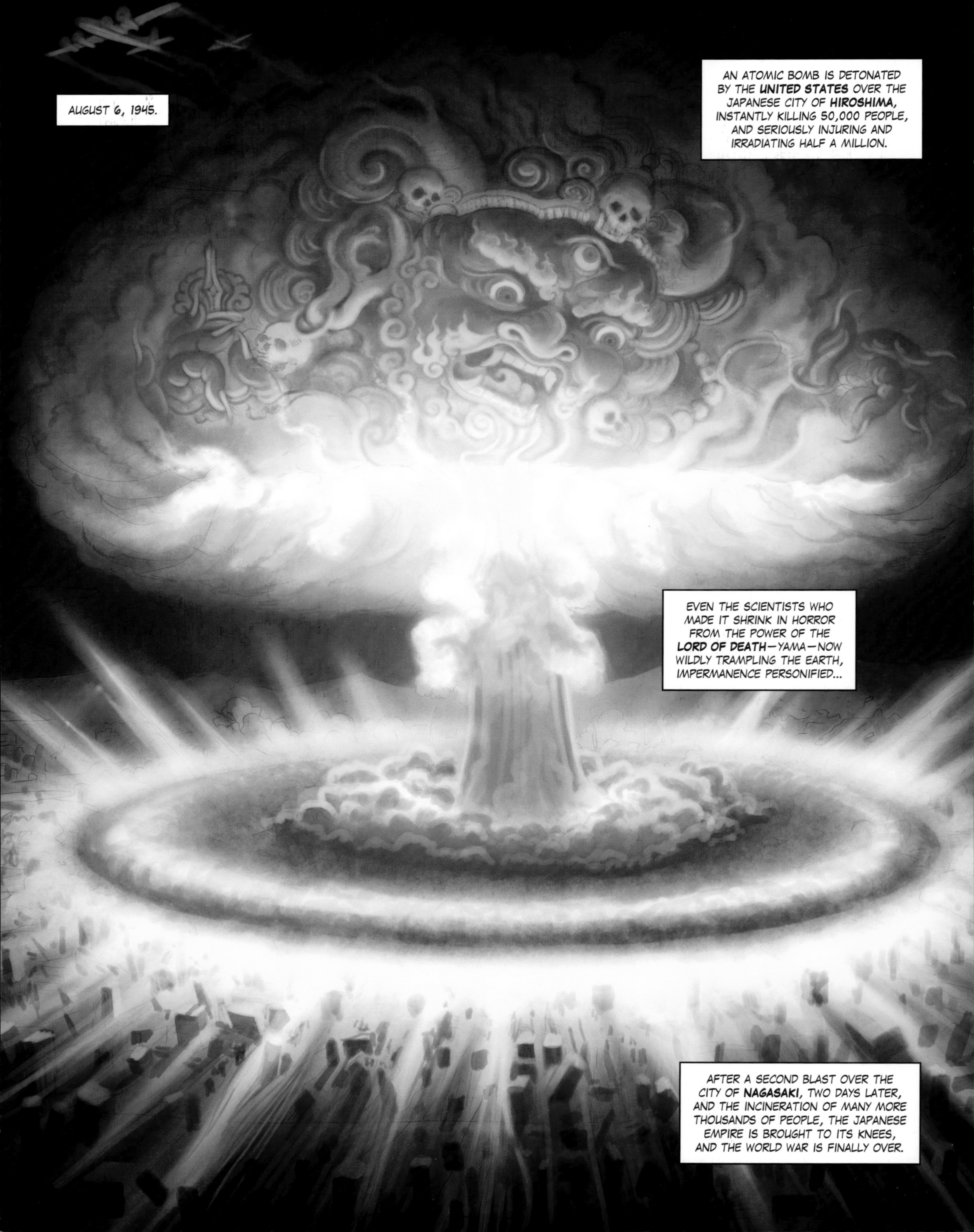
AUGUST 6, 1945.
AN ATOMIC BOMB IS DETONATED BY THE **UNITED STATES** OVER THE JAPANESE CITY OF **HIROSHIMA,** INSTANTLY KILLING 50,000 PEOPLE, AND SERIOUSLY INJURING AND IRRADIATING HALF A MILLION.
EVEN THE SCIENTISTS WHO MADE IT SHRINK IN HORROR FROM THE POWER OF THE **LORD OF DEATH**—YAMA—NOW WILDLY TRAMPLING THE EARTH, IMPERMANENCE PERSONIFIED...
AFTER A SECOND BLAST OVER THE CITY OF **NAGASAKI,** TWO DAYS LATER, AND THE INCINERATION OF MANY MORE THOUSANDS OF PEOPLE, THE JAPANESE EMPIRE IS BROUGHT TO ITS KNEES, AND THE WORLD WAR IS FINALLY OVER.

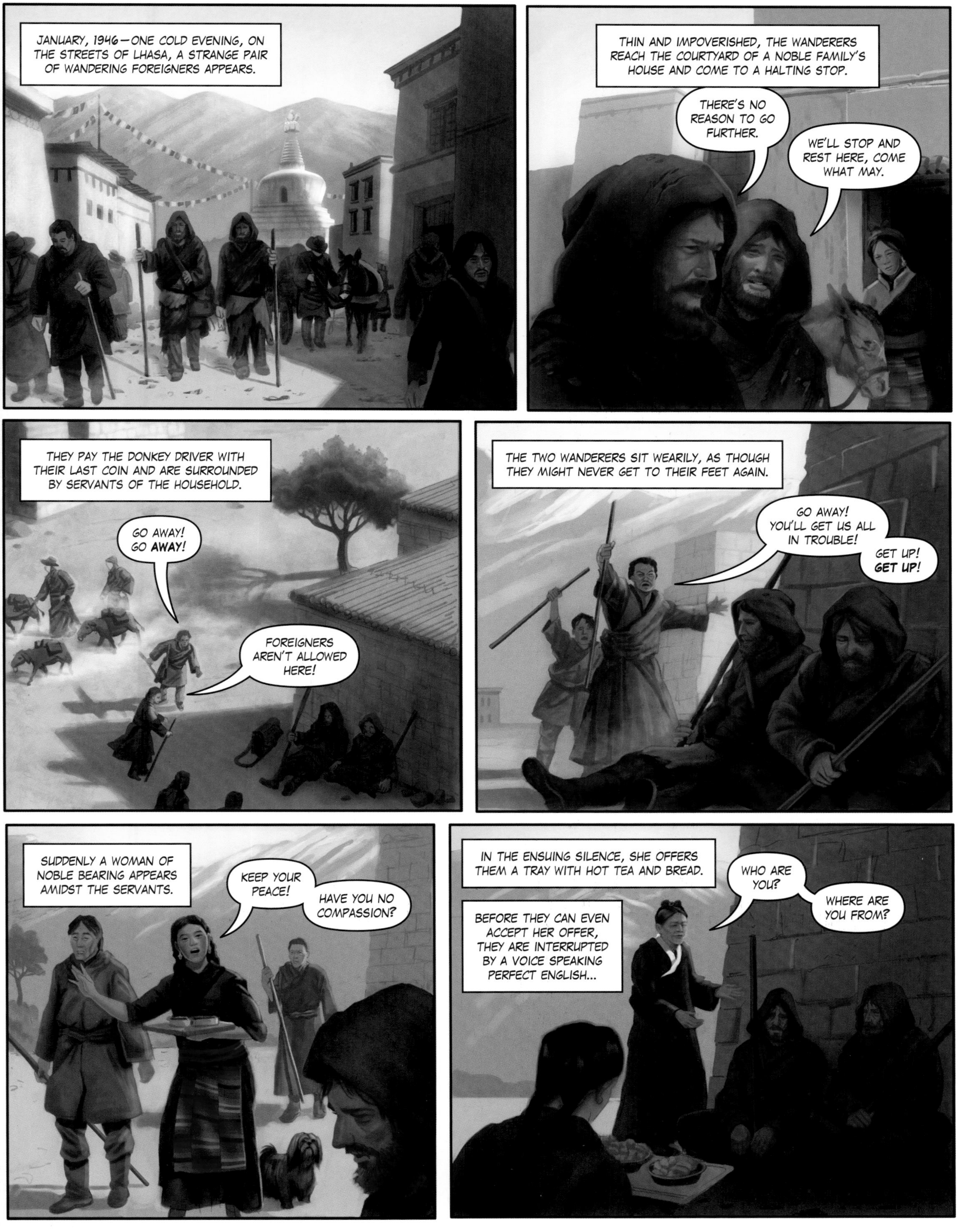

JANUARY, 1946—ONE COLD EVENING, ON THE STREETS OF LHASA, A STRANGE PAIR OF WANDERING FOREIGNERS APPEARS.
THIN AND IMPOVERISHED, THE WANDERERS REACH THE COURTYARD OF A NOBLE FAMILY'S HOUSE AND COME TO A HALTING STOP.
THERE'S NO REASON TO GO FURTHER.
WE'LL STOP AND REST HERE, COME WHAT MAY.
THEY PAY THE DONKEY DRIVER WITH THEIR LAST COIN AND ARE SURROUNDED BY SERVANTS OF THE HOUSEHOLD.
GO AWAY! GO **AWAY!**
FOREIGNERS AREN'T ALLOWED HERE!
THE TWO WANDERERS SIT WEARILY, AS THOUGH THEY MIGHT NEVER GET TO THEIR FEET AGAIN.
GO AWAY! YOU'LL GET US ALL IN TROUBLE!
GET UP! **GET UP!**
SUDDENLY A WOMAN OF NOBLE BEARING APPEARS AMIDST THE SERVANTS.
KEEP YOUR PEACE!
HAVE YOU NO COMPASSION?
IN THE ENSUING SILENCE, SHE OFFERS THEM A TRAY WITH HOT TEA AND BREAD.
BEFORE THEY CAN EVEN ACCEPT HER OFFER, THEY ARE INTERRUPTED BY A VOICE SPEAKING PERFECT ENGLISH...
WHO ARE YOU?
WHERE ARE YOU FROM?

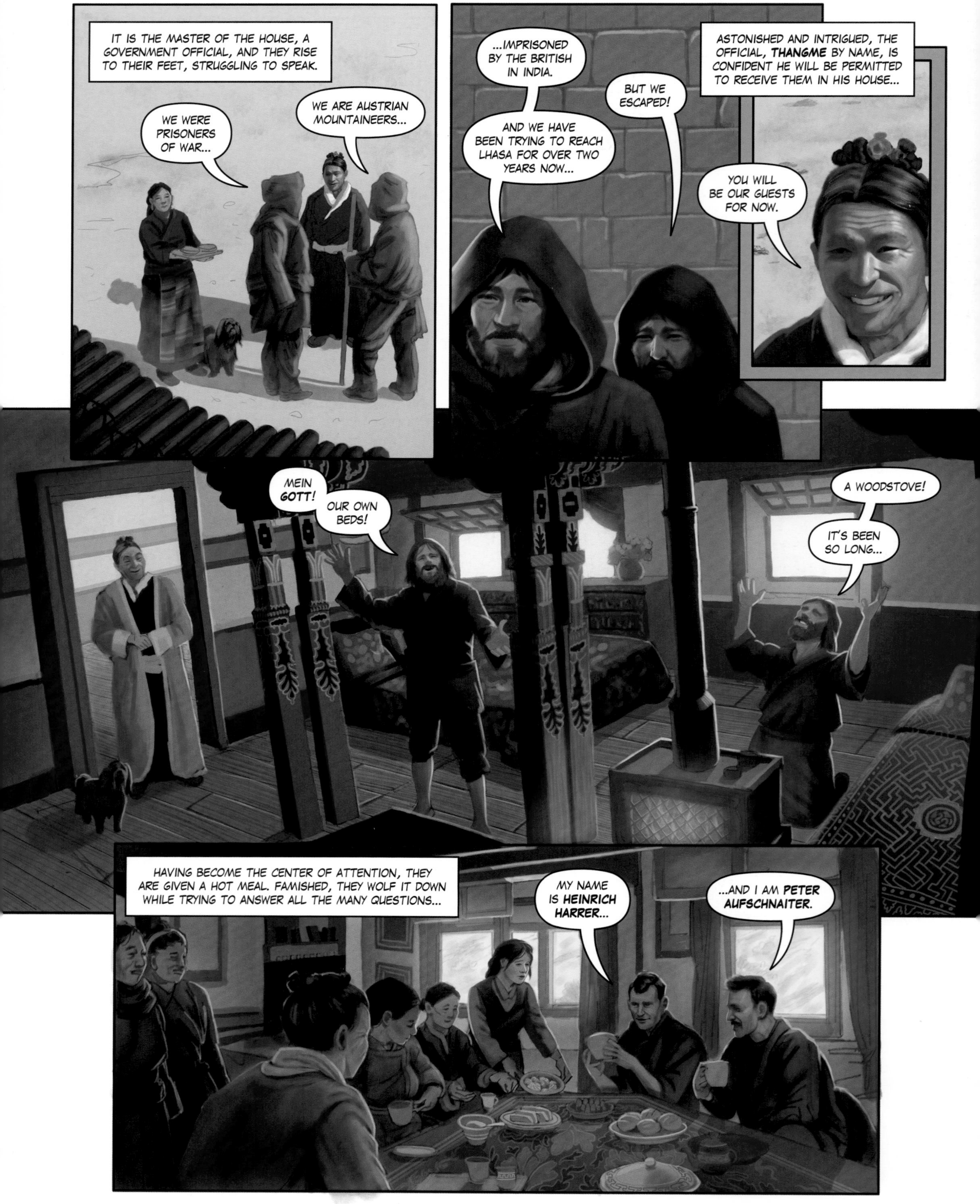
IT IS THE MASTER OF THE HOUSE, A GOVERNMENT OFFICIAL, AND THEY RISE TO THEIR FEET, STRUGGLING TO SPEAK.
WE ARE AUSTRIAN MOUNTAINEERS...
WE WERE PRISONERS OF WAR...
...IMPRISONED BY THE BRITISH IN INDIA.
AND WE HAVE BEEN TRYING TO REACH LHASA FOR OVER TWO YEARS NOW...
BUT WE ESCAPED!
ASTONISHED AND INTRIGUED, THE OFFICIAL, **THANGME** BY NAME, IS CONFIDENT HE WILL BE PERMITTED TO RECEIVE THEM IN HIS HOUSE...
YOU WILL BE OUR GUESTS FOR NOW.
MEIN **GOTT**!
OUR OWN BEDS!
A WOODSTOVE!
IT'S BEEN SO LONG...
HAVING BECOME THE CENTER OF ATTENTION, THEY ARE GIVEN A HOT MEAL. FAMISHED, THEY WOLF IT DOWN WHILE TRYING TO ANSWER ALL THE MANY QUESTIONS...
MY NAME IS **HEINRICH HARRER**...
...AND I AM **PETER AUFSCHNAITER**.

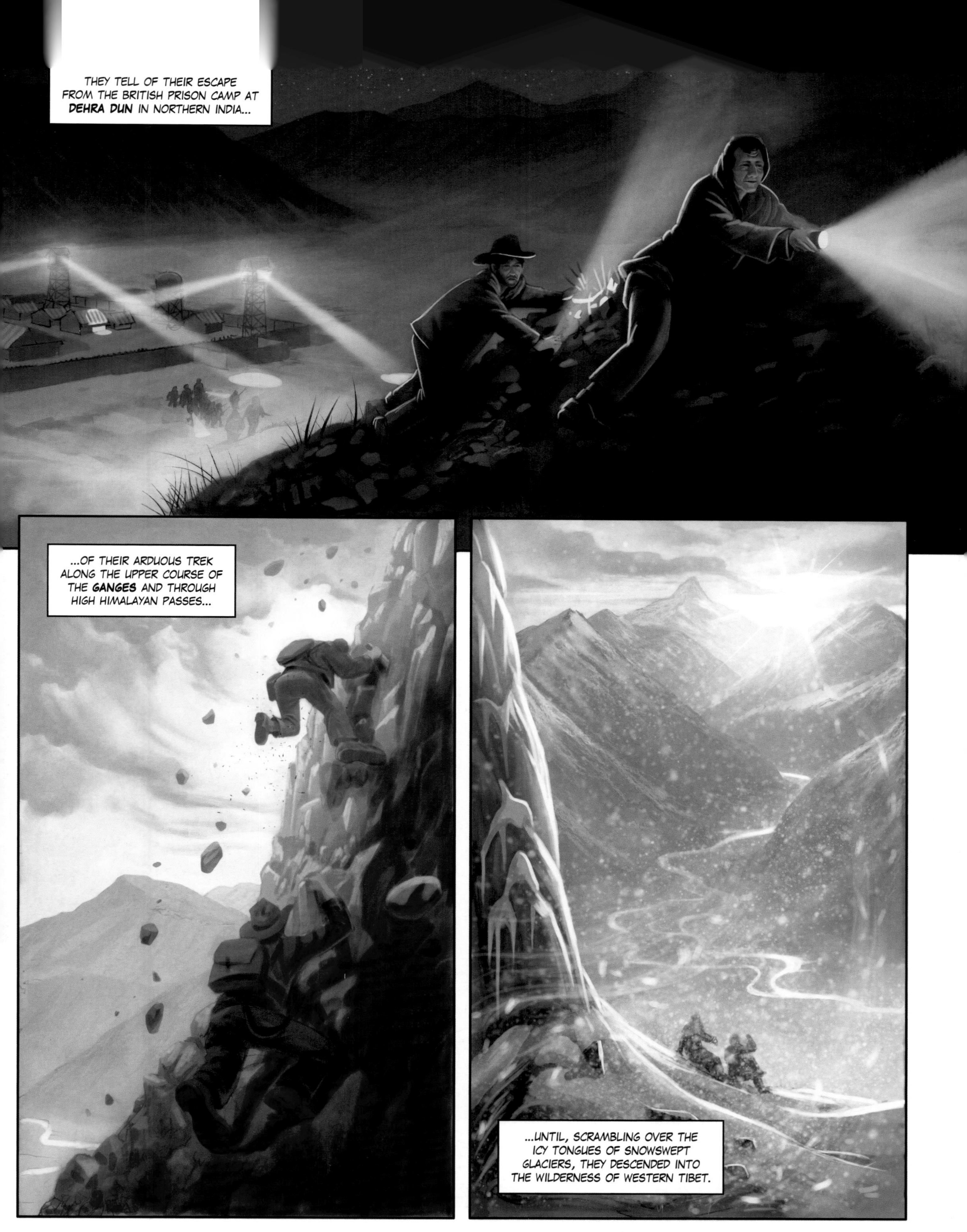
THEY TELL OF THEIR ESCAPE FROM THE BRITISH PRISON CAMP AT DEHRA DUN IN NORTHERN INDIA...
...OF THEIR ARDUOUS TREK ALONG THE UPPER COURSE OF THE GANGES AND THROUGH HIGH HIMALAYAN PASSES...
...UNTIL, SCRAMBLING OVER THE ICY TONGUES OF SNOWSWEPT GLACIERS, THEY DESCENDED INTO THE WILDERNESS OF WESTERN TIBET.

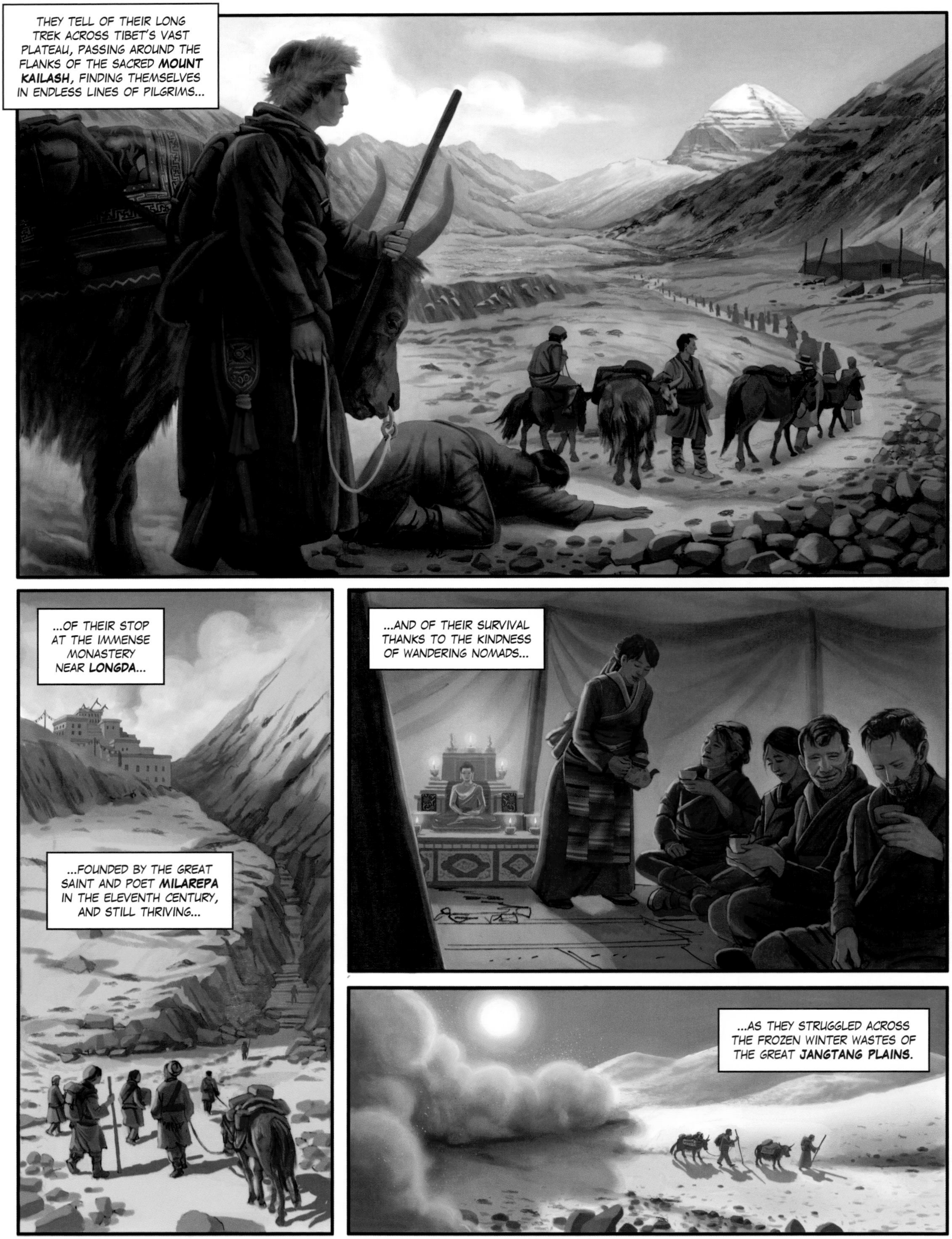
THEY TELL OF THEIR LONG TREK ACROSS TIBET'S VAST PLATEAU, PASSING AROUND THE FLANKS OF THE SACRED MOUNT KAILASH, FINDING THEMSELVES IN ENDLESS LINES OF PILGRIMS...
...OF THEIR STOP AT THE IMMENSE MONASTERY NEAR LONGDA...
...FOUNDED BY THE GREAT SAINT AND POET MILAREPA IN THE ELEVENTH CENTURY, AND STILL THRIVING...
...AND OF THEIR SURVIVAL THANKS TO THE KINDNESS OF WANDERING NOMADS...
...AS THEY STRUGGLED ACROSS THE FROZEN WINTER WASTES OF THE GREAT JANGTANG PLAINS.

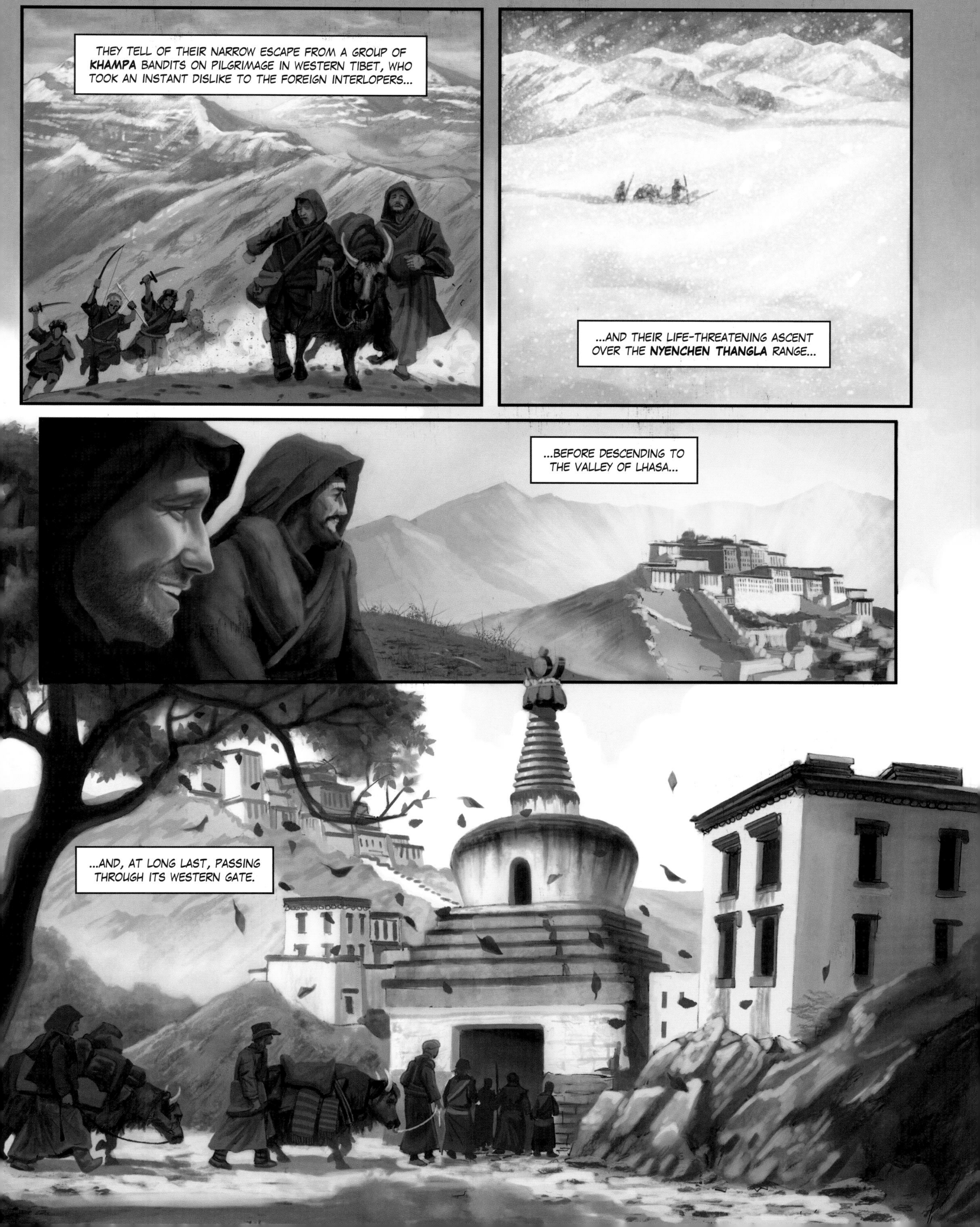
THEY TELL OF THEIR NARROW ESCAPE FROM A GROUP OF KHAMPA BANDITS ON PILGRIMAGE IN WESTERN TIBET, WHO TOOK AN INSTANT DISLIKE TO THE FOREIGN INTERLOPERS...
...AND THEIR LIFE-THREATENING ASCENT OVER THE NYENCHEN THANGLA RANGE...
...BEFORE DESCENDING TO THE VALLEY OF LHASA...
...AND, AT LONG LAST, PASSING THROUGH ITS WESTERN GATE.

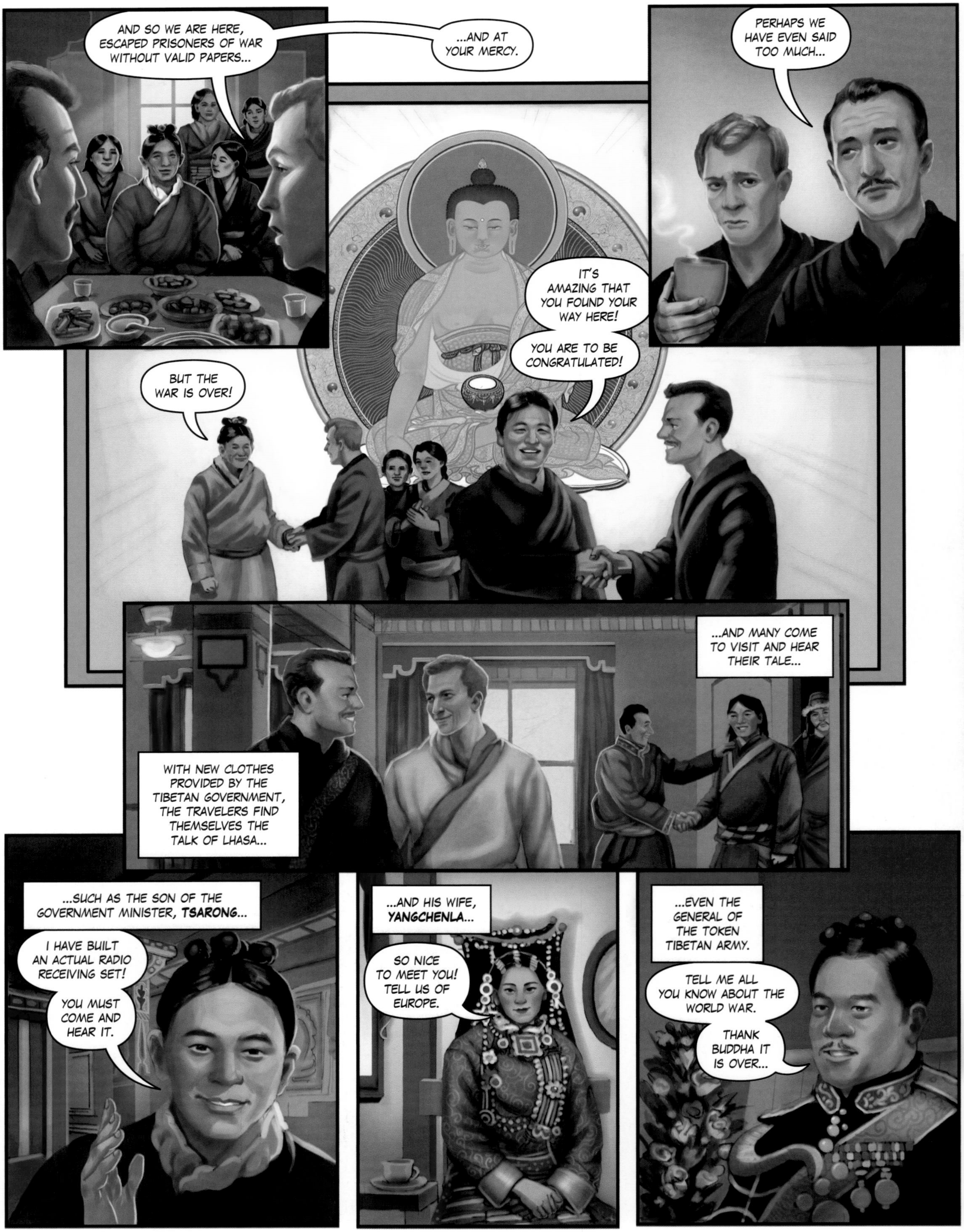
AND SO WE ARE HERE, ESCAPED PRISONERS OF WAR WITHOUT VALID PAPERS...
...AND AT YOUR MERCY.
PERHAPS WE HAVE EVEN SAID TOO MUCH...
BUT THE WAR IS OVER!
IT'S AMAZING THAT YOU FOUND YOUR WAY HERE!
YOU ARE TO BE CONGRATULATED!
WITH NEW CLOTHES PROVIDED BY THE TIBETAN GOVERNMENT, THE TRAVELERS FIND THEMSELVES THE TALK OF LHASA...
...AND MANY COME TO VISIT AND HEAR THEIR TALE...
...SUCH AS THE SON OF THE GOVERNMENT MINISTER, **TSARONG**...
I HAVE BUILT AN ACTUAL RADIO RECEIVING SET!
YOU MUST COME AND HEAR IT.
...AND HIS WIFE, **YANGCHENLA**...
SO NICE TO MEET YOU! TELL US OF EUROPE.
...EVEN THE GENERAL OF THE TOKEN TIBETAN ARMY.
TELL ME ALL YOU KNOW ABOUT THE WORLD WAR.
THANK BUDDHA IT IS OVER...

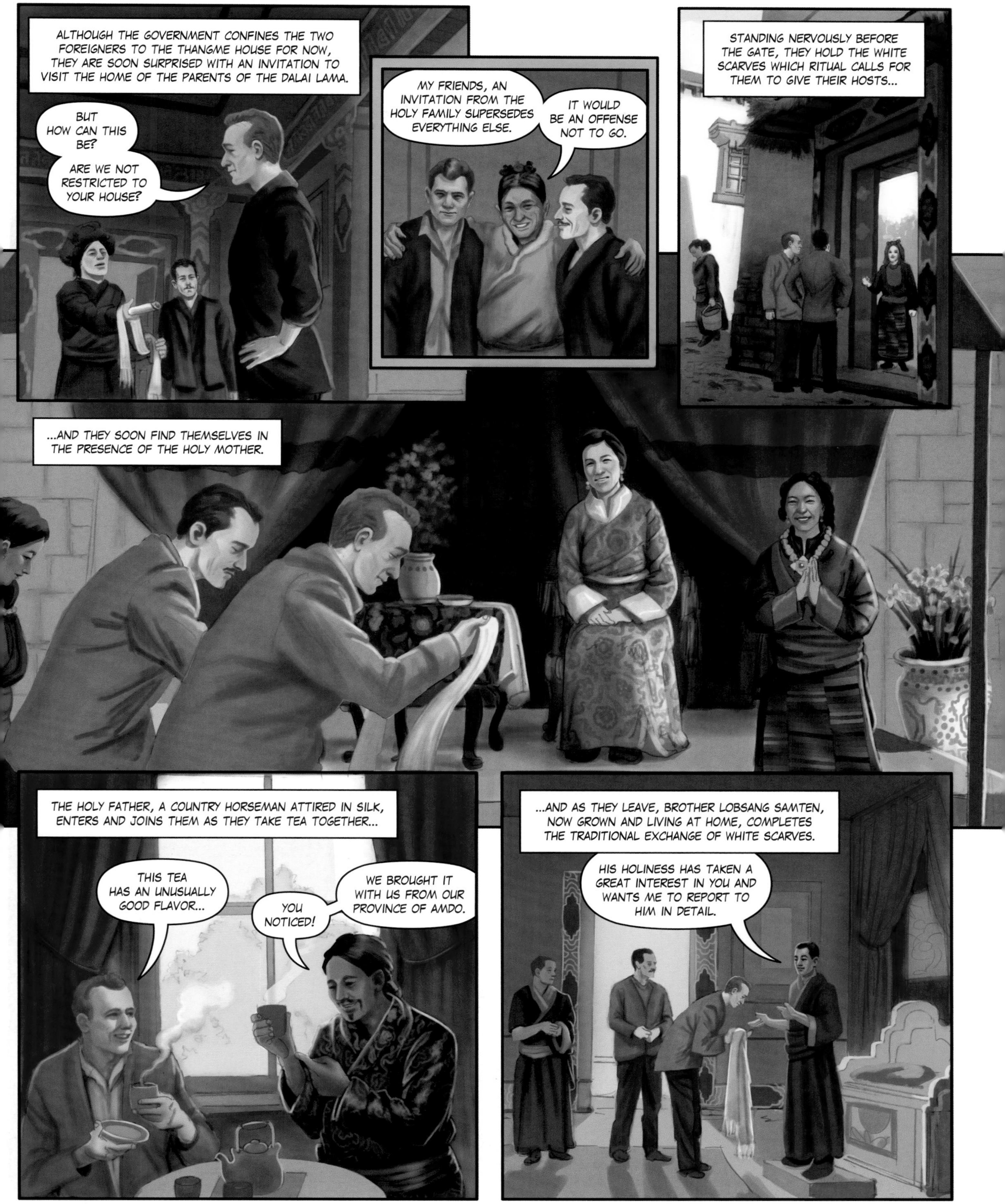

ALTHOUGH THE GOVERNMENT CONFINES THE TWO FOREIGNERS TO THE THANGME HOUSE FOR NOW, THEY ARE SOON SURPRISED WITH AN INVITATION TO VISIT THE HOME OF THE PARENTS OF THE DALAI LAMA.
BUT HOW CAN THIS BE?
ARE WE NOT RESTRICTED TO YOUR HOUSE?
MY FRIENDS, AN INVITATION FROM THE HOLY FAMILY SUPERSEDES EVERYTHING ELSE.
IT WOULD BE AN OFFENSE NOT TO GO.
STANDING NERVOUSLY BEFORE THE GATE, THEY HOLD THE WHITE SCARVES WHICH RITUAL CALLS FOR THEM TO GIVE THEIR HOSTS...
...AND THEY SOON FIND THEMSELVES IN THE PRESENCE OF THE HOLY MOTHER.
THE HOLY FATHER, A COUNTRY HORSEMAN ATTIRED IN SILK, ENTERS AND JOINS THEM AS THEY TAKE TEA TOGETHER...
THIS TEA HAS AN UNUSUALLY GOOD FLAVOR...
YOU NOTICED!
WE BROUGHT IT WITH US FROM OUR PROVINCE OF AMDO.
...AND AS THEY LEAVE, BROTHER LOBSANG SAMTEN, NOW GROWN AND LIVING AT HOME, COMPLETES THE TRADITIONAL EXCHANGE OF WHITE SCARVES.
HIS HOLINESS HAS TAKEN A GREAT INTEREST IN YOU AND WANTS ME TO REPORT TO HIM IN DETAIL.

HARRER AND AUFSCHNAITER ARE SOON GIVEN THEIR OWN APARTMENT IN THE HOME OF TSARONG, THE WEALTHY CABINET MINISTER.

FROM A WINDOW THEY CAN SEE THE POTALA PALACE IN THE DISTANCE...

...WHERE THE YOUNG DALAI LAMA IS SAID TO BE OFTEN SEEN WITH A TELESCOPE OR HIGH-POWERED BINOCULARS, OBSERVING HIS PEOPLE...

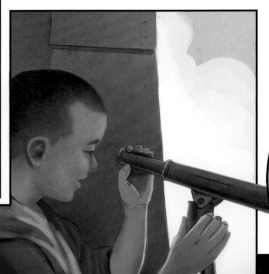

...WHO STOP WHATEVER THEY ARE DOING AND PROSTRATE THEMSELVES IN HIS DIRECTION, CONSIDERING IT GREATLY MERITORIOUS TO BOW DIRECTLY BEFORE THE HOLY REINCARNATION OF THEIR BODHISATTVA SAVIOR.

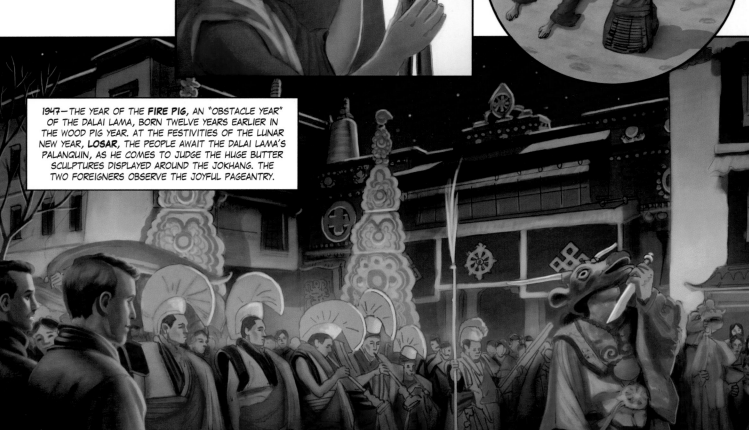

1947—THE YEAR OF THE **FIRE PIG**, AN "OBSTACLE YEAR" OF THE DALAI LAMA, BORN TWELVE YEARS EARLIER IN THE WOOD PIG YEAR. AT THE FESTIVITIES OF THE LUNAR NEW YEAR, **LOSAR**, THE PEOPLE AWAIT THE DALAI LAMA'S PALANQUIN, AS HE COMES TO JUDGE THE HUGE BUTTER SCULPTURES DISPLAYED AROUND THE JOKHANG. THE TWO FOREIGNERS OBSERVE THE JOYFUL PAGEANTRY.

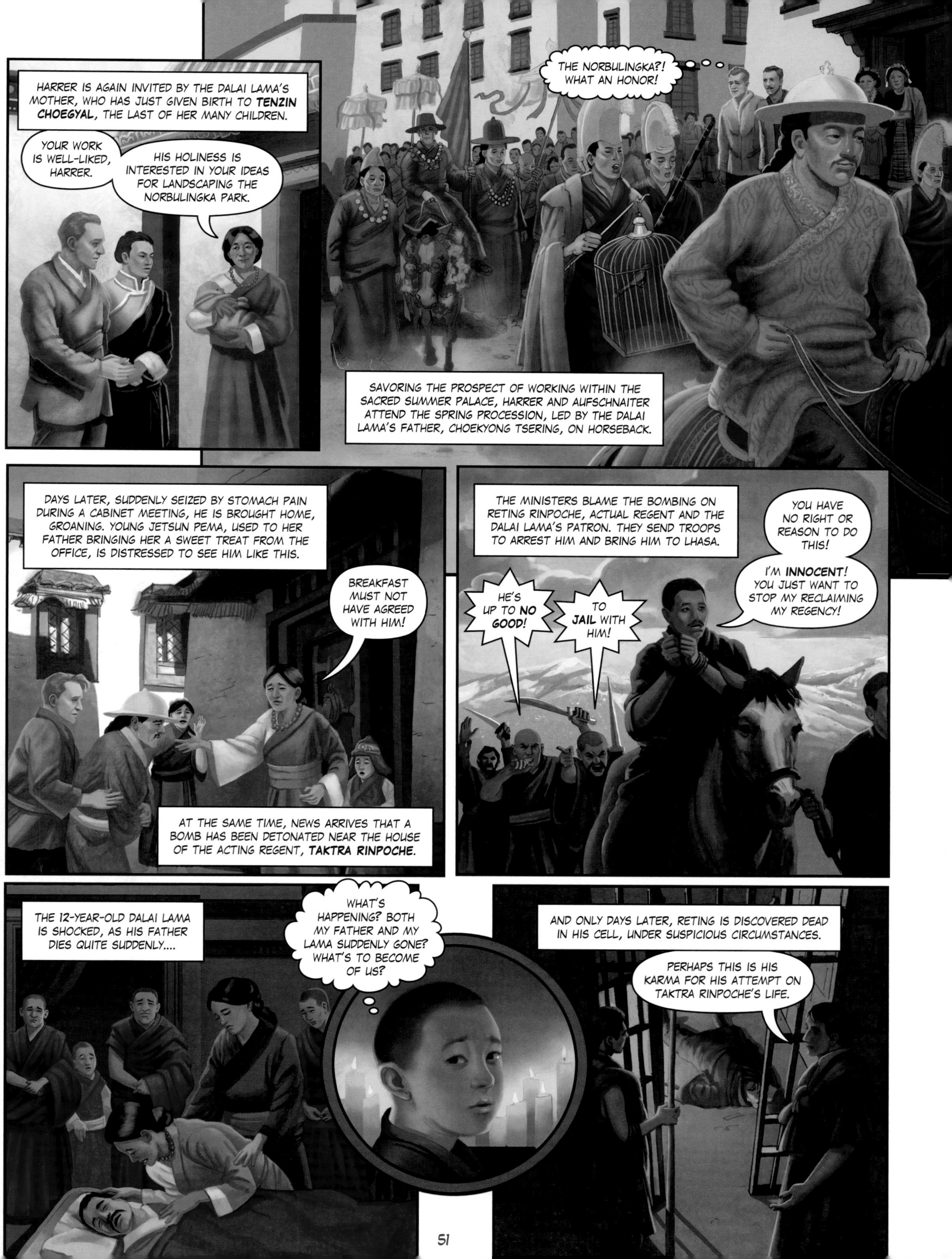
HARRER IS AGAIN INVITED BY THE DALAI LAMA'S MOTHER, WHO HAS JUST GIVEN BIRTH TO **TENZIN CHOEGYAL**, THE LAST OF HER MANY CHILDREN.
YOUR WORK IS WELL-LIKED, HARRER.
HIS HOLINESS IS INTERESTED IN YOUR IDEAS FOR LANDSCAPING THE NORBULINGKA PARK.
THE NORBULINGKA?! WHAT AN HONOR!
SAVORING THE PROSPECT OF WORKING WITHIN THE SACRED SUMMER PALACE, HARRER AND AUFSCHNAITER ATTEND THE SPRING PROCESSION, LED BY THE DALAI LAMA'S FATHER, CHOEKYONG TSERING, ON HORSEBACK.
DAYS LATER, SUDDENLY SEIZED BY STOMACH PAIN DURING A CABINET MEETING, HE IS BROUGHT HOME, GROANING. YOUNG JETSUN PEMA, USED TO HER FATHER BRINGING HER A SWEET TREAT FROM THE OFFICE, IS DISTRESSED TO SEE HIM LIKE THIS.
BREAKFAST MUST NOT HAVE AGREED WITH HIM!
AT THE SAME TIME, NEWS ARRIVES THAT A BOMB HAS BEEN DETONATED NEAR THE HOUSE OF THE ACTING REGENT, **TAKTRA RINPOCHE**.
THE MINISTERS BLAME THE BOMBING ON RETING RINPOCHE, ACTUAL REGENT AND THE DALAI LAMA'S PATRON. THEY SEND TROOPS TO ARREST HIM AND BRING HIM TO LHASA.
YOU HAVE NO RIGHT OR REASON TO DO THIS!
I'M **INNOCENT**! YOU JUST WANT TO STOP MY RECLAIMING MY REGENCY!
HE'S UP TO **NO GOOD**!
TO **JAIL** WITH HIM!
THE 12-YEAR-OLD DALAI LAMA IS SHOCKED, AS HIS FATHER DIES QUITE SUDDENLY....
WHAT'S HAPPENING? BOTH MY FATHER AND MY LAMA SUDDENLY GONE? WHAT'S TO BECOME OF US?
AND ONLY DAYS LATER, RETING IS DISCOVERED DEAD IN HIS CELL, UNDER SUSPICIOUS CIRCUMSTANCES.
PERHAPS THIS IS HIS KARMA FOR HIS ATTEMPT ON TAKTRA RINPOCHE'S LIFE.

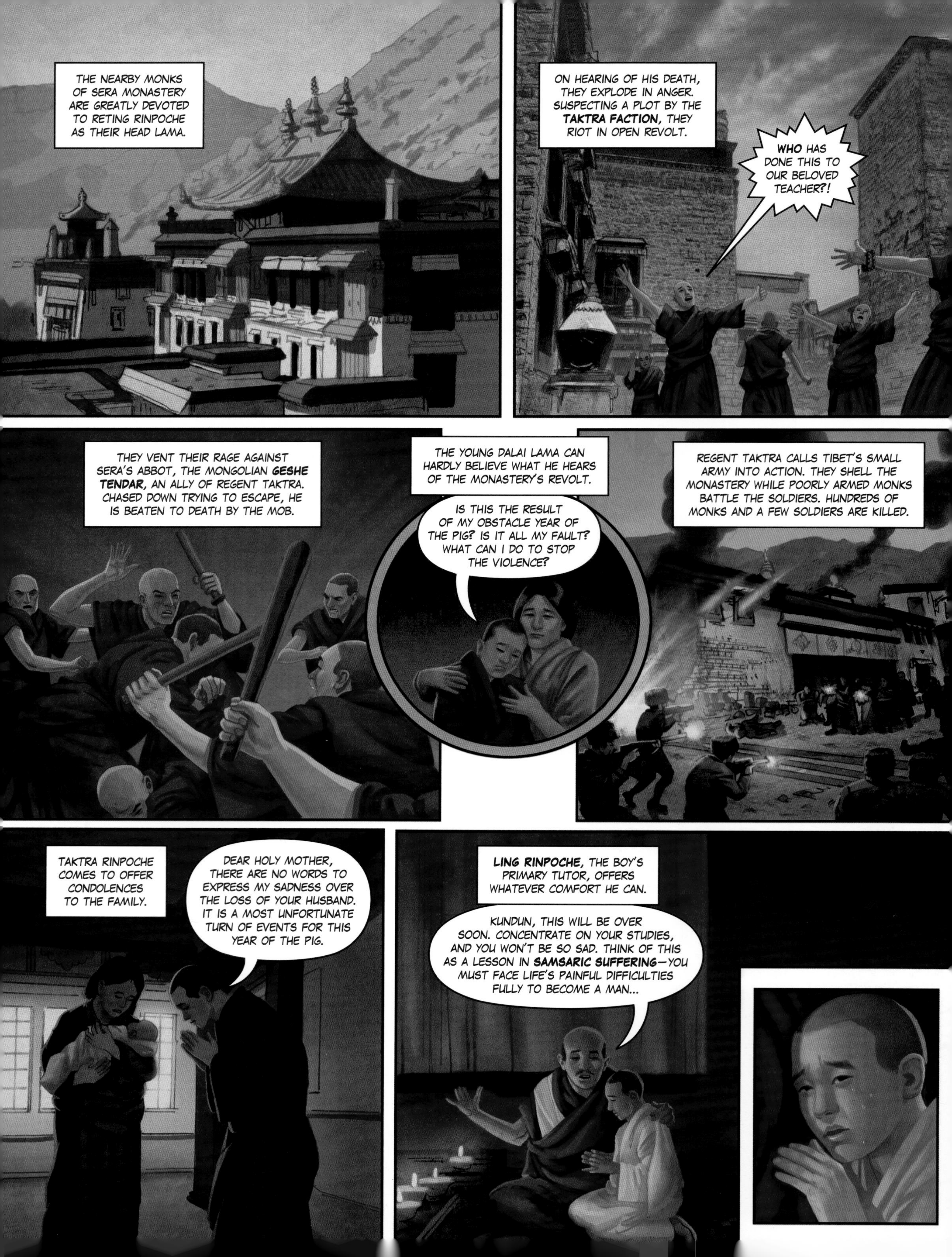
THE NEARBY MONKS OF SERA MONASTERY ARE GREATLY DEVOTED TO RETING RINPOCHE AS THEIR HEAD LAMA.
ON HEARING OF HIS DEATH, THEY EXPLODE IN ANGER. SUSPECTING A PLOT BY THE **TAKTRA FACTION,** THEY RIOT IN OPEN REVOLT.
WHO HAS DONE THIS TO OUR BELOVED TEACHER?!
THEY VENT THEIR RAGE AGAINST SERA'S ABBOT, THE MONGOLIAN **GESHE TENDAR,** AN ALLY OF REGENT TAKTRA. CHASED DOWN TRYING TO ESCAPE, HE IS BEATEN TO DEATH BY THE MOB.
THE YOUNG DALAI LAMA CAN HARDLY BELIEVE WHAT HE HEARS OF THE MONASTERY'S REVOLT.
IS THIS THE RESULT OF MY OBSTACLE YEAR OF THE PIG? IS IT ALL MY FAULT? WHAT CAN I DO TO STOP THE VIOLENCE?
REGENT TAKTRA CALLS TIBET'S SMALL ARMY INTO ACTION. THEY SHELL THE MONASTERY WHILE POORLY ARMED MONKS BATTLE THE SOLDIERS. HUNDREDS OF MONKS AND A FEW SOLDIERS ARE KILLED.
TAKTRA RINPOCHE COMES TO OFFER CONDOLENCES TO THE FAMILY.
DEAR HOLY MOTHER, THERE ARE NO WORDS TO EXPRESS MY SADNESS OVER THE LOSS OF YOUR HUSBAND. IT IS A MOST UNFORTUNATE TURN OF EVENTS FOR THIS YEAR OF THE PIG.
LING RINPOCHE, THE BOY'S PRIMARY TUTOR, OFFERS WHATEVER COMFORT HE CAN.
KUNDUN, THIS WILL BE OVER SOON. CONCENTRATE ON YOUR STUDIES, AND YOU WON'T BE SO SAD. THINK OF THIS AS A LESSON IN **SAMSARIC SUFFERING**—YOU MUST FACE LIFE'S PAINFUL DIFFICULTIES FULLY TO BECOME A MAN...

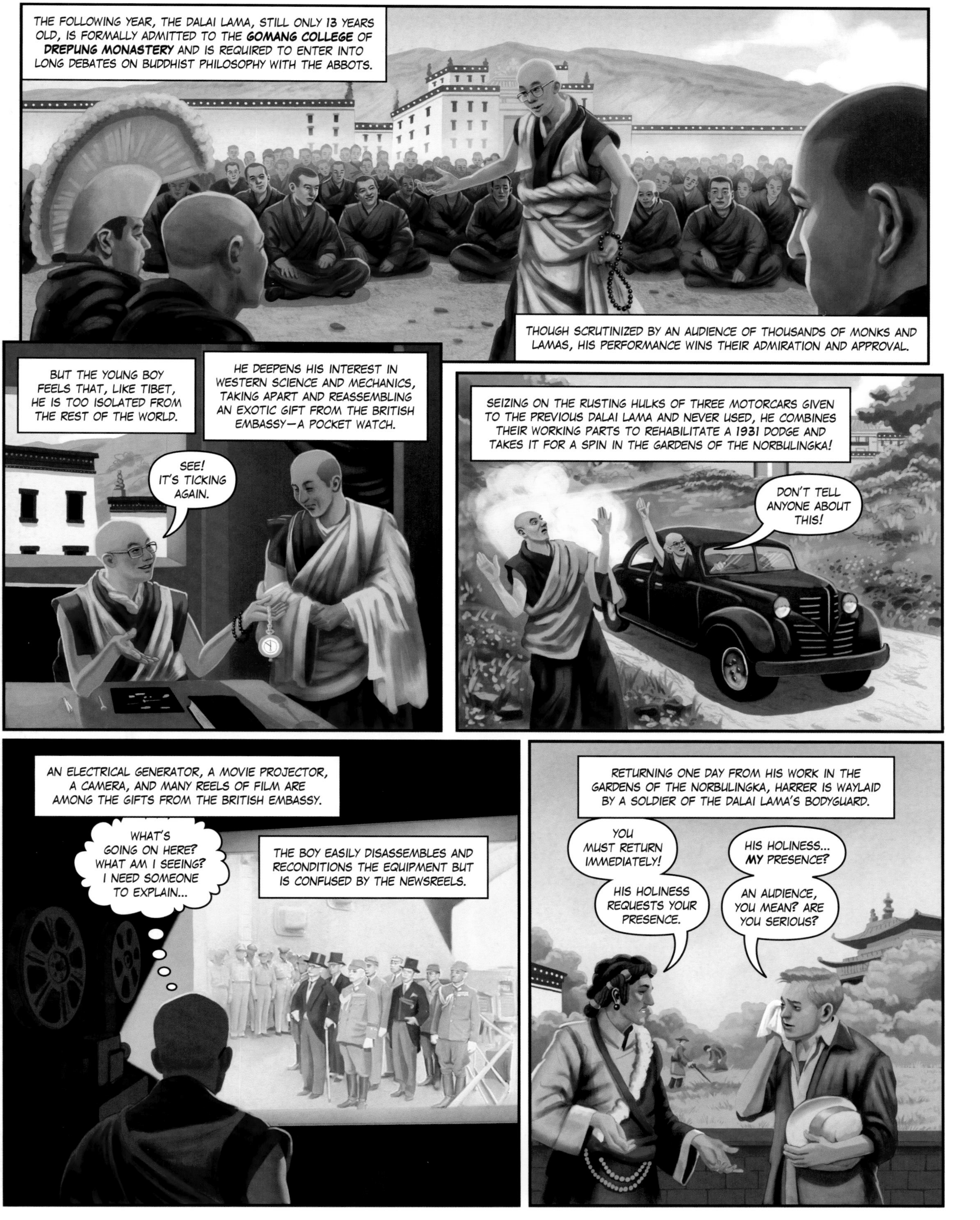
THE FOLLOWING YEAR, THE DALAI LAMA, STILL ONLY 13 YEARS OLD, IS FORMALLY ADMITTED TO THE **GOMANG COLLEGE** OF **DREPUNG MONASTERY** AND IS REQUIRED TO ENTER INTO LONG DEBATES ON BUDDHIST PHILOSOPHY WITH THE ABBOTS.
THOUGH SCRUTINIZED BY AN AUDIENCE OF THOUSANDS OF MONKS AND LAMAS, HIS PERFORMANCE WINS THEIR ADMIRATION AND APPROVAL.
BUT THE YOUNG BOY FEELS THAT, LIKE TIBET, HE IS TOO ISOLATED FROM THE REST OF THE WORLD.
HE DEEPENS HIS INTEREST IN WESTERN SCIENCE AND MECHANICS, TAKING APART AND REASSEMBLING AN EXOTIC GIFT FROM THE BRITISH EMBASSY—A POCKET WATCH.
SEE! IT'S TICKING AGAIN.
SEIZING ON THE RUSTING HULKS OF THREE MOTORCARS GIVEN TO THE PREVIOUS DALAI LAMA AND NEVER USED, HE COMBINES THEIR WORKING PARTS TO REHABILITATE A 1931 DODGE AND TAKES IT FOR A SPIN IN THE GARDENS OF THE NORBULINGKA!
DON'T TELL ANYONE ABOUT THIS!
AN ELECTRICAL GENERATOR, A MOVIE PROJECTOR, A CAMERA, AND MANY REELS OF FILM ARE AMONG THE GIFTS FROM THE BRITISH EMBASSY.
WHAT'S GOING ON HERE? WHAT AM I SEEING? I NEED SOMEONE TO EXPLAIN...
THE BOY EASILY DISASSEMBLES AND RECONDITIONS THE EQUIPMENT BUT IS CONFUSED BY THE NEWSREELS.
RETURNING ONE DAY FROM HIS WORK IN THE GARDENS OF THE NORBULINGKA, HARRER IS WAYLAID BY A SOLDIER OF THE DALAI LAMA'S BODYGUARD.
YOU MUST RETURN IMMEDIATELY!
HIS HOLINESS REQUESTS YOUR PRESENCE.
HIS HOLINESS... **MY** PRESENCE?
AN AUDIENCE, YOU MEAN? ARE YOU SERIOUS?

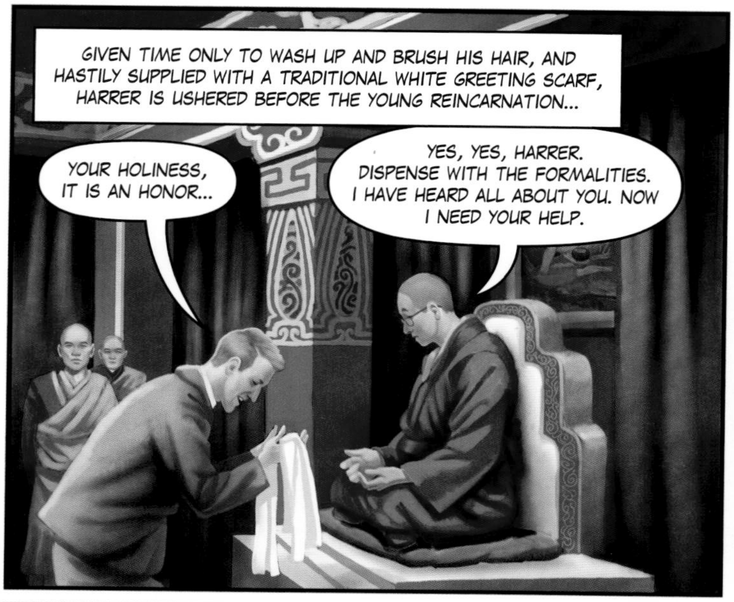
GIVEN TIME ONLY TO WASH UP AND BRUSH HIS HAIR, AND HASTILY SUPPLIED WITH A TRADITIONAL WHITE GREETING SCARF, HARRER IS USHERED BEFORE THE YOUNG REINCARNATION...
YOUR HOLINESS, IT IS AN HONOR...
YES, YES, HARRER. DISPENSE WITH THE FORMALITIES. I HAVE HEARD ALL ABOUT YOU. NOW I NEED YOUR HELP.

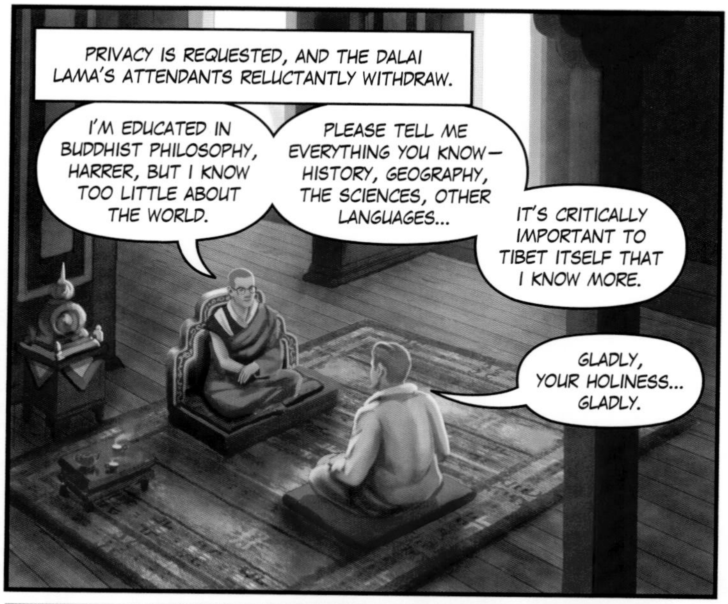
PRIVACY IS REQUESTED, AND THE DALAI LAMA'S ATTENDANTS RELUCTANTLY WITHDRAW.
I'M EDUCATED IN BUDDHIST PHILOSOPHY, HARRER, BUT I KNOW TOO LITTLE ABOUT THE WORLD.
PLEASE TELL ME EVERYTHING YOU KNOW—HISTORY, GEOGRAPHY, THE SCIENCES, OTHER LANGUAGES...
IT'S CRITICALLY IMPORTANT TO TIBET ITSELF THAT I KNOW MORE.
GLADLY, YOUR HOLINESS... GLADLY.

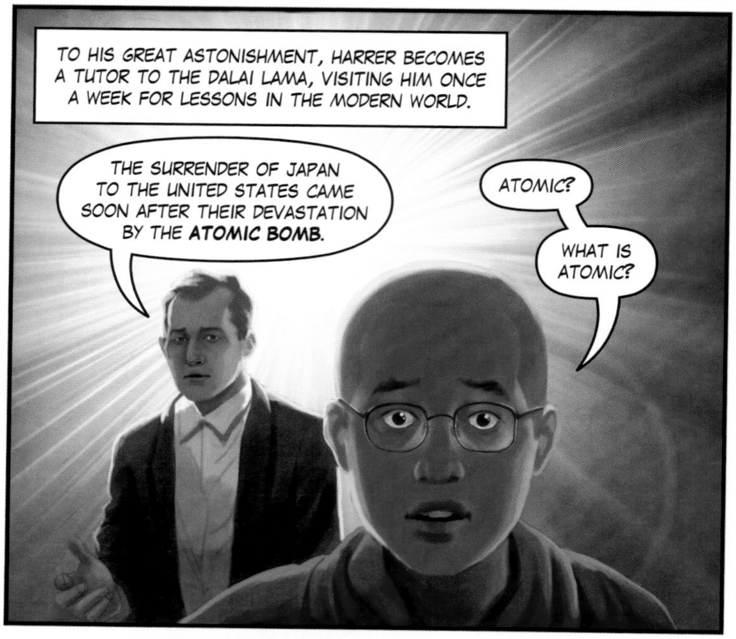
TO HIS GREAT ASTONISHMENT, HARRER BECOMES A TUTOR TO THE DALAI LAMA, VISITING HIM ONCE A WEEK FOR LESSONS IN THE MODERN WORLD.
THE SURRENDER OF JAPAN TO THE UNITED STATES CAME SOON AFTER THEIR DEVASTATION BY THE **ATOMIC BOMB**.
ATOMIC?
WHAT IS ATOMIC?

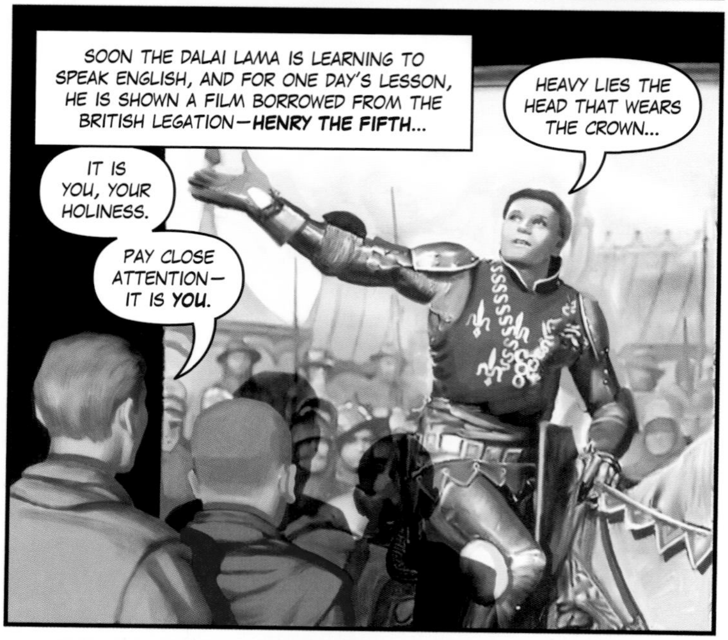
SOON THE DALAI LAMA IS LEARNING TO SPEAK ENGLISH, AND FOR ONE DAY'S LESSON, HE IS SHOWN A FILM BORROWED FROM THE BRITISH LEGATION—**HENRY THE FIFTH**...
HEAVY LIES THE HEAD THAT WEARS THE CROWN...
IT IS YOU, YOUR HOLINESS.
PAY CLOSE ATTENTION—IT IS **YOU**.

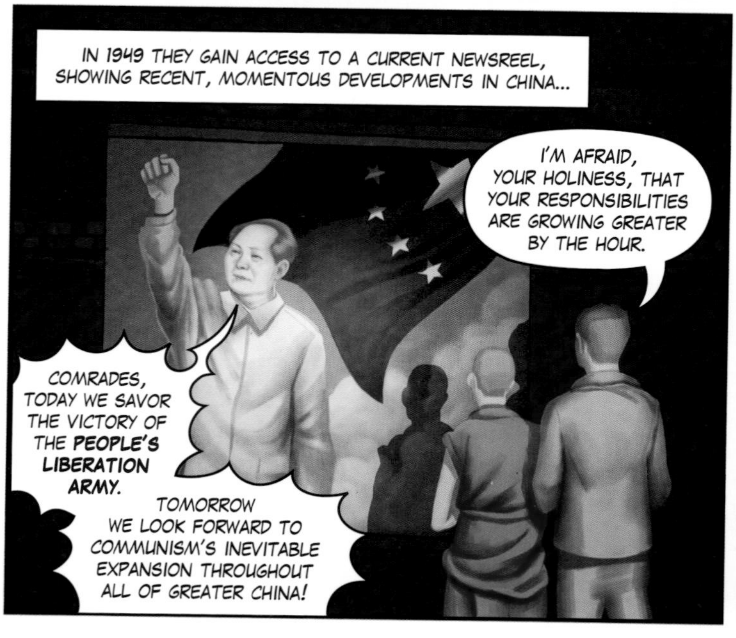
IN 1949 THEY GAIN ACCESS TO A CURRENT NEWSREEL, SHOWING RECENT, MOMENTOUS DEVELOPMENTS IN CHINA...
I'M AFRAID, YOUR HOLINESS, THAT YOUR RESPONSIBILITIES ARE GROWING GREATER BY THE HOUR.
COMRADES, TODAY WE SAVOR THE VICTORY OF THE **PEOPLE'S LIBERATION ARMY**.
TOMORROW WE LOOK FORWARD TO COMMUNISM'S INEVITABLE EXPANSION THROUGHOUT ALL OF GREATER CHINA!

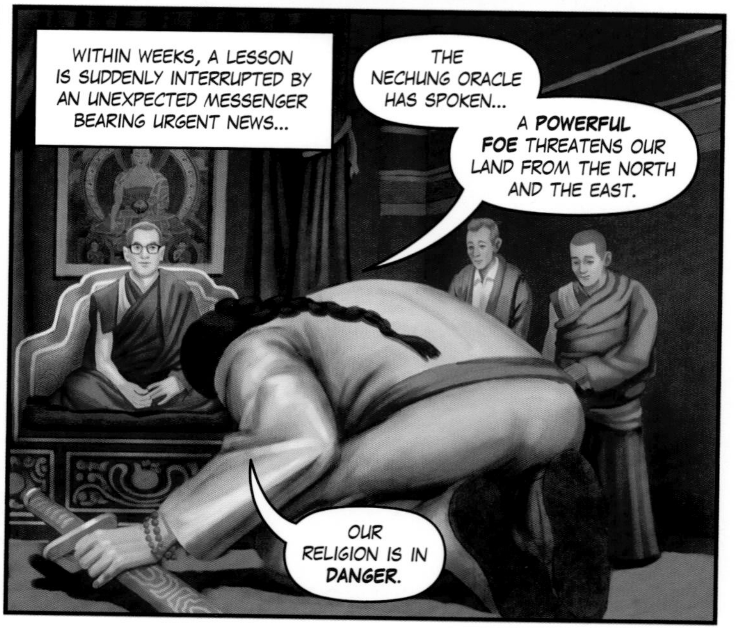
WITHIN WEEKS, A LESSON IS SUDDENLY INTERRUPTED BY AN UNEXPECTED MESSENGER BEARING URGENT NEWS...
THE NECHUNG ORACLE HAS SPOKEN...
A **POWERFUL FOE** THREATENS OUR LAND FROM THE NORTH AND THE EAST.
OUR RELIGION IS IN **DANGER**.

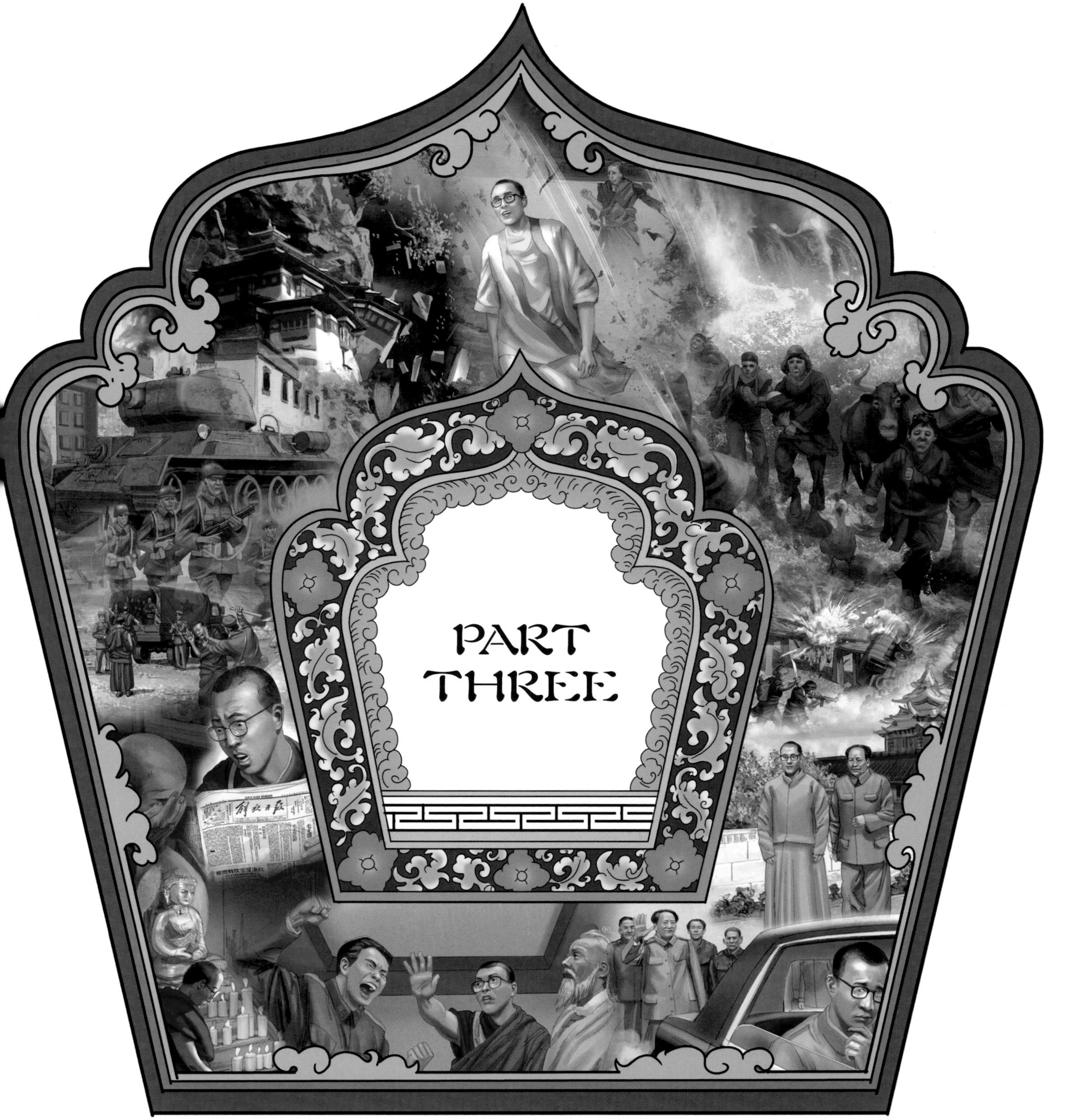

PART THREE

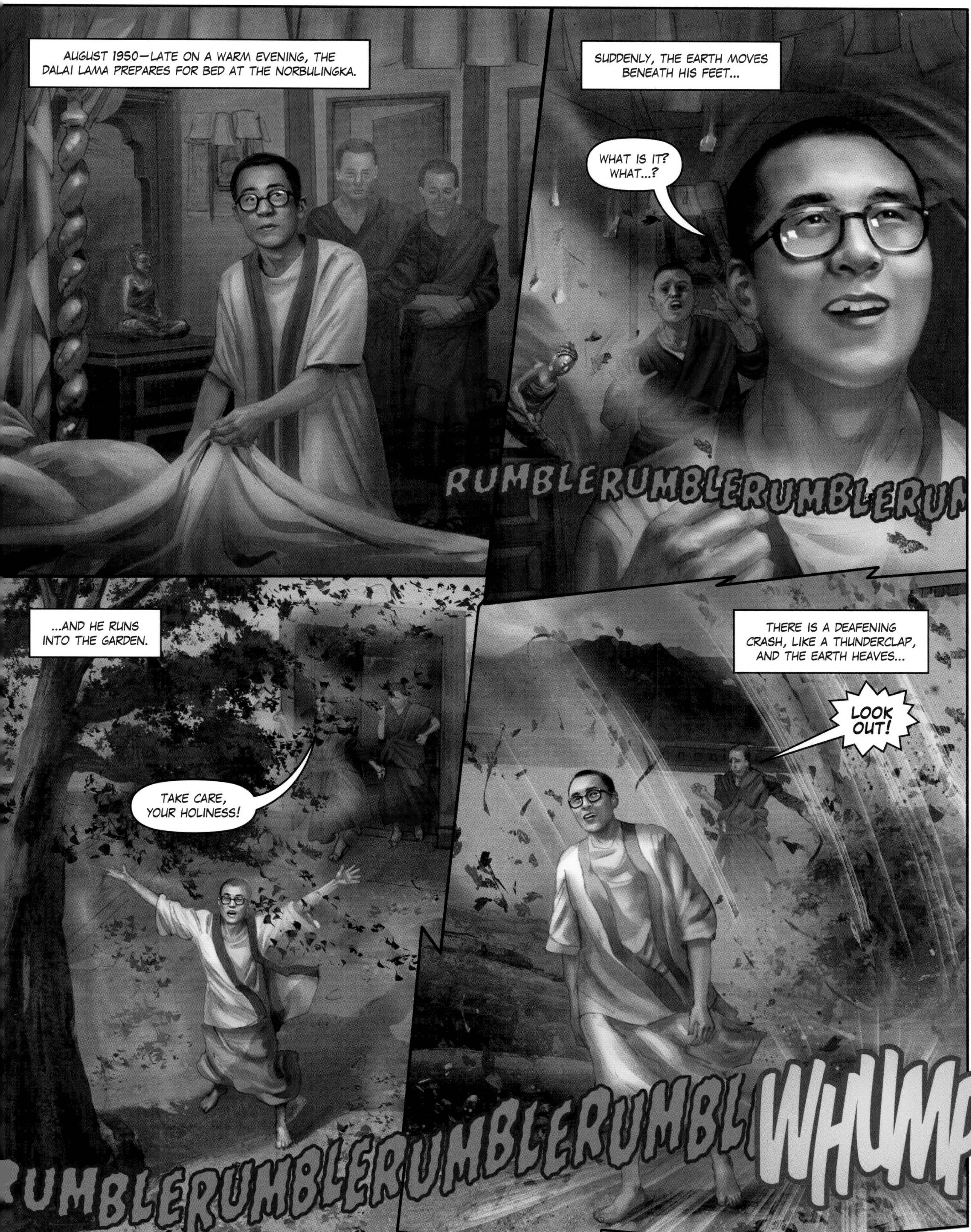
AUGUST 1950—LATE ON A WARM EVENING, THE DALAI LAMA PREPARES FOR BED AT THE NORBULINGKA.
SUDDENLY, THE EARTH MOVES BENEATH HIS FEET...
WHAT IS IT? WHAT...?
RUMBLERUMBLERUMBLERUM
...AND HE RUNS INTO THE GARDEN.
TAKE CARE, YOUR HOLINESS!
THERE IS A DEAFENING CRASH, LIKE A THUNDERCLAP, AND THE EARTH HEAVES...
LOOK OUT!
RUMBLERUMBLERUMBLERUMBL
WHUMP

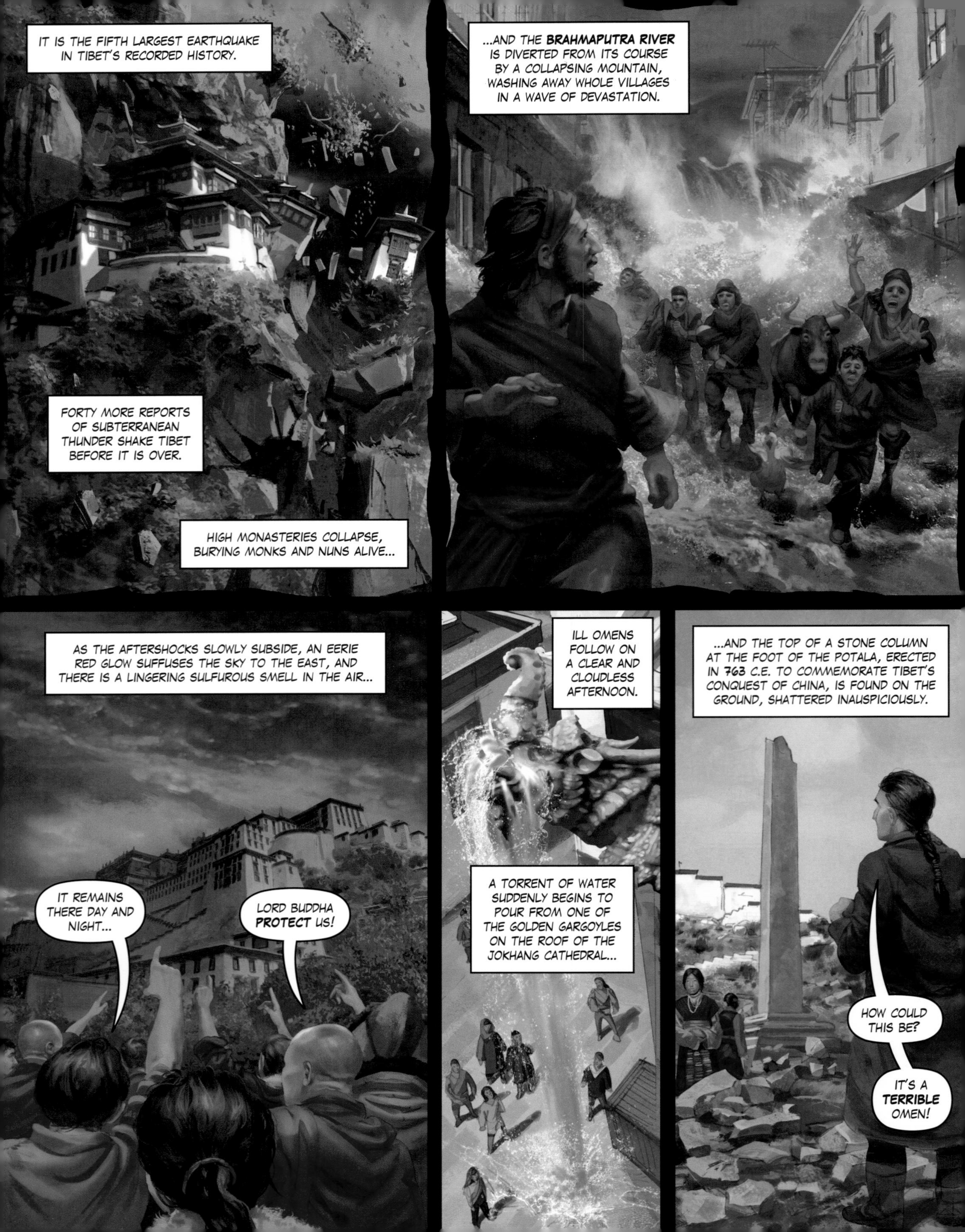

IT IS THE FIFTH LARGEST EARTHQUAKE IN TIBET'S RECORDED HISTORY.
FORTY MORE REPORTS OF SUBTERRANEAN THUNDER SHAKE TIBET BEFORE IT IS OVER.
HIGH MONASTERIES COLLAPSE, BURYING MONKS AND NUNS ALIVE...
...AND THE **BRAHMAPUTRA RIVER** IS DIVERTED FROM ITS COURSE BY A COLLAPSING MOUNTAIN, WASHING AWAY WHOLE VILLAGES IN A WAVE OF DEVASTATION.
AS THE AFTERSHOCKS SLOWLY SUBSIDE, AN EERIE RED GLOW SUFFUSES THE SKY TO THE EAST, AND THERE IS A LINGERING SULFUROUS SMELL IN THE AIR...
IT REMAINS THERE DAY AND NIGHT...
LORD BUDDHA **PROTECT** US!
ILL OMENS FOLLOW ON A CLEAR AND CLOUDLESS AFTERNOON.
A TORRENT OF WATER SUDDENLY BEGINS TO POUR FROM ONE OF THE GOLDEN GARGOYLES ON THE ROOF OF THE JOKHANG CATHEDRAL...
...AND THE TOP OF A STONE COLUMN AT THE FOOT OF THE POTALA, ERECTED IN **763** C.E. TO COMMEMORATE TIBET'S CONQUEST OF CHINA, IS FOUND ON THE GROUND, SHATTERED INAUSPICIOUSLY.
HOW COULD THIS BE?
IT'S A **TERRIBLE** OMEN!

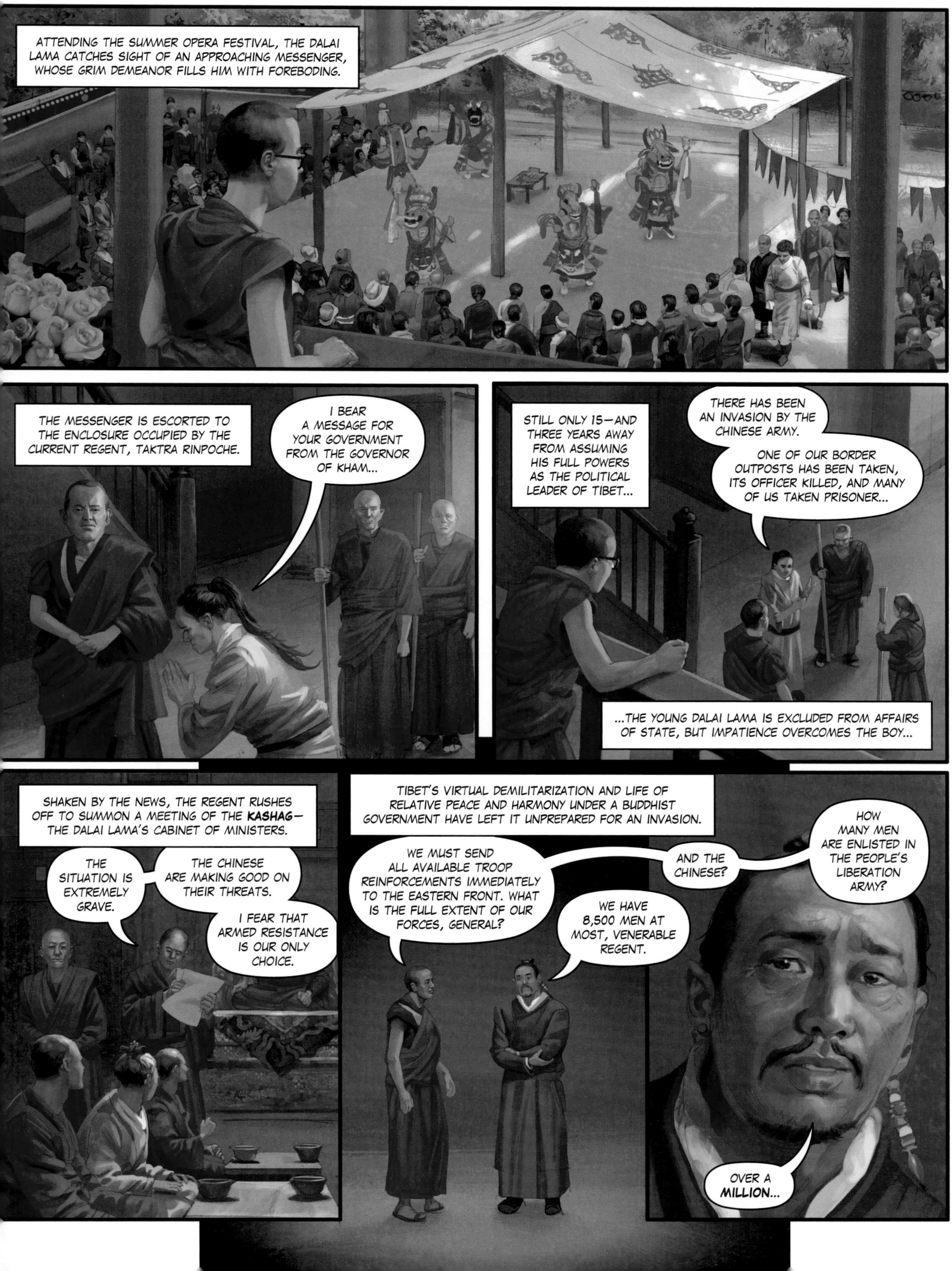

ATTENDING THE SUMMER OPERA FESTIVAL, THE DALAI LAMA CATCHES SIGHT OF AN APPROACHING MESSENGER, WHOSE GRIM DEMEANOR FILLS HIM WITH FOREBODING.
THE MESSENGER IS ESCORTED TO THE ENCLOSURE OCCUPIED BY THE CURRENT REGENT, TAKTRA RINPOCHE.
I BEAR A MESSAGE FOR YOUR GOVERNMENT FROM THE GOVERNOR OF KHAM...
STILL ONLY 15—AND THREE YEARS AWAY FROM ASSUMING HIS FULL POWERS AS THE POLITICAL LEADER OF TIBET...
THERE HAS BEEN AN INVASION BY THE CHINESE ARMY.
ONE OF OUR BORDER OUTPOSTS HAS BEEN TAKEN, ITS OFFICER KILLED, AND MANY OF US TAKEN PRISONER...
...THE YOUNG DALAI LAMA IS EXCLUDED FROM AFFAIRS OF STATE, BUT IMPATIENCE OVERCOMES THE BOY...
SHAKEN BY THE NEWS, THE REGENT RUSHES OFF TO SUMMON A MEETING OF THE **KASHAG**—THE DALAI LAMA'S CABINET OF MINISTERS.
THE SITUATION IS EXTREMELY GRAVE.
THE CHINESE ARE MAKING GOOD ON THEIR THREATS.
I FEAR THAT ARMED RESISTANCE IS OUR ONLY CHOICE.
TIBET'S VIRTUAL DEMILITARIZATION AND LIFE OF RELATIVE PEACE AND HARMONY UNDER A BUDDHIST GOVERNMENT HAVE LEFT IT UNPREPARED FOR AN INVASION.
WE MUST SEND ALL AVAILABLE TROOP REINFORCEMENTS IMMEDIATELY TO THE EASTERN FRONT. WHAT IS THE FULL EXTENT OF OUR FORCES, GENERAL?
WE HAVE 8,500 MEN AT MOST, VENERABLE REGENT.
AND THE CHINESE?
HOW MANY MEN ARE ENLISTED IN THE PEOPLE'S LIBERATION ARMY?
OVER A **MILLION**...

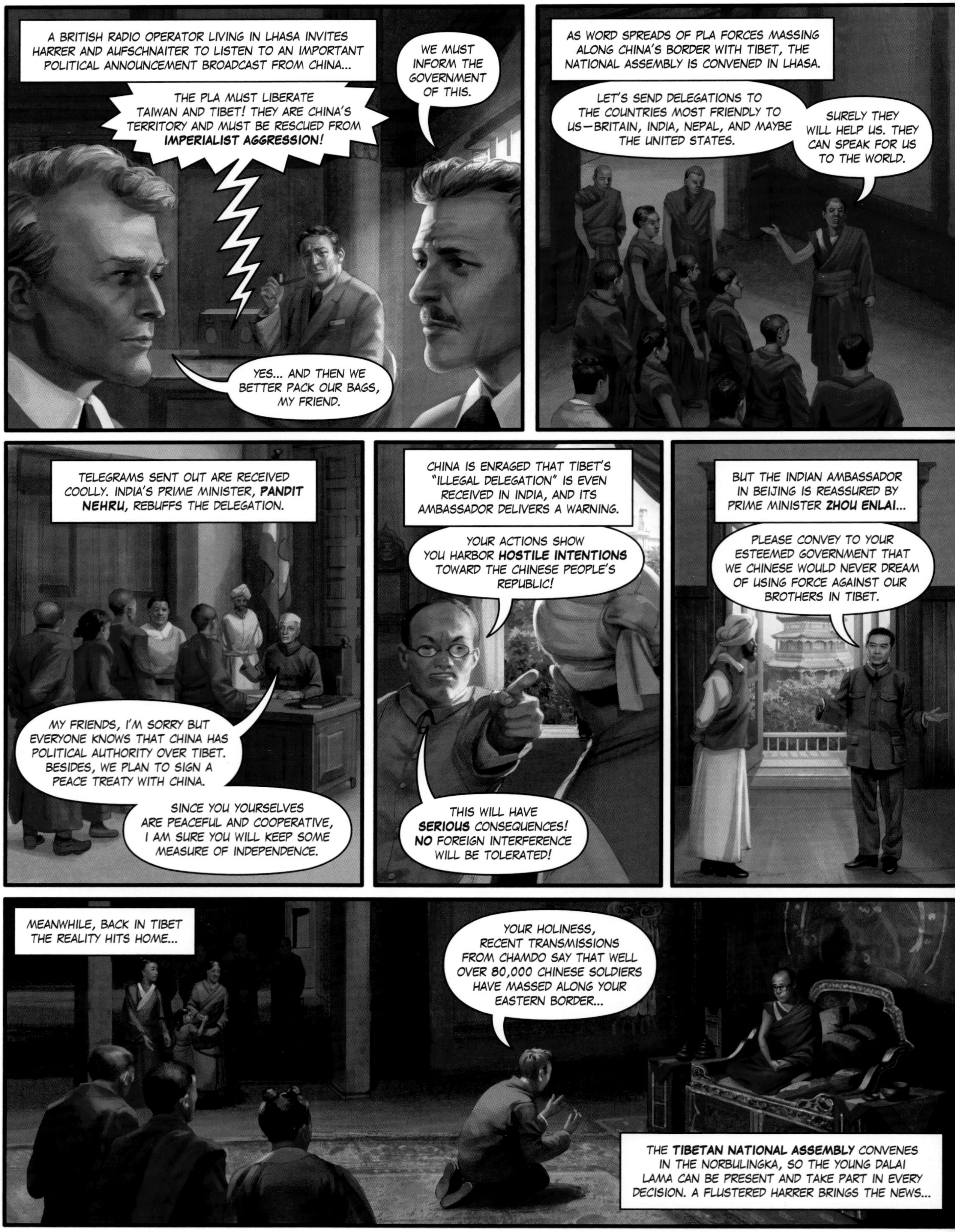

A BRITISH RADIO OPERATOR LIVING IN LHASA INVITES HARRER AND AUFSCHNAITER TO LISTEN TO AN IMPORTANT POLITICAL ANNOUNCEMENT BROADCAST FROM CHINA...
THE PLA MUST LIBERATE TAIWAN AND TIBET! THEY ARE CHINA'S TERRITORY AND MUST BE RESCUED FROM **IMPERIALIST AGGRESSION**!
WE MUST INFORM THE GOVERNMENT OF THIS.
YES... AND THEN WE BETTER PACK OUR BAGS, MY FRIEND.
AS WORD SPREADS OF PLA FORCES MASSING ALONG CHINA'S BORDER WITH TIBET, THE NATIONAL ASSEMBLY IS CONVENED IN LHASA.
LET'S SEND DELEGATIONS TO THE COUNTRIES MOST FRIENDLY TO US—BRITAIN, INDIA, NEPAL, AND MAYBE THE UNITED STATES.
SURELY THEY WILL HELP US. THEY CAN SPEAK FOR US TO THE WORLD.
TELEGRAMS SENT OUT ARE RECEIVED COOLLY. INDIA'S PRIME MINISTER, **PANDIT NEHRU**, REBUFFS THE DELEGATION.
MY FRIENDS, I'M SORRY BUT EVERYONE KNOWS THAT CHINA HAS POLITICAL AUTHORITY OVER TIBET. BESIDES, WE PLAN TO SIGN A PEACE TREATY WITH CHINA.
SINCE YOU YOURSELVES ARE PEACEFUL AND COOPERATIVE, I AM SURE YOU WILL KEEP SOME MEASURE OF INDEPENDENCE.
CHINA IS ENRAGED THAT TIBET'S "ILLEGAL DELEGATION" IS EVEN RECEIVED IN INDIA, AND ITS AMBASSADOR DELIVERS A WARNING.
YOUR ACTIONS SHOW YOU HARBOR **HOSTILE INTENTIONS** TOWARD THE CHINESE PEOPLE'S REPUBLIC!
THIS WILL HAVE **SERIOUS** CONSEQUENCES! **NO** FOREIGN INTERFERENCE WILL BE TOLERATED!
BUT THE INDIAN AMBASSADOR IN BEIJING IS REASSURED BY PRIME MINISTER **ZHOU ENLAI**...
PLEASE CONVEY TO YOUR ESTEEMED GOVERNMENT THAT WE CHINESE WOULD NEVER DREAM OF USING FORCE AGAINST OUR BROTHERS IN TIBET.
MEANWHILE, BACK IN TIBET THE REALITY HITS HOME...
YOUR HOLINESS, RECENT TRANSMISSIONS FROM CHAMDO SAY THAT WELL OVER 80,000 CHINESE SOLDIERS HAVE MASSED ALONG YOUR EASTERN BORDER...
THE **TIBETAN NATIONAL ASSEMBLY** CONVENES IN THE NORBULINGKA, SO THE YOUNG DALAI LAMA CAN BE PRESENT AND TAKE PART IN EVERY DECISION. A FLUSTERED HARRER BRINGS THE NEWS...

OCTOBER 7, 1950—THE COMMUNIST CHINESE PEOPLE'S LIBERATION ARMY INVADES TIBET, SIMULTANEOUSLY ATTACKING SIX PLACES ALONG ITS EASTERN BORDER.

JOINED IN BATTLE BY THE KHAMPAS—ARMED HORSEMEN OF MOUNTAINOUS KHAM, FAMOUS FOR THEIR FEROCITY—THE TIBETAN ARMY IN **DENGKOG** HOLDS OUT AGAINST THE ONSLAUGHT AND TURNS BACK THE INVADERS.

BUT ELSEWHERE, THE TIBETANS ARE CONFUSED, OVERRUN, AND DEFEATED. **CHAMDO**, THE CAPITAL OF KHAM, IS SURROUNDED, ITS PEOPLE GRIPPED BY FEAR.

DESPERATE, THEY PROSTRATE THEMSELVES, CHANT MANTRAS, TURN PRAYER WHEELS, AND THROW EFFIGIES OF THE CHINESE INTO THE FLAMES...

WHO CAN SAVE US?

WE MUST FLEE!

PRAY TO LORD BUDDHA!

THE NEW GOVERNOR OF KHAM, **NGABO NGAWANG JIGME**, ARRIVES FROM LHASA AND SUCCUMBS TO THE PANIC. HE REQUESTS PERMISSION FROM LHASA TO SURRENDER—BUT IS TURNED DOWN.

IT'S NO USE!

RETREAT TO LHASA!

THEY MUST **FEND** FOR THEMSELVES!

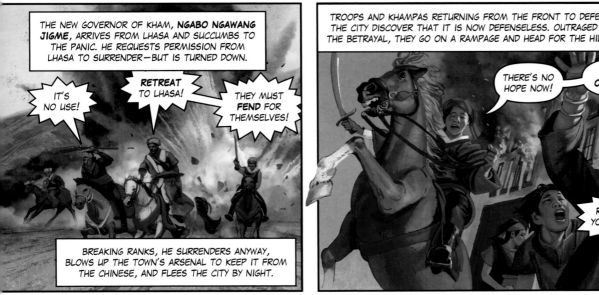

TROOPS AND KHAMPAS RETURNING FROM THE FRONT TO DEFEND THE CITY DISCOVER THAT IT IS NOW DEFENSELESS. OUTRAGED BY THE BETRAYAL, THEY GO ON A RAMPAGE AND HEAD FOR THE HILLS.

THERE'S NO HOPE NOW!

IT'S THE **END OF EVERYTHING!**

RUN FOR YOUR **LIFE!**

BREAKING RANKS, HE SURRENDERS ANYWAY, BLOWS UP THE TOWN'S ARSENAL TO KEEP IT FROM THE CHINESE, AND FLEES THE CITY BY NIGHT.

PANIC-STRICKEN, THE PEOPLE FLEE...

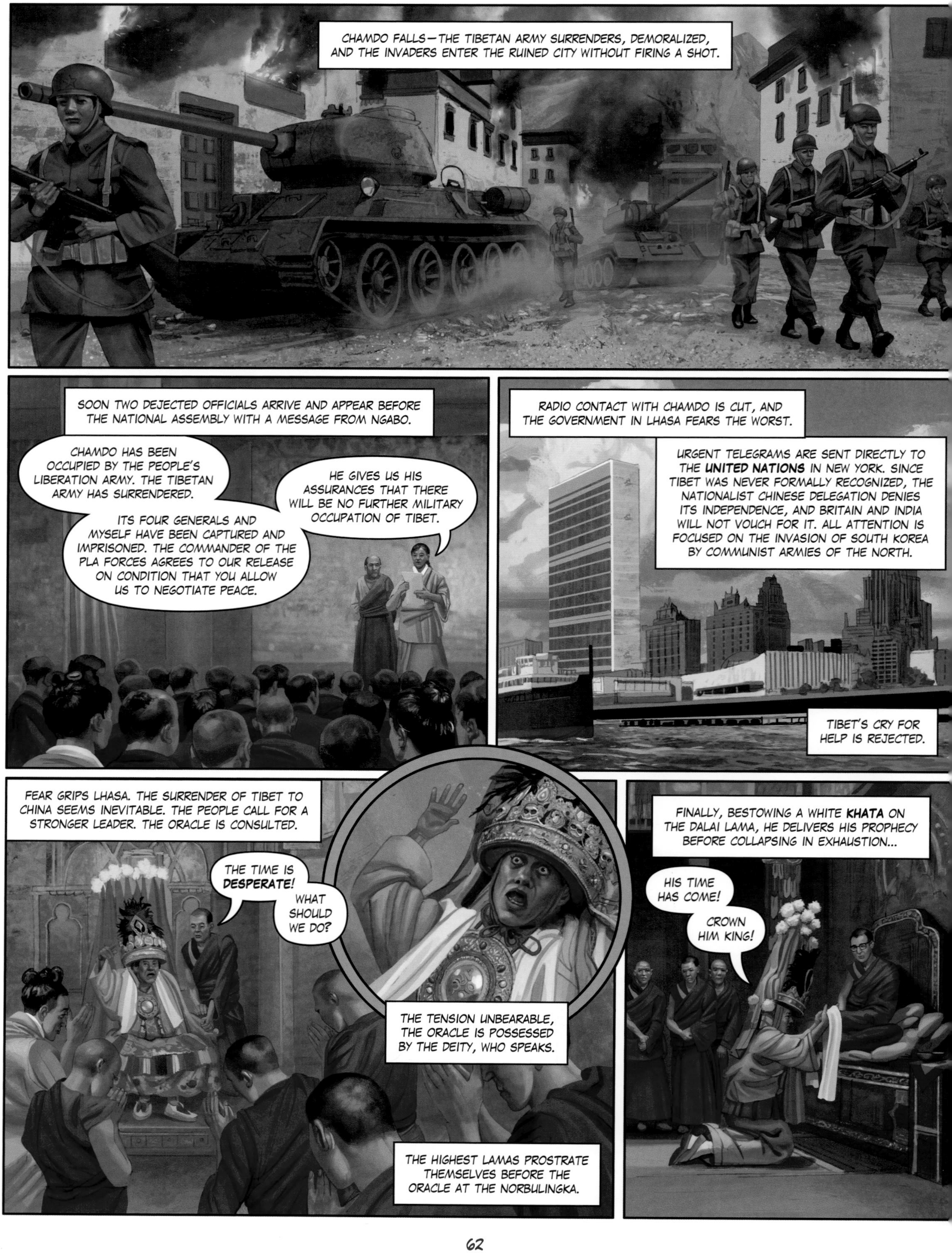
CHAMDO FALLS—THE TIBETAN ARMY SURRENDERS, DEMORALIZED, AND THE INVADERS ENTER THE RUINED CITY WITHOUT FIRING A SHOT.
SOON TWO DEJECTED OFFICIALS ARRIVE AND APPEAR BEFORE THE NATIONAL ASSEMBLY WITH A MESSAGE FROM NGABO.
CHAMDO HAS BEEN OCCUPIED BY THE PEOPLE'S LIBERATION ARMY. THE TIBETAN ARMY HAS SURRENDERED.
ITS FOUR GENERALS AND MYSELF HAVE BEEN CAPTURED AND IMPRISONED. THE COMMANDER OF THE PLA FORCES AGREES TO OUR RELEASE ON CONDITION THAT YOU ALLOW US TO NEGOTIATE PEACE.
HE GIVES US HIS ASSURANCES THAT THERE WILL BE NO FURTHER MILITARY OCCUPATION OF TIBET.
RADIO CONTACT WITH CHAMDO IS CUT, AND THE GOVERNMENT IN LHASA FEARS THE WORST.
URGENT TELEGRAMS ARE SENT DIRECTLY TO THE **UNITED NATIONS** IN NEW YORK. SINCE TIBET WAS NEVER FORMALLY RECOGNIZED, THE NATIONALIST CHINESE DELEGATION DENIES ITS INDEPENDENCE, AND BRITAIN AND INDIA WILL NOT VOUCH FOR IT. ALL ATTENTION IS FOCUSED ON THE INVASION OF SOUTH KOREA BY COMMUNIST ARMIES OF THE NORTH.
TIBET'S CRY FOR HELP IS REJECTED.
FEAR GRIPS LHASA. THE SURRENDER OF TIBET TO CHINA SEEMS INEVITABLE. THE PEOPLE CALL FOR A STRONGER LEADER. THE ORACLE IS CONSULTED.
THE TIME IS **DESPERATE!**
WHAT SHOULD WE DO?
THE HIGHEST LAMAS PROSTRATE THEMSELVES BEFORE THE ORACLE AT THE NORBULINGKA.
THE TENSION UNBEARABLE, THE ORACLE IS POSSESSED BY THE DEITY, WHO SPEAKS.
FINALLY, BESTOWING A WHITE **KHATA** ON THE DALAI LAMA, HE DELIVERS HIS PROPHECY BEFORE COLLAPSING IN EXHAUSTION...
HIS TIME HAS COME!
CROWN HIM KING!

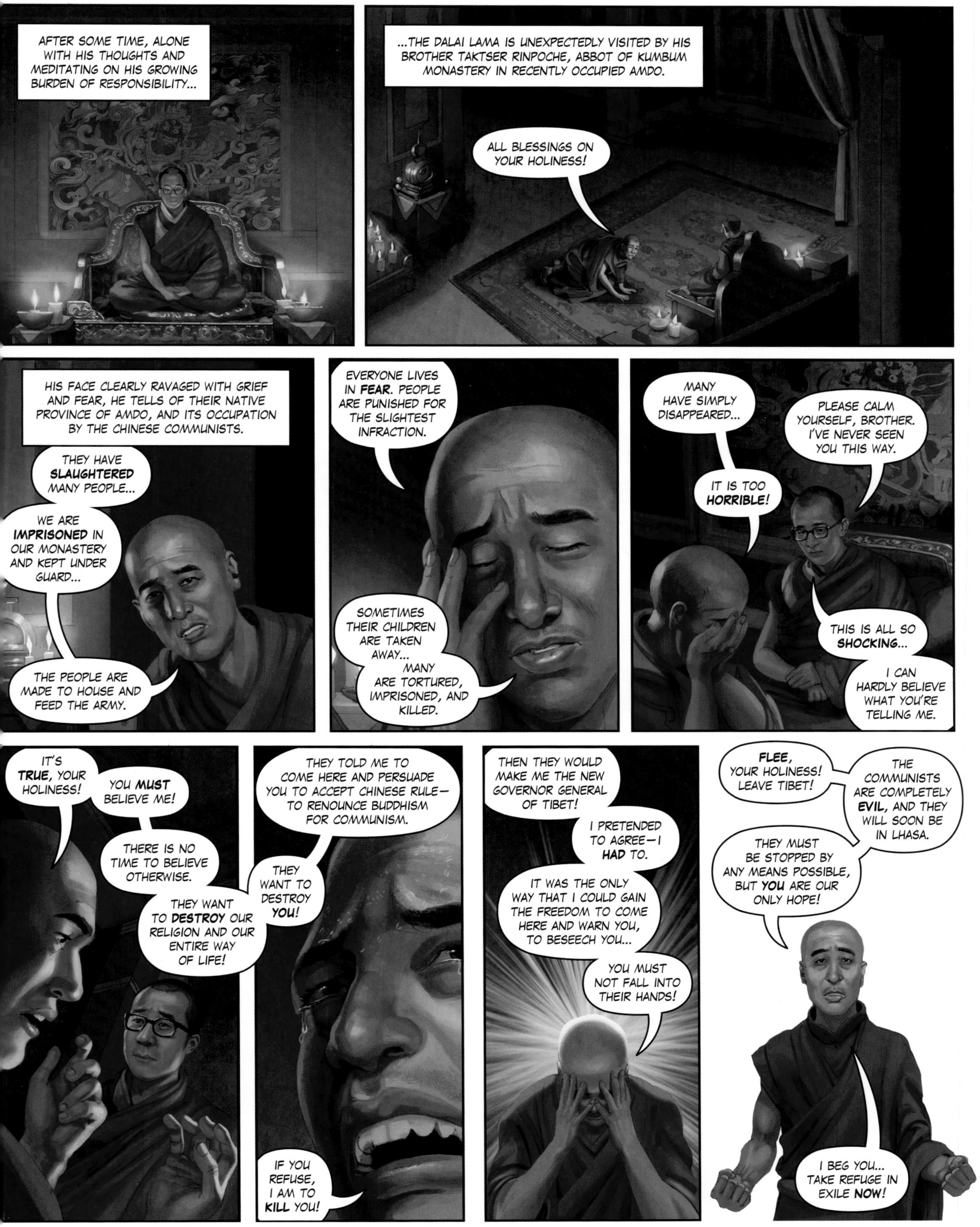
AFTER SOME TIME, ALONE WITH HIS THOUGHTS AND MEDITATING ON HIS GROWING BURDEN OF RESPONSIBILITY...
...THE DALAI LAMA IS UNEXPECTEDLY VISITED BY HIS BROTHER TAKTSER RINPOCHE, ABBOT OF KUMBUM MONASTERY IN RECENTLY OCCUPIED AMDO.
ALL BLESSINGS ON YOUR HOLINESS!
HIS FACE CLEARLY RAVAGED WITH GRIEF AND FEAR, HE TELLS OF THEIR NATIVE PROVINCE OF AMDO, AND ITS OCCUPATION BY THE CHINESE COMMUNISTS.
THEY HAVE **SLAUGHTERED** MANY PEOPLE...
WE ARE **IMPRISONED** IN OUR MONASTERY AND KEPT UNDER GUARD...
THE PEOPLE ARE MADE TO HOUSE AND FEED THE ARMY.
EVERYONE LIVES IN **FEAR**. PEOPLE ARE PUNISHED FOR THE SLIGHTEST INFRACTION.
SOMETIMES THEIR CHILDREN ARE TAKEN AWAY...
MANY ARE TORTURED, IMPRISONED, AND KILLED.
MANY HAVE SIMPLY DISAPPEARED...
IT IS TOO **HORRIBLE!**
PLEASE CALM YOURSELF, BROTHER. I'VE NEVER SEEN YOU THIS WAY.
THIS IS ALL SO **SHOCKING...**
I CAN HARDLY BELIEVE WHAT YOU'RE TELLING ME.
IT'S **TRUE**, YOUR HOLINESS!
YOU **MUST** BELIEVE ME!
THERE IS NO TIME TO BELIEVE OTHERWISE.
THEY WANT TO **DESTROY** OUR RELIGION AND OUR ENTIRE WAY OF LIFE!
THEY TOLD ME TO COME HERE AND PERSUADE YOU TO ACCEPT CHINESE RULE—TO RENOUNCE BUDDHISM FOR COMMUNISM.
THEY WANT TO DESTROY **YOU!**
IF YOU REFUSE, I AM TO **KILL** YOU!
THEN THEY WOULD MAKE ME THE NEW GOVERNOR GENERAL OF TIBET!
I PRETENDED TO AGREE—I **HAD** TO.
IT WAS THE ONLY WAY THAT I COULD GAIN THE FREEDOM TO COME HERE AND WARN YOU, TO BESEECH YOU...
YOU MUST NOT FALL INTO THEIR HANDS!
FLEE, YOUR HOLINESS! LEAVE TIBET!
THE COMMUNISTS ARE COMPLETELY **EVIL**, AND THEY WILL SOON BE IN LHASA.
THEY MUST BE STOPPED BY ANY MEANS POSSIBLE, BUT **YOU** ARE OUR ONLY HOPE!
I BEG YOU... TAKE REFUGE IN EXILE **NOW!**

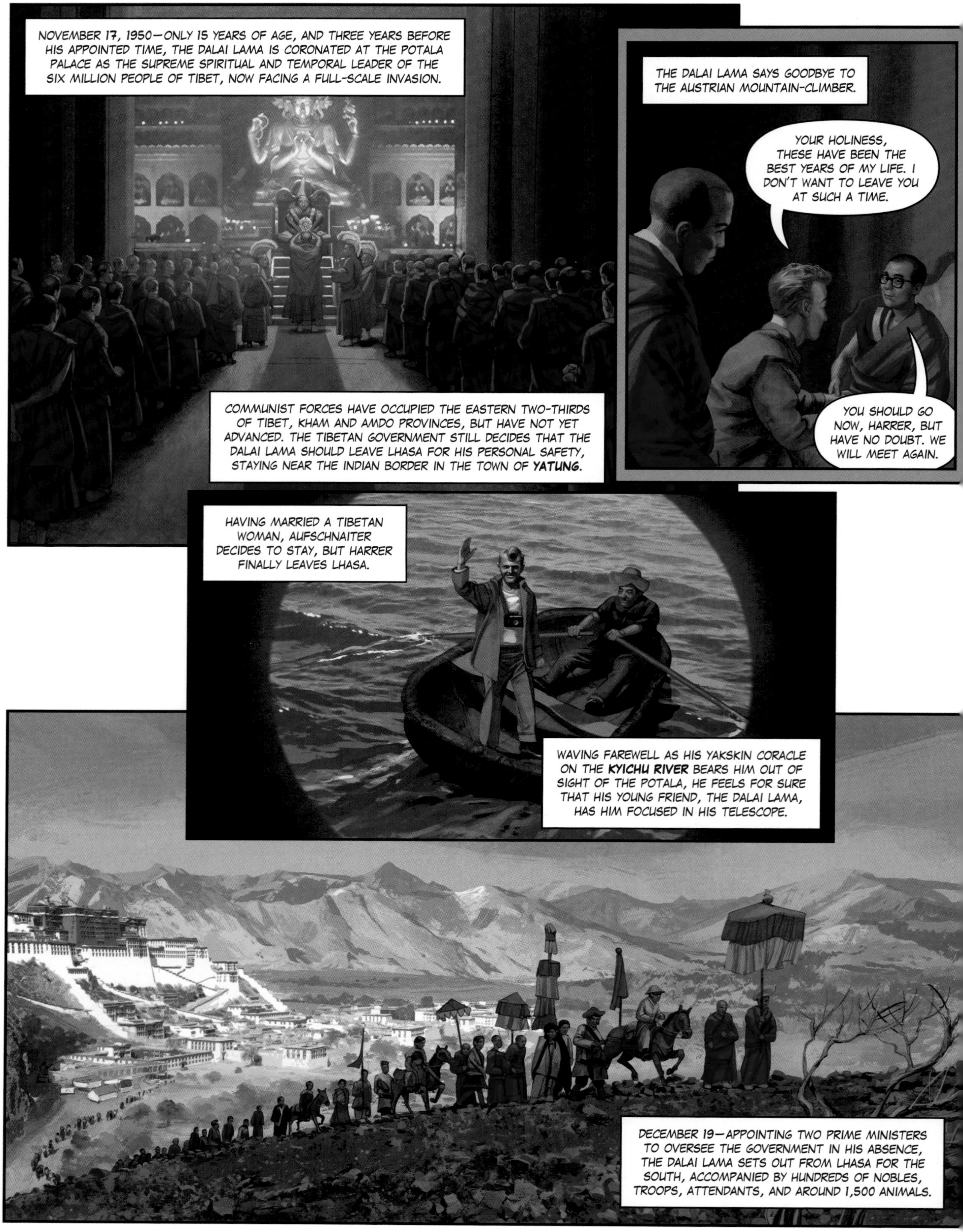

NOVEMBER 17, 1950—ONLY 15 YEARS OF AGE, AND THREE YEARS BEFORE HIS APPOINTED TIME, THE DALAI LAMA IS CORONATED AT THE POTALA PALACE AS THE SUPREME SPIRITUAL AND TEMPORAL LEADER OF THE SIX MILLION PEOPLE OF TIBET, NOW FACING A FULL-SCALE INVASION.
COMMUNIST FORCES HAVE OCCUPIED THE EASTERN TWO-THIRDS OF TIBET, KHAM AND AMDO PROVINCES, BUT HAVE NOT YET ADVANCED. THE TIBETAN GOVERNMENT STILL DECIDES THAT THE DALAI LAMA SHOULD LEAVE LHASA FOR HIS PERSONAL SAFETY, STAYING NEAR THE INDIAN BORDER IN THE TOWN OF YATUNG.
THE DALAI LAMA SAYS GOODBYE TO THE AUSTRIAN MOUNTAIN-CLIMBER.
YOUR HOLINESS, THESE HAVE BEEN THE BEST YEARS OF MY LIFE. I DON'T WANT TO LEAVE YOU AT SUCH A TIME.
YOU SHOULD GO NOW, HARRER, BUT HAVE NO DOUBT. WE WILL MEET AGAIN.
HAVING MARRIED A TIBETAN WOMAN, AUFSCHNAITER DECIDES TO STAY, BUT HARRER FINALLY LEAVES LHASA.
WAVING FAREWELL AS HIS YAKSKIN CORACLE ON THE KYICHU RIVER BEARS HIM OUT OF SIGHT OF THE POTALA, HE FEELS FOR SURE THAT HIS YOUNG FRIEND, THE DALAI LAMA, HAS HIM FOCUSED IN HIS TELESCOPE.
DECEMBER 19—APPOINTING TWO PRIME MINISTERS TO OVERSEE THE GOVERNMENT IN HIS ABSENCE, THE DALAI LAMA SETS OUT FROM LHASA FOR THE SOUTH, ACCOMPANIED BY HUNDREDS OF NOBLES, TROOPS, ATTENDANTS, AND AROUND 1,500 ANIMALS.

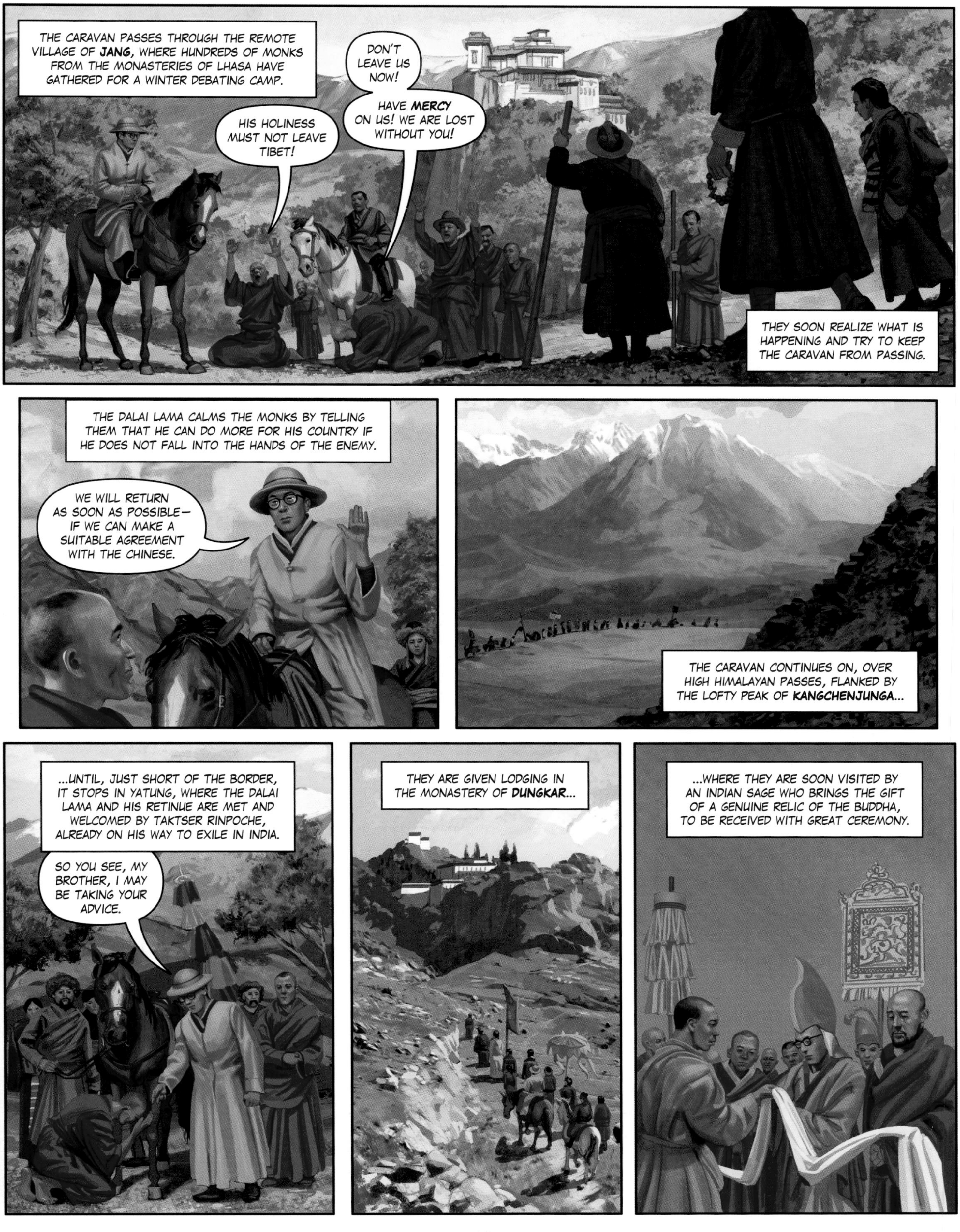
THE CARAVAN PASSES THROUGH THE REMOTE VILLAGE OF JANG, WHERE HUNDREDS OF MONKS FROM THE MONASTERIES OF LHASA HAVE GATHERED FOR A WINTER DEBATING CAMP.
HIS HOLINESS MUST NOT LEAVE TIBET!
DON'T LEAVE US NOW!
HAVE MERCY ON US! WE ARE LOST WITHOUT YOU!
THEY SOON REALIZE WHAT IS HAPPENING AND TRY TO KEEP THE CARAVAN FROM PASSING.
THE DALAI LAMA CALMS THE MONKS BY TELLING THEM THAT HE CAN DO MORE FOR HIS COUNTRY IF HE DOES NOT FALL INTO THE HANDS OF THE ENEMY.
WE WILL RETURN AS SOON AS POSSIBLE— IF WE CAN MAKE A SUITABLE AGREEMENT WITH THE CHINESE.
THE CARAVAN CONTINUES ON, OVER HIGH HIMALAYAN PASSES, FLANKED BY THE LOFTY PEAK OF KANGCHENJUNGA...
...UNTIL, JUST SHORT OF THE BORDER, IT STOPS IN YATUNG, WHERE THE DALAI LAMA AND HIS RETINUE ARE MET AND WELCOMED BY TAKTSER RINPOCHE, ALREADY ON HIS WAY TO EXILE IN INDIA.
SO YOU SEE, MY BROTHER, I MAY BE TAKING YOUR ADVICE.
THEY ARE GIVEN LODGING IN THE MONASTERY OF DUNGKAR...
...WHERE THEY ARE SOON VISITED BY AN INDIAN SAGE WHO BRINGS THE GIFT OF A GENUINE RELIC OF THE BUDDHA, TO BE RECEIVED WITH GREAT CEREMONY.

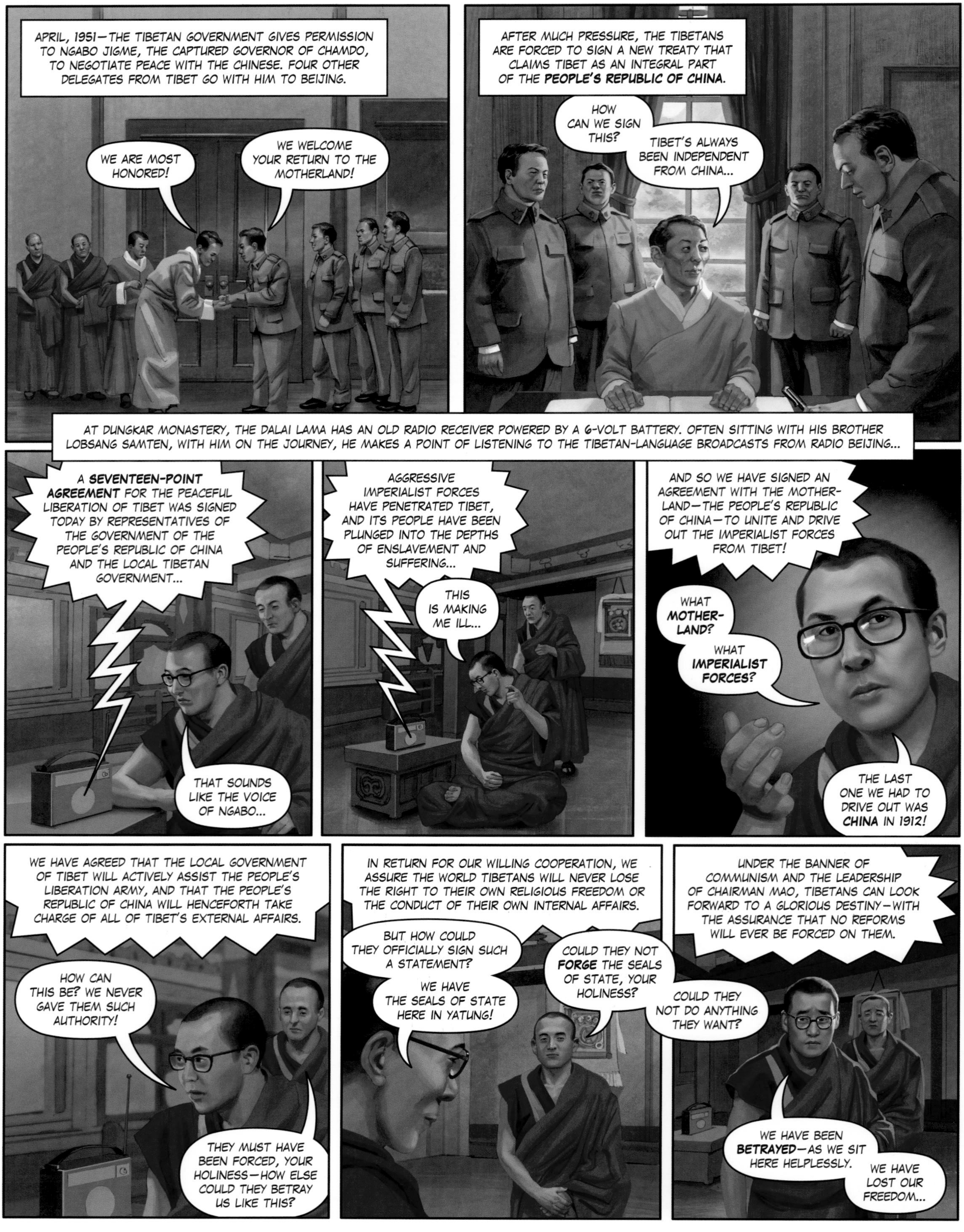

APRIL, 1951—THE TIBETAN GOVERNMENT GIVES PERMISSION TO NGABO JIGME, THE CAPTURED GOVERNOR OF CHAMDO, TO NEGOTIATE PEACE WITH THE CHINESE. FOUR OTHER DELEGATES FROM TIBET GO WITH HIM TO BEIJING.
WE ARE MOST HONORED!
WE WELCOME YOUR RETURN TO THE MOTHERLAND!
AFTER MUCH PRESSURE, THE TIBETANS ARE FORCED TO SIGN A NEW TREATY THAT CLAIMS TIBET AS AN INTEGRAL PART OF THE **PEOPLE'S REPUBLIC OF CHINA**.
HOW CAN WE SIGN THIS?
TIBET'S ALWAYS BEEN INDEPENDENT FROM CHINA...
AT DUNGKAR MONASTERY, THE DALAI LAMA HAS AN OLD RADIO RECEIVER POWERED BY A 6-VOLT BATTERY. OFTEN SITTING WITH HIS BROTHER LOBSANG SAMTEN, WITH HIM ON THE JOURNEY, HE MAKES A POINT OF LISTENING TO THE TIBETAN-LANGUAGE BROADCASTS FROM RADIO BEIJING...
A **SEVENTEEN-POINT AGREEMENT** FOR THE PEACEFUL LIBERATION OF TIBET WAS SIGNED TODAY BY REPRESENTATIVES OF THE GOVERNMENT OF THE PEOPLE'S REPUBLIC OF CHINA AND THE LOCAL TIBETAN GOVERNMENT...
THAT SOUNDS LIKE THE VOICE OF NGABO...
AGGRESSIVE IMPERIALIST FORCES HAVE PENETRATED TIBET, AND ITS PEOPLE HAVE BEEN PLUNGED INTO THE DEPTHS OF ENSLAVEMENT AND SUFFERING...
THIS IS MAKING ME ILL...
AND SO WE HAVE SIGNED AN AGREEMENT WITH THE MOTHER-LAND—THE PEOPLE'S REPUBLIC OF CHINA—TO UNITE AND DRIVE OUT THE IMPERIALIST FORCES FROM TIBET!
WHAT **MOTHER-LAND?**
WHAT **IMPERIALIST FORCES?**
THE LAST ONE WE HAD TO DRIVE OUT WAS **CHINA** IN 1912!
WE HAVE AGREED THAT THE LOCAL GOVERNMENT OF TIBET WILL ACTIVELY ASSIST THE PEOPLE'S LIBERATION ARMY, AND THAT THE PEOPLE'S REPUBLIC OF CHINA WILL HENCEFORTH TAKE CHARGE OF ALL OF TIBET'S EXTERNAL AFFAIRS.
HOW CAN THIS BE? WE NEVER GAVE THEM SUCH AUTHORITY!
THEY MUST HAVE BEEN FORCED, YOUR HOLINESS—HOW ELSE COULD THEY BETRAY US LIKE THIS?
IN RETURN FOR OUR WILLING COOPERATION, WE ASSURE THE WORLD TIBETANS WILL NEVER LOSE THE RIGHT TO THEIR OWN RELIGIOUS FREEDOM OR THE CONDUCT OF THEIR OWN INTERNAL AFFAIRS.
BUT HOW COULD THEY OFFICIALLY SIGN SUCH A STATEMENT?
WE HAVE THE SEALS OF STATE HERE IN YATUNG!
COULD THEY NOT **FORGE** THE SEALS OF STATE, YOUR HOLINESS?
UNDER THE BANNER OF COMMUNISM AND THE LEADERSHIP OF CHAIRMAN MAO, TIBETANS CAN LOOK FORWARD TO A GLORIOUS DESTINY—WITH THE ASSURANCE THAT NO REFORMS WILL EVER BE FORCED ON THEM.
COULD THEY NOT DO ANYTHING THEY WANT?
WE HAVE BEEN **BETRAYED**—AS WE SIT HERE HELPLESSLY.
WE HAVE LOST OUR FREEDOM...

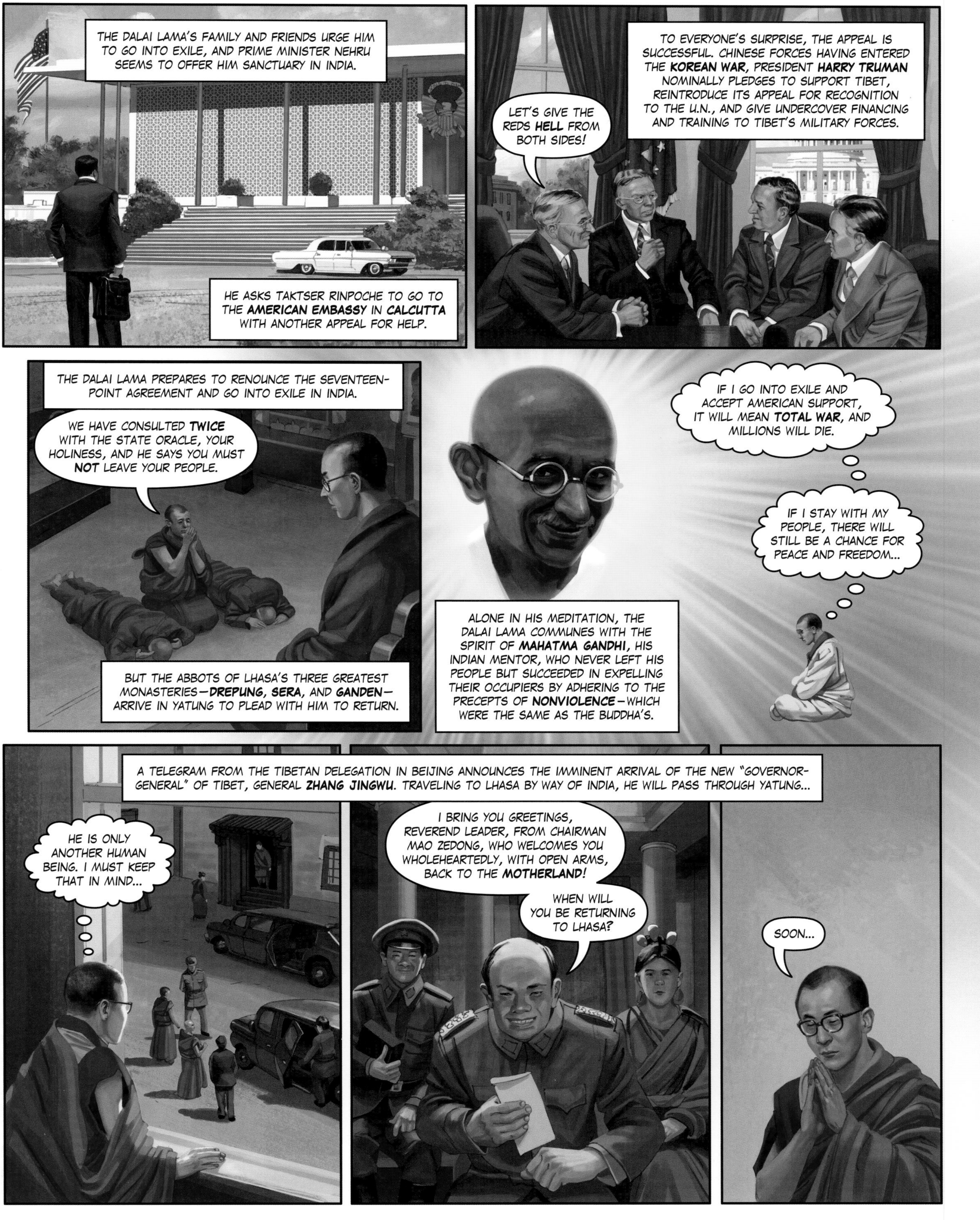
THE DALAI LAMA'S FAMILY AND FRIENDS URGE HIM TO GO INTO EXILE, AND PRIME MINISTER NEHRU SEEMS TO OFFER HIM SANCTUARY IN INDIA.
HE ASKS TAKTSER RINPOCHE TO GO TO THE **AMERICAN EMBASSY** IN **CALCUTTA** WITH ANOTHER APPEAL FOR HELP.
TO EVERYONE'S SURPRISE, THE APPEAL IS SUCCESSFUL. CHINESE FORCES HAVING ENTERED THE **KOREAN WAR**, PRESIDENT **HARRY TRUMAN** NOMINALLY PLEDGES TO SUPPORT TIBET, REINTRODUCE ITS APPEAL FOR RECOGNITION TO THE U.N., AND GIVE UNDERCOVER FINANCING AND TRAINING TO TIBET'S MILITARY FORCES.
LET'S GIVE THE REDS **HELL** FROM BOTH SIDES!
THE DALAI LAMA PREPARES TO RENOUNCE THE SEVENTEEN-POINT AGREEMENT AND GO INTO EXILE IN INDIA.
WE HAVE CONSULTED **TWICE** WITH THE STATE ORACLE, YOUR HOLINESS, AND HE SAYS YOU MUST **NOT** LEAVE YOUR PEOPLE.
BUT THE ABBOTS OF LHASA'S THREE GREATEST MONASTERIES—**DREPUNG, SERA,** AND **GANDEN**—ARRIVE IN YATUNG TO PLEAD WITH HIM TO RETURN.
ALONE IN HIS MEDITATION, THE DALAI LAMA COMMUNES WITH THE SPIRIT OF **MAHATMA GANDHI**, HIS INDIAN MENTOR, WHO NEVER LEFT HIS PEOPLE BUT SUCCEEDED IN EXPELLING THEIR OCCUPIERS BY ADHERING TO THE PRECEPTS OF **NONVIOLENCE**—WHICH WERE THE SAME AS THE BUDDHA'S.
IF I GO INTO EXILE AND ACCEPT AMERICAN SUPPORT, IT WILL MEAN **TOTAL WAR**, AND MILLIONS WILL DIE.
IF I STAY WITH MY PEOPLE, THERE WILL STILL BE A CHANCE FOR PEACE AND FREEDOM...
A TELEGRAM FROM THE TIBETAN DELEGATION IN BEIJING ANNOUNCES THE IMMINENT ARRIVAL OF THE NEW "GOVERNOR-GENERAL" OF TIBET, GENERAL **ZHANG JINGWU**. TRAVELING TO LHASA BY WAY OF INDIA, HE WILL PASS THROUGH YATUNG...
HE IS ONLY ANOTHER HUMAN BEING. I MUST KEEP THAT IN MIND...
I BRING YOU GREETINGS, REVEREND LEADER, FROM CHAIRMAN MAO ZEDONG, WHO WELCOMES YOU WHOLEHEARTEDLY, WITH OPEN ARMS, BACK TO THE **MOTHERLAND**!
WHEN WILL YOU BE RETURNING TO LHASA?
SOON...

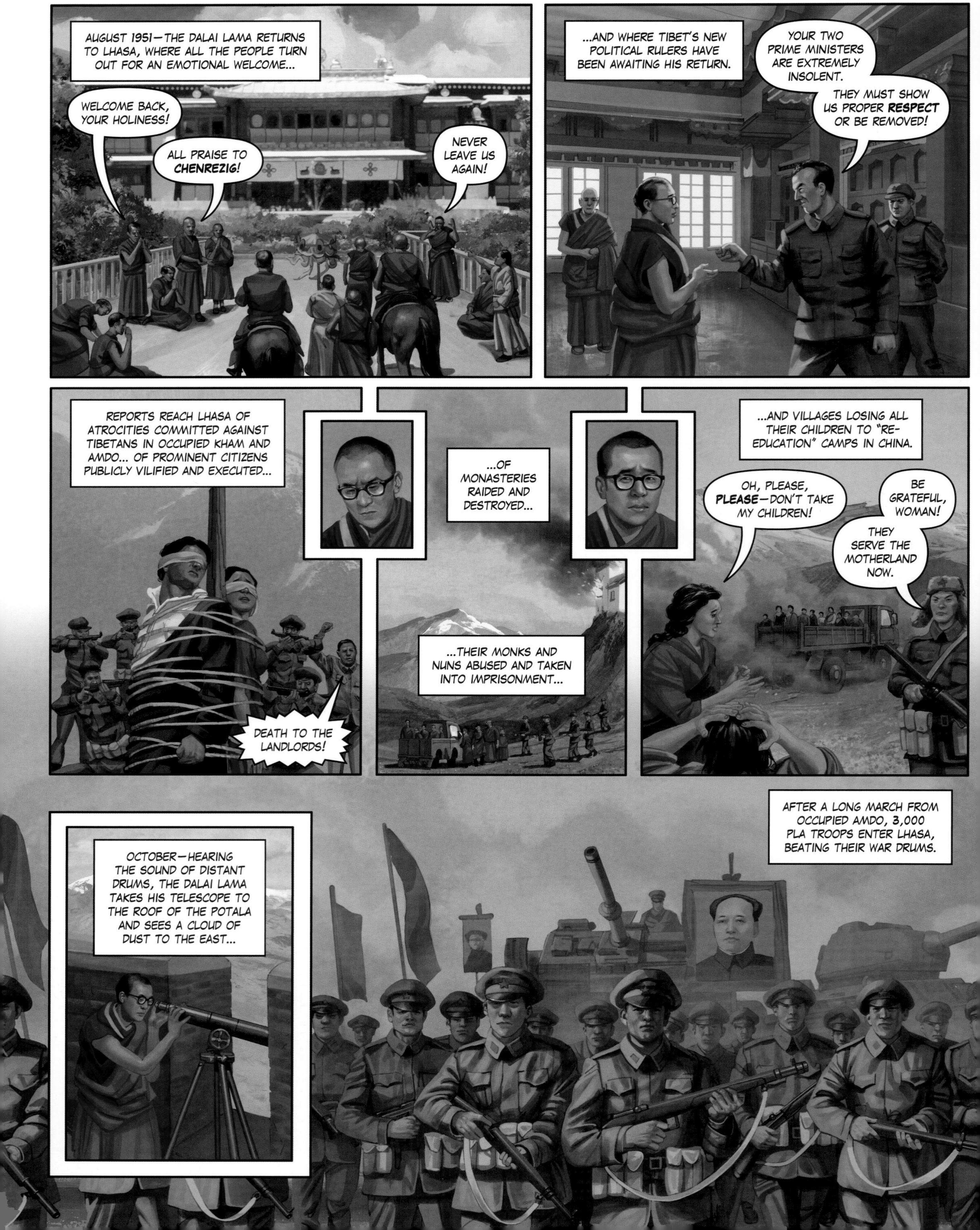
AUGUST 1951—THE DALAI LAMA RETURNS TO LHASA, WHERE ALL THE PEOPLE TURN OUT FOR AN EMOTIONAL WELCOME...
WELCOME BACK, YOUR HOLINESS!
ALL PRAISE TO CHENREZIG!
NEVER LEAVE US AGAIN!
...AND WHERE TIBET'S NEW POLITICAL RULERS HAVE BEEN AWAITING HIS RETURN.
YOUR TWO PRIME MINISTERS ARE EXTREMELY INSOLENT.
THEY MUST SHOW US PROPER RESPECT OR BE REMOVED!
REPORTS REACH LHASA OF ATROCITIES COMMITTED AGAINST TIBETANS IN OCCUPIED KHAM AND AMDO... OF PROMINENT CITIZENS PUBLICLY VILIFIED AND EXECUTED...
DEATH TO THE LANDLORDS!
...OF MONASTERIES RAIDED AND DESTROYED...
...THEIR MONKS AND NUNS ABUSED AND TAKEN INTO IMPRISONMENT...
...AND VILLAGES LOSING ALL THEIR CHILDREN TO "RE-EDUCATION" CAMPS IN CHINA.
OH, PLEASE, PLEASE—DON'T TAKE MY CHILDREN!
BE GRATEFUL, WOMAN!
THEY SERVE THE MOTHERLAND NOW.
OCTOBER—HEARING THE SOUND OF DISTANT DRUMS, THE DALAI LAMA TAKES HIS TELESCOPE TO THE ROOF OF THE POTALA AND SEES A CLOUD OF DUST TO THE EAST...
AFTER A LONG MARCH FROM OCCUPIED AMDO, 3,000 PLA TROOPS ENTER LHASA, BEATING THEIR WAR DRUMS.

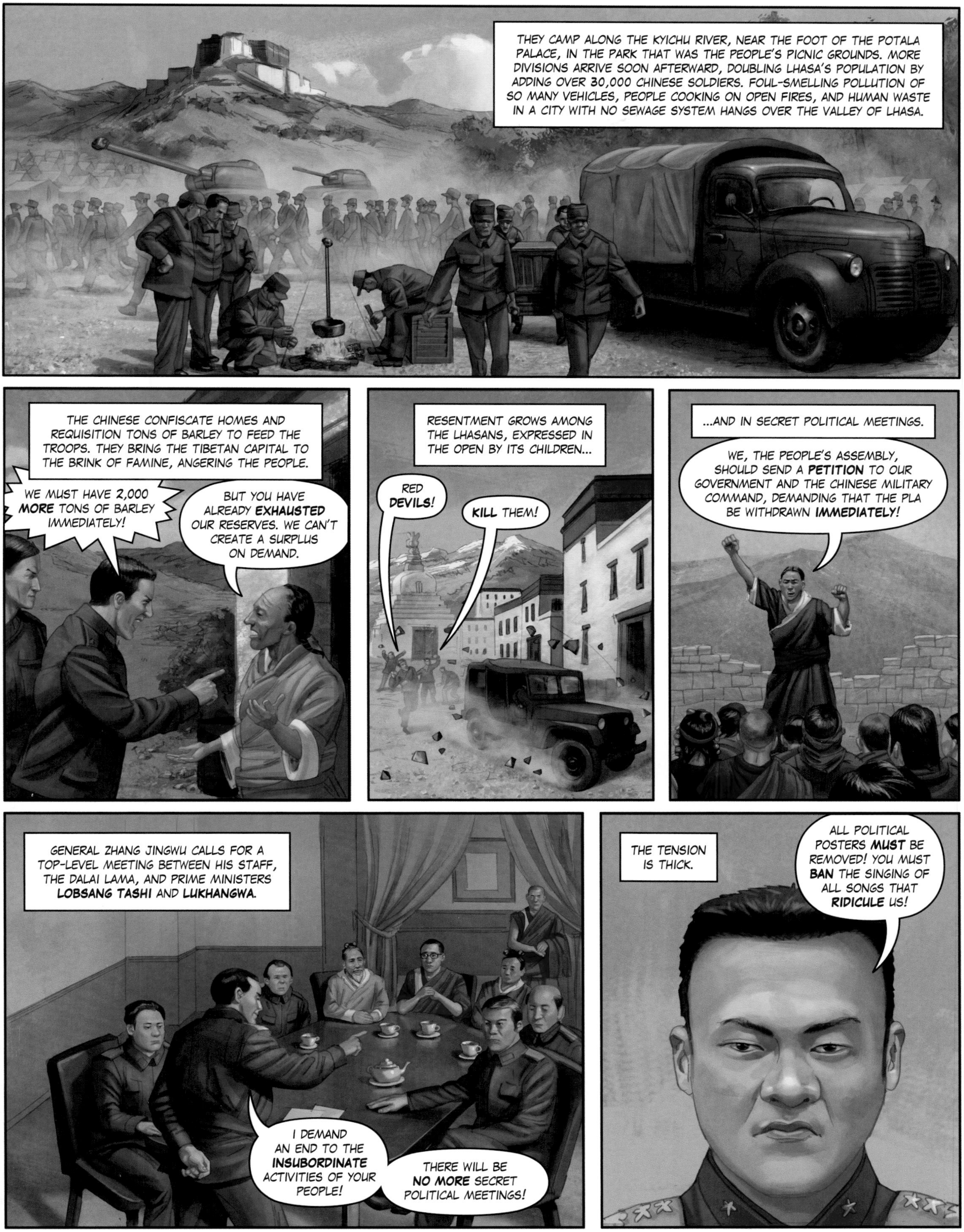

THEY CAMP ALONG THE KYICHU RIVER, NEAR THE FOOT OF THE POTALA PALACE, IN THE PARK THAT WAS THE PEOPLE'S PICNIC GROUNDS. MORE DIVISIONS ARRIVE SOON AFTERWARD, DOUBLING LHASA'S POPULATION BY ADDING OVER 30,000 CHINESE SOLDIERS. FOUL-SMELLING POLLUTION OF SO MANY VEHICLES, PEOPLE COOKING ON OPEN FIRES, AND HUMAN WASTE IN A CITY WITH NO SEWAGE SYSTEM HANGS OVER THE VALLEY OF LHASA.
THE CHINESE CONFISCATE HOMES AND REQUISITION TONS OF BARLEY TO FEED THE TROOPS. THEY BRING THE TIBETAN CAPITAL TO THE BRINK OF FAMINE, ANGERING THE PEOPLE.
WE MUST HAVE 2,000 **MORE** TONS OF BARLEY IMMEDIATELY!
BUT YOU HAVE ALREADY **EXHAUSTED** OUR RESERVES. WE CAN'T CREATE A SURPLUS ON DEMAND.
RESENTMENT GROWS AMONG THE LHASANS, EXPRESSED IN THE OPEN BY ITS CHILDREN...
RED **DEVILS**!
KILL THEM!
...AND IN SECRET POLITICAL MEETINGS.
WE, THE PEOPLE'S ASSEMBLY, SHOULD SEND A **PETITION** TO OUR GOVERNMENT AND THE CHINESE MILITARY COMMAND, DEMANDING THAT THE PLA BE WITHDRAWN **IMMEDIATELY**!
GENERAL ZHANG JINGWU CALLS FOR A TOP-LEVEL MEETING BETWEEN HIS STAFF, THE DALAI LAMA, AND PRIME MINISTERS **LOBSANG TASHI** AND **LUKHANGWA**.
I DEMAND AN END TO THE **INSUBORDINATE** ACTIVITIES OF YOUR PEOPLE!
THERE WILL BE **NO MORE** SECRET POLITICAL MEETINGS!
THE TENSION IS THICK.
ALL POLITICAL POSTERS **MUST** BE REMOVED! YOU MUST **BAN** THE SINGING OF ALL SONGS THAT **RIDICULE** US!

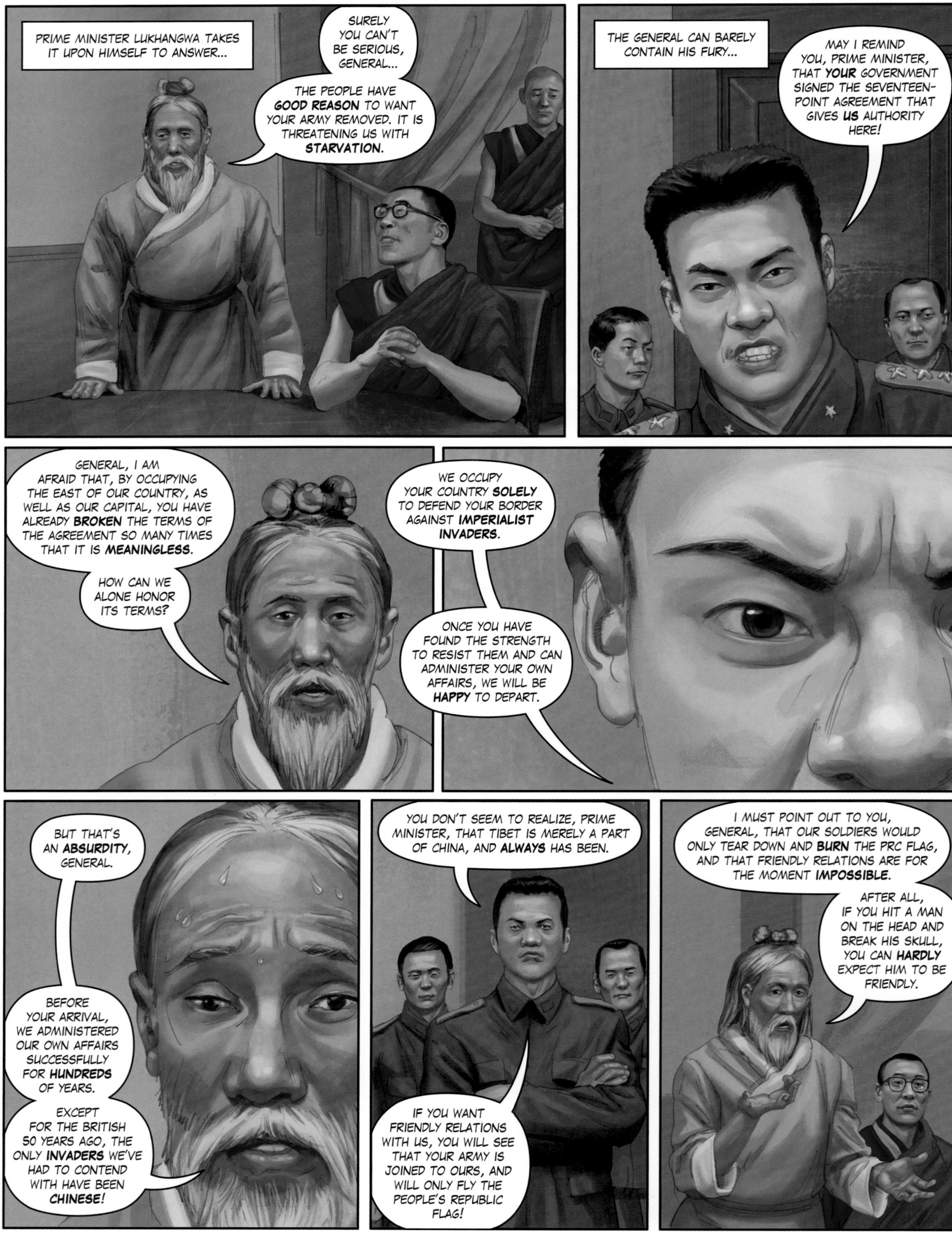
PRIME MINISTER LUKHANGWA TAKES IT UPON HIMSELF TO ANSWER...
SURELY YOU CAN'T BE SERIOUS, GENERAL...
THE PEOPLE HAVE **GOOD REASON** TO WANT YOUR ARMY REMOVED. IT IS THREATENING US WITH **STARVATION**.
THE GENERAL CAN BARELY CONTAIN HIS FURY...
MAY I REMIND YOU, PRIME MINISTER, THAT **YOUR** GOVERNMENT SIGNED THE SEVENTEEN-POINT AGREEMENT THAT GIVES **US** AUTHORITY HERE!
GENERAL, I AM AFRAID THAT, BY OCCUPYING THE EAST OF OUR COUNTRY, AS WELL AS OUR CAPITAL, YOU HAVE ALREADY **BROKEN** THE TERMS OF THE AGREEMENT SO MANY TIMES THAT IT IS **MEANINGLESS**.
HOW CAN WE ALONE HONOR ITS TERMS?
WE OCCUPY YOUR COUNTRY **SOLELY** TO DEFEND YOUR BORDER AGAINST **IMPERIALIST INVADERS**.
ONCE YOU HAVE FOUND THE STRENGTH TO RESIST THEM AND CAN ADMINISTER YOUR OWN AFFAIRS, WE WILL BE **HAPPY** TO DEPART.
BUT THAT'S AN **ABSURDITY**, GENERAL.
BEFORE YOUR ARRIVAL, WE ADMINISTERED OUR OWN AFFAIRS SUCCESSFULLY FOR **HUNDREDS** OF YEARS.
EXCEPT FOR THE BRITISH 50 YEARS AGO, THE ONLY **INVADERS** WE'VE HAD TO CONTEND WITH HAVE BEEN **CHINESE**!
YOU DON'T SEEM TO REALIZE, PRIME MINISTER, THAT TIBET IS MERELY A PART OF CHINA, AND **ALWAYS** HAS BEEN.
IF YOU WANT FRIENDLY RELATIONS WITH US, YOU WILL SEE THAT YOUR ARMY IS JOINED TO OURS, AND WILL ONLY FLY THE PEOPLE'S REPUBLIC FLAG!
I MUST POINT OUT TO YOU, GENERAL, THAT OUR SOLDIERS WOULD ONLY TEAR DOWN AND **BURN** THE PRC FLAG, AND THAT FRIENDLY RELATIONS ARE FOR THE MOMENT **IMPOSSIBLE**.
AFTER ALL, IF YOU HIT A MAN ON THE HEAD AND BREAK HIS SKULL, YOU CAN **HARDLY** EXPECT HIM TO BE FRIENDLY.

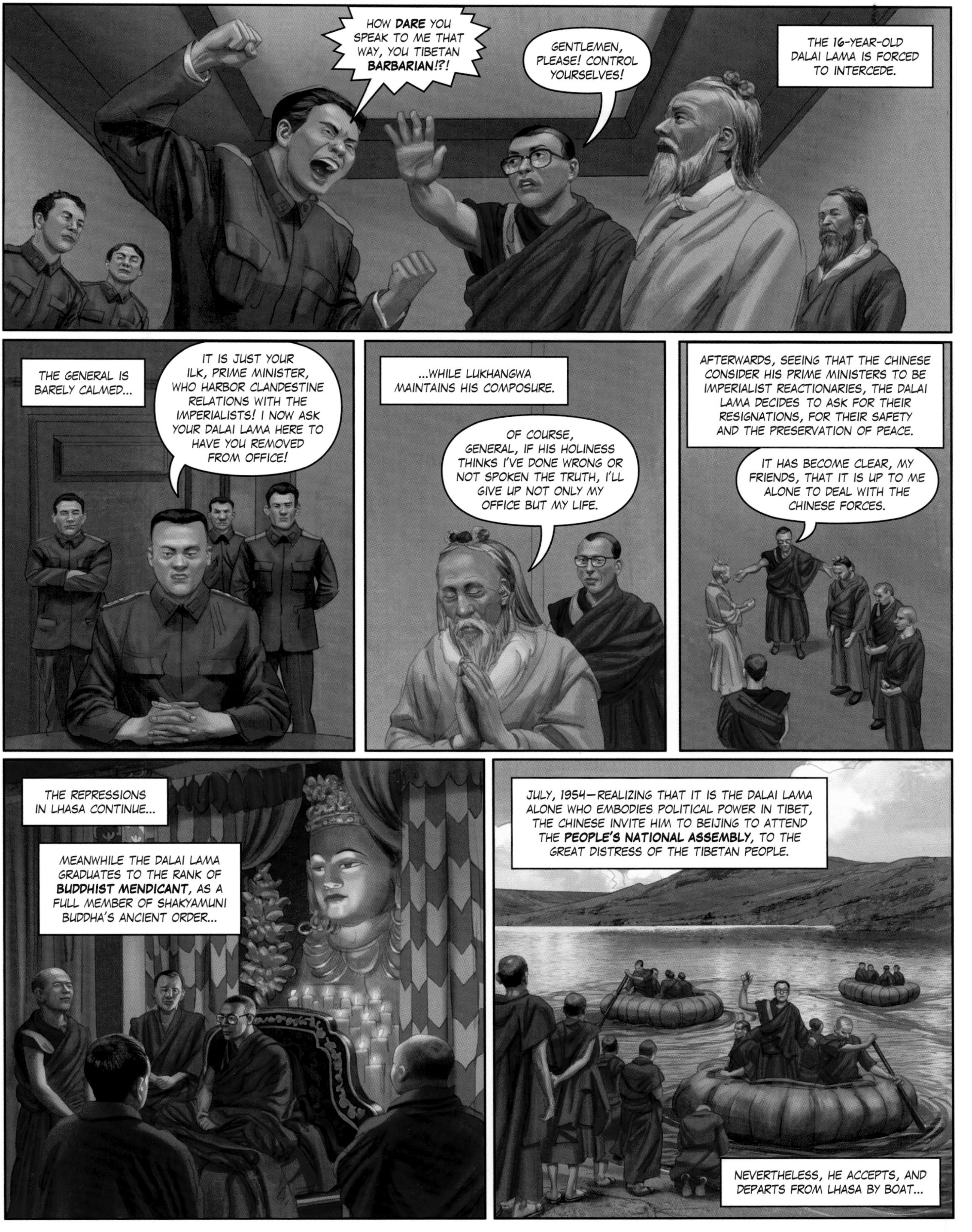
HOW DARE YOU SPEAK TO ME THAT WAY, YOU TIBETAN BARBARIAN!?!
GENTLEMEN, PLEASE! CONTROL YOURSELVES!
THE 16-YEAR-OLD DALAI LAMA IS FORCED TO INTERCEDE.
THE GENERAL IS BARELY CALMED...
IT IS JUST YOUR ILK, PRIME MINISTER, WHO HARBOR CLANDESTINE RELATIONS WITH THE IMPERIALISTS! I NOW ASK YOUR DALAI LAMA HERE TO HAVE YOU REMOVED FROM OFFICE!
...WHILE LUKHANGWA MAINTAINS HIS COMPOSURE.
OF COURSE, GENERAL, IF HIS HOLINESS THINKS I'VE DONE WRONG OR NOT SPOKEN THE TRUTH, I'LL GIVE UP NOT ONLY MY OFFICE BUT MY LIFE.
AFTERWARDS, SEEING THAT THE CHINESE CONSIDER HIS PRIME MINISTERS TO BE IMPERIALIST REACTIONARIES, THE DALAI LAMA DECIDES TO ASK FOR THEIR RESIGNATIONS, FOR THEIR SAFETY AND THE PRESERVATION OF PEACE.
IT HAS BECOME CLEAR, MY FRIENDS, THAT IT IS UP TO ME ALONE TO DEAL WITH THE CHINESE FORCES.
THE REPRESSIONS IN LHASA CONTINUE...
MEANWHILE THE DALAI LAMA GRADUATES TO THE RANK OF BUDDHIST MENDICANT, AS A FULL MEMBER OF SHAKYAMUNI BUDDHA'S ANCIENT ORDER...
JULY, 1954—REALIZING THAT IT IS THE DALAI LAMA ALONE WHO EMBODIES POLITICAL POWER IN TIBET, THE CHINESE INVITE HIM TO BEIJING TO ATTEND THE PEOPLE'S NATIONAL ASSEMBLY, TO THE GREAT DISTRESS OF THE TIBETAN PEOPLE.
NEVERTHELESS, HE ACCEPTS, AND DEPARTS FROM LHASA BY BOAT...

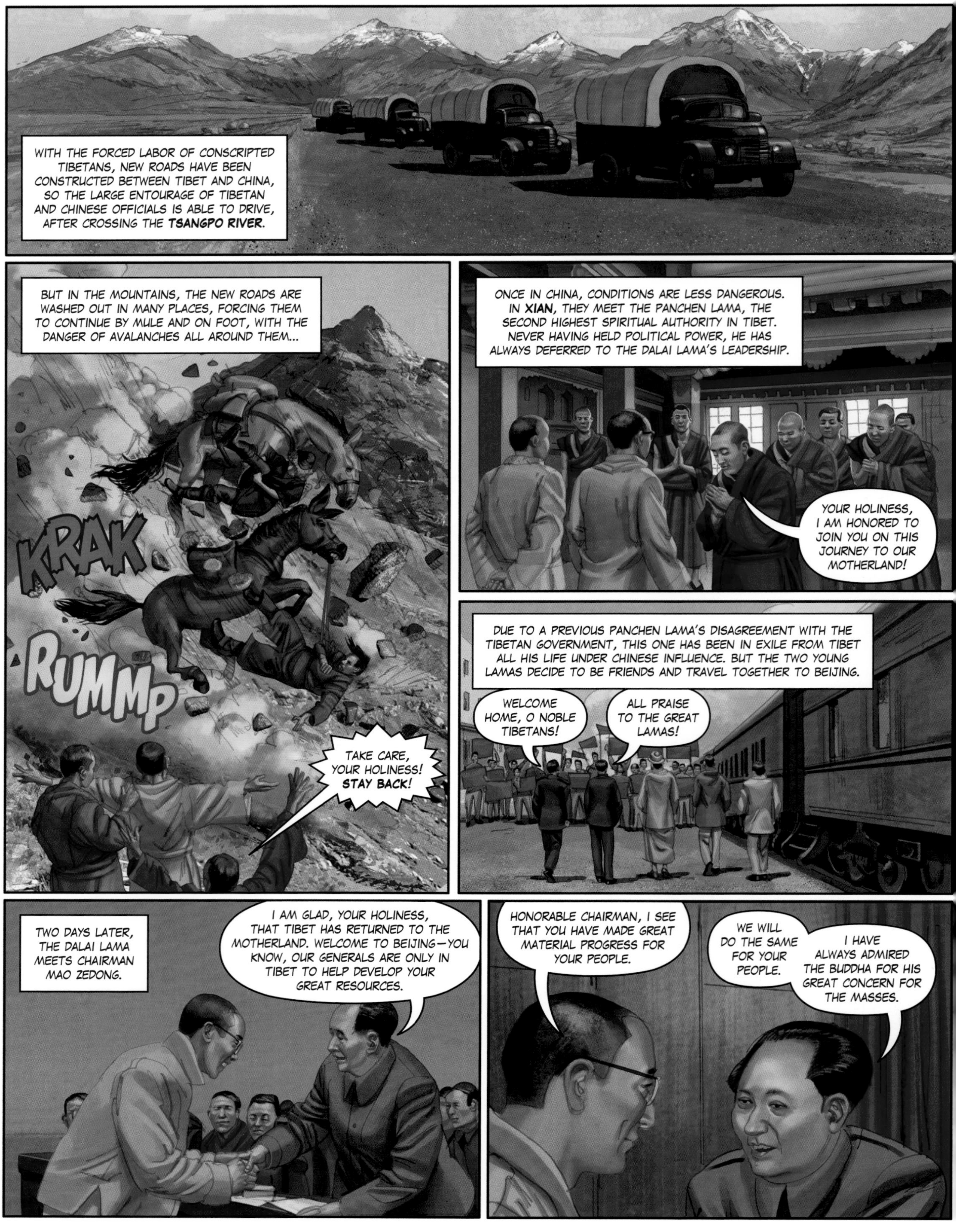
WITH THE FORCED LABOR OF CONSCRIPTED TIBETANS, NEW ROADS HAVE BEEN CONSTRUCTED BETWEEN TIBET AND CHINA, SO THE LARGE ENTOURAGE OF TIBETAN AND CHINESE OFFICIALS IS ABLE TO DRIVE, AFTER CROSSING THE **TSANGPO RIVER**.
BUT IN THE MOUNTAINS, THE NEW ROADS ARE WASHED OUT IN MANY PLACES, FORCING THEM TO CONTINUE BY MULE AND ON FOOT, WITH THE DANGER OF AVALANCHES ALL AROUND THEM...
KRAK
RUMMP
TAKE CARE, YOUR HOLINESS! **STAY BACK!**
ONCE IN CHINA, CONDITIONS ARE LESS DANGEROUS. IN **XIAN**, THEY MEET THE PANCHEN LAMA, THE SECOND HIGHEST SPIRITUAL AUTHORITY IN TIBET. NEVER HAVING HELD POLITICAL POWER, HE HAS ALWAYS DEFERRED TO THE DALAI LAMA'S LEADERSHIP.
YOUR HOLINESS, I AM HONORED TO JOIN YOU ON THIS JOURNEY TO OUR MOTHERLAND!
DUE TO A PREVIOUS PANCHEN LAMA'S DISAGREEMENT WITH THE TIBETAN GOVERNMENT, THIS ONE HAS BEEN IN EXILE FROM TIBET ALL HIS LIFE UNDER CHINESE INFLUENCE. BUT THE TWO YOUNG LAMAS DECIDE TO BE FRIENDS AND TRAVEL TOGETHER TO BEIJING.
WELCOME HOME, O NOBLE TIBETANS!
ALL PRAISE TO THE GREAT LAMAS!
TWO DAYS LATER, THE DALAI LAMA MEETS CHAIRMAN MAO ZEDONG.
I AM GLAD, YOUR HOLINESS, THAT TIBET HAS RETURNED TO THE MOTHERLAND. WELCOME TO BEIJING—YOU KNOW, OUR GENERALS ARE ONLY IN TIBET TO HELP DEVELOP YOUR GREAT RESOURCES.
HONORABLE CHAIRMAN, I SEE THAT YOU HAVE MADE GREAT MATERIAL PROGRESS FOR YOUR PEOPLE.
WE WILL DO THE SAME FOR YOUR PEOPLE.
I HAVE ALWAYS ADMIRED THE BUDDHA FOR HIS GREAT CONCERN FOR THE MASSES.

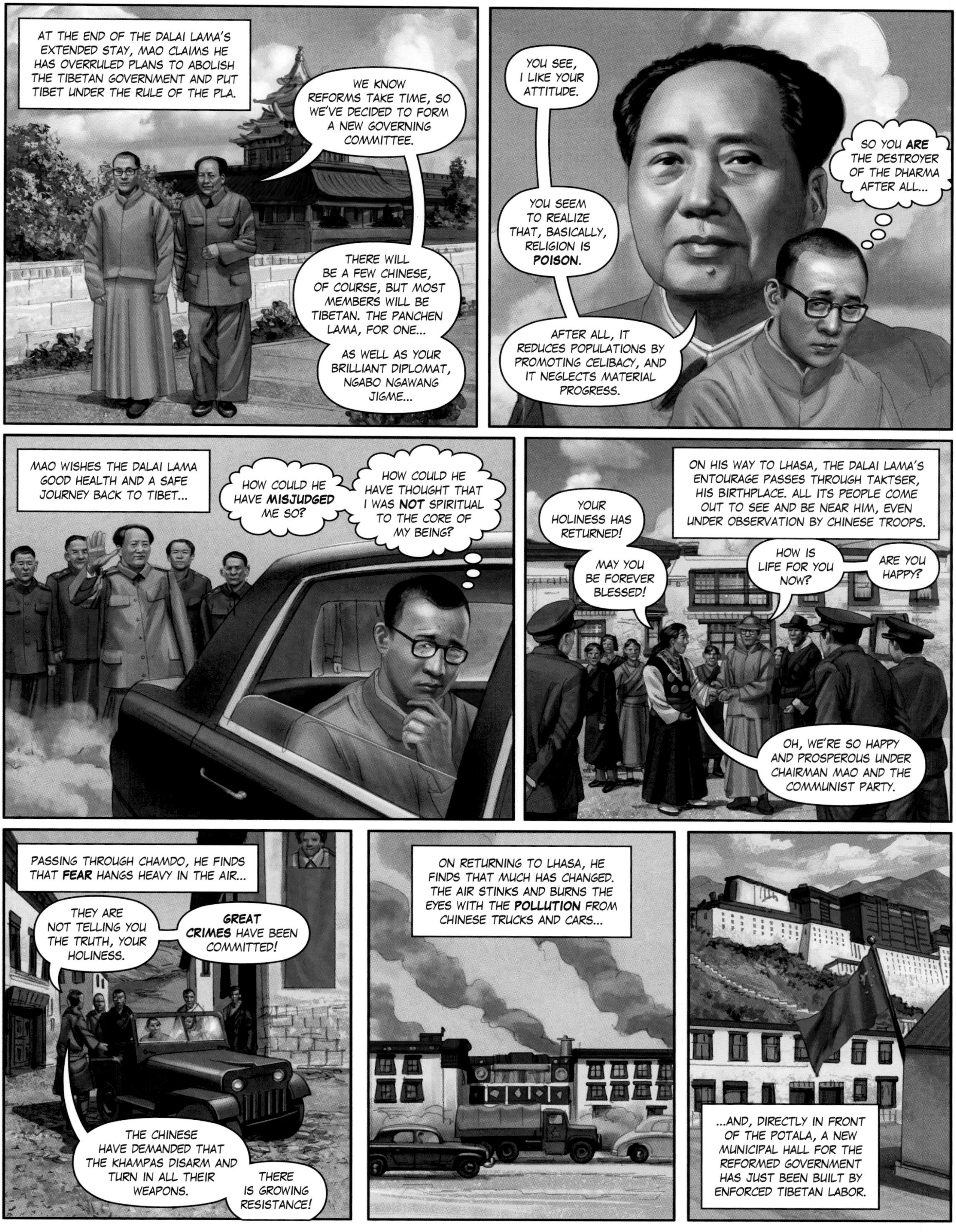
AT THE END OF THE DALAI LAMA'S EXTENDED STAY, MAO CLAIMS HE HAS OVERRULED PLANS TO ABOLISH THE TIBETAN GOVERNMENT AND PUT TIBET UNDER THE RULE OF THE PLA.
WE KNOW REFORMS TAKE TIME, SO WE'VE DECIDED TO FORM A NEW GOVERNING COMMITTEE.
THERE WILL BE A FEW CHINESE, OF COURSE, BUT MOST MEMBERS WILL BE TIBETAN. THE PANCHEN LAMA, FOR ONE...
AS WELL AS YOUR BRILLIANT DIPLOMAT, NGABO NGAWANG JIGME...
YOU SEE, I LIKE YOUR ATTITUDE.
YOU SEEM TO REALIZE THAT, BASICALLY, RELIGION IS **POISON**.
AFTER ALL, IT REDUCES POPULATIONS BY PROMOTING CELIBACY, AND IT NEGLECTS MATERIAL PROGRESS.
SO YOU **ARE** THE DESTROYER OF THE DHARMA AFTER ALL...
MAO WISHES THE DALAI LAMA GOOD HEALTH AND A SAFE JOURNEY BACK TO TIBET...
HOW COULD HE HAVE **MISJUDGED** ME SO?
HOW COULD HE HAVE THOUGHT THAT I WAS **NOT** SPIRITUAL TO THE CORE OF MY BEING?
ON HIS WAY TO LHASA, THE DALAI LAMA'S ENTOURAGE PASSES THROUGH TAKTSER, HIS BIRTHPLACE. ALL ITS PEOPLE COME OUT TO SEE AND BE NEAR HIM, EVEN UNDER OBSERVATION BY CHINESE TROOPS.
YOUR HOLINESS HAS RETURNED!
MAY YOU BE FOREVER BLESSED!
HOW IS LIFE FOR YOU NOW?
ARE YOU HAPPY?
OH, WE'RE SO HAPPY AND PROSPEROUS UNDER CHAIRMAN MAO AND THE COMMUNIST PARTY.
PASSING THROUGH CHAMDO, HE FINDS THAT **FEAR** HANGS HEAVY IN THE AIR...
THEY ARE NOT TELLING YOU THE TRUTH, YOUR HOLINESS.
GREAT CRIMES HAVE BEEN COMMITTED!
THE CHINESE HAVE DEMANDED THAT THE KHAMPAS DISARM AND TURN IN ALL THEIR WEAPONS.
THERE IS GROWING RESISTANCE!
ON RETURNING TO LHASA, HE FINDS THAT MUCH HAS CHANGED. THE AIR STINKS AND BURNS THE EYES WITH THE **POLLUTION** FROM CHINESE TRUCKS AND CARS...
...AND, DIRECTLY IN FRONT OF THE POTALA, A NEW MUNICIPAL HALL FOR THE REFORMED GOVERNMENT HAS JUST BEEN BUILT BY ENFORCED TIBETAN LABOR.

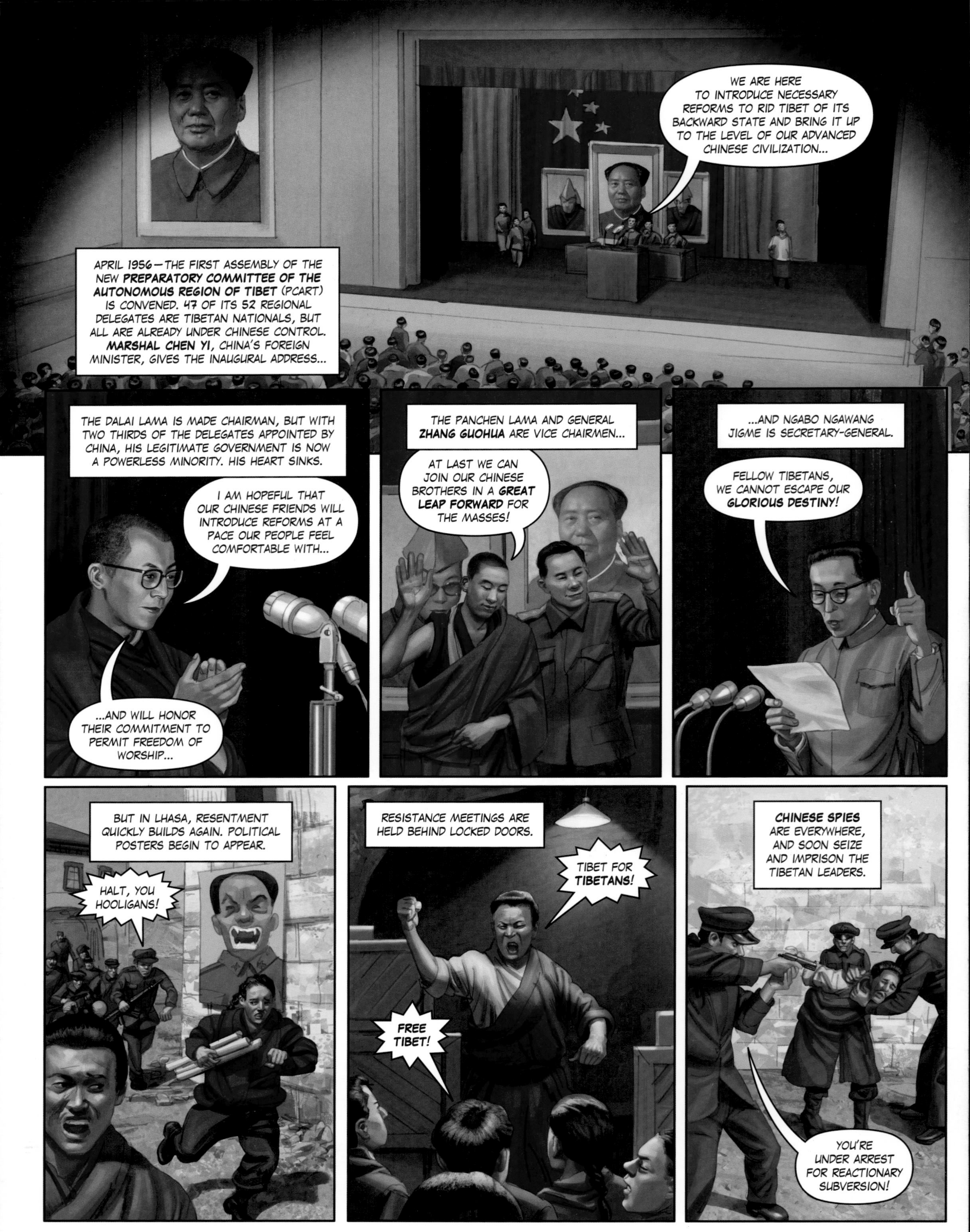

APRIL 1956—THE FIRST ASSEMBLY OF THE NEW PREPARATORY COMMITTEE OF THE AUTONOMOUS REGION OF TIBET (PCART) IS CONVENED. 47 OF ITS 52 REGIONAL DELEGATES ARE TIBETAN NATIONALS, BUT ALL ARE ALREADY UNDER CHINESE CONTROL. MARSHAL CHEN YI, CHINA'S FOREIGN MINISTER, GIVES THE INAUGURAL ADDRESS...
WE ARE HERE TO INTRODUCE NECESSARY REFORMS TO RID TIBET OF ITS BACKWARD STATE AND BRING IT UP TO THE LEVEL OF OUR ADVANCED CHINESE CIVILIZATION...
THE DALAI LAMA IS MADE CHAIRMAN, BUT WITH TWO THIRDS OF THE DELEGATES APPOINTED BY CHINA, HIS LEGITIMATE GOVERNMENT IS NOW A POWERLESS MINORITY. HIS HEART SINKS.
I AM HOPEFUL THAT OUR CHINESE FRIENDS WILL INTRODUCE REFORMS AT A PACE OUR PEOPLE FEEL COMFORTABLE WITH...
...AND WILL HONOR THEIR COMMITMENT TO PERMIT FREEDOM OF WORSHIP...
THE PANCHEN LAMA AND GENERAL ZHANG GUOHUA ARE VICE CHAIRMEN...
AT LAST WE CAN JOIN OUR CHINESE BROTHERS IN A GREAT LEAP FORWARD FOR THE MASSES!
...AND NGABO NGAWANG JIGME IS SECRETARY-GENERAL.
FELLOW TIBETANS, WE CANNOT ESCAPE OUR GLORIOUS DESTINY!
BUT IN LHASA, RESENTMENT QUICKLY BUILDS AGAIN. POLITICAL POSTERS BEGIN TO APPEAR.
HALT, YOU HOOLIGANS!
RESISTANCE MEETINGS ARE HELD BEHIND LOCKED DOORS.
TIBET FOR TIBETANS!
FREE TIBET!
CHINESE SPIES ARE EVERYWHERE, AND SOON SEIZE AND IMPRISON THE TIBETAN LEADERS.
YOU'RE UNDER ARREST FOR REACTIONARY SUBVERSION!

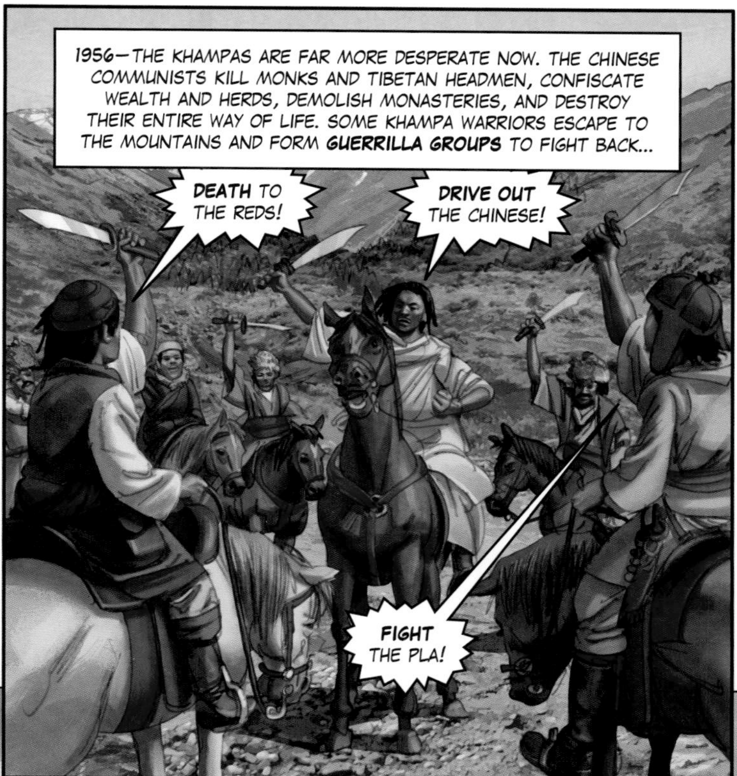
1956—THE KHAMPAS ARE FAR MORE DESPERATE NOW. THE CHINESE COMMUNISTS KILL MONKS AND TIBETAN HEADMEN, CONFISCATE WEALTH AND HERDS, DEMOLISH MONASTERIES, AND DESTROY THEIR ENTIRE WAY OF LIFE. SOME KHAMPA WARRIORS ESCAPE TO THE MOUNTAINS AND FORM **GUERRILLA GROUPS** TO FIGHT BACK...
DEATH TO THE REDS!
DRIVE OUT THE CHINESE!
FIGHT THE PLA!

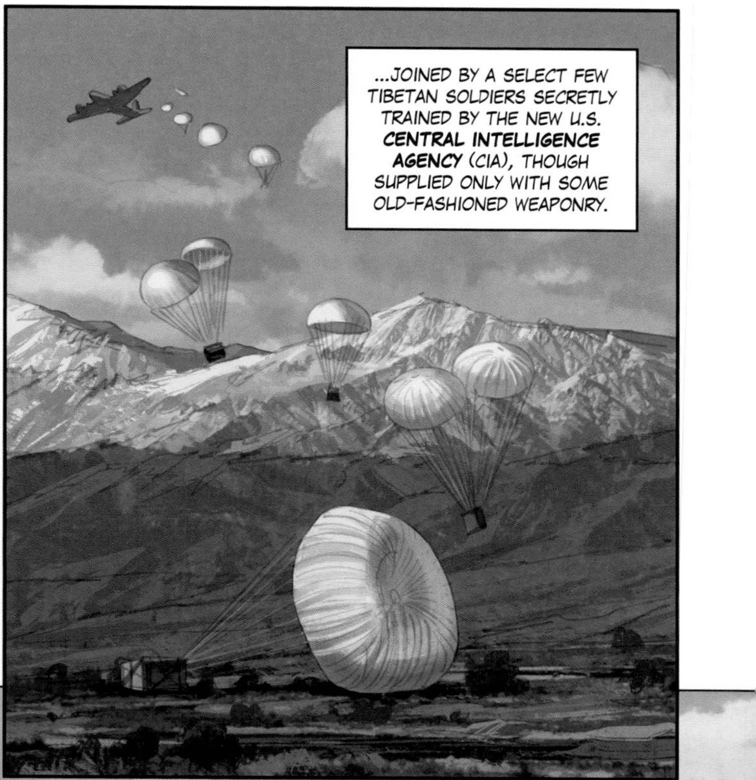
...JOINED BY A SELECT FEW TIBETAN SOLDIERS SECRETLY TRAINED BY THE NEW U.S. **CENTRAL INTELLIGENCE AGENCY** (CIA), THOUGH SUPPLIED ONLY WITH SOME OLD-FASHIONED WEAPONRY.

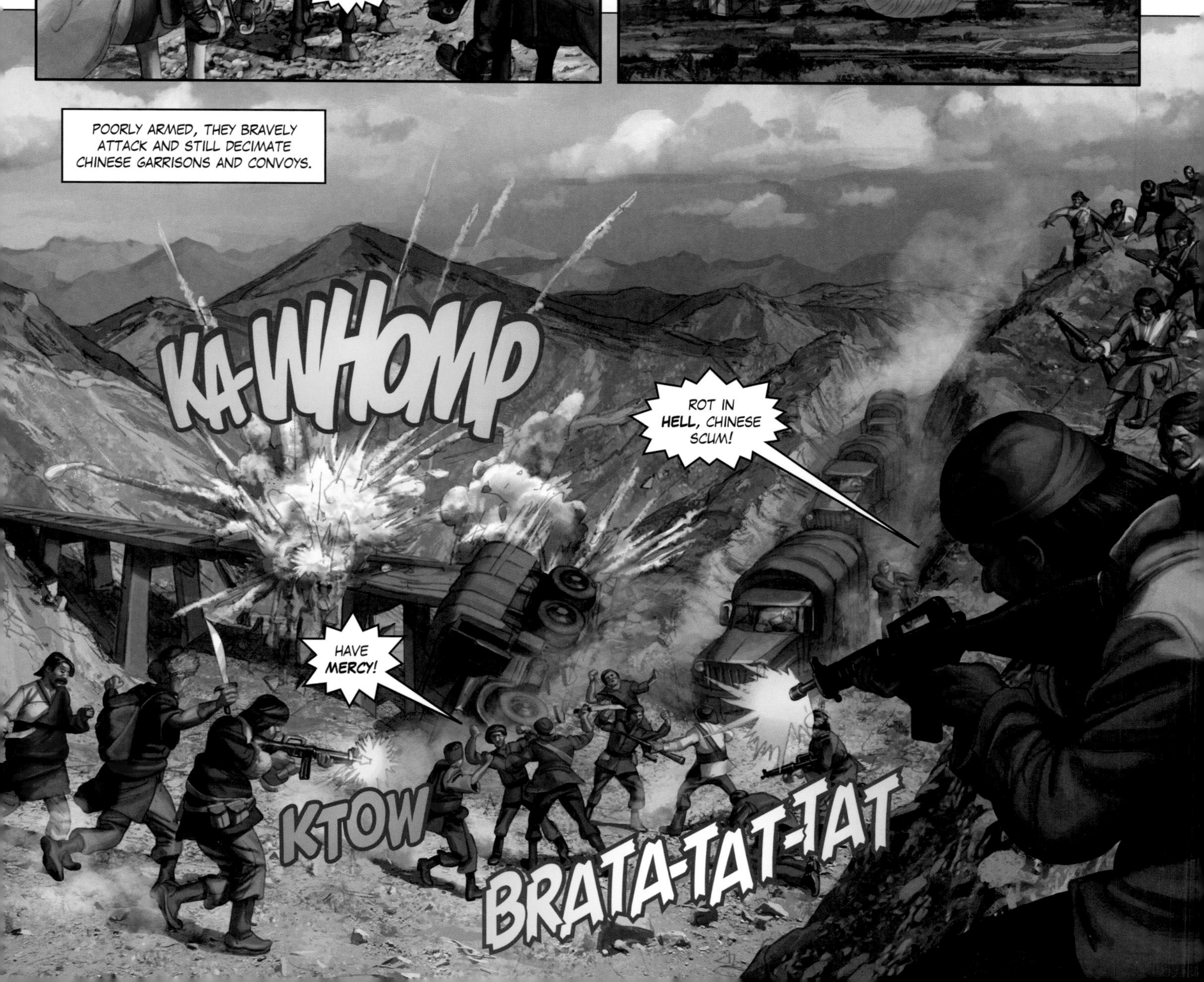
POORLY ARMED, THEY BRAVELY ATTACK AND STILL DECIMATE CHINESE GARRISONS AND CONVOYS.
KA-WHOMP
ROT IN **HELL**, CHINESE SCUM!
HAVE **MERCY**!
KTOW
BRATA-TAT-TAT

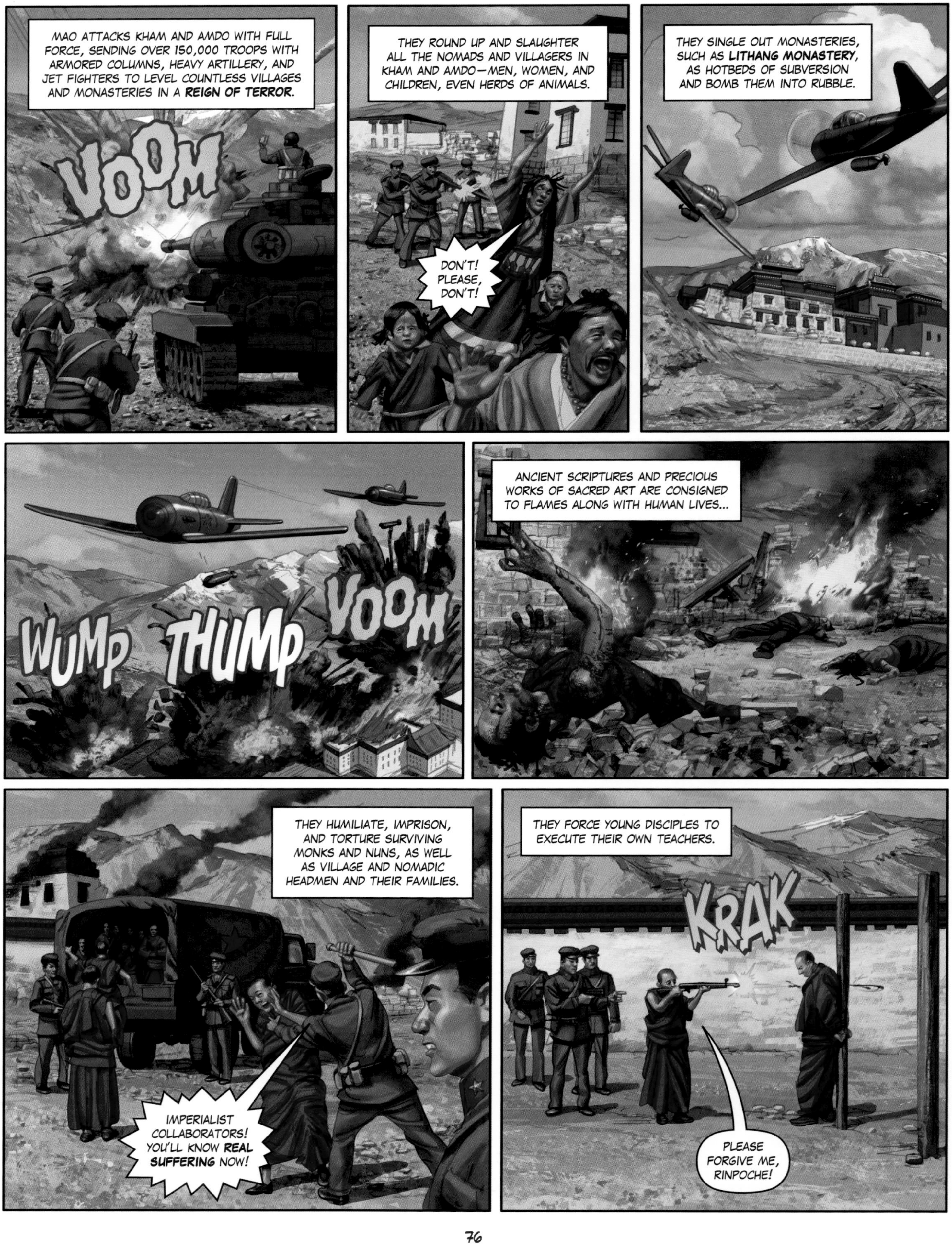
MAO ATTACKS KHAM AND AMDO WITH FULL FORCE, SENDING OVER 150,000 TROOPS WITH ARMORED COLUMNS, HEAVY ARTILLERY, AND JET FIGHTERS TO LEVEL COUNTLESS VILLAGES AND MONASTERIES IN A **REIGN OF TERROR**.
VOOM
THEY ROUND UP AND SLAUGHTER ALL THE NOMADS AND VILLAGERS IN KHAM AND AMDO—MEN, WOMEN, AND CHILDREN, EVEN HERDS OF ANIMALS.
DON'T! PLEASE, DON'T!
THEY SINGLE OUT MONASTERIES, SUCH AS **LITHANG MONASTERY**, AS HOTBEDS OF SUBVERSION AND BOMB THEM INTO RUBBLE.
WUMP
THUMP
VOOM
ANCIENT SCRIPTURES AND PRECIOUS WORKS OF SACRED ART ARE CONSIGNED TO FLAMES ALONG WITH HUMAN LIVES...
THEY HUMILIATE, IMPRISON, AND TORTURE SURVIVING MONKS AND NUNS, AS WELL AS VILLAGE AND NOMADIC HEADMEN AND THEIR FAMILIES.
IMPERIALIST COLLABORATORS! YOU'LL KNOW **REAL SUFFERING** NOW!
THEY FORCE YOUNG DISCIPLES TO EXECUTE THEIR OWN TEACHERS.
KRAK
PLEASE FORGIVE ME, RINPOCHE!

OUTRAGED BY A NEWSPAPER ACCOUNT OF THE ATROCITIES IN AMDO AND KHAM, THE DALAI LAMA DEMANDS A MEETING WITH VICE-CHAIRMAN GENERAL ZHANG GUOHUA...

GENERAL, THIS MUST BE **STOPPED**!

I AM WRITING PERSONALLY TO CHAIRMAN MAO ABOUT THE EVENTS IN THE EAST. HOW ARE TIBETANS SUPPOSED TO TRUST THE CHINESE IF **THIS** IS HOW YOU BEHAVE?

CALM YOURSELF, YOUR EXCELLENCY! WHAT COULD POSSIBLY HAVE UPSET YOU SO?

SEE FOR YOURSELF.

IT IS ENTIRELY WRONG FOR YOU TO DO SUCH THINGS!

A PHOTOGRAPH IN A TIBETAN NEWSPAPER PUBLISHED BY THE CHINESE SHOWS THE SEVERED HEADS OF KHAMPA RESISTANCE LEADERS ON PUBLIC DISPLAY.

I MUST INFORM YOU, YOUR EXCELLENCY...

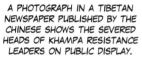

THE GENERAL IS UNPERTURBED...

IF ANY OF YOUR PEOPLE RESIST OUR PROTECTION AND ASSISTANCE, WHICH BENEFIT THE MASSES BY PREVENTING THEIR EXPLOITATION, THEY CAN EXPECT TO BE **PUNISHED**.

YOUR CRITICISMS OF OUR ACTIONS ARE AN **INSULT** TO THE MOTHERLAND.

THE FULL TRUTH FINALLY BEGINS TO DAWN...

BY **BOMBING** AND **BEHEADING** THEM?

I MUST INFORM YOU THAT YOUR REASONING IS COMPLETELY LUNATIC! YOU CAN IN NO WAY JUSTIFY THE **TORTURE** OF INNOCENT PEOPLE.

SURELY CHAIRMAN MAO WOULD **NOT** CONDONE THESE ACTIONS...

DEVASTATED, HE RETURNS TO HIS QUARTERS.

I HAVE NEVER BEFORE BELIEVED THAT HUMAN BEINGS COULD BE CAPABLE OF SUCH **CRUELTY**.

AND YET I CAN DO NOTHING.

I SHOULD RESIGN ENTIRELY FROM OFFICE.

I HAVE NEVER BEFORE FELT SO **DELUDED**!

THE WHOLE "LOCAL GOVERNMENT" IS JUST A SHAM.

WE HAVE NO REAL POWER HERE. WE'RE TOTALLY OUTNUMBERED BY THE CHINESE AND A FEW COLLABORATORS.

I WOULD HAVE TO AGREE, YOUR HOLINESS.

IT SEEMS THEY ONLY APPLY IT TO WHAT THEY CALL "OUTER TIBET," WHAT WE USED TO CALL OUR "CENTRAL PROVINCE."

EVEN THE SEVENTEEN-POINT AGREEMENT, FLAWED AS IT IS, HAS NOT REALLY BEEN HONORED. IT IS A WORTHLESS DOCUMENT.

THEY'VE PUT KHAM AND AMDO INTO "**INNER TIBET**..."

...WHICH THEY CLAIM AS THEIR OWN, TO DEAL WITH AS THEY SEE FIT...

...WHICH MEANS THEY HAVE **STOLEN** YOUR AUTHORITY FROM OVER TWO-THIRDS OF YOUR PEOPLE.

I WILL WRITE TO MAO PERSONALLY.

HE'S BEING KEPT IN THE DARK ABOUT THESE THINGS, BUT HE KNOWS ME AND TRUSTS ME.

HE WILL LISTEN TO ME...

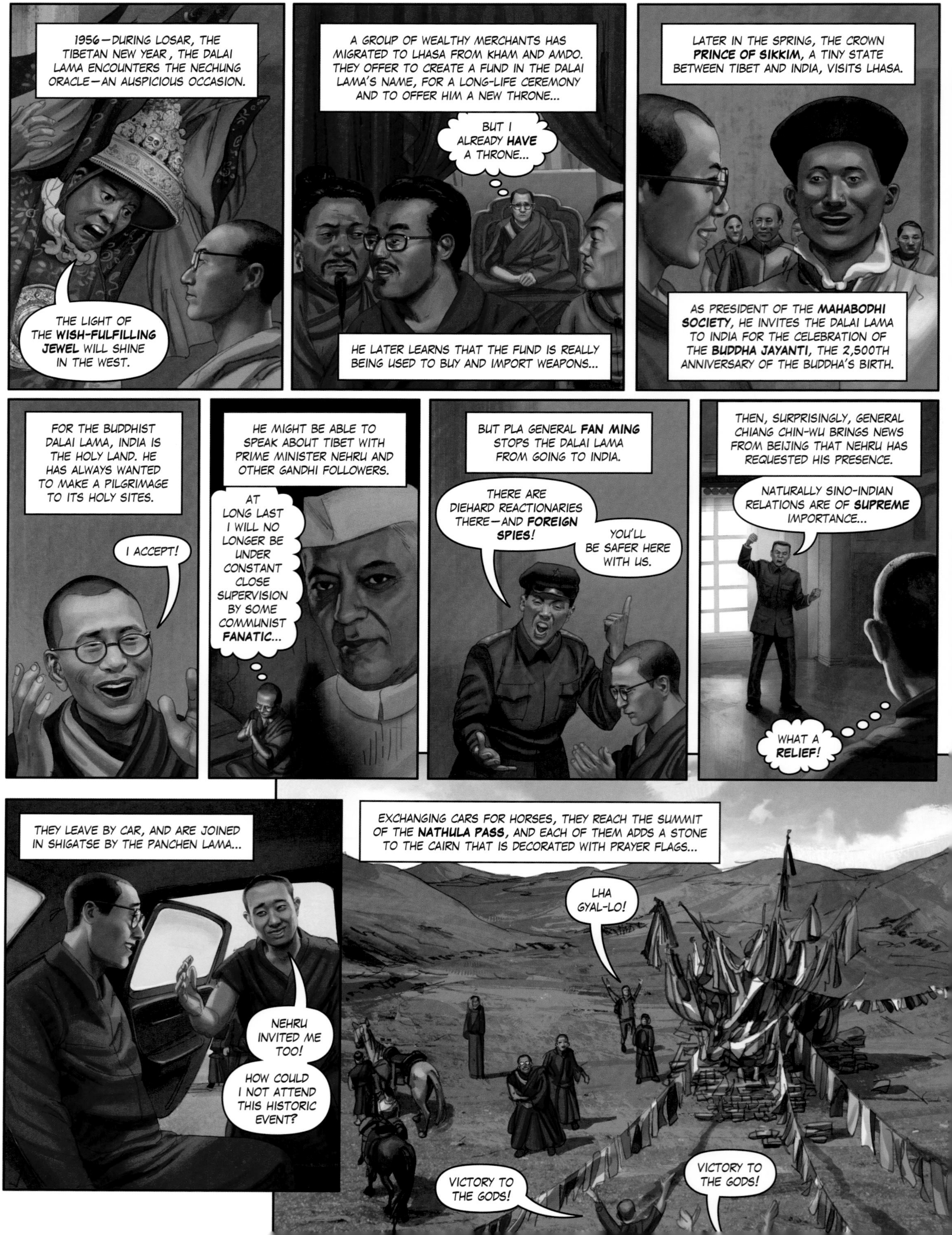
1956—DURING LOSAR, THE TIBETAN NEW YEAR, THE DALAI LAMA ENCOUNTERS THE NECHUNG ORACLE—AN AUSPICIOUS OCCASION.
THE LIGHT OF THE WISH-FULFILLING JEWEL WILL SHINE IN THE WEST.
A GROUP OF WEALTHY MERCHANTS HAS MIGRATED TO LHASA FROM KHAM AND AMDO. THEY OFFER TO CREATE A FUND IN THE DALAI LAMA'S NAME, FOR A LONG-LIFE CEREMONY AND TO OFFER HIM A NEW THRONE...
BUT I ALREADY HAVE A THRONE...
HE LATER LEARNS THAT THE FUND IS REALLY BEING USED TO BUY AND IMPORT WEAPONS...
LATER IN THE SPRING, THE CROWN PRINCE OF SIKKIM, A TINY STATE BETWEEN TIBET AND INDIA, VISITS LHASA.
AS PRESIDENT OF THE MAHABODHI SOCIETY, HE INVITES THE DALAI LAMA TO INDIA FOR THE CELEBRATION OF THE BUDDHA JAYANTI, THE 2,500TH ANNIVERSARY OF THE BUDDHA'S BIRTH.
FOR THE BUDDHIST DALAI LAMA, INDIA IS THE HOLY LAND. HE HAS ALWAYS WANTED TO MAKE A PILGRIMAGE TO ITS HOLY SITES.
I ACCEPT!
HE MIGHT BE ABLE TO SPEAK ABOUT TIBET WITH PRIME MINISTER NEHRU AND OTHER GANDHI FOLLOWERS.
AT LONG LAST I WILL NO LONGER BE UNDER CONSTANT CLOSE SUPERVISION BY SOME COMMUNIST FANATIC...
BUT PLA GENERAL FAN MING STOPS THE DALAI LAMA FROM GOING TO INDIA.
THERE ARE DIEHARD REACTIONARIES THERE—AND FOREIGN SPIES!
YOU'LL BE SAFER HERE WITH US.
THEN, SURPRISINGLY, GENERAL CHIANG CHIN-WU BRINGS NEWS FROM BEIJING THAT NEHRU HAS REQUESTED HIS PRESENCE.
NATURALLY SINO-INDIAN RELATIONS ARE OF SUPREME IMPORTANCE...
WHAT A RELIEF!
THEY LEAVE BY CAR, AND ARE JOINED IN SHIGATSE BY THE PANCHEN LAMA...
NEHRU INVITED ME TOO!
HOW COULD I NOT ATTEND THIS HISTORIC EVENT?
EXCHANGING CARS FOR HORSES, THEY REACH THE SUMMIT OF THE NATHULA PASS, AND EACH OF THEM ADDS A STONE TO THE CAIRN THAT IS DECORATED WITH PRAYER FLAGS...
LHA GYAL-LO!
VICTORY TO THE GODS!
VICTORY TO THE GODS!

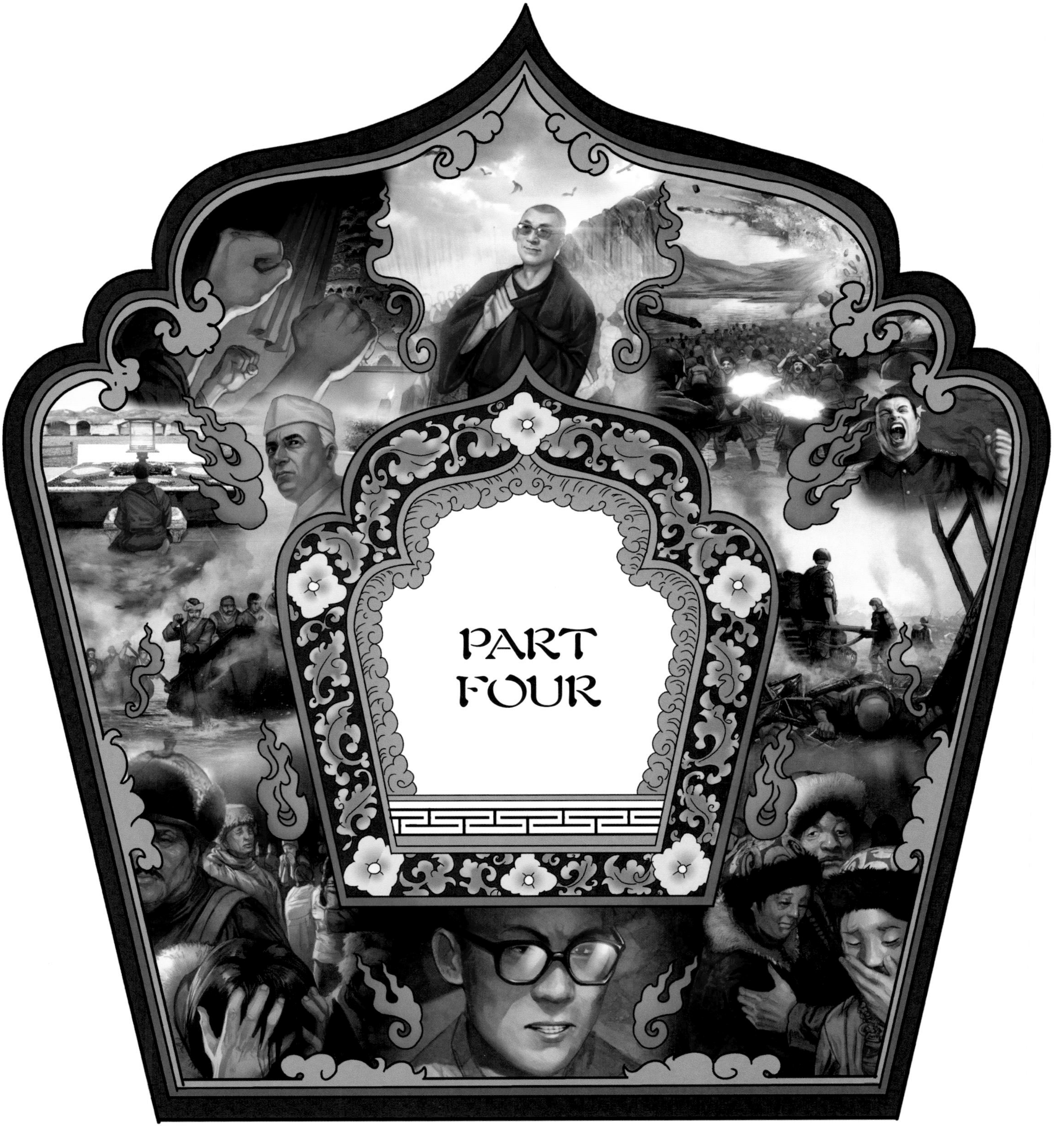
PART
FOUR

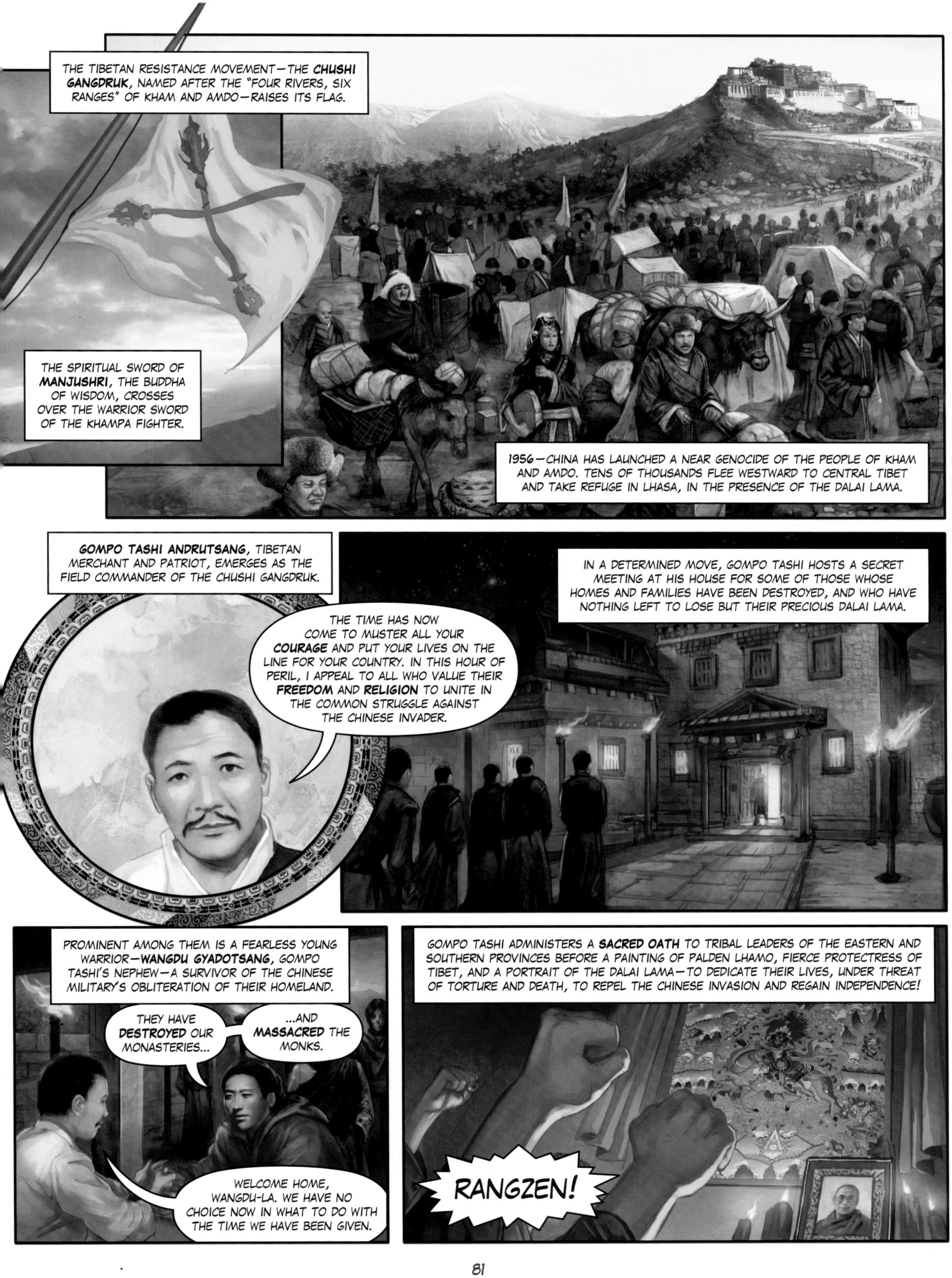
THE TIBETAN RESISTANCE MOVEMENT—THE CHUSHI GANGDRUK, NAMED AFTER THE "FOUR RIVERS, SIX RANGES" OF KHAM AND AMDO—RAISES ITS FLAG.
THE SPIRITUAL SWORD OF MANJUSHRI, THE BUDDHA OF WISDOM, CROSSES OVER THE WARRIOR SWORD OF THE KHAMPA FIGHTER.
1956—CHINA HAS LAUNCHED A NEAR GENOCIDE OF THE PEOPLE OF KHAM AND AMDO. TENS OF THOUSANDS FLEE WESTWARD TO CENTRAL TIBET AND TAKE REFUGE IN LHASA, IN THE PRESENCE OF THE DALAI LAMA.
GOMPO TASHI ANDRUTSANG, TIBETAN MERCHANT AND PATRIOT, EMERGES AS THE FIELD COMMANDER OF THE CHUSHI GANGDRUK.
THE TIME HAS NOW COME TO MUSTER ALL YOUR COURAGE AND PUT YOUR LIVES ON THE LINE FOR YOUR COUNTRY. IN THIS HOUR OF PERIL, I APPEAL TO ALL WHO VALUE THEIR FREEDOM AND RELIGION TO UNITE IN THE COMMON STRUGGLE AGAINST THE CHINESE INVADER.
IN A DETERMINED MOVE, GOMPO TASHI HOSTS A SECRET MEETING AT HIS HOUSE FOR SOME OF THOSE WHOSE HOMES AND FAMILIES HAVE BEEN DESTROYED, AND WHO HAVE NOTHING LEFT TO LOSE BUT THEIR PRECIOUS DALAI LAMA.
PROMINENT AMONG THEM IS A FEARLESS YOUNG WARRIOR—WANGDU GYADOTSANG, GOMPO TASHI'S NEPHEW—A SURVIVOR OF THE CHINESE MILITARY'S OBLITERATION OF THEIR HOMELAND.
THEY HAVE DESTROYED OUR MONASTERIES...
...AND MASSACRED THE MONKS.
WELCOME HOME, WANGDU-LA. WE HAVE NO CHOICE NOW IN WHAT TO DO WITH THE TIME WE HAVE BEEN GIVEN.
GOMPO TASHI ADMINISTERS A SACRED OATH TO TRIBAL LEADERS OF THE EASTERN AND SOUTHERN PROVINCES BEFORE A PAINTING OF PALDEN LHAMO, FIERCE PROTECTRESS OF TIBET, AND A PORTRAIT OF THE DALAI LAMA—TO DEDICATE THEIR LIVES, UNDER THREAT OF TORTURE AND DEATH, TO REPEL THE CHINESE INVASION AND REGAIN INDEPENDENCE!
RANGZEN!

MET AT THE BORDER BY A DELEGATION FROM **GANGTOK**, THE DALAI LAMA'S PARTY DESCENDS FROM THE HIMALAYAN SUMMIT IN HEAVY SNOWFALL AND IS WELCOMED TO SIKKIM.

LODGED BESIDE A FROZEN LAKE IN A HIDDEN VALLEY, THE DALAI LAMA MEETS HIS ELDER BROTHERS, TAKTSER RINPOCHE AND GYALO THONDUP.

YOUR HOLINESS, WE ARE NOT RETURNING.

WE THINK YOU ALSO SHOULD STAY IN INDIA.

IN A RARE MOMENT, THREE OF THE DALAI LAMA'S BROTHERS AND HIS TWO SISTERS REUNITE WITH HIM.

ON THE PLANE FROM BAGDOGRA TO DELHI, BOTH THE DALAI LAMA AND THE PANCHEN LAMA MARVEL AT THE BEAUTY OF THE LAND THEY REVERE AS THE BIRTHPLACE OF THE BUDDHA BUT HAVE NEVER SEEN.

SO THIS IS THE LAND OF TOLERANCE AND FREEDOM.

PRIME MINISTER NEHRU MEETS THEM AT THE NEW DELHI AIRFIELD...

WE ARE HONORED BY YOUR PRESENCE, YOUR HOLINESS.

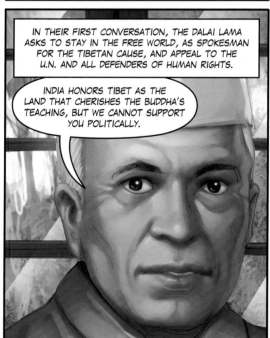

IN THEIR FIRST CONVERSATION, THE DALAI LAMA ASKS TO STAY IN THE FREE WORLD, AS SPOKESMAN FOR THE TIBETAN CAUSE, AND APPEAL TO THE U.N. AND ALL DEFENDERS OF HUMAN RIGHTS.

INDIA HONORS TIBET AS THE LAND THAT CHERISHES THE BUDDHA'S TEACHING, BUT WE CANNOT SUPPORT YOU POLITICALLY.

BUT THE COMMUNISTS HATE OUR RELIGION AND HARM OUR PEOPLE. IT IS SO DIFFICULT...

I KNOW, YOUR HOLINESS, BUT YOU MUST RETURN TO LHASA TO HELP US KEEP THE PEACE.

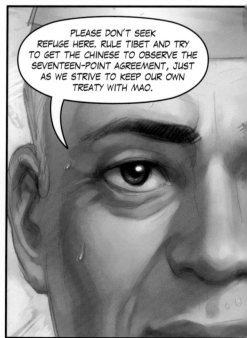

PLEASE DON'T SEEK REFUGE HERE. RULE TIBET AND TRY TO GET THE CHINESE TO OBSERVE THE SEVENTEEN-POINT AGREEMENT, JUST AS WE STRIVE TO KEEP OUR OWN TREATY WITH MAO.

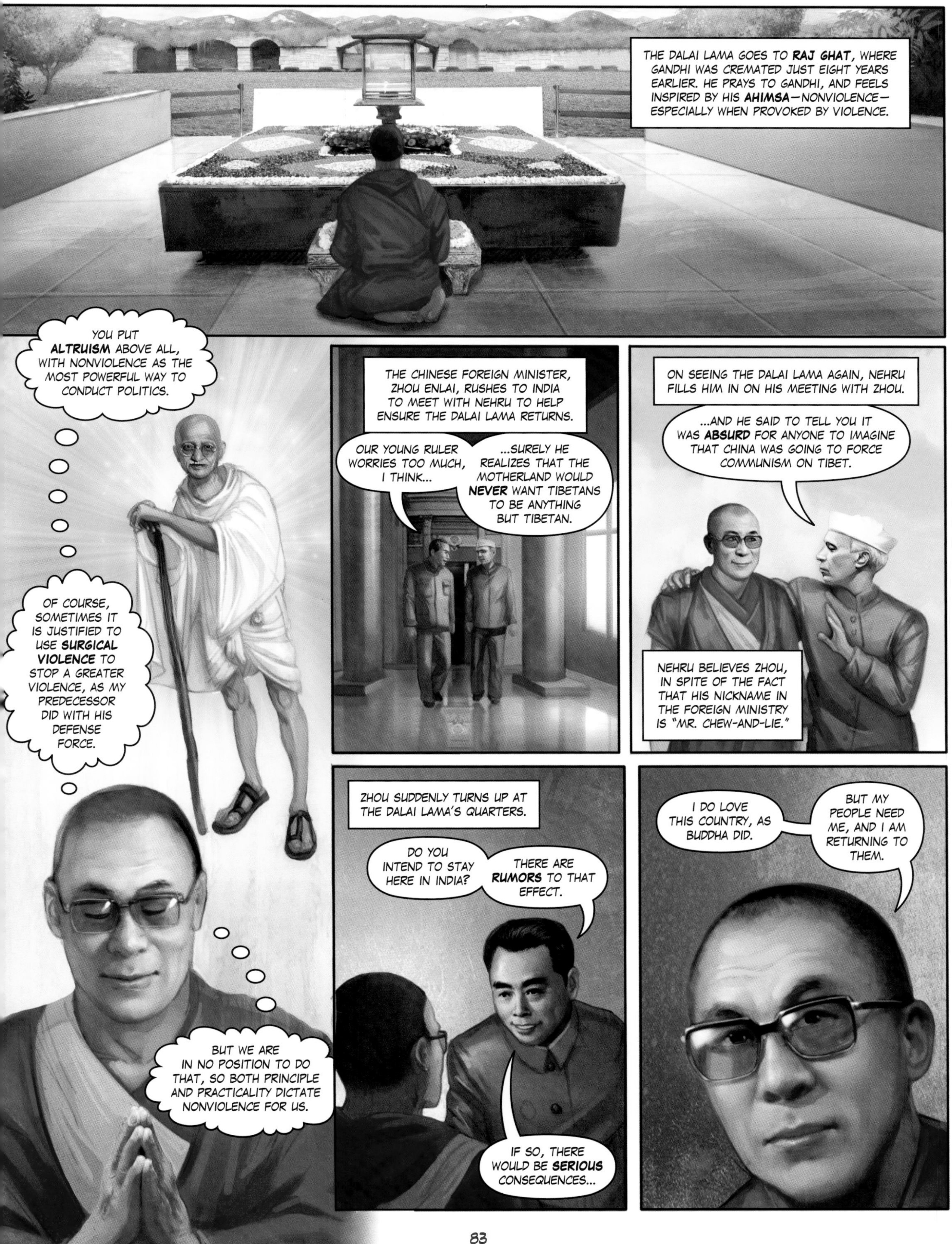
THE DALAI LAMA GOES TO RAJ GHAT, WHERE GANDHI WAS CREMATED JUST EIGHT YEARS EARLIER. HE PRAYS TO GANDHI, AND FEELS INSPIRED BY HIS AHIMSA—NONVIOLENCE—ESPECIALLY WHEN PROVOKED BY VIOLENCE.
YOU PUT ALTRUISM ABOVE ALL, WITH NONVIOLENCE AS THE MOST POWERFUL WAY TO CONDUCT POLITICS.
OF COURSE, SOMETIMES IT IS JUSTIFIED TO USE SURGICAL VIOLENCE TO STOP A GREATER VIOLENCE, AS MY PREDECESSOR DID WITH HIS DEFENSE FORCE.
BUT WE ARE IN NO POSITION TO DO THAT, SO BOTH PRINCIPLE AND PRACTICALITY DICTATE NONVIOLENCE FOR US.
THE CHINESE FOREIGN MINISTER, ZHOU ENLAI, RUSHES TO INDIA TO MEET WITH NEHRU TO HELP ENSURE THE DALAI LAMA RETURNS.
OUR YOUNG RULER WORRIES TOO MUCH, I THINK...
...SURELY HE REALIZES THAT THE MOTHERLAND WOULD NEVER WANT TIBETANS TO BE ANYTHING BUT TIBETAN.
ON SEEING THE DALAI LAMA AGAIN, NEHRU FILLS HIM IN ON HIS MEETING WITH ZHOU.
...AND HE SAID TO TELL YOU IT WAS ABSURD FOR ANYONE TO IMAGINE THAT CHINA WAS GOING TO FORCE COMMUNISM ON TIBET.
NEHRU BELIEVES ZHOU, IN SPITE OF THE FACT THAT HIS NICKNAME IN THE FOREIGN MINISTRY IS "MR. CHEW-AND-LIE."
ZHOU SUDDENLY TURNS UP AT THE DALAI LAMA'S QUARTERS.
DO YOU INTEND TO STAY HERE IN INDIA?
THERE ARE RUMORS TO THAT EFFECT.
IF SO, THERE WOULD BE SERIOUS CONSEQUENCES...
I DO LOVE THIS COUNTRY, AS BUDDHA DID.
BUT MY PEOPLE NEED ME, AND I AM RETURNING TO THEM.

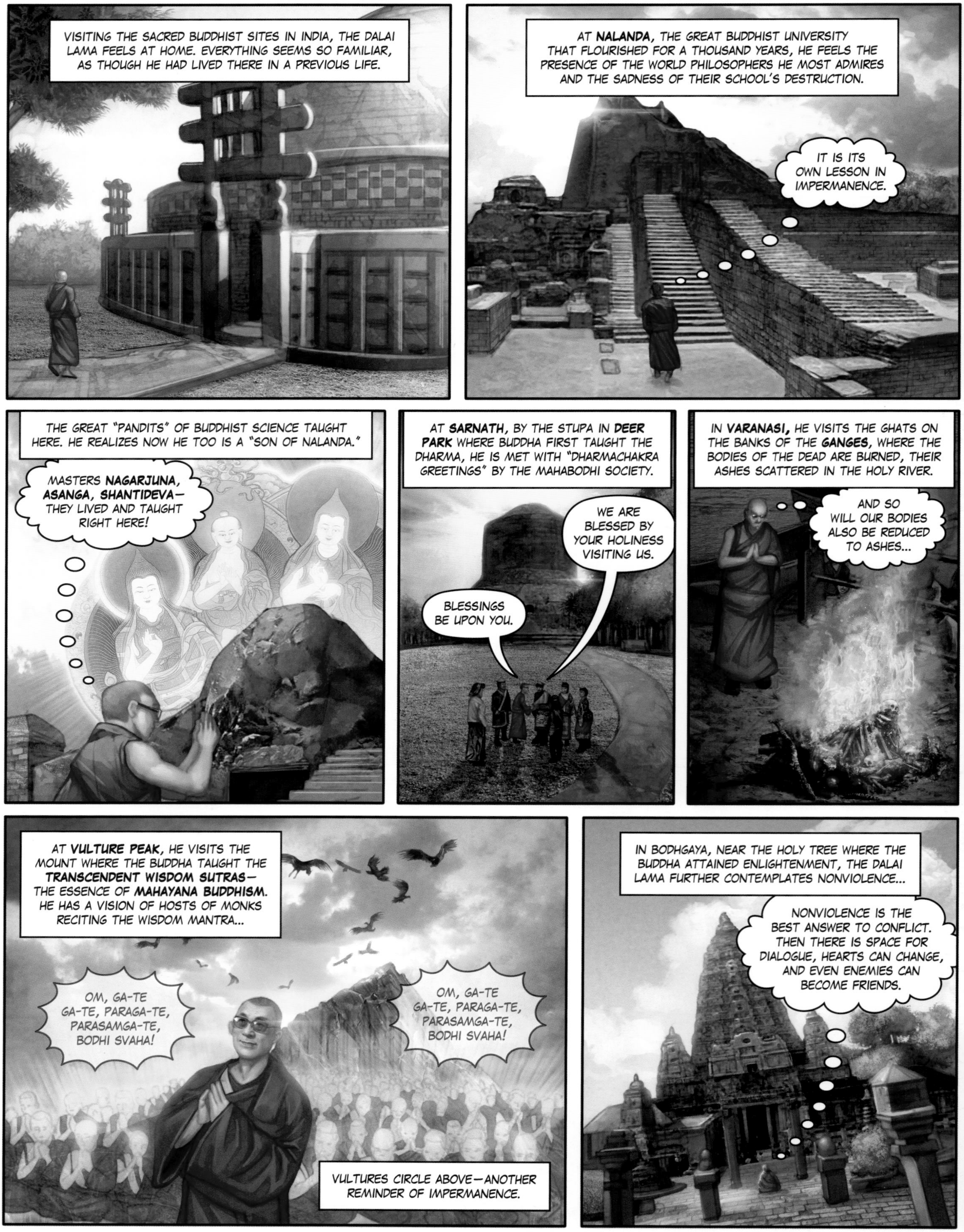
VISITING THE SACRED BUDDHIST SITES IN INDIA, THE DALAI LAMA FEELS AT HOME. EVERYTHING SEEMS SO FAMILIAR, AS THOUGH HE HAD LIVED THERE IN A PREVIOUS LIFE.
AT NALANDA, THE GREAT BUDDHIST UNIVERSITY THAT FLOURISHED FOR A THOUSAND YEARS, HE FEELS THE PRESENCE OF THE WORLD PHILOSOPHERS HE MOST ADMIRES AND THE SADNESS OF THEIR SCHOOL'S DESTRUCTION.
IT IS ITS OWN LESSON IN IMPERMANENCE.
THE GREAT "PANDITS" OF BUDDHIST SCIENCE TAUGHT HERE. HE REALIZES NOW HE TOO IS A "SON OF NALANDA."
MASTERS NAGARJUNA, ASANGA, SHANTIDEVA—THEY LIVED AND TAUGHT RIGHT HERE!
AT SARNATH, BY THE STUPA IN DEER PARK WHERE BUDDHA FIRST TAUGHT THE DHARMA, HE IS MET WITH "DHARMACHAKRA GREETINGS" BY THE MAHABODHI SOCIETY.
WE ARE BLESSED BY YOUR HOLINESS VISITING US.
BLESSINGS BE UPON YOU.
IN VARANASI, HE VISITS THE GHATS ON THE BANKS OF THE GANGES, WHERE THE BODIES OF THE DEAD ARE BURNED, THEIR ASHES SCATTERED IN THE HOLY RIVER.
AND SO WILL OUR BODIES ALSO BE REDUCED TO ASHES...
AT VULTURE PEAK, HE VISITS THE MOUNT WHERE THE BUDDHA TAUGHT THE TRANSCENDENT WISDOM SUTRAS—THE ESSENCE OF MAHAYANA BUDDHISM. HE HAS A VISION OF HOSTS OF MONKS RECITING THE WISDOM MANTRA...
OM, GA-TE GA-TE, PARAGA-TE, PARASAMGA-TE, BODHI SVAHA!
OM, GA-TE GA-TE, PARAGA-TE, PARASAMGA-TE, BODHI SVAHA!
VULTURES CIRCLE ABOVE—ANOTHER REMINDER OF IMPERMANENCE.
IN BODHGAYA, NEAR THE HOLY TREE WHERE THE BUDDHA ATTAINED ENLIGHTENMENT, THE DALAI LAMA FURTHER CONTEMPLATES NONVIOLENCE...
NONVIOLENCE IS THE BEST ANSWER TO CONFLICT. THEN THERE IS SPACE FOR DIALOGUE, HEARTS CAN CHANGE, AND EVEN ENEMIES CAN BECOME FRIENDS.

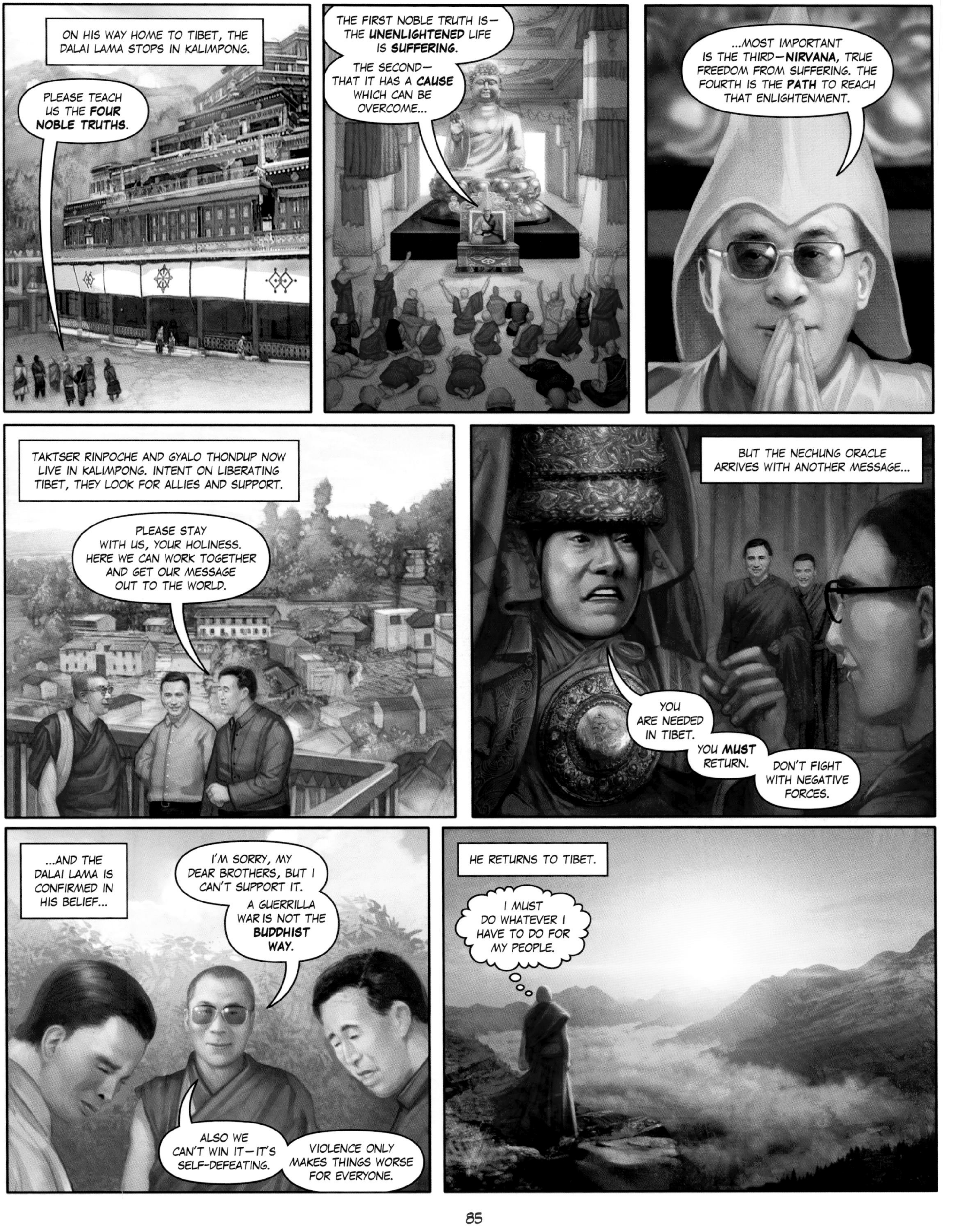
ON HIS WAY HOME TO TIBET, THE DALAI LAMA STOPS IN KALIMPONG.
PLEASE TEACH US THE **FOUR NOBLE TRUTHS**.
THE FIRST NOBLE TRUTH IS— THE **UNENLIGHTENED** LIFE IS **SUFFERING**.
THE SECOND— THAT IT HAS A **CAUSE** WHICH CAN BE OVERCOME...
...MOST IMPORTANT IS THE THIRD—**NIRVANA**, TRUE FREEDOM FROM SUFFERING. THE FOURTH IS THE **PATH** TO REACH THAT ENLIGHTENMENT.
TAKTSER RINPOCHE AND GYALO THONDUP NOW LIVE IN KALIMPONG. INTENT ON LIBERATING TIBET, THEY LOOK FOR ALLIES AND SUPPORT.
PLEASE STAY WITH US, YOUR HOLINESS. HERE WE CAN WORK TOGETHER AND GET OUR MESSAGE OUT TO THE WORLD.
BUT THE NECHUNG ORACLE ARRIVES WITH ANOTHER MESSAGE...
YOU ARE NEEDED IN TIBET.
YOU **MUST** RETURN.
DON'T FIGHT WITH NEGATIVE FORCES.
...AND THE DALAI LAMA IS CONFIRMED IN HIS BELIEF...
I'M SORRY, MY DEAR BROTHERS, BUT I CAN'T SUPPORT IT.
A GUERRILLA WAR IS NOT THE **BUDDHIST WAY**.
ALSO WE CAN'T WIN IT—IT'S SELF-DEFEATING.
VIOLENCE ONLY MAKES THINGS WORSE FOR EVERYONE.
HE RETURNS TO TIBET.
I MUST DO WHATEVER I HAVE TO DO FOR MY PEOPLE.

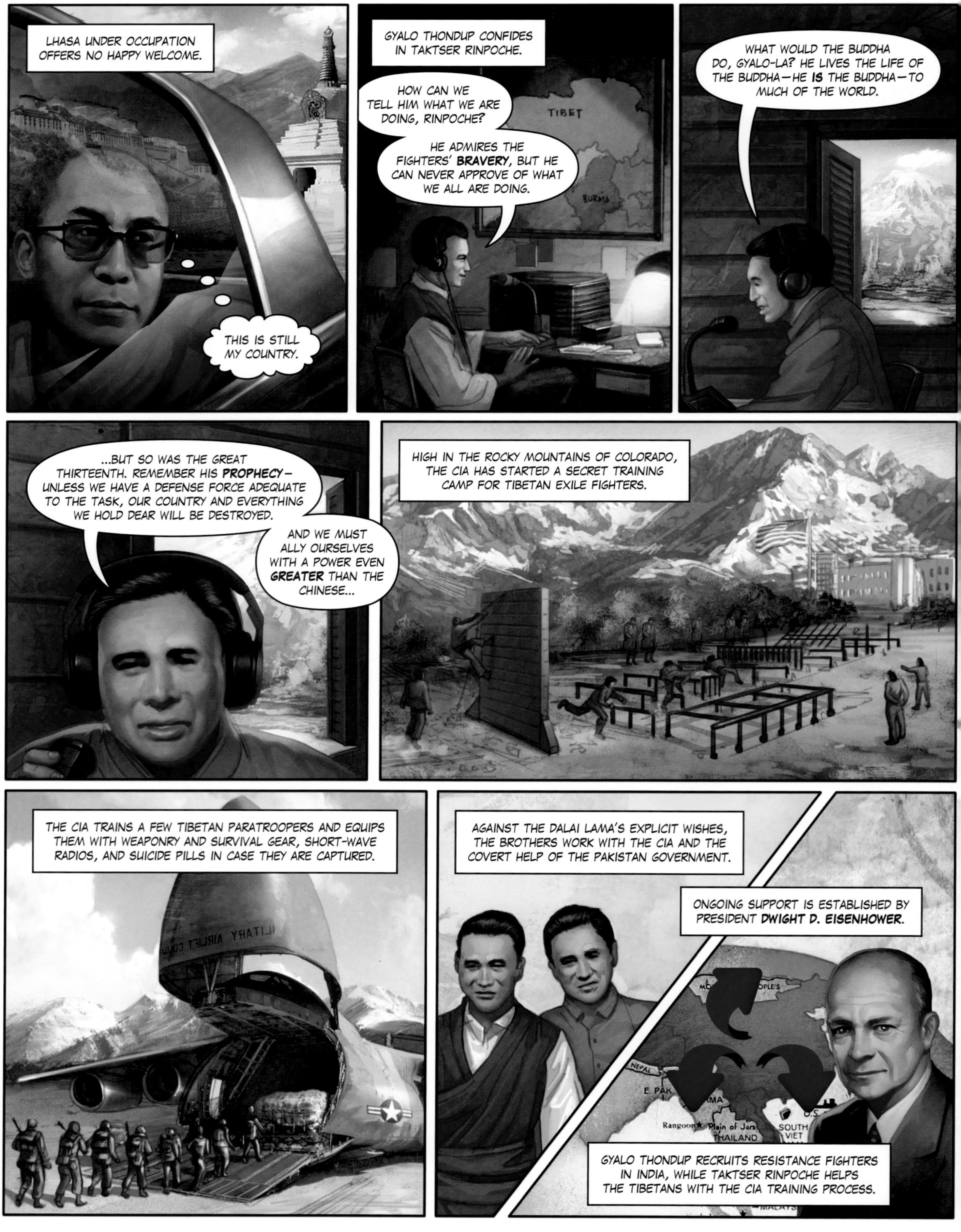
LHASA UNDER OCCUPATION OFFERS NO HAPPY WELCOME.
THIS IS STILL MY COUNTRY.
GYALO THONDUP CONFIDES IN TAKTSER RINPOCHE.
TIBET
BURMA
HOW CAN WE TELL HIM WHAT WE ARE DOING, RINPOCHE?
HE ADMIRES THE FIGHTERS' **BRAVERY**, BUT HE CAN NEVER APPROVE OF WHAT WE ALL ARE DOING.
WHAT WOULD THE BUDDHA DO, GYALO-LA? HE LIVES THE LIFE OF THE BUDDHA—HE **IS** THE BUDDHA—TO MUCH OF THE WORLD.
...BUT SO WAS THE GREAT THIRTEENTH. REMEMBER HIS **PROPHECY**—UNLESS WE HAVE A DEFENSE FORCE ADEQUATE TO THE TASK, OUR COUNTRY AND EVERYTHING WE HOLD DEAR WILL BE DESTROYED.
AND WE MUST ALLY OURSELVES WITH A POWER EVEN **GREATER** THAN THE CHINESE...
HIGH IN THE ROCKY MOUNTAINS OF COLORADO, THE CIA HAS STARTED A SECRET TRAINING CAMP FOR TIBETAN EXILE FIGHTERS.
THE CIA TRAINS A FEW TIBETAN PARATROOPERS AND EQUIPS THEM WITH WEAPONRY AND SURVIVAL GEAR, SHORT-WAVE RADIOS, AND SUICIDE PILLS IN CASE THEY ARE CAPTURED.
AGAINST THE DALAI LAMA'S EXPLICIT WISHES, THE BROTHERS WORK WITH THE CIA AND THE COVERT HELP OF THE PAKISTAN GOVERNMENT.
ONGOING SUPPORT IS ESTABLISHED BY PRESIDENT **DWIGHT D. EISENHOWER**.
NEPAL
Rangoon
Plain of Jars
THAILAND
SOUTH VIET
GYALO THONDUP RECRUITS RESISTANCE FIGHTERS IN INDIA, WHILE TAKTSER RINPOCHE HELPS THE TIBETANS WITH THE CIA TRAINING PROCESS.

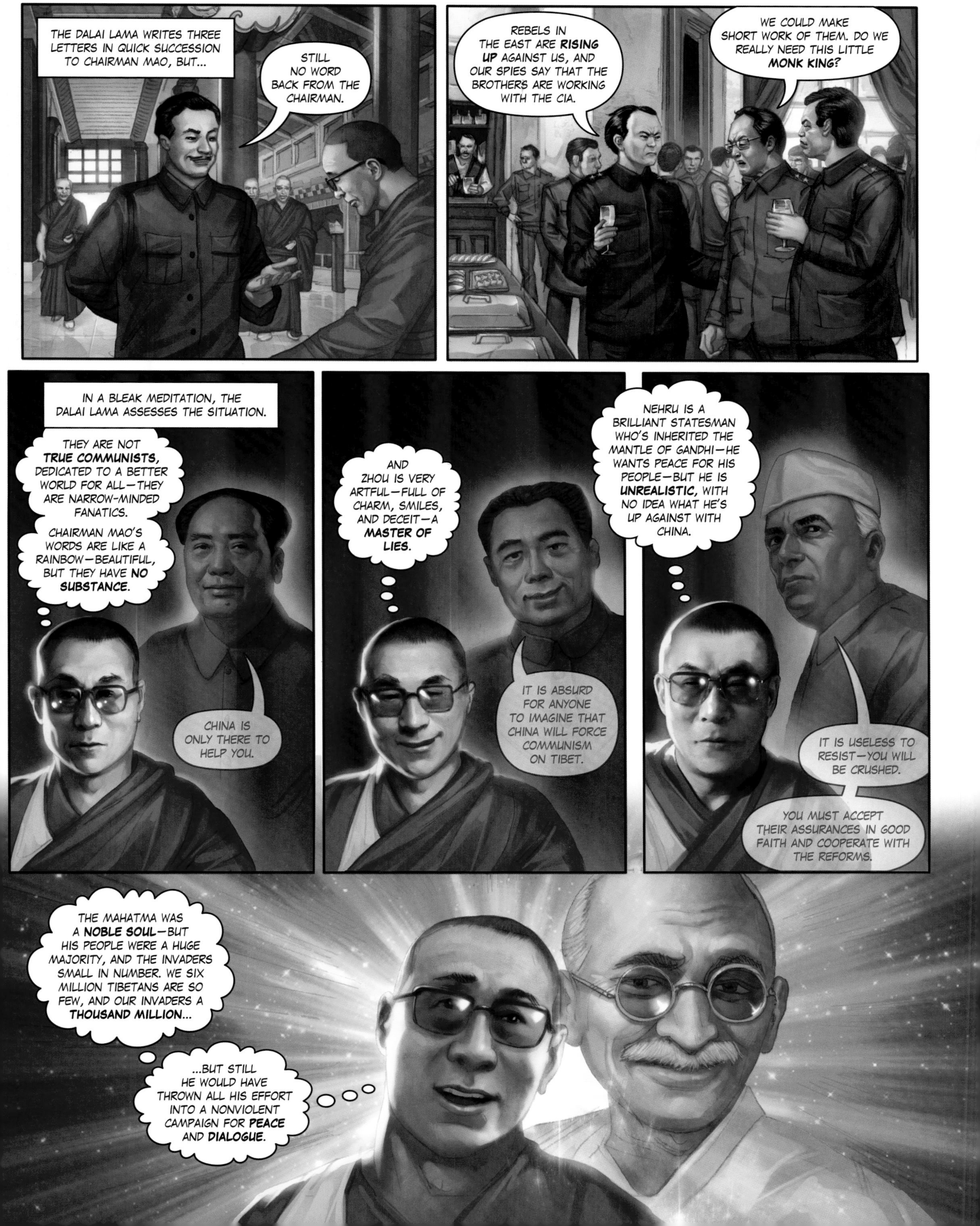

THE DALAI LAMA WRITES THREE LETTERS IN QUICK SUCCESSION TO CHAIRMAN MAO, BUT...
STILL NO WORD BACK FROM THE CHAIRMAN.
REBELS IN THE EAST ARE **RISING UP** AGAINST US, AND OUR SPIES SAY THAT THE BROTHERS ARE WORKING WITH THE CIA.
WE COULD MAKE SHORT WORK OF THEM. DO WE REALLY NEED THIS LITTLE **MONK KING?**
IN A BLEAK MEDITATION, THE DALAI LAMA ASSESSES THE SITUATION.
THEY ARE NOT **TRUE COMMUNISTS,** DEDICATED TO A BETTER WORLD FOR ALL—THEY ARE NARROW-MINDED FANATICS.
CHAIRMAN MAO'S WORDS ARE LIKE A RAINBOW—BEAUTIFUL, BUT THEY HAVE **NO SUBSTANCE.**
CHINA IS ONLY THERE TO HELP YOU.
AND ZHOU IS VERY ARTFUL—FULL OF CHARM, SMILES, AND DECEIT—A **MASTER OF LIES.**
IT IS ABSURD FOR ANYONE TO IMAGINE THAT CHINA WILL FORCE COMMUNISM ON TIBET.
NEHRU IS A BRILLIANT STATESMAN WHO'S INHERITED THE MANTLE OF GANDHI—HE WANTS PEACE FOR HIS PEOPLE—BUT HE IS **UNREALISTIC,** WITH NO IDEA WHAT HE'S UP AGAINST WITH CHINA.
IT IS USELESS TO RESIST—YOU WILL BE CRUSHED.
YOU MUST ACCEPT THEIR ASSURANCES IN GOOD FAITH AND COOPERATE WITH THE REFORMS.
THE MAHATMA WAS A **NOBLE SOUL**—BUT HIS PEOPLE WERE A HUGE MAJORITY, AND THE INVADERS SMALL IN NUMBER. WE SIX MILLION TIBETANS ARE SO FEW, AND OUR INVADERS A **THOUSAND MILLION...**
...BUT STILL HE WOULD HAVE THROWN ALL HIS EFFORT INTO A NONVIOLENT CAMPAIGN FOR **PEACE** AND **DIALOGUE.**

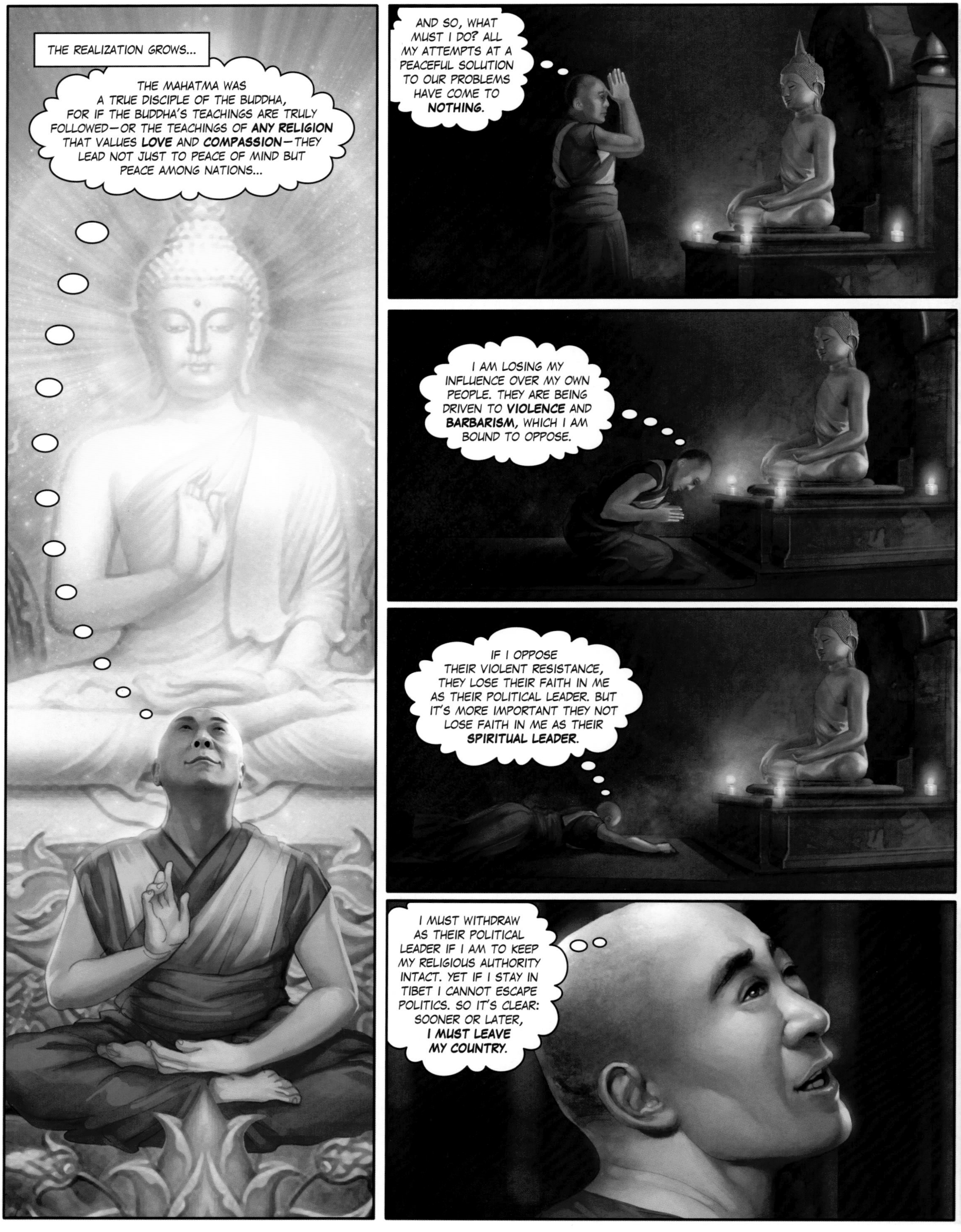
THE REALIZATION GROWS...
THE MAHATMA WAS A TRUE DISCIPLE OF THE BUDDHA, FOR IF THE BUDDHA'S TEACHINGS ARE TRULY FOLLOWED—OR THE TEACHINGS OF **ANY RELIGION** THAT VALUES **LOVE** AND **COMPASSION**—THEY LEAD NOT JUST TO PEACE OF MIND BUT PEACE AMONG NATIONS...
AND SO, WHAT MUST I DO? ALL MY ATTEMPTS AT A PEACEFUL SOLUTION TO OUR PROBLEMS HAVE COME TO **NOTHING**.
I AM LOSING MY INFLUENCE OVER MY OWN PEOPLE. THEY ARE BEING DRIVEN TO **VIOLENCE** AND **BARBARISM**, WHICH I AM BOUND TO OPPOSE.
IF I OPPOSE THEIR VIOLENT RESISTANCE, THEY LOSE THEIR FAITH IN ME AS THEIR POLITICAL LEADER. BUT IT'S MORE IMPORTANT THEY NOT LOSE FAITH IN ME AS THEIR **SPIRITUAL LEADER**.
I MUST WITHDRAW AS THEIR POLITICAL LEADER IF I AM TO KEEP MY RELIGIOUS AUTHORITY INTACT. YET IF I STAY IN TIBET I CANNOT ESCAPE POLITICS. SO IT'S CLEAR: SOONER OR LATER, **I MUST LEAVE MY COUNTRY**.

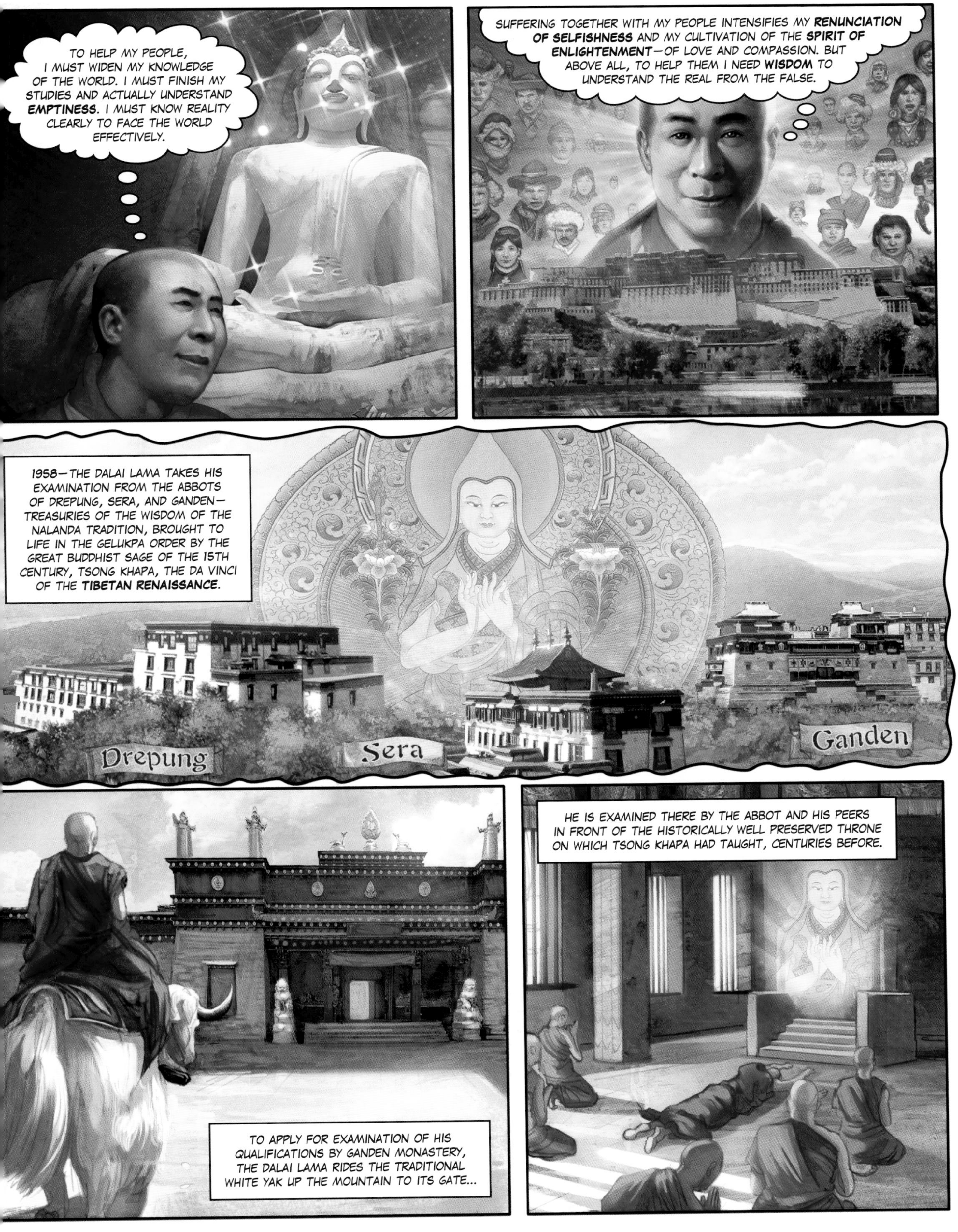
TO HELP MY PEOPLE, I MUST WIDEN MY KNOWLEDGE OF THE WORLD. I MUST FINISH MY STUDIES AND ACTUALLY UNDERSTAND **EMPTINESS**. I MUST KNOW REALITY CLEARLY TO FACE THE WORLD EFFECTIVELY.
SUFFERING TOGETHER WITH MY PEOPLE INTENSIFIES MY **RENUNCIATION OF SELFISHNESS** AND MY CULTIVATION OF THE **SPIRIT OF ENLIGHTENMENT**—OF LOVE AND COMPASSION. BUT ABOVE ALL, TO HELP THEM I NEED **WISDOM** TO UNDERSTAND THE REAL FROM THE FALSE.
1958—THE DALAI LAMA TAKES HIS EXAMINATION FROM THE ABBOTS OF DREPUNG, SERA, AND GANDEN—TREASURIES OF THE WISDOM OF THE NALANDA TRADITION, BROUGHT TO LIFE IN THE GELUKPA ORDER BY THE GREAT BUDDHIST SAGE OF THE 15TH CENTURY, TSONG KHAPA, THE DA VINCI OF THE **TIBETAN RENAISSANCE**.
Drepung
Sera
Ganden
TO APPLY FOR EXAMINATION OF HIS QUALIFICATIONS BY GANDEN MONASTERY, THE DALAI LAMA RIDES THE TRADITIONAL WHITE YAK UP THE MOUNTAIN TO ITS GATE...
HE IS EXAMINED THERE BY THE ABBOT AND HIS PEERS IN FRONT OF THE HISTORICALLY WELL PRESERVED THRONE ON WHICH TSONG KHAPA HAD TAUGHT, CENTURIES BEFORE.

JUNE 1958—THE GUERRILLA WAR IN THE EAST INTENSIFIES. SURVIVORS OF CHINESE ATROCITIES JOIN THE CHUSHI GANGDRUK MOVEMENT. THE OVERPOWERING PLA HAS DRIVEN THEM WEST TO LHASA. OVER 10,000 REFUGEES ARE ENCAMPED AROUND THE CITY.

THE CHINESE INFILTRATE THE CAMPS, "TAKING A CENSUS." THEY RECORD DETAILED PERSONAL HISTORIES....

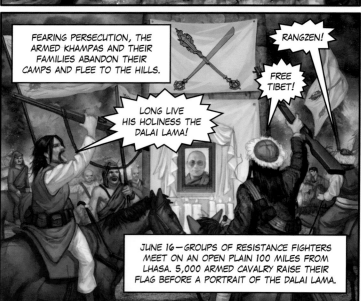

FEARING PERSECUTION, THE ARMED KHAMPAS AND THEIR FAMILIES ABANDON THEIR CAMPS AND FLEE TO THE HILLS.

RANGZEN!

FREE TIBET!

LONG LIVE HIS HOLINESS THE DALAI LAMA!

JUNE 16—GROUPS OF RESISTANCE FIGHTERS MEET ON AN OPEN PLAIN 100 MILES FROM LHASA. 5,000 ARMED CAVALRY RAISE THEIR FLAG BEFORE A PORTRAIT OF THE DALAI LAMA.

THE KHAMPAS OVERRUN AND DESTROY THE 3,000-MAN PLA GARRISON AT **TSETHANG**, ONLY 30 MILES FROM LHASA. ARMED CHINESE GENERALS, LIVID WITH RAGE, RUSH TO MEET WITH THE DALAI LAMA.

YOU MUST DEPLOY THE ENTIRE TIBETAN ARMY AGAINST THESE **REACTIONARIES!**

WITH RESPECT, THAT WOULD NOT BE WISE.

SEND OUR ARMY OUT THERE, AND THEY WILL ONLY JOIN THE KHAMPAS.

THE CHINESE ARM ALL THEIR CIVILIANS AND BARRICADE THEIR OWN ENCAMPMENTS BEHIND BARBED WIRE AND MACHINE-GUN EMPLACEMENTS.

TENSIONS IN LHASA ARE AT THE BREAKING POINT...

GENERAL **TAN GUANSAN** ADDRESSES A PUBLIC MEETING IN LHASA, THREATENING TO EXECUTE THE ENTIRE TIBETAN GOVERNMENT...

WHERE THERE IS **ROTTEN MEAT**, FLIES GATHER! BUT GET RID OF THE MEAT, AND THE FLIES ARE **NO MORE TROUBLE!**

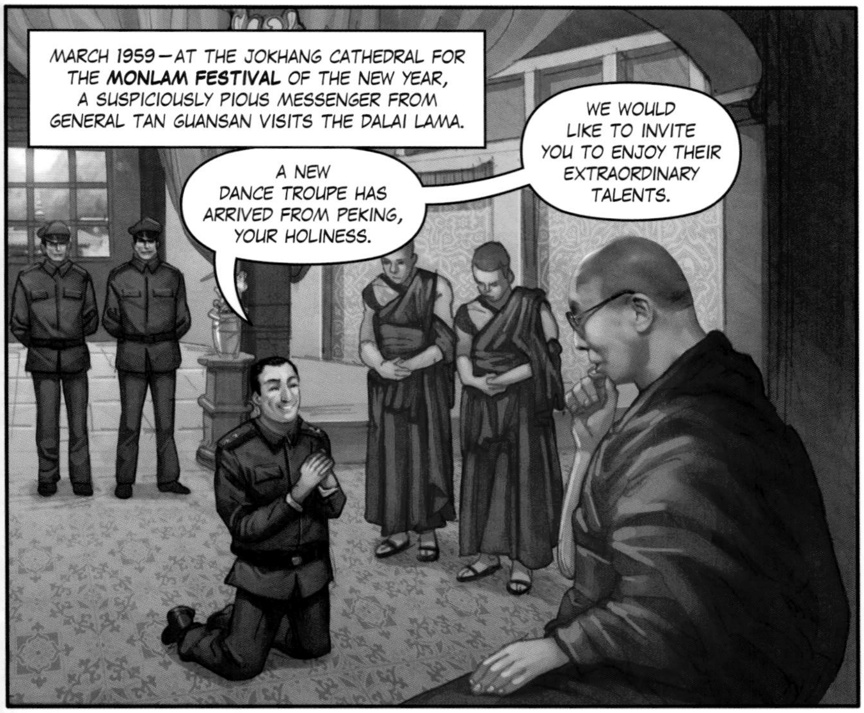
MARCH 1959—AT THE JOKHANG CATHEDRAL FOR THE **MONLAM FESTIVAL** OF THE NEW YEAR, A SUSPICIOUSLY PIOUS MESSENGER FROM GENERAL TAN GUANSAN VISITS THE DALAI LAMA.
A NEW DANCE TROUPE HAS ARRIVED FROM PEKING, YOUR HOLINESS.
WE WOULD LIKE TO INVITE YOU TO ENJOY THEIR EXTRAORDINARY TALENTS.

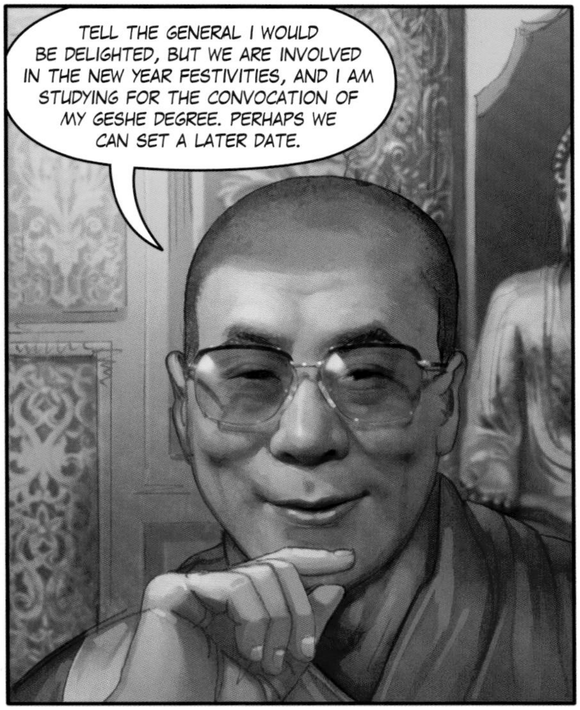
TELL THE GENERAL I WOULD BE DELIGHTED, BUT WE ARE INVOLVED IN THE NEW YEAR FESTIVITIES, AND I AM STUDYING FOR THE CONVOCATION OF MY GESHE DEGREE. PERHAPS WE CAN SET A LATER DATE.

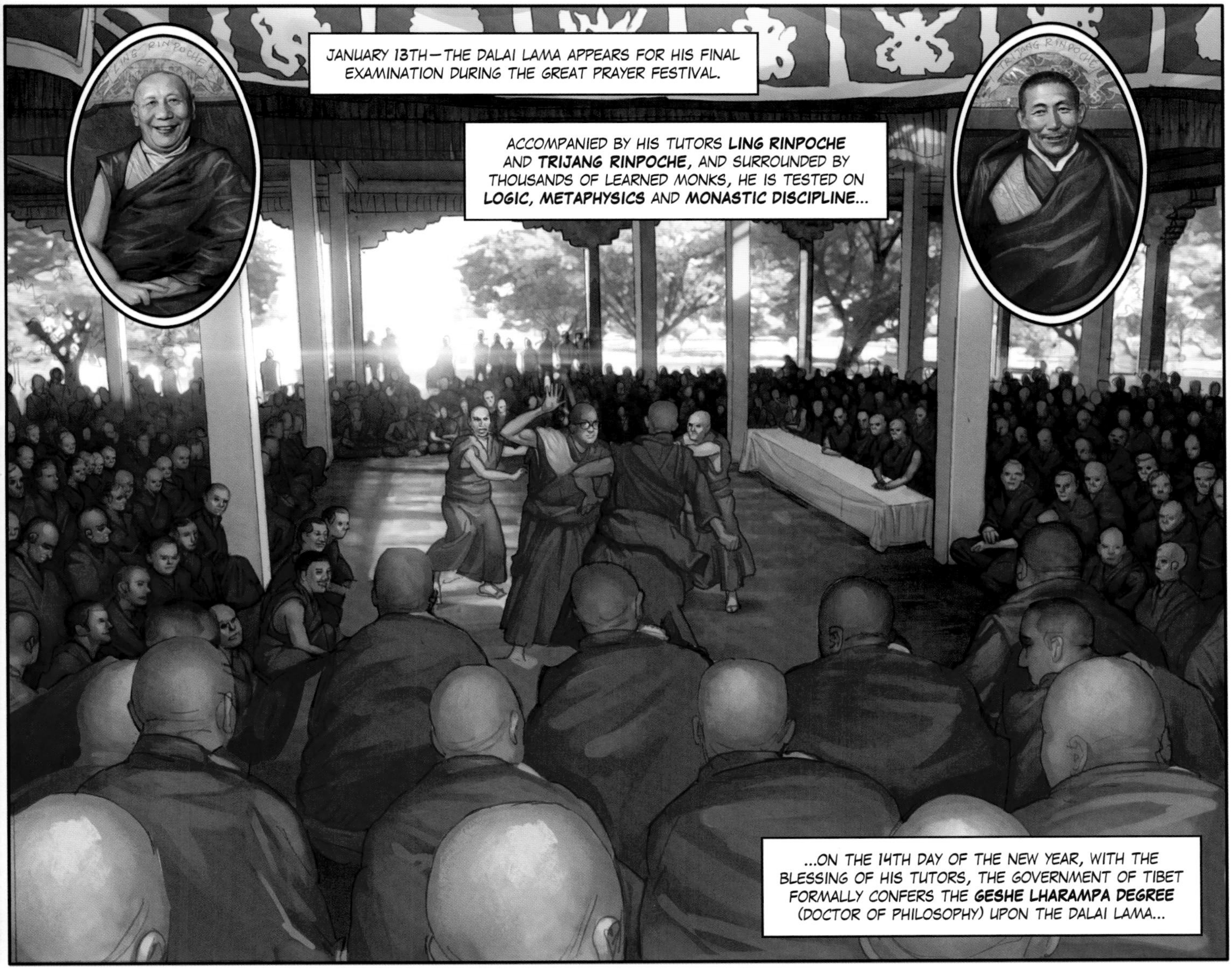
JANUARY 13TH—THE DALAI LAMA APPEARS FOR HIS FINAL EXAMINATION DURING THE GREAT PRAYER FESTIVAL.
ACCOMPANIED BY HIS TUTORS **LING RINPOCHE** AND **TRIJANG RINPOCHE**, AND SURROUNDED BY THOUSANDS OF LEARNED MONKS, HE IS TESTED ON **LOGIC, METAPHYSICS** AND **MONASTIC DISCIPLINE**...
...ON THE 14TH DAY OF THE NEW YEAR, WITH THE BLESSING OF HIS TUTORS, THE GOVERNMENT OF TIBET FORMALLY CONFERS THE **GESHE LHARAMPA DEGREE** (DOCTOR OF PHILOSOPHY) UPON THE DALAI LAMA...

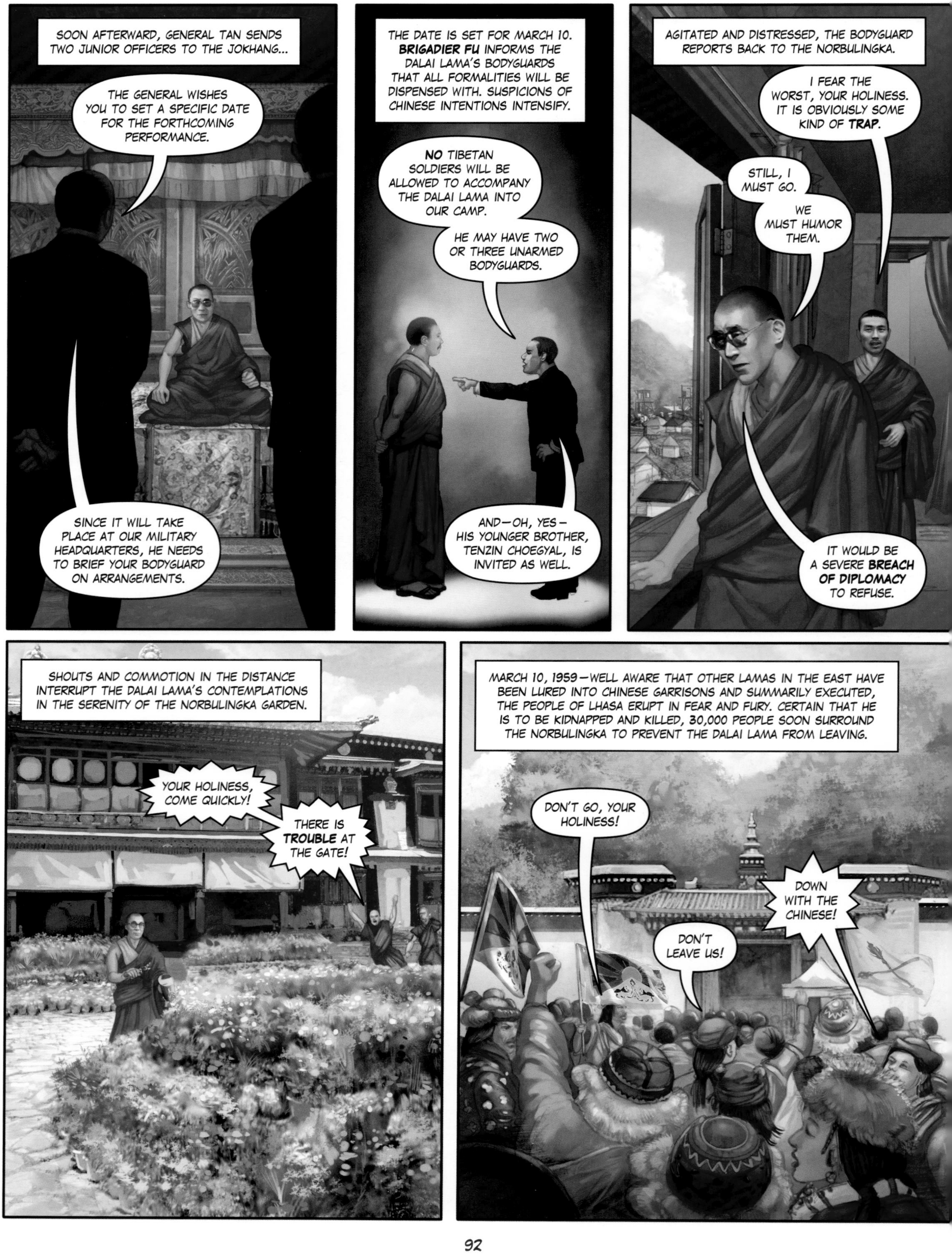
SOON AFTERWARD, GENERAL TAN SENDS TWO JUNIOR OFFICERS TO THE JOKHANG...
THE GENERAL WISHES YOU TO SET A SPECIFIC DATE FOR THE FORTHCOMING PERFORMANCE.
SINCE IT WILL TAKE PLACE AT OUR MILITARY HEADQUARTERS, HE NEEDS TO BRIEF YOUR BODYGUARD ON ARRANGEMENTS.
THE DATE IS SET FOR MARCH 10. BRIGADIER FU INFORMS THE DALAI LAMA'S BODYGUARDS THAT ALL FORMALITIES WILL BE DISPENSED WITH. SUSPICIONS OF CHINESE INTENTIONS INTENSIFY.
NO TIBETAN SOLDIERS WILL BE ALLOWED TO ACCOMPANY THE DALAI LAMA INTO OUR CAMP.
HE MAY HAVE TWO OR THREE UNARMED BODYGUARDS.
AND—OH, YES—HIS YOUNGER BROTHER, TENZIN CHOEGYAL, IS INVITED AS WELL.
AGITATED AND DISTRESSED, THE BODYGUARD REPORTS BACK TO THE NORBULINGKA.
I FEAR THE WORST, YOUR HOLINESS. IT IS OBVIOUSLY SOME KIND OF TRAP.
STILL, I MUST GO.
WE MUST HUMOR THEM.
IT WOULD BE A SEVERE BREACH OF DIPLOMACY TO REFUSE.
SHOUTS AND COMMOTION IN THE DISTANCE INTERRUPT THE DALAI LAMA'S CONTEMPLATIONS IN THE SERENITY OF THE NORBULINGKA GARDEN.
YOUR HOLINESS, COME QUICKLY!
THERE IS TROUBLE AT THE GATE!
MARCH 10, 1959—WELL AWARE THAT OTHER LAMAS IN THE EAST HAVE BEEN LURED INTO CHINESE GARRISONS AND SUMMARILY EXECUTED, THE PEOPLE OF LHASA ERUPT IN FEAR AND FURY. CERTAIN THAT HE IS TO BE KIDNAPPED AND KILLED, 30,000 PEOPLE SOON SURROUND THE NORBULINGKA TO PREVENT THE DALAI LAMA FROM LEAVING.
DON'T GO, YOUR HOLINESS!
DOWN WITH THE CHINESE!
DON'T LEAVE US!

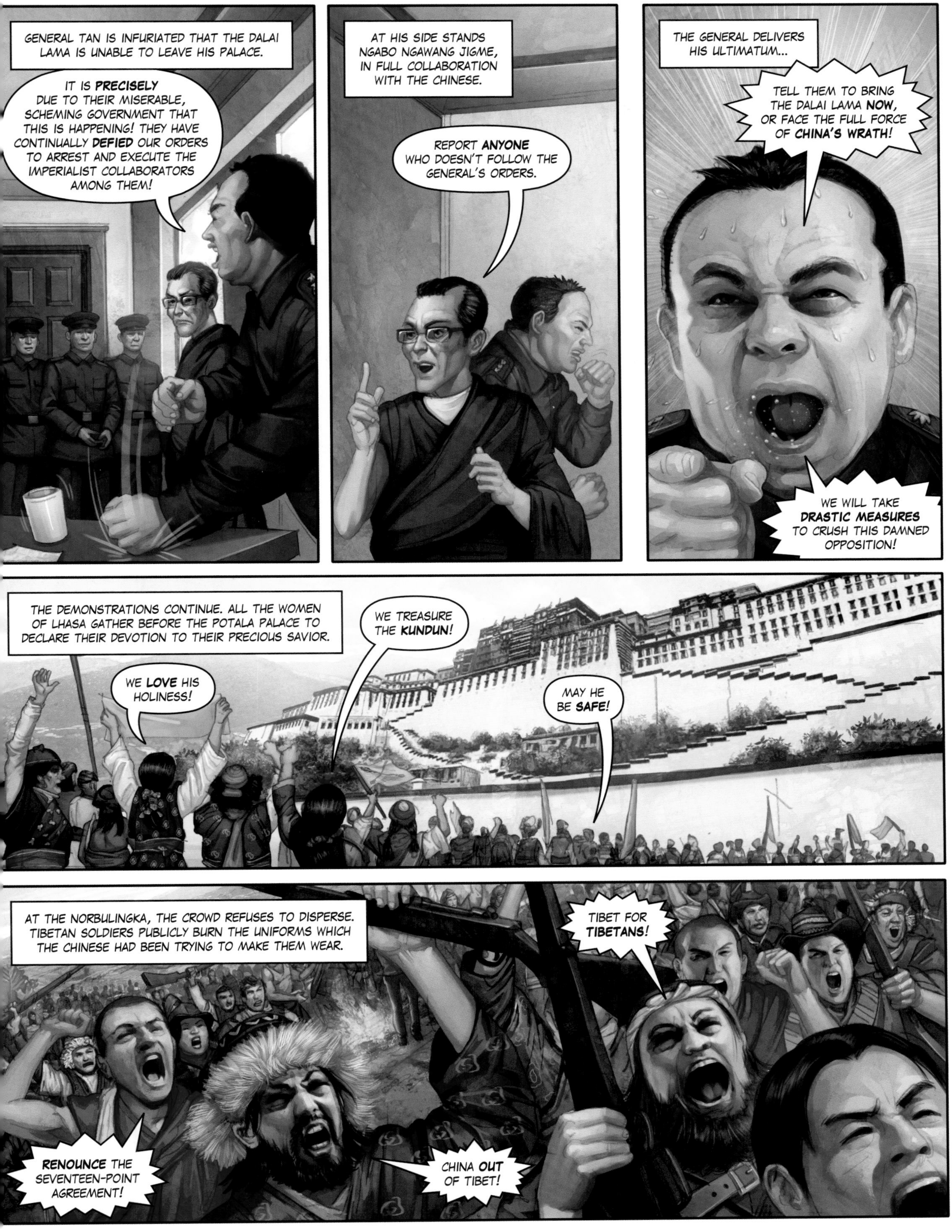
GENERAL TAN IS INFURIATED THAT THE DALAI LAMA IS UNABLE TO LEAVE HIS PALACE.
IT IS **PRECISELY** DUE TO THEIR MISERABLE, SCHEMING GOVERNMENT THAT THIS IS HAPPENING! THEY HAVE CONTINUALLY **DEFIED** OUR ORDERS TO ARREST AND EXECUTE THE IMPERIALIST COLLABORATORS AMONG THEM!
AT HIS SIDE STANDS NGABO NGAWANG JIGME, IN FULL COLLABORATION WITH THE CHINESE.
REPORT **ANYONE** WHO DOESN'T FOLLOW THE GENERAL'S ORDERS.
THE GENERAL DELIVERS HIS ULTIMATUM...
TELL THEM TO BRING THE DALAI LAMA **NOW**, OR FACE THE FULL FORCE OF **CHINA'S WRATH**!
WE WILL TAKE **DRASTIC MEASURES** TO CRUSH THIS DAMNED OPPOSITION!
THE DEMONSTRATIONS CONTINUE. ALL THE WOMEN OF LHASA GATHER BEFORE THE POTALA PALACE TO DECLARE THEIR DEVOTION TO THEIR PRECIOUS SAVIOR.
WE **LOVE** HIS HOLINESS!
WE TREASURE THE **KUNDUN**!
MAY HE BE **SAFE**!
AT THE NORBULINGKA, THE CROWD REFUSES TO DISPERSE. TIBETAN SOLDIERS PUBLICLY BURN THE UNIFORMS WHICH THE CHINESE HAD BEEN TRYING TO MAKE THEM WEAR.
TIBET FOR **TIBETANS**!
RENOUNCE THE SEVENTEEN-POINT AGREEMENT!
CHINA **OUT** OF TIBET!

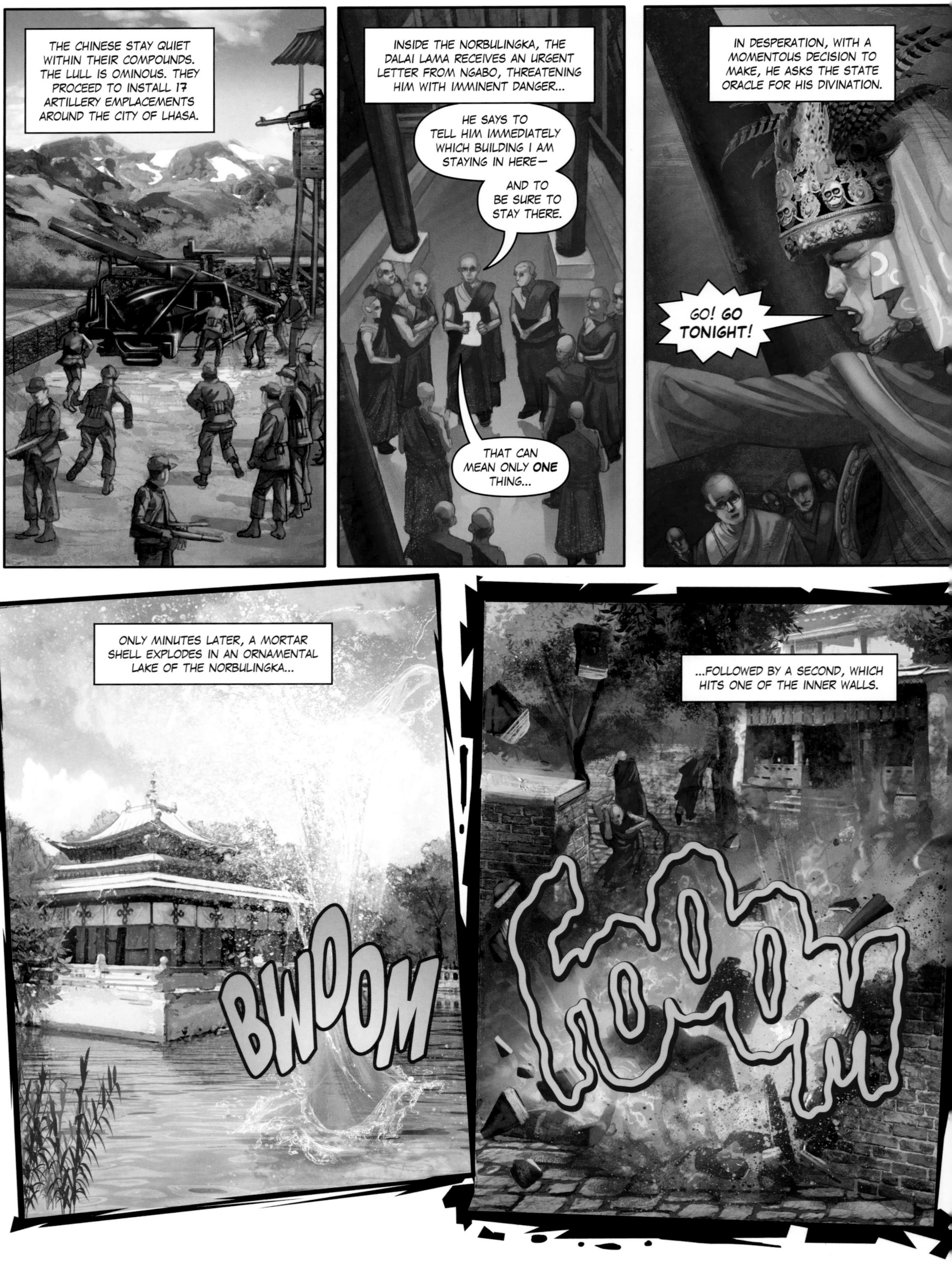
THE CHINESE STAY QUIET WITHIN THEIR COMPOUNDS. THE LULL IS OMINOUS. THEY PROCEED TO INSTALL 17 ARTILLERY EMPLACEMENTS AROUND THE CITY OF LHASA.
INSIDE THE NORBULINGKA, THE DALAI LAMA RECEIVES AN URGENT LETTER FROM NGABO, THREATENING HIM WITH IMMINENT DANGER...
HE SAYS TO TELL HIM IMMEDIATELY WHICH BUILDING I AM STAYING IN HERE—
AND TO BE SURE TO STAY THERE.
THAT CAN MEAN ONLY ONE THING...
IN DESPERATION, WITH A MOMENTOUS DECISION TO MAKE, HE ASKS THE STATE ORACLE FOR HIS DIVINATION.
GO! GO TONIGHT!
ONLY MINUTES LATER, A MORTAR SHELL EXPLODES IN AN ORNAMENTAL LAKE OF THE NORBULINGKA...
BWOOM
...FOLLOWED BY A SECOND, WHICH HITS ONE OF THE INNER WALLS.

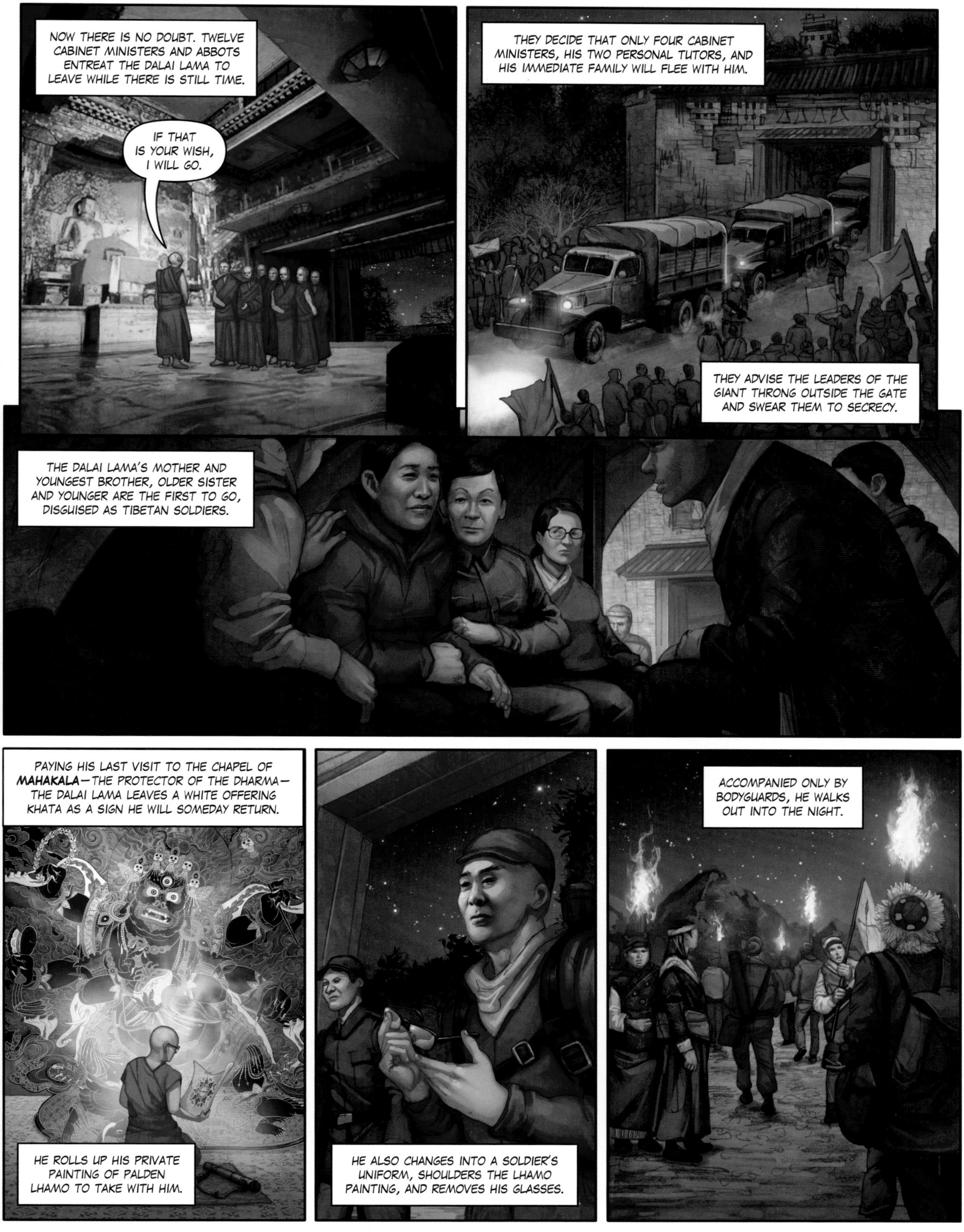

NOW THERE IS NO DOUBT. TWELVE CABINET MINISTERS AND ABBOTS ENTREAT THE DALAI LAMA TO LEAVE WHILE THERE IS STILL TIME.
IF THAT IS YOUR WISH, I WILL GO.
THEY DECIDE THAT ONLY FOUR CABINET MINISTERS, HIS TWO PERSONAL TUTORS, AND HIS IMMEDIATE FAMILY WILL FLEE WITH HIM.
THEY ADVISE THE LEADERS OF THE GIANT THRONG OUTSIDE THE GATE AND SWEAR THEM TO SECRECY.
THE DALAI LAMA'S MOTHER AND YOUNGEST BROTHER, OLDER SISTER AND YOUNGER ARE THE FIRST TO GO, DISGUISED AS TIBETAN SOLDIERS.
PAYING HIS LAST VISIT TO THE CHAPEL OF **MAHAKALA**—THE PROTECTOR OF THE DHARMA—THE DALAI LAMA LEAVES A WHITE OFFERING KHATA AS A SIGN HE WILL SOMEDAY RETURN.
HE ROLLS UP HIS PRIVATE PAINTING OF PALDEN LHAMO TO TAKE WITH HIM.
HE ALSO CHANGES INTO A SOLDIER'S UNIFORM, SHOULDERS THE LHAMO PAINTING, AND REMOVES HIS GLASSES.
ACCOMPANIED ONLY BY BODYGUARDS, HE WALKS OUT INTO THE NIGHT.

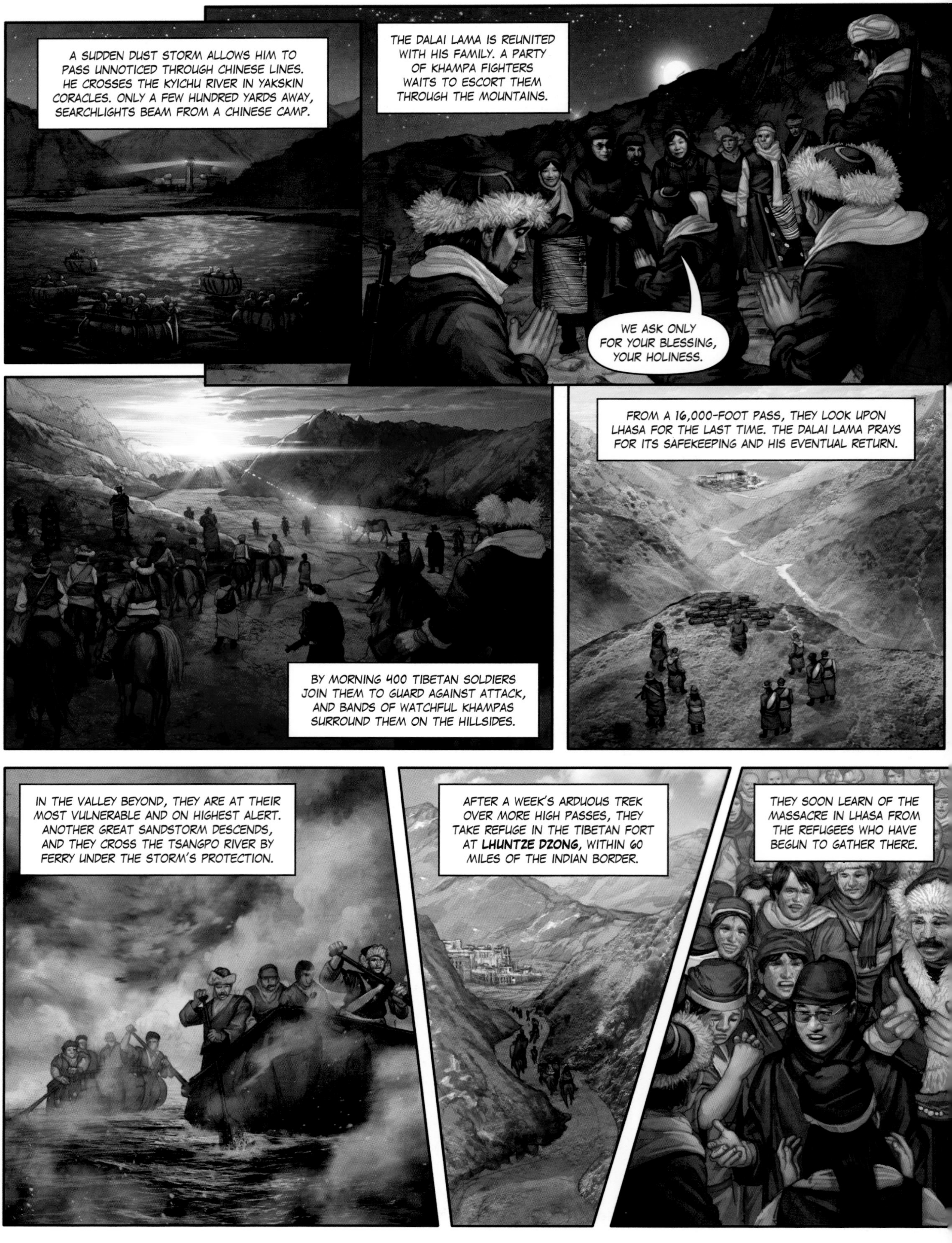
A SUDDEN DUST STORM ALLOWS HIM TO PASS UNNOTICED THROUGH CHINESE LINES. HE CROSSES THE KYICHU RIVER IN YAKSKIN CORACLES. ONLY A FEW HUNDRED YARDS AWAY, SEARCHLIGHTS BEAM FROM A CHINESE CAMP.
THE DALAI LAMA IS REUNITED WITH HIS FAMILY. A PARTY OF KHAMPA FIGHTERS WAITS TO ESCORT THEM THROUGH THE MOUNTAINS.
WE ASK ONLY FOR YOUR BLESSING, YOUR HOLINESS.
BY MORNING 400 TIBETAN SOLDIERS JOIN THEM TO GUARD AGAINST ATTACK, AND BANDS OF WATCHFUL KHAMPAS SURROUND THEM ON THE HILLSIDES.
FROM A 16,000-FOOT PASS, THEY LOOK UPON LHASA FOR THE LAST TIME. THE DALAI LAMA PRAYS FOR ITS SAFEKEEPING AND HIS EVENTUAL RETURN.
IN THE VALLEY BEYOND, THEY ARE AT THEIR MOST VULNERABLE AND ON HIGHEST ALERT. ANOTHER GREAT SANDSTORM DESCENDS, AND THEY CROSS THE TSANGPO RIVER BY FERRY UNDER THE STORM'S PROTECTION.
AFTER A WEEK'S ARDUOUS TREK OVER MORE HIGH PASSES, THEY TAKE REFUGE IN THE TIBETAN FORT AT **LHUNTZE DZONG**, WITHIN 60 MILES OF THE INDIAN BORDER.
THEY SOON LEARN OF THE MASSACRE IN LHASA FROM THE REFUGEES WHO HAVE BEGUN TO GATHER THERE.

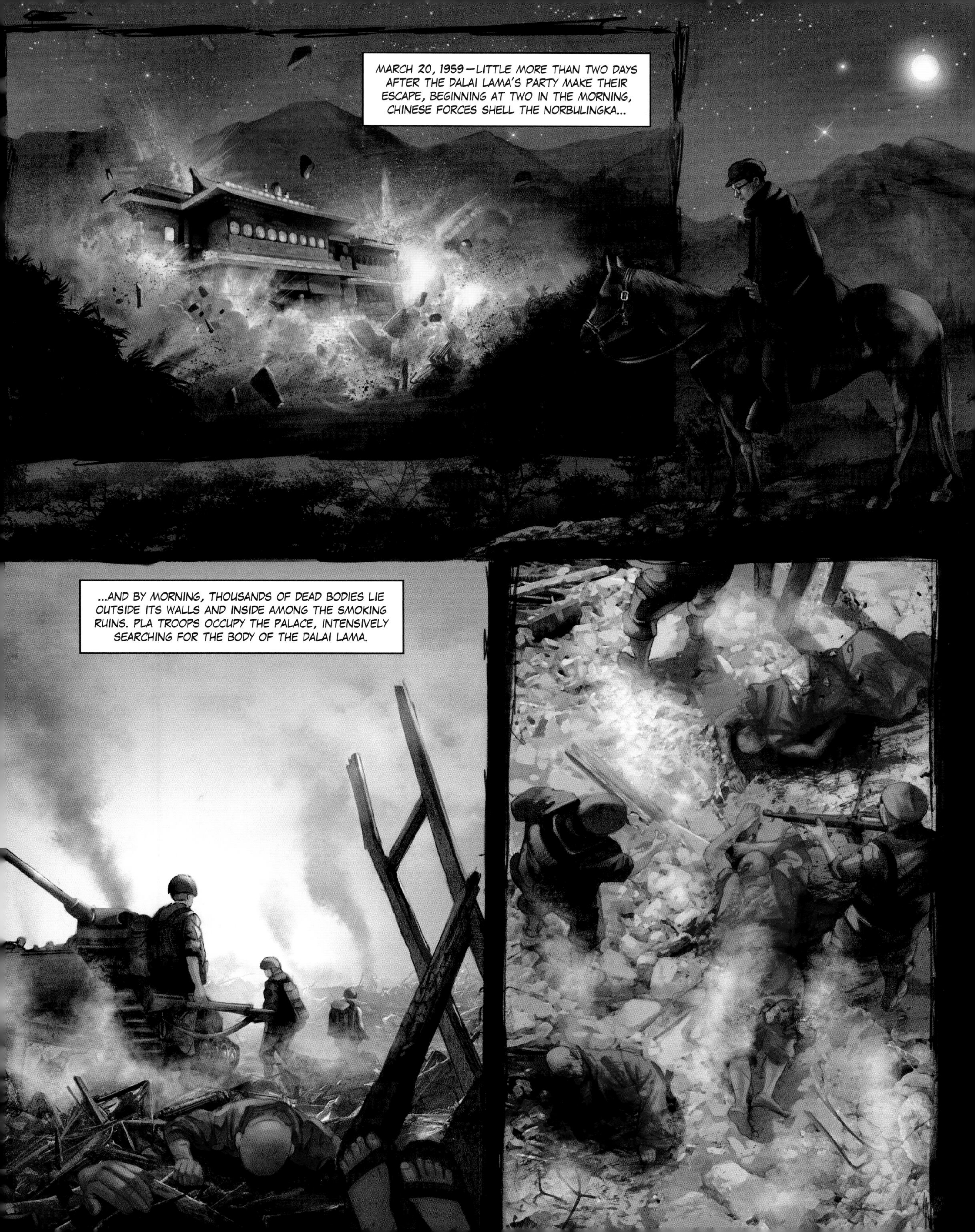
MARCH 20, 1959—LITTLE MORE THAN TWO DAYS AFTER THE DALAI LAMA'S PARTY MAKE THEIR ESCAPE, BEGINNING AT TWO IN THE MORNING, CHINESE FORCES SHELL THE NORBULINGKA...
...AND BY MORNING, THOUSANDS OF DEAD BODIES LIE OUTSIDE ITS WALLS AND INSIDE AMONG THE SMOKING RUINS. PLA TROOPS OCCUPY THE PALACE, INTENSIVELY SEARCHING FOR THE BODY OF THE DALAI LAMA.

REALIZING HE ALREADY MADE HIS ESCAPE, THE CHINESE UNLEASH THEIR WRATH ON THE HELPLESS CITIZENS OF LHASA, IMPOSING A RUTHLESS REIGN OF TERROR, SHELLING EVEN THE POTALA PALACE.

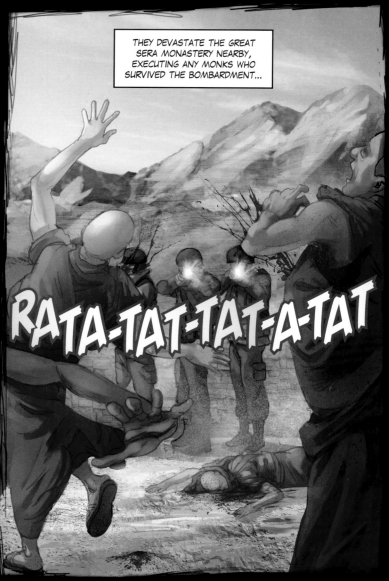

THEY DEVASTATE THE GREAT SERA MONASTERY NEARBY, EXECUTING ANY MONKS WHO SURVIVED THE BOMBARDMENT...

RATA-TAT-TAT-A-TAT

VOOM

KA-TOOM

THEY KILL TO THE LAST MAN THE DEFENDERS OF THE **CHAKPORI MEDICAL COLLEGE**, ONE OF THE EARLIEST SCHOOLS OF TIBETAN MEDICINE, REDUCING IT TO RUBBLE.

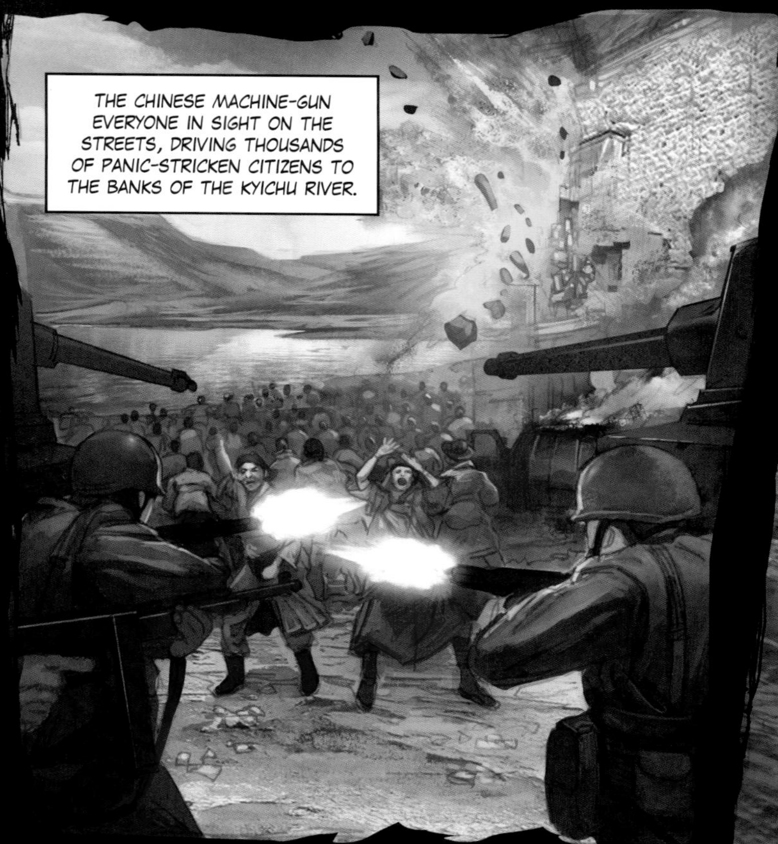
THE CHINESE MACHINE-GUN EVERYONE IN SIGHT ON THE STREETS, DRIVING THOUSANDS OF PANIC-STRICKEN CITIZENS TO THE BANKS OF THE KYICHU RIVER.

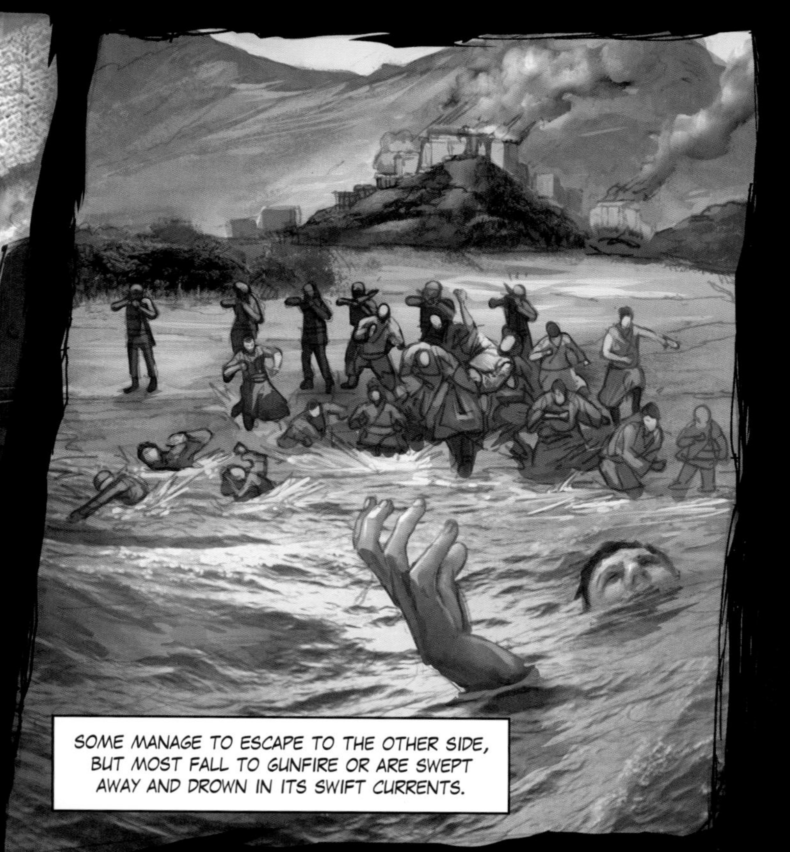
SOME MANAGE TO ESCAPE TO THE OTHER SIDE, BUT MOST FALL TO GUNFIRE OR ARE SWEPT AWAY AND DROWN IN ITS SWIFT CURRENTS.

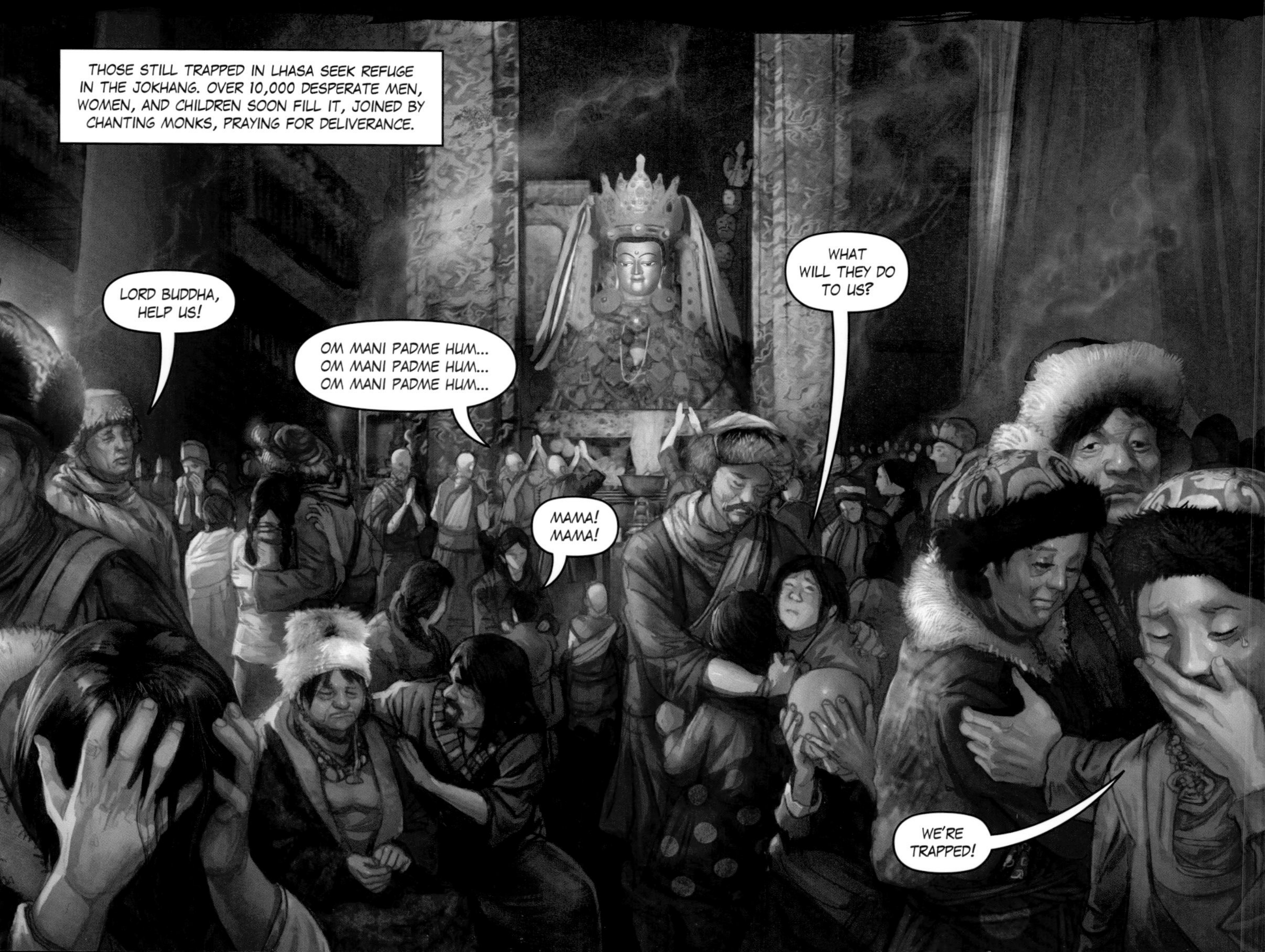
THOSE STILL TRAPPED IN LHASA SEEK REFUGE IN THE JOKHANG. OVER 10,000 DESPERATE MEN, WOMEN, AND CHILDREN SOON FILL IT, JOINED BY CHANTING MONKS, PRAYING FOR DELIVERANCE.
LORD BUDDHA, HELP US!
OM MANI PADME HUM... OM MANI PADME HUM... OM MANI PADME HUM...
WHAT WILL THEY DO TO US?
MAMA! MAMA!
WE'RE TRAPPED!

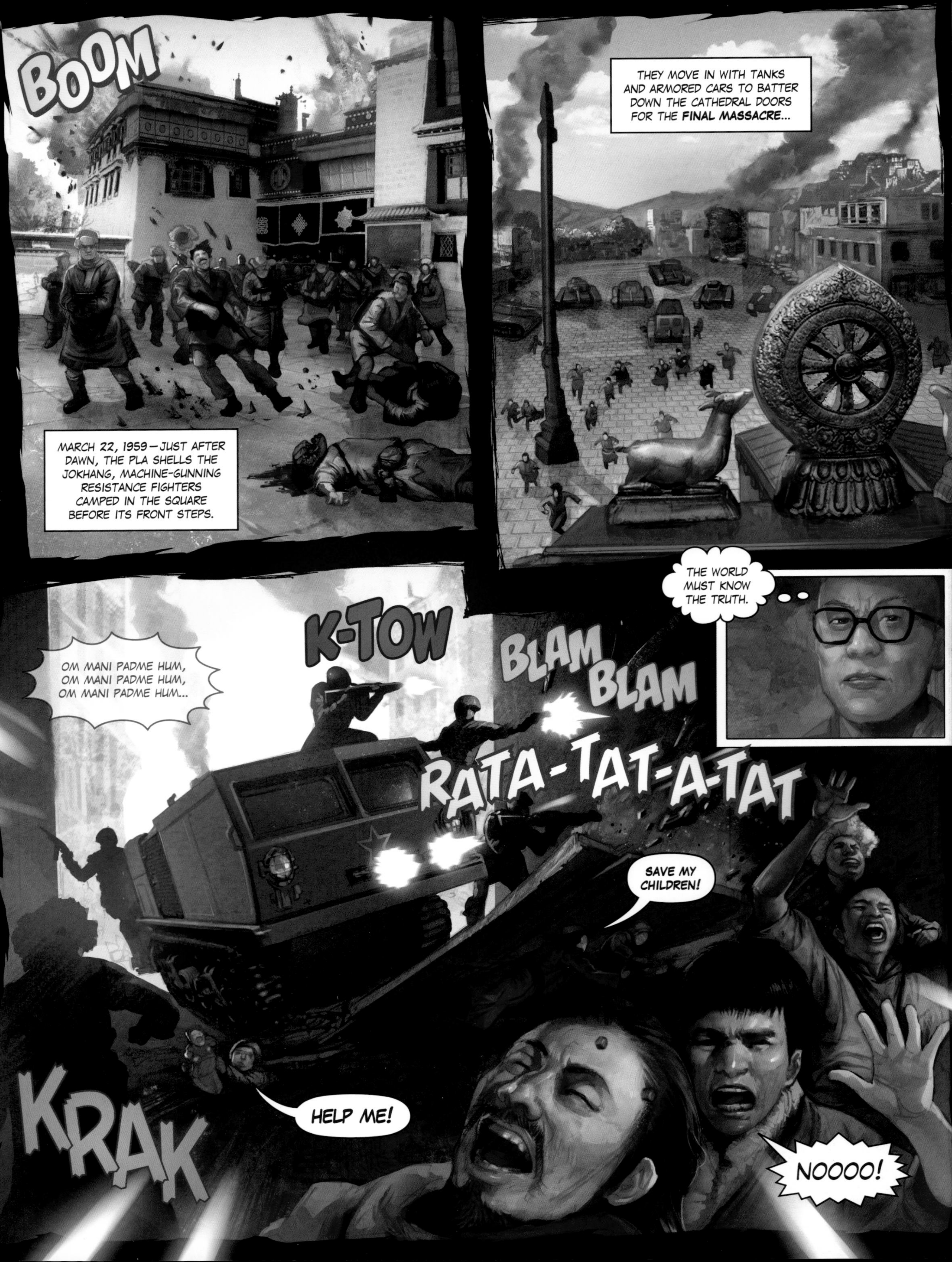
BOOM
MARCH 22, 1959—JUST AFTER DAWN, THE PLA SHELLS THE JOKHANG, MACHINE-GUNNING RESISTANCE FIGHTERS CAMPED IN THE SQUARE BEFORE ITS FRONT STEPS.
THEY MOVE IN WITH TANKS AND ARMORED CARS TO BATTER DOWN THE CATHEDRAL DOORS FOR THE FINAL MASSACRE...
OM MANI PADME HUM, OM MANI PADME HUM, OM MANI PADME HUM...
K-TOW
BLAM BLAM
THE WORLD MUST KNOW THE TRUTH.
RATA-TAT-A-TAT
SAVE MY CHILDREN!
KRAK
HELP ME!
NOOOO!

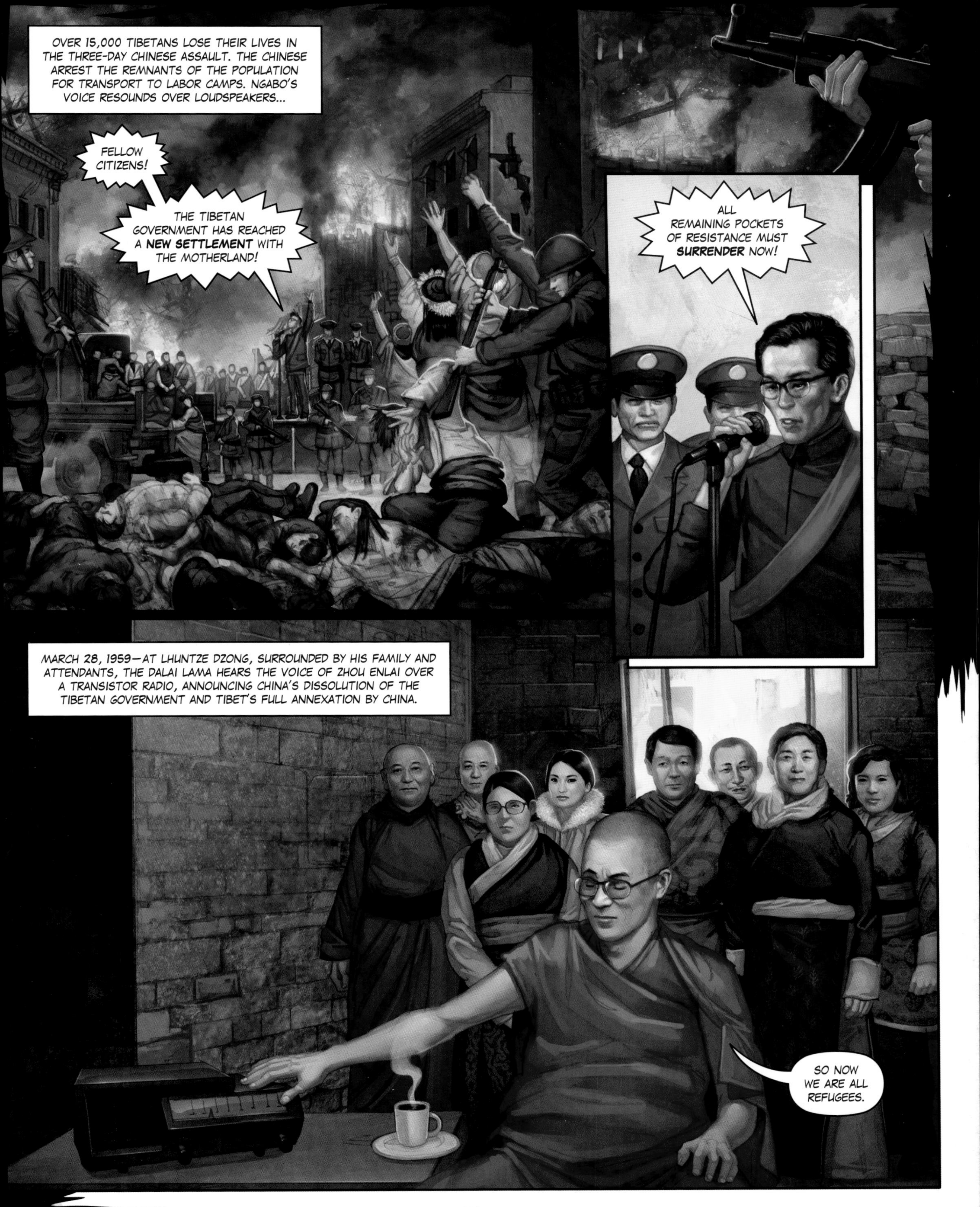
OVER 15,000 TIBETANS LOSE THEIR LIVES IN THE THREE-DAY CHINESE ASSAULT. THE CHINESE ARREST THE REMNANTS OF THE POPULATION FOR TRANSPORT TO LABOR CAMPS. NGABO'S VOICE RESOUNDS OVER LOUDSPEAKERS...
FELLOW CITIZENS!
THE TIBETAN GOVERNMENT HAS REACHED A **NEW SETTLEMENT** WITH THE MOTHERLAND!
ALL REMAINING POCKETS OF RESISTANCE MUST **SURRENDER** NOW!
MARCH 28, 1959—AT LHUNTZE DZONG, SURROUNDED BY HIS FAMILY AND ATTENDANTS, THE DALAI LAMA HEARS THE VOICE OF ZHOU ENLAI OVER A TRANSISTOR RADIO, ANNOUNCING CHINA'S DISSOLUTION OF THE TIBETAN GOVERNMENT AND TIBET'S FULL ANNEXATION BY CHINA.
SO NOW WE ARE ALL REFUGEES.

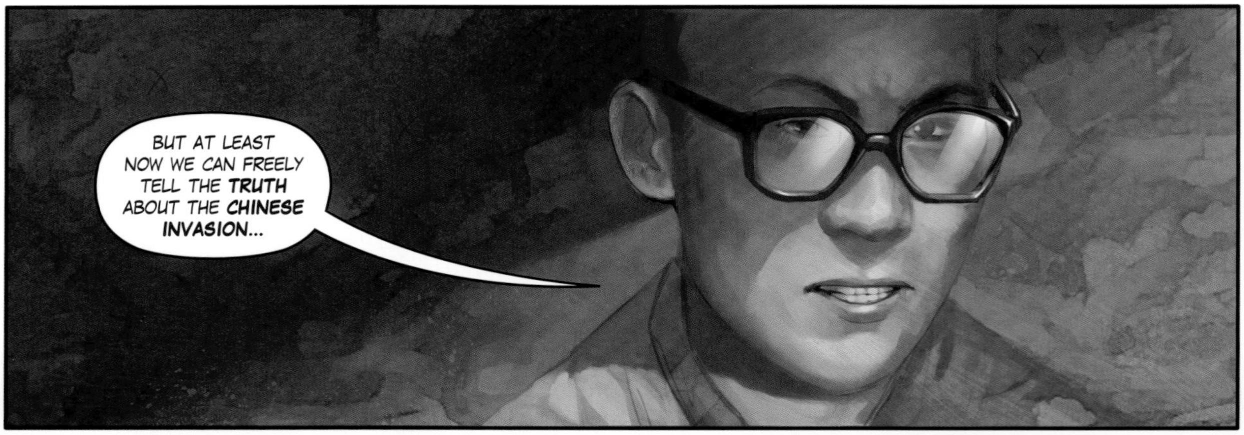
BUT AT LEAST NOW WE CAN FREELY TELL THE **TRUTH** ABOUT THE **CHINESE INVASION**...

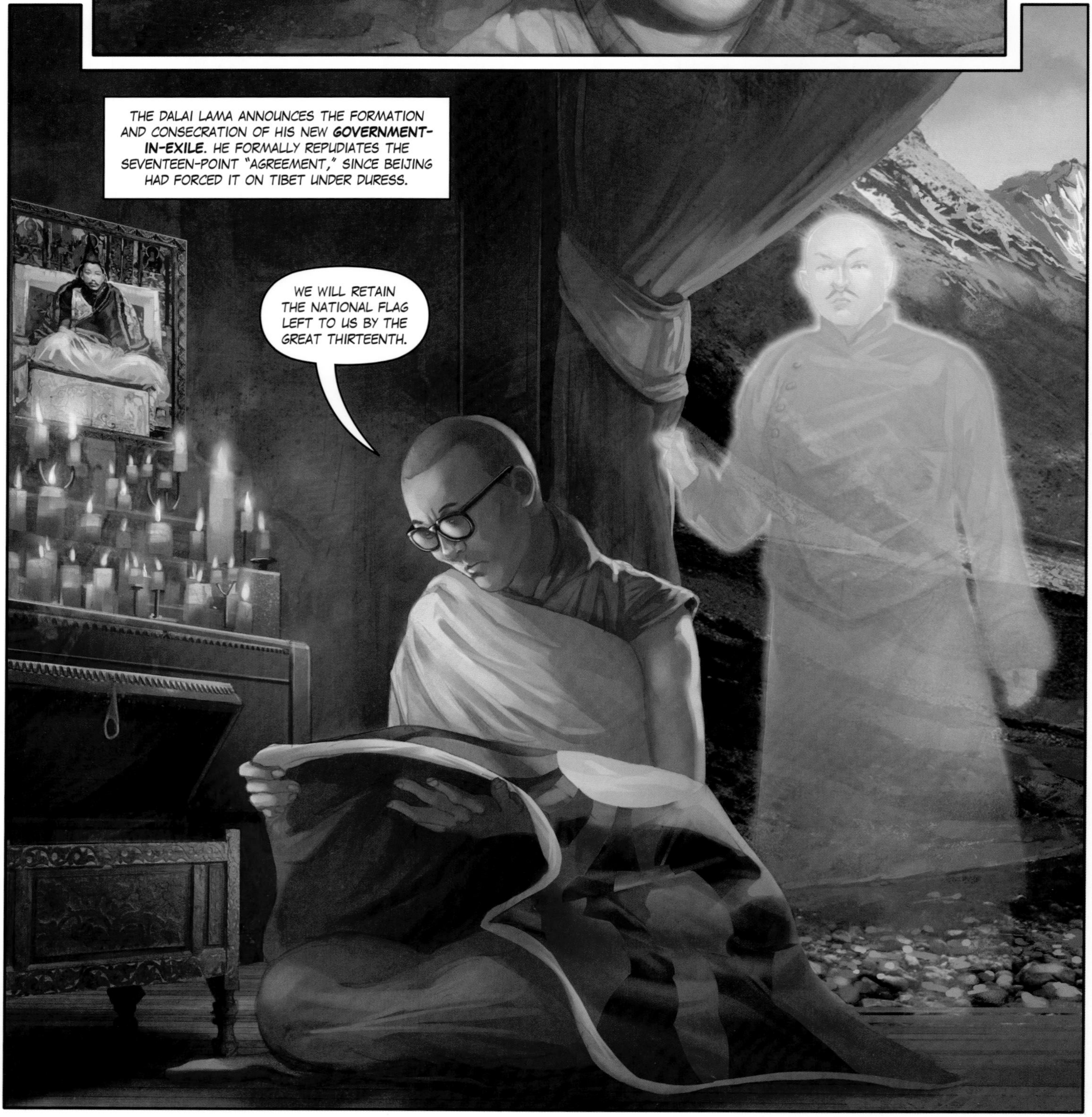
THE DALAI LAMA ANNOUNCES THE FORMATION AND CONSECRATION OF HIS NEW **GOVERNMENT-IN-EXILE**. HE FORMALLY REPUDIATES THE SEVENTEEN-POINT "AGREEMENT," SINCE BEIJING HAD FORCED IT ON TIBET UNDER DURESS.
WE WILL RETAIN THE NATIONAL FLAG LEFT TO US BY THE GREAT THIRTEENTH.

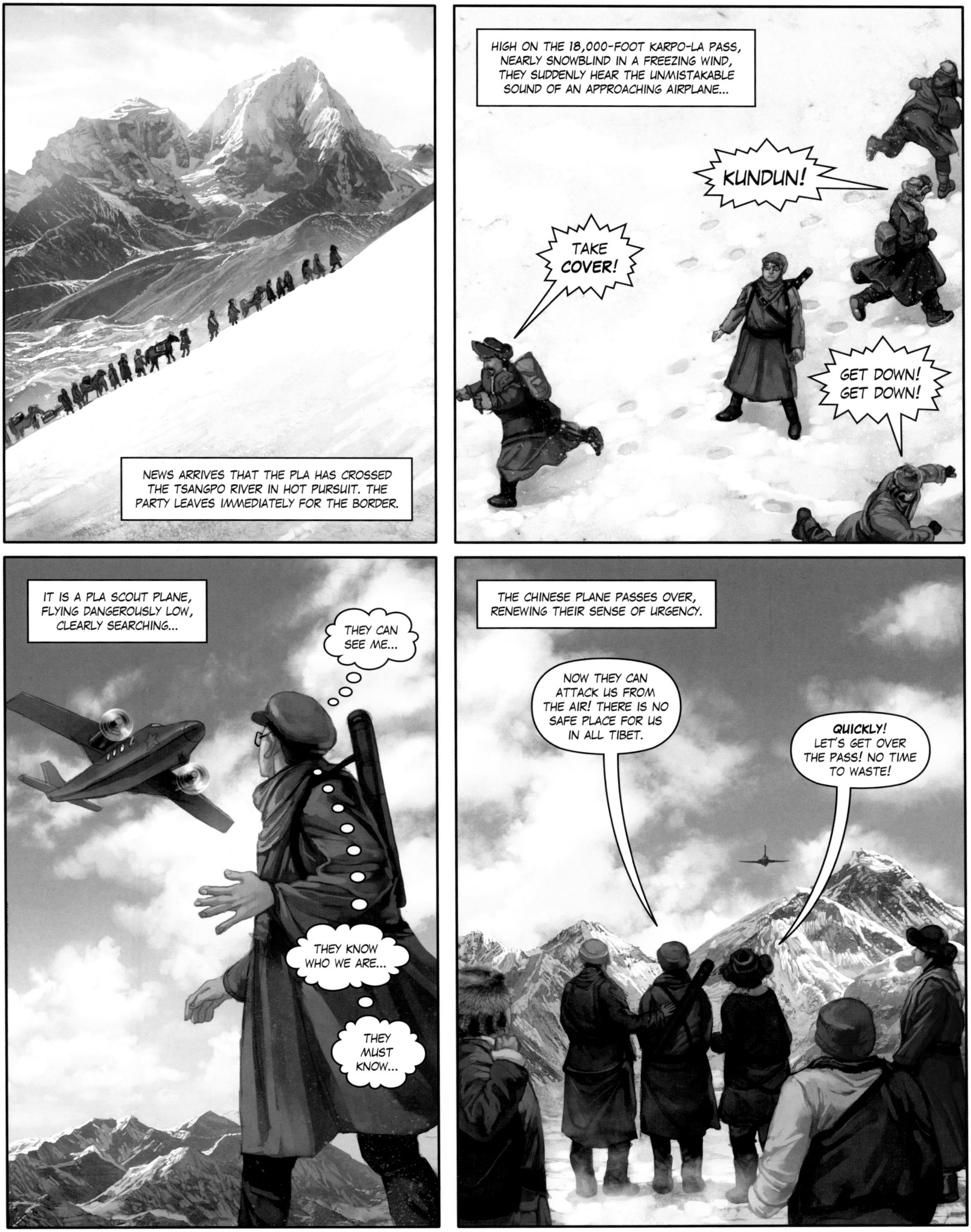
NEWS ARRIVES THAT THE PLA HAS CROSSED THE TSANGPO RIVER IN HOT PURSUIT. THE PARTY LEAVES IMMEDIATELY FOR THE BORDER.
HIGH ON THE 18,000-FOOT KARPO-LA PASS, NEARLY SNOWBLIND IN A FREEZING WIND, THEY SUDDENLY HEAR THE UNMISTAKABLE SOUND OF AN APPROACHING AIRPLANE...
KUNDUN!
TAKE COVER!
GET DOWN! GET DOWN!
IT IS A PLA SCOUT PLANE, FLYING DANGEROUSLY LOW, CLEARLY SEARCHING...
THEY CAN SEE ME...
THEY KNOW WHO WE ARE...
THEY MUST KNOW...
THE CHINESE PLANE PASSES OVER, RENEWING THEIR SENSE OF URGENCY.
NOW THEY CAN ATTACK US FROM THE AIR! THERE IS NO SAFE PLACE FOR US IN ALL TIBET.
QUICKLY! LET'S GET OVER THE PASS! NO TIME TO WASTE!

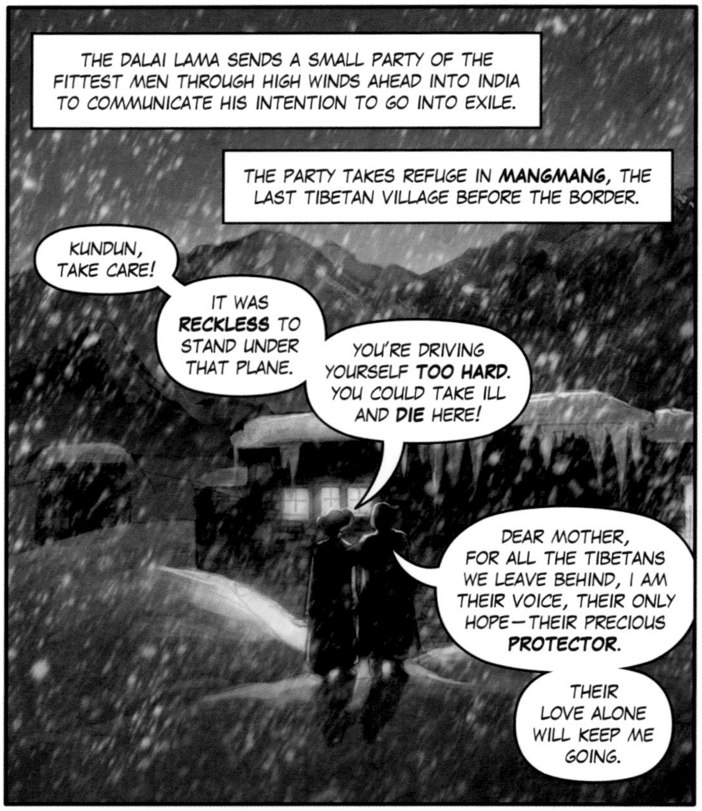
THE DALAI LAMA SENDS A SMALL PARTY OF THE FITTEST MEN THROUGH HIGH WINDS AHEAD INTO INDIA TO COMMUNICATE HIS INTENTION TO GO INTO EXILE.
THE PARTY TAKES REFUGE IN **MANGMANG**, THE LAST TIBETAN VILLAGE BEFORE THE BORDER.
KUNDUN, TAKE CARE!
IT WAS **RECKLESS** TO STAND UNDER THAT PLANE.
YOU'RE DRIVING YOURSELF **TOO HARD**. YOU COULD TAKE ILL AND **DIE** HERE!
DEAR MOTHER, FOR ALL THE TIBETANS WE LEAVE BEHIND, I AM THEIR VOICE, THEIR ONLY HOPE—THEIR PRECIOUS **PROTECTOR**.
THEIR LOVE ALONE WILL KEEP ME GOING.

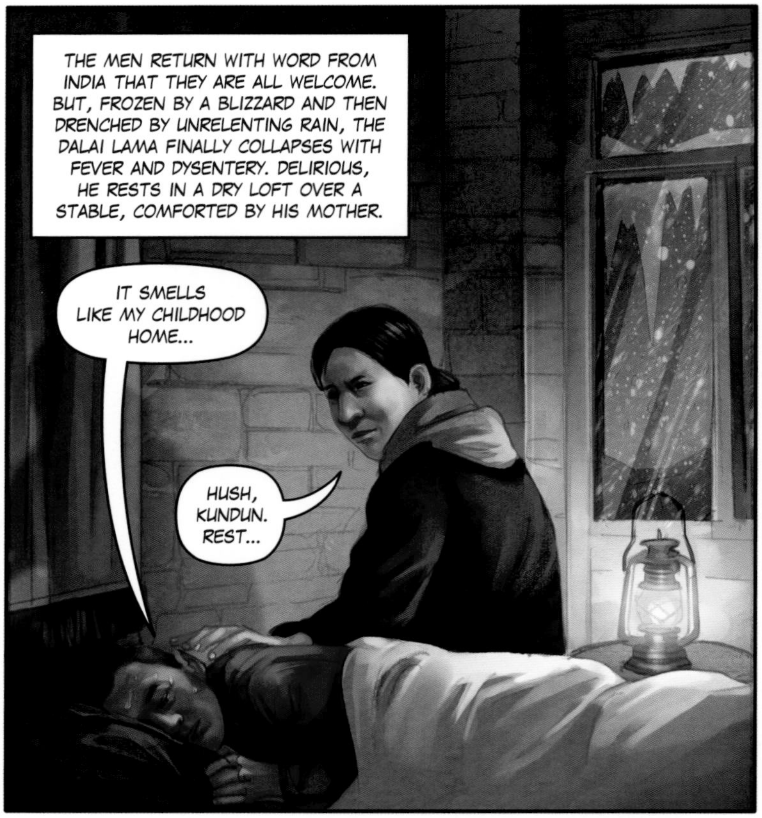
THE MEN RETURN WITH WORD FROM INDIA THAT THEY ARE ALL WELCOME. BUT, FROZEN BY A BLIZZARD AND THEN DRENCHED BY UNRELENTING RAIN, THE DALAI LAMA FINALLY COLLAPSES WITH FEVER AND DYSENTERY. DELIRIOUS, HE RESTS IN A DRY LOFT OVER A STABLE, COMFORTED BY HIS MOTHER.
IT SMELLS LIKE MY CHILDHOOD HOME...
HUSH, KUNDUN. REST...

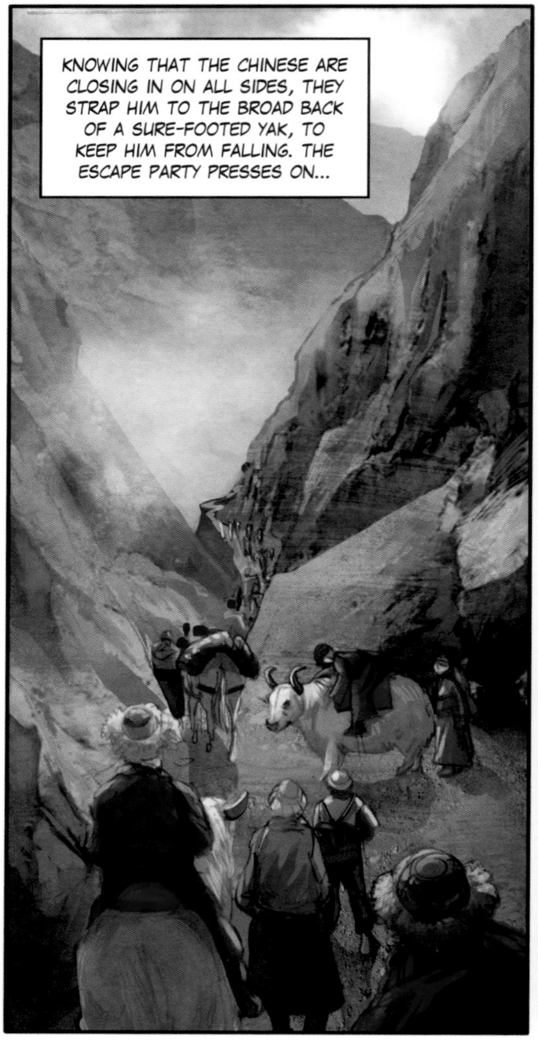
KNOWING THAT THE CHINESE ARE CLOSING IN ON ALL SIDES, THEY STRAP HIM TO THE BROAD BACK OF A SURE-FOOTED YAK, TO KEEP HIM FROM FALLING. THE ESCAPE PARTY PRESSES ON...

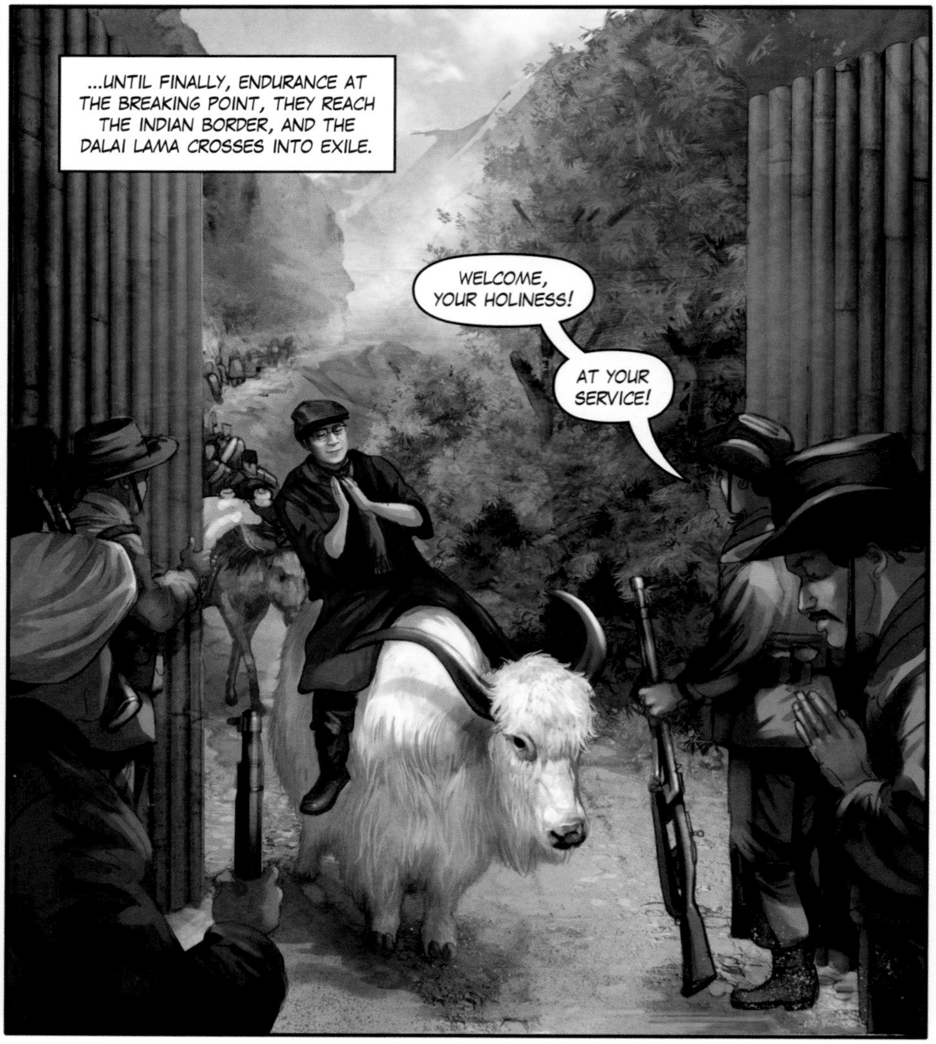
...UNTIL FINALLY, ENDURANCE AT THE BREAKING POINT, THEY REACH THE INDIAN BORDER, AND THE DALAI LAMA CROSSES INTO EXILE.
WELCOME, YOUR HOLINESS!
AT YOUR SERVICE!

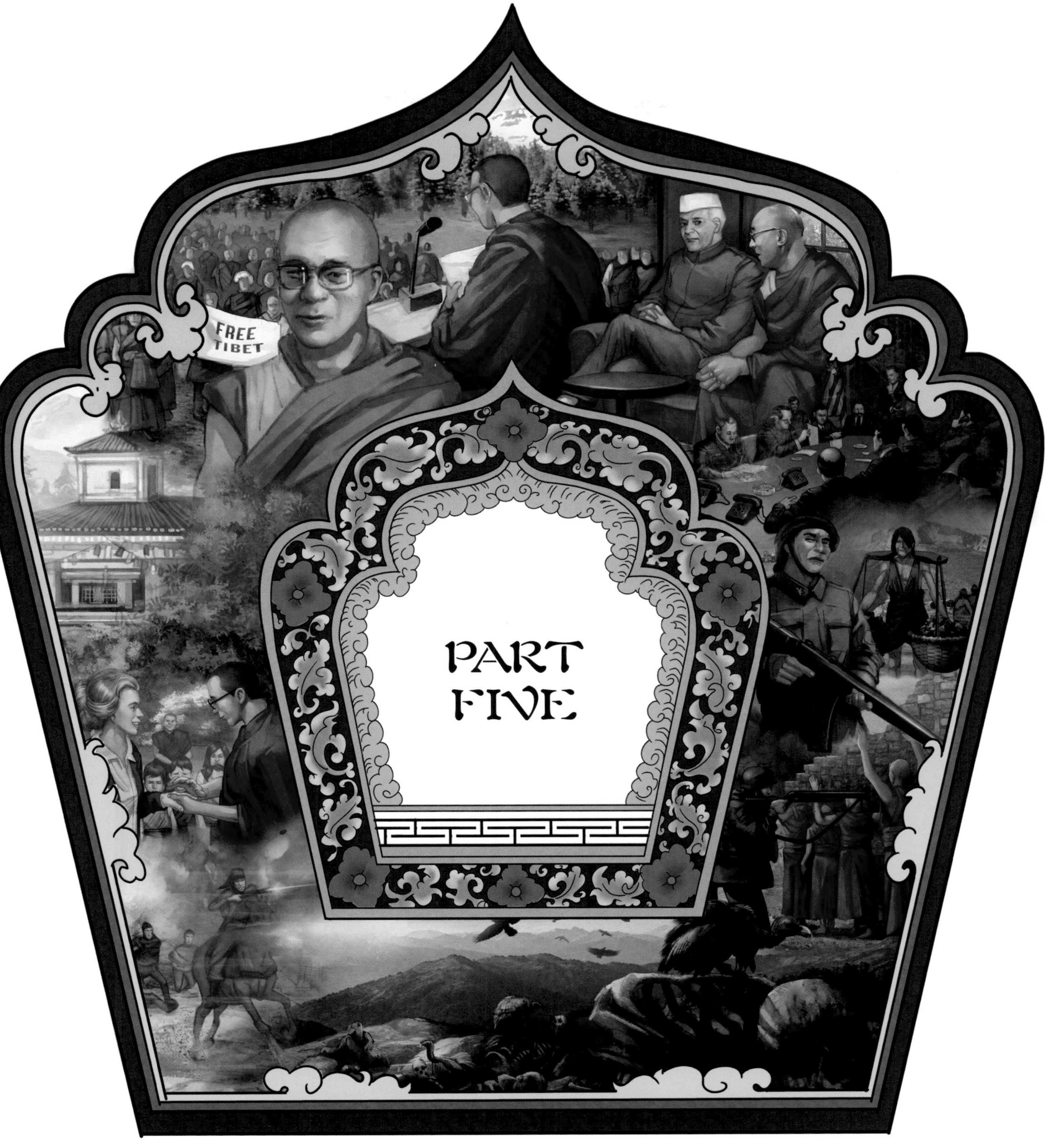
FREE TIBET

PART FIVE

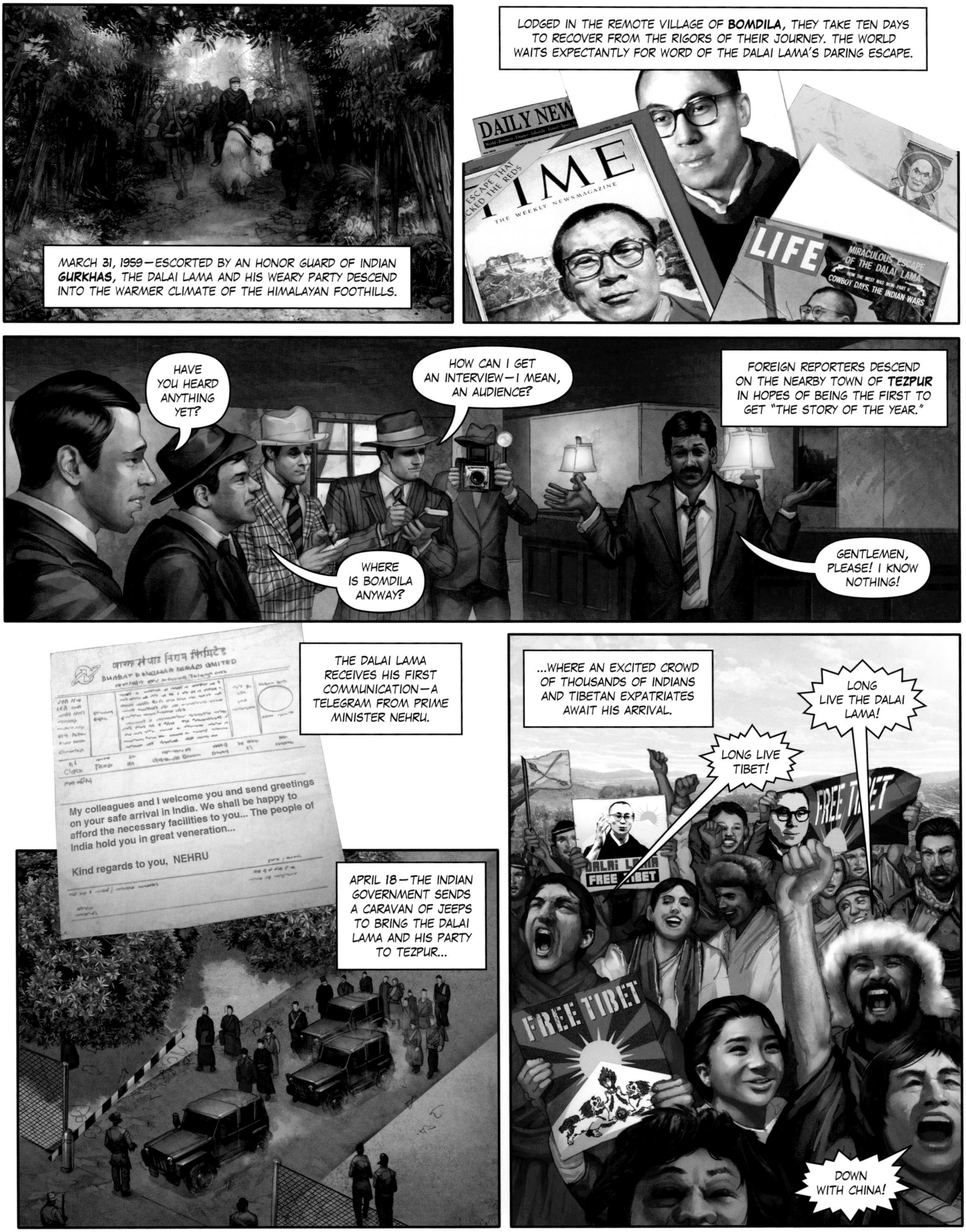
MARCH 31, 1959—ESCORTED BY AN HONOR GUARD OF INDIAN **GURKHAS,** THE DALAI LAMA AND HIS WEARY PARTY DESCEND INTO THE WARMER CLIMATE OF THE HIMALAYAN FOOTHILLS.
LODGED IN THE REMOTE VILLAGE OF **BOMDILA,** THEY TAKE TEN DAYS TO RECOVER FROM THE RIGORS OF THEIR JOURNEY. THE WORLD WAITS EXPECTANTLY FOR WORD OF THE DALAI LAMA'S DARING ESCAPE.
DAILY NEW
TIME
THE WEEKLY NEWSMAGAZINE
LIFE
MIRACULOUS ESCAPE OF THE DALAI LAMA
COWBOY DAYS, THE INDIAN WARS
HAVE YOU HEARD ANYTHING YET?
HOW CAN I GET AN INTERVIEW—I MEAN, AN AUDIENCE?
FOREIGN REPORTERS DESCEND ON THE NEARBY TOWN OF **TEZPUR** IN HOPES OF BEING THE FIRST TO GET "THE STORY OF THE YEAR."
WHERE IS BOMDILA ANYWAY?
GENTLEMEN, PLEASE! I KNOW NOTHING!
THE DALAI LAMA RECEIVES HIS FIRST COMMUNICATION—A TELEGRAM FROM PRIME MINISTER NEHRU.
My colleagues and I welcome you and send greetings on your safe arrival in India. We shall be happy to afford the necessary facilities to you... The people of India hold you in great veneration...
Kind regards to you, NEHRU
APRIL 18—THE INDIAN GOVERNMENT SENDS A CARAVAN OF JEEPS TO BRING THE DALAI LAMA AND HIS PARTY TO TEZPUR...
...WHERE AN EXCITED CROWD OF THOUSANDS OF INDIANS AND TIBETAN EXPATRIATES AWAIT HIS ARRIVAL.
LONG LIVE THE DALAI LAMA!
LONG LIVE TIBET!
FREE TIBET
DALAI LAMA
FREE TIBET
FREE TIBET
DOWN WITH CHINA!

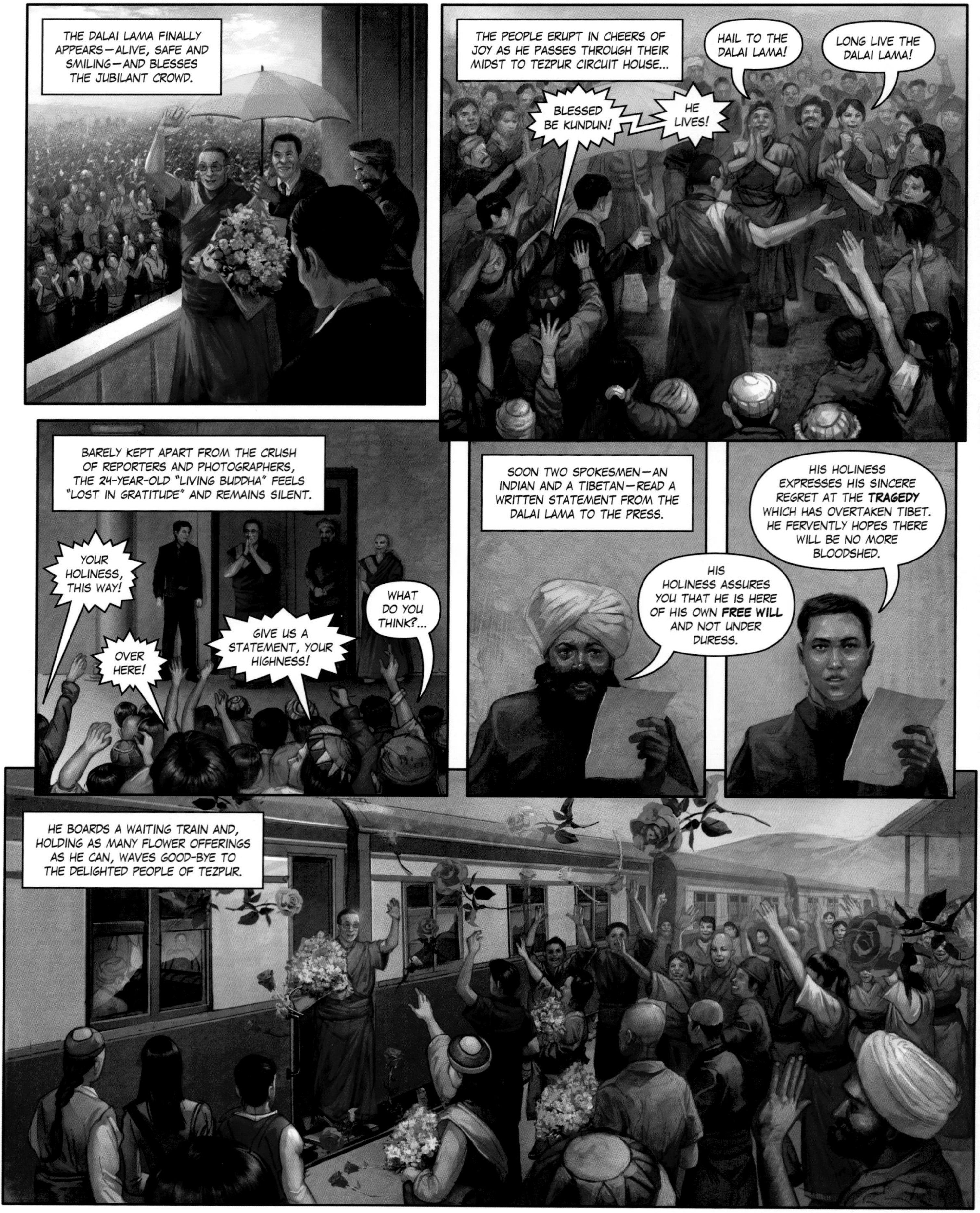

THE DALAI LAMA FINALLY APPEARS—ALIVE, SAFE AND SMILING—AND BLESSES THE JUBILANT CROWD.
THE PEOPLE ERUPT IN CHEERS OF JOY AS HE PASSES THROUGH THEIR MIDST TO TEZPUR CIRCUIT HOUSE...
HAIL TO THE DALAI LAMA!
LONG LIVE THE DALAI LAMA!
BLESSED BE KUNDUN!
HE LIVES!
BARELY KEPT APART FROM THE CRUSH OF REPORTERS AND PHOTOGRAPHERS, THE 24-YEAR-OLD "LIVING BUDDHA" FEELS "LOST IN GRATITUDE" AND REMAINS SILENT.
YOUR HOLINESS, THIS WAY!
OVER HERE!
GIVE US A STATEMENT, YOUR HIGHNESS!
WHAT DO YOU THINK?...
SOON TWO SPOKESMEN—AN INDIAN AND A TIBETAN—READ A WRITTEN STATEMENT FROM THE DALAI LAMA TO THE PRESS.
HIS HOLINESS ASSURES YOU THAT HE IS HERE OF HIS OWN FREE WILL AND NOT UNDER DURESS.
HIS HOLINESS EXPRESSES HIS SINCERE REGRET AT THE TRAGEDY WHICH HAS OVERTAKEN TIBET. HE FERVENTLY HOPES THERE WILL BE NO MORE BLOODSHED.
HE BOARDS A WAITING TRAIN AND, HOLDING AS MANY FLOWER OFFERINGS AS HE CAN, WAVES GOOD-BYE TO THE DELIGHTED PEOPLE OF TEZPUR.

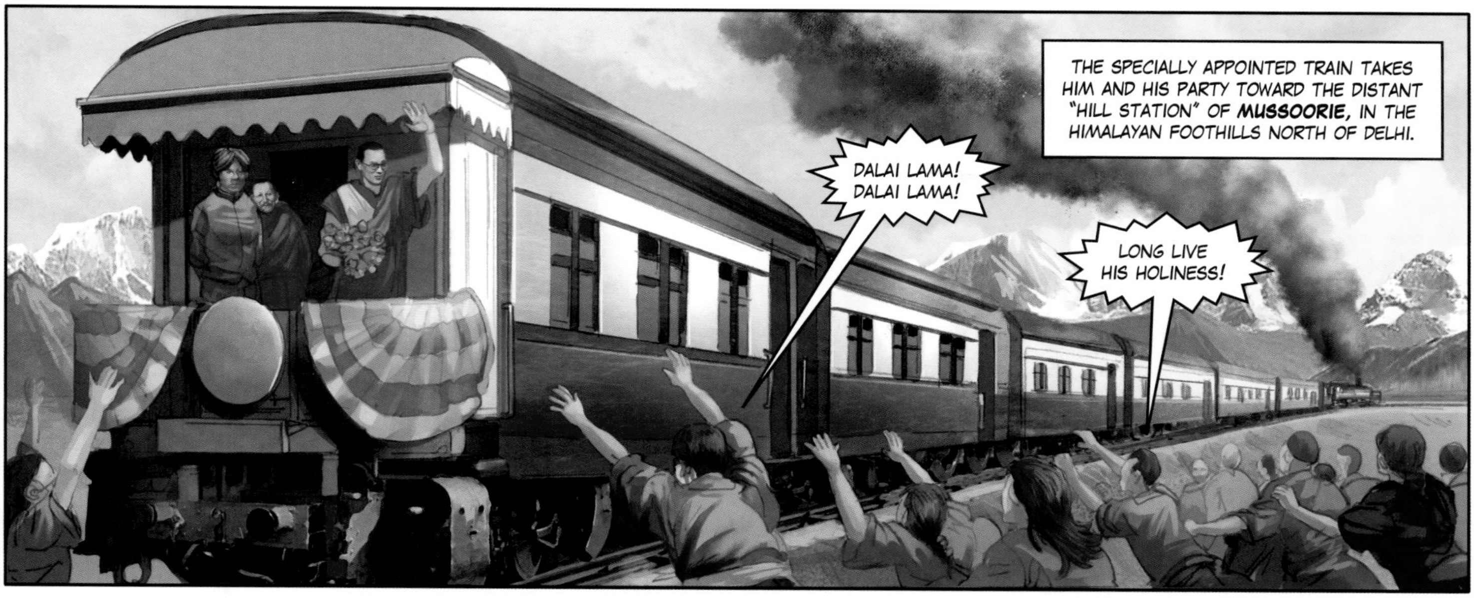
THE SPECIALLY APPOINTED TRAIN TAKES HIM AND HIS PARTY TOWARD THE DISTANT "HILL STATION" OF MUSSOORIE, IN THE HIMALAYAN FOOTHILLS NORTH OF DELHI.
DALAI LAMA! DALAI LAMA!
LONG LIVE HIS HOLINESS!

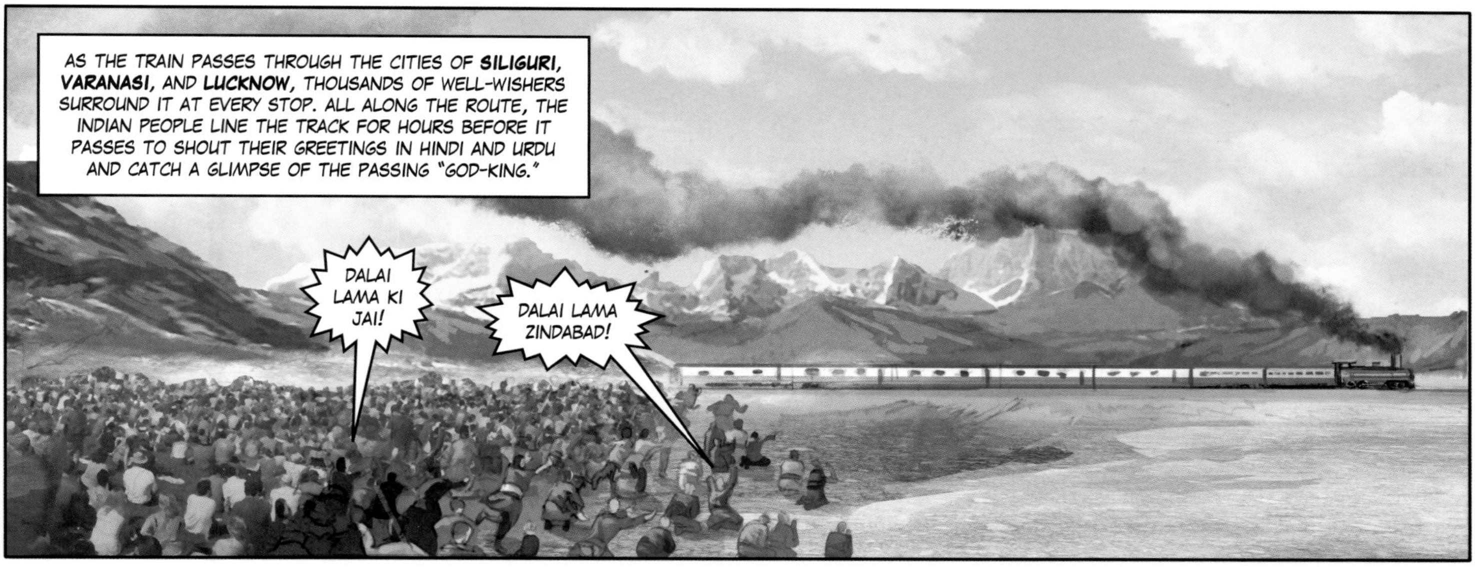
AS THE TRAIN PASSES THROUGH THE CITIES OF SILIGURI, VARANASI, AND LUCKNOW, THOUSANDS OF WELL-WISHERS SURROUND IT AT EVERY STOP. ALL ALONG THE ROUTE, THE INDIAN PEOPLE LINE THE TRACK FOR HOURS BEFORE IT PASSES TO SHOUT THEIR GREETINGS IN HINDI AND URDU AND CATCH A GLIMPSE OF THE PASSING "GOD-KING."
DALAI LAMA KI JAI!
DALAI LAMA ZINDABAD!

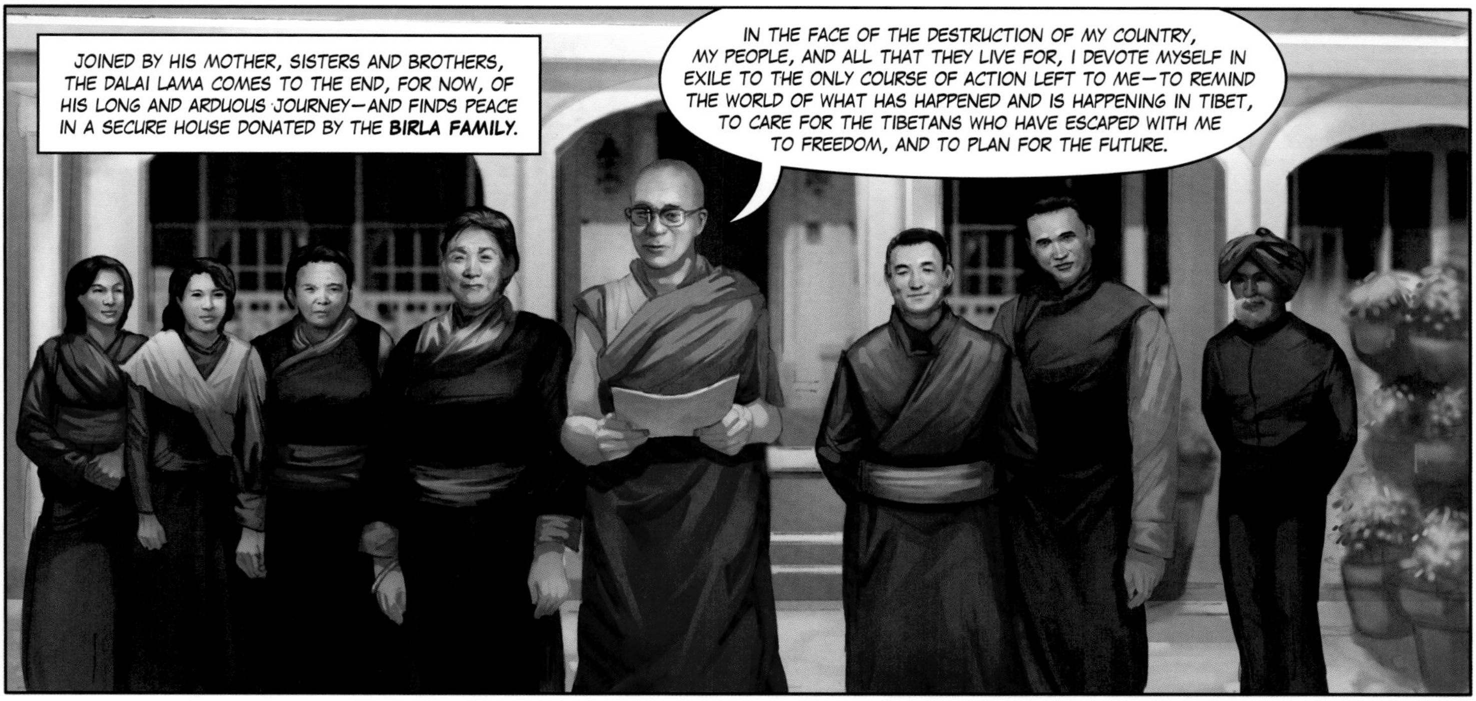
JOINED BY HIS MOTHER, SISTERS AND BROTHERS, THE DALAI LAMA COMES TO THE END, FOR NOW, OF HIS LONG AND ARDUOUS JOURNEY—AND FINDS PEACE IN A SECURE HOUSE DONATED BY THE BIRLA FAMILY.
IN THE FACE OF THE DESTRUCTION OF MY COUNTRY, MY PEOPLE, AND ALL THAT THEY LIVE FOR, I DEVOTE MYSELF IN EXILE TO THE ONLY COURSE OF ACTION LEFT TO ME—TO REMIND THE WORLD OF WHAT HAS HAPPENED AND IS HAPPENING IN TIBET, TO CARE FOR THE TIBETANS WHO HAVE ESCAPED WITH ME TO FREEDOM, AND TO PLAN FOR THE FUTURE.

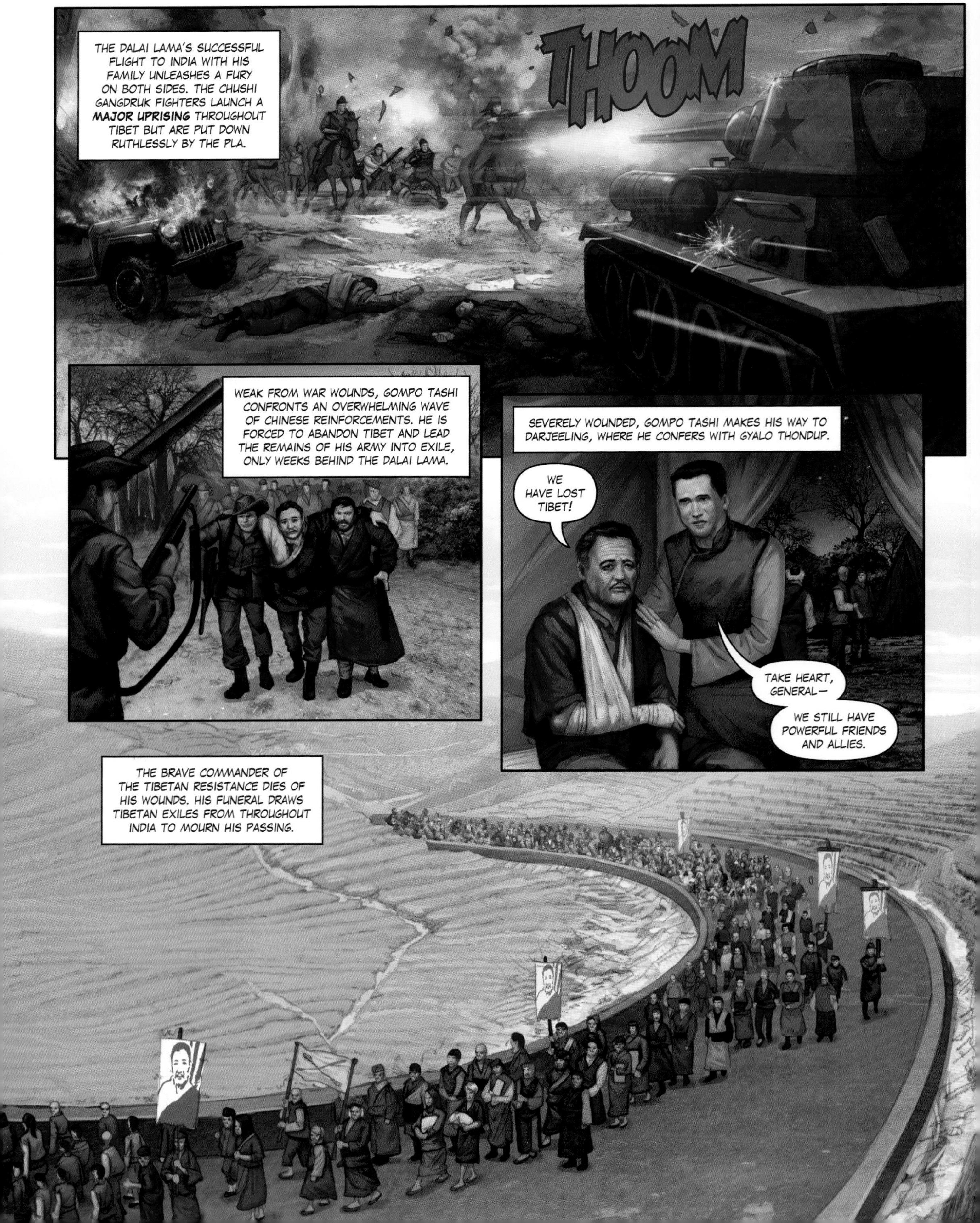
THE DALAI LAMA'S SUCCESSFUL FLIGHT TO INDIA WITH HIS FAMILY UNLEASHES A FURY ON BOTH SIDES. THE CHUSHI GANGDRUK FIGHTERS LAUNCH A MAJOR UPRISING THROUGHOUT TIBET BUT ARE PUT DOWN RUTHLESSLY BY THE PLA.
THOOM
WEAK FROM WAR WOUNDS, GOMPO TASHI CONFRONTS AN OVERWHELMING WAVE OF CHINESE REINFORCEMENTS. HE IS FORCED TO ABANDON TIBET AND LEAD THE REMAINS OF HIS ARMY INTO EXILE, ONLY WEEKS BEHIND THE DALAI LAMA.
SEVERELY WOUNDED, GOMPO TASHI MAKES HIS WAY TO DARJEELING, WHERE HE CONFERS WITH GYALO THONDUP.
WE HAVE LOST TIBET!
TAKE HEART, GENERAL—
WE STILL HAVE POWERFUL FRIENDS AND ALLIES.
THE BRAVE COMMANDER OF THE TIBETAN RESISTANCE DIES OF HIS WOUNDS. HIS FUNERAL DRAWS TIBETAN EXILES FROM THROUGHOUT INDIA TO MOURN HIS PASSING.

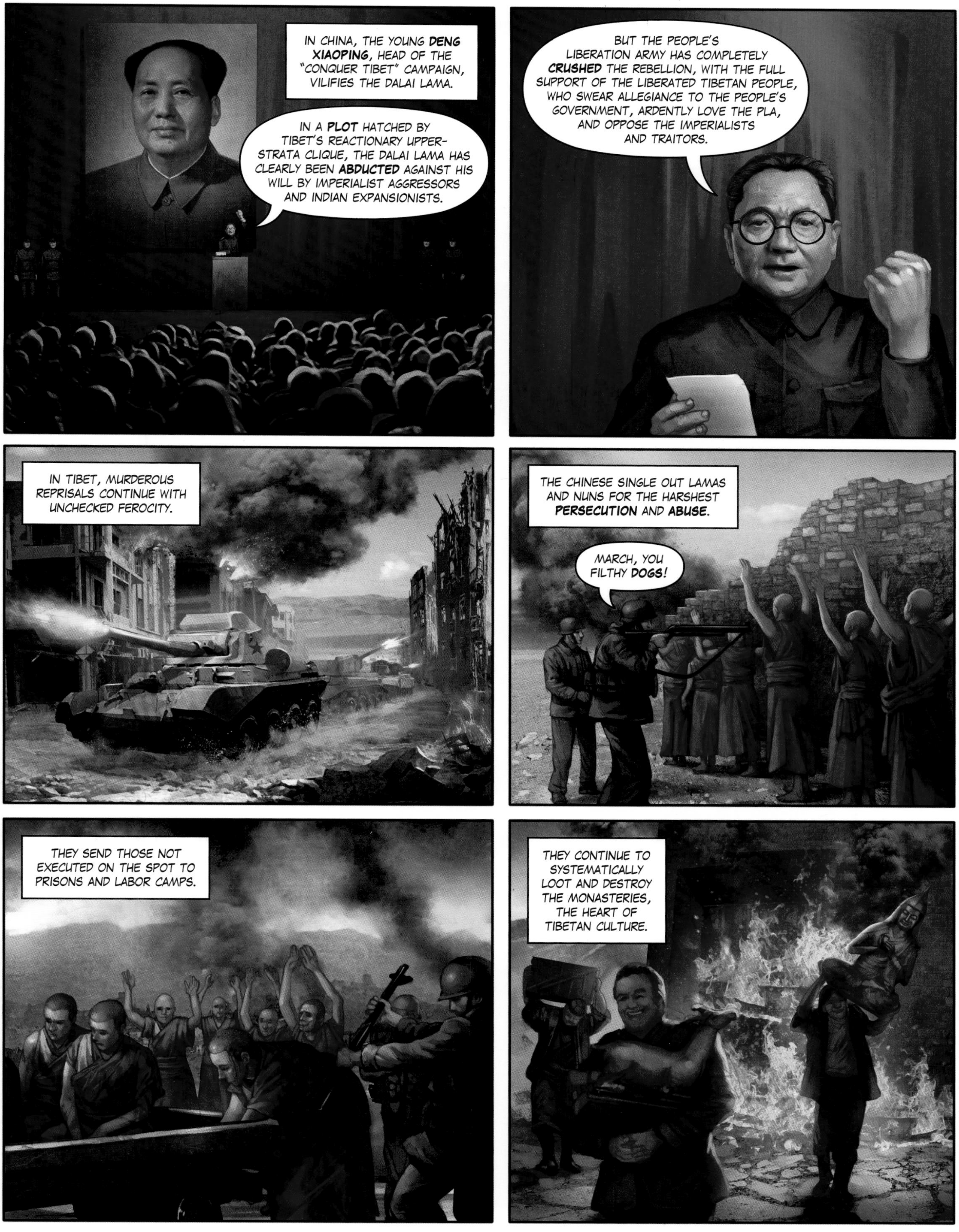
IN CHINA, THE YOUNG **DENG XIAOPING**, HEAD OF THE "CONQUER TIBET" CAMPAIGN, VILIFIES THE DALAI LAMA.
IN A **PLOT** HATCHED BY TIBET'S REACTIONARY UPPER-STRATA CLIQUE, THE DALAI LAMA HAS CLEARLY BEEN **ABDUCTED** AGAINST HIS WILL BY IMPERIALIST AGGRESSORS AND INDIAN EXPANSIONISTS.
BUT THE PEOPLE'S LIBERATION ARMY HAS COMPLETELY **CRUSHED** THE REBELLION, WITH THE FULL SUPPORT OF THE LIBERATED TIBETAN PEOPLE, WHO SWEAR ALLEGIANCE TO THE PEOPLE'S GOVERNMENT, ARDENTLY LOVE THE PLA, AND OPPOSE THE IMPERIALISTS AND TRAITORS.
IN TIBET, MURDEROUS REPRISALS CONTINUE WITH UNCHECKED FEROCITY.
THE CHINESE SINGLE OUT LAMAS AND NUNS FOR THE HARSHEST **PERSECUTION** AND **ABUSE**.
MARCH, YOU FILTHY **DOGS**!
THEY SEND THOSE NOT EXECUTED ON THE SPOT TO PRISONS AND LABOR CAMPS.
THEY CONTINUE TO SYSTEMATICALLY LOOT AND DESTROY THE MONASTERIES, THE HEART OF TIBETAN CULTURE.

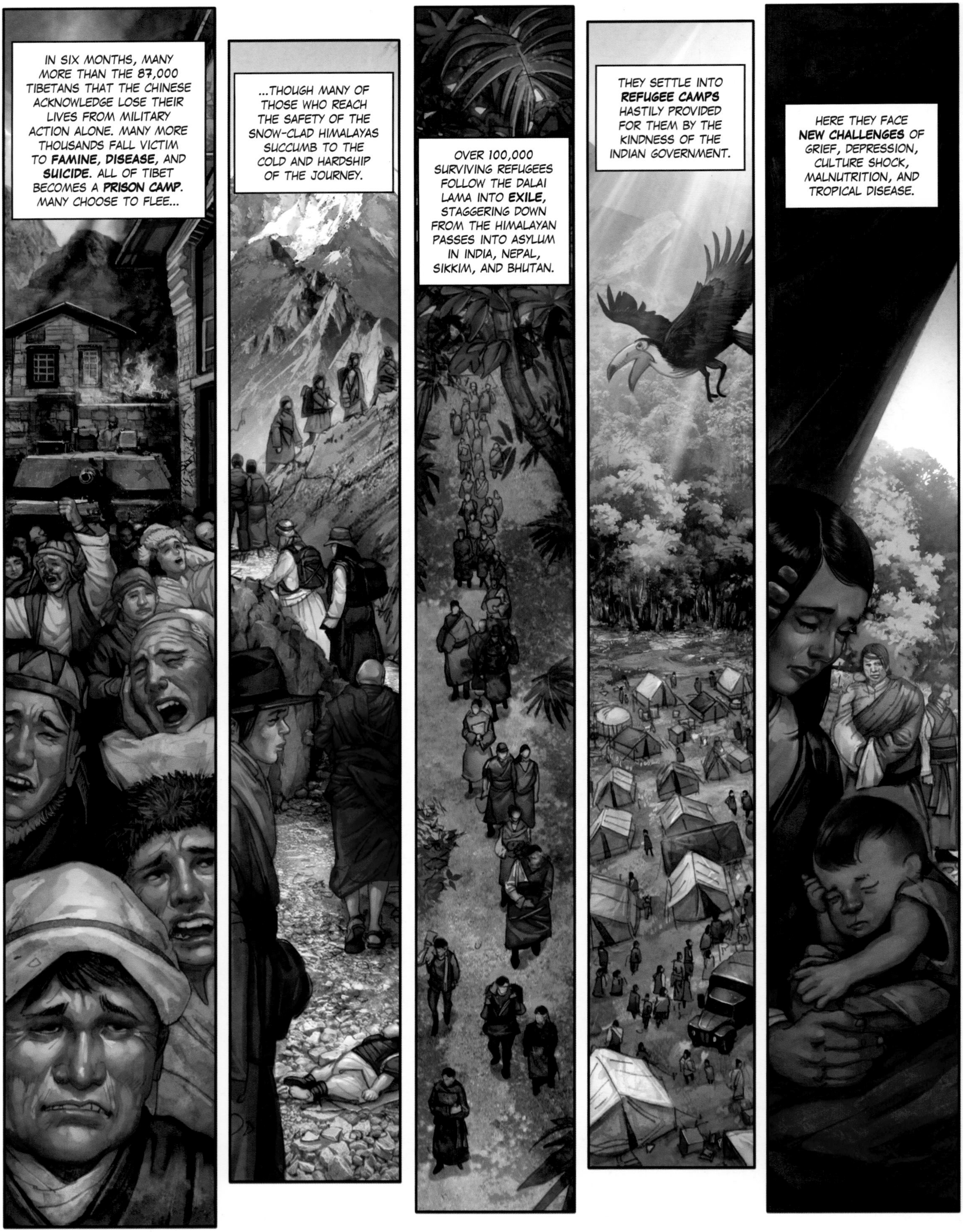
IN SIX MONTHS, MANY MORE THAN THE 87,000 TIBETANS THAT THE CHINESE ACKNOWLEDGE LOSE THEIR LIVES FROM MILITARY ACTION ALONE. MANY MORE THOUSANDS FALL VICTIM TO **FAMINE, DISEASE,** AND **SUICIDE**. ALL OF TIBET BECOMES A **PRISON CAMP**. MANY CHOOSE TO FLEE...
...THOUGH MANY OF THOSE WHO REACH THE SAFETY OF THE SNOW-CLAD HIMALAYAS SUCCUMB TO THE COLD AND HARDSHIP OF THE JOURNEY.
OVER 100,000 SURVIVING REFUGEES FOLLOW THE DALAI LAMA INTO **EXILE**, STAGGERING DOWN FROM THE HIMALAYAN PASSES INTO ASYLUM IN INDIA, NEPAL, SIKKIM, AND BHUTAN.
THEY SETTLE INTO **REFUGEE CAMPS** HASTILY PROVIDED FOR THEM BY THE KINDNESS OF THE INDIAN GOVERNMENT.
HERE THEY FACE **NEW CHALLENGES** OF GRIEF, DEPRESSION, CULTURE SHOCK, MALNUTRITION, AND TROPICAL DISEASE.

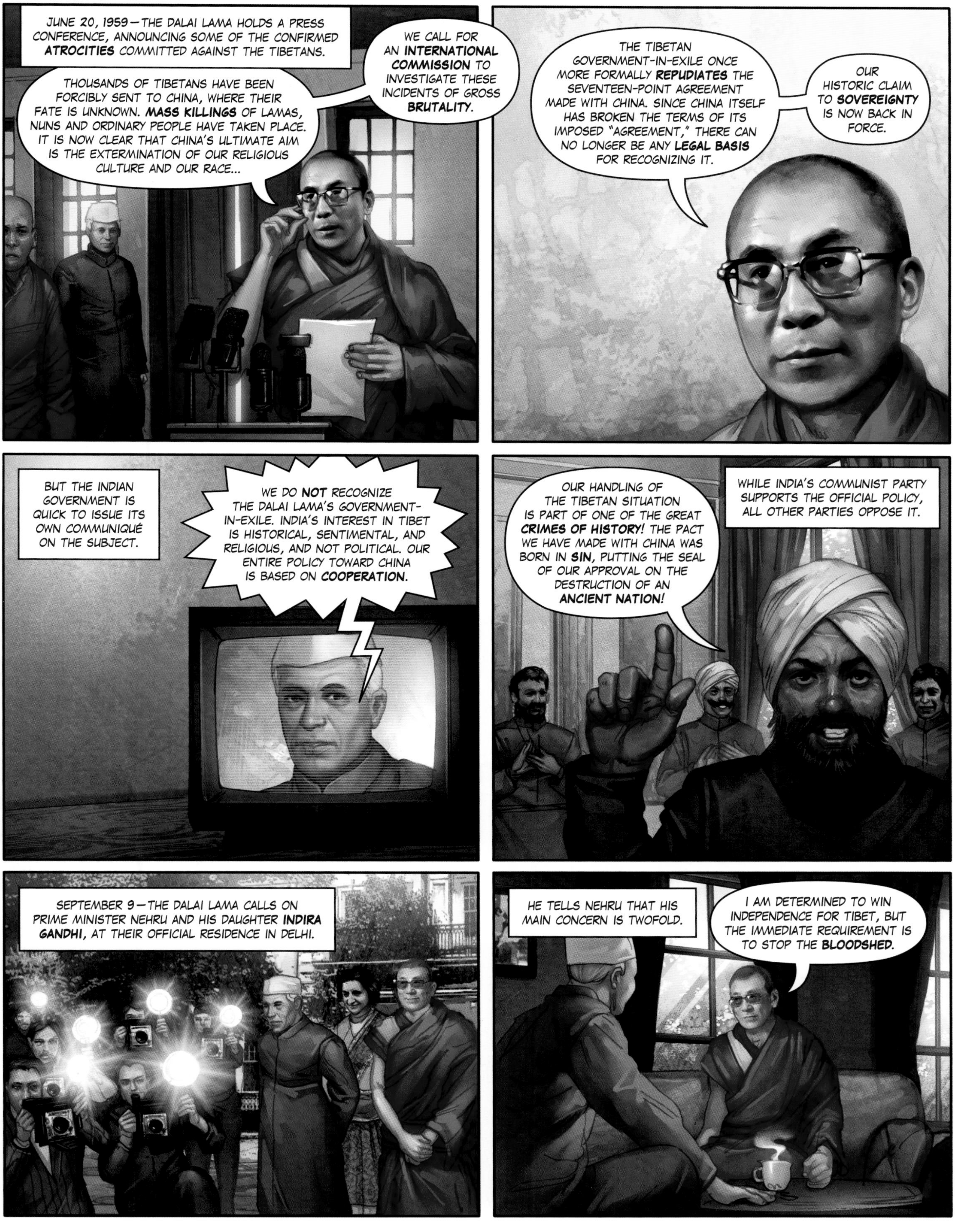

JUNE 20, 1959—THE DALAI LAMA HOLDS A PRESS CONFERENCE, ANNOUNCING SOME OF THE CONFIRMED ATROCITIES COMMITTED AGAINST THE TIBETANS.
THOUSANDS OF TIBETANS HAVE BEEN FORCIBLY SENT TO CHINA, WHERE THEIR FATE IS UNKNOWN. MASS KILLINGS OF LAMAS, NUNS AND ORDINARY PEOPLE HAVE TAKEN PLACE. IT IS NOW CLEAR THAT CHINA'S ULTIMATE AIM IS THE EXTERMINATION OF OUR RELIGIOUS CULTURE AND OUR RACE...
WE CALL FOR AN INTERNATIONAL COMMISSION TO INVESTIGATE THESE INCIDENTS OF GROSS BRUTALITY.
THE TIBETAN GOVERNMENT-IN-EXILE ONCE MORE FORMALLY REPUDIATES THE SEVENTEEN-POINT AGREEMENT MADE WITH CHINA. SINCE CHINA ITSELF HAS BROKEN THE TERMS OF ITS IMPOSED "AGREEMENT," THERE CAN NO LONGER BE ANY LEGAL BASIS FOR RECOGNIZING IT.
OUR HISTORIC CLAIM TO SOVEREIGNTY IS NOW BACK IN FORCE.
BUT THE INDIAN GOVERNMENT IS QUICK TO ISSUE ITS OWN COMMUNIQUÉ ON THE SUBJECT.
WE DO NOT RECOGNIZE THE DALAI LAMA'S GOVERNMENT-IN-EXILE. INDIA'S INTEREST IN TIBET IS HISTORICAL, SENTIMENTAL, AND RELIGIOUS, AND NOT POLITICAL. OUR ENTIRE POLICY TOWARD CHINA IS BASED ON COOPERATION.
OUR HANDLING OF THE TIBETAN SITUATION IS PART OF ONE OF THE GREAT CRIMES OF HISTORY! THE PACT WE HAVE MADE WITH CHINA WAS BORN IN SIN, PUTTING THE SEAL OF OUR APPROVAL ON THE DESTRUCTION OF AN ANCIENT NATION!
WHILE INDIA'S COMMUNIST PARTY SUPPORTS THE OFFICIAL POLICY, ALL OTHER PARTIES OPPOSE IT.
SEPTEMBER 9—THE DALAI LAMA CALLS ON PRIME MINISTER NEHRU AND HIS DAUGHTER INDIRA GANDHI, AT THEIR OFFICIAL RESIDENCE IN DELHI.
HE TELLS NEHRU THAT HIS MAIN CONCERN IS TWOFOLD.
I AM DETERMINED TO WIN INDEPENDENCE FOR TIBET, BUT THE IMMEDIATE REQUIREMENT IS TO STOP THE BLOODSHED.

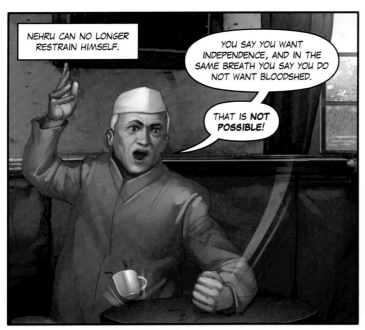

NEHRU CAN NO LONGER RESTRAIN HIMSELF.

YOU SAY YOU WANT INDEPENDENCE, AND IN THE SAME BREATH YOU SAY YOU DO NOT WANT BLOODSHED.

THAT IS **NOT POSSIBLE!**

MY YOUNG FRIEND, DON'T BE **HASTY.** CONSIDER WELL THE REALITY OF THE SITUATION.

WE ARE SYMPATHETIC TO YOUR CAUSE, BUT WE CANNOT RECOGNIZE YOUR GOVERNMENT.

INDIA CANNOT AFFORD TO TAKE SIDES AGAINST CHINA.

WE ARE UTTERLY **UNPREPARED** FOR WAR.

THE DALAI LAMA REALIZES NOW THAT THE FUTURE OF HIS PEOPLE IS FAR LESS CERTAIN THAN HE HAD IMAGINED.

THEN I MUST DO WHAT I CAN TO HAVE THE QUESTION OF TIBET'S INDEPENDENCE RAISED AT THE UNITED NATIONS.

IT IS CLEARLY OUR **ONLY** HOPE.

SINCE NEITHER TIBET NOR CHINA IS A MEMBER STATE, IT IS HIGHLY **UNLIKELY** THAT YOU WILL SUCCEED.

AND EVEN IF YOU DO, IT WILL HAVE NO EFFECT. THE WORLD IS NOW DIVIDED INTO TWO CAMPS—AND ONE IS **AGAINST YOU.**

IT WILL BE **IMPOSSIBLE** TO FORGE THE AGREEMENT THAT YOU WANT.

I AM AWARE OF THE DIFFICULTIES, BUT THE WORLD MUST BE CONSTANTLY REMINDED OF WHAT HAS HAPPENED IN TIBET—WHAT IS **STILL** HAPPENING.

IT IS VITAL THAT MY PEOPLE ARE NOT **FORGOTTEN** IN THEIR MISERY.

THE WAY TO KEEP THE TIBETAN QUESTION ALIVE IS NOT THROUGH THE U.N., MY FRIEND, BUT THROUGH THE **EDUCATION** OF YOUR **CHILDREN** AND THE **PRESERVATION** OF YOUR **CULTURE.**

BUT NOW THAT YOU'VE DECIDED TO APPEAL—GO AHEAD. IT'S UP TO YOU. YOU LIVE IN A **FREE COUNTRY** NOW.

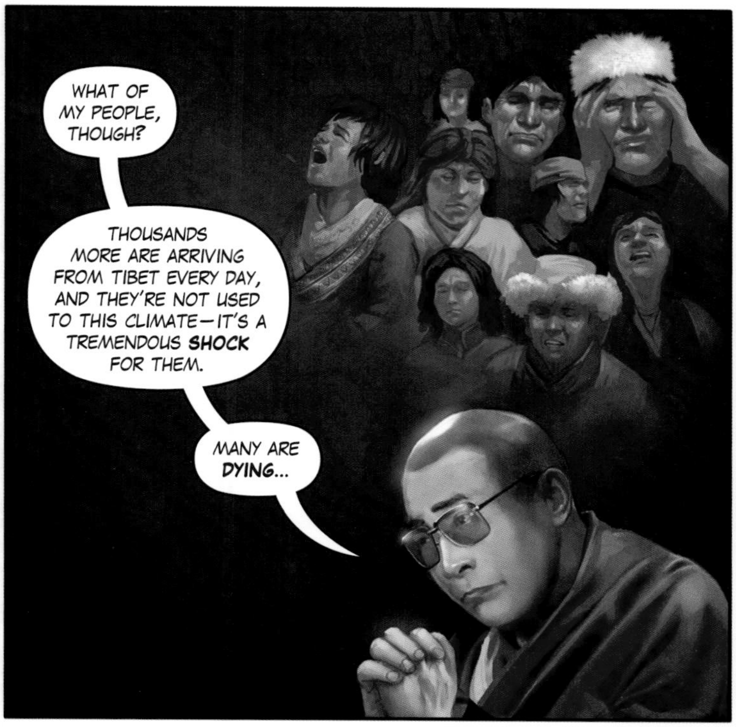
WHAT OF MY PEOPLE, THOUGH?
THOUSANDS MORE ARE ARRIVING FROM TIBET EVERY DAY, AND THEY'RE NOT USED TO THIS CLIMATE—IT'S A TREMENDOUS **SHOCK** FOR THEM.
MANY ARE **DYING**...

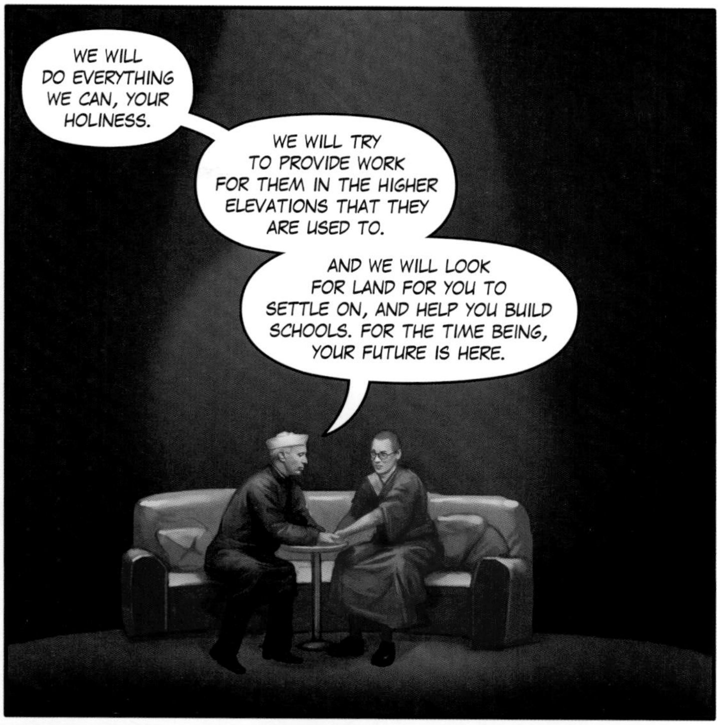
WE WILL DO EVERYTHING WE CAN, YOUR HOLINESS.
WE WILL TRY TO PROVIDE WORK FOR THEM IN THE HIGHER ELEVATIONS THAT THEY ARE USED TO.
AND WE WILL LOOK FOR LAND FOR YOU TO SETTLE ON, AND HELP YOU BUILD SCHOOLS. FOR THE TIME BEING, YOUR FUTURE IS HERE.

THE INTERNATIONAL COMMISSION OF JURISTS SOON PUBLISHES A REPORT, CONCLUDING THAT TIBET IS A TRULY SOVEREIGN STATE, INDEPENDENT OF CHINESE CONTROL IN LEGAL FACT. IT ACCUSES THE CHINESE GOVERNMENT OF COMMITTING **GENOCIDE** IN TIBET.

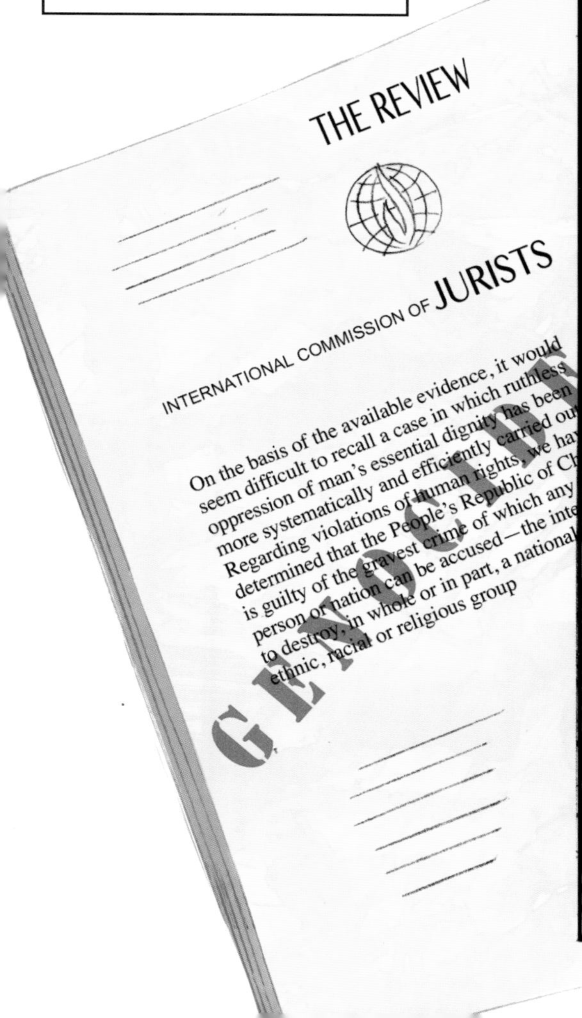
THE REVIEW
INTERNATIONAL COMMISSION OF JURISTS
On the basis of the available evidence, it would
seem difficult to recall a case in which ruthless
oppression of man's essential dignity has been
more systematically and efficiently carried ou
Regarding violations of human rights, we ha
determined that the People's Republic of Ch
is guilty of the gravest crime of which any
person or nation can be accused—the inte
to destroy, in whole or in part, a national
ethnic, racial or religious group

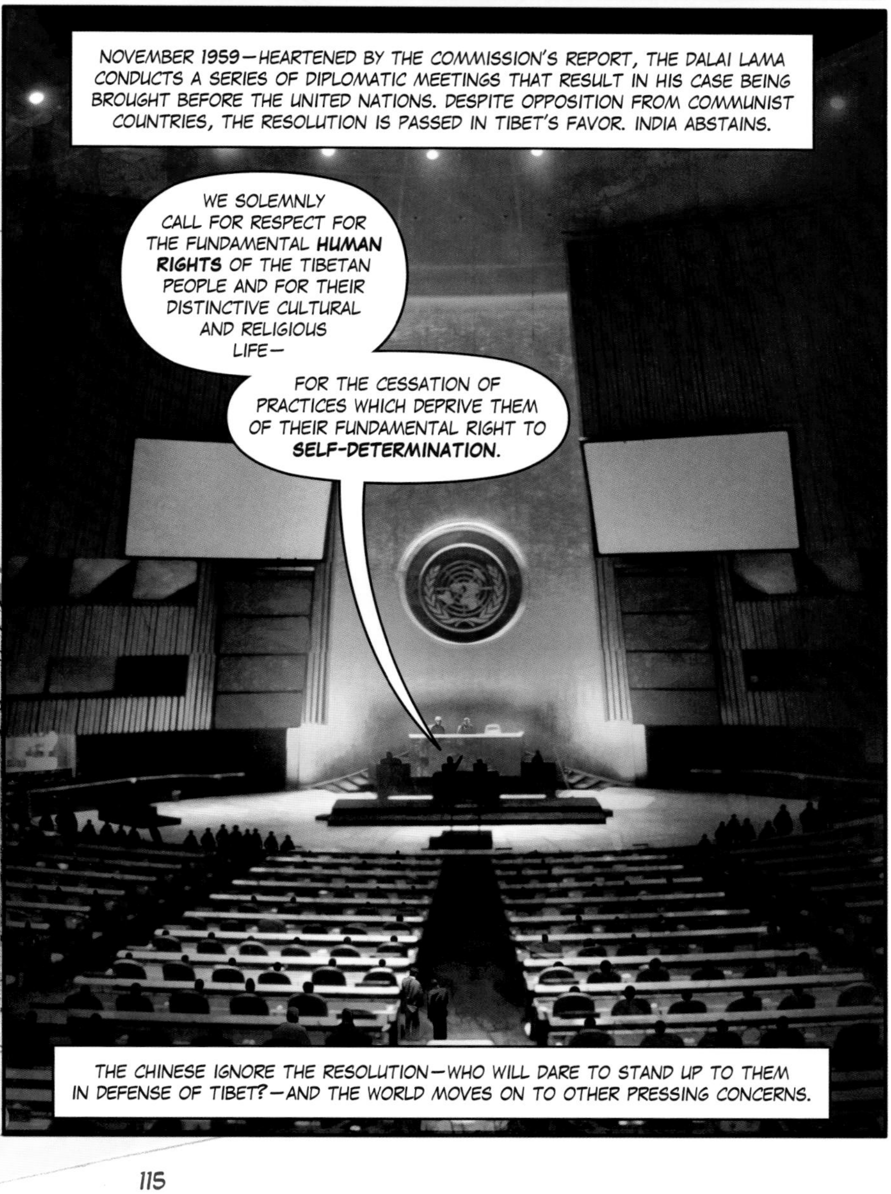
NOVEMBER 1959—HEARTENED BY THE COMMISSION'S REPORT, THE DALAI LAMA CONDUCTS A SERIES OF DIPLOMATIC MEETINGS THAT RESULT IN HIS CASE BEING BROUGHT BEFORE THE UNITED NATIONS. DESPITE OPPOSITION FROM COMMUNIST COUNTRIES, THE RESOLUTION IS PASSED IN TIBET'S FAVOR. INDIA ABSTAINS.
WE SOLEMNLY CALL FOR RESPECT FOR THE FUNDAMENTAL **HUMAN RIGHTS** OF THE TIBETAN PEOPLE AND FOR THEIR DISTINCTIVE CULTURAL AND RELIGIOUS LIFE—
FOR THE CESSATION OF PRACTICES WHICH DEPRIVE THEM OF THEIR FUNDAMENTAL RIGHT TO **SELF-DETERMINATION**.
THE CHINESE IGNORE THE RESOLUTION—WHO WILL DARE TO STAND UP TO THEM IN DEFENSE OF TIBET?—AND THE WORLD MOVES ON TO OTHER PRESSING CONCERNS.

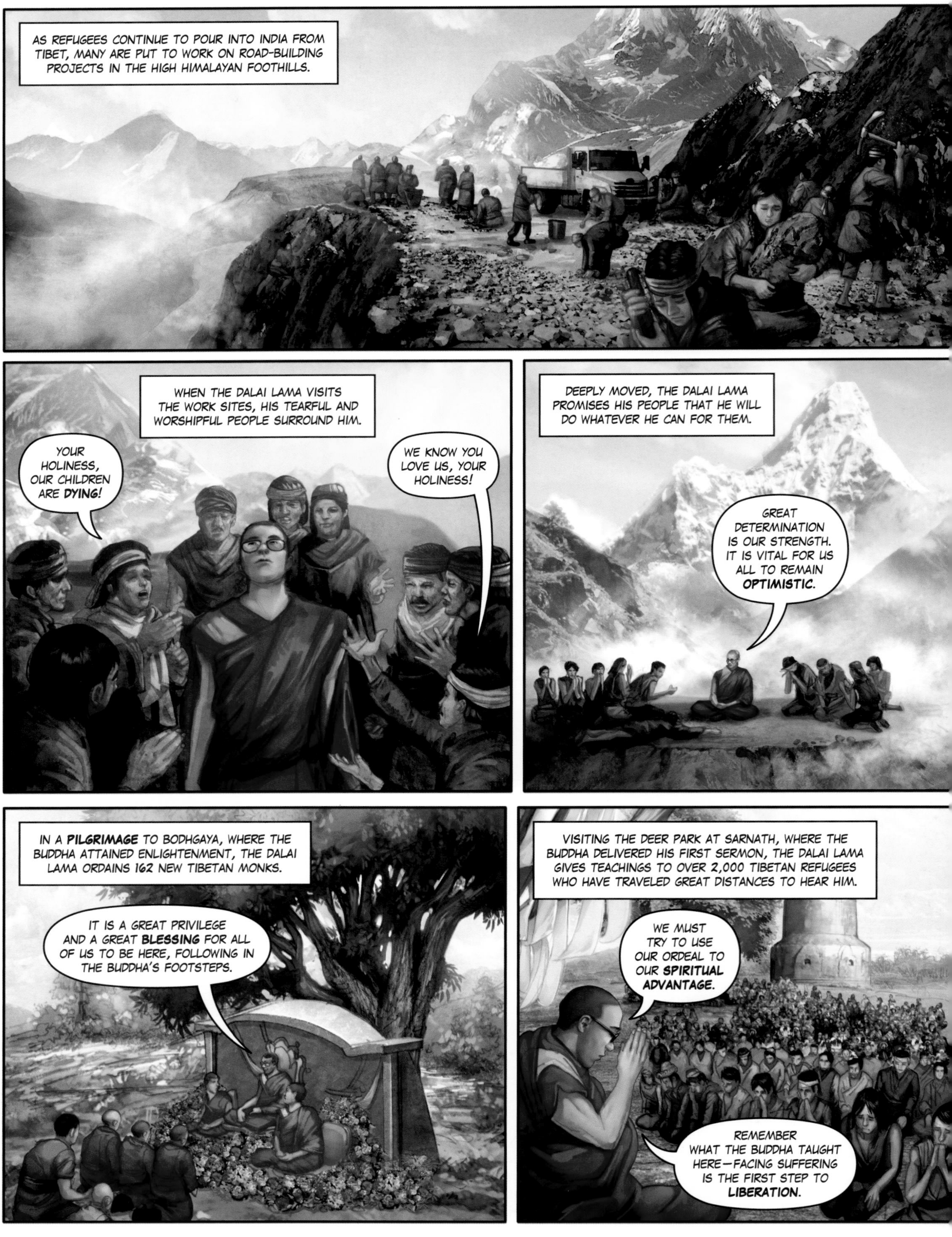
AS REFUGEES CONTINUE TO POUR INTO INDIA FROM TIBET, MANY ARE PUT TO WORK ON ROAD-BUILDING PROJECTS IN THE HIGH HIMALAYAN FOOTHILLS.
WHEN THE DALAI LAMA VISITS THE WORK SITES, HIS TEARFUL AND WORSHIPFUL PEOPLE SURROUND HIM.
YOUR HOLINESS, OUR CHILDREN ARE DYING!
WE KNOW YOU LOVE US, YOUR HOLINESS!
DEEPLY MOVED, THE DALAI LAMA PROMISES HIS PEOPLE THAT HE WILL DO WHATEVER HE CAN FOR THEM.
GREAT DETERMINATION IS OUR STRENGTH. IT IS VITAL FOR US ALL TO REMAIN OPTIMISTIC.
IN A PILGRIMAGE TO BODHGAYA, WHERE THE BUDDHA ATTAINED ENLIGHTENMENT, THE DALAI LAMA ORDAINS 162 NEW TIBETAN MONKS.
IT IS A GREAT PRIVILEGE AND A GREAT BLESSING FOR ALL OF US TO BE HERE, FOLLOWING IN THE BUDDHA'S FOOTSTEPS.
VISITING THE DEER PARK AT SARNATH, WHERE THE BUDDHA DELIVERED HIS FIRST SERMON, THE DALAI LAMA GIVES TEACHINGS TO OVER 2,000 TIBETAN REFUGEES WHO HAVE TRAVELED GREAT DISTANCES TO HEAR HIM.
WE MUST TRY TO USE OUR ORDEAL TO OUR SPIRITUAL ADVANTAGE.
REMEMBER WHAT THE BUDDHA TAUGHT HERE—FACING SUFFERING IS THE FIRST STEP TO LIBERATION.

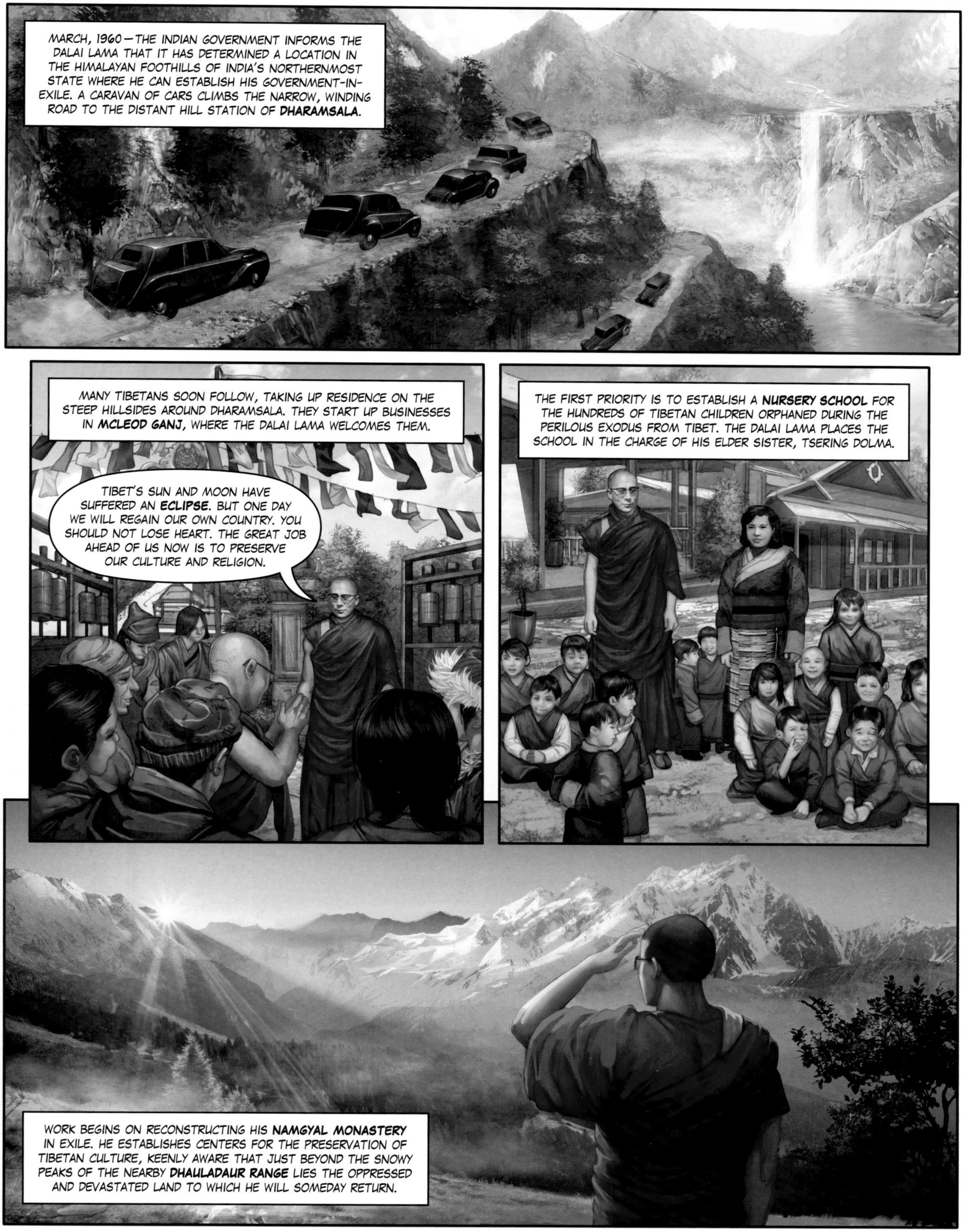
MARCH, 1960—THE INDIAN GOVERNMENT INFORMS THE DALAI LAMA THAT IT HAS DETERMINED A LOCATION IN THE HIMALAYAN FOOTHILLS OF INDIA'S NORTHERNMOST STATE WHERE HE CAN ESTABLISH HIS GOVERNMENT-IN-EXILE. A CARAVAN OF CARS CLIMBS THE NARROW, WINDING ROAD TO THE DISTANT HILL STATION OF DHARAMSALA.
MANY TIBETANS SOON FOLLOW, TAKING UP RESIDENCE ON THE STEEP HILLSIDES AROUND DHARAMSALA. THEY START UP BUSINESSES IN MCLEOD GANJ, WHERE THE DALAI LAMA WELCOMES THEM.
TIBET'S SUN AND MOON HAVE SUFFERED AN ECLIPSE. BUT ONE DAY WE WILL REGAIN OUR OWN COUNTRY. YOU SHOULD NOT LOSE HEART. THE GREAT JOB AHEAD OF US NOW IS TO PRESERVE OUR CULTURE AND RELIGION.
THE FIRST PRIORITY IS TO ESTABLISH A NURSERY SCHOOL FOR THE HUNDREDS OF TIBETAN CHILDREN ORPHANED DURING THE PERILOUS EXODUS FROM TIBET. THE DALAI LAMA PLACES THE SCHOOL IN THE CHARGE OF HIS ELDER SISTER, TSERING DOLMA.
WORK BEGINS ON RECONSTRUCTING HIS NAMGYAL MONASTERY IN EXILE. HE ESTABLISHES CENTERS FOR THE PRESERVATION OF TIBETAN CULTURE, KEENLY AWARE THAT JUST BEYOND THE SNOWY PEAKS OF THE NEARBY DHAULADAUR RANGE LIES THE OPPRESSED AND DEVASTATED LAND TO WHICH HE WILL SOMEDAY RETURN.

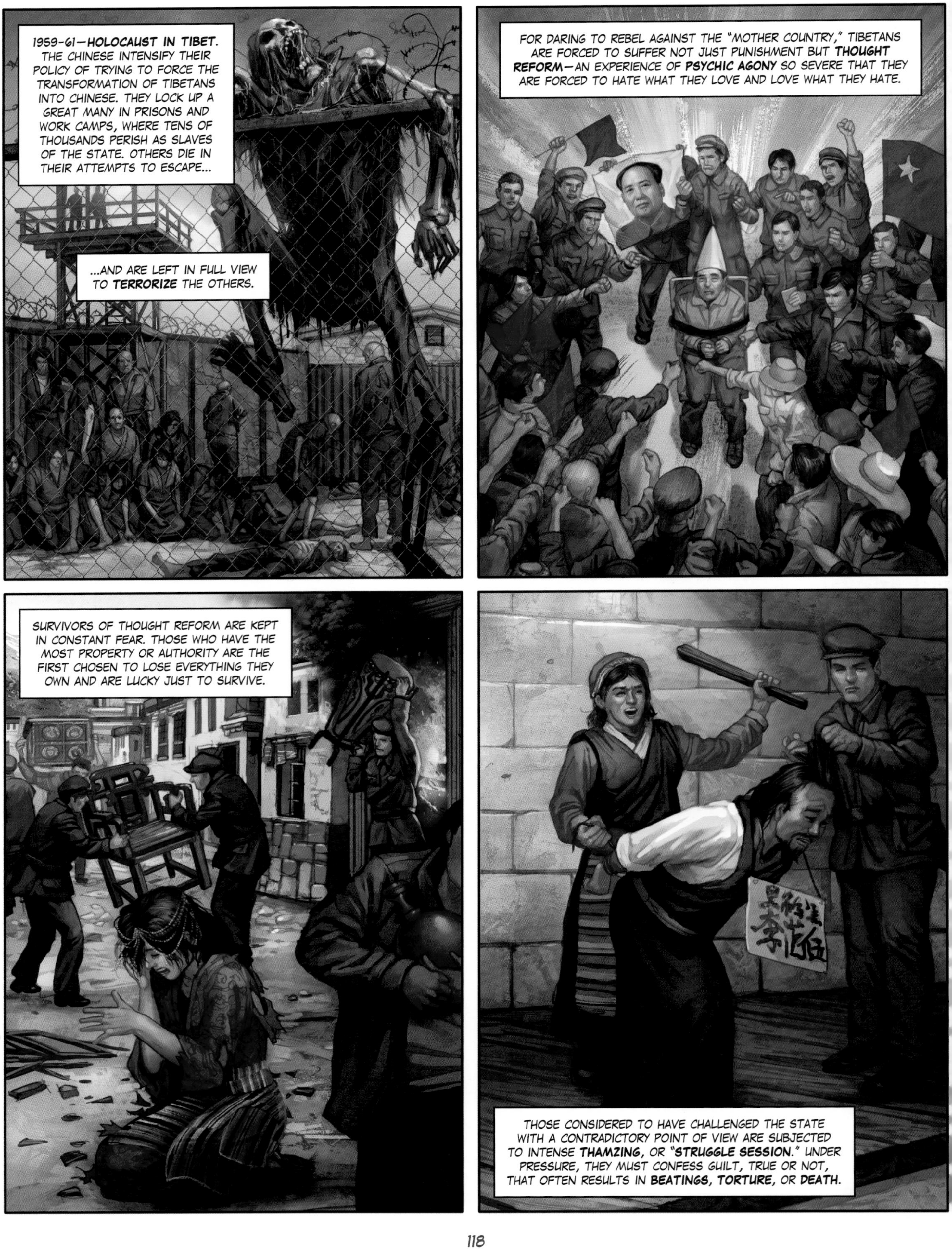
1959-61—HOLOCAUST IN TIBET. THE CHINESE INTENSIFY THEIR POLICY OF TRYING TO FORCE THE TRANSFORMATION OF TIBETANS INTO CHINESE. THEY LOCK UP A GREAT MANY IN PRISONS AND WORK CAMPS, WHERE TENS OF THOUSANDS PERISH AS SLAVES OF THE STATE. OTHERS DIE IN THEIR ATTEMPTS TO ESCAPE...
...AND ARE LEFT IN FULL VIEW TO TERRORIZE THE OTHERS.
FOR DARING TO REBEL AGAINST THE "MOTHER COUNTRY," TIBETANS ARE FORCED TO SUFFER NOT JUST PUNISHMENT BUT THOUGHT REFORM—AN EXPERIENCE OF PSYCHIC AGONY SO SEVERE THAT THEY ARE FORCED TO HATE WHAT THEY LOVE AND LOVE WHAT THEY HATE.
SURVIVORS OF THOUGHT REFORM ARE KEPT IN CONSTANT FEAR. THOSE WHO HAVE THE MOST PROPERTY OR AUTHORITY ARE THE FIRST CHOSEN TO LOSE EVERYTHING THEY OWN AND ARE LUCKY JUST TO SURVIVE.
THOSE CONSIDERED TO HAVE CHALLENGED THE STATE WITH A CONTRADICTORY POINT OF VIEW ARE SUBJECTED TO INTENSE THAMZING, OR "STRUGGLE SESSION." UNDER PRESSURE, THEY MUST CONFESS GUILT, TRUE OR NOT, THAT OFTEN RESULTS IN BEATINGS, TORTURE, OR DEATH.

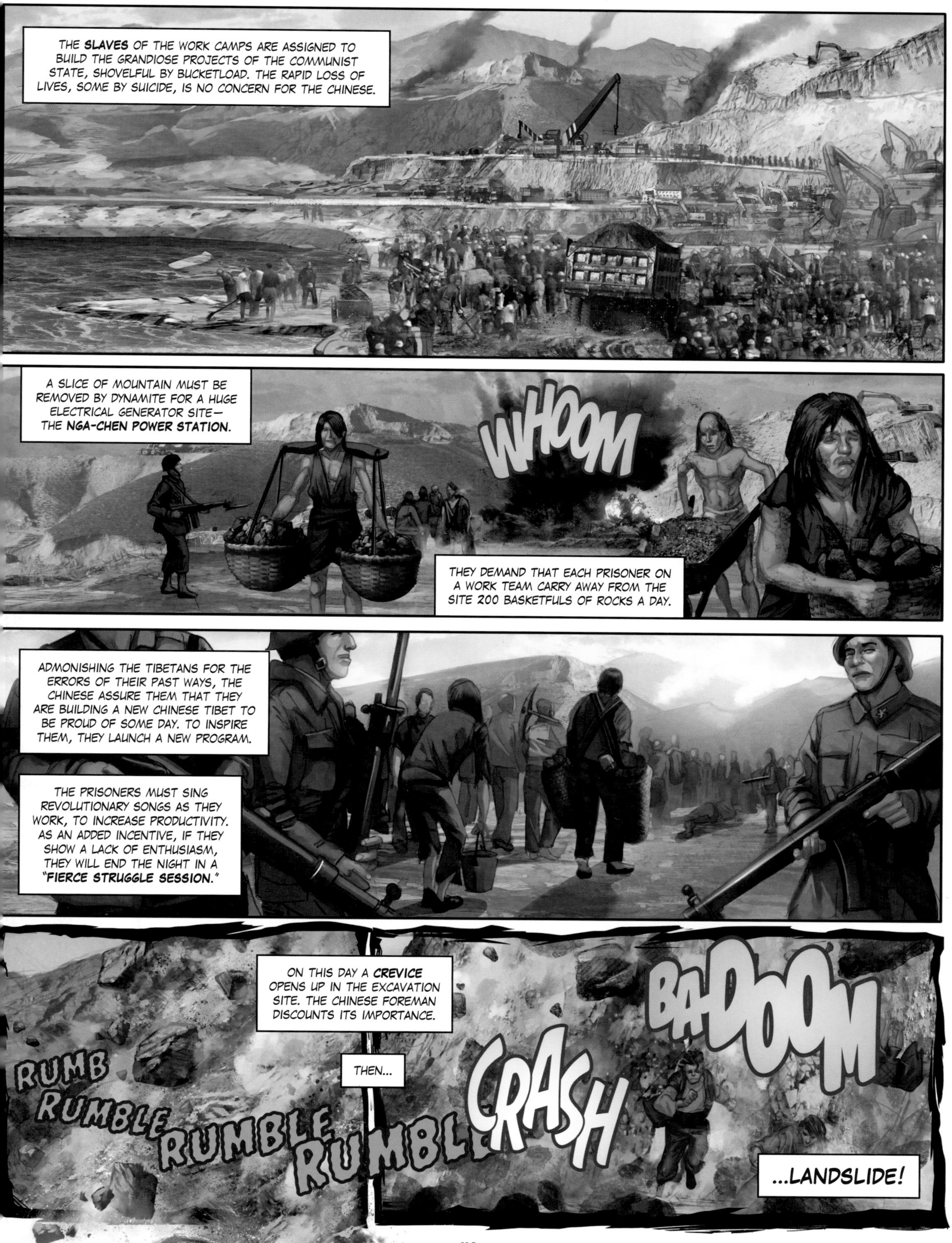
THE SLAVES OF THE WORK CAMPS ARE ASSIGNED TO BUILD THE GRANDIOSE PROJECTS OF THE COMMUNIST STATE, SHOVELFUL BY BUCKETLOAD. THE RAPID LOSS OF LIVES, SOME BY SUICIDE, IS NO CONCERN FOR THE CHINESE.
A SLICE OF MOUNTAIN MUST BE REMOVED BY DYNAMITE FOR A HUGE ELECTRICAL GENERATOR SITE— THE NGA-CHEN POWER STATION.
WHOOM
THEY DEMAND THAT EACH PRISONER ON A WORK TEAM CARRY AWAY FROM THE SITE 200 BASKETFULS OF ROCKS A DAY.
ADMONISHING THE TIBETANS FOR THE ERRORS OF THEIR PAST WAYS, THE CHINESE ASSURE THEM THAT THEY ARE BUILDING A NEW CHINESE TIBET TO BE PROUD OF SOME DAY. TO INSPIRE THEM, THEY LAUNCH A NEW PROGRAM.
THE PRISONERS MUST SING REVOLUTIONARY SONGS AS THEY WORK, TO INCREASE PRODUCTIVITY. AS AN ADDED INCENTIVE, IF THEY SHOW A LACK OF ENTHUSIASM, THEY WILL END THE NIGHT IN A "FIERCE STRUGGLE SESSION."
ON THIS DAY A CREVICE OPENS UP IN THE EXCAVATION SITE. THE CHINESE FOREMAN DISCOUNTS ITS IMPORTANCE.
BA-DOOM
RUMB
RUMBLE RUMBLE RUMBL
THEN...
CRASH
...LANDSLIDE!

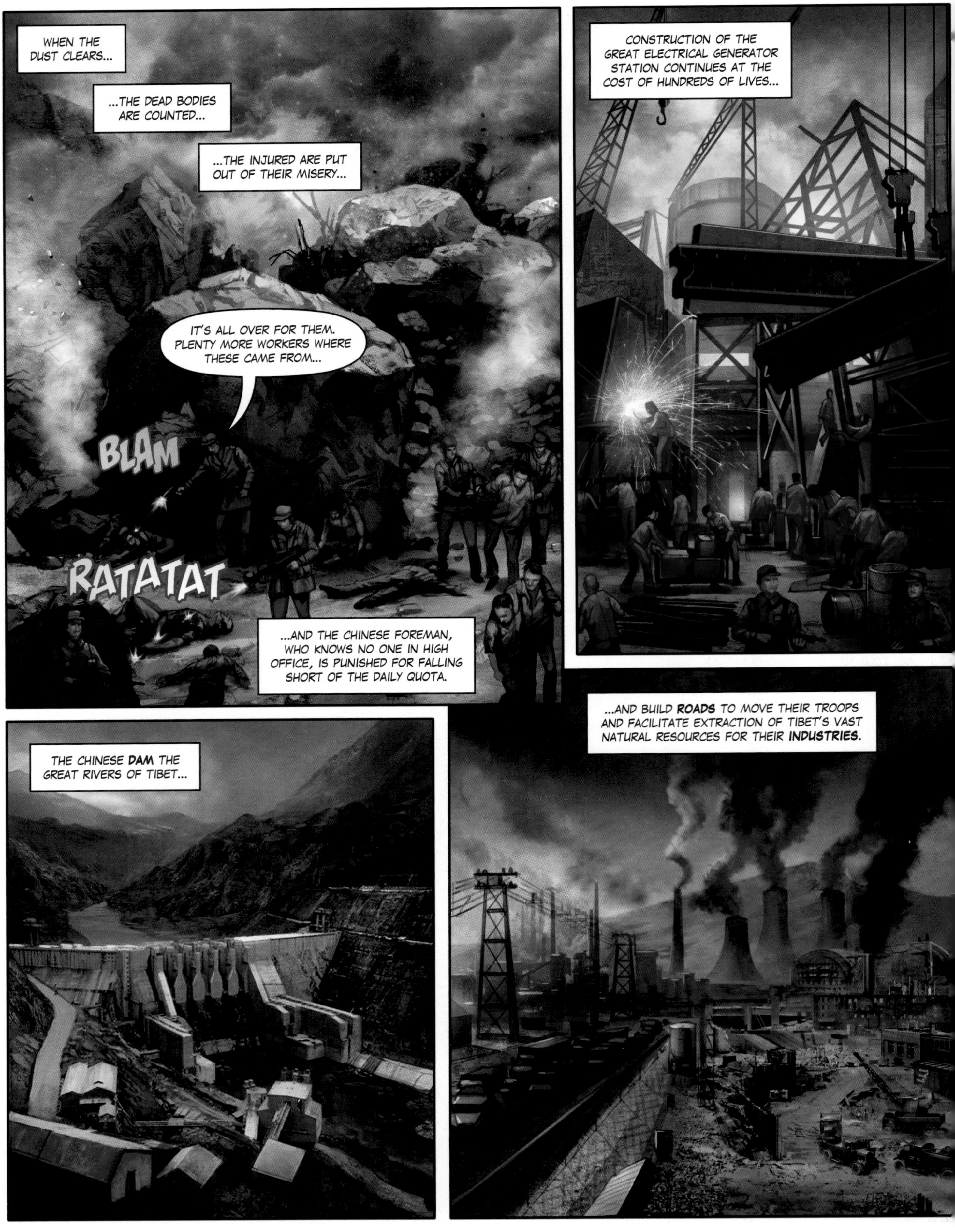
WHEN THE DUST CLEARS...
...THE DEAD BODIES ARE COUNTED...
...THE INJURED ARE PUT OUT OF THEIR MISERY...
IT'S ALL OVER FOR THEM. PLENTY MORE WORKERS WHERE THESE CAME FROM...
BLAM
RATATAT
...AND THE CHINESE FOREMAN, WHO KNOWS NO ONE IN HIGH OFFICE, IS PUNISHED FOR FALLING SHORT OF THE DAILY QUOTA.
CONSTRUCTION OF THE GREAT ELECTRICAL GENERATOR STATION CONTINUES AT THE COST OF HUNDREDS OF LIVES...
THE CHINESE **DAM** THE GREAT RIVERS OF TIBET...
...AND BUILD **ROADS** TO MOVE THEIR TROOPS AND FACILITATE EXTRACTION OF TIBET'S VAST NATURAL RESOURCES FOR THEIR **INDUSTRIES**.

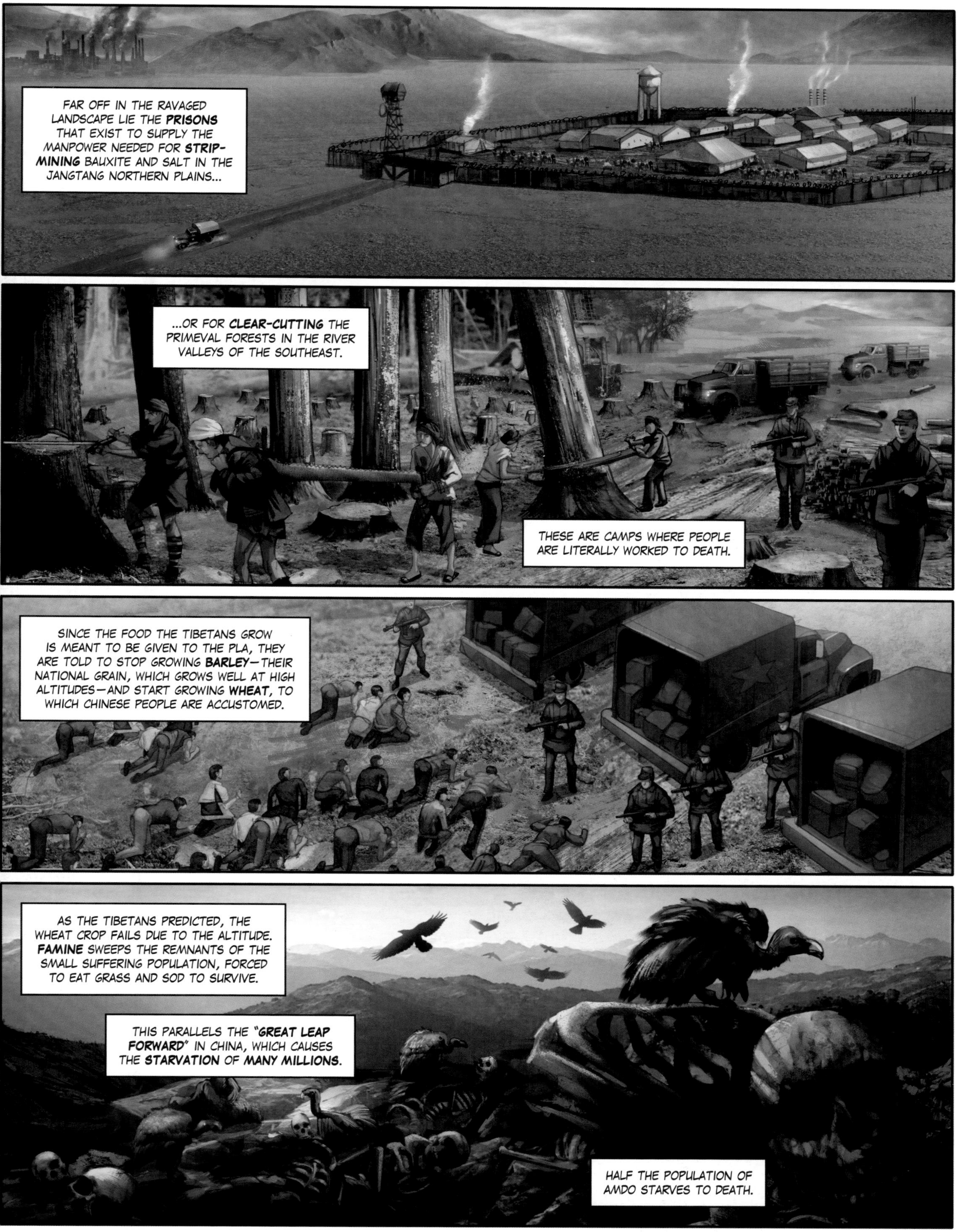
FAR OFF IN THE RAVAGED LANDSCAPE LIE THE **PRISONS** THAT EXIST TO SUPPLY THE MANPOWER NEEDED FOR **STRIP-MINING** BAUXITE AND SALT IN THE JANGTANG NORTHERN PLAINS...
...OR FOR **CLEAR-CUTTING** THE PRIMEVAL FORESTS IN THE RIVER VALLEYS OF THE SOUTHEAST.
THESE ARE CAMPS WHERE PEOPLE ARE LITERALLY WORKED TO DEATH.
SINCE THE FOOD THE TIBETANS GROW IS MEANT TO BE GIVEN TO THE PLA, THEY ARE TOLD TO STOP GROWING **BARLEY**—THEIR NATIONAL GRAIN, WHICH GROWS WELL AT HIGH ALTITUDES—AND START GROWING **WHEAT**, TO WHICH CHINESE PEOPLE ARE ACCUSTOMED.
AS THE TIBETANS PREDICTED, THE WHEAT CROP FAILS DUE TO THE ALTITUDE. **FAMINE** SWEEPS THE REMNANTS OF THE SMALL SUFFERING POPULATION, FORCED TO EAT GRASS AND SOD TO SURVIVE.
THIS PARALLELS THE **"GREAT LEAP FORWARD"** IN CHINA, WHICH CAUSES THE **STARVATION** OF **MANY MILLIONS**.
HALF THE POPULATION OF AMDO STARVES TO DEATH.

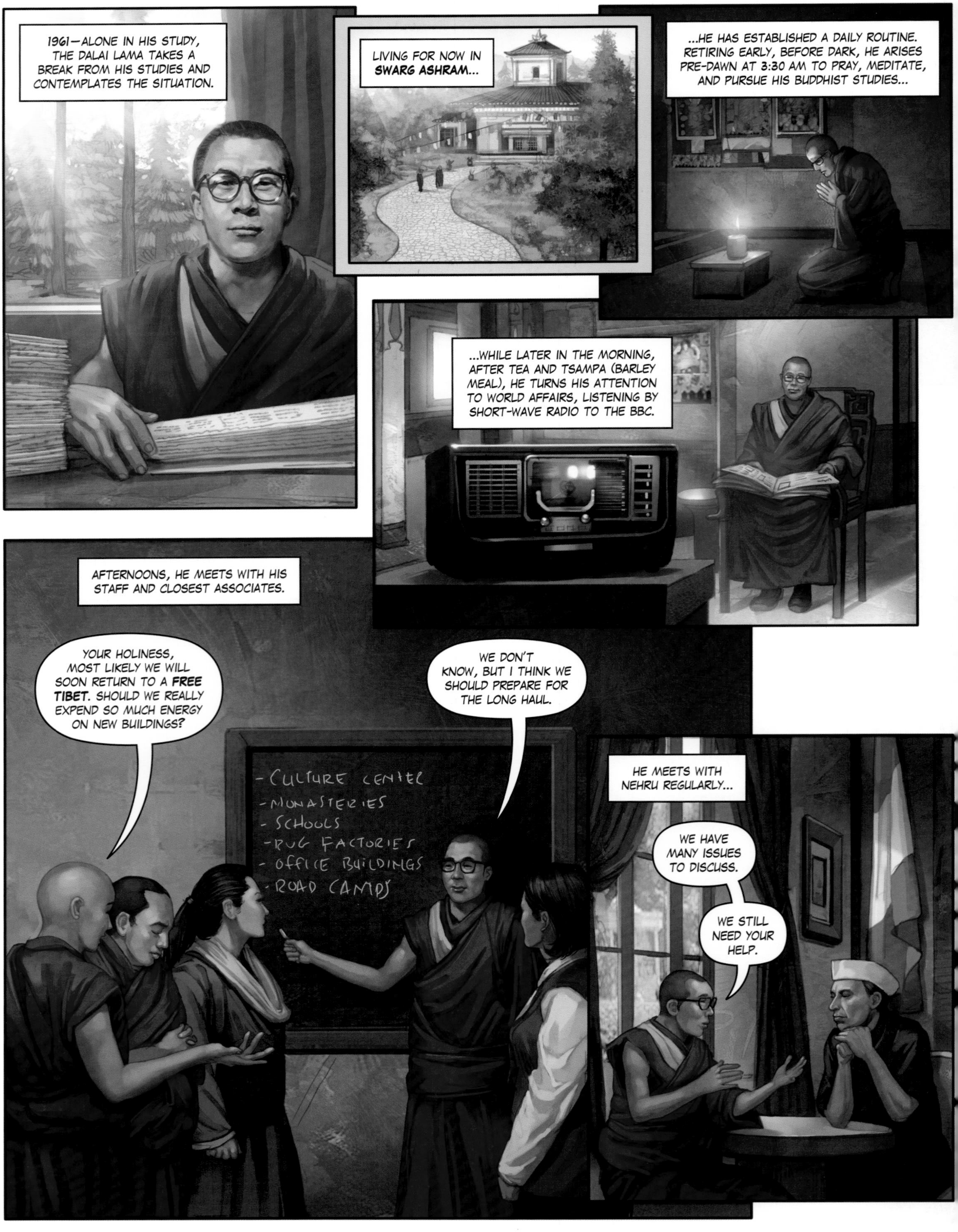
1961—ALONE IN HIS STUDY, THE DALAI LAMA TAKES A BREAK FROM HIS STUDIES AND CONTEMPLATES THE SITUATION.
LIVING FOR NOW IN **SWARG ASHRAM**...
...HE HAS ESTABLISHED A DAILY ROUTINE. RETIRING EARLY, BEFORE DARK, HE ARISES PRE-DAWN AT 3:30 AM TO PRAY, MEDITATE, AND PURSUE HIS BUDDHIST STUDIES...
...WHILE LATER IN THE MORNING, AFTER TEA AND TSAMPA (BARLEY MEAL), HE TURNS HIS ATTENTION TO WORLD AFFAIRS, LISTENING BY SHORT-WAVE RADIO TO THE BBC.
AFTERNOONS, HE MEETS WITH HIS STAFF AND CLOSEST ASSOCIATES.
YOUR HOLINESS, MOST LIKELY WE WILL SOON RETURN TO A **FREE TIBET**. SHOULD WE REALLY EXPEND SO MUCH ENERGY ON NEW BUILDINGS?
WE DON'T KNOW, BUT I THINK WE SHOULD PREPARE FOR THE LONG HAUL.
-CULTURE CENTER
-MONASTERIES
-SCHOOLS
-RUG FACTORIES
-OFFICE BUILDINGS
-ROAD CAMPS
HE MEETS WITH NEHRU REGULARLY...
WE HAVE MANY ISSUES TO DISCUSS.
WE STILL NEED YOUR HELP.

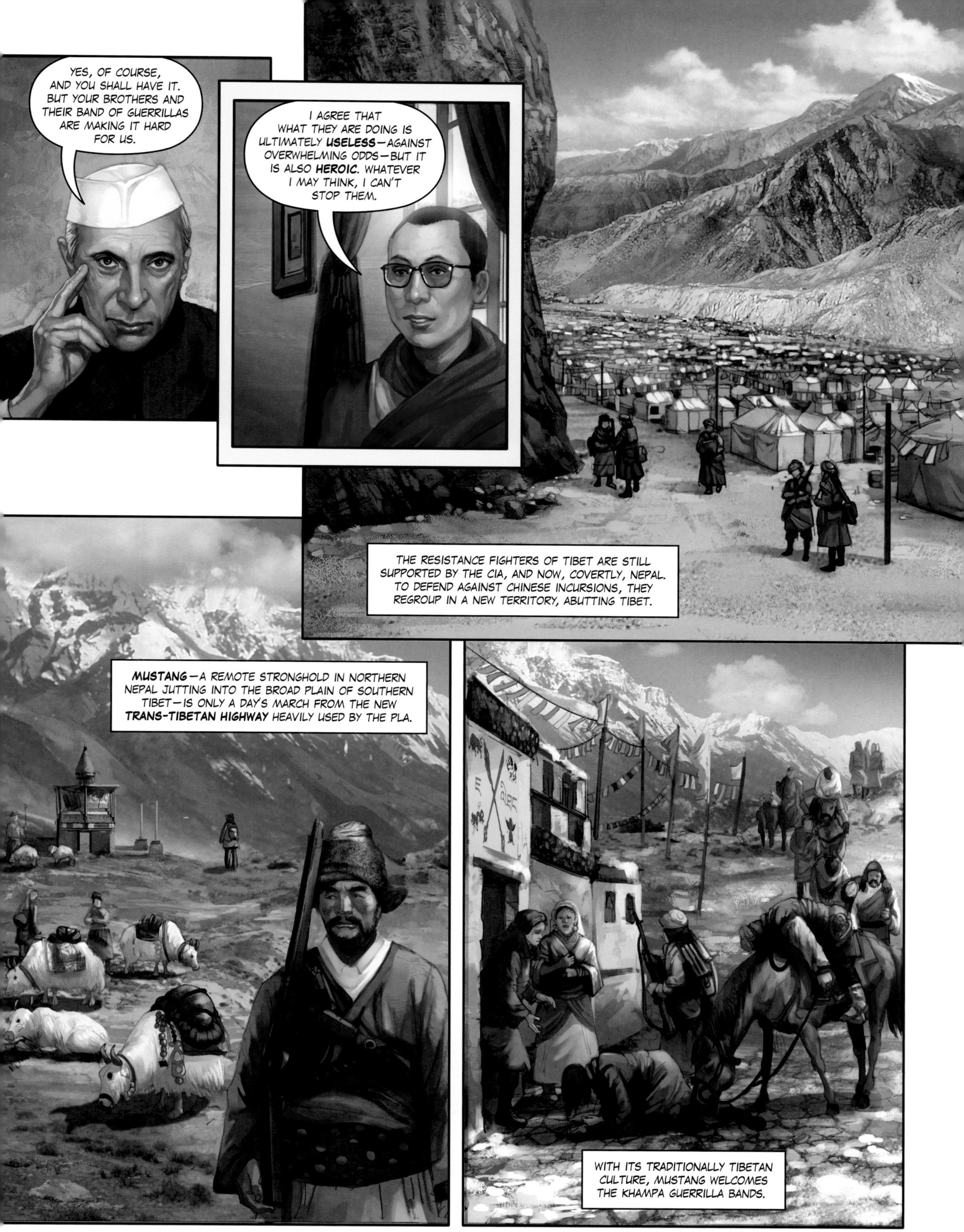
YES, OF COURSE, AND YOU SHALL HAVE IT. BUT YOUR BROTHERS AND THEIR BAND OF GUERRILLAS ARE MAKING IT HARD FOR US.
I AGREE THAT WHAT THEY ARE DOING IS ULTIMATELY USELESS—AGAINST OVERWHELMING ODDS—BUT IT IS ALSO HEROIC. WHATEVER I MAY THINK, I CAN'T STOP THEM.
THE RESISTANCE FIGHTERS OF TIBET ARE STILL SUPPORTED BY THE CIA, AND NOW, COVERTLY, NEPAL. TO DEFEND AGAINST CHINESE INCURSIONS, THEY REGROUP IN A NEW TERRITORY, ABUTTING TIBET.
MUSTANG—A REMOTE STRONGHOLD IN NORTHERN NEPAL JUTTING INTO THE BROAD PLAIN OF SOUTHERN TIBET—IS ONLY A DAY'S MARCH FROM THE NEW TRANS-TIBETAN HIGHWAY HEAVILY USED BY THE PLA.
WITH ITS TRADITIONALLY TIBETAN CULTURE, MUSTANG WELCOMES THE KHAMPA GUERRILLA BANDS.

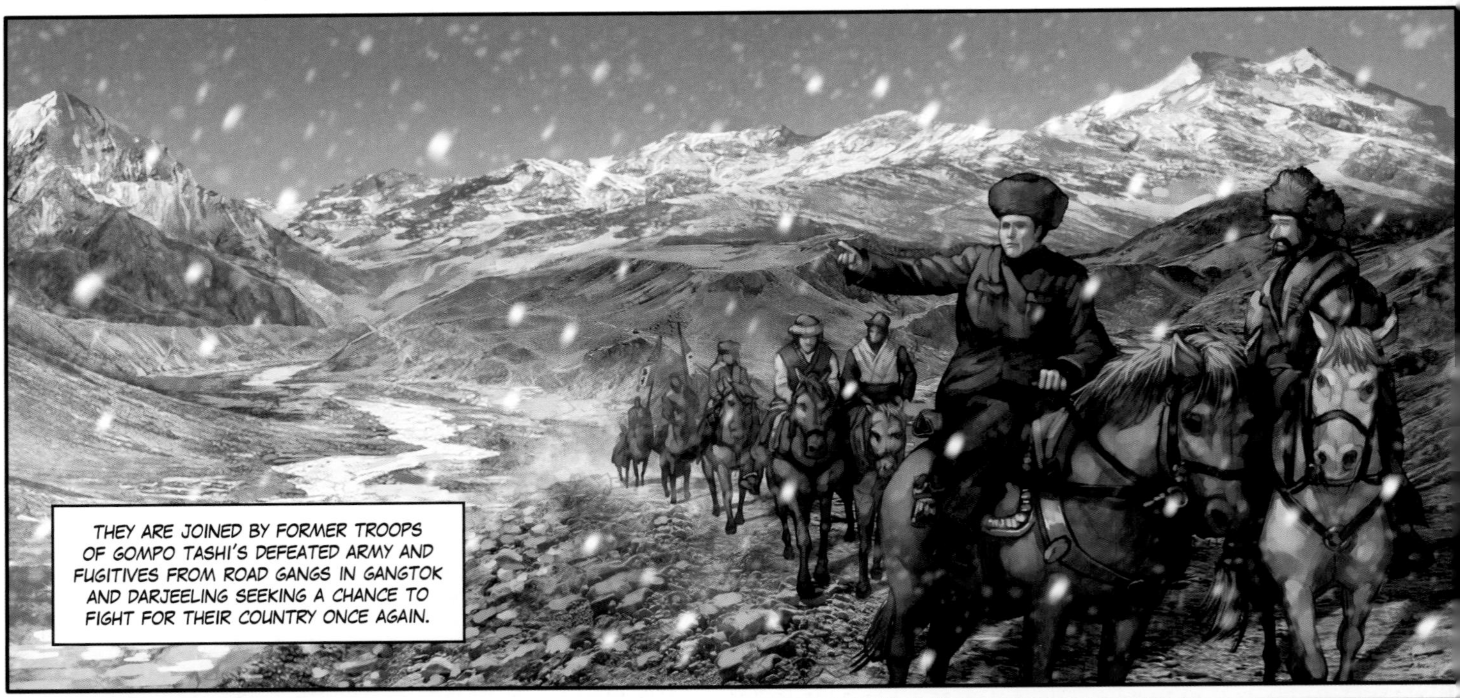
THEY ARE JOINED BY FORMER TROOPS OF GOMPO TASHI'S DEFEATED ARMY AND FUGITIVES FROM ROAD GANGS IN GANGTOK AND DARJEELING SEEKING A CHANCE TO FIGHT FOR THEIR COUNTRY ONCE AGAIN.

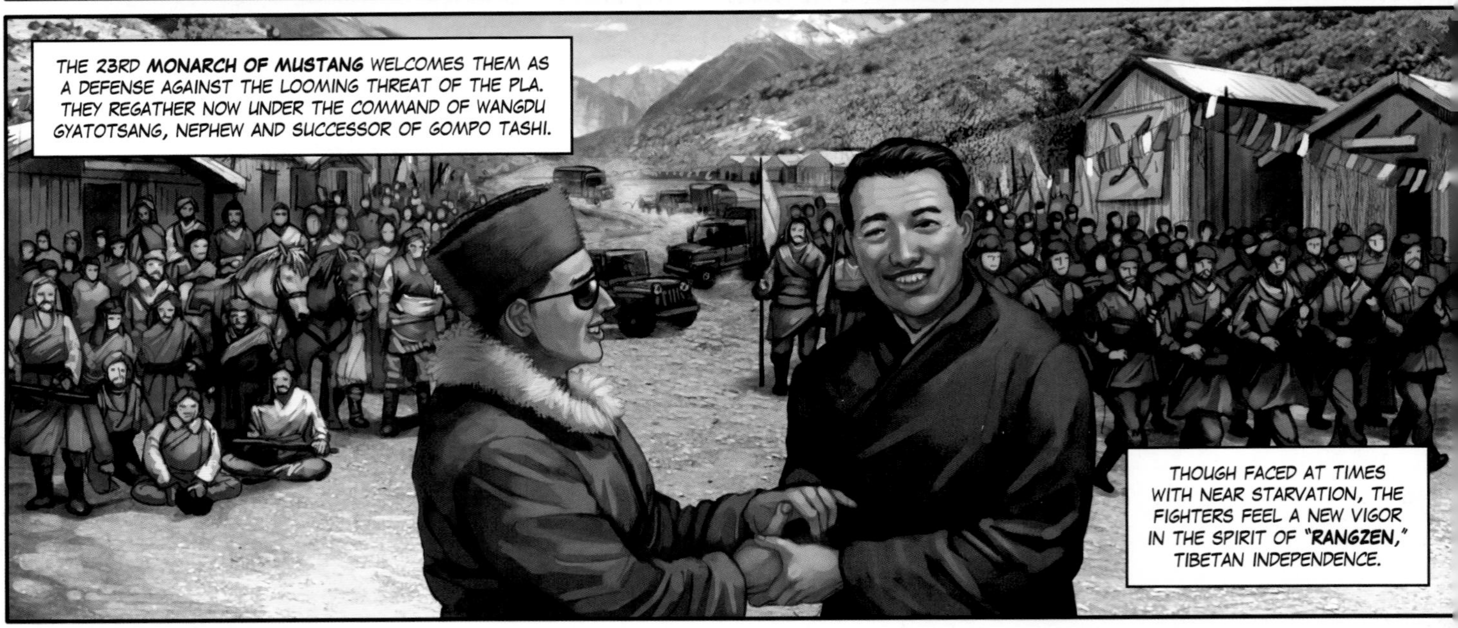
THE 23RD **MONARCH OF MUSTANG** WELCOMES THEM AS A DEFENSE AGAINST THE LOOMING THREAT OF THE PLA. THEY REGATHER NOW UNDER THE COMMAND OF WANGDU GYATOTSANG, NEPHEW AND SUCCESSOR OF GOMPO TASHI.
THOUGH FACED AT TIMES WITH NEAR STARVATION, THE FIGHTERS FEEL A NEW VIGOR IN THE SPIRIT OF **"RANGZEN,"** TIBETAN INDEPENDENCE.

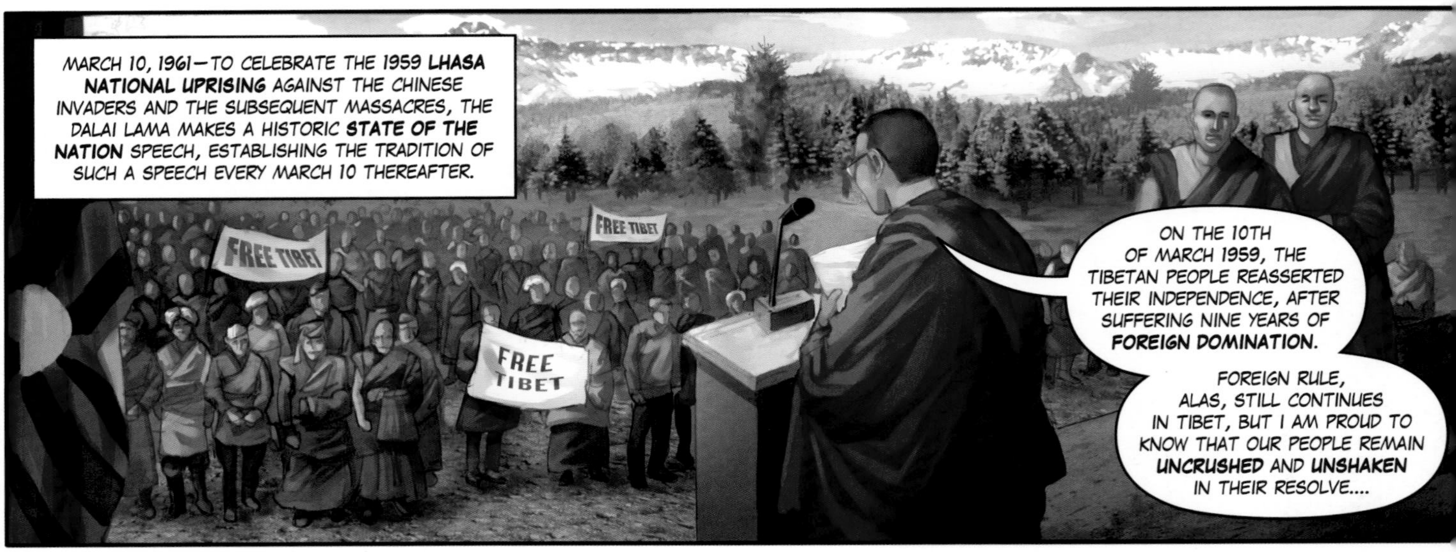
MARCH 10, 1961—TO CELEBRATE THE 1959 **LHASA NATIONAL UPRISING** AGAINST THE CHINESE INVADERS AND THE SUBSEQUENT MASSACRES, THE DALAI LAMA MAKES A HISTORIC **STATE OF THE NATION** SPEECH, ESTABLISHING THE TRADITION OF SUCH A SPEECH EVERY MARCH 10 THEREAFTER.
FREE TIBET
FREE TIBET
FREE TIBET
ON THE 10TH OF MARCH 1959, THE TIBETAN PEOPLE REASSERTED THEIR INDEPENDENCE, AFTER SUFFERING NINE YEARS OF **FOREIGN DOMINATION.**
FOREIGN RULE, ALAS, STILL CONTINUES IN TIBET, BUT I AM PROUD TO KNOW THAT OUR PEOPLE REMAIN **UNCRUSHED** AND **UNSHAKEN** IN THEIR RESOLVE....

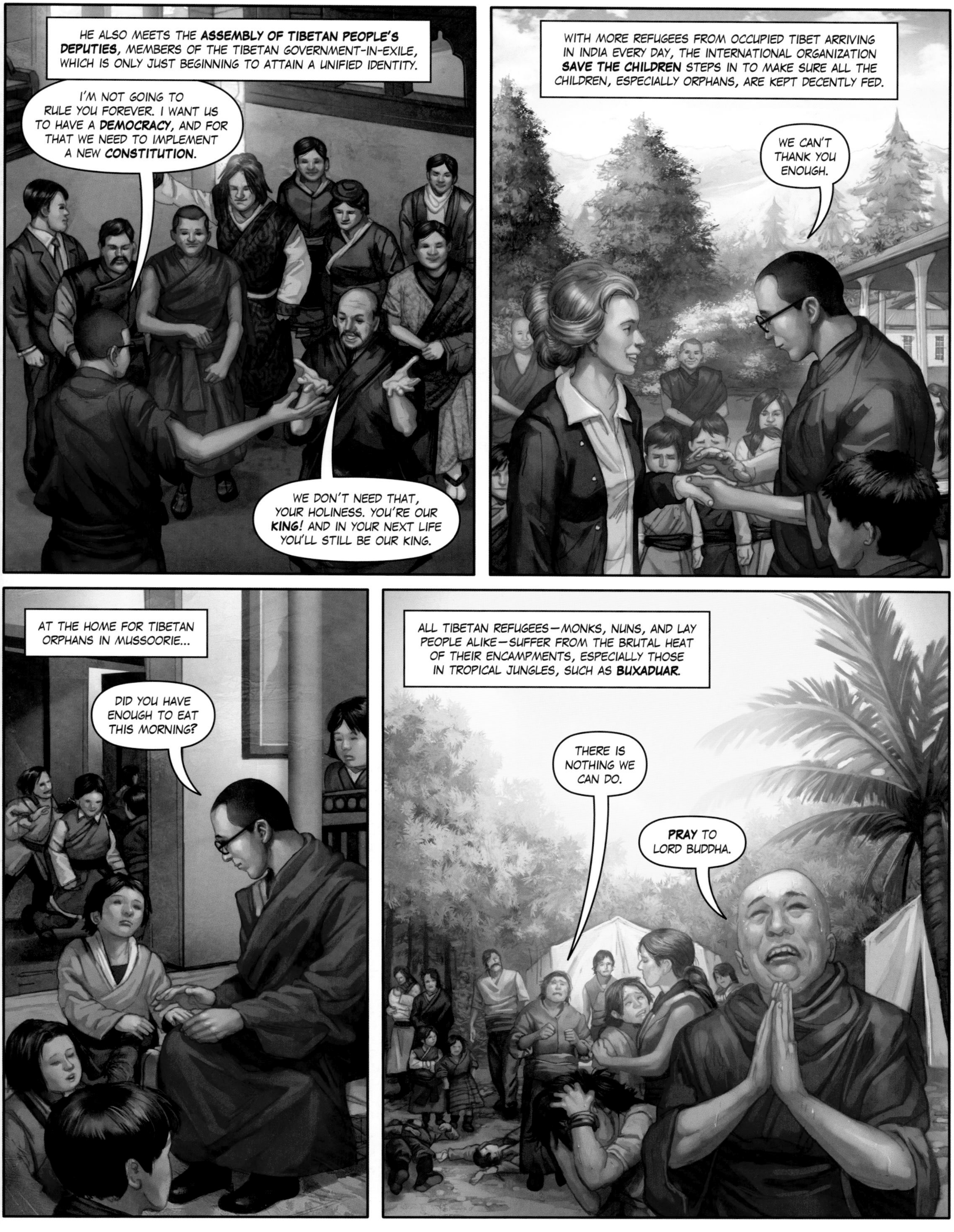
HE ALSO MEETS THE **ASSEMBLY OF TIBETAN PEOPLE'S DEPUTIES**, MEMBERS OF THE TIBETAN GOVERNMENT-IN-EXILE, WHICH IS ONLY JUST BEGINNING TO ATTAIN A UNIFIED IDENTITY.
I'M NOT GOING TO RULE YOU FOREVER. I WANT US TO HAVE A **DEMOCRACY**, AND FOR THAT WE NEED TO IMPLEMENT A NEW **CONSTITUTION**.
WE DON'T NEED THAT, YOUR HOLINESS. YOU'RE OUR **KING!** AND IN YOUR NEXT LIFE YOU'LL STILL BE OUR KING.
WITH MORE REFUGEES FROM OCCUPIED TIBET ARRIVING IN INDIA EVERY DAY, THE INTERNATIONAL ORGANIZATION **SAVE THE CHILDREN** STEPS IN TO MAKE SURE ALL THE CHILDREN, ESPECIALLY ORPHANS, ARE KEPT DECENTLY FED.
WE CAN'T THANK YOU ENOUGH.
AT THE HOME FOR TIBETAN ORPHANS IN MUSSOORIE...
DID YOU HAVE ENOUGH TO EAT THIS MORNING?
ALL TIBETAN REFUGEES—MONKS, NUNS, AND LAY PEOPLE ALIKE—SUFFER FROM THE BRUTAL HEAT OF THEIR ENCAMPMENTS, ESPECIALLY THOSE IN TROPICAL JUNGLES, SUCH AS **BUXADUAR**.
THERE IS NOTHING WE CAN DO.
PRAY TO LORD BUDDHA.

MARCH 10, 1961: *"I know that the struggle which began a few years ago is still being waged in Tibet against the invader and the oppressor, who masquerades under the name and guise of 'liberator.' I can confidently assert that the civilized world is, every day, becoming more and more aware of those who, in the name of liberation, are crushing out the freedom of defenseless neighbors."* —HH the Dalai Lama

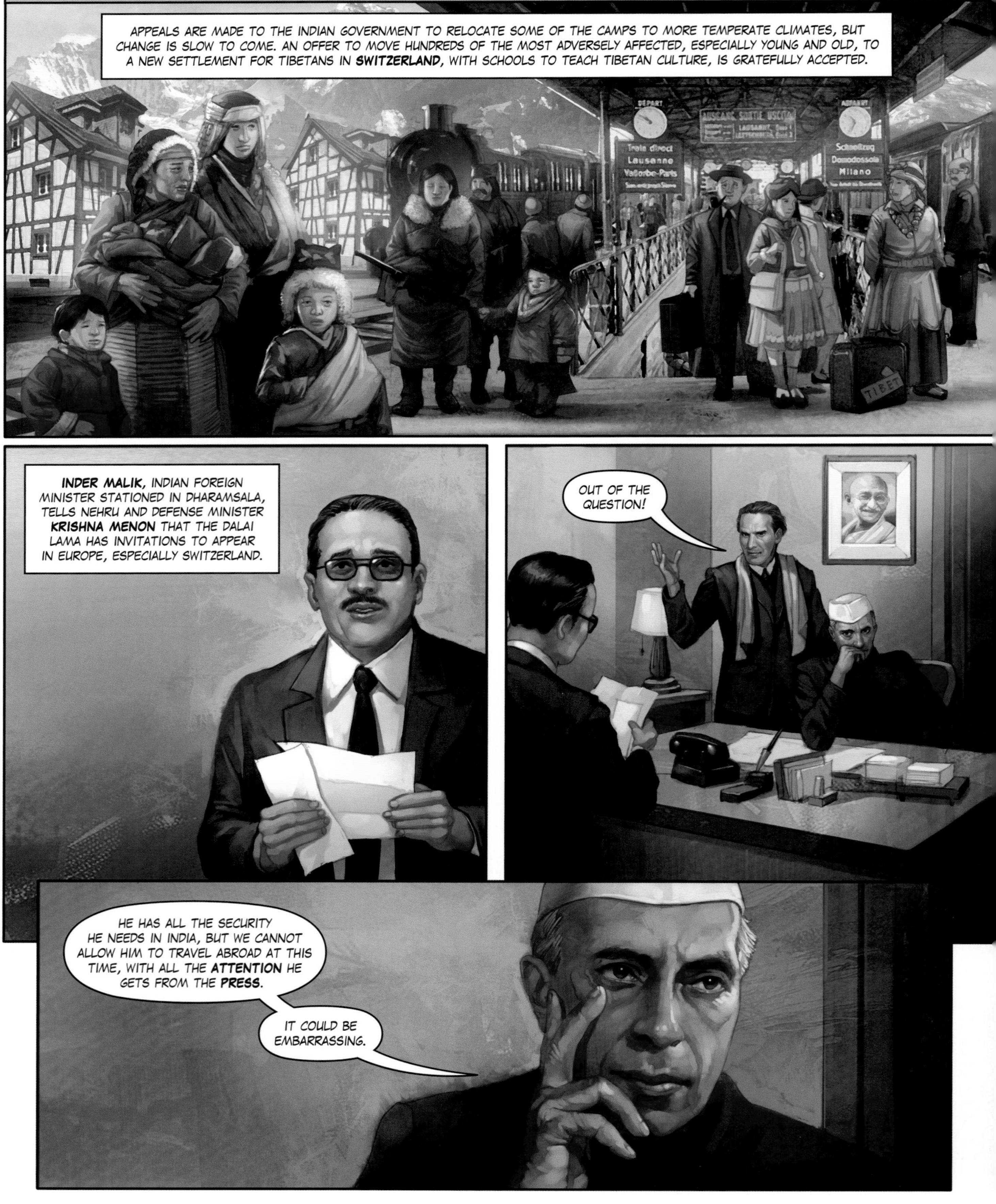
APPEALS ARE MADE TO THE INDIAN GOVERNMENT TO RELOCATE SOME OF THE CAMPS TO MORE TEMPERATE CLIMATES, BUT CHANGE IS SLOW TO COME. AN OFFER TO MOVE HUNDREDS OF THE MOST ADVERSELY AFFECTED, ESPECIALLY YOUNG AND OLD, TO A NEW SETTLEMENT FOR TIBETANS IN **SWITZERLAND,** WITH SCHOOLS TO TEACH TIBETAN CULTURE, IS GRATEFULLY ACCEPTED.
Lausanne
Schnellzug
Domodossola
Milano
TIBET
INDER MALIK, INDIAN FOREIGN MINISTER STATIONED IN DHARAMSALA, TELLS NEHRU AND DEFENSE MINISTER **KRISHNA MENON** THAT THE DALAI LAMA HAS INVITATIONS TO APPEAR IN EUROPE, ESPECIALLY SWITZERLAND.
OUT OF THE QUESTION!
HE HAS ALL THE SECURITY HE NEEDS IN INDIA, BUT WE CANNOT ALLOW HIM TO TRAVEL ABROAD AT THIS TIME, WITH ALL THE **ATTENTION** HE GETS FROM THE **PRESS.**
IT COULD BE EMBARRASSING.

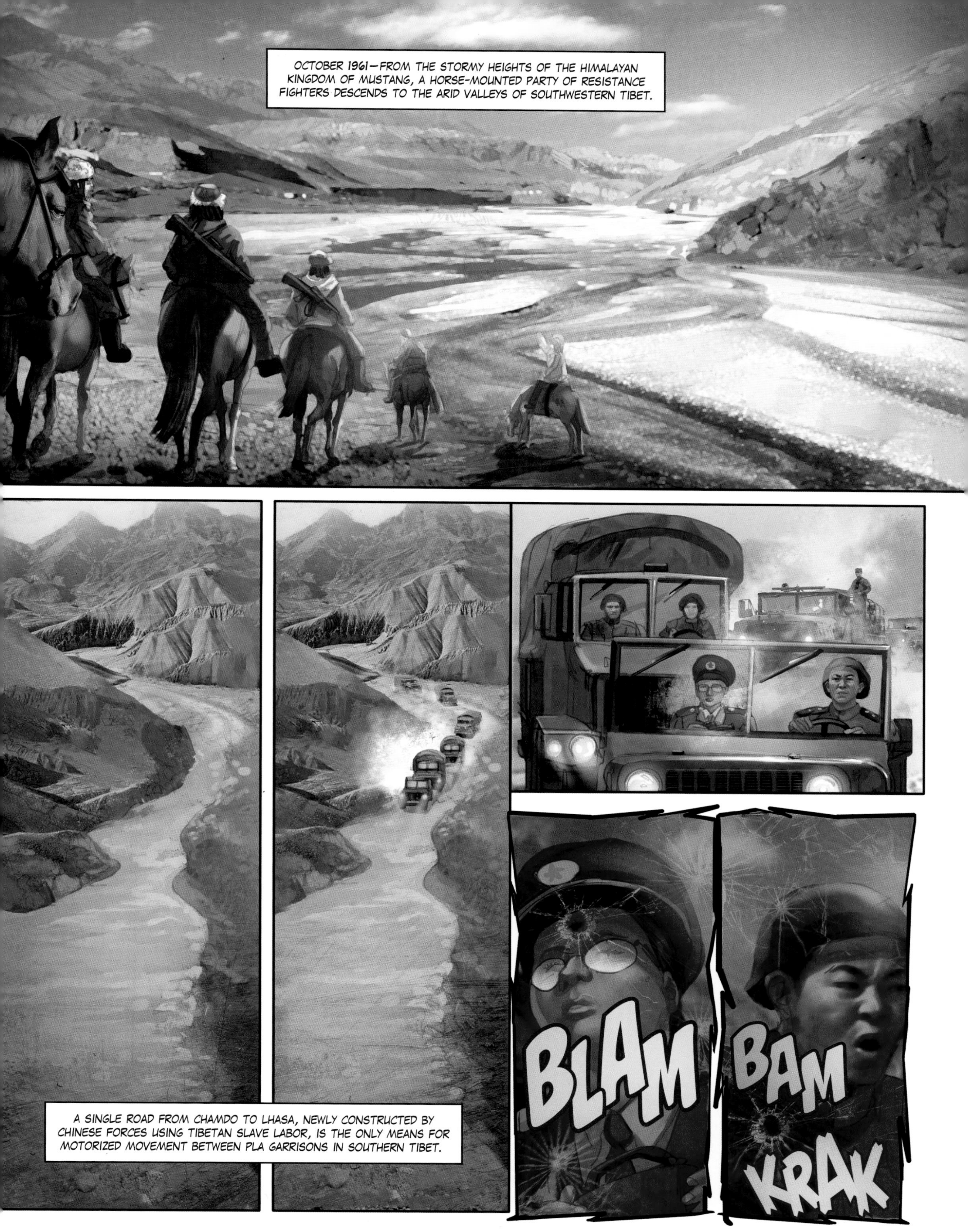

OCTOBER 1961—FROM THE STORMY HEIGHTS OF THE HIMALAYAN KINGDOM OF MUSTANG, A HORSE-MOUNTED PARTY OF RESISTANCE FIGHTERS DESCENDS TO THE ARID VALLEYS OF SOUTHWESTERN TIBET.
A SINGLE ROAD FROM CHAMDO TO LHASA, NEWLY CONSTRUCTED BY CHINESE FORCES USING TIBETAN SLAVE LABOR, IS THE ONLY MEANS FOR MOTORIZED MOVEMENT BETWEEN PLA GARRISONS IN SOUTHERN TIBET.
BLAM
BAM
KRAK

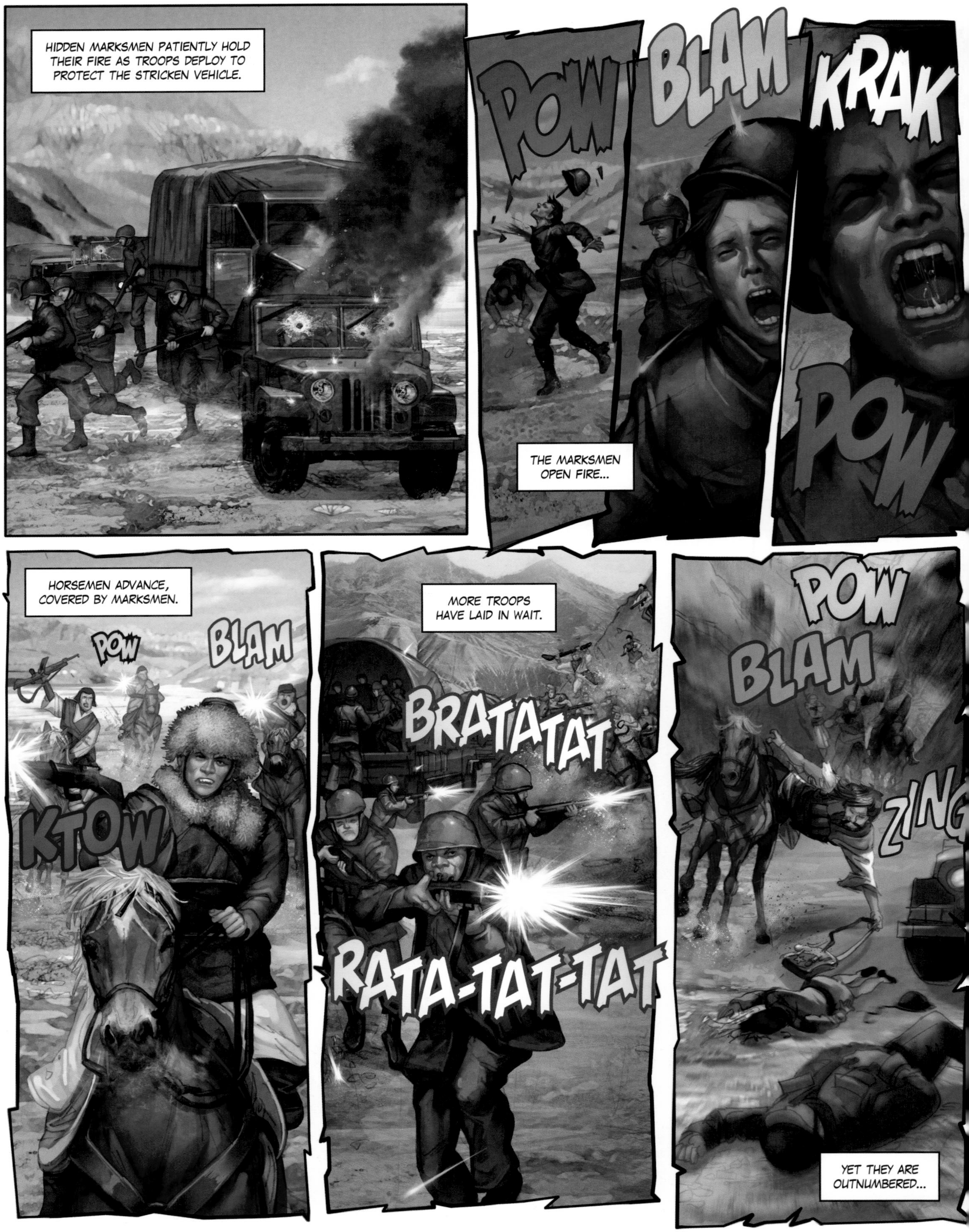

HIDDEN MARKSMEN PATIENTLY HOLD THEIR FIRE AS TROOPS DEPLOY TO PROTECT THE STRICKEN VEHICLE.
POW
BLAM
KRAK
POW
THE MARKSMEN OPEN FIRE...
HORSEMEN ADVANCE, COVERED BY MARKSMEN.
POW
BLAM
KTOW
MORE TROOPS HAVE LAID IN WAIT.
BRATATAT
RATA-TAT-TAT
POW
BLAM
YET THEY ARE OUTNUMBERED...

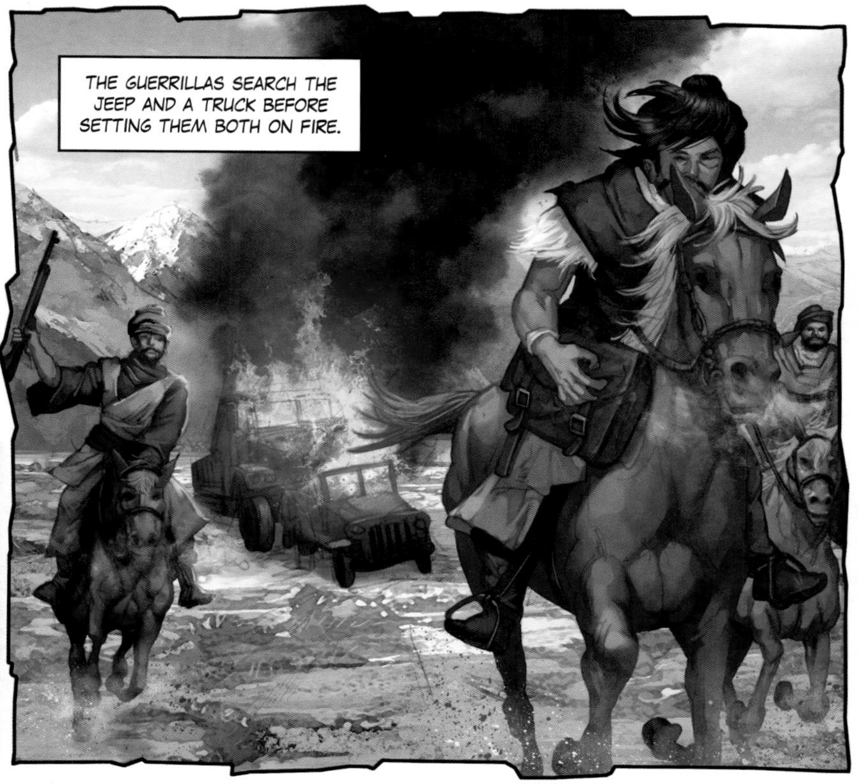
THE GUERRILLAS SEARCH THE JEEP AND A TRUCK BEFORE SETTING THEM BOTH ON FIRE.

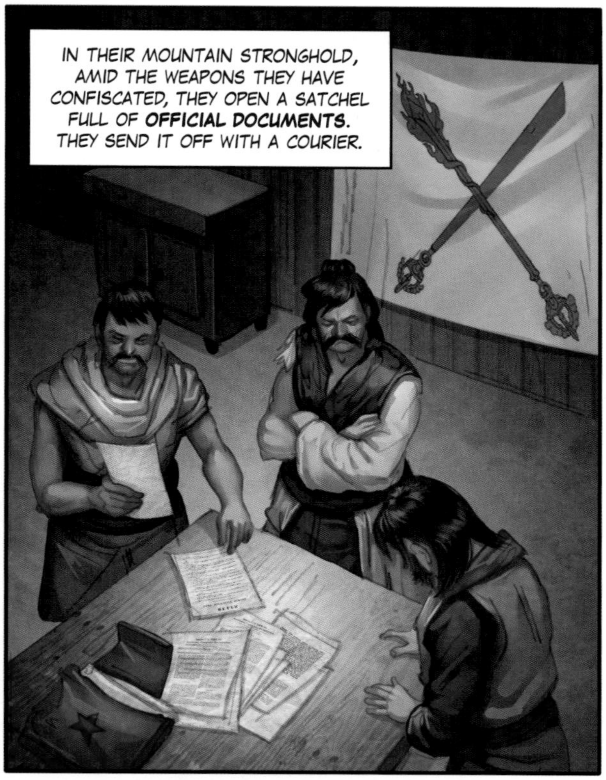
IN THEIR MOUNTAIN STRONGHOLD, AMID THE WEAPONS THEY HAVE CONFISCATED, THEY OPEN A SATCHEL FULL OF **OFFICIAL DOCUMENTS**. THEY SEND IT OFF WITH A COURIER.

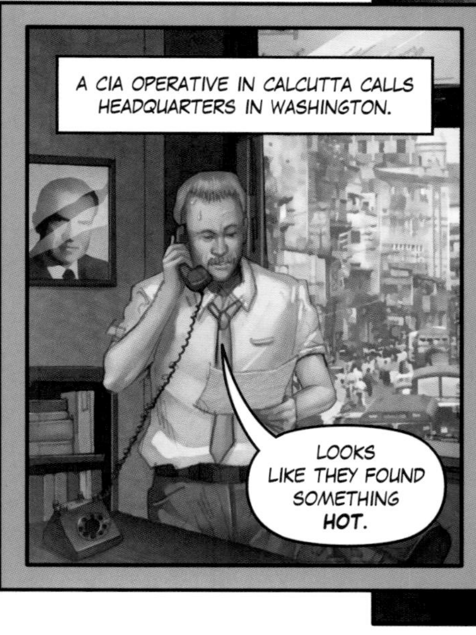
A CIA OPERATIVE IN CALCUTTA CALLS HEADQUARTERS IN WASHINGTON.
LOOKS LIKE THEY FOUND SOMETHING **HOT**.

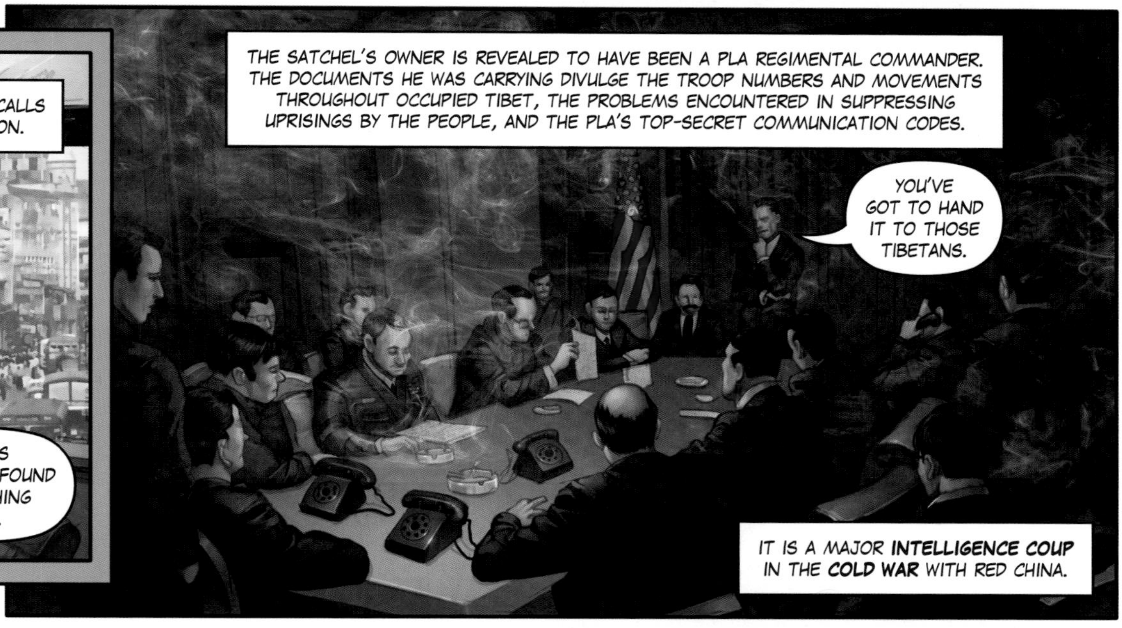
THE SATCHEL'S OWNER IS REVEALED TO HAVE BEEN A PLA REGIMENTAL COMMANDER. THE DOCUMENTS HE WAS CARRYING DIVULGE THE TROOP NUMBERS AND MOVEMENTS THROUGHOUT OCCUPIED TIBET, THE PROBLEMS ENCOUNTERED IN SUPPRESSING UPRISINGS BY THE PEOPLE, AND THE PLA'S TOP-SECRET COMMUNICATION CODES.
YOU'VE GOT TO HAND IT TO THOSE TIBETANS.
IT IS A MAJOR **INTELLIGENCE COUP** IN THE **COLD WAR** WITH RED CHINA.

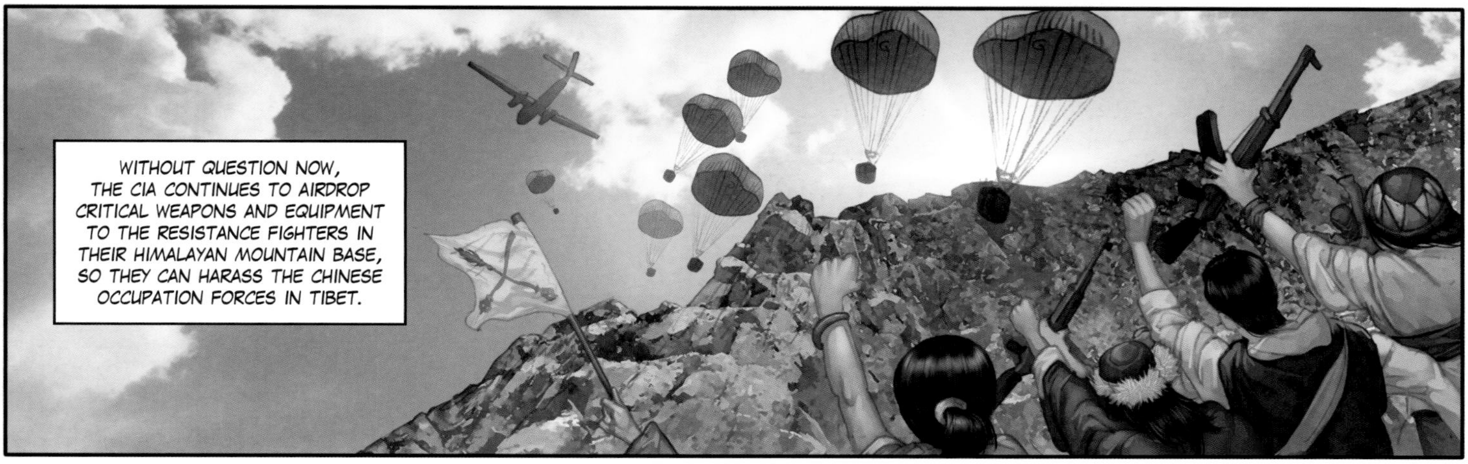
WITHOUT QUESTION NOW, THE CIA CONTINUES TO AIRDROP CRITICAL WEAPONS AND EQUIPMENT TO THE RESISTANCE FIGHTERS IN THEIR HIMALAYAN MOUNTAIN BASE, SO THEY CAN HARASS THE CHINESE OCCUPATION FORCES IN TIBET.

MARCH 10, 1962: *"Every day that passes, more and more refugees are fleeing to the neighboring states to escape from inhuman treatment and persecution. But the spirit of the people has not been and cannot be crushed. Those who cannot escape are there still offering their passive resistance to the unwelcome measures of the authorities in the military occupation of Tibet."* —HH the Dalai Lama

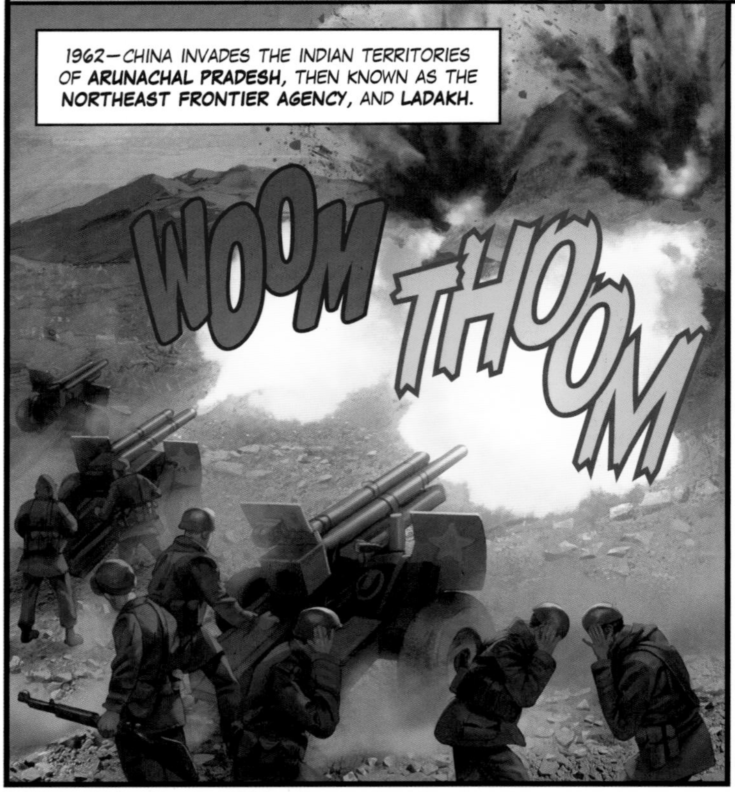
1962—CHINA INVADES THE INDIAN TERRITORIES OF **ARUNACHAL PRADESH**, THEN KNOWN AS THE **NORTHEAST FRONTIER AGENCY**, AND **LADAKH**.
WOOM
THOOM

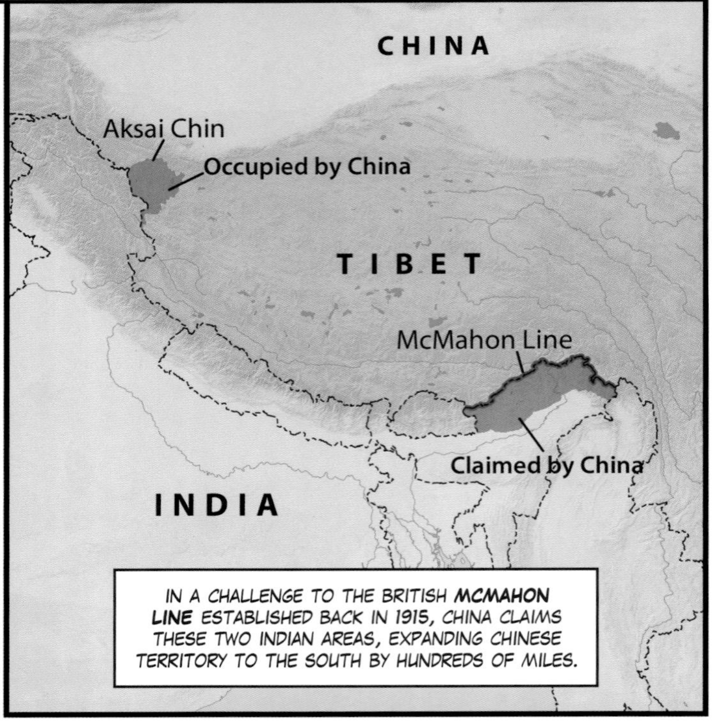
CHINA
Aksai Chin
Occupied by China
TIBET
McMahon Line
Claimed by China
INDIA
IN A CHALLENGE TO THE BRITISH **MCMAHON LINE** ESTABLISHED BACK IN 1915, CHINA CLAIMS THESE TWO INDIAN AREAS, EXPANDING CHINESE TERRITORY TO THE SOUTH BY HUNDREDS OF MILES.

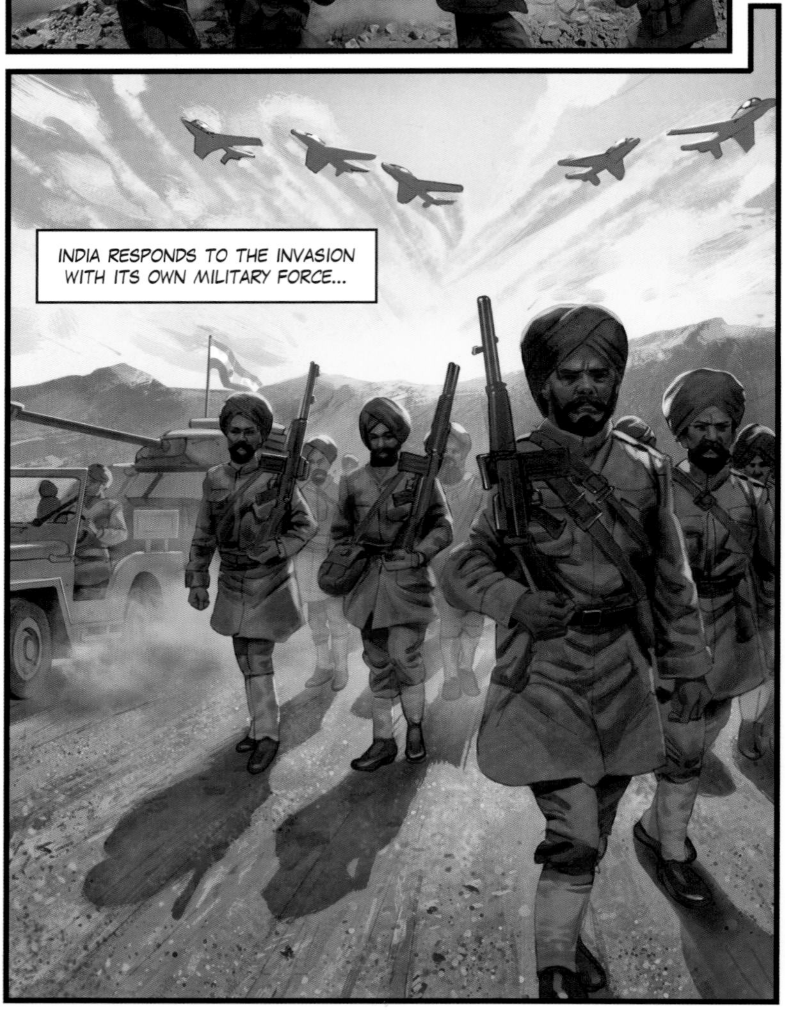
INDIA RESPONDS TO THE INVASION WITH ITS OWN MILITARY FORCE...

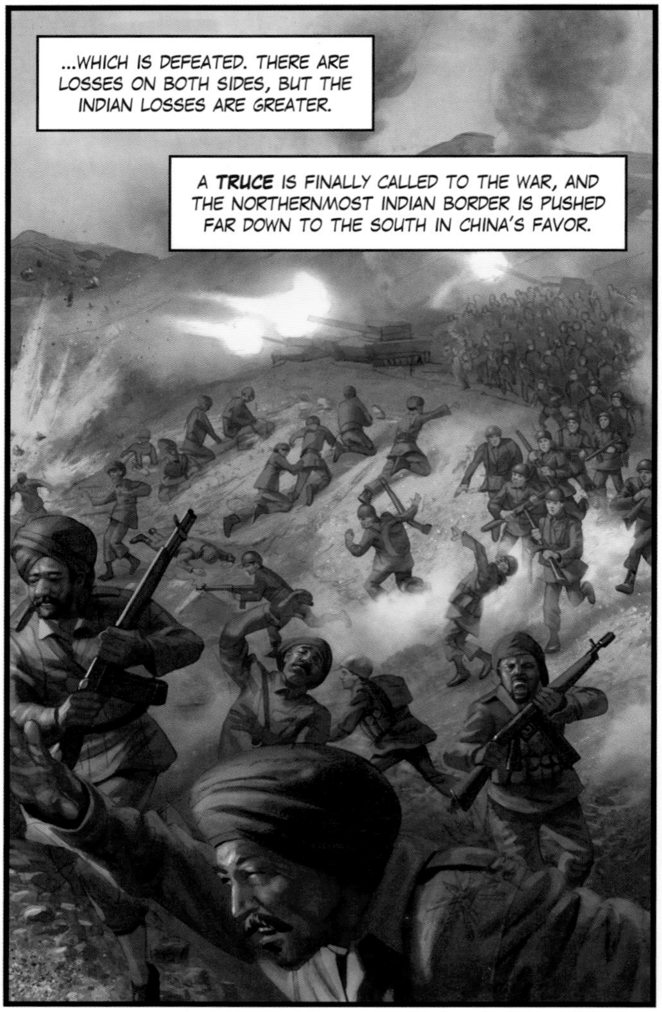
...WHICH IS DEFEATED. THERE ARE LOSSES ON BOTH SIDES, BUT THE INDIAN LOSSES ARE GREATER.
A **TRUCE** IS FINALLY CALLED TO THE WAR, AND THE NORTHERNMOST INDIAN BORDER IS PUSHED FAR DOWN TO THE SOUTH IN CHINA'S FAVOR.

PRIME MINISTER NEHRU IS HUMILIATED BY THE MASSIVE LOSSES. HIS DAUGHTER INDIRA TRIES TO COMFORT HIM IN HIS DESPAIR.

MAO HAS DESTROYED THE VERY HEART OF OUR BROTHERHOOD—OUR **SINO-INDIAN PEACE.**

THEY ARE SEEING JUST HOW FAR THEY CAN GO, FATHER. TAKE CARE TO SEE THAT THE DALAI LAMA IS EVEN BETTER PROTECTED.

NOW FINALLY ALERT TO THE HEIGHTENED DANGER, NEHRU AUTHORIZES THE FORMATION OF A SPECIAL **FRONTIER FORCE,** COMPRISED OF 10,000 TIBETAN MEN AND WOMEN, TO PATROL THE INDIAN BORDER ALONG THE HIMALAYAN RANGE BETWEEN ARUNACHAL AND LADAKH. IN DHARAMSALA, THE DALAI LAMA WRITES A LETTER OF ACQUIESCENCE....

My dear Prime Minister,

Your idea of including our Tibetan resistance fighters in a new defense force for India – the Special Frontier Force – as a means of discouraging future incursions from the North, has met with my full approval. You are now our patron, as India is Tibet's, and so the defense of your nation becomes our own. I would hope that this new military relationship will allay some of your concerns about our brave and impetuous fighters. That some of them choose to remain independent of our direct control in order to pursue their determined effort to regain our homeland is a matter which I can hardly excuse but cannot prevent (I admire their human heroism, but cannot condone their violent ethic or approve the practicality of their strategy against the overwhelming odds).

AT SWARG ASHRAM, HIGH ABOVE DHARAMSALA, THE DALAI LAMA TRIES TO REASON WITH HIS OLDER BROTHER...

AS YOU CAN SEE, GYALO-LA, VIOLENT RESISTANCE WILL ONLY RESULT IN **MORE** VIOLENCE.

NEHRU'S MENTOR GANDHI SHOWED US THE WAY—AHIMSA. **MORAL FORCE** MAKES NONVIOLENT RESISTANCE **POSSIBLE** AND **POWERFUL.**

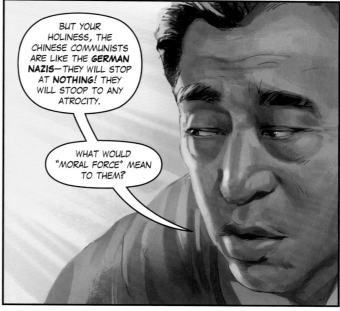

BUT YOUR HOLINESS, THE CHINESE COMMUNISTS ARE LIKE THE **GERMAN NAZIS**—THEY WILL STOP AT **NOTHING!** THEY WILL STOOP TO ANY ATROCITY.

WHAT WOULD "MORAL FORCE" MEAN TO THEM?

IT'S A **TRAP,** GYALO-LA! **BEWARE** OF FALLING INTO IT. THEY WOULD HAVE YOU AT THEIR LEVEL. WHATEVER ANY OF THEM DOES TO YOU, HE IS STILL YOUR BROTHER.

IN PAST LIFETIMES HE HAS EVEN BEEN YOUR **MOTHER!**

ALL HUMAN BEINGS ARE BASICALLY THE SAME.

TO REGARD YOUR **TORTURER** AS YOUR **TEACHER**—TO FORGIVE HIM—MOVES YOU BOTH TOWARD ENLIGHTENMENT.

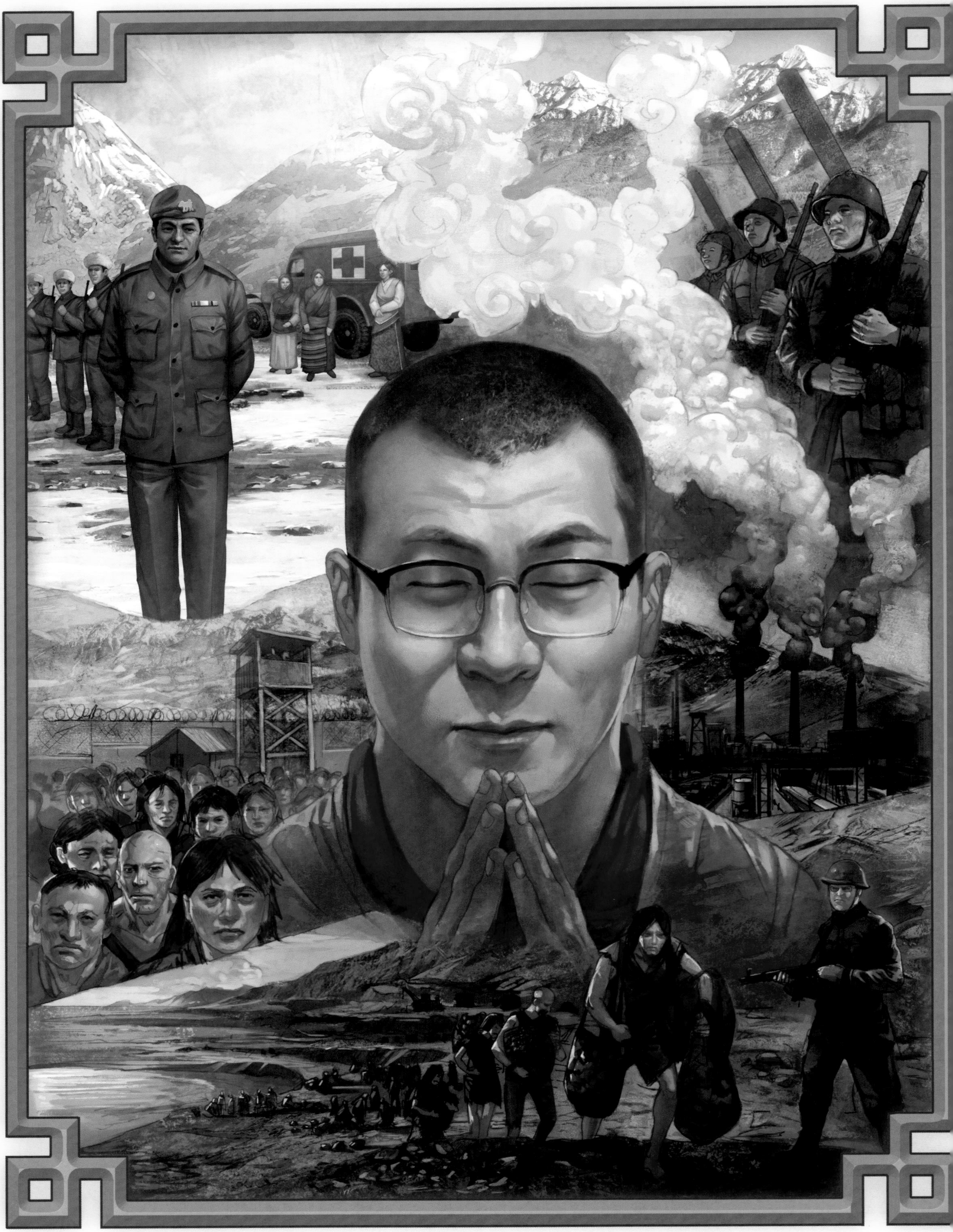

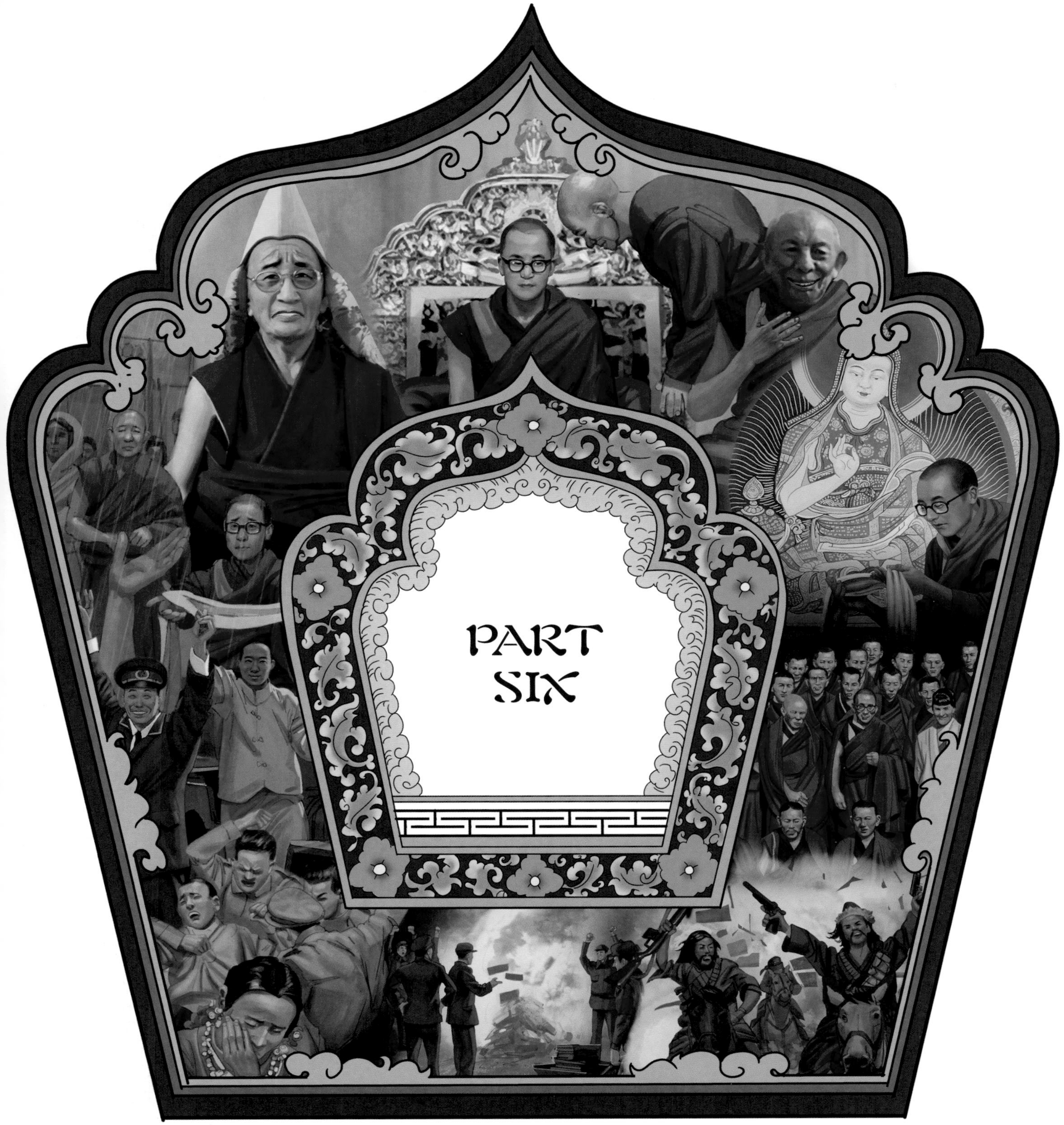
PART
SIX

MARCH 10, 1963: *"China does not hear the voice of the world. The passive resistance of our people still continues. Vivid accounts of unspeakable misery are still being brought to us in exile. The situation continues to be desperate and hopeless. But those of our unfortunate brothers and sisters who remain in Tibet must not lose their faith in the ultimate victory of truth...."* —HH the Dalai Lama

THE DALAI LAMA CONTINUES HIS PERSONAL STUDY AND PRACTICE OF MAHAYANA BUDDHISM, IN THE TRADITION OF INDIA'S NALANDA SCHOOL AND HIS OWN **GELUKPA ORDER**, FOUNDED BY JEY TSONG KHAPA, AND NOW TRANSMITTED TO HIM BY HIS SENIOR TUTOR, LING RINPOCHE.

LING RINPOCHE TELLS HIM HE SHOULD FURTHER STUDY THE **KALACHAKRA**, THE **"TIME MACHINE"** TANTRA, INTO WHICH LING HAD INITIATED HIM IN 1953. HE URGES THE DALAI LAMA TO SEEK INSTRUCTION FROM A LIVING MASTER OF THE ANCIENT TRADITION, **KIRTI TSENSHAB RINPOCHE**.

TEACH HIS HOLINESS THE KALACHAKRA TANTRA? NOT **ME**! I WOULD NEVER **DARE** TO DO THAT.

FOCUSING ON ITS **TANTRIC TEACHINGS**, THE DALAI LAMA REALIZES THAT HE HAS A SPECIAL AFFINITY WITH THE KALACHAKRA. HE RESOLVES TO SERVE AS THE **VAJRA MENTOR** IN TRANSMITTING THE TIME MACHINE BUDDHA VISION.

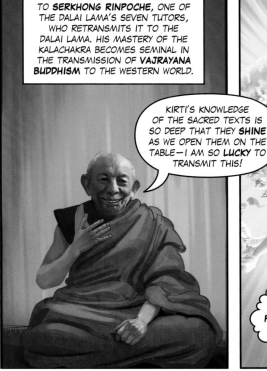

KIRTI RINPOCHE TRANSMITS HIS KNOWLEDGE OF THE KALACHAKRA TO **SERKHONG RINPOCHE**, ONE OF THE DALAI LAMA'S SEVEN TUTORS, WHO RETRANSMITS IT TO THE DALAI LAMA. HIS MASTERY OF THE KALACHAKRA BECOMES SEMINAL IN THE TRANSMISSION OF **VAJRAYANA BUDDHISM** TO THE WESTERN WORLD.

KIRTI'S KNOWLEDGE OF THE SACRED TEXTS IS SO DEEP THAT THEY **SHINE** AS WE OPEN THEM ON THE TABLE—I AM SO **LUCKY** TO TRANSMIT THIS!

ON RETREAT, THE YOUNG DALAI LAMA DISCOVERS IN A VISION HE HAS THE POWERFUL BACKING OF **VAJRAVEGA**—KALACHAKRA AS THE DIAMOND FORCE OF **LOVE** AND **BLISS**—WHO IS MORE THAN A MATCH FOR THE DARK SIDE.

THANKS TO BUDDHA, THE **FORCE OF TRUTH** IS A FORCE OF **LIGHT**.

MARCH 10, 1963: *"… This memorable day as on other days, I pray with all earnestness and fervor that the great Avalokiteshvara may grant my beloved people courage and determination to enable them to continue their passive struggle against tyranny and oppression…."*

SERKHONG RINPOCHE TELLS THE DALAI LAMA ABOUT A SPECIAL TEACHER HE SHOULD MEET.

YOUR HOLINESS, I KNOW THE LINEAGE-HOLDING MASTER OF THE **EXCHANGE-OF-SELF-AND-OTHER** COMPASSION PRECEPT PASSED DOWN FROM MANJUSHRI, NAGARJUNA, SHANTIDEVA, AND THE GREAT **NYINGMA** MASTER, **PATRUL RINPOCHE.**

HE IS A LIVING TREASURE IN UNCONVENTIONAL GARB, NAMED **KHUNU LAMA RINPOCHE,** AND I **URGENTLY** ADVISE YOU TO SEEK HIM OUT.

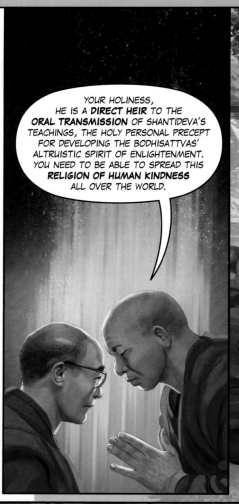

YOUR HOLINESS, HE IS A **DIRECT HEIR** TO THE **ORAL TRANSMISSION** OF SHANTIDEVA'S TEACHINGS, THE HOLY PERSONAL PRECEPT FOR DEVELOPING THE BODHISATTVAS' ALTRUISTIC SPIRIT OF ENLIGHTENMENT. YOU NEED TO BE ABLE TO SPREAD THIS **RELIGION OF HUMAN KINDNESS** ALL OVER THE WORLD.

KHUNU LAMA TEACHES INFORMALLY NEAR THE BODHI TREE IN BODHGAYA.

I MUST FIND THIS REMARKABLE KHUNU LAMA AND REQUEST HIS TRANSMISSION OF THE LIVING TEACHING.

THE SEARCH IS ON…

THE DALAI LAMA'S MOTORCADE THREADS THROUGH THE NARROW STREETS OF VARANASI, WHERE KHUNU LAMA LIVES. THE TRANSLATOR **KAZI SONAM TOBGYAL** AND SERKHONG RINPOCHE ACCOMPANY THE DALAI LAMA.

THIS IS IT—THE NEIGHBORHOOD WHERE HE WAS LAST REPORTED TO BE LIVING.

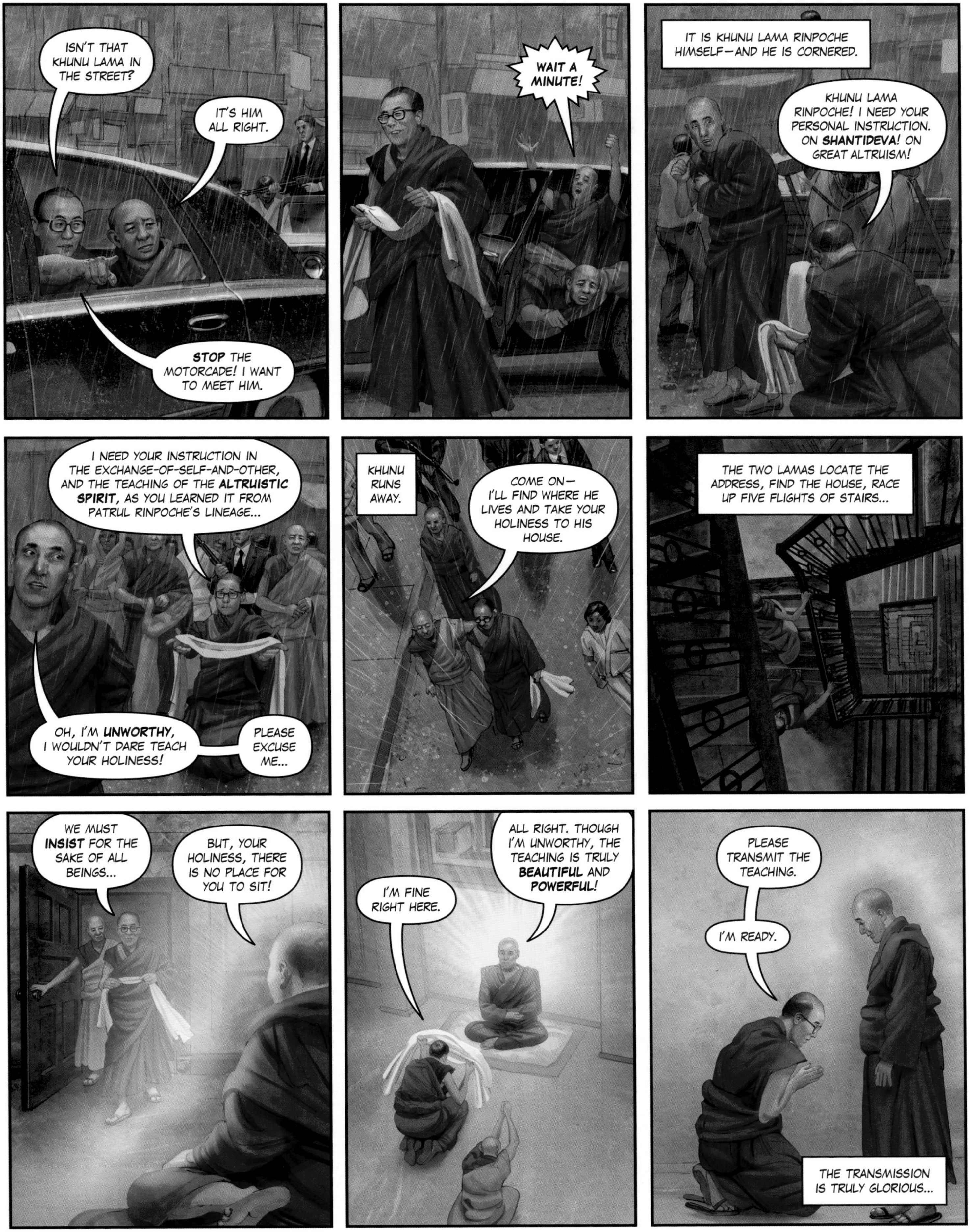
ISN'T THAT KHUNU LAMA IN THE STREET?
IT'S HIM ALL RIGHT.
STOP THE MOTORCADE! I WANT TO MEET HIM.
WAIT A MINUTE!
IT IS KHUNU LAMA RINPOCHE HIMSELF—AND HE IS CORNERED.
KHUNU LAMA RINPOCHE! I NEED YOUR PERSONAL INSTRUCTION. ON SHANTIDEVA! ON GREAT ALTRUISM!
I NEED YOUR INSTRUCTION IN THE EXCHANGE-OF-SELF-AND-OTHER, AND THE TEACHING OF THE ALTRUISTIC SPIRIT, AS YOU LEARNED IT FROM PATRUL RINPOCHE'S LINEAGE...
OH, I'M UNWORTHY, I WOULDN'T DARE TEACH YOUR HOLINESS!
PLEASE EXCUSE ME...
KHUNU RUNS AWAY.
COME ON— I'LL FIND WHERE HE LIVES AND TAKE YOUR HOLINESS TO HIS HOUSE.
THE TWO LAMAS LOCATE THE ADDRESS, FIND THE HOUSE, RACE UP FIVE FLIGHTS OF STAIRS...
WE MUST INSIST FOR THE SAKE OF ALL BEINGS...
BUT, YOUR HOLINESS, THERE IS NO PLACE FOR YOU TO SIT!
I'M FINE RIGHT HERE.
ALL RIGHT. THOUGH I'M UNWORTHY, THE TEACHING IS TRULY BEAUTIFUL AND POWERFUL!
PLEASE TRANSMIT THE TEACHING.
I'M READY.
THE TRANSMISSION IS TRULY GLORIOUS...

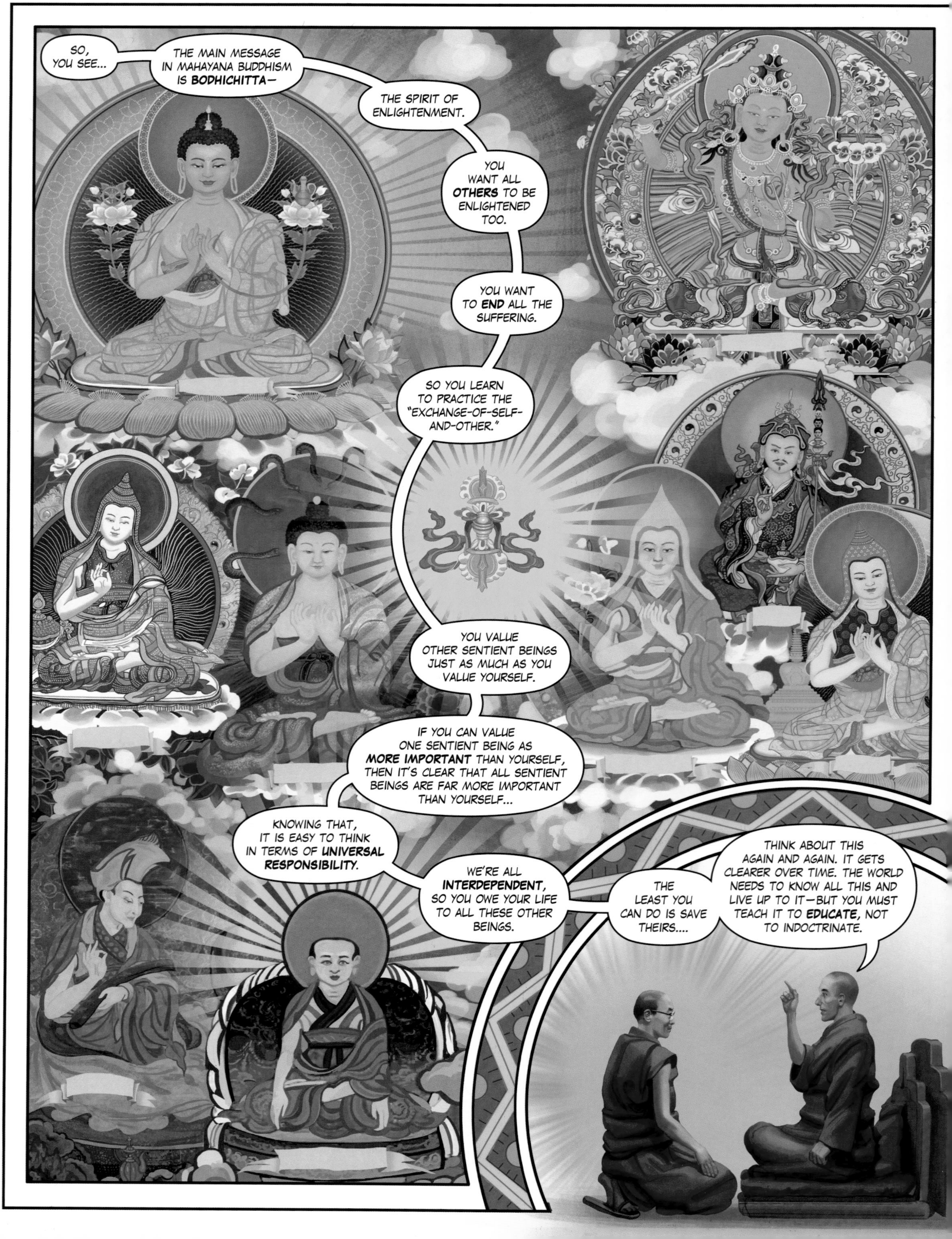

SO, YOU SEE...
THE MAIN MESSAGE IN MAHAYANA BUDDHISM IS **BODHICHITTA**—
THE SPIRIT OF ENLIGHTENMENT.
YOU WANT ALL **OTHERS** TO BE ENLIGHTENED TOO.
YOU WANT TO **END** ALL THE SUFFERING.
SO YOU LEARN TO PRACTICE THE "EXCHANGE-OF-SELF-AND-OTHER."
YOU VALUE OTHER SENTIENT BEINGS JUST AS MUCH AS YOU VALUE YOURSELF.
IF YOU CAN VALUE ONE SENTIENT BEING AS **MORE IMPORTANT** THAN YOURSELF, THEN IT'S CLEAR THAT ALL SENTIENT BEINGS ARE FAR MORE IMPORTANT THAN YOURSELF...
KNOWING THAT, IT IS EASY TO THINK IN TERMS OF **UNIVERSAL RESPONSIBILITY**.
WE'RE ALL **INTERDEPENDENT**, SO YOU OWE YOUR LIFE TO ALL THESE OTHER BEINGS.
THE LEAST YOU CAN DO IS SAVE THEIRS....
THINK ABOUT THIS AGAIN AND AGAIN. IT GETS CLEARER OVER TIME. THE WORLD NEEDS TO KNOW ALL THIS AND LIVE UP TO IT—BUT YOU MUST TEACH IT TO **EDUCATE**, NOT TO INDOCTRINATE.

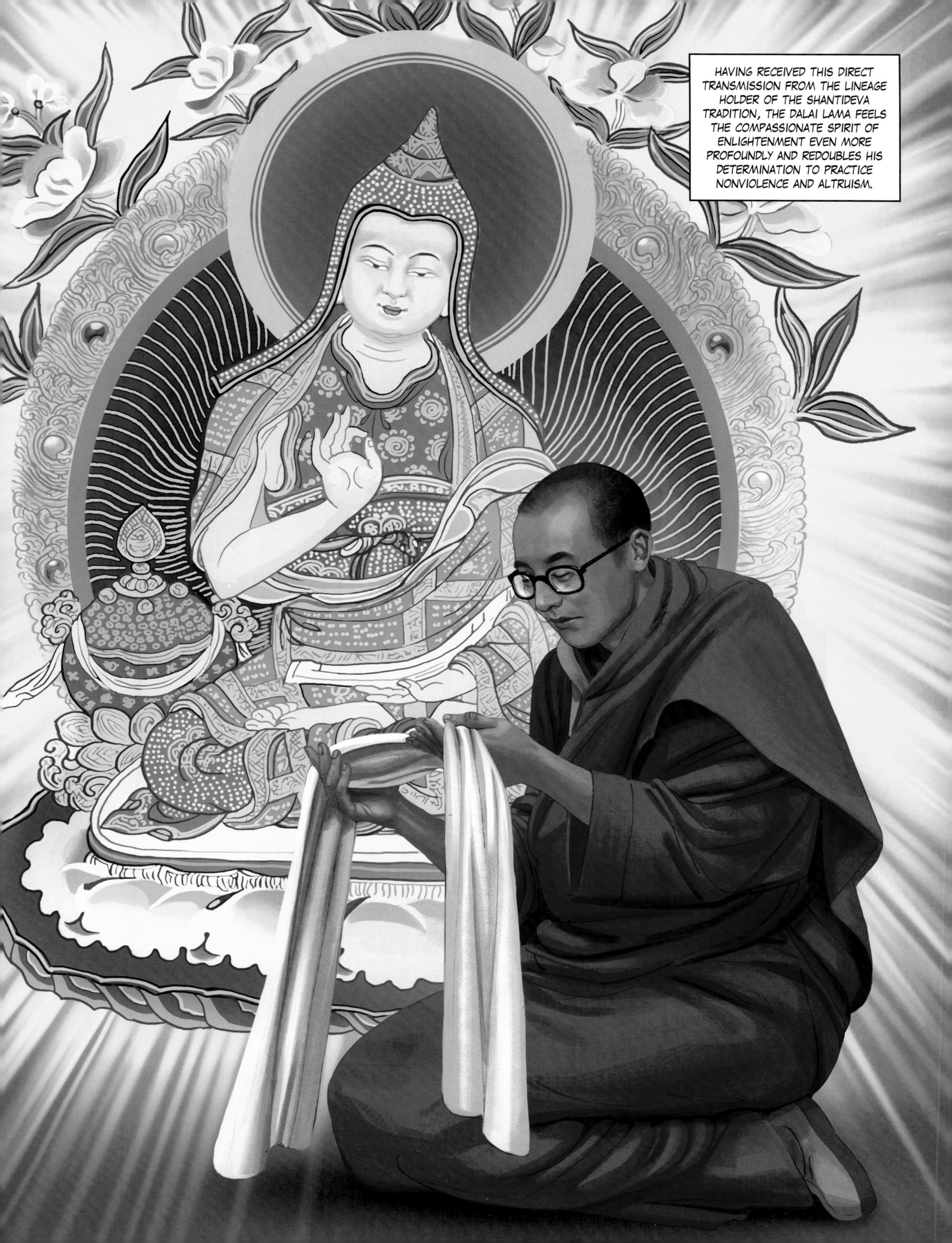
HAVING RECEIVED THIS DIRECT TRANSMISSION FROM THE LINEAGE HOLDER OF THE SHANTIDEVA TRADITION, THE DALAI LAMA FEELS THE COMPASSIONATE SPIRIT OF ENLIGHTENMENT EVEN MORE PROFOUNDLY AND REDOUBLES HIS DETERMINATION TO PRACTICE NONVIOLENCE AND ALTRUISM.

MARCH 10, 1963: *"... We must all, with unshaken faith, continue to struggle for the not too distant day of regaining freedom of our country. To build and prepare for the future is one of our primary responsibilities. For this purpose, I have prepared a future Constitution for Tibet which is consistent with the teachings of Lord Buddha and with the rich spiritual and temporal heritage of our history and democracy."*

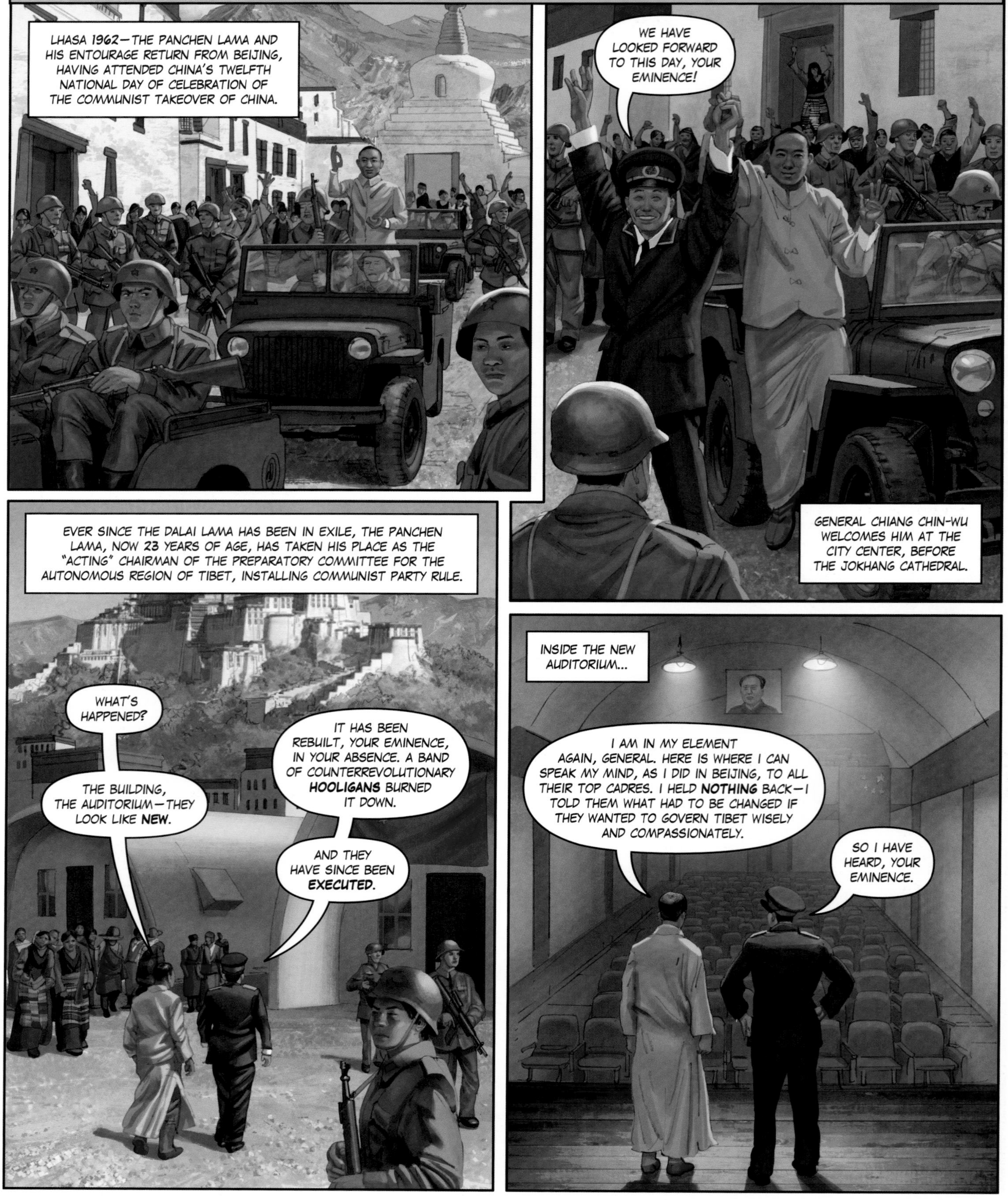

LHASA 1962—THE PANCHEN LAMA AND HIS ENTOURAGE RETURN FROM BEIJING, HAVING ATTENDED CHINA'S TWELFTH NATIONAL DAY OF CELEBRATION OF THE COMMUNIST TAKEOVER OF CHINA.
WE HAVE LOOKED FORWARD TO THIS DAY, YOUR EMINENCE!
GENERAL CHIANG CHIN-WU WELCOMES HIM AT THE CITY CENTER, BEFORE THE JOKHANG CATHEDRAL.
EVER SINCE THE DALAI LAMA HAS BEEN IN EXILE, THE PANCHEN LAMA, NOW 23 YEARS OF AGE, HAS TAKEN HIS PLACE AS THE "ACTING" CHAIRMAN OF THE PREPARATORY COMMITTEE FOR THE AUTONOMOUS REGION OF TIBET, INSTALLING COMMUNIST PARTY RULE.
WHAT'S HAPPENED?
THE BUILDING, THE AUDITORIUM—THEY LOOK LIKE **NEW**.
IT HAS BEEN REBUILT, YOUR EMINENCE, IN YOUR ABSENCE. A BAND OF COUNTERREVOLUTIONARY **HOOLIGANS** BURNED IT DOWN.
AND THEY HAVE SINCE BEEN **EXECUTED**.
INSIDE THE NEW AUDITORIUM...
I AM IN MY ELEMENT AGAIN, GENERAL. HERE IS WHERE I CAN SPEAK MY MIND, AS I DID IN BEIJING, TO ALL THEIR TOP CADRES. I HELD **NOTHING** BACK—I TOLD THEM WHAT HAD TO BE CHANGED IF THEY WANTED TO GOVERN TIBET WISELY AND COMPASSIONATELY.
SO I HAVE HEARD, YOUR EMINENCE.

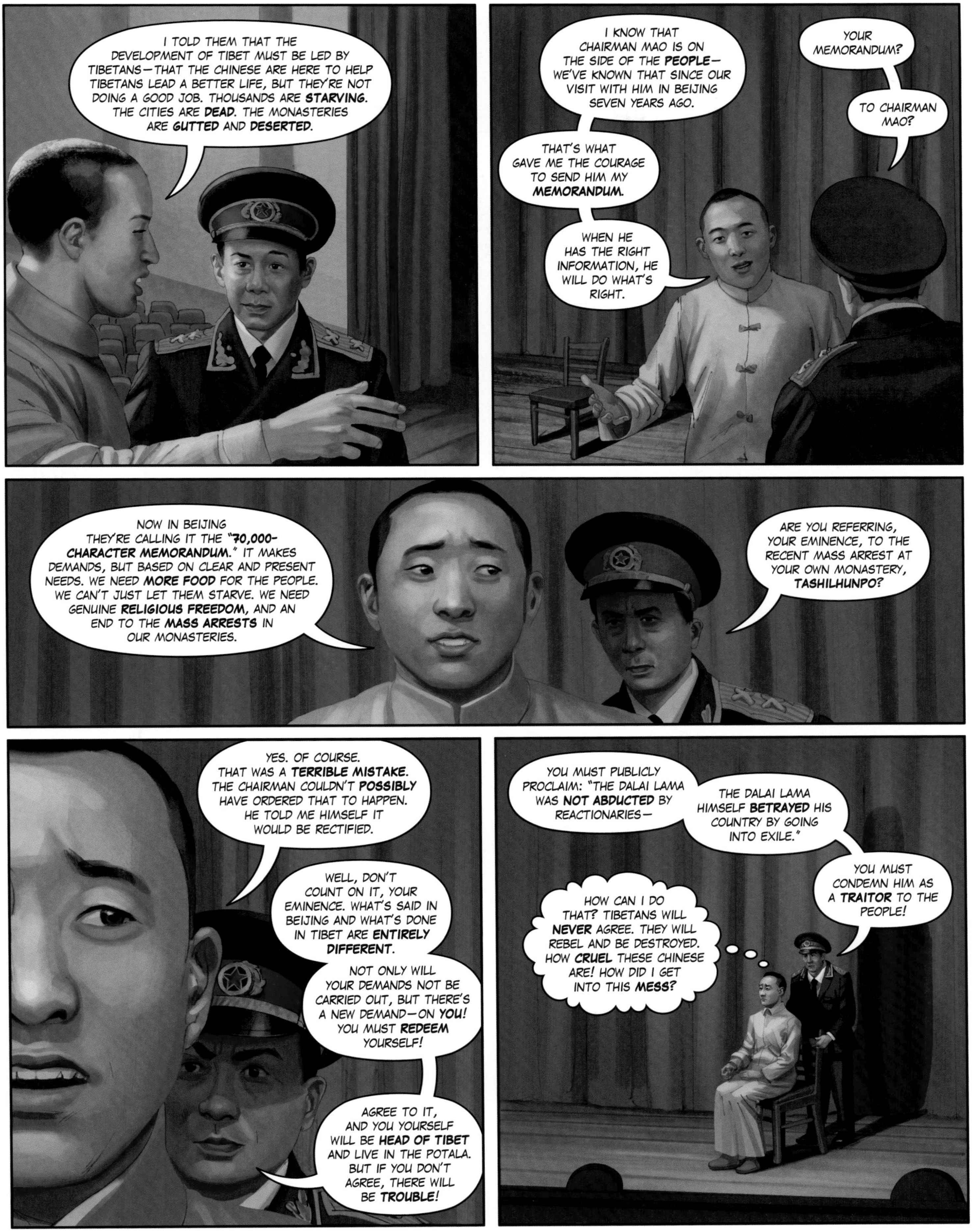
I TOLD THEM THAT THE DEVELOPMENT OF TIBET MUST BE LED BY TIBETANS—THAT THE CHINESE ARE HERE TO HELP TIBETANS LEAD A BETTER LIFE, BUT THEY'RE NOT DOING A GOOD JOB. THOUSANDS ARE **STARVING**. THE CITIES ARE **DEAD**. THE MONASTERIES ARE **GUTTED** AND **DESERTED**.
I KNOW THAT CHAIRMAN MAO IS ON THE SIDE OF THE **PEOPLE**—WE'VE KNOWN THAT SINCE OUR VISIT WITH HIM IN BEIJING SEVEN YEARS AGO.
THAT'S WHAT GAVE ME THE COURAGE TO SEND HIM MY **MEMORANDUM**.
WHEN HE HAS THE RIGHT INFORMATION, HE WILL DO WHAT'S RIGHT.
YOUR MEMORANDUM?
TO CHAIRMAN MAO?
NOW IN BEIJING THEY'RE CALLING IT THE **"70,000-CHARACTER MEMORANDUM."** IT MAKES DEMANDS, BUT BASED ON CLEAR AND PRESENT NEEDS. WE NEED **MORE FOOD** FOR THE PEOPLE. WE CAN'T JUST LET THEM STARVE. WE NEED GENUINE **RELIGIOUS FREEDOM**, AND AN END TO THE **MASS ARRESTS** IN OUR MONASTERIES.
ARE YOU REFERRING, YOUR EMINENCE, TO THE RECENT MASS ARREST AT YOUR OWN MONASTERY, **TASHILHUNPO?**
YES. OF COURSE. THAT WAS A **TERRIBLE MISTAKE**. THE CHAIRMAN COULDN'T **POSSIBLY** HAVE ORDERED THAT TO HAPPEN. HE TOLD ME HIMSELF IT WOULD BE RECTIFIED.
WELL, DON'T COUNT ON IT, YOUR EMINENCE. WHAT'S SAID IN BEIJING AND WHAT'S DONE IN TIBET ARE **ENTIRELY DIFFERENT**.
NOT ONLY WILL YOUR DEMANDS NOT BE CARRIED OUT, BUT THERE'S A NEW DEMAND—ON **YOU**! YOU MUST **REDEEM** YOURSELF!
AGREE TO IT, AND YOU YOURSELF WILL BE **HEAD OF TIBET** AND LIVE IN THE POTALA. BUT IF YOU DON'T AGREE, THERE WILL BE **TROUBLE**!
YOU MUST PUBLICLY PROCLAIM: "THE DALAI LAMA WAS **NOT ABDUCTED** BY REACTIONARIES—
THE DALAI LAMA HIMSELF **BETRAYED** HIS COUNTRY BY GOING INTO EXILE."
YOU MUST CONDEMN HIM AS A **TRAITOR** TO THE PEOPLE!
HOW CAN I DO THAT? TIBETANS WILL **NEVER** AGREE. THEY WILL REBEL AND BE DESTROYED. HOW **CRUEL** THESE CHINESE ARE! HOW DID I GET INTO THIS **MESS?**

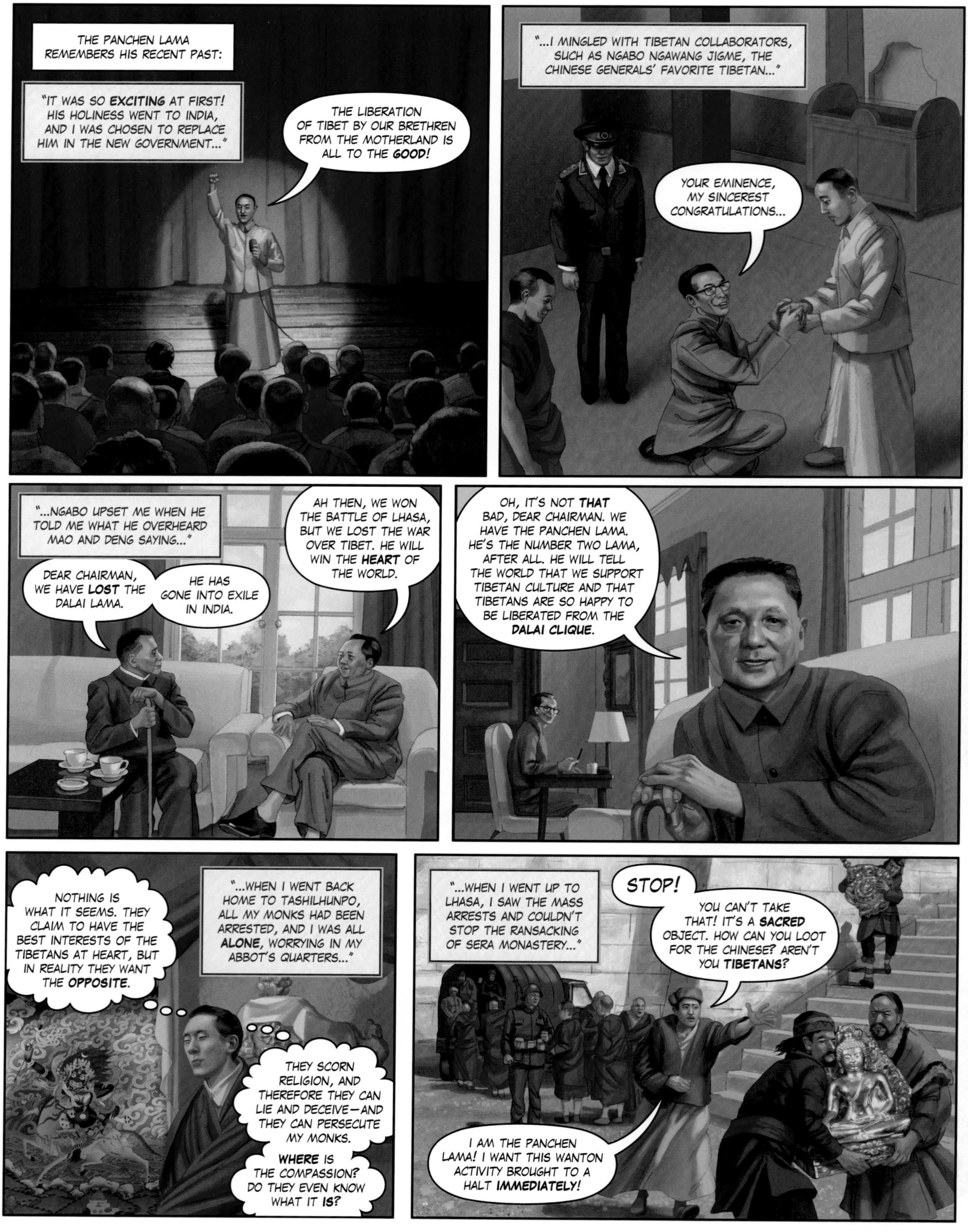
THE PANCHEN LAMA REMEMBERS HIS RECENT PAST:
"IT WAS SO EXCITING AT FIRST! HIS HOLINESS WENT TO INDIA, AND I WAS CHOSEN TO REPLACE HIM IN THE NEW GOVERNMENT..."
THE LIBERATION OF TIBET BY OUR BRETHREN FROM THE MOTHERLAND IS ALL TO THE GOOD!
"...I MINGLED WITH TIBETAN COLLABORATORS, SUCH AS NGABO NGAWANG JIGME, THE CHINESE GENERALS' FAVORITE TIBETAN..."
YOUR EMINENCE, MY SINCEREST CONGRATULATIONS...
"...NGABO UPSET ME WHEN HE TOLD ME WHAT HE OVERHEARD MAO AND DENG SAYING..."
DEAR CHAIRMAN, WE HAVE LOST THE DALAI LAMA.
HE HAS GONE INTO EXILE IN INDIA.
AH THEN, WE WON THE BATTLE OF LHASA, BUT WE LOST THE WAR OVER TIBET. HE WILL WIN THE HEART OF THE WORLD.
OH, IT'S NOT THAT BAD, DEAR CHAIRMAN. WE HAVE THE PANCHEN LAMA. HE'S THE NUMBER TWO LAMA, AFTER ALL. HE WILL TELL THE WORLD THAT WE SUPPORT TIBETAN CULTURE AND THAT TIBETANS ARE SO HAPPY TO BE LIBERATED FROM THE DALAI CLIQUE.
NOTHING IS WHAT IT SEEMS. THEY CLAIM TO HAVE THE BEST INTERESTS OF THE TIBETANS AT HEART, BUT IN REALITY THEY WANT THE OPPOSITE.
"...WHEN I WENT BACK HOME TO TASHILHUNPO, ALL MY MONKS HAD BEEN ARRESTED, AND I WAS ALL ALONE, WORRYING IN MY ABBOT'S QUARTERS..."
THEY SCORN RELIGION, AND THEREFORE THEY CAN LIE AND DECEIVE—AND THEY CAN PERSECUTE MY MONKS.
WHERE IS THE COMPASSION? DO THEY EVEN KNOW WHAT IT IS?
"...WHEN I WENT UP TO LHASA, I SAW THE MASS ARRESTS AND COULDN'T STOP THE RANSACKING OF SERA MONASTERY..."
STOP!
YOU CAN'T TAKE THAT! IT'S A SACRED OBJECT. HOW CAN YOU LOOT FOR THE CHINESE? AREN'T YOU TIBETANS?
I AM THE PANCHEN LAMA! I WANT THIS WANTON ACTIVITY BROUGHT TO A HALT IMMEDIATELY!

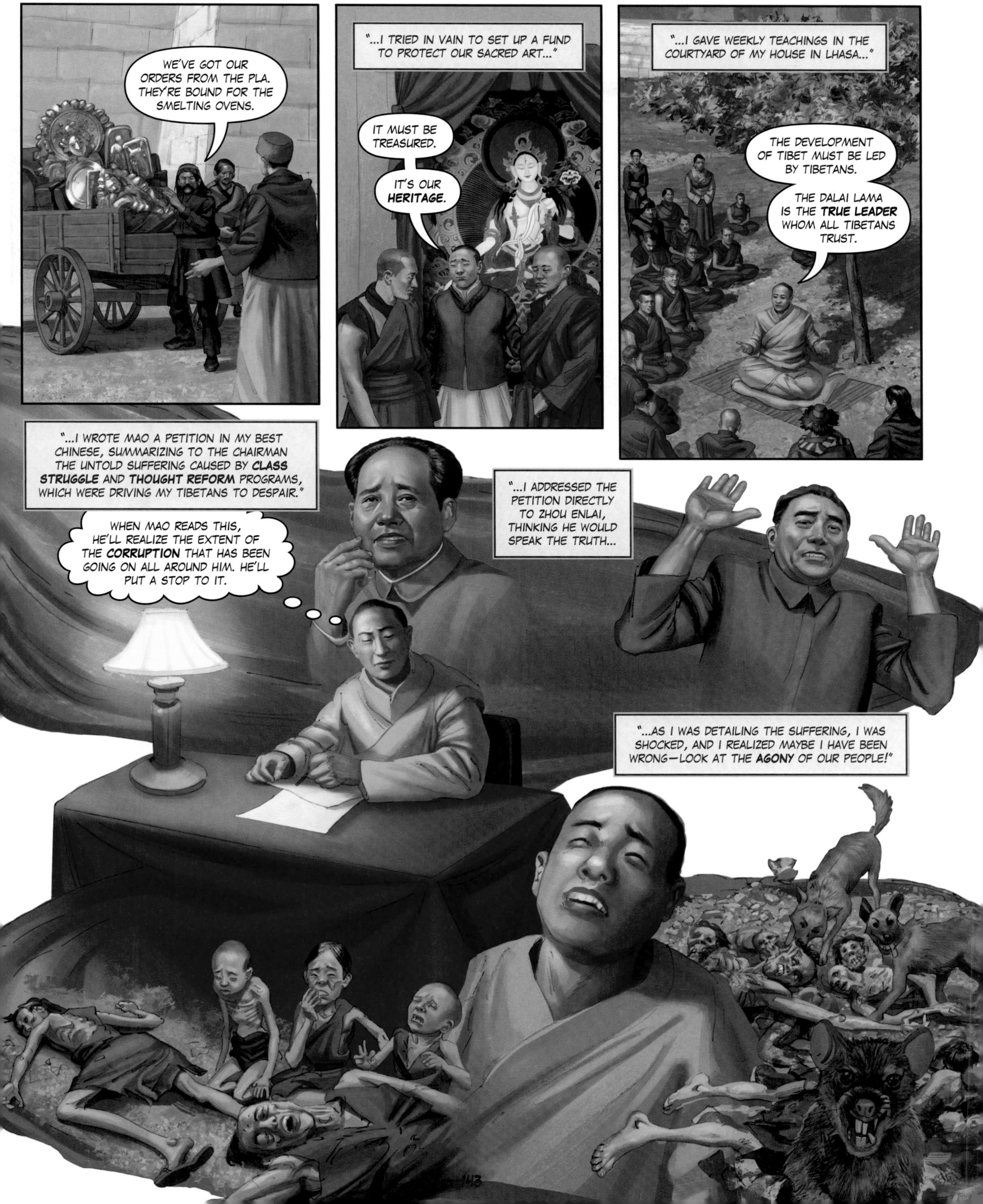
WE'VE GOT OUR ORDERS FROM THE PLA. THEY'RE BOUND FOR THE SMELTING OVENS.
"...I TRIED IN VAIN TO SET UP A FUND TO PROTECT OUR SACRED ART..."
IT MUST BE TREASURED.
IT'S OUR **HERITAGE**.
"...I GAVE WEEKLY TEACHINGS IN THE COURTYARD OF MY HOUSE IN LHASA..."
THE DEVELOPMENT OF TIBET MUST BE LED BY TIBETANS.
THE DALAI LAMA IS THE **TRUE LEADER** WHOM ALL TIBETANS TRUST.
"...I WROTE MAO A PETITION IN MY BEST CHINESE, SUMMARIZING TO THE CHAIRMAN THE UNTOLD SUFFERING CAUSED BY **CLASS STRUGGLE** AND **THOUGHT REFORM** PROGRAMS, WHICH WERE DRIVING MY TIBETANS TO DESPAIR."
WHEN MAO READS THIS, HE'LL REALIZE THE EXTENT OF THE **CORRUPTION** THAT HAS BEEN GOING ON ALL AROUND HIM. HE'LL PUT A STOP TO IT.
"...I ADDRESSED THE PETITION DIRECTLY TO ZHOU ENLAI, THINKING HE WOULD SPEAK THE TRUTH...
"...AS I WAS DETAILING THE SUFFERING, I WAS SHOCKED, AND I REALIZED MAYBE I HAVE BEEN WRONG—LOOK AT THE **AGONY** OF OUR PEOPLE!"

MARCH 10, 1964: *"The barbarous atrocities, even to the extent of exterminating the race and religious belief of the Tibetans, still continue, and the struggle of the people still goes on. Our way may be a hard and long one, but I believe that truth and faith must ultimately prevail."*

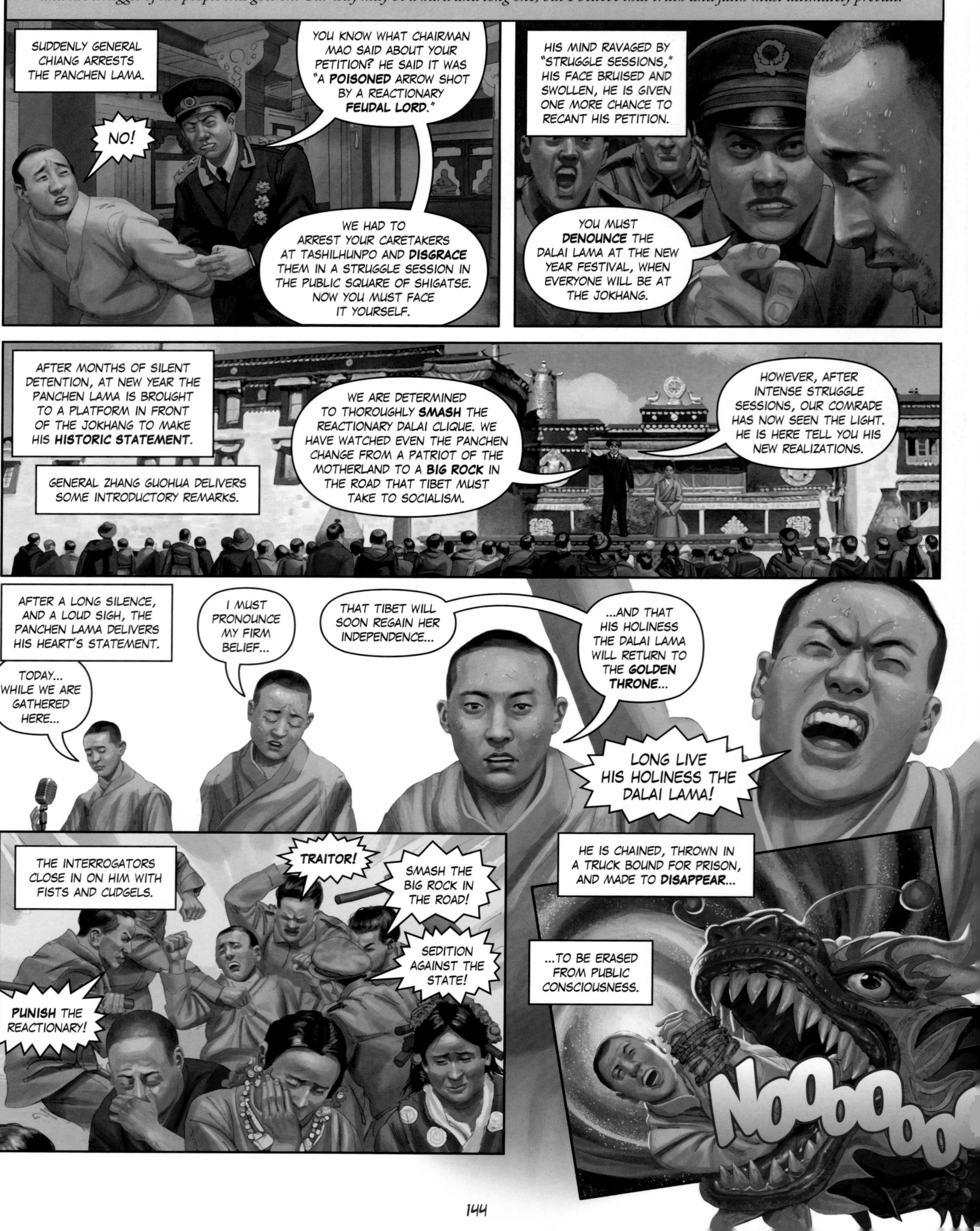
SUDDENLY GENERAL CHIANG ARRESTS THE PANCHEN LAMA.
NO!
YOU KNOW WHAT CHAIRMAN MAO SAID ABOUT YOUR PETITION? HE SAID IT WAS "A POISONED ARROW SHOT BY A REACTIONARY FEUDAL LORD."
WE HAD TO ARREST YOUR CARETAKERS AT TASHILHUNPO AND DISGRACE THEM IN A STRUGGLE SESSION IN THE PUBLIC SQUARE OF SHIGATSE. NOW YOU MUST FACE IT YOURSELF.
HIS MIND RAVAGED BY "STRUGGLE SESSIONS," HIS FACE BRUISED AND SWOLLEN, HE IS GIVEN ONE MORE CHANCE TO RECANT HIS PETITION.
YOU MUST DENOUNCE THE DALAI LAMA AT THE NEW YEAR FESTIVAL, WHEN EVERYONE WILL BE AT THE JOKHANG.
AFTER MONTHS OF SILENT DETENTION, AT NEW YEAR THE PANCHEN LAMA IS BROUGHT TO A PLATFORM IN FRONT OF THE JOKHANG TO MAKE HIS HISTORIC STATEMENT.
GENERAL ZHANG GUOHUA DELIVERS SOME INTRODUCTORY REMARKS.
WE ARE DETERMINED TO THOROUGHLY SMASH THE REACTIONARY DALAI CLIQUE. WE HAVE WATCHED EVEN THE PANCHEN CHANGE FROM A PATRIOT OF THE MOTHERLAND TO A BIG ROCK IN THE ROAD THAT TIBET MUST TAKE TO SOCIALISM.
HOWEVER, AFTER INTENSE STRUGGLE SESSIONS, OUR COMRADE HAS NOW SEEN THE LIGHT. HE IS HERE TELL YOU HIS NEW REALIZATIONS.
AFTER A LONG SILENCE, AND A LOUD SIGH, THE PANCHEN LAMA DELIVERS HIS HEART'S STATEMENT.
TODAY... WHILE WE ARE GATHERED HERE...
I MUST PRONOUNCE MY FIRM BELIEF...
THAT TIBET WILL SOON REGAIN HER INDEPENDENCE...
...AND THAT HIS HOLINESS THE DALAI LAMA WILL RETURN TO THE GOLDEN THRONE...
LONG LIVE HIS HOLINESS THE DALAI LAMA!
THE INTERROGATORS CLOSE IN ON HIM WITH FISTS AND CUDGELS.
TRAITOR!
SMASH THE BIG ROCK IN THE ROAD!
SEDITION AGAINST THE STATE!
PUNISH THE REACTIONARY!
HE IS CHAINED, THROWN IN A TRUCK BOUND FOR PRISON, AND MADE TO DISAPPEAR...
...TO BE ERASED FROM PUBLIC CONSCIOUSNESS.
NOOOOOOO

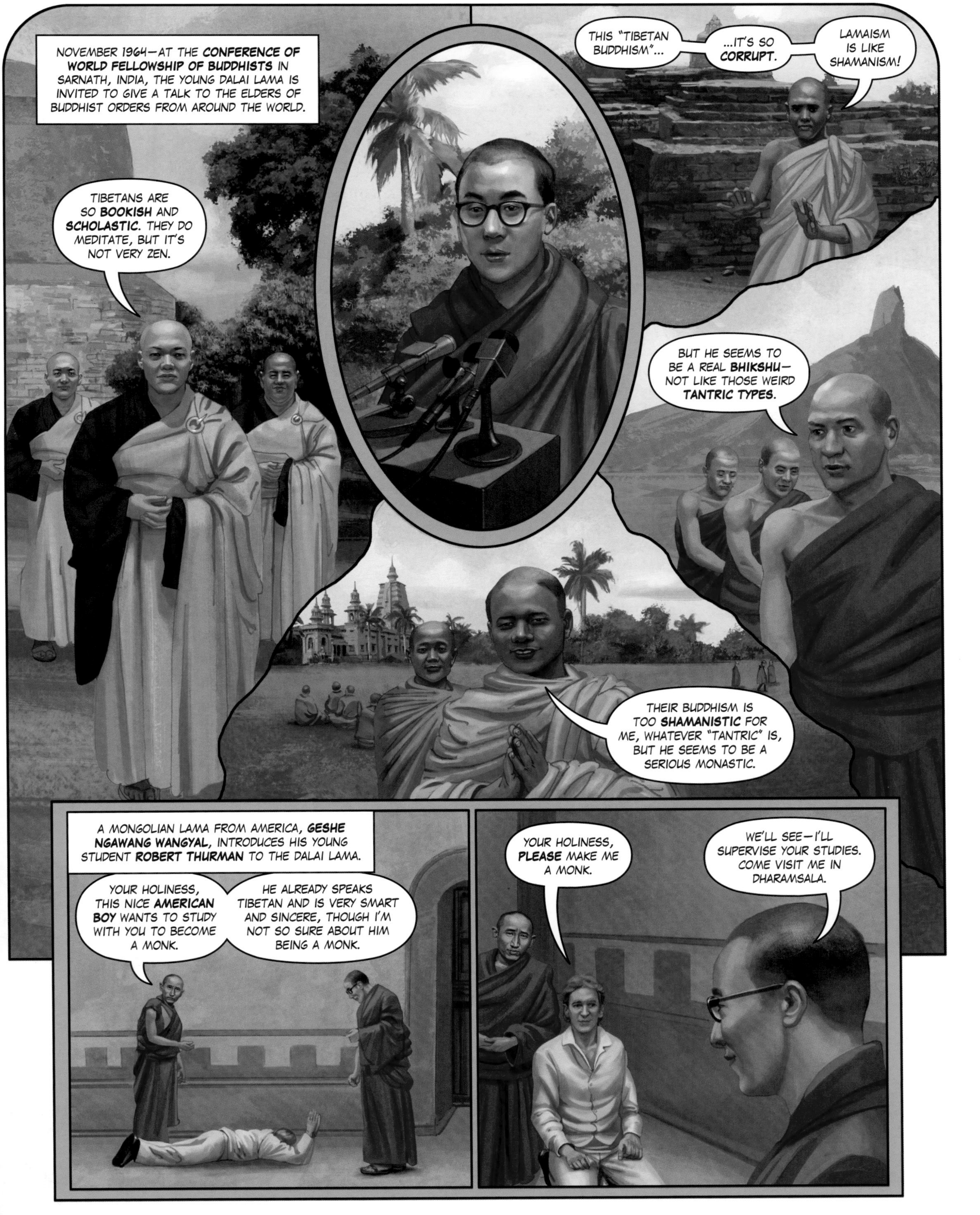

NOVEMBER 1964—AT THE **CONFERENCE OF WORLD FELLOWSHIP OF BUDDHISTS** IN SARNATH, INDIA, THE YOUNG DALAI LAMA IS INVITED TO GIVE A TALK TO THE ELDERS OF BUDDHIST ORDERS FROM AROUND THE WORLD.
TIBETANS ARE SO **BOOKISH** AND **SCHOLASTIC**. THEY DO MEDITATE, BUT IT'S NOT VERY ZEN.
THIS "TIBETAN BUDDHISM"...
...IT'S SO **CORRUPT**.
LAMAISM IS LIKE SHAMANISM!
BUT HE SEEMS TO BE A REAL **BHIKSHU**—NOT LIKE THOSE WEIRD **TANTRIC TYPES**.
THEIR BUDDHISM IS TOO **SHAMANISTIC** FOR ME, WHATEVER "TANTRIC" IS, BUT HE SEEMS TO BE A SERIOUS MONASTIC.
A MONGOLIAN LAMA FROM AMERICA, **GESHE NGAWANG WANGYAL**, INTRODUCES HIS YOUNG STUDENT **ROBERT THURMAN** TO THE DALAI LAMA.
YOUR HOLINESS, THIS NICE **AMERICAN BOY** WANTS TO STUDY WITH YOU TO BECOME A MONK.
HE ALREADY SPEAKS TIBETAN AND IS VERY SMART AND SINCERE, THOUGH I'M NOT SO SURE ABOUT HIM BEING A MONK.
YOUR HOLINESS, **PLEASE** MAKE ME A MONK.
WE'LL SEE—I'LL SUPERVISE YOUR STUDIES. COME VISIT ME IN DHARAMSALA.

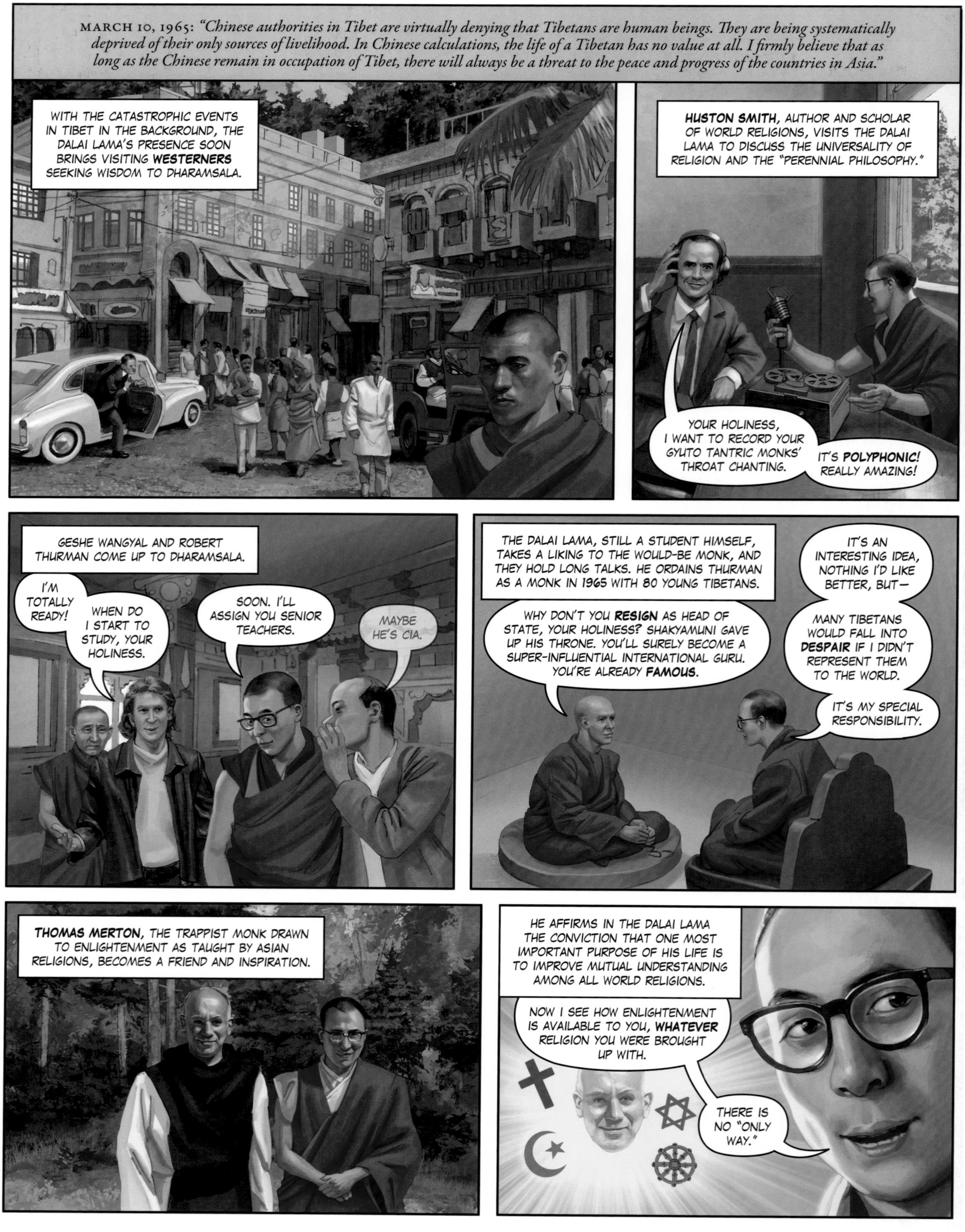
MARCH 10, 1965: "Chinese authorities in Tibet are virtually denying that Tibetans are human beings. They are being systematically deprived of their only sources of livelihood. In Chinese calculations, the life of a Tibetan has no value at all. I firmly believe that as long as the Chinese remain in occupation of Tibet, there will always be a threat to the peace and progress of the countries in Asia."
WITH THE CATASTROPHIC EVENTS IN TIBET IN THE BACKGROUND, THE DALAI LAMA'S PRESENCE SOON BRINGS VISITING **WESTERNERS** SEEKING WISDOM TO DHARAMSALA.
HUSTON SMITH, AUTHOR AND SCHOLAR OF WORLD RELIGIONS, VISITS THE DALAI LAMA TO DISCUSS THE UNIVERSALITY OF RELIGION AND THE "PERENNIAL PHILOSOPHY."
YOUR HOLINESS, I WANT TO RECORD YOUR GYUTO TANTRIC MONKS' THROAT CHANTING.
IT'S **POLYPHONIC!** REALLY AMAZING!
GESHE WANGYAL AND ROBERT THURMAN COME UP TO DHARAMSALA.
I'M TOTALLY READY!
WHEN DO I START TO STUDY, YOUR HOLINESS.
SOON. I'LL ASSIGN YOU SENIOR TEACHERS.
MAYBE HE'S CIA.
THE DALAI LAMA, STILL A STUDENT HIMSELF, TAKES A LIKING TO THE WOULD-BE MONK, AND THEY HOLD LONG TALKS. HE ORDAINS THURMAN AS A MONK IN 1965 WITH 80 YOUNG TIBETANS.
WHY DON'T YOU **RESIGN** AS HEAD OF STATE, YOUR HOLINESS? SHAKYAMUNI GAVE UP HIS THRONE. YOU'LL SURELY BECOME A SUPER-INFLUENTIAL INTERNATIONAL GURU. YOU'RE ALREADY **FAMOUS**.
IT'S AN INTERESTING IDEA, NOTHING I'D LIKE BETTER, BUT—
MANY TIBETANS WOULD FALL INTO **DESPAIR** IF I DIDN'T REPRESENT THEM TO THE WORLD.
IT'S MY SPECIAL RESPONSIBILITY.
THOMAS MERTON, THE TRAPPIST MONK DRAWN TO ENLIGHTENMENT AS TAUGHT BY ASIAN RELIGIONS, BECOMES A FRIEND AND INSPIRATION.
HE AFFIRMS IN THE DALAI LAMA THE CONVICTION THAT ONE MOST IMPORTANT PURPOSE OF HIS LIFE IS TO IMPROVE MUTUAL UNDERSTANDING AMONG ALL WORLD RELIGIONS.
NOW I SEE HOW ENLIGHTENMENT IS AVAILABLE TO YOU, **WHATEVER** RELIGION YOU WERE BROUGHT UP WITH.
THERE IS NO "ONLY WAY."

MARCH 10, 1966: *"It is now seven years since that historic day when the people of Tibet rose in spontaneous revolt against the tyranny and oppression of the Chinese Communist military occupation. Against fearful odds and in utter self-sacrifice, our people stood up as one against the might of their conquerors. Many died in the struggle and others suffered torture and humiliation before being killed. It is to the memory of these martyrs of Tibetan nationalism and the cause for which they have made their supreme sacrifice that we dedicate this day. . . ."*

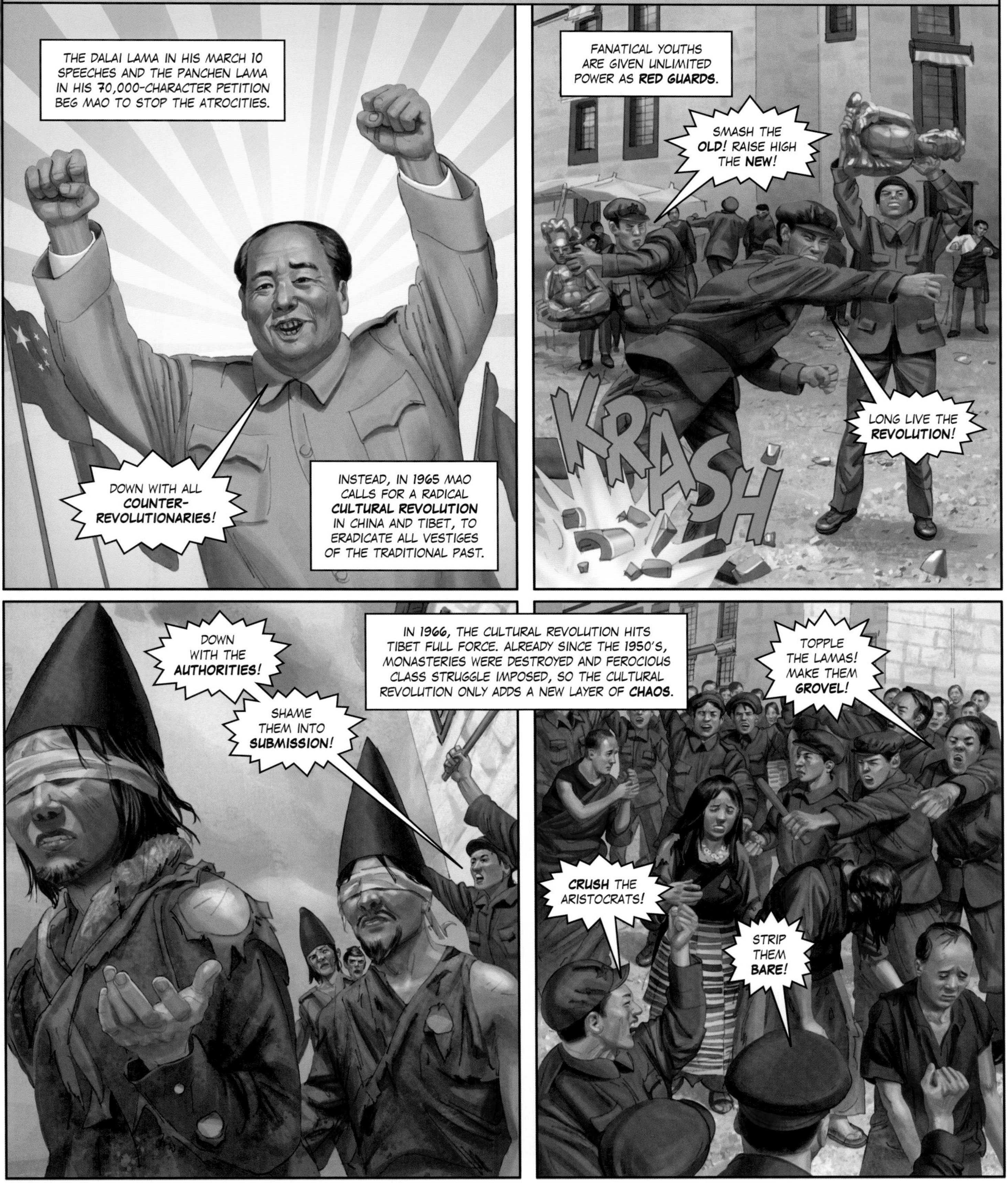

THE DALAI LAMA IN HIS MARCH 10 SPEECHES AND THE PANCHEN LAMA IN HIS 70,000-CHARACTER PETITION BEG MAO TO STOP THE ATROCITIES.
DOWN WITH ALL COUNTER-REVOLUTIONARIES!
INSTEAD, IN 1965 MAO CALLS FOR A RADICAL CULTURAL REVOLUTION IN CHINA AND TIBET, TO ERADICATE ALL VESTIGES OF THE TRADITIONAL PAST.
FANATICAL YOUTHS ARE GIVEN UNLIMITED POWER AS RED GUARDS.
SMASH THE OLD! RAISE HIGH THE NEW!
KRASH
LONG LIVE THE REVOLUTION!
IN 1966, THE CULTURAL REVOLUTION HITS TIBET FULL FORCE. ALREADY SINCE THE 1950'S, MONASTERIES WERE DESTROYED AND FEROCIOUS CLASS STRUGGLE IMPOSED, SO THE CULTURAL REVOLUTION ONLY ADDS A NEW LAYER OF CHAOS.
DOWN WITH THE AUTHORITIES!
SHAME THEM INTO SUBMISSION!
TOPPLE THE LAMAS! MAKE THEM GROVEL!
CRUSH THE ARISTOCRATS!
STRIP THEM BARE!

MARCH 10, 1966: *"... Since the invasion of Tibet in 1949, our people were reduced to the status of a subject race under the shackles of an alien conqueror bent on wiping out every vestige of our national and cultural heritage. They have killed and tortured our people; they looted the ancient treasures of Tibet; they have deprived our people of even the smallest traces of fundamental freedom...."*

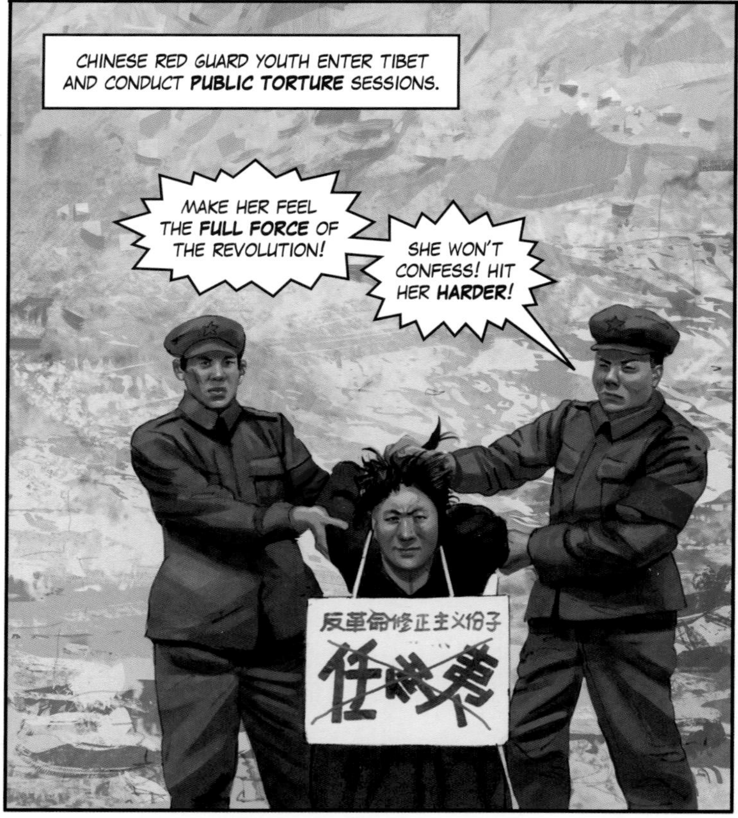
CHINESE RED GUARD YOUTH ENTER TIBET AND CONDUCT **PUBLIC TORTURE** SESSIONS.
MAKE HER FEEL THE **FULL FORCE** OF THE REVOLUTION!
SHE WON'T CONFESS! HIT HER **HARDER**!
反革命修正主义份子

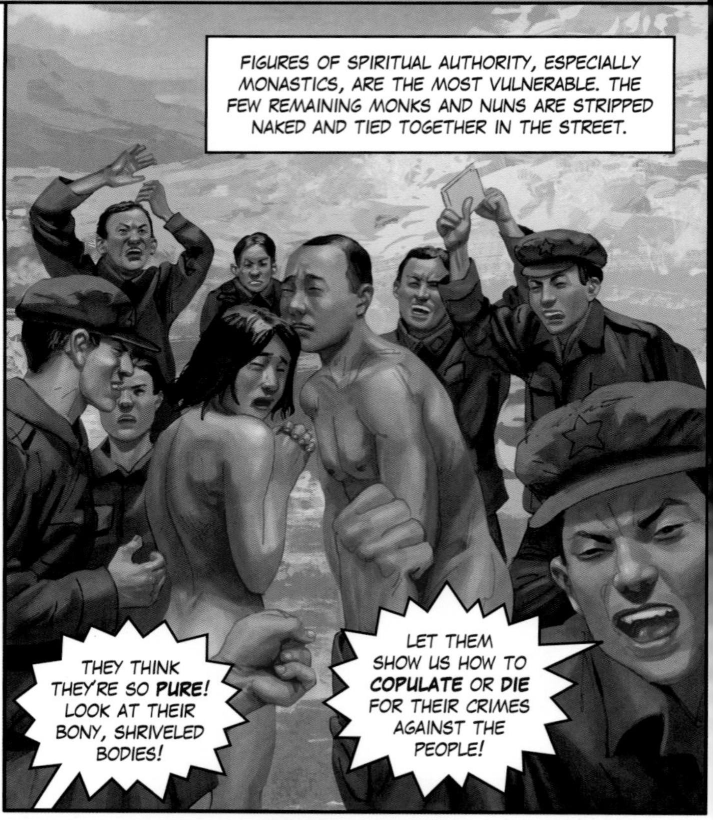
FIGURES OF SPIRITUAL AUTHORITY, ESPECIALLY MONASTICS, ARE THE MOST VULNERABLE. THE FEW REMAINING MONKS AND NUNS ARE STRIPPED NAKED AND TIED TOGETHER IN THE STREET.
THEY THINK THEY'RE SO **PURE**! LOOK AT THEIR BONY, SHRIVELED BODIES!
LET THEM SHOW US HOW TO **COPULATE** OR **DIE** FOR THEIR CRIMES AGAINST THE PEOPLE!

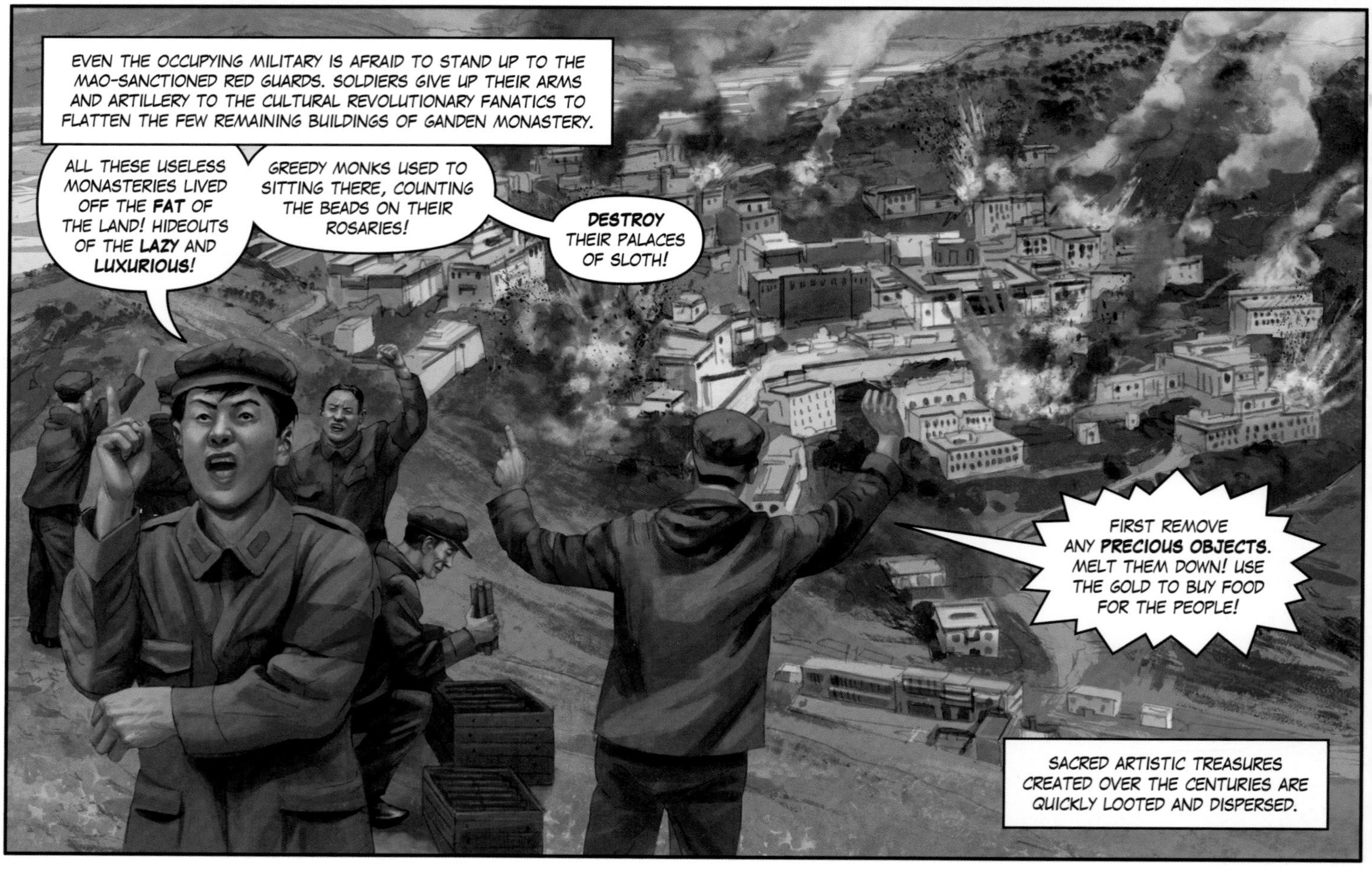
EVEN THE OCCUPYING MILITARY IS AFRAID TO STAND UP TO THE MAO-SANCTIONED RED GUARDS. SOLDIERS GIVE UP THEIR ARMS AND ARTILLERY TO THE CULTURAL REVOLUTIONARY FANATICS TO FLATTEN THE FEW REMAINING BUILDINGS OF GANDEN MONASTERY.
ALL THESE USELESS MONASTERIES LIVED OFF THE **FAT** OF THE LAND! HIDEOUTS OF THE **LAZY** AND **LUXURIOUS**!
GREEDY MONKS USED TO SITTING THERE, COUNTING THE BEADS ON THEIR ROSARIES!
DESTROY THEIR PALACES OF SLOTH!
FIRST REMOVE ANY **PRECIOUS OBJECTS**. MELT THEM DOWN! USE THE GOLD TO BUY FOOD FOR THE PEOPLE!
SACRED ARTISTIC TREASURES CREATED OVER THE CENTURIES ARE QUICKLY LOOTED AND DISPERSED.

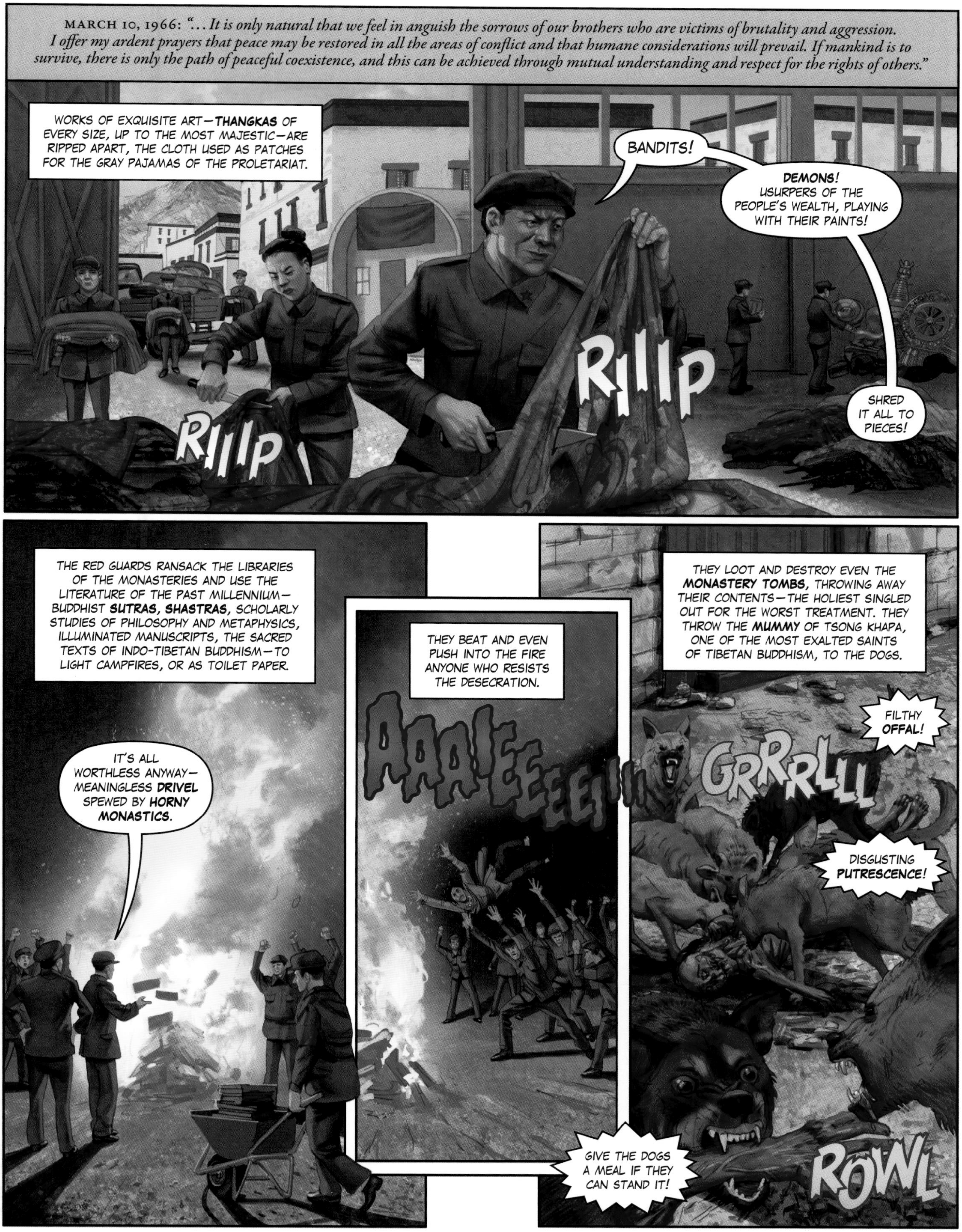
MARCH 10, 1966: "...It is only natural that we feel in anguish the sorrows of our brothers who are victims of brutality and aggression. I offer my ardent prayers that peace may be restored in all the areas of conflict and that humane considerations will prevail. If mankind is to survive, there is only the path of peaceful coexistence, and this can be achieved through mutual understanding and respect for the rights of others."
WORKS OF EXQUISITE ART—THANGKAS OF EVERY SIZE, UP TO THE MOST MAJESTIC—ARE RIPPED APART, THE CLOTH USED AS PATCHES FOR THE GRAY PAJAMAS OF THE PROLETARIAT.
BANDITS!
DEMONS! USURPERS OF THE PEOPLE'S WEALTH, PLAYING WITH THEIR PAINTS!
RIIIP
RIIIP
SHRED IT ALL TO PIECES!
THE RED GUARDS RANSACK THE LIBRARIES OF THE MONASTERIES AND USE THE LITERATURE OF THE PAST MILLENNIUM—BUDDHIST SUTRAS, SHASTRAS, SCHOLARLY STUDIES OF PHILOSOPHY AND METAPHYSICS, ILLUMINATED MANUSCRIPTS, THE SACRED TEXTS OF INDO-TIBETAN BUDDHISM—TO LIGHT CAMPFIRES, OR AS TOILET PAPER.
IT'S ALL WORTHLESS ANYWAY—MEANINGLESS DRIVEL SPEWED BY HORNY MONASTICS.
THEY BEAT AND EVEN PUSH INTO THE FIRE ANYONE WHO RESISTS THE DESECRATION.
AAAIEEEIIII
THEY LOOT AND DESTROY EVEN THE MONASTERY TOMBS, THROWING AWAY THEIR CONTENTS—THE HOLIEST SINGLED OUT FOR THE WORST TREATMENT. THEY THROW THE MUMMY OF TSONG KHAPA, ONE OF THE MOST EXALTED SAINTS OF TIBETAN BUDDHISM, TO THE DOGS.
FILTHY OFFAL!
GRRRLLL
DISGUSTING PUTRESCENCE!
GIVE THE DOGS A MEAL IF THEY CAN STAND IT!
ROWL

MARCH 10, 1967: *"The Communist Chinese occupation is one long catalogue of untold miseries and sufferings. Farmers and herdsmen are deprived of the fruits of their labor. Many Tibetans on meager rations are forced to construct military roads and fortifications. Countless numbers are victims of 'public trials' and 'purging sessions' in which all manner of public humiliation and brutalities have been inflicted. . . ."*

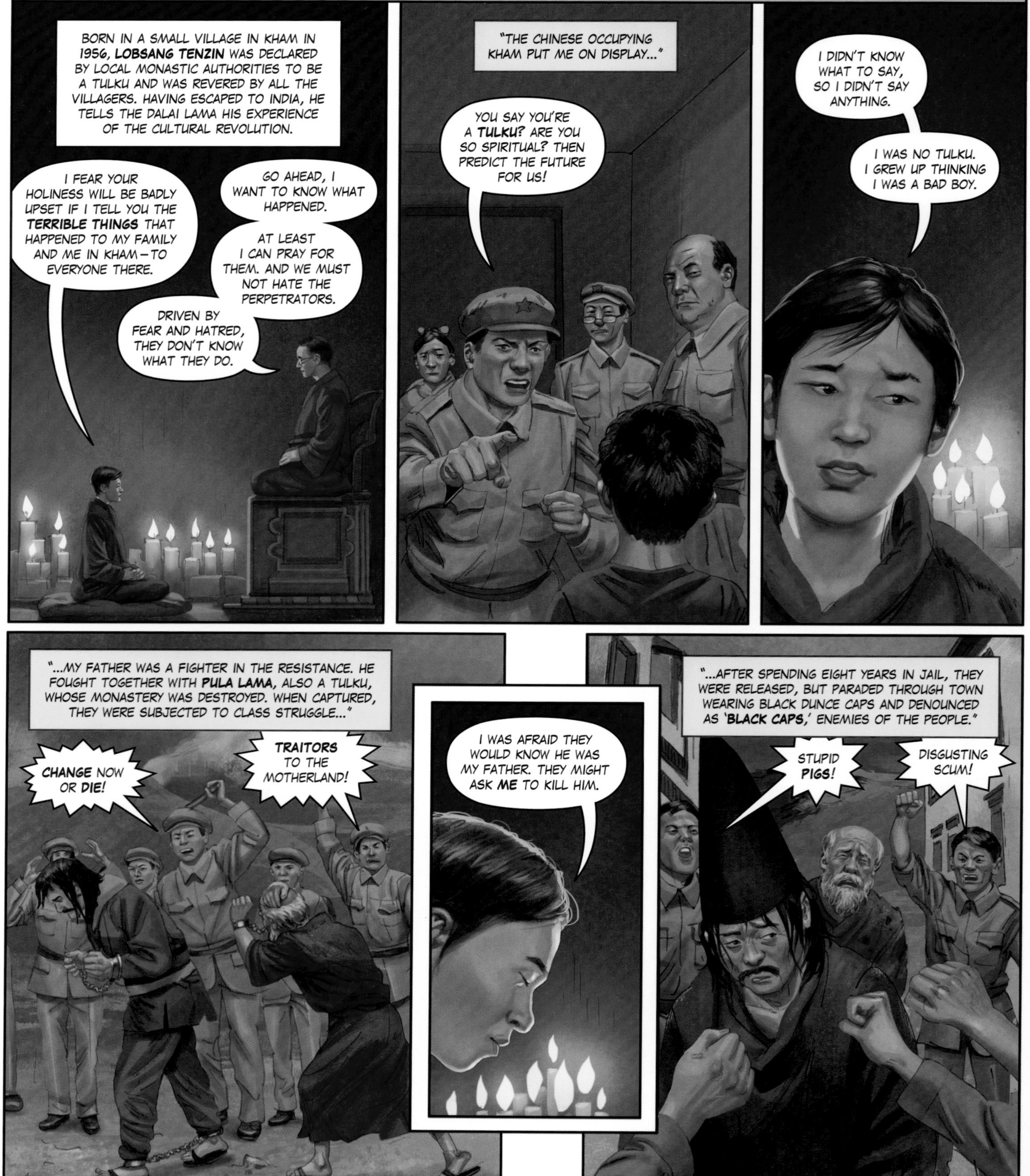
BORN IN A SMALL VILLAGE IN KHAM IN 1956, LOBSANG TENZIN WAS DECLARED BY LOCAL MONASTIC AUTHORITIES TO BE A TULKU AND WAS REVERED BY ALL THE VILLAGERS. HAVING ESCAPED TO INDIA, HE TELLS THE DALAI LAMA HIS EXPERIENCE OF THE CULTURAL REVOLUTION.
I FEAR YOUR HOLINESS WILL BE BADLY UPSET IF I TELL YOU THE TERRIBLE THINGS THAT HAPPENED TO MY FAMILY AND ME IN KHAM—TO EVERYONE THERE.
GO AHEAD, I WANT TO KNOW WHAT HAPPENED.
AT LEAST I CAN PRAY FOR THEM. AND WE MUST NOT HATE THE PERPETRATORS.
DRIVEN BY FEAR AND HATRED, THEY DON'T KNOW WHAT THEY DO.
"THE CHINESE OCCUPYING KHAM PUT ME ON DISPLAY..."
YOU SAY YOU'RE A TULKU? ARE YOU SO SPIRITUAL? THEN PREDICT THE FUTURE FOR US!
I DIDN'T KNOW WHAT TO SAY, SO I DIDN'T SAY ANYTHING.
I WAS NO TULKU. I GREW UP THINKING I WAS A BAD BOY.
"...MY FATHER WAS A FIGHTER IN THE RESISTANCE. HE FOUGHT TOGETHER WITH PULA LAMA, ALSO A TULKU, WHOSE MONASTERY WAS DESTROYED. WHEN CAPTURED, THEY WERE SUBJECTED TO CLASS STRUGGLE..."
CHANGE NOW OR DIE!
TRAITORS TO THE MOTHERLAND!
I WAS AFRAID THEY WOULD KNOW HE WAS MY FATHER. THEY MIGHT ASK ME TO KILL HIM.
"...AFTER SPENDING EIGHT YEARS IN JAIL, THEY WERE RELEASED, BUT PARADED THROUGH TOWN WEARING BLACK DUNCE CAPS AND DENOUNCED AS 'BLACK CAPS,' ENEMIES OF THE PEOPLE."
STUPID PIGS!
DISGUSTING SCUM!

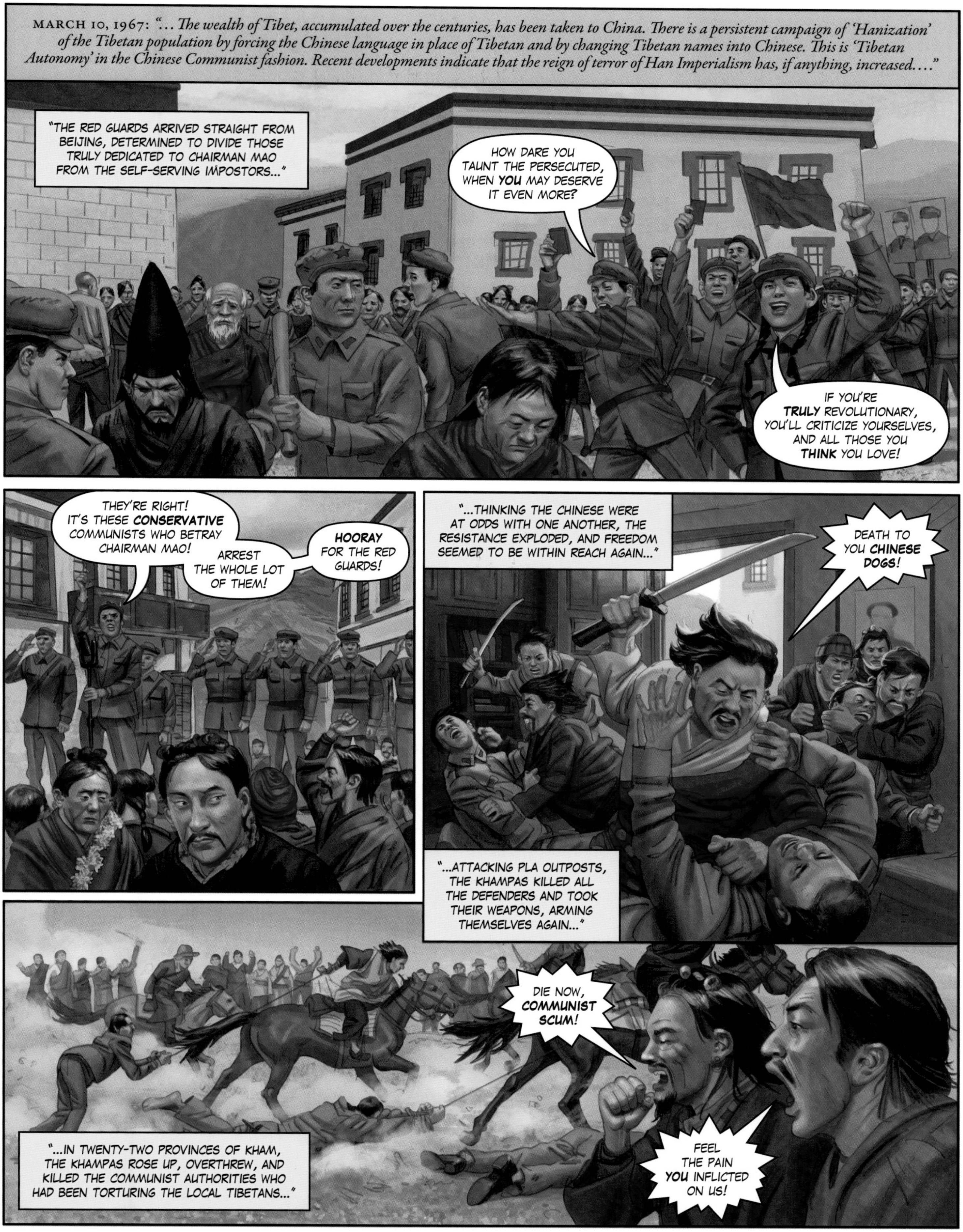
MARCH 10, 1967: "... The wealth of Tibet, accumulated over the centuries, has been taken to China. There is a persistent campaign of 'Hanization' of the Tibetan population by forcing the Chinese language in place of Tibetan and by changing Tibetan names into Chinese. This is 'Tibetan Autonomy' in the Chinese Communist fashion. Recent developments indicate that the reign of terror of Han Imperialism has, if anything, increased...."
"THE RED GUARDS ARRIVED STRAIGHT FROM BEIJING, DETERMINED TO DIVIDE THOSE TRULY DEDICATED TO CHAIRMAN MAO FROM THE SELF-SERVING IMPOSTORS..."
HOW DARE YOU TAUNT THE PERSECUTED, WHEN YOU MAY DESERVE IT EVEN MORE?
IF YOU'RE TRULY REVOLUTIONARY, YOU'LL CRITICIZE YOURSELVES, AND ALL THOSE YOU THINK YOU LOVE!
THEY'RE RIGHT! IT'S THESE CONSERVATIVE COMMUNISTS WHO BETRAY CHAIRMAN MAO!
ARREST THE WHOLE LOT OF THEM!
HOORAY FOR THE RED GUARDS!
"...THINKING THE CHINESE WERE AT ODDS WITH ONE ANOTHER, THE RESISTANCE EXPLODED, AND FREEDOM SEEMED TO BE WITHIN REACH AGAIN..."
DEATH TO YOU CHINESE DOGS!
"...ATTACKING PLA OUTPOSTS, THE KHAMPAS KILLED ALL THE DEFENDERS AND TOOK THEIR WEAPONS, ARMING THEMSELVES AGAIN..."
DIE NOW, COMMUNIST SCUM!
"...IN TWENTY-TWO PROVINCES OF KHAM, THE KHAMPAS ROSE UP, OVERTHREW, AND KILLED THE COMMUNIST AUTHORITIES WHO HAD BEEN TORTURING THE LOCAL TIBETANS..."
FEEL THE PAIN YOU INFLICTED ON US!

MARCH 10, 1967: *"… While we look with profound sorrow at the abject misery and suffering of our people in Tibet, we cannot but renew our firm determination to regain their freedom. During our exile, we have made every effort to prepare ourselves for the day when we can return to a free Tibet. To this end we have promulgated a provisional constitution for Tibet based on justice, equality and democracy, as laid down by Lord Buddha."*

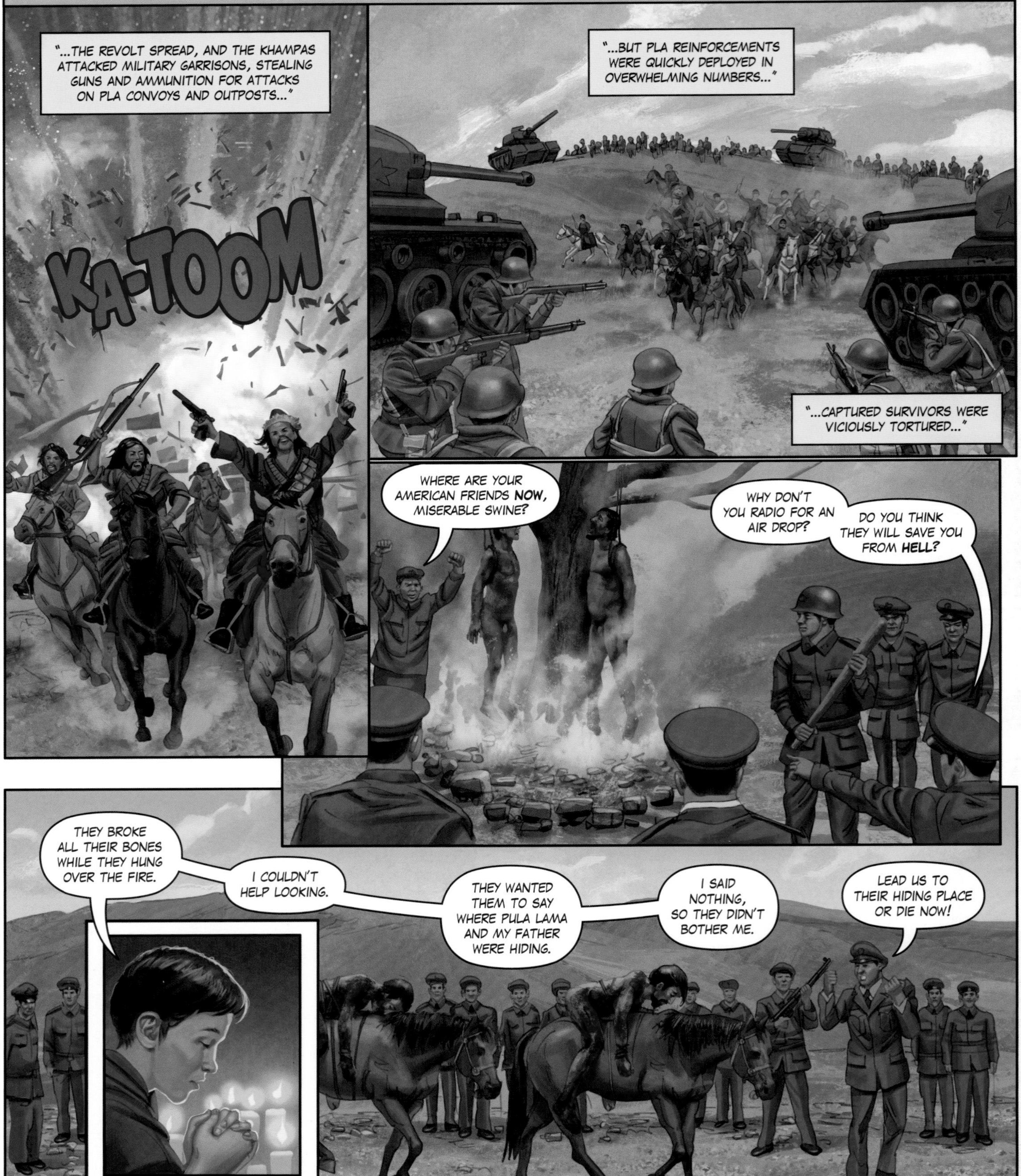

"...THE REVOLT SPREAD, AND THE KHAMPAS ATTACKED MILITARY GARRISONS, STEALING GUNS AND AMMUNITION FOR ATTACKS ON PLA CONVOYS AND OUTPOSTS..."
KA-TOOM
"...BUT PLA REINFORCEMENTS WERE QUICKLY DEPLOYED IN OVERWHELMING NUMBERS..."
"...CAPTURED SURVIVORS WERE VICIOUSLY TORTURED..."
WHERE ARE YOUR AMERICAN FRIENDS **NOW,** MISERABLE SWINE?
WHY DON'T YOU RADIO FOR AN AIR DROP?
DO YOU THINK THEY WILL SAVE YOU FROM **HELL?**
THEY BROKE ALL THEIR BONES WHILE THEY HUNG OVER THE FIRE.
I COULDN'T HELP LOOKING.
THEY WANTED THEM TO SAY WHERE PULA LAMA AND MY FATHER WERE HIDING.
I SAID NOTHING, SO THEY DIDN'T BOTHER ME.
LEAD US TO THEIR HIDING PLACE OR DIE NOW!

MARCH 10, 1968: *"We firmly believe that for the lasting peace of Asia and of the world, India and China should remain at peace. We believe that, unless Tibet is restored her freedom and created into a demilitarized zone, peace will not be achieved. We also believe that the mighty voice and support of India will hasten the day when the anguish of the people of Tibet will come to an end, with freedom, dignity and peace restored."*

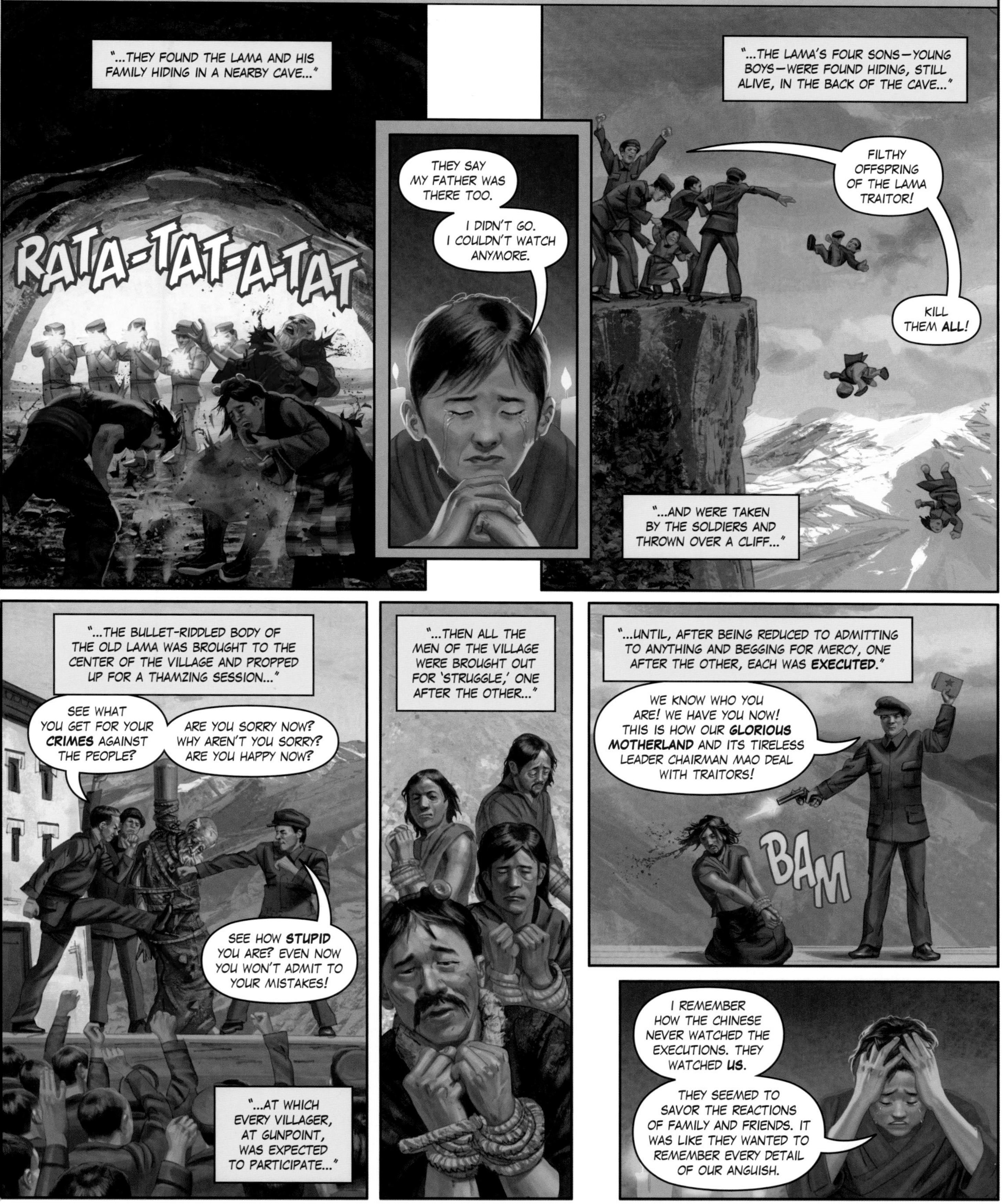

"...THEY FOUND THE LAMA AND HIS FAMILY HIDING IN A NEARBY CAVE..."
RATA-TAT-A-TAT
THEY SAY MY FATHER WAS THERE TOO.
I DIDN'T GO. I COULDN'T WATCH ANYMORE.
"...THE LAMA'S FOUR SONS—YOUNG BOYS—WERE FOUND HIDING, STILL ALIVE, IN THE BACK OF THE CAVE..."
FILTHY OFFSPRING OF THE LAMA TRAITOR!
KILL THEM ALL!
"...AND WERE TAKEN BY THE SOLDIERS AND THROWN OVER A CLIFF..."
"...THE BULLET-RIDDLED BODY OF THE OLD LAMA WAS BROUGHT TO THE CENTER OF THE VILLAGE AND PROPPED UP FOR A THAMZING SESSION..."
SEE WHAT YOU GET FOR YOUR CRIMES AGAINST THE PEOPLE?
ARE YOU SORRY NOW? WHY AREN'T YOU SORRY? ARE YOU HAPPY NOW?
SEE HOW STUPID YOU ARE? EVEN NOW YOU WON'T ADMIT TO YOUR MISTAKES!
"...AT WHICH EVERY VILLAGER, AT GUNPOINT, WAS EXPECTED TO PARTICIPATE..."
"...THEN ALL THE MEN OF THE VILLAGE WERE BROUGHT OUT FOR 'STRUGGLE,' ONE AFTER THE OTHER..."
"...UNTIL, AFTER BEING REDUCED TO ADMITTING TO ANYTHING AND BEGGING FOR MERCY, ONE AFTER THE OTHER, EACH WAS EXECUTED."
WE KNOW WHO YOU ARE! WE HAVE YOU NOW! THIS IS HOW OUR GLORIOUS MOTHERLAND AND ITS TIRELESS LEADER CHAIRMAN MAO DEAL WITH TRAITORS!
BAM
I REMEMBER HOW THE CHINESE NEVER WATCHED THE EXECUTIONS. THEY WATCHED US.
THEY SEEMED TO SAVOR THE REACTIONS OF FAMILY AND FRIENDS. IT WAS LIKE THEY WANTED TO REMEMBER EVERY DETAIL OF OUR ANGUISH.

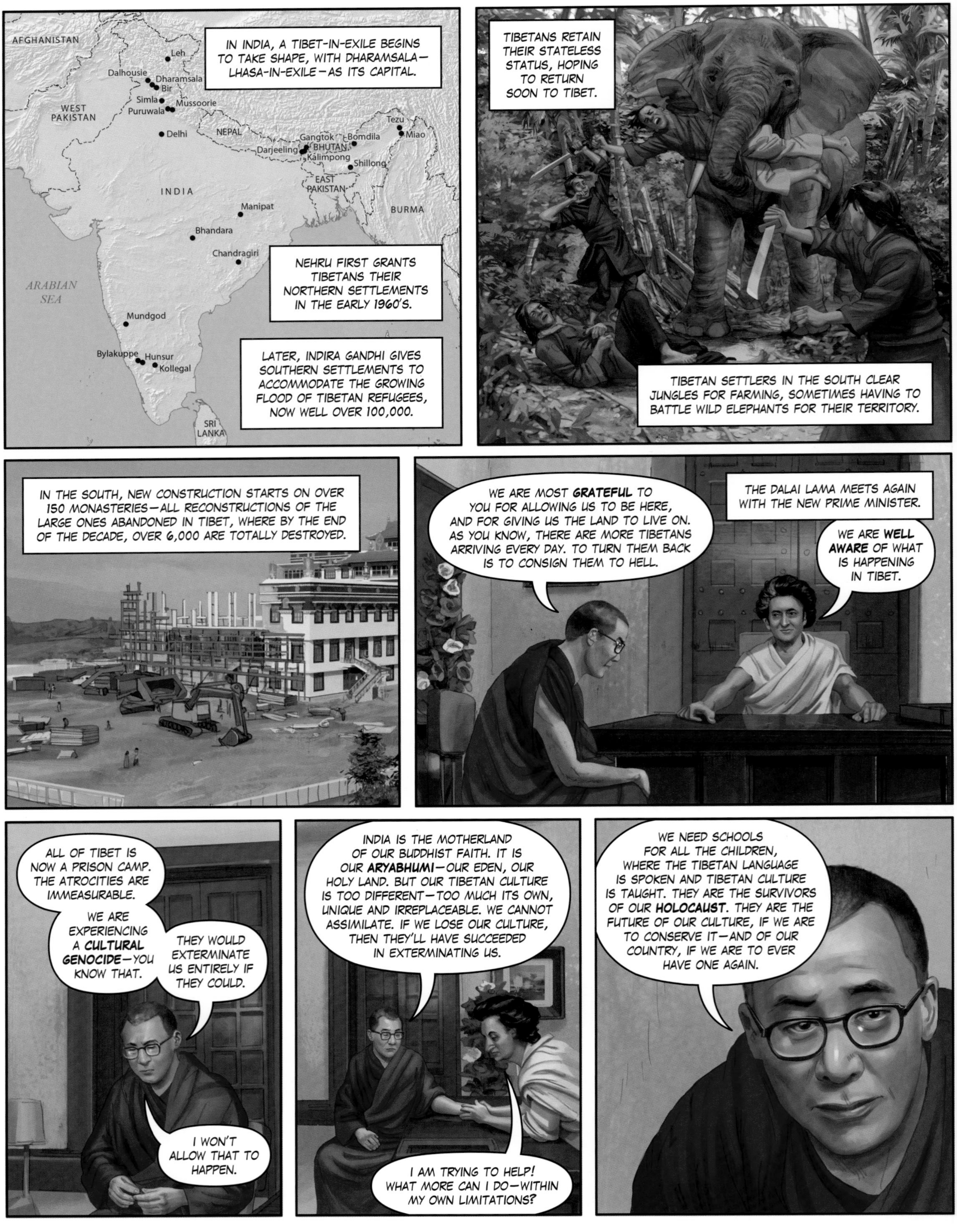
IN INDIA, A TIBET-IN-EXILE BEGINS TO TAKE SHAPE, WITH DHARAMSALA—LHASA-IN-EXILE—AS ITS CAPITAL.
AFGHANISTAN
Leh
Dalhousie
Dharamsala
Bir
Simla
Mussoorie
Puruwala
WEST PAKISTAN
Delhi
NEPAL
Tezu
Miao
Gangtok
Bomdila
Darjeeling
BHUTAN
Kalimpong
Shillong
EAST PAKISTAN
INDIA
Manipat
BURMA
Bhandara
Chandragiri
ARABIAN SEA
NEHRU FIRST GRANTS TIBETANS THEIR NORTHERN SETTLEMENTS IN THE EARLY 1960'S.
Mundgod
Bylakuppe
Hunsur
Kollegal
LATER, INDIRA GANDHI GIVES SOUTHERN SETTLEMENTS TO ACCOMMODATE THE GROWING FLOOD OF TIBETAN REFUGEES, NOW WELL OVER 100,000.
SRI LANKA
TIBETANS RETAIN THEIR STATELESS STATUS, HOPING TO RETURN SOON TO TIBET.
TIBETAN SETTLERS IN THE SOUTH CLEAR JUNGLES FOR FARMING, SOMETIMES HAVING TO BATTLE WILD ELEPHANTS FOR THEIR TERRITORY.
IN THE SOUTH, NEW CONSTRUCTION STARTS ON OVER 150 MONASTERIES—ALL RECONSTRUCTIONS OF THE LARGE ONES ABANDONED IN TIBET, WHERE BY THE END OF THE DECADE, OVER 6,000 ARE TOTALLY DESTROYED.
THE DALAI LAMA MEETS AGAIN WITH THE NEW PRIME MINISTER.
WE ARE MOST **GRATEFUL** TO YOU FOR ALLOWING US TO BE HERE, AND FOR GIVING US THE LAND TO LIVE ON. AS YOU KNOW, THERE ARE MORE TIBETANS ARRIVING EVERY DAY. TO TURN THEM BACK IS TO CONSIGN THEM TO HELL.
WE ARE **WELL AWARE** OF WHAT IS HAPPENING IN TIBET.
ALL OF TIBET IS NOW A PRISON CAMP. THE ATROCITIES ARE IMMEASURABLE.
WE ARE EXPERIENCING A **CULTURAL GENOCIDE**—YOU KNOW THAT.
THEY WOULD EXTERMINATE US ENTIRELY IF THEY COULD.
I WON'T ALLOW THAT TO HAPPEN.
INDIA IS THE MOTHERLAND OF OUR BUDDHIST FAITH. IT IS OUR **ARYABHUMI**—OUR EDEN, OUR HOLY LAND. BUT OUR TIBETAN CULTURE IS TOO DIFFERENT—TOO MUCH ITS OWN, UNIQUE AND IRREPLACEABLE. WE CANNOT ASSIMILATE. IF WE LOSE OUR CULTURE, THEN THEY'LL HAVE SUCCEEDED IN EXTERMINATING US.
I AM TRYING TO HELP! WHAT MORE CAN I DO—WITHIN MY OWN LIMITATIONS?
WE NEED SCHOOLS FOR ALL THE CHILDREN, WHERE THE TIBETAN LANGUAGE IS SPOKEN AND TIBETAN CULTURE IS TAUGHT. THEY ARE THE SURVIVORS OF OUR **HOLOCAUST**. THEY ARE THE FUTURE OF OUR CULTURE, IF WE ARE TO CONSERVE IT—AND OF OUR COUNTRY, IF WE ARE TO EVER HAVE ONE AGAIN.

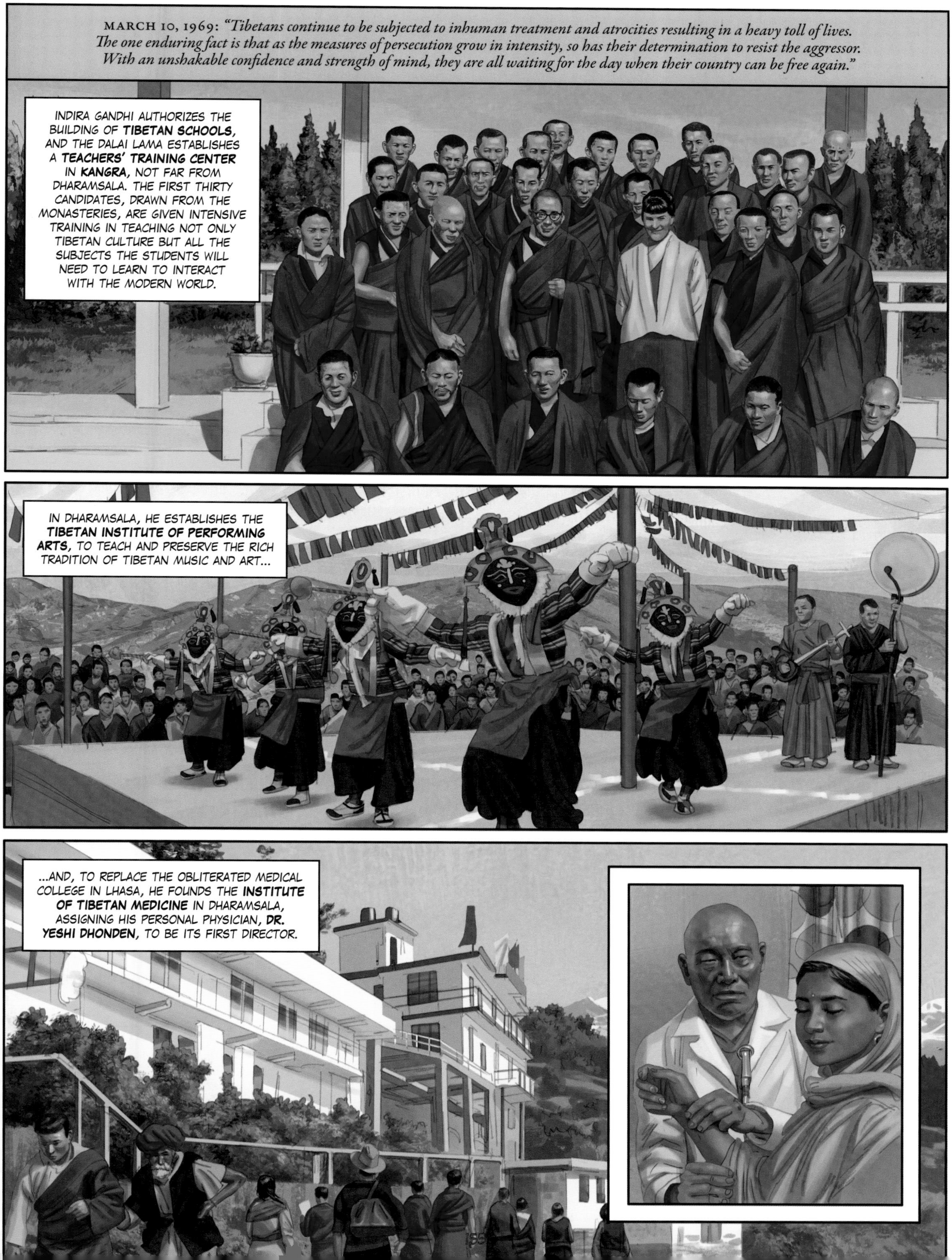
MARCH 10, 1969: "Tibetans continue to be subjected to inhuman treatment and atrocities resulting in a heavy toll of lives. The one enduring fact is that as the measures of persecution grow in intensity, so has their determination to resist the aggressor. With an unshakable confidence and strength of mind, they are all waiting for the day when their country can be free again."
INDIRA GANDHI AUTHORIZES THE BUILDING OF TIBETAN SCHOOLS, AND THE DALAI LAMA ESTABLISHES A TEACHERS' TRAINING CENTER IN KANGRA, NOT FAR FROM DHARAMSALA. THE FIRST THIRTY CANDIDATES, DRAWN FROM THE MONASTERIES, ARE GIVEN INTENSIVE TRAINING IN TEACHING NOT ONLY TIBETAN CULTURE BUT ALL THE SUBJECTS THE STUDENTS WILL NEED TO LEARN TO INTERACT WITH THE MODERN WORLD.
IN DHARAMSALA, HE ESTABLISHES THE TIBETAN INSTITUTE OF PERFORMING ARTS, TO TEACH AND PRESERVE THE RICH TRADITION OF TIBETAN MUSIC AND ART...
...AND, TO REPLACE THE OBLITERATED MEDICAL COLLEGE IN LHASA, HE FOUNDS THE INSTITUTE OF TIBETAN MEDICINE IN DHARAMSALA, ASSIGNING HIS PERSONAL PHYSICIAN, DR. YESHI DHONDEN, TO BE ITS FIRST DIRECTOR.

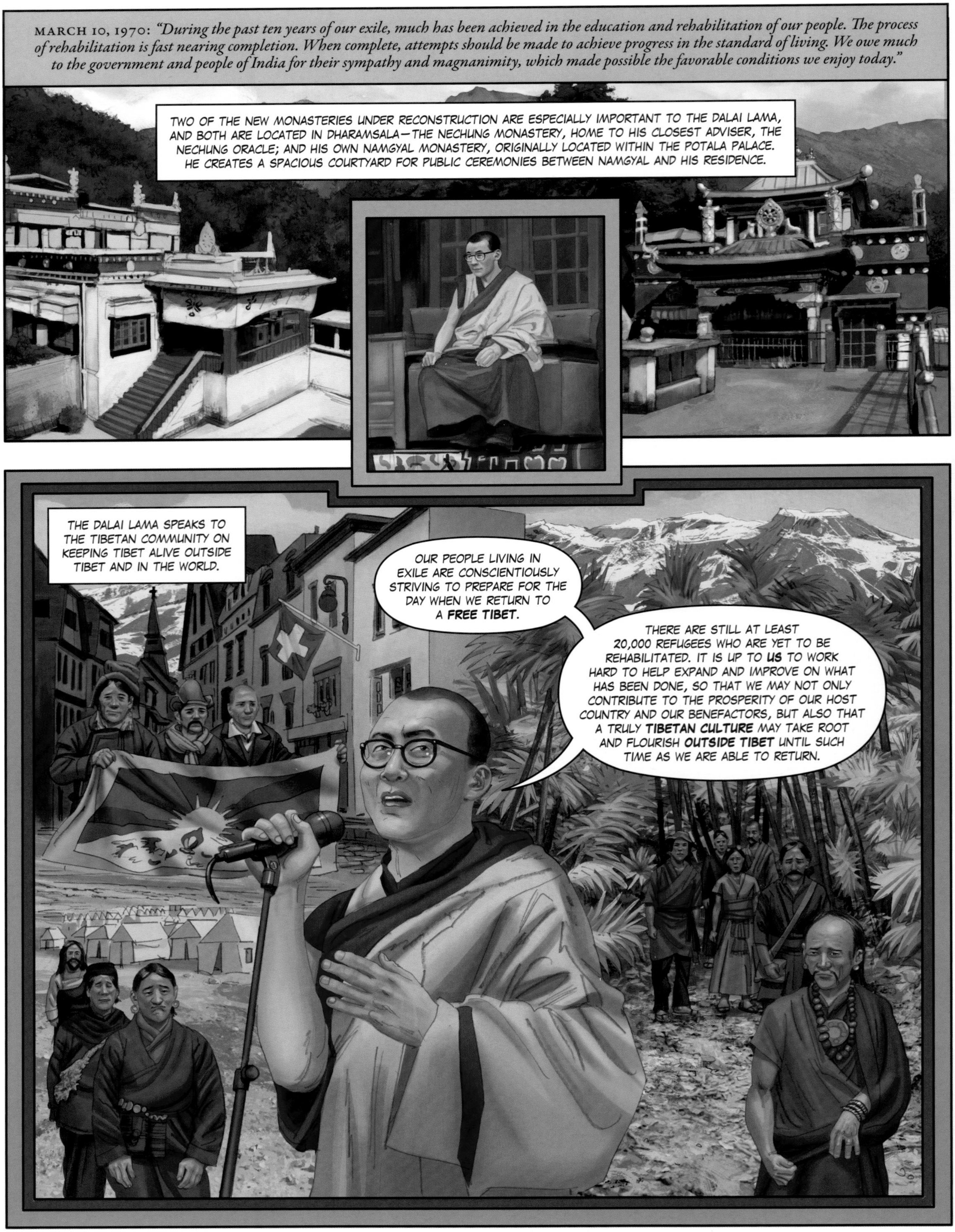
MARCH 10, 1970: "During the past ten years of our exile, much has been achieved in the education and rehabilitation of our people. The process of rehabilitation is fast nearing completion. When complete, attempts should be made to achieve progress in the standard of living. We owe much to the government and people of India for their sympathy and magnanimity, which made possible the favorable conditions we enjoy today."
TWO OF THE NEW MONASTERIES UNDER RECONSTRUCTION ARE ESPECIALLY IMPORTANT TO THE DALAI LAMA, AND BOTH ARE LOCATED IN DHARAMSALA—THE NECHUNG MONASTERY, HOME TO HIS CLOSEST ADVISER, THE NECHUNG ORACLE; AND HIS OWN NAMGYAL MONASTERY, ORIGINALLY LOCATED WITHIN THE POTALA PALACE. HE CREATES A SPACIOUS COURTYARD FOR PUBLIC CEREMONIES BETWEEN NAMGYAL AND HIS RESIDENCE.
THE DALAI LAMA SPEAKS TO THE TIBETAN COMMUNITY ON KEEPING TIBET ALIVE OUTSIDE TIBET AND IN THE WORLD.
OUR PEOPLE LIVING IN EXILE ARE CONSCIENTIOUSLY STRIVING TO PREPARE FOR THE DAY WHEN WE RETURN TO A **FREE TIBET**.
THERE ARE STILL AT LEAST 20,000 REFUGEES WHO ARE YET TO BE REHABILITATED. IT IS UP TO **US** TO WORK HARD TO HELP EXPAND AND IMPROVE ON WHAT HAS BEEN DONE, SO THAT WE MAY NOT ONLY CONTRIBUTE TO THE PROSPERITY OF OUR HOST COUNTRY AND OUR BENEFACTORS, BUT ALSO THAT A TRULY **TIBETAN CULTURE** MAY TAKE ROOT AND FLOURISH **OUTSIDE TIBET** UNTIL SUCH TIME AS WE ARE ABLE TO RETURN.

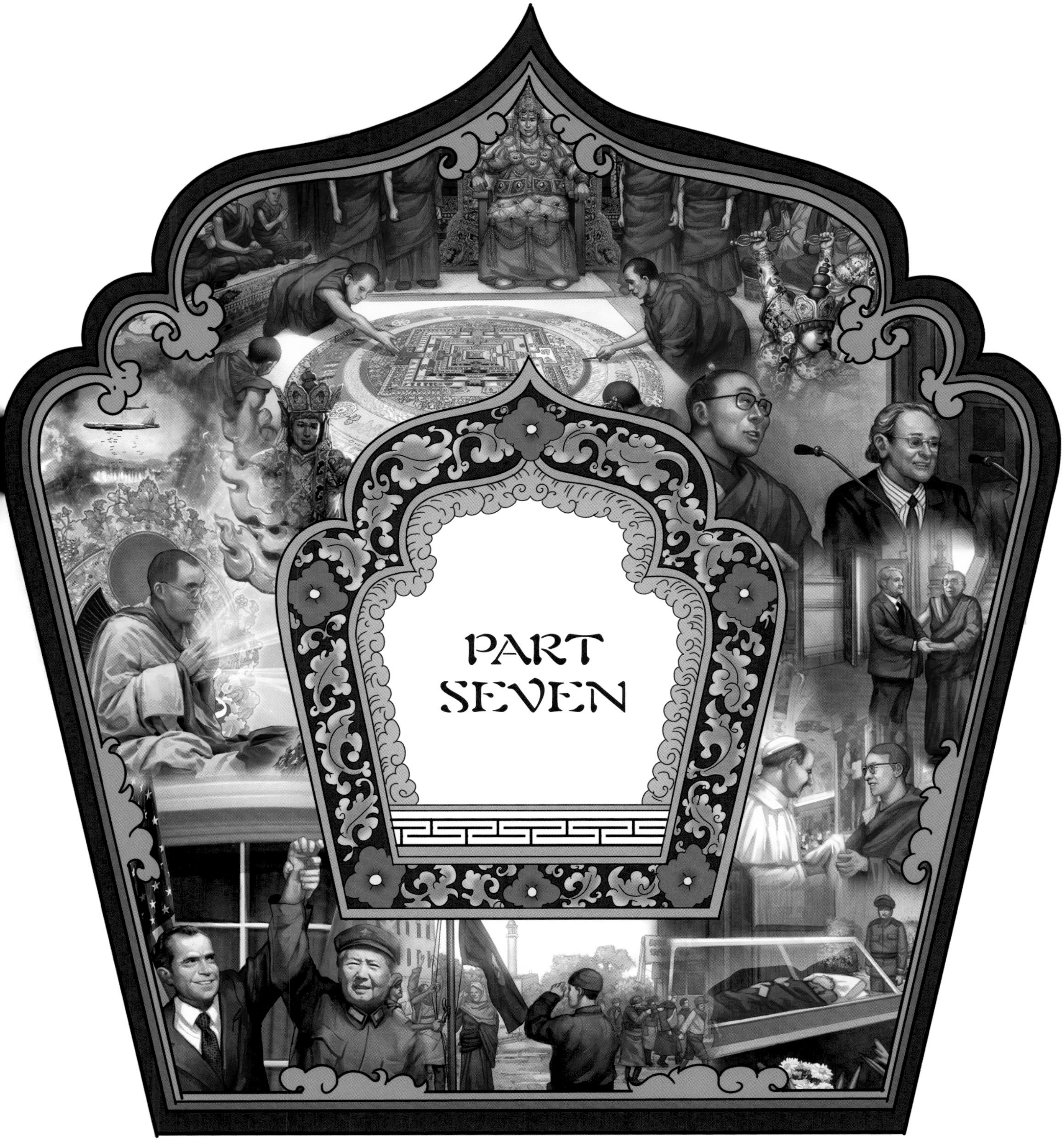
PART
SEVEN

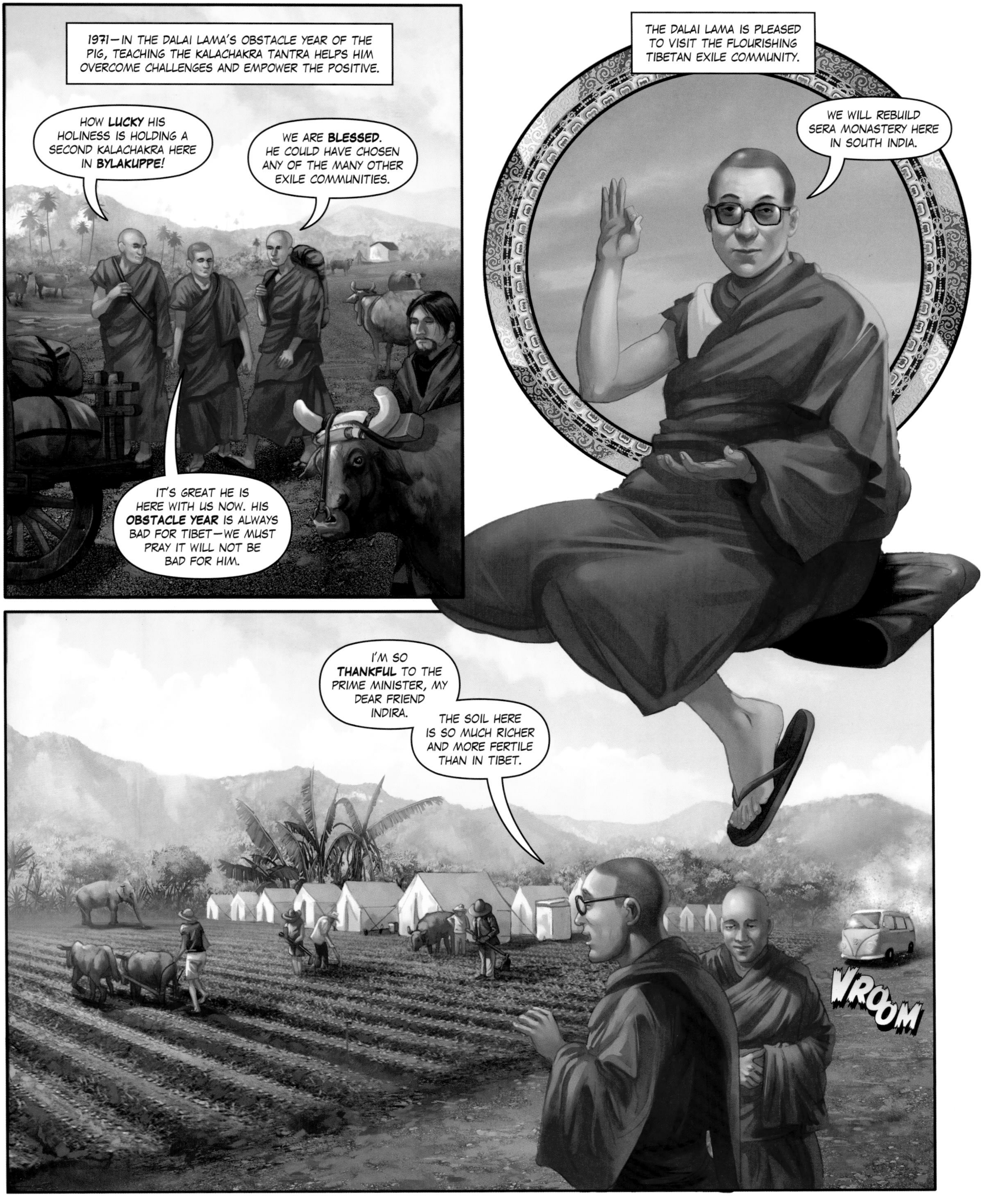
1971—IN THE DALAI LAMA'S OBSTACLE YEAR OF THE PIG, TEACHING THE KALACHAKRA TANTRA HELPS HIM OVERCOME CHALLENGES AND EMPOWER THE POSITIVE.
HOW LUCKY HIS HOLINESS IS HOLDING A SECOND KALACHAKRA HERE IN BYLAKUPPE!
WE ARE BLESSED. HE COULD HAVE CHOSEN ANY OF THE MANY OTHER EXILE COMMUNITIES.
IT'S GREAT HE IS HERE WITH US NOW. HIS OBSTACLE YEAR IS ALWAYS BAD FOR TIBET—WE MUST PRAY IT WILL NOT BE BAD FOR HIM.
THE DALAI LAMA IS PLEASED TO VISIT THE FLOURISHING TIBETAN EXILE COMMUNITY.
WE WILL REBUILD SERA MONASTERY HERE IN SOUTH INDIA.
I'M SO THANKFUL TO THE PRIME MINISTER, MY DEAR FRIEND INDIRA.
THE SOIL HERE IS SO MUCH RICHER AND MORE FERTILE THAN IN TIBET.
VROOM

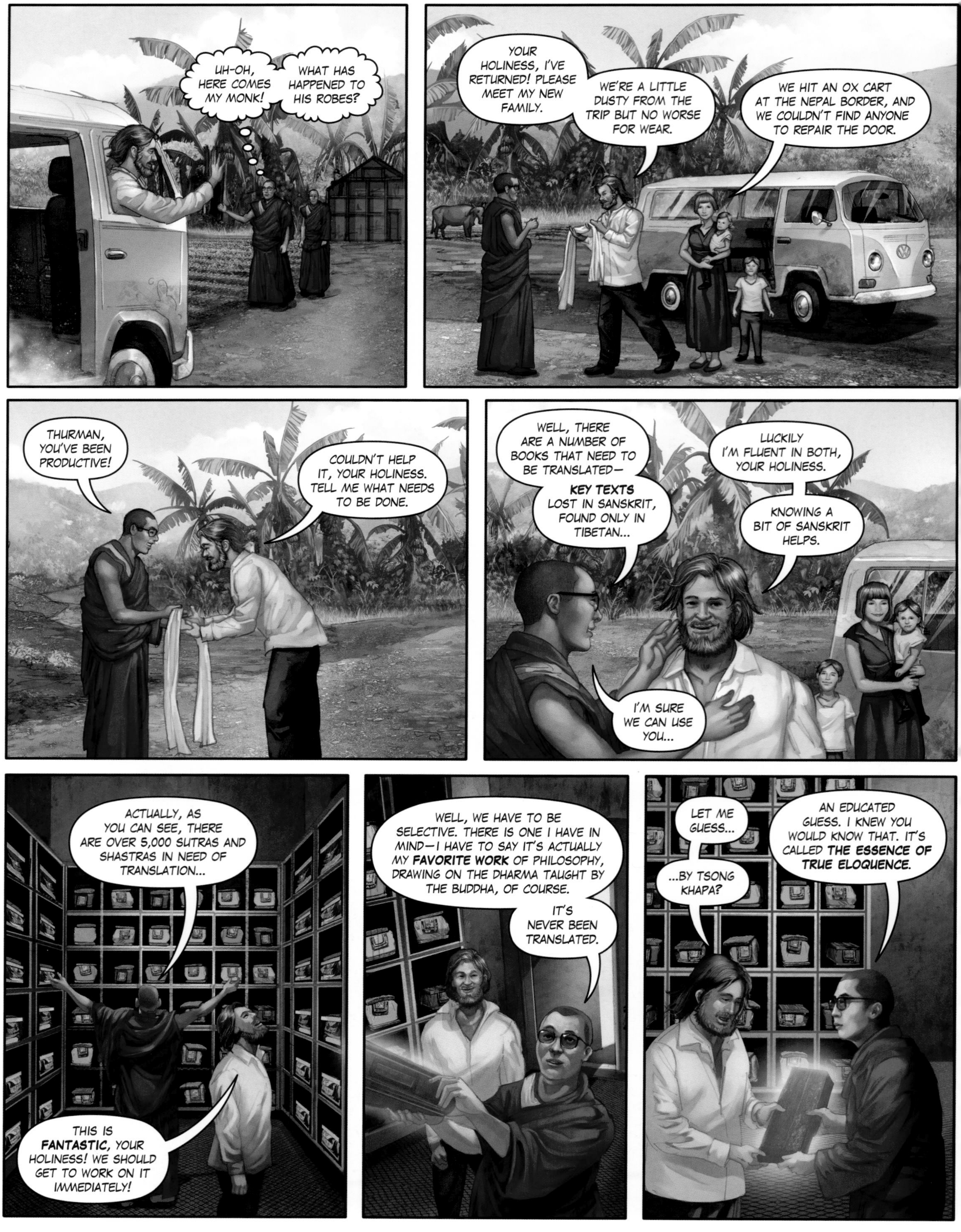
UH-OH, HERE COMES MY MONK!
WHAT HAS HAPPENED TO HIS ROBES?
YOUR HOLINESS, I'VE RETURNED! PLEASE MEET MY NEW FAMILY.
WE'RE A LITTLE DUSTY FROM THE TRIP BUT NO WORSE FOR WEAR.
WE HIT AN OX CART AT THE NEPAL BORDER, AND WE COULDN'T FIND ANYONE TO REPAIR THE DOOR.
THURMAN, YOU'VE BEEN PRODUCTIVE!
COULDN'T HELP IT, YOUR HOLINESS. TELL ME WHAT NEEDS TO BE DONE.
WELL, THERE ARE A NUMBER OF BOOKS THAT NEED TO BE TRANSLATED— **KEY TEXTS** LOST IN SANSKRIT, FOUND ONLY IN TIBETAN...
LUCKILY I'M FLUENT IN BOTH, YOUR HOLINESS.
KNOWING A BIT OF SANSKRIT HELPS.
I'M SURE WE CAN USE YOU...
ACTUALLY, AS YOU CAN SEE, THERE ARE OVER 5,000 SUTRAS AND SHASTRAS IN NEED OF TRANSLATION...
THIS IS **FANTASTIC,** YOUR HOLINESS! WE SHOULD GET TO WORK ON IT IMMEDIATELY!
WELL, WE HAVE TO BE SELECTIVE. THERE IS ONE I HAVE IN MIND—I HAVE TO SAY IT'S ACTUALLY MY **FAVORITE WORK** OF PHILOSOPHY, DRAWING ON THE DHARMA TAUGHT BY THE BUDDHA, OF COURSE.
IT'S NEVER BEEN TRANSLATED.
LET ME GUESS...
...BY TSONG KHAPA?
AN EDUCATED GUESS. I KNEW YOU WOULD KNOW THAT. IT'S CALLED **THE ESSENCE OF TRUE ELOQUENCE**.

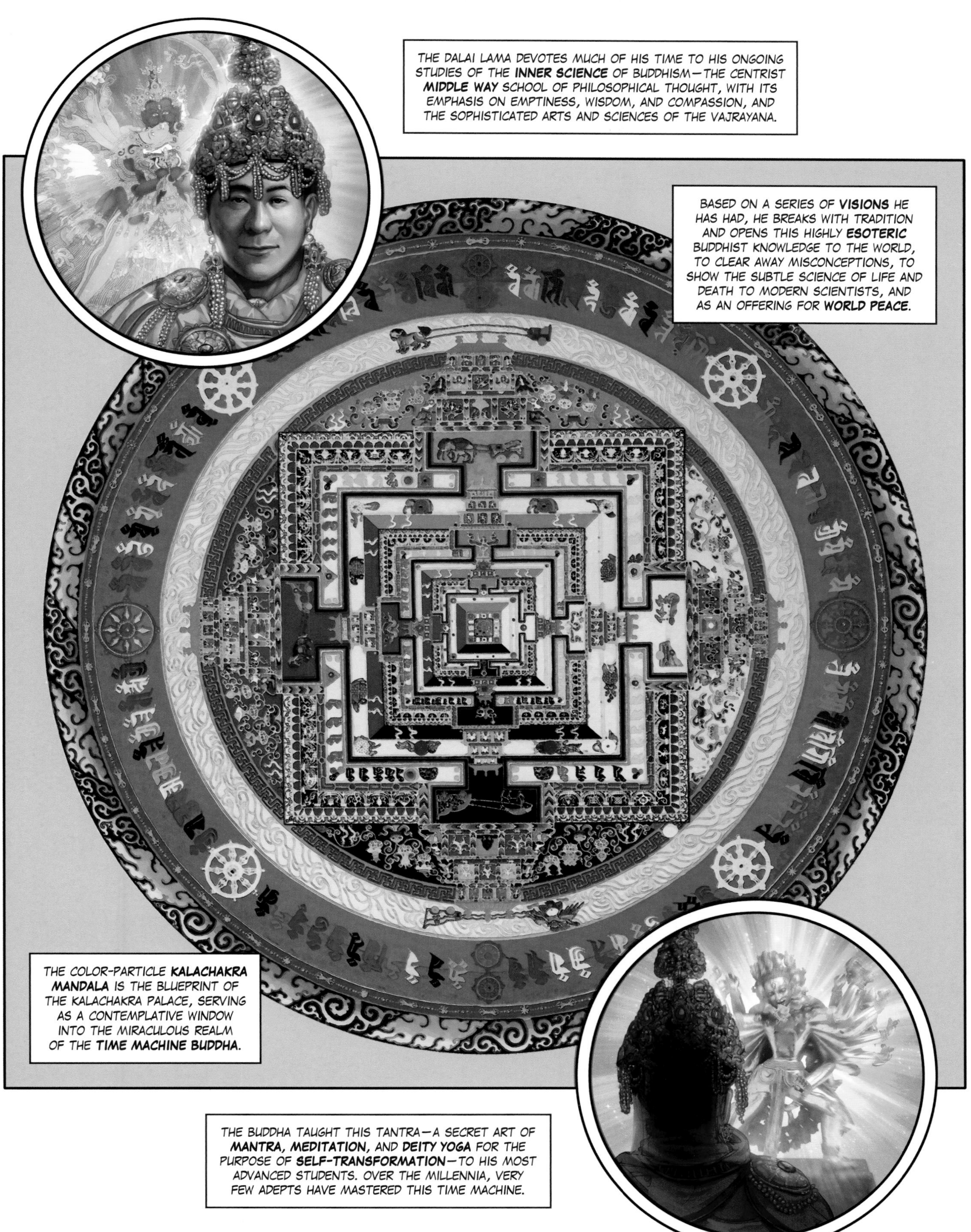
THE DALAI LAMA DEVOTES MUCH OF HIS TIME TO HIS ONGOING STUDIES OF THE **INNER SCIENCE** OF BUDDHISM—THE CENTRIST **MIDDLE WAY** SCHOOL OF PHILOSOPHICAL THOUGHT, WITH ITS EMPHASIS ON EMPTINESS, WISDOM, AND COMPASSION, AND THE SOPHISTICATED ARTS AND SCIENCES OF THE VAJRAYANA.
BASED ON A SERIES OF **VISIONS** HE HAS HAD, HE BREAKS WITH TRADITION AND OPENS THIS HIGHLY **ESOTERIC** BUDDHIST KNOWLEDGE TO THE WORLD, TO CLEAR AWAY MISCONCEPTIONS, TO SHOW THE SUBTLE SCIENCE OF LIFE AND DEATH TO MODERN SCIENTISTS, AND AS AN OFFERING FOR **WORLD PEACE**.
THE COLOR-PARTICLE **KALACHAKRA MANDALA** IS THE BLUEPRINT OF THE KALACHAKRA PALACE, SERVING AS A CONTEMPLATIVE WINDOW INTO THE MIRACULOUS REALM OF THE **TIME MACHINE BUDDHA**.
THE BUDDHA TAUGHT THIS TANTRA—A SECRET ART OF **MANTRA, MEDITATION,** AND **DEITY YOGA** FOR THE PURPOSE OF **SELF-TRANSFORMATION**—TO HIS MOST ADVANCED STUDENTS. OVER THE MILLENNIA, VERY FEW ADEPTS HAVE MASTERED THIS TIME MACHINE.

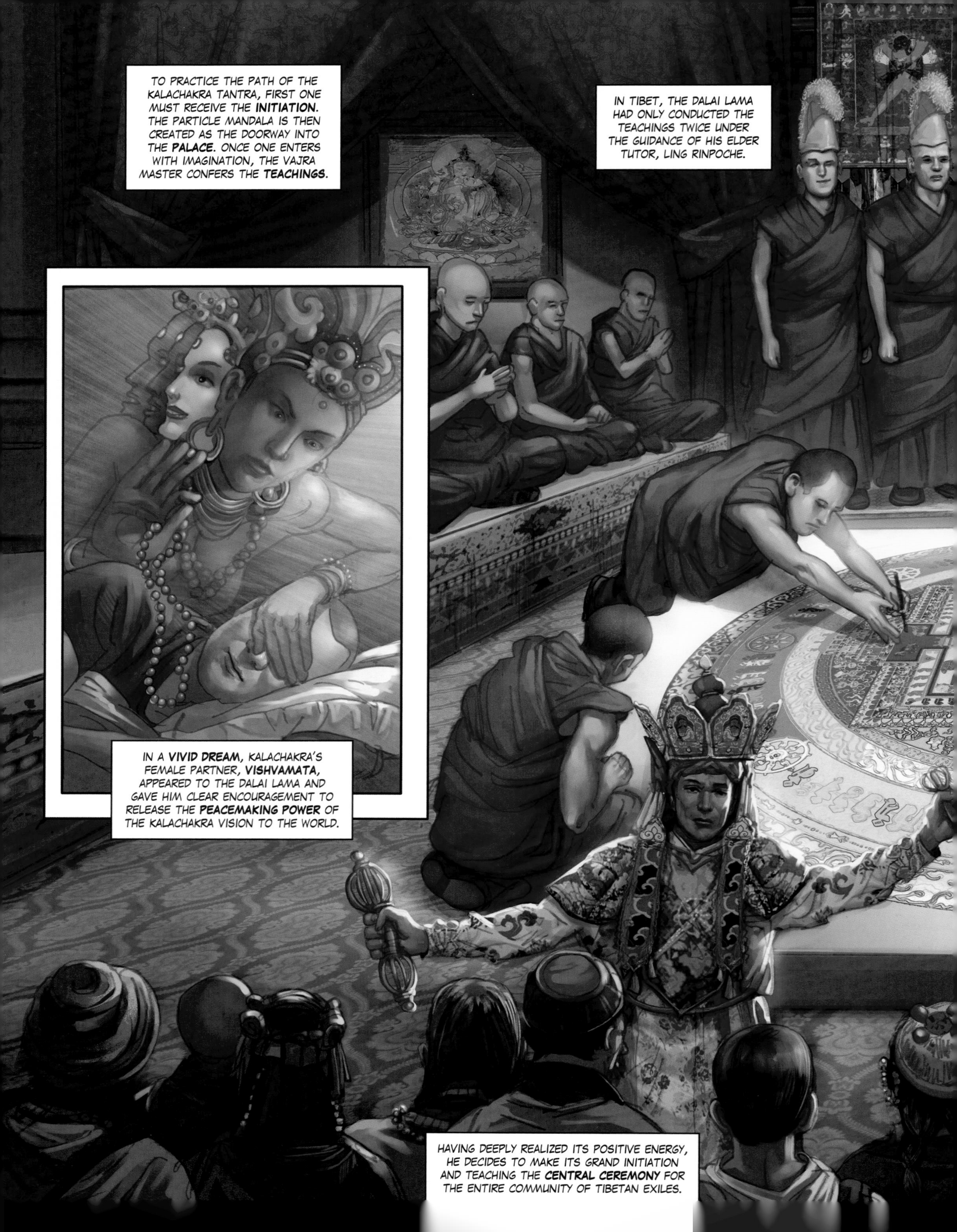
TO PRACTICE THE PATH OF THE KALACHAKRA TANTRA, FIRST ONE MUST RECEIVE THE **INITIATION**. THE PARTICLE MANDALA IS THEN CREATED AS THE DOORWAY INTO THE **PALACE**. ONCE ONE ENTERS WITH IMAGINATION, THE VAJRA MASTER CONFERS THE **TEACHINGS**.
IN TIBET, THE DALAI LAMA HAD ONLY CONDUCTED THE TEACHINGS TWICE UNDER THE GUIDANCE OF HIS ELDER TUTOR, LING RINPOCHE.
IN A **VIVID DREAM**, KALACHAKRA'S FEMALE PARTNER, **VISHVAMATA**, APPEARED TO THE DALAI LAMA AND GAVE HIM CLEAR ENCOURAGEMENT TO RELEASE THE **PEACEMAKING POWER** OF THE KALACHAKRA VISION TO THE WORLD.
HAVING DEEPLY REALIZED ITS POSITIVE ENERGY, HE DECIDES TO MAKE ITS GRAND INITIATION AND TEACHING THE **CENTRAL CEREMONY** FOR THE ENTIRE COMMUNITY OF TIBETAN EXILES.

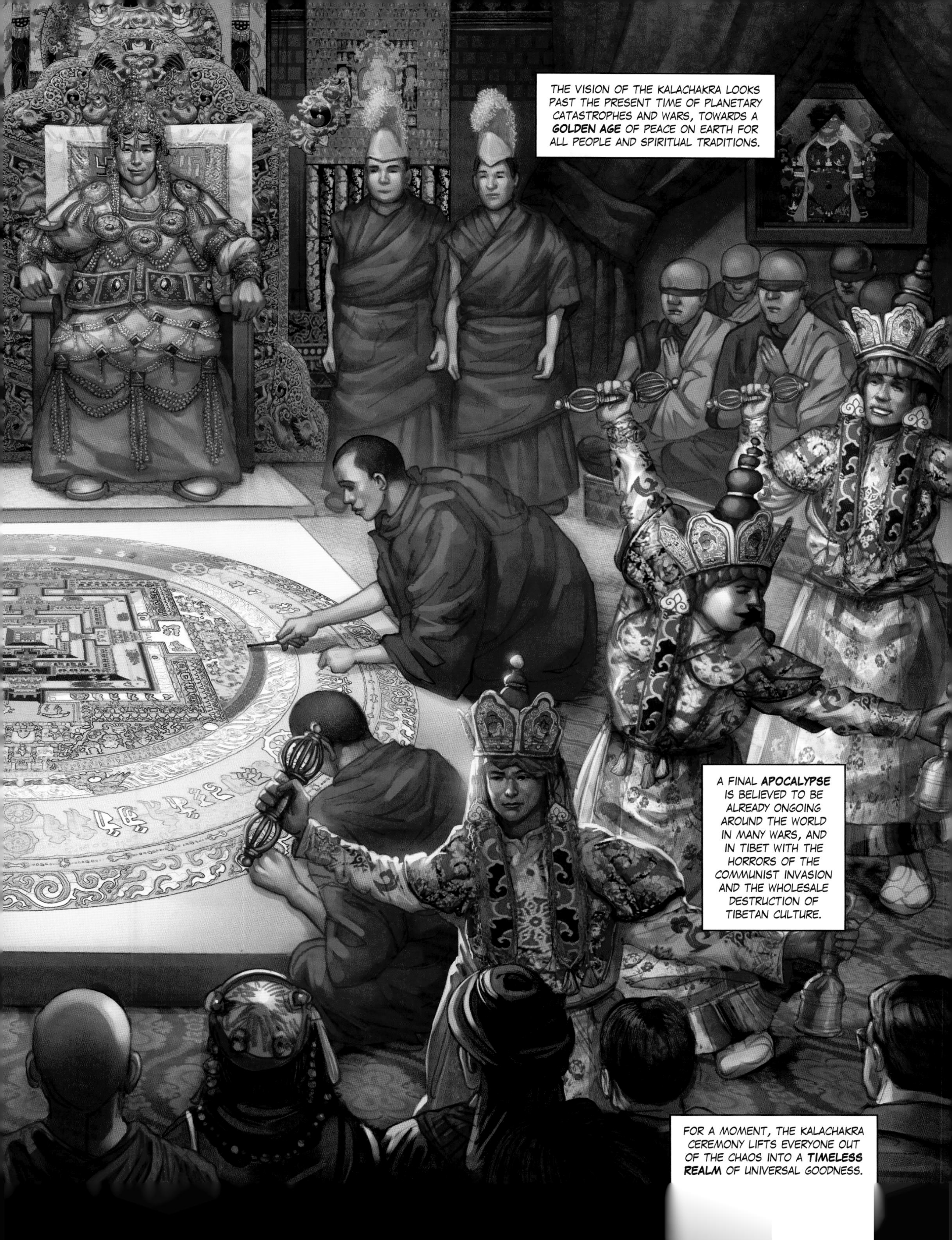
THE VISION OF THE KALACHAKRA LOOKS PAST THE PRESENT TIME OF PLANETARY CATASTROPHES AND WARS, TOWARDS A **GOLDEN AGE** OF PEACE ON EARTH FOR ALL PEOPLE AND SPIRITUAL TRADITIONS.
A FINAL **APOCALYPSE** IS BELIEVED TO BE ALREADY ONGOING AROUND THE WORLD IN MANY WARS, AND IN TIBET WITH THE HORRORS OF THE COMMUNIST INVASION AND THE WHOLESALE DESTRUCTION OF TIBETAN CULTURE.
FOR A MOMENT, THE KALACHAKRA CEREMONY LIFTS EVERYONE OUT OF THE CHAOS INTO A **TIMELESS REALM** OF UNIVERSAL GOODNESS.

THE KALACHAKRA INITIATION WAS FIRST PERFORMED BY THE BUDDHA OVER 2,500 YEARS AGO FOR VISITORS FROM THE MAGICAL COUNTRY OF **SHAMBHALA.** IT HAS BEEN PRACTICED OVER THE CENTURIES BY THE MOST ADVANCED STUDENTS TO COMPRESS MANY LIFETIMES OF KARMIC EVOLUTION, TO ATTAIN **ENLIGHTENMENT IN A SINGLE LIFE.** THE DALAI LAMA SITS ENTHRONED AS THE VAJRA MENTOR, A MEDIUM FOR KALACHAKRA BUDDHA, SINCE THE INITIATION INVOLVES SEEING THE HUMAN TEACHER AS THE BUDDHA HIMSELF.

KALACHAKRA MEANS **"TIME WHEEL,"** REFERRING TO THE BUDDHA'S PROGRESSIVE VISION OF HISTORY AS A MACHINE OF TIME IN WHICH HUMAN BEINGS DO EVOLVE FROM OUR PRESENT INDUSTRIAL SAVAGERY OF IGNORANCE, GREED, AND VIOLENCE TOWARD WISDOM, GENEROSITY, AND KINDNESS. THE GOLDEN AGE WHEN WE ALL LIVE TOGETHER TOLERANTLY, SUSTAINABLY, AND PEACEFULLY IS PREDICTED TO COME 400 YEARS FROM NOW. TIBETAN BUDDHISTS HOPE THAT THE DALAI LAMA'S TEACHINGS WILL ACCELERATE ITS COMING.

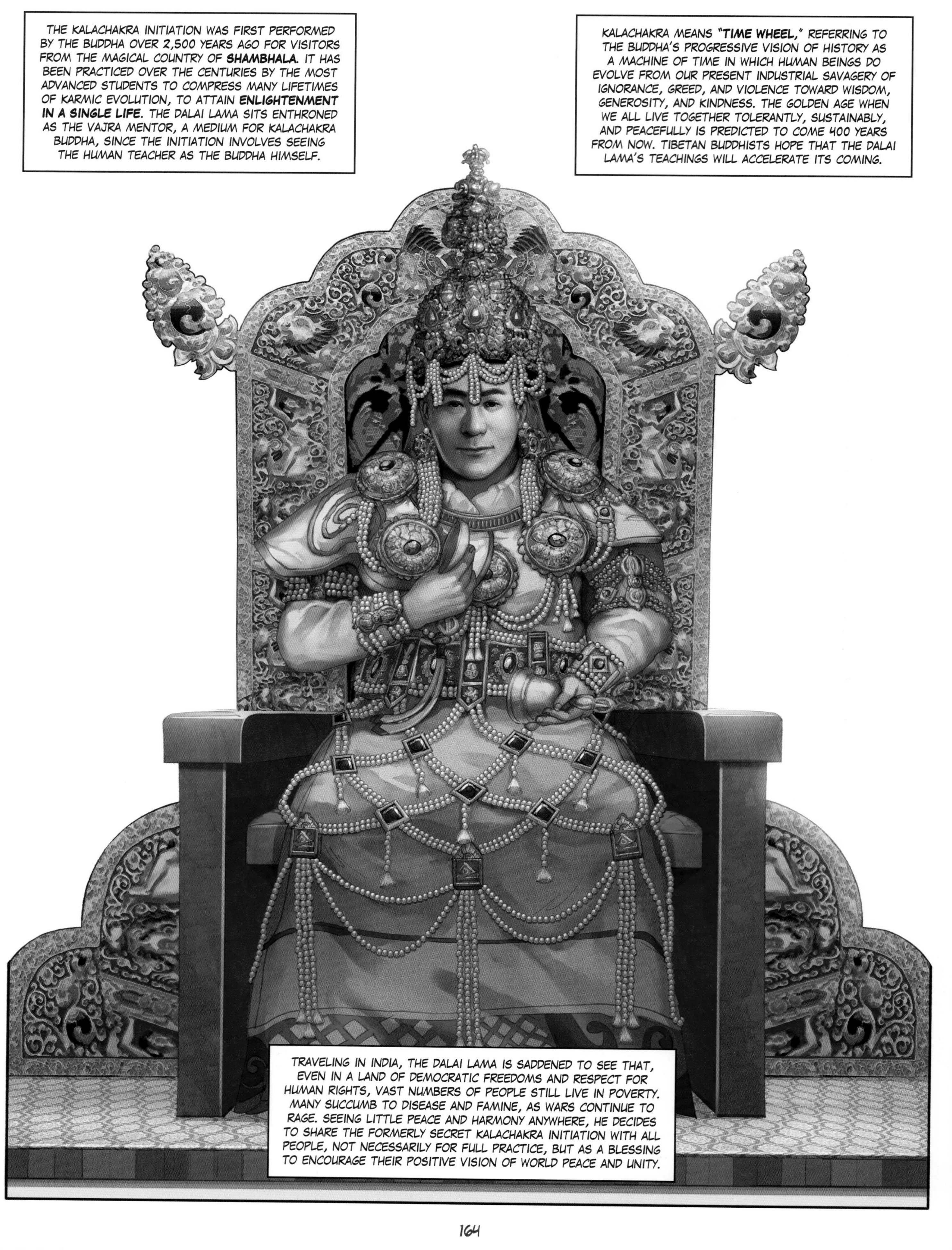
TRAVELING IN INDIA, THE DALAI LAMA IS SADDENED TO SEE THAT, EVEN IN A LAND OF DEMOCRATIC FREEDOMS AND RESPECT FOR HUMAN RIGHTS, VAST NUMBERS OF PEOPLE STILL LIVE IN POVERTY. MANY SUCCUMB TO DISEASE AND FAMINE, AS WARS CONTINUE TO RAGE. SEEING LITTLE PEACE AND HARMONY ANYWHERE, HE DECIDES TO SHARE THE FORMERLY SECRET KALACHAKRA INITIATION WITH ALL PEOPLE, NOT NECESSARILY FOR FULL PRACTICE, BUT AS A BLESSING TO ENCOURAGE THEIR POSITIVE VISION OF WORLD PEACE AND UNITY.

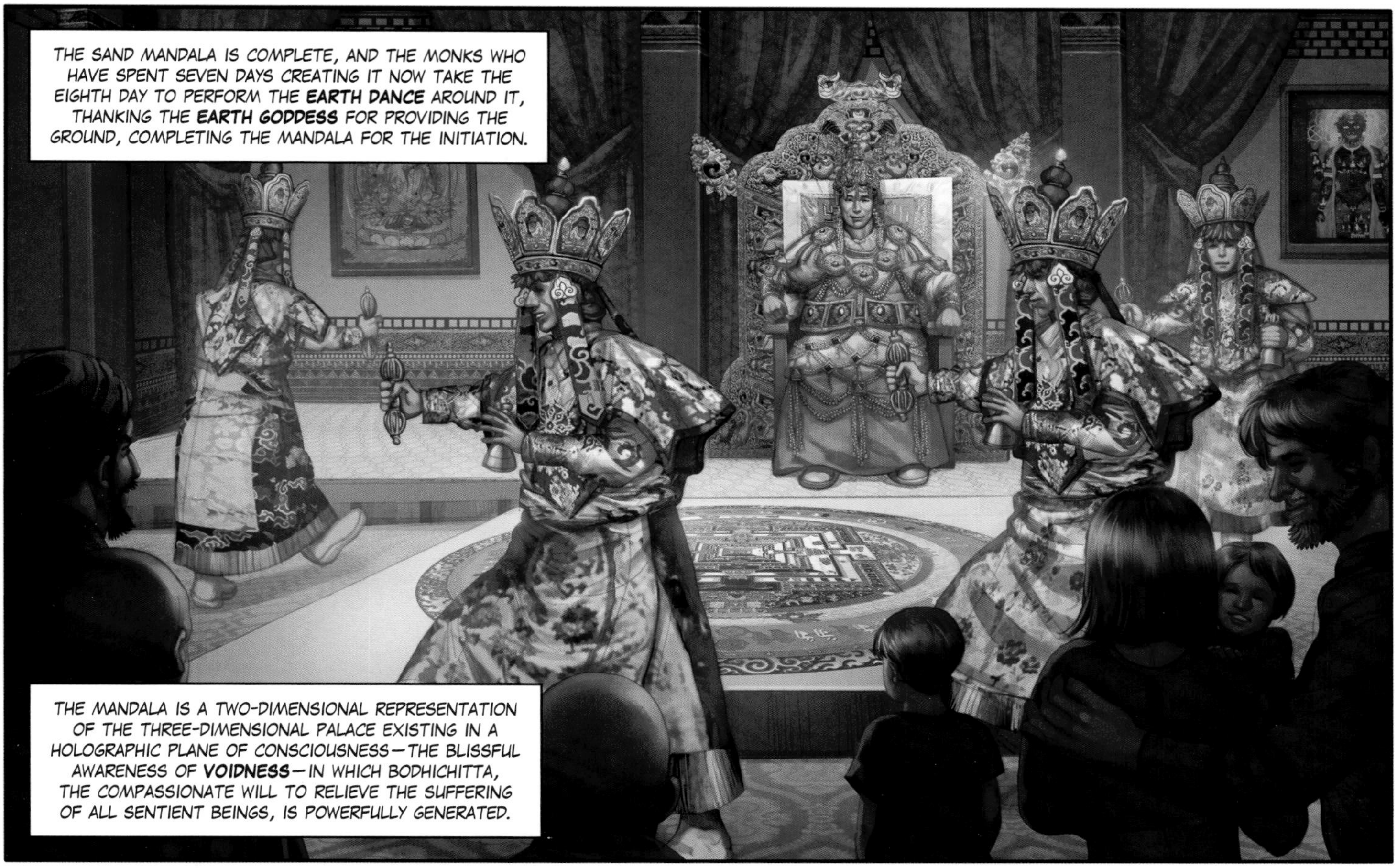
THE SAND MANDALA IS COMPLETE, AND THE MONKS WHO HAVE SPENT SEVEN DAYS CREATING IT NOW TAKE THE EIGHTH DAY TO PERFORM THE **EARTH DANCE** AROUND IT, THANKING THE **EARTH GODDESS** FOR PROVIDING THE GROUND, COMPLETING THE MANDALA FOR THE INITIATION.
THE MANDALA IS A TWO-DIMENSIONAL REPRESENTATION OF THE THREE-DIMENSIONAL PALACE EXISTING IN A HOLOGRAPHIC PLANE OF CONSCIOUSNESS—THE BLISSFUL AWARENESS OF **VOIDNESS**—IN WHICH BODHICHITTA, THE COMPASSIONATE WILL TO RELIEVE THE SUFFERING OF ALL SENTIENT BEINGS, IS POWERFULLY GENERATED.

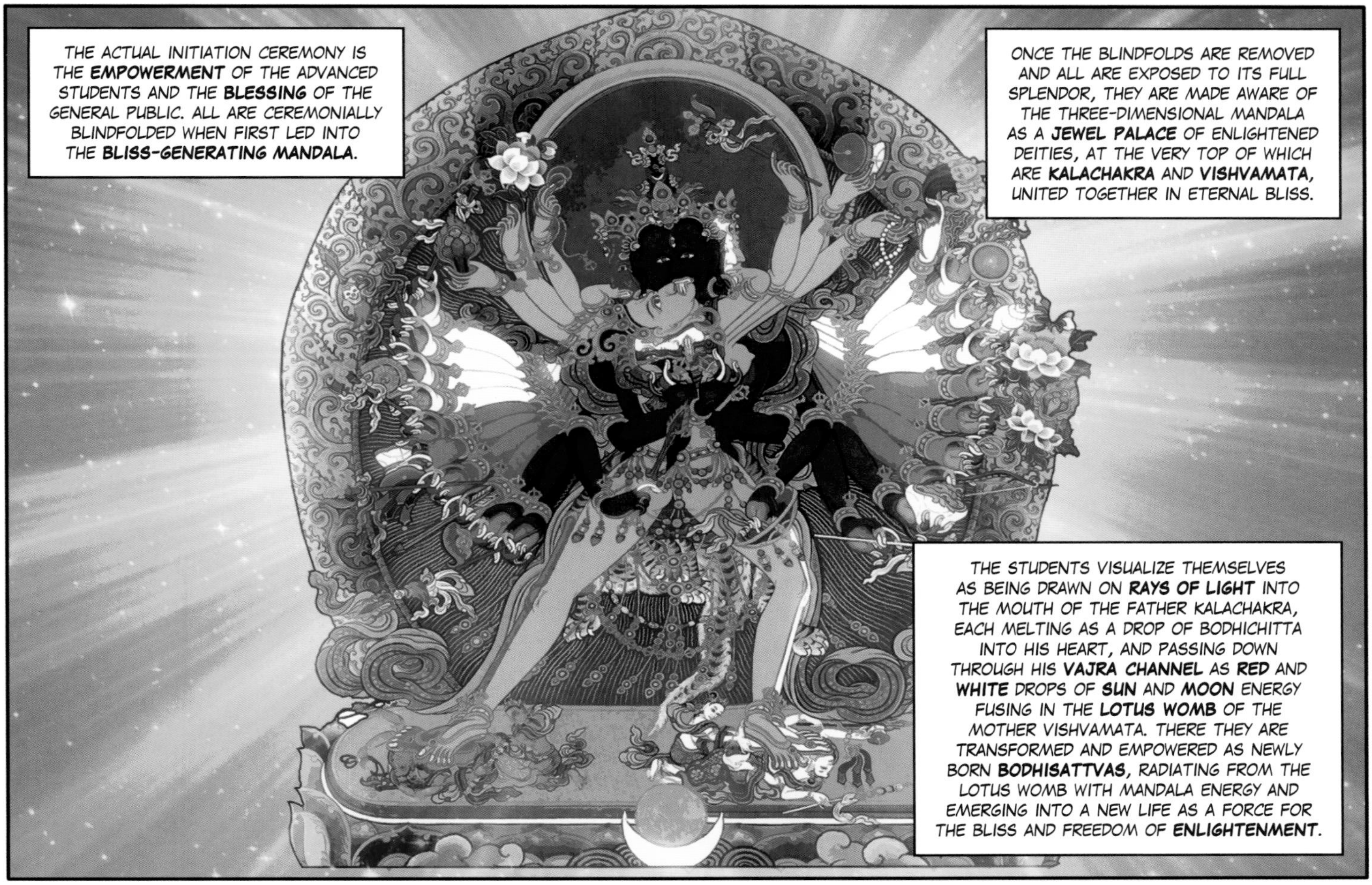
THE ACTUAL INITIATION CEREMONY IS THE **EMPOWERMENT** OF THE ADVANCED STUDENTS AND THE **BLESSING** OF THE GENERAL PUBLIC. ALL ARE CEREMONIALLY BLINDFOLDED WHEN FIRST LED INTO THE **BLISS-GENERATING MANDALA**.
ONCE THE BLINDFOLDS ARE REMOVED AND ALL ARE EXPOSED TO ITS FULL SPLENDOR, THEY ARE MADE AWARE OF THE THREE-DIMENSIONAL MANDALA AS A **JEWEL PALACE** OF ENLIGHTENED DEITIES, AT THE VERY TOP OF WHICH ARE **KALACHAKRA** AND **VISHVAMATA**, UNITED TOGETHER IN ETERNAL BLISS.
THE STUDENTS VISUALIZE THEMSELVES AS BEING DRAWN ON **RAYS OF LIGHT** INTO THE MOUTH OF THE FATHER KALACHAKRA, EACH MELTING AS A DROP OF BODHICHITTA INTO HIS HEART, AND PASSING DOWN THROUGH HIS **VAJRA CHANNEL** AS **RED** AND **WHITE** DROPS OF **SUN** AND **MOON** ENERGY FUSING IN THE **LOTUS WOMB** OF THE MOTHER VISHVAMATA. THERE THEY ARE TRANSFORMED AND EMPOWERED AS NEWLY BORN **BODHISATTVAS**, RADIATING FROM THE LOTUS WOMB WITH MANDALA ENERGY AND EMERGING INTO A NEW LIFE AS A FORCE FOR THE BLISS AND FREEDOM OF **ENLIGHTENMENT**.

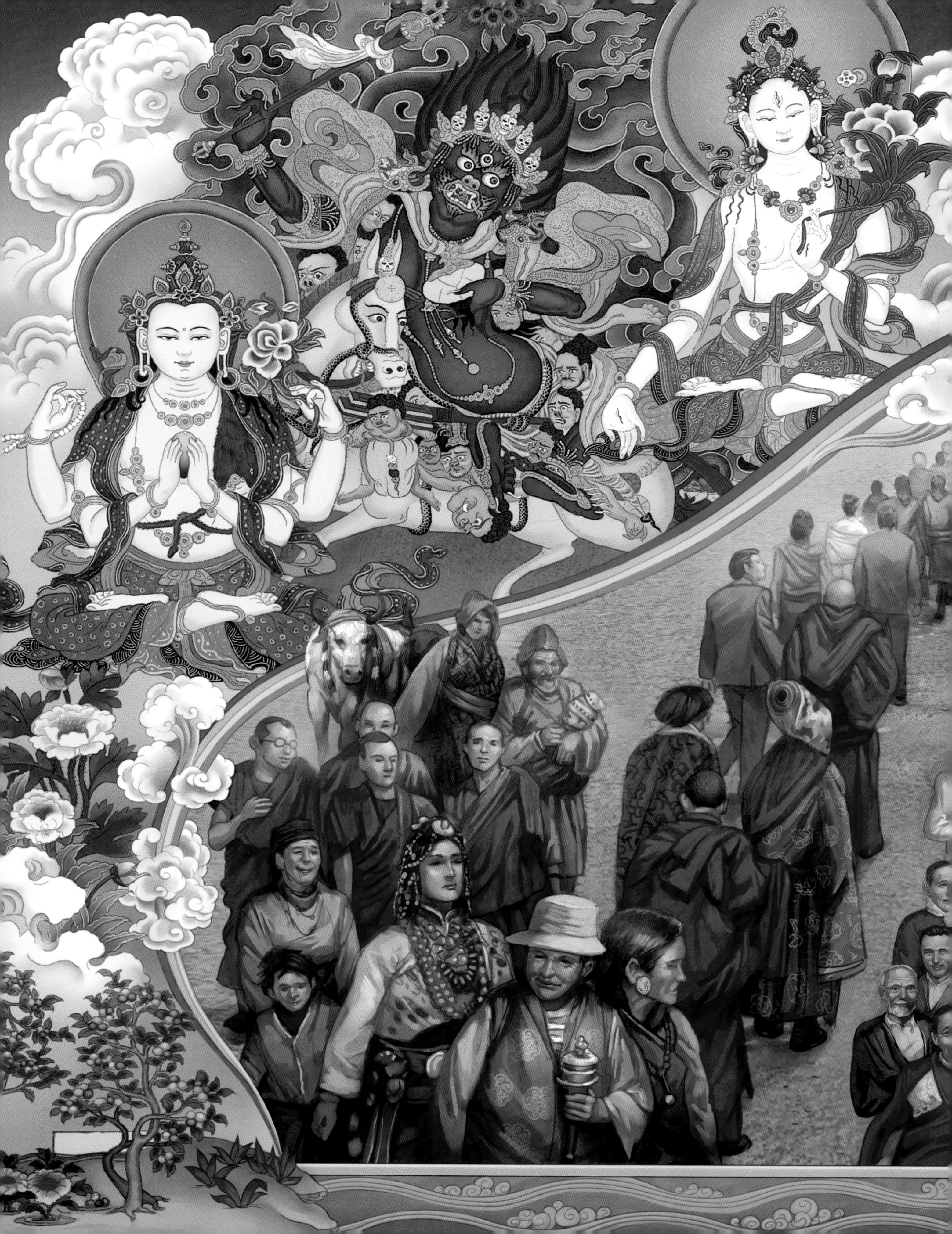

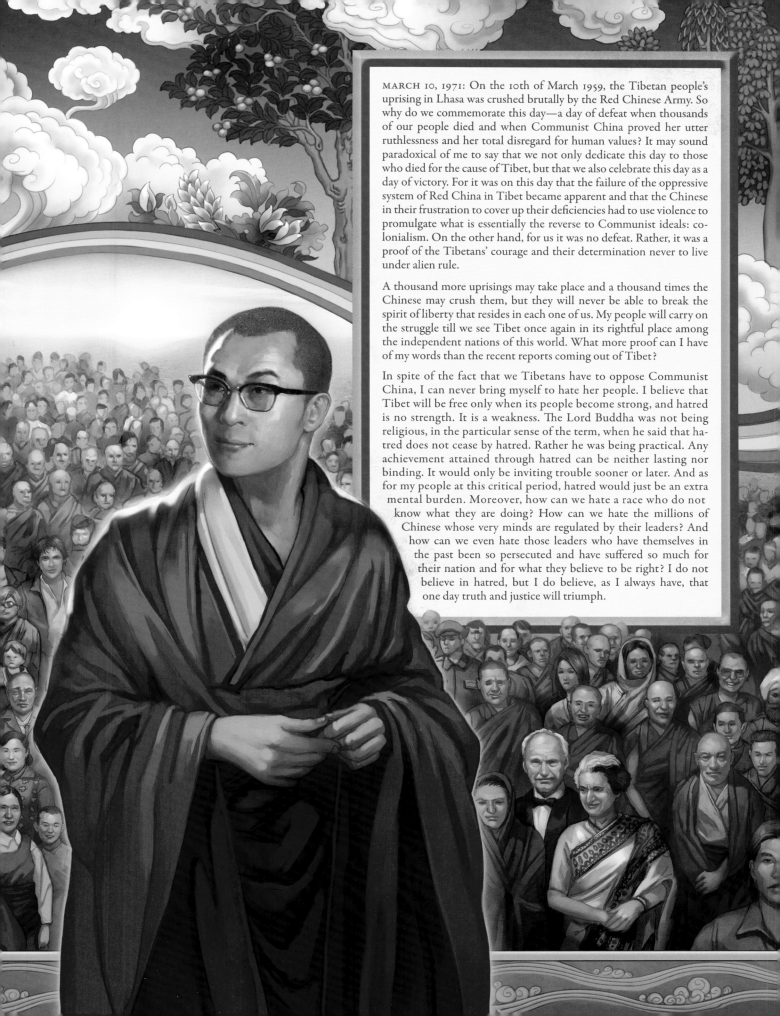

MARCH 10, 1971: On the 10th of March 1959, the Tibetan people's uprising in Lhasa was crushed brutally by the Red Chinese Army. So why do we commemorate this day—a day of defeat when thousands of our people died and when Communist China proved her utter ruthlessness and her total disregard for human values? It may sound paradoxical of me to say that we not only dedicate this day to those who died for the cause of Tibet, but that we also celebrate this day as a day of victory. For it was on this day that the failure of the oppressive system of Red China in Tibet became apparent and that the Chinese in their frustration to cover up their deficiencies had to use violence to promulgate what is essentially the reverse to Communist ideals: colonialism. On the other hand, for us it was no defeat. Rather, it was a proof of the Tibetans' courage and their determination never to live under alien rule.

A thousand more uprisings may take place and a thousand times the Chinese may crush them, but they will never be able to break the spirit of liberty that resides in each one of us. My people will carry on the struggle till we see Tibet once again in its rightful place among the independent nations of this world. What more proof can I have of my words than the recent reports coming out of Tibet?

In spite of the fact that we Tibetans have to oppose Communist China, I can never bring myself to hate her people. I believe that Tibet will be free only when its people become strong, and hatred is no strength. It is a weakness. The Lord Buddha was not being religious, in the particular sense of the term, when he said that hatred does not cease by hatred. Rather he was being practical. Any achievement attained through hatred can be neither lasting nor binding. It would only be inviting trouble sooner or later. And as for my people at this critical period, hatred would just be an extra mental burden. Moreover, how can we hate a race who do not know what they are doing? How can we hate the millions of Chinese whose very minds are regulated by their leaders? And how can we even hate those leaders who have themselves in the past been so persecuted and have suffered so much for their nation and for what they believe to be right? I do not believe in hatred, but I do believe, as I always have, that one day truth and justice will triumph.

MARCH 10, 1972: *"The past decade has been a great test for the people of Tibet, still the victims of this monstrous and alien onslaught on the very way of life that Tibetans cherish. Young Tibetans, both under Chinese control and in the lands where they have sought refuge, are becoming more conscious of their national identity—there is this new awareness in them of the Tibetan nation and the culture that once flourished there. . . ."*

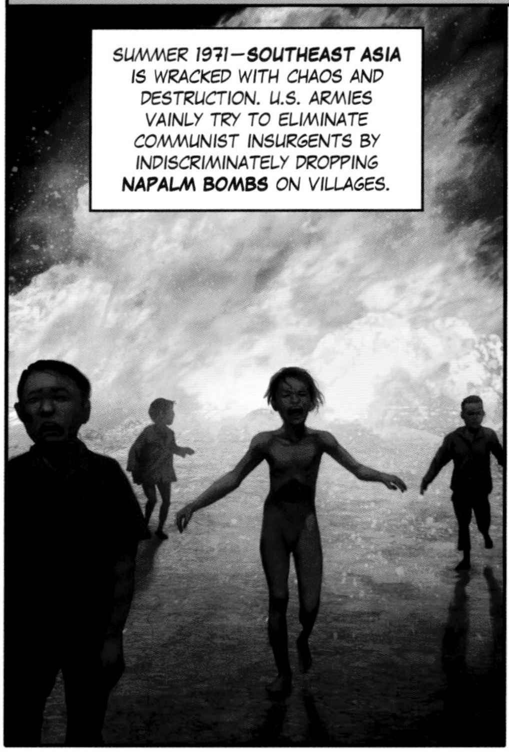
SUMMER 1971—SOUTHEAST ASIA IS WRACKED WITH CHAOS AND DESTRUCTION. U.S. ARMIES VAINLY TRY TO ELIMINATE COMMUNIST INSURGENTS BY INDISCRIMINATELY DROPPING NAPALM BOMBS ON VILLAGES.

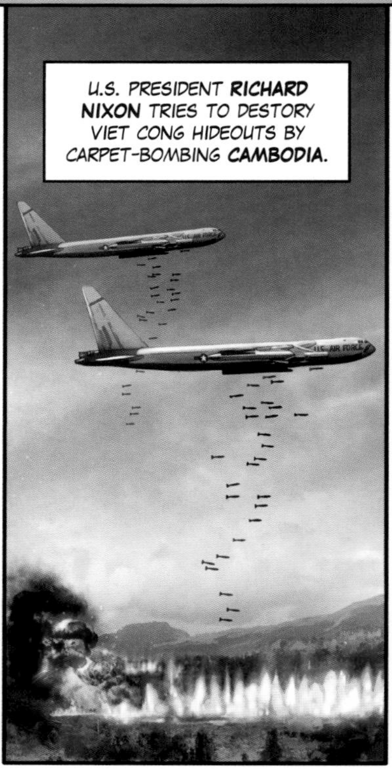
U.S. PRESIDENT RICHARD NIXON TRIES TO DESTORY VIET CONG HIDEOUTS BY CARPET-BOMBING CAMBODIA.

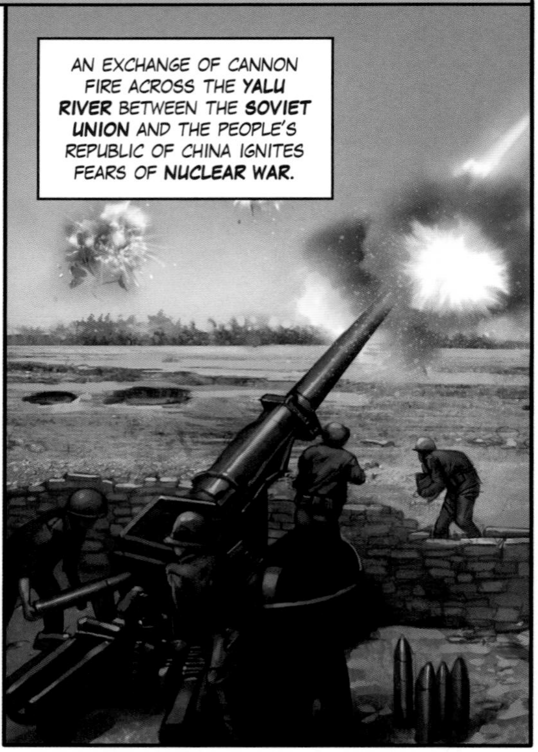
AN EXCHANGE OF CANNON FIRE ACROSS THE YALU RIVER BETWEEN THE SOVIET UNION AND THE PEOPLE'S REPUBLIC OF CHINA IGNITES FEARS OF NUCLEAR WAR.

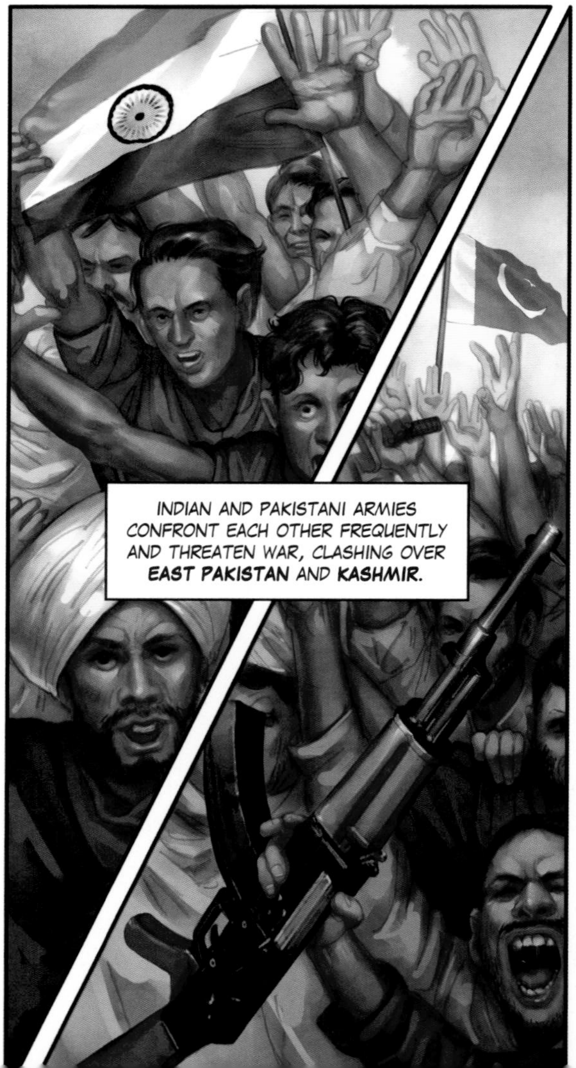
INDIAN AND PAKISTANI ARMIES CONFRONT EACH OTHER FREQUENTLY AND THREATEN WAR, CLASHING OVER EAST PAKISTAN AND KASHMIR.

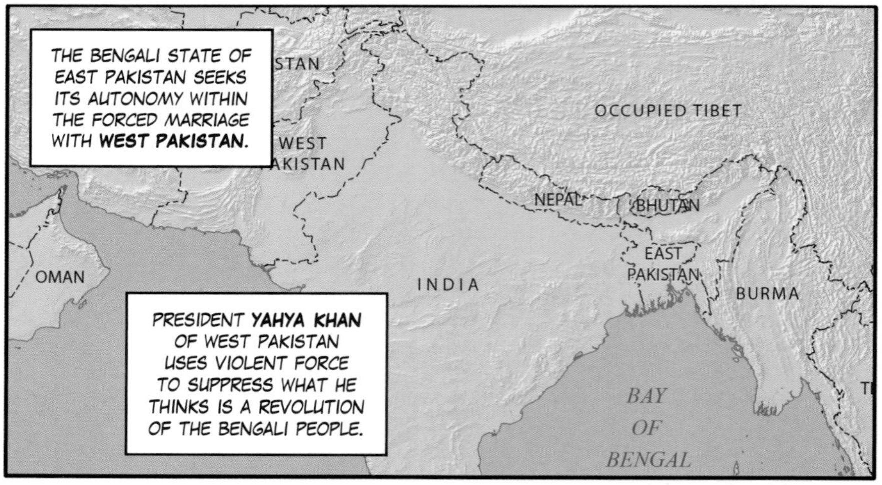
THE BENGALI STATE OF EAST PAKISTAN SEEKS ITS AUTONOMY WITHIN THE FORCED MARRIAGE WITH WEST PAKISTAN.
OCCUPIED TIBET
WEST
NEPAL
BHUTAN
EAST PAKISTAN
OMAN
INDIA
BURMA
BAY OF BENGAL
PRESIDENT YAHYA KHAN OF WEST PAKISTAN USES VIOLENT FORCE TO SUPPRESS WHAT HE THINKS IS A REVOLUTION OF THE BENGALI PEOPLE.

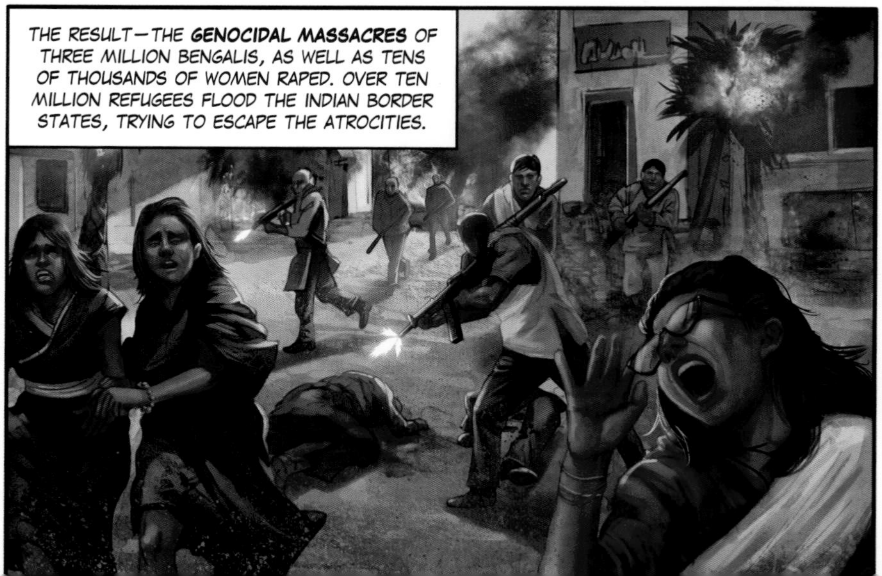
THE RESULT—THE GENOCIDAL MASSACRES OF THREE MILLION BENGALIS, AS WELL AS TENS OF THOUSANDS OF WOMEN RAPED. OVER TEN MILLION REFUGEES FLOOD THE INDIAN BORDER STATES, TRYING TO ESCAPE THE ATROCITIES.

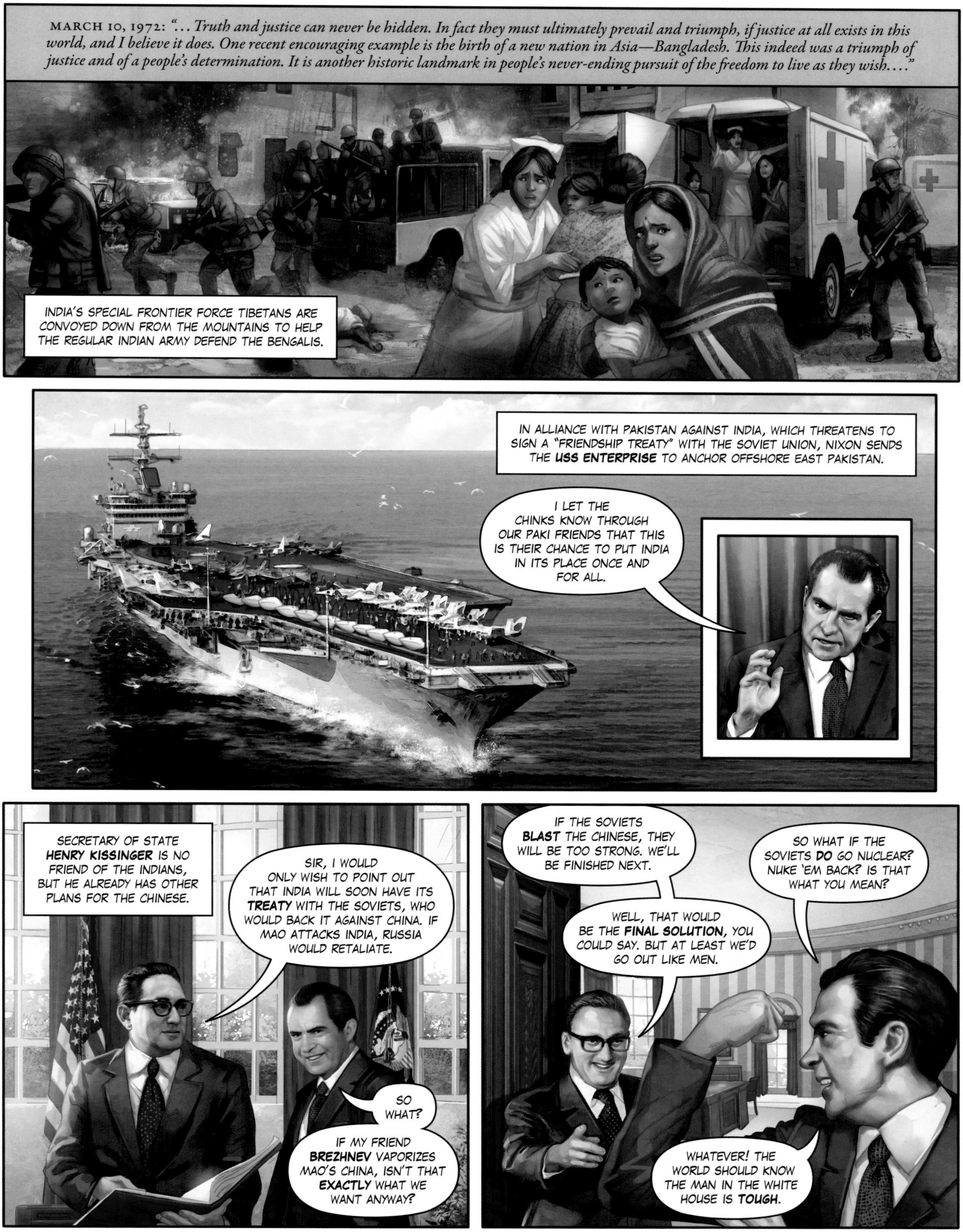
MARCH 10, 1972: "... Truth and justice can never be hidden. In fact they must ultimately prevail and triumph, if justice at all exists in this world, and I believe it does. One recent encouraging example is the birth of a new nation in Asia—Bangladesh. This indeed was a triumph of justice and of a people's determination. It is another historic landmark in people's never-ending pursuit of the freedom to live as they wish...."
INDIA'S SPECIAL FRONTIER FORCE TIBETANS ARE CONVOYED DOWN FROM THE MOUNTAINS TO HELP THE REGULAR INDIAN ARMY DEFEND THE BENGALIS.
IN ALLIANCE WITH PAKISTAN AGAINST INDIA, WHICH THREATENS TO SIGN A "FRIENDSHIP TREATY" WITH THE SOVIET UNION, NIXON SENDS THE USS ENTERPRISE TO ANCHOR OFFSHORE EAST PAKISTAN.
I LET THE CHINKS KNOW THROUGH OUR PAKI FRIENDS THAT THIS IS THEIR CHANCE TO PUT INDIA IN ITS PLACE ONCE AND FOR ALL.
SECRETARY OF STATE HENRY KISSINGER IS NO FRIEND OF THE INDIANS, BUT HE ALREADY HAS OTHER PLANS FOR THE CHINESE.
SIR, I WOULD ONLY WISH TO POINT OUT THAT INDIA WILL SOON HAVE ITS TREATY WITH THE SOVIETS, WHO WOULD BACK IT AGAINST CHINA. IF MAO ATTACKS INDIA, RUSSIA WOULD RETALIATE.
SO WHAT?
IF MY FRIEND BREZHNEV VAPORIZES MAO'S CHINA, ISN'T THAT EXACTLY WHAT WE WANT ANYWAY?
IF THE SOVIETS BLAST THE CHINESE, THEY WILL BE TOO STRONG. WE'LL BE FINISHED NEXT.
SO WHAT IF THE SOVIETS DO GO NUCLEAR? NUKE 'EM BACK? IS THAT WHAT YOU MEAN?
WELL, THAT WOULD BE THE FINAL SOLUTION, YOU COULD SAY. BUT AT LEAST WE'D GO OUT LIKE MEN.
WHATEVER! THE WORLD SHOULD KNOW THE MAN IN THE WHITE HOUSE IS TOUGH.

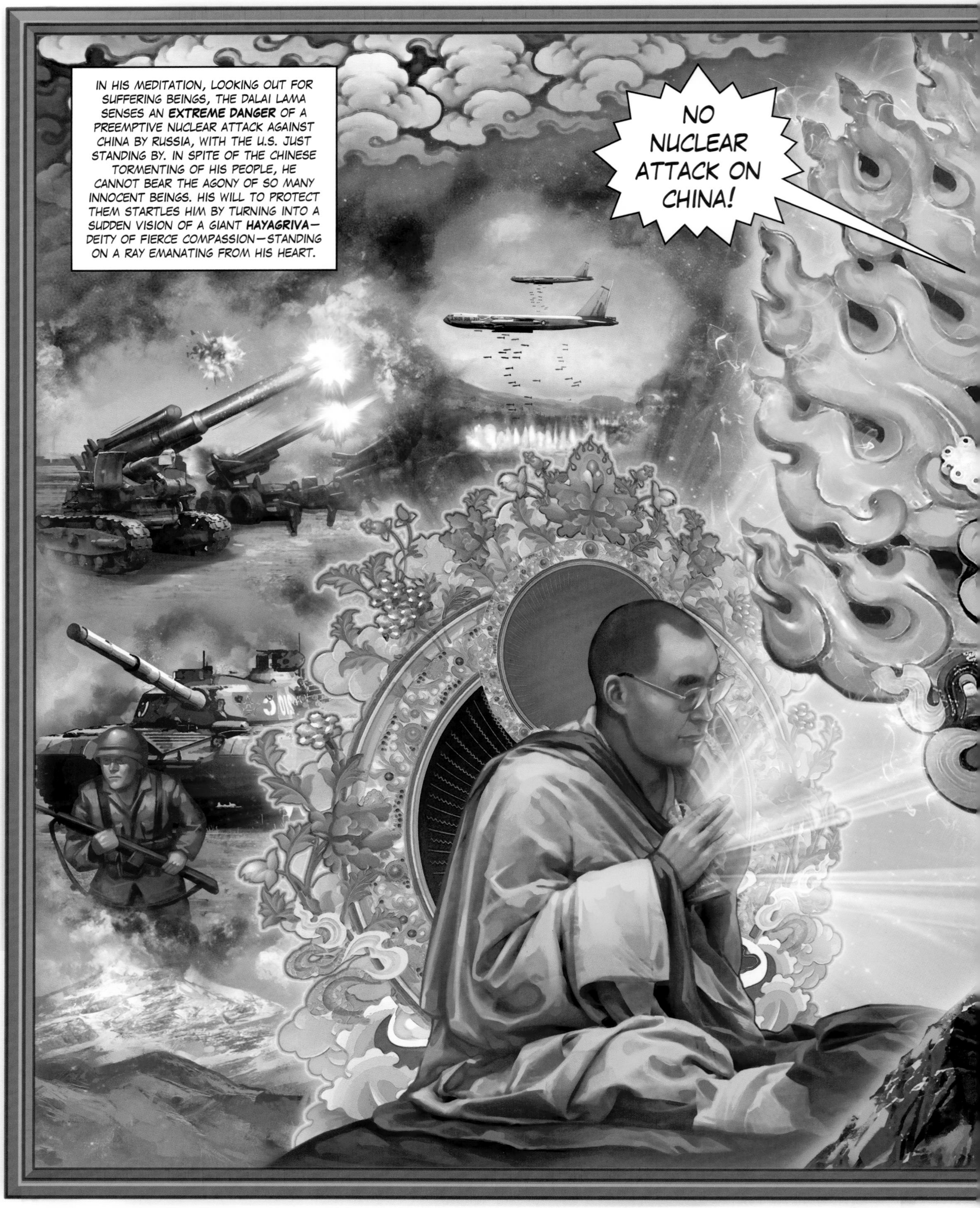
IN HIS MEDITATION, LOOKING OUT FOR SUFFERING BEINGS, THE DALAI LAMA SENSES AN **EXTREME DANGER** OF A PREEMPTIVE NUCLEAR ATTACK AGAINST CHINA BY RUSSIA, WITH THE U.S. JUST STANDING BY. IN SPITE OF THE CHINESE TORMENTING OF HIS PEOPLE, HE CANNOT BEAR THE AGONY OF SO MANY INNOCENT BEINGS. HIS WILL TO PROTECT THEM STARTLES HIM BY TURNING INTO A SUDDEN VISION OF A GIANT **HAYAGRIVA**—DEITY OF FIERCE COMPASSION—STANDING ON A RAY EMANATING FROM HIS HEART.
NO NUCLEAR ATTACK ON CHINA!

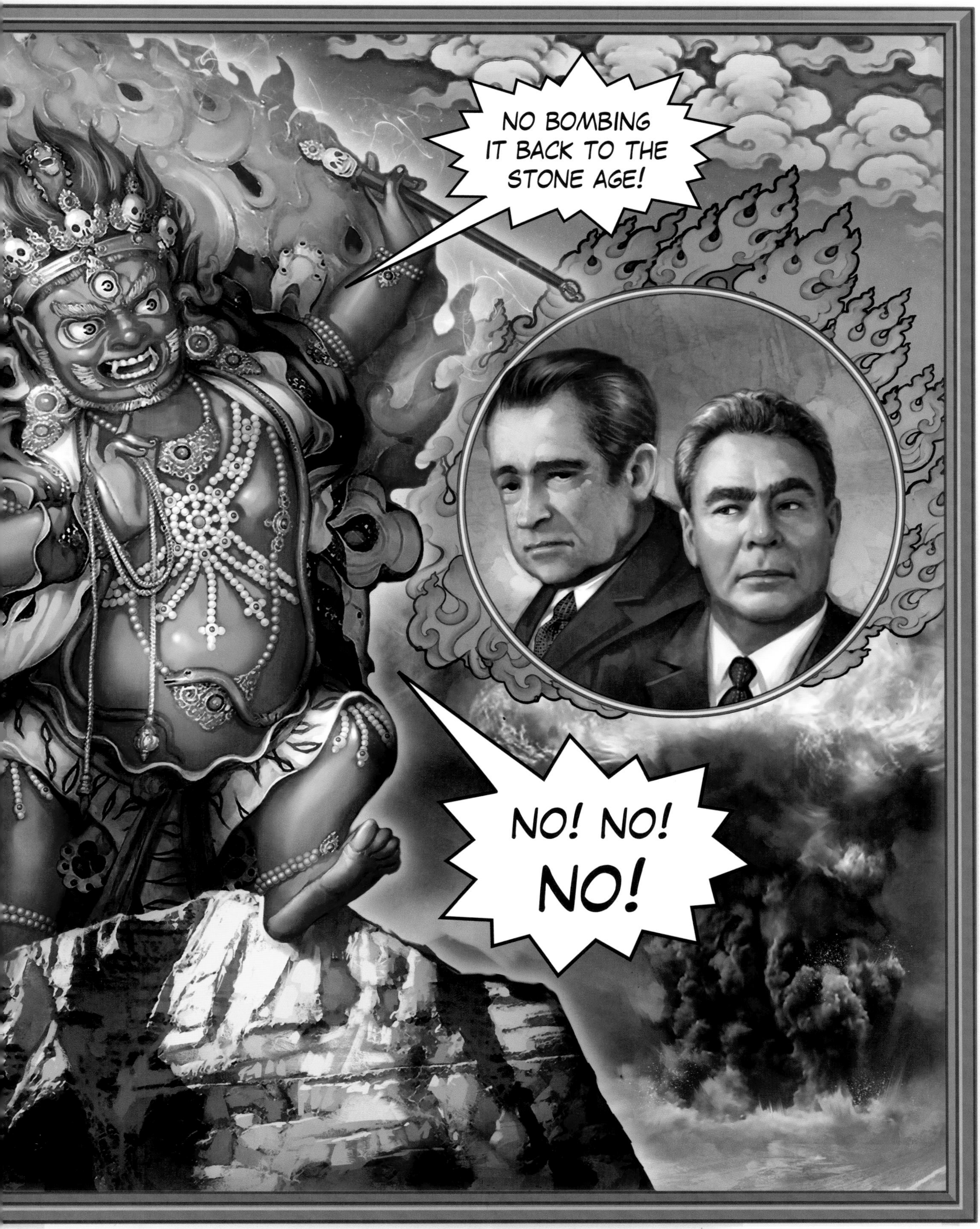
NO BOMBING IT BACK TO THE STONE AGE!
NO! NO! NO!

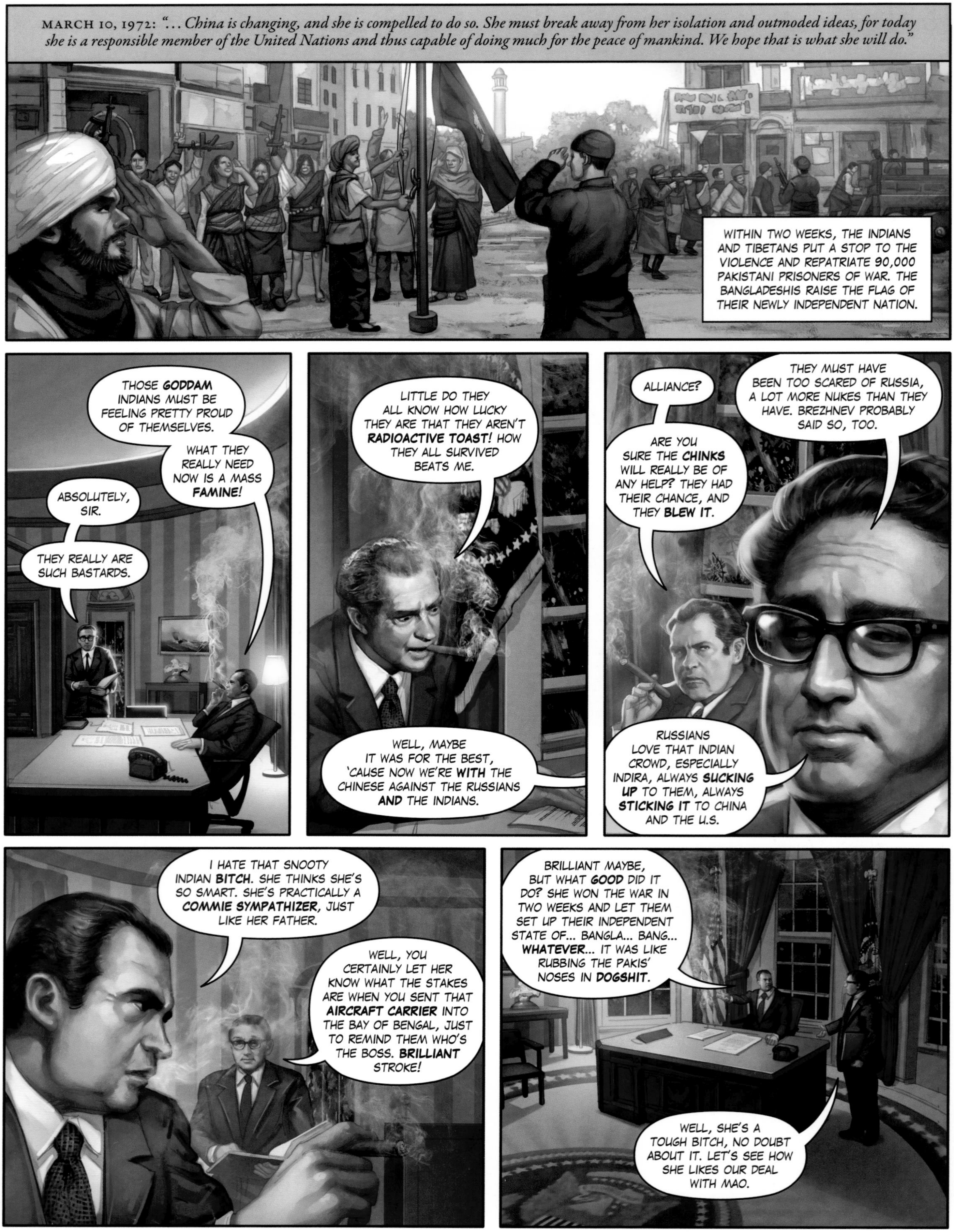
MARCH 10, 1972: "... China is changing, and she is compelled to do so. She must break away from her isolation and outmoded ideas, for today she is a responsible member of the United Nations and thus capable of doing much for the peace of mankind. We hope that is what she will do."
WITHIN TWO WEEKS, THE INDIANS AND TIBETANS PUT A STOP TO THE VIOLENCE AND REPATRIATE 90,000 PAKISTANI PRISONERS OF WAR. THE BANGLADESHIS RAISE THE FLAG OF THEIR NEWLY INDEPENDENT NATION.
THOSE GODDAM INDIANS MUST BE FEELING PRETTY PROUD OF THEMSELVES.
WHAT THEY REALLY NEED NOW IS A MASS FAMINE!
ABSOLUTELY, SIR.
THEY REALLY ARE SUCH BASTARDS.
LITTLE DO THEY ALL KNOW HOW LUCKY THEY ARE THAT THEY AREN'T RADIOACTIVE TOAST! HOW THEY ALL SURVIVED BEATS ME.
WELL, MAYBE IT WAS FOR THE BEST, 'CAUSE NOW WE'RE WITH THE CHINESE AGAINST THE RUSSIANS AND THE INDIANS.
ALLIANCE?
THEY MUST HAVE BEEN TOO SCARED OF RUSSIA, A LOT MORE NUKES THAN THEY HAVE. BREZHNEV PROBABLY SAID SO, TOO.
ARE YOU SURE THE CHINKS WILL REALLY BE OF ANY HELP? THEY HAD THEIR CHANCE, AND THEY BLEW IT.
RUSSIANS LOVE THAT INDIAN CROWD, ESPECIALLY INDIRA, ALWAYS SUCKING UP TO THEM, ALWAYS STICKING IT TO CHINA AND THE U.S.
I HATE THAT SNOOTY INDIAN BITCH. SHE THINKS SHE'S SO SMART. SHE'S PRACTICALLY A COMMIE SYMPATHIZER, JUST LIKE HER FATHER.
WELL, YOU CERTAINLY LET HER KNOW WHAT THE STAKES ARE WHEN YOU SENT THAT AIRCRAFT CARRIER INTO THE BAY OF BENGAL, JUST TO REMIND THEM WHO'S THE BOSS. BRILLIANT STROKE!
BRILLIANT MAYBE, BUT WHAT GOOD DID IT DO? SHE WON THE WAR IN TWO WEEKS AND LET THEM SET UP THEIR INDEPENDENT STATE OF... BANGLA... BANG... WHATEVER... IT WAS LIKE RUBBING THE PAKIS' NOSES IN DOGSHIT.
WELL, SHE'S A TOUGH BITCH, NO DOUBT ABOUT IT. LET'S SEE HOW SHE LIKES OUR DEAL WITH MAO.

MARCH 10, 1973: *"Many changes have been occurring in the international political scene, and I hope the Chinese leaders will discard their present narrow-minded policy and listen to reason, and see the reality that is lying all around them. There will be a satisfactory conclusion."*

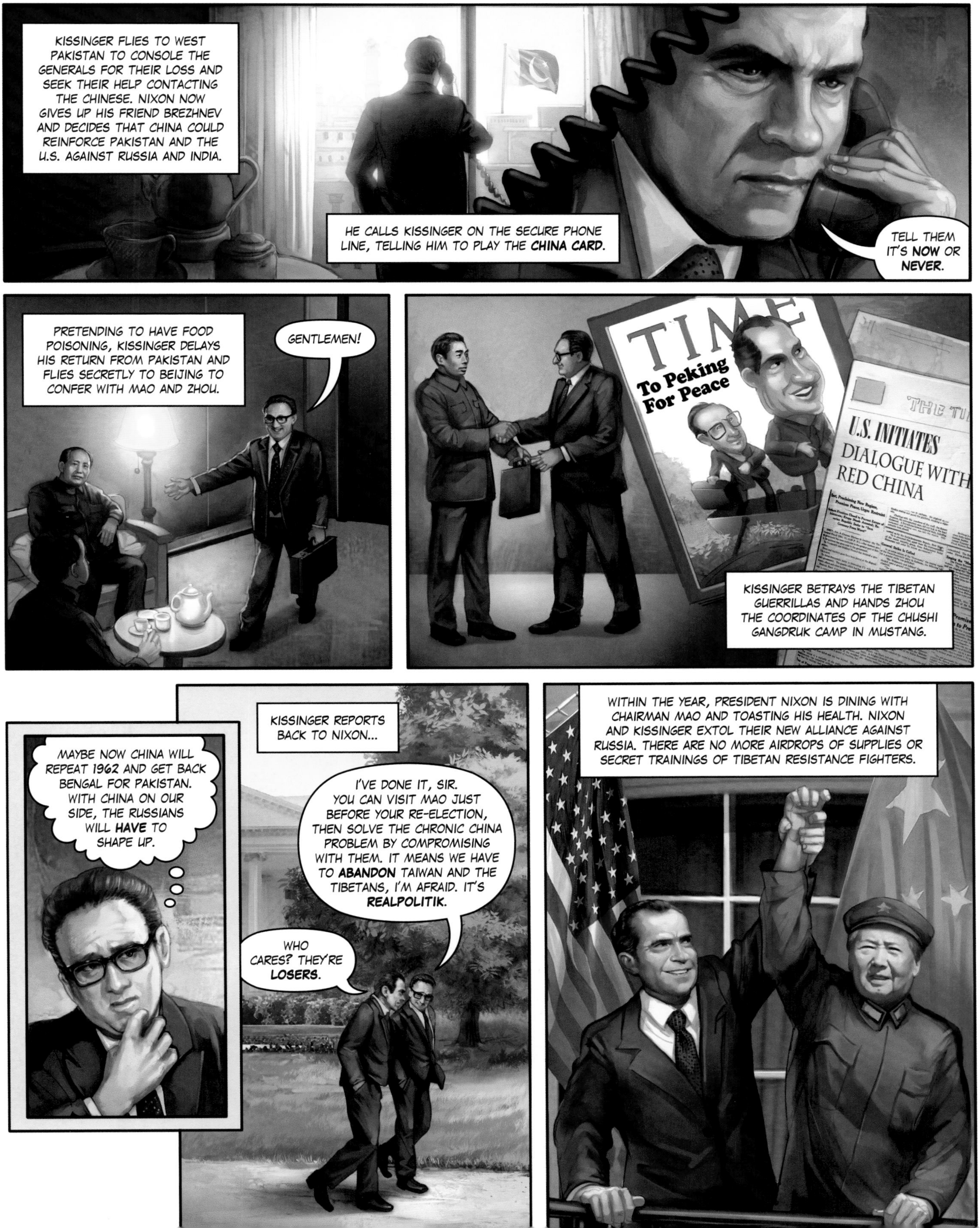

KISSINGER FLIES TO WEST PAKISTAN TO CONSOLE THE GENERALS FOR THEIR LOSS AND SEEK THEIR HELP CONTACTING THE CHINESE. NIXON NOW GIVES UP HIS FRIEND BREZHNEV AND DECIDES THAT CHINA COULD REINFORCE PAKISTAN AND THE U.S. AGAINST RUSSIA AND INDIA.
HE CALLS KISSINGER ON THE SECURE PHONE LINE, TELLING HIM TO PLAY THE **CHINA CARD**.
TELL THEM IT'S **NOW** OR **NEVER**.
PRETENDING TO HAVE FOOD POISONING, KISSINGER DELAYS HIS RETURN FROM PAKISTAN AND FLIES SECRETLY TO BEIJING TO CONFER WITH MAO AND ZHOU.
GENTLEMEN!
TIME
To Peking For Peace
U.S. INITIATES DIALOGUE WITH RED CHINA
KISSINGER BETRAYS THE TIBETAN GUERRILLAS AND HANDS ZHOU THE COORDINATES OF THE CHUSHI GANGDRUK CAMP IN MUSTANG.
MAYBE NOW CHINA WILL REPEAT 1962 AND GET BACK BENGAL FOR PAKISTAN. WITH CHINA ON OUR SIDE, THE RUSSIANS WILL **HAVE** TO SHAPE UP.
KISSINGER REPORTS BACK TO NIXON...
I'VE DONE IT, SIR. YOU CAN VISIT MAO JUST BEFORE YOUR RE-ELECTION, THEN SOLVE THE CHRONIC CHINA PROBLEM BY COMPROMISING WITH THEM. IT MEANS WE HAVE TO **ABANDON** TAIWAN AND THE TIBETANS, I'M AFRAID. IT'S **REALPOLITIK**.
WHO CARES? THEY'RE **LOSERS**.
WITHIN THE YEAR, PRESIDENT NIXON IS DINING WITH CHAIRMAN MAO AND TOASTING HIS HEALTH. NIXON AND KISSINGER EXTOL THEIR NEW ALLIANCE AGAINST RUSSIA. THERE ARE NO MORE AIRDROPS OF SUPPLIES OR SECRET TRAININGS OF TIBETAN RESISTANCE FIGHTERS.

MARCH 10, 1974: *"What is the spirit of March 10? We say it is the cause of Tibet. But what is the cause of Tibet? Is it a struggle against a race, a nation and an ideology? Or is it an unreasonable struggle waged by a minority in exile for their own interests? It is none of these. The cause of Tibet is the cause of the Tibetan people; it is the cause of six million people. It is the struggle of a people to determine their own identity. Until they are satisfied, the struggle for Tibet will continue. I believe in justice and truth, without which there is no basis for human hope. I also believe in the right of every nation to struggle for its freedom, including Tibet and its neighboring states that have fallen victim to Chinese aggression. Although there are signs of liberalization in Lhasa itself and some border areas, this has in no way alleviated the suffering of the vast majority of the people. Refugees still report that the overall situation in Tibet continues to be very grave."*

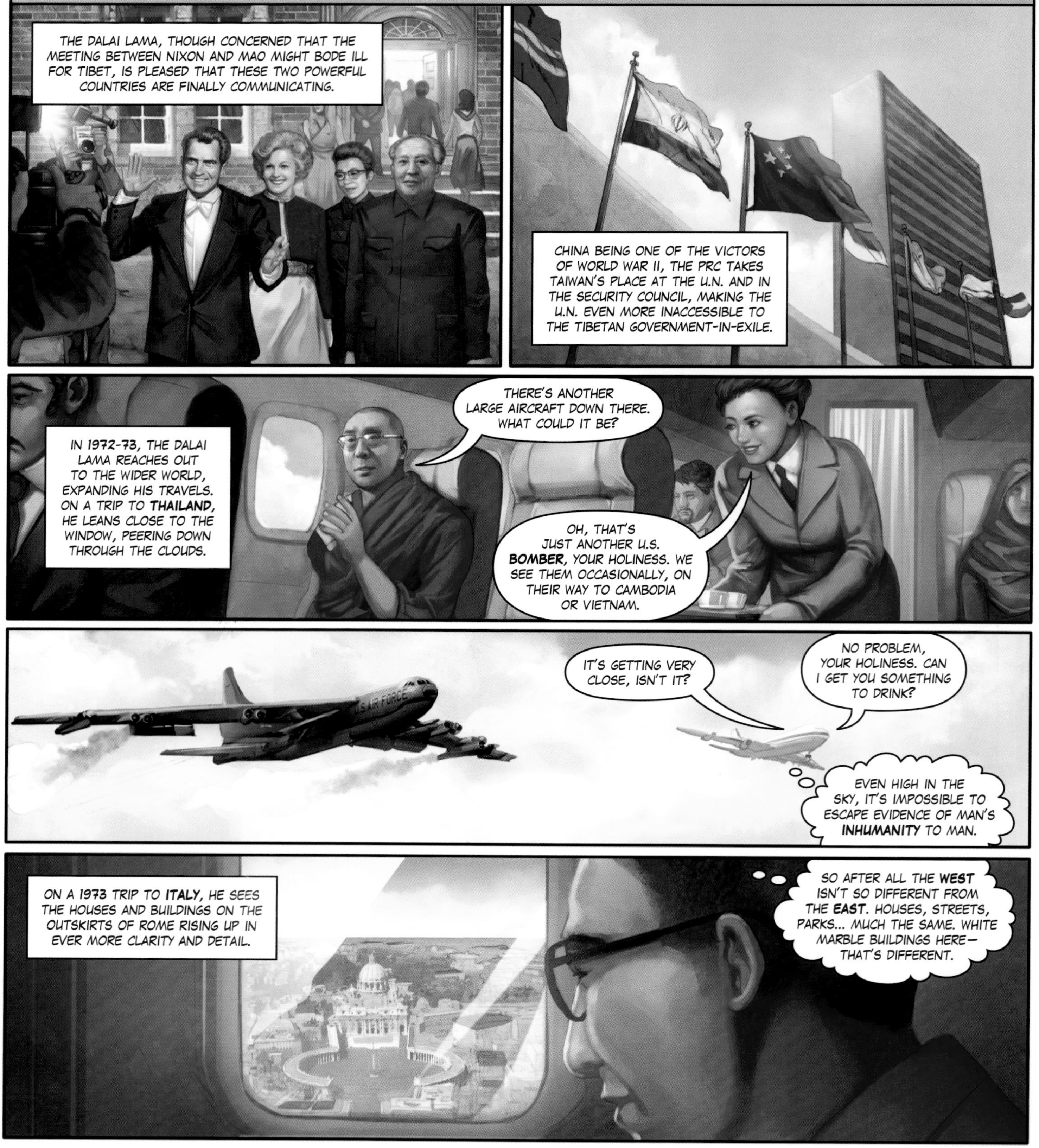
THE DALAI LAMA, THOUGH CONCERNED THAT THE MEETING BETWEEN NIXON AND MAO MIGHT BODE ILL FOR TIBET, IS PLEASED THAT THESE TWO POWERFUL COUNTRIES ARE FINALLY COMMUNICATING.
CHINA BEING ONE OF THE VICTORS OF WORLD WAR II, THE PRC TAKES TAIWAN'S PLACE AT THE U.N. AND IN THE SECURITY COUNCIL, MAKING THE U.N. EVEN MORE INACCESSIBLE TO THE TIBETAN GOVERNMENT-IN-EXILE.
IN 1972-73, THE DALAI LAMA REACHES OUT TO THE WIDER WORLD, EXPANDING HIS TRAVELS. ON A TRIP TO **THAILAND**, HE LEANS CLOSE TO THE WINDOW, PEERING DOWN THROUGH THE CLOUDS.
THERE'S ANOTHER LARGE AIRCRAFT DOWN THERE. WHAT COULD IT BE?
OH, THAT'S JUST ANOTHER U.S. **BOMBER**, YOUR HOLINESS. WE SEE THEM OCCASIONALLY, ON THEIR WAY TO CAMBODIA OR VIETNAM.
U.S. AIR FORCE
IT'S GETTING VERY CLOSE, ISN'T IT?
NO PROBLEM, YOUR HOLINESS. CAN I GET YOU SOMETHING TO DRINK?
EVEN HIGH IN THE SKY, IT'S IMPOSSIBLE TO ESCAPE EVIDENCE OF MAN'S **INHUMANITY** TO MAN.
ON A **1973** TRIP TO **ITALY**, HE SEES THE HOUSES AND BUILDINGS ON THE OUTSKIRTS OF ROME RISING UP IN EVER MORE CLARITY AND DETAIL.
SO AFTER ALL THE **WEST** ISN'T SO DIFFERENT FROM THE **EAST**. HOUSES, STREETS, PARKS... MUCH THE SAME. WHITE MARBLE BUILDINGS HERE—THAT'S DIFFERENT.

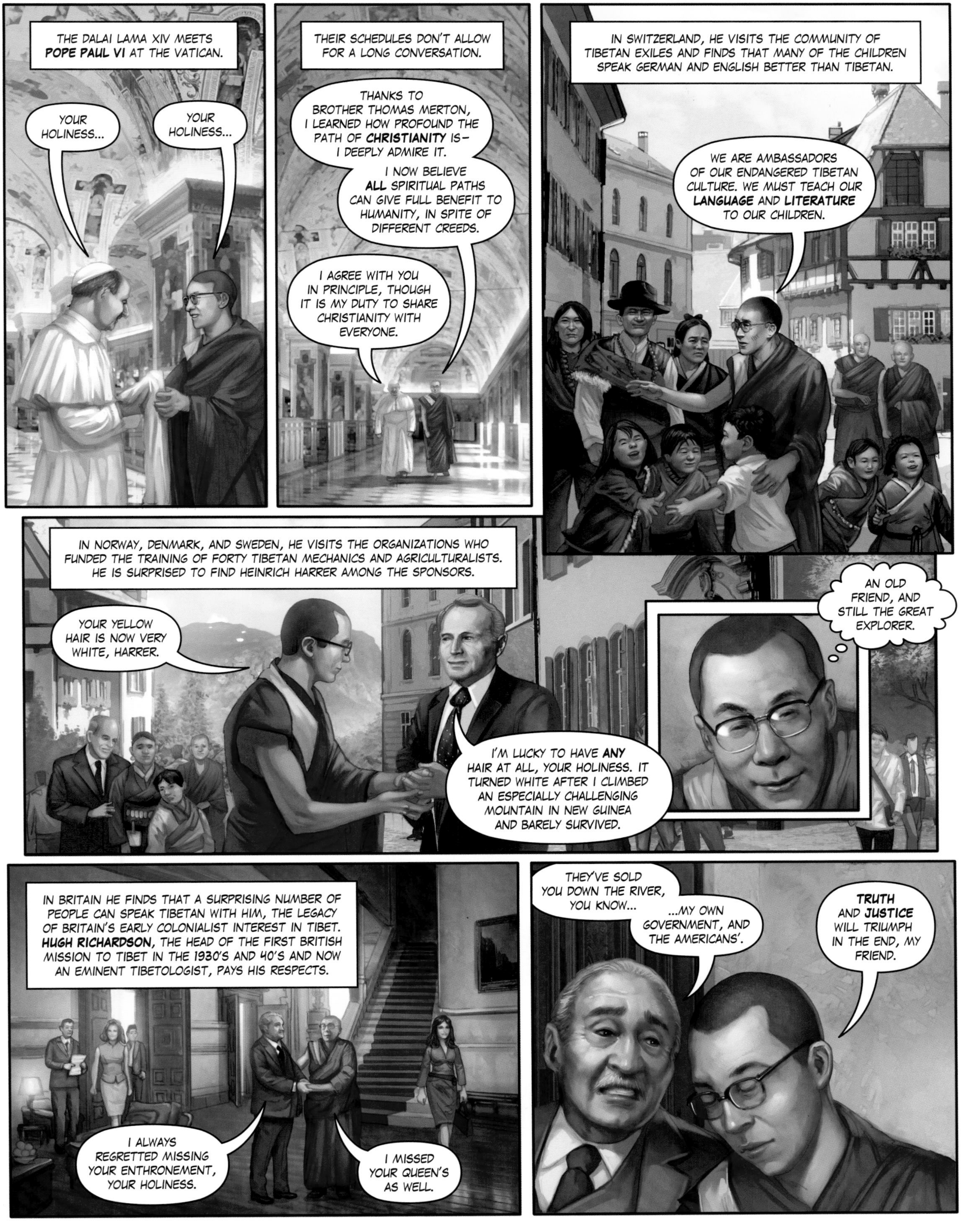
THE DALAI LAMA XIV MEETS POPE PAUL VI AT THE VATICAN.
YOUR HOLINESS...
YOUR HOLINESS...
THEIR SCHEDULES DON'T ALLOW FOR A LONG CONVERSATION.
THANKS TO BROTHER THOMAS MERTON, I LEARNED HOW PROFOUND THE PATH OF CHRISTIANITY IS– I DEEPLY ADMIRE IT.
I NOW BELIEVE ALL SPIRITUAL PATHS CAN GIVE FULL BENEFIT TO HUMANITY, IN SPITE OF DIFFERENT CREEDS.
I AGREE WITH YOU IN PRINCIPLE, THOUGH IT IS MY DUTY TO SHARE CHRISTIANITY WITH EVERYONE.
IN SWITZERLAND, HE VISITS THE COMMUNITY OF TIBETAN EXILES AND FINDS THAT MANY OF THE CHILDREN SPEAK GERMAN AND ENGLISH BETTER THAN TIBETAN.
WE ARE AMBASSADORS OF OUR ENDANGERED TIBETAN CULTURE. WE MUST TEACH OUR LANGUAGE AND LITERATURE TO OUR CHILDREN.
IN NORWAY, DENMARK, AND SWEDEN, HE VISITS THE ORGANIZATIONS WHO FUNDED THE TRAINING OF FORTY TIBETAN MECHANICS AND AGRICULTURALISTS. HE IS SURPRISED TO FIND HEINRICH HARRER AMONG THE SPONSORS.
YOUR YELLOW HAIR IS NOW VERY WHITE, HARRER.
I'M LUCKY TO HAVE ANY HAIR AT ALL, YOUR HOLINESS. IT TURNED WHITE AFTER I CLIMBED AN ESPECIALLY CHALLENGING MOUNTAIN IN NEW GUINEA AND BARELY SURVIVED.
AN OLD FRIEND, AND STILL THE GREAT EXPLORER.
IN BRITAIN HE FINDS THAT A SURPRISING NUMBER OF PEOPLE CAN SPEAK TIBETAN WITH HIM, THE LEGACY OF BRITAIN'S EARLY COLONIALIST INTEREST IN TIBET. HUGH RICHARDSON, THE HEAD OF THE FIRST BRITISH MISSION TO TIBET IN THE 1930'S AND 40'S AND NOW AN EMINENT TIBETOLOGIST, PAYS HIS RESPECTS.
I ALWAYS REGRETTED MISSING YOUR ENTHRONEMENT, YOUR HOLINESS.
I MISSED YOUR QUEEN'S AS WELL.
THEY'VE SOLD YOU DOWN THE RIVER, YOU KNOW...
...MY OWN GOVERNMENT, AND THE AMERICANS'.
TRUTH AND JUSTICE WILL TRIUMPH IN THE END, MY FRIEND.

MARCH 10, 1975: *"We Tibetans in exile have made commendable progress in material well-being, both individually and collectively. Especially in the education of our youth, we have done remarkably. We enjoy full rights and live as complete human beings, as others do in the rest of the world. . . ."*

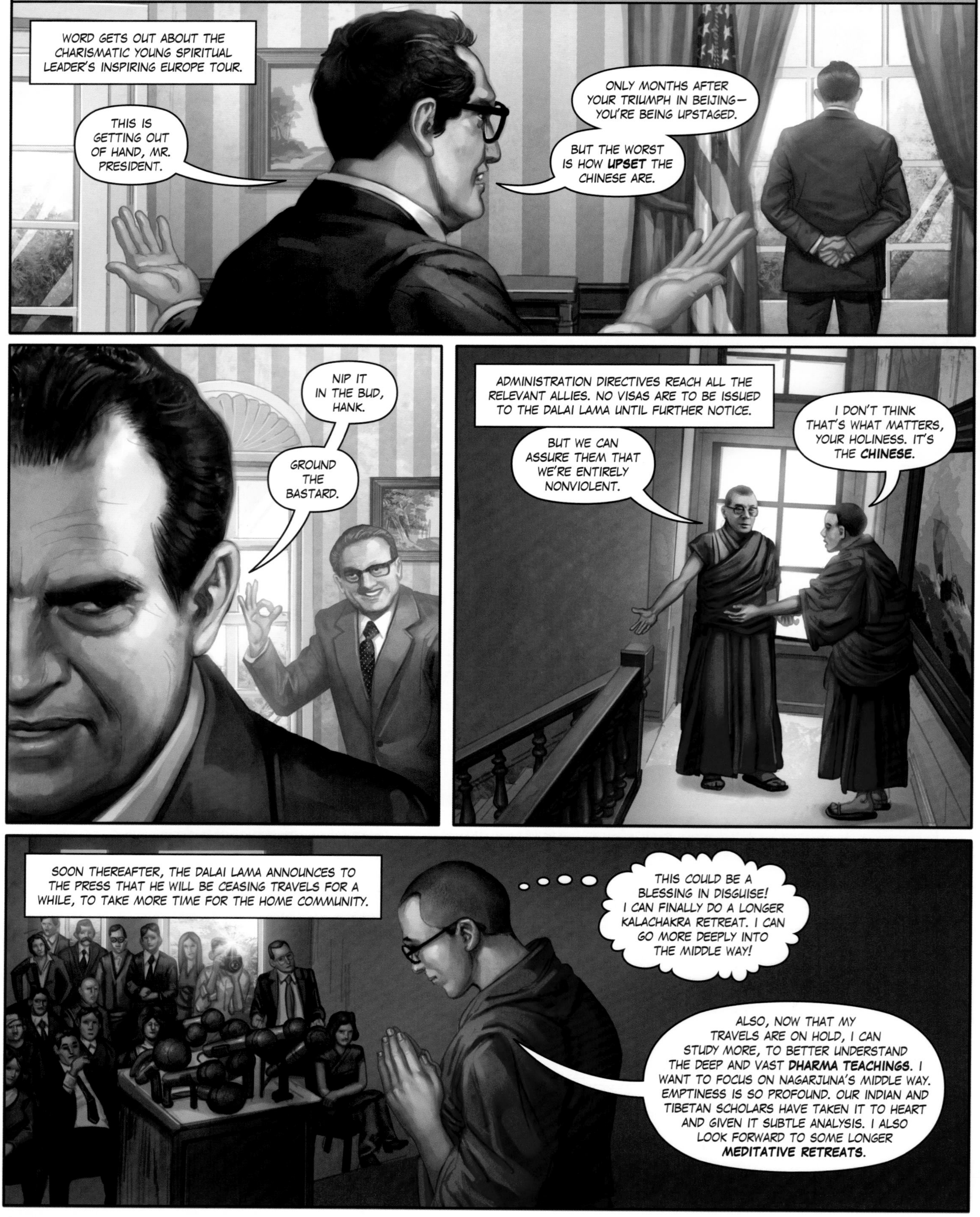
WORD GETS OUT ABOUT THE CHARISMATIC YOUNG SPIRITUAL LEADER'S INSPIRING EUROPE TOUR.
THIS IS GETTING OUT OF HAND, MR. PRESIDENT.
ONLY MONTHS AFTER YOUR TRIUMPH IN BEIJING—YOU'RE BEING UPSTAGED.
BUT THE WORST IS HOW **UPSET** THE CHINESE ARE.
NIP IT IN THE BUD, HANK.
GROUND THE BASTARD.
ADMINISTRATION DIRECTIVES REACH ALL THE RELEVANT ALLIES. NO VISAS ARE TO BE ISSUED TO THE DALAI LAMA UNTIL FURTHER NOTICE.
BUT WE CAN ASSURE THEM THAT WE'RE ENTIRELY NONVIOLENT.
I DON'T THINK THAT'S WHAT MATTERS, YOUR HOLINESS. IT'S THE **CHINESE**.
SOON THEREAFTER, THE DALAI LAMA ANNOUNCES TO THE PRESS THAT HE WILL BE CEASING TRAVELS FOR A WHILE, TO TAKE MORE TIME FOR THE HOME COMMUNITY.
THIS COULD BE A BLESSING IN DISGUISE! I CAN FINALLY DO A LONGER KALACHAKRA RETREAT. I CAN GO MORE DEEPLY INTO THE MIDDLE WAY!
ALSO, NOW THAT MY TRAVELS ARE ON HOLD, I CAN STUDY MORE, TO BETTER UNDERSTAND THE DEEP AND VAST **DHARMA TEACHINGS**. I WANT TO FOCUS ON NAGARJUNA'S MIDDLE WAY. EMPTINESS IS SO PROFOUND. OUR INDIAN AND TIBETAN SCHOLARS HAVE TAKEN IT TO HEART AND GIVEN IT SUBTLE ANALYSIS. I ALSO LOOK FORWARD TO SOME LONGER **MEDITATIVE RETREATS**.

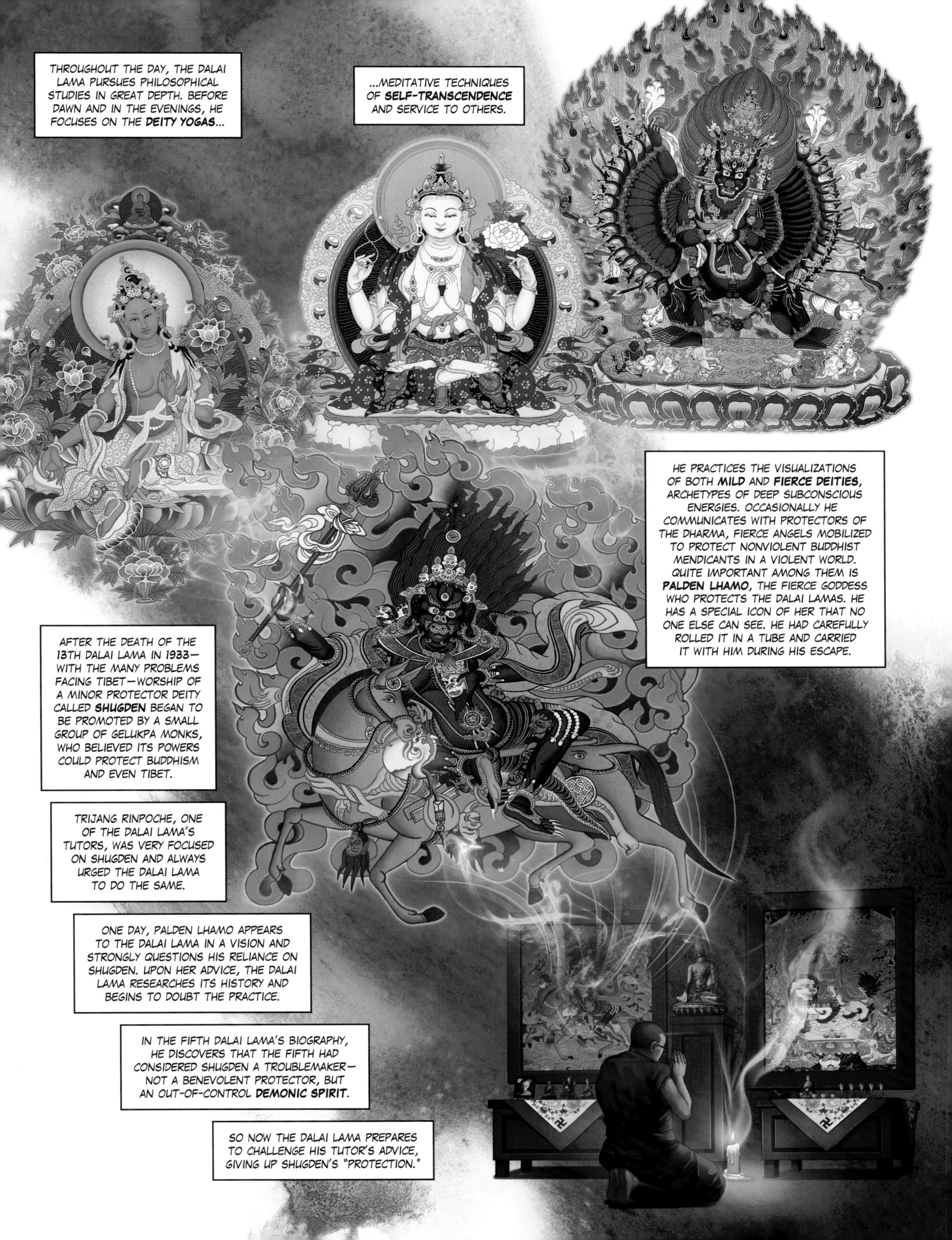
THROUGHOUT THE DAY, THE DALAI LAMA PURSUES PHILOSOPHICAL STUDIES IN GREAT DEPTH. BEFORE DAWN AND IN THE EVENINGS, HE FOCUSES ON THE DEITY YOGAS...
...MEDITATIVE TECHNIQUES OF SELF-TRANSCENDENCE AND SERVICE TO OTHERS.
HE PRACTICES THE VISUALIZATIONS OF BOTH MILD AND FIERCE DEITIES, ARCHETYPES OF DEEP SUBCONSCIOUS ENERGIES. OCCASIONALLY HE COMMUNICATES WITH PROTECTORS OF THE DHARMA, FIERCE ANGELS MOBILIZED TO PROTECT NONVIOLENT BUDDHIST MENDICANTS IN A VIOLENT WORLD. QUITE IMPORTANT AMONG THEM IS PALDEN LHAMO, THE FIERCE GODDESS WHO PROTECTS THE DALAI LAMAS. HE HAS A SPECIAL ICON OF HER THAT NO ONE ELSE CAN SEE. HE HAD CAREFULLY ROLLED IT IN A TUBE AND CARRIED IT WITH HIM DURING HIS ESCAPE.
AFTER THE DEATH OF THE 13TH DALAI LAMA IN 1933—WITH THE MANY PROBLEMS FACING TIBET—WORSHIP OF A MINOR PROTECTOR DEITY CALLED SHUGDEN BEGAN TO BE PROMOTED BY A SMALL GROUP OF GELUKPA MONKS, WHO BELIEVED ITS POWERS COULD PROTECT BUDDHISM AND EVEN TIBET.
TRIJANG RINPOCHE, ONE OF THE DALAI LAMA'S TUTORS, WAS VERY FOCUSED ON SHUGDEN AND ALWAYS URGED THE DALAI LAMA TO DO THE SAME.
ONE DAY, PALDEN LHAMO APPEARS TO THE DALAI LAMA IN A VISION AND STRONGLY QUESTIONS HIS RELIANCE ON SHUGDEN. UPON HER ADVICE, THE DALAI LAMA RESEARCHES ITS HISTORY AND BEGINS TO DOUBT THE PRACTICE.
IN THE FIFTH DALAI LAMA'S BIOGRAPHY, HE DISCOVERS THAT THE FIFTH HAD CONSIDERED SHUGDEN A TROUBLEMAKER—NOT A BENEVOLENT PROTECTOR, BUT AN OUT-OF-CONTROL DEMONIC SPIRIT.
SO NOW THE DALAI LAMA PREPARES TO CHALLENGE HIS TUTOR'S ADVICE, GIVING UP SHUGDEN'S "PROTECTION."

MARCH 10, 1975: *"... The issue of Tibet is deeply linked with the changes in international politics and especially with the progress of the peace process in Asia. As such, we must steer the ship of our struggle according to the shifting directions of the winds of international relations to reach the shore of Tibetan freedom and happiness. To attain this goal, we must persevere and become ever more united."*

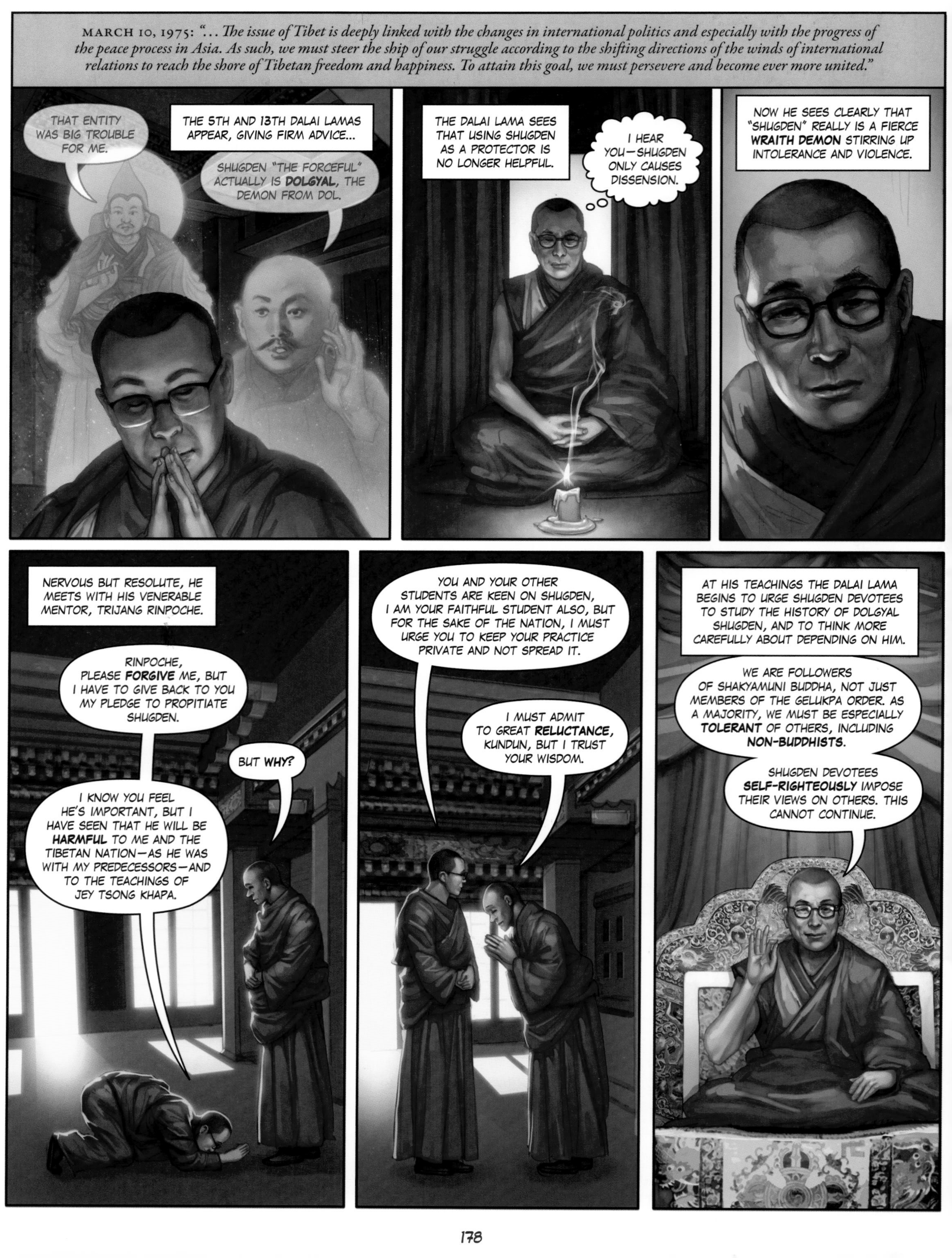

THAT ENTITY WAS BIG TROUBLE FOR ME.
THE 5TH AND 13TH DALAI LAMAS APPEAR, GIVING FIRM ADVICE...
SHUGDEN "THE FORCEFUL" ACTUALLY IS DOLGYAL, THE DEMON FROM DOL.
THE DALAI LAMA SEES THAT USING SHUGDEN AS A PROTECTOR IS NO LONGER HELPFUL.
I HEAR YOU—SHUGDEN ONLY CAUSES DISSENSION.
NOW HE SEES CLEARLY THAT "SHUGDEN" REALLY IS A FIERCE WRAITH DEMON STIRRING UP INTOLERANCE AND VIOLENCE.
NERVOUS BUT RESOLUTE, HE MEETS WITH HIS VENERABLE MENTOR, TRIJANG RINPOCHE.
RINPOCHE, PLEASE FORGIVE ME, BUT I HAVE TO GIVE BACK TO YOU MY PLEDGE TO PROPITIATE SHUGDEN.
BUT WHY?
I KNOW YOU FEEL HE'S IMPORTANT, BUT I HAVE SEEN THAT HE WILL BE HARMFUL TO ME AND THE TIBETAN NATION—AS HE WAS WITH MY PREDECESSORS—AND TO THE TEACHINGS OF JEY TSONG KHAPA.
YOU AND YOUR OTHER STUDENTS ARE KEEN ON SHUGDEN, I AM YOUR FAITHFUL STUDENT ALSO, BUT FOR THE SAKE OF THE NATION, I MUST URGE YOU TO KEEP YOUR PRACTICE PRIVATE AND NOT SPREAD IT.
I MUST ADMIT TO GREAT RELUCTANCE, KUNDUN, BUT I TRUST YOUR WISDOM.
AT HIS TEACHINGS THE DALAI LAMA BEGINS TO URGE SHUGDEN DEVOTEES TO STUDY THE HISTORY OF DOLGYAL SHUGDEN, AND TO THINK MORE CAREFULLY ABOUT DEPENDING ON HIM.
WE ARE FOLLOWERS OF SHAKYAMUNI BUDDHA, NOT JUST MEMBERS OF THE GELUKPA ORDER. AS A MAJORITY, WE MUST BE ESPECIALLY TOLERANT OF OTHERS, INCLUDING NON-BUDDHISTS.
SHUGDEN DEVOTEES SELF-RIGHTEOUSLY IMPOSE THEIR VIEWS ON OTHERS. THIS CANNOT CONTINUE.

MARCH 10, 1976: *"In this twentieth century, the world has witnessed the rise of the sun of equal freedom. People of many nations are enjoying the warmth of freedom, which they did not have before. In ancient times, we Tibetans were known for our high degree of civilization and courage in all Asia. Should we always remain slaves of the barbarous, suffering under their cruel domination? Those of our unfortunate brothers and sisters who remain in Tibet must not lose their faith in the ultimate victory of truth. . . ."*

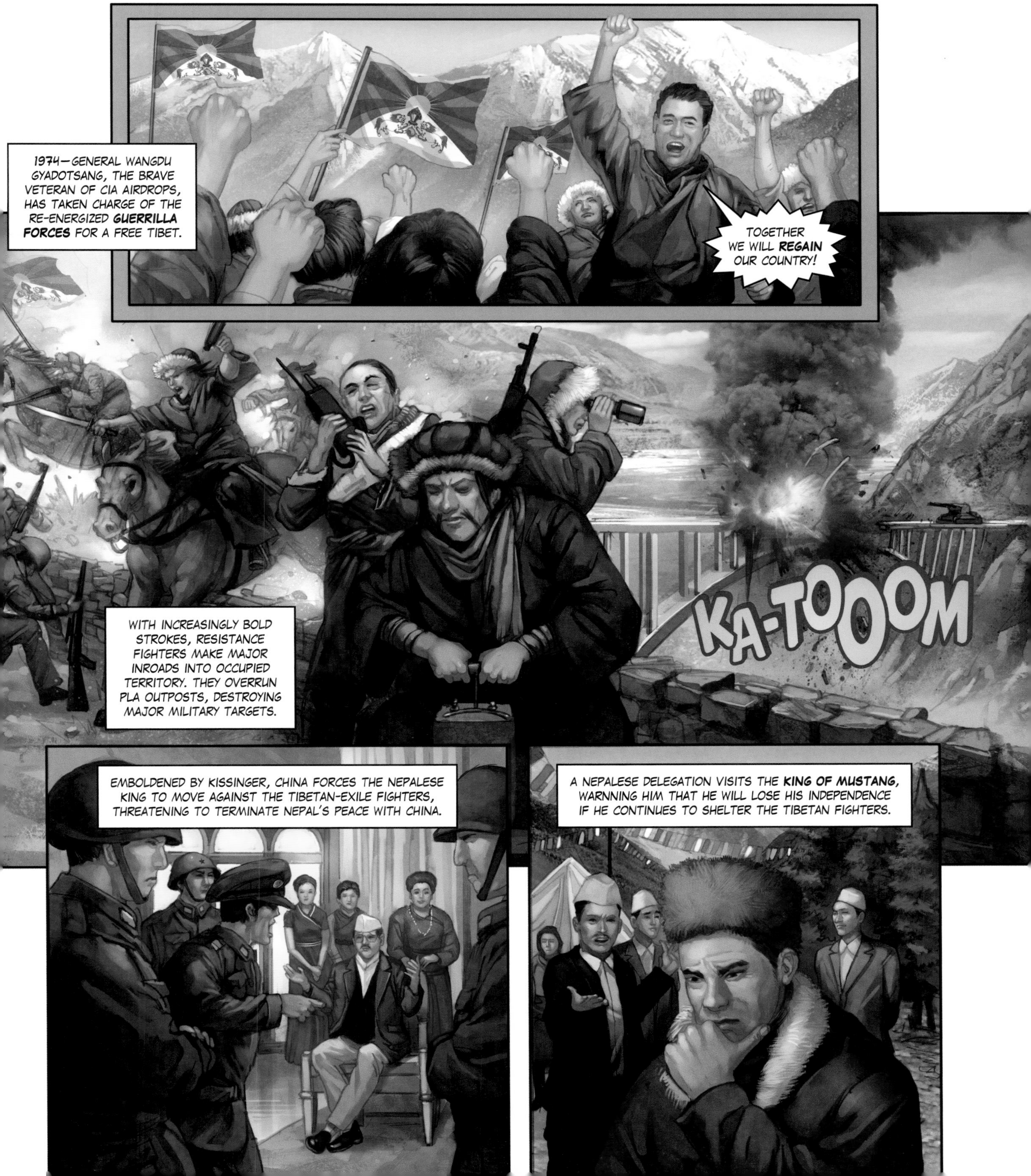

1974—GENERAL WANGDU GYADOTSANG, THE BRAVE VETERAN OF CIA AIRDROPS, HAS TAKEN CHARGE OF THE RE-ENERGIZED **GUERRILLA FORCES** FOR A FREE TIBET.
TOGETHER WE WILL **REGAIN** OUR COUNTRY!
WITH INCREASINGLY BOLD STROKES, RESISTANCE FIGHTERS MAKE MAJOR INROADS INTO OCCUPIED TERRITORY. THEY OVERRUN PLA OUTPOSTS, DESTROYING MAJOR MILITARY TARGETS.
KA-TOOOM
EMBOLDENED BY KISSINGER, CHINA FORCES THE NEPALESE KING TO MOVE AGAINST THE TIBETAN-EXILE FIGHTERS, THREATENING TO TERMINATE NEPAL'S PEACE WITH CHINA.
A NEPALESE DELEGATION VISITS THE **KING OF MUSTANG**, WARNNING HIM THAT HE WILL LOSE HIS INDEPENDENCE IF HE CONTINUES TO SHELTER THE TIBETAN FIGHTERS.

MARCH 10, 1976: *"... Tibet is blessed with bountiful wealth and rich natural beauty. Should our country be converted to a war-machinery manufacturing fortress, and the Tibetan people, its rightful owners, reduced to criminals perpetually subjected to oppression and humiliation?"*

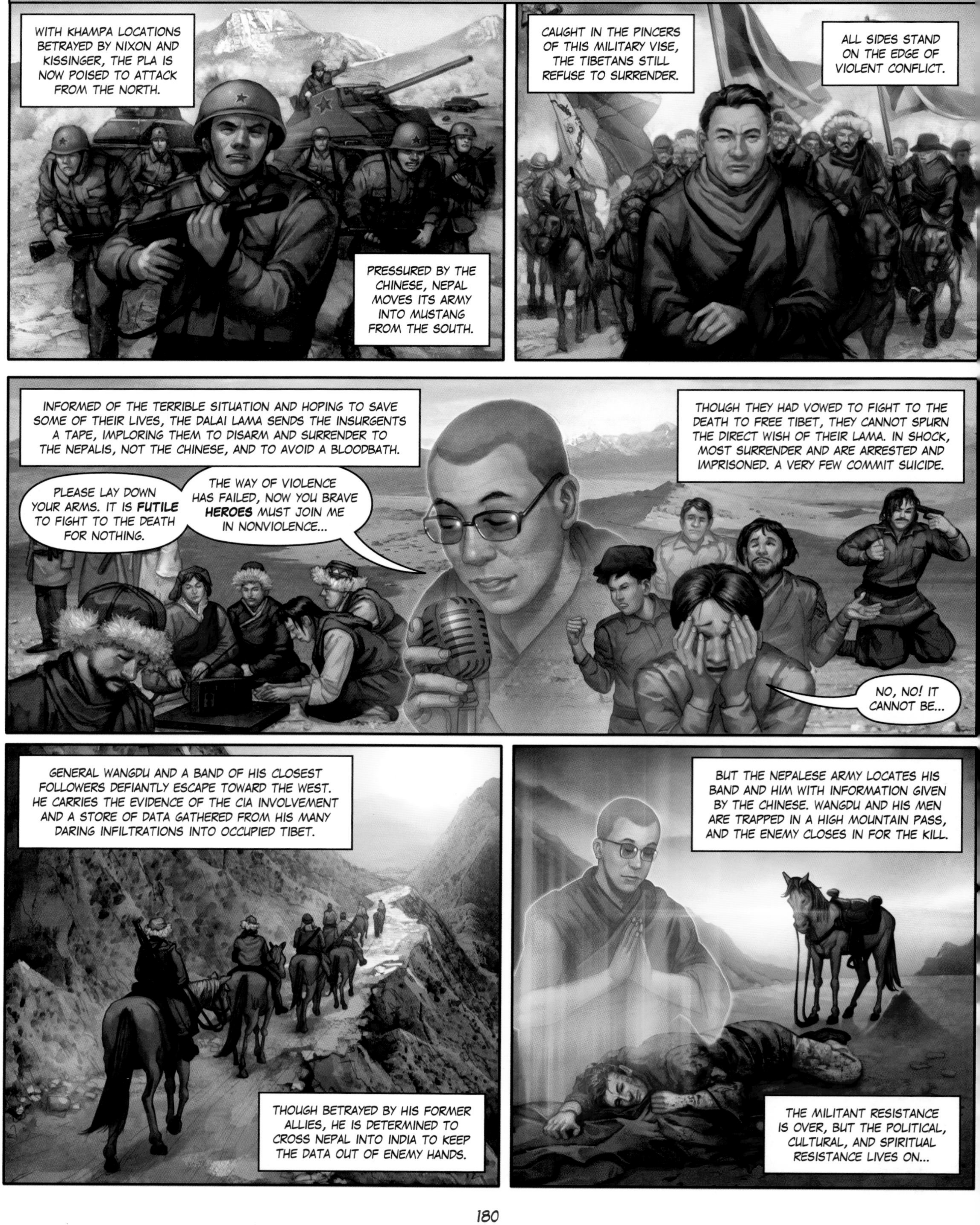

WITH KHAMPA LOCATIONS BETRAYED BY NIXON AND KISSINGER, THE PLA IS NOW POISED TO ATTACK FROM THE NORTH.
PRESSURED BY THE CHINESE, NEPAL MOVES ITS ARMY INTO MUSTANG FROM THE SOUTH.
CAUGHT IN THE PINCERS OF THIS MILITARY VISE, THE TIBETANS STILL REFUSE TO SURRENDER.
ALL SIDES STAND ON THE EDGE OF VIOLENT CONFLICT.
INFORMED OF THE TERRIBLE SITUATION AND HOPING TO SAVE SOME OF THEIR LIVES, THE DALAI LAMA SENDS THE INSURGENTS A TAPE, IMPLORING THEM TO DISARM AND SURRENDER TO THE NEPALIS, NOT THE CHINESE, AND TO AVOID A BLOODBATH.
PLEASE LAY DOWN YOUR ARMS. IT IS **FUTILE** TO FIGHT TO THE DEATH FOR NOTHING.
THE WAY OF VIOLENCE HAS FAILED, NOW YOU BRAVE **HEROES** MUST JOIN ME IN NONVIOLENCE...
THOUGH THEY HAD VOWED TO FIGHT TO THE DEATH TO FREE TIBET, THEY CANNOT SPURN THE DIRECT WISH OF THEIR LAMA. IN SHOCK, MOST SURRENDER AND ARE ARRESTED AND IMPRISONED. A VERY FEW COMMIT SUICIDE.
NO, NO! IT CANNOT BE...
GENERAL WANGDU AND A BAND OF HIS CLOSEST FOLLOWERS DEFIANTLY ESCAPE TOWARD THE WEST. HE CARRIES THE EVIDENCE OF THE CIA INVOLVEMENT AND A STORE OF DATA GATHERED FROM HIS MANY DARING INFILTRATIONS INTO OCCUPIED TIBET.
THOUGH BETRAYED BY HIS FORMER ALLIES, HE IS DETERMINED TO CROSS NEPAL INTO INDIA TO KEEP THE DATA OUT OF ENEMY HANDS.
BUT THE NEPALESE ARMY LOCATES HIS BAND AND HIM WITH INFORMATION GIVEN BY THE CHINESE. WANGDU AND HIS MEN ARE TRAPPED IN A HIGH MOUNTAIN PASS, AND THE ENEMY CLOSES IN FOR THE KILL.
THE MILITANT RESISTANCE IS OVER, BUT THE POLITICAL, CULTURAL, AND SPIRITUAL RESISTANCE LIVES ON...

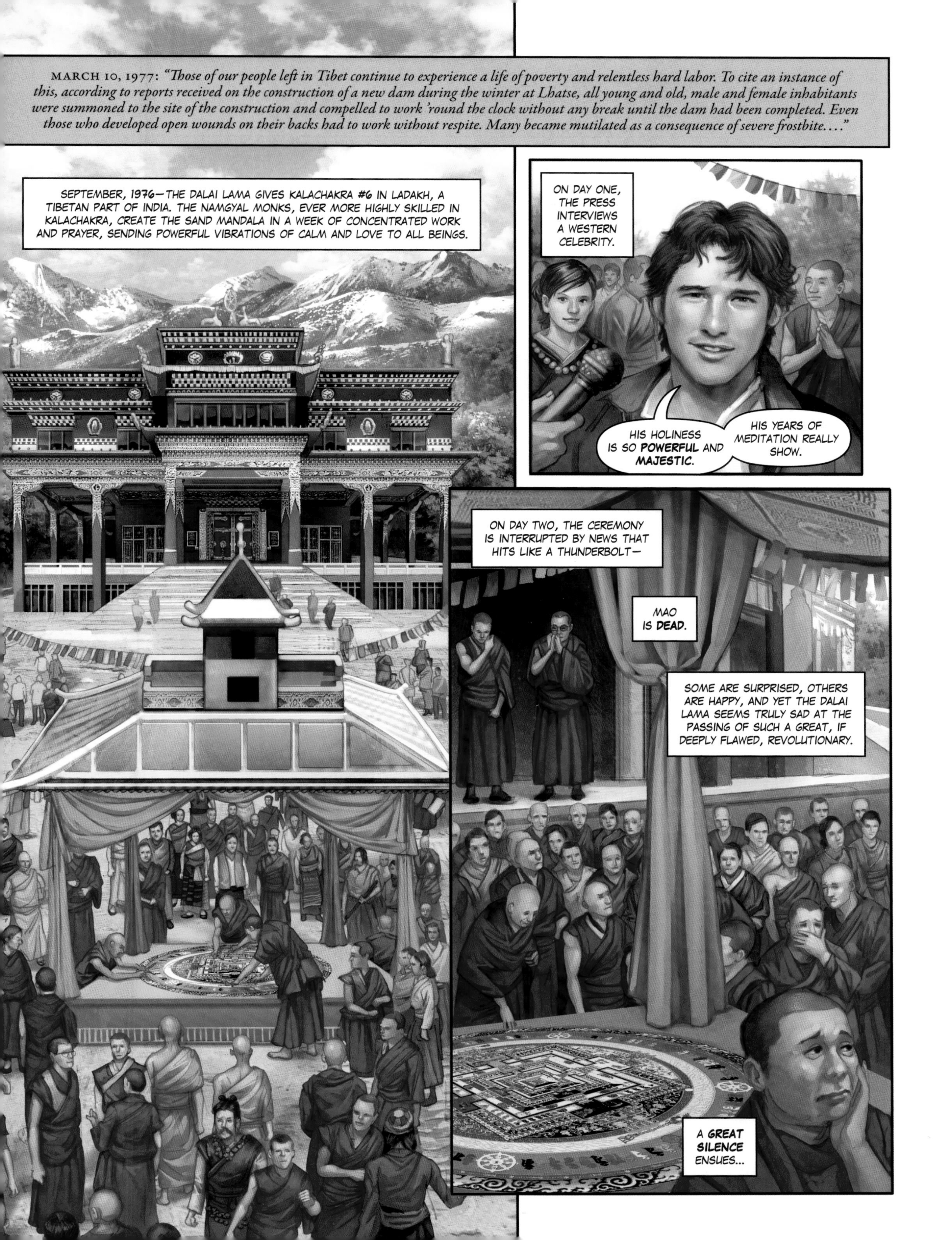
MARCH 10, 1977: "Those of our people left in Tibet continue to experience a life of poverty and relentless hard labor. To cite an instance of this, according to reports received on the construction of a new dam during the winter at Lhatse, all young and old, male and female inhabitants were summoned to the site of the construction and compelled to work 'round the clock without any break until the dam had been completed. Even those who developed open wounds on their backs had to work without respite. Many became mutilated as a consequence of severe frostbite...."
SEPTEMBER, 1976—THE DALAI LAMA GIVES KALACHAKRA #6 IN LADAKH, A TIBETAN PART OF INDIA. THE NAMGYAL MONKS, EVER MORE HIGHLY SKILLED IN KALACHAKRA, CREATE THE SAND MANDALA IN A WEEK OF CONCENTRATED WORK AND PRAYER, SENDING POWERFUL VIBRATIONS OF CALM AND LOVE TO ALL BEINGS.
ON DAY ONE, THE PRESS INTERVIEWS A WESTERN CELEBRITY.
HIS HOLINESS IS SO **POWERFUL** AND **MAJESTIC**.
HIS YEARS OF MEDITATION REALLY SHOW.
ON DAY TWO, THE CEREMONY IS INTERRUPTED BY NEWS THAT HITS LIKE A THUNDERBOLT—
MAO IS **DEAD**.
SOME ARE SURPRISED, OTHERS ARE HAPPY, AND YET THE DALAI LAMA SEEMS TRULY SAD AT THE PASSING OF SUCH A GREAT, IF DEEPLY FLAWED, REVOLUTIONARY.
A **GREAT SILENCE** ENSUES...

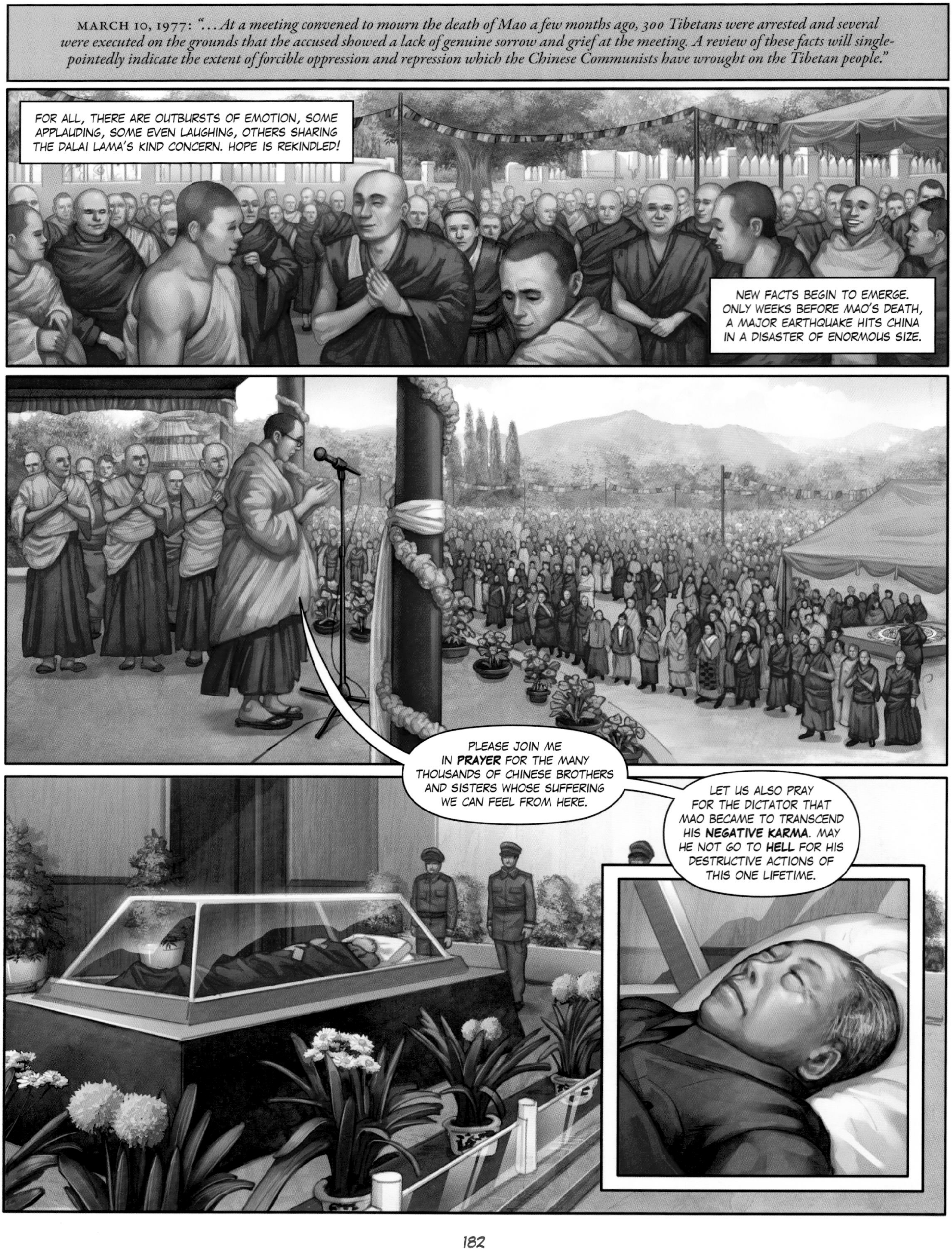
MARCH 10, 1977: "... At a meeting convened to mourn the death of Mao a few months ago, 300 Tibetans were arrested and several were executed on the grounds that the accused showed a lack of genuine sorrow and grief at the meeting. A review of these facts will single-pointedly indicate the extent of forcible oppression and repression which the Chinese Communists have wrought on the Tibetan people."
FOR ALL, THERE ARE OUTBURSTS OF EMOTION, SOME APPLAUDING, SOME EVEN LAUGHING, OTHERS SHARING THE DALAI LAMA'S KIND CONCERN. HOPE IS REKINDLED!
NEW FACTS BEGIN TO EMERGE. ONLY WEEKS BEFORE MAO'S DEATH, A MAJOR EARTHQUAKE HITS CHINA IN A DISASTER OF ENORMOUS SIZE.
PLEASE JOIN ME IN PRAYER FOR THE MANY THOUSANDS OF CHINESE BROTHERS AND SISTERS WHOSE SUFFERING WE CAN FEEL FROM HERE.
LET US ALSO PRAY FOR THE DICTATOR THAT MAO BECAME TO TRANSCEND HIS NEGATIVE KARMA. MAY HE NOT GO TO HELL FOR HIS DESTRUCTIVE ACTIONS OF THIS ONE LIFETIME.

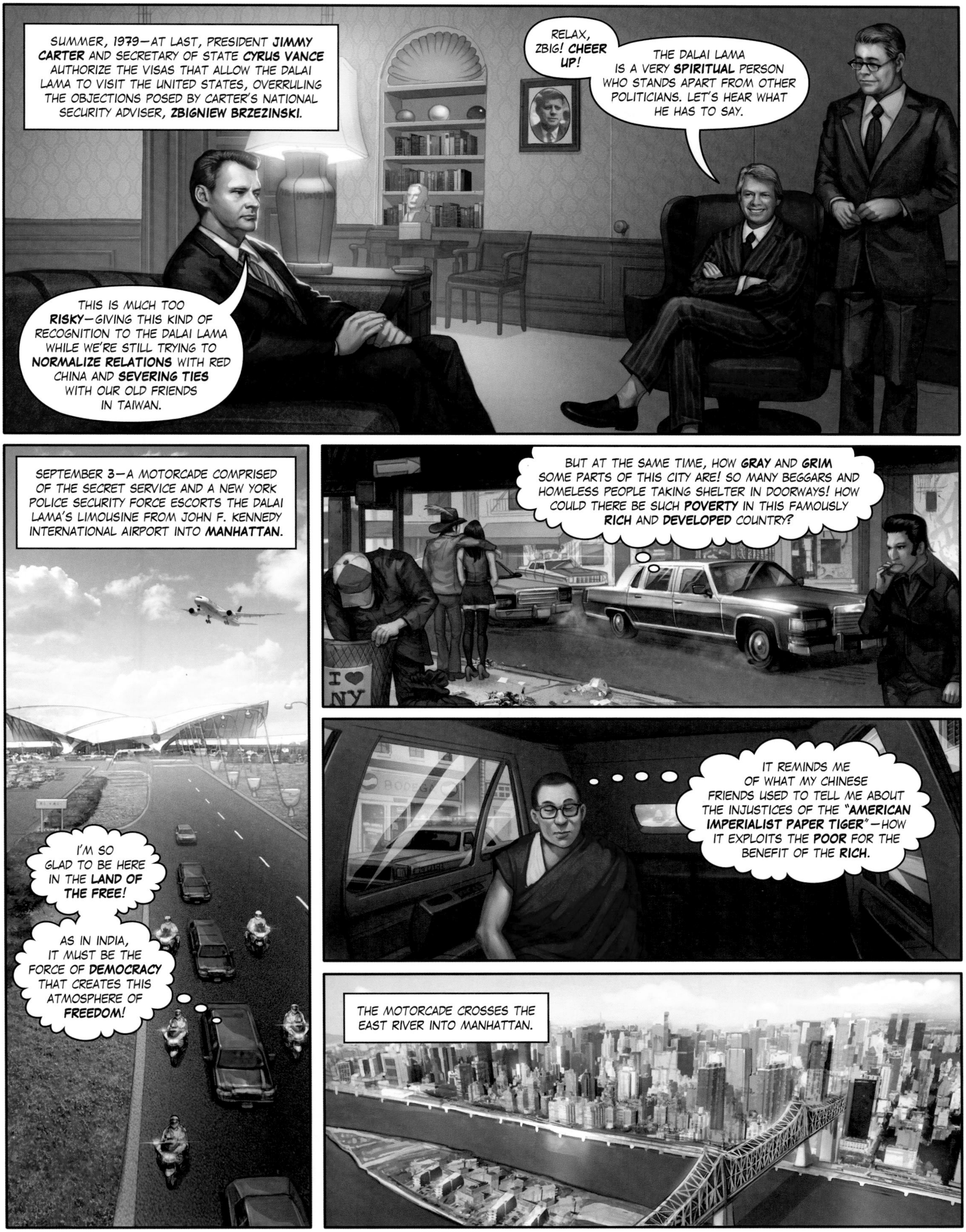

SUMMER, 1979—AT LAST, PRESIDENT **JIMMY CARTER** AND SECRETARY OF STATE **CYRUS VANCE** AUTHORIZE THE VISAS THAT ALLOW THE DALAI LAMA TO VISIT THE UNITED STATES, OVERRULING THE OBJECTIONS POSED BY CARTER'S NATIONAL SECURITY ADVISER, **ZBIGNIEW BRZEZINSKI**.
RELAX, ZBIG! **CHEER UP**!
THE DALAI LAMA IS A VERY **SPIRITUAL** PERSON WHO STANDS APART FROM OTHER POLITICIANS. LET'S HEAR WHAT HE HAS TO SAY.
THIS IS MUCH TOO **RISKY**—GIVING THIS KIND OF RECOGNITION TO THE DALAI LAMA WHILE WE'RE STILL TRYING TO **NORMALIZE RELATIONS** WITH RED CHINA AND **SEVERING TIES** WITH OUR OLD FRIENDS IN TAIWAN.
SEPTEMBER 3—A MOTORCADE COMPRISED OF THE SECRET SERVICE AND A NEW YORK POLICE SECURITY FORCE ESCORTS THE DALAI LAMA'S LIMOUSINE FROM JOHN F. KENNEDY INTERNATIONAL AIRPORT INTO **MANHATTAN**.
I'M SO GLAD TO BE HERE IN THE **LAND OF THE FREE**!
AS IN INDIA, IT MUST BE THE FORCE OF **DEMOCRACY** THAT CREATES THIS ATMOSPHERE OF **FREEDOM**!
BUT AT THE SAME TIME, HOW **GRAY** AND **GRIM** SOME PARTS OF THIS CITY ARE! SO MANY BEGGARS AND HOMELESS PEOPLE TAKING SHELTER IN DOORWAYS! HOW COULD THERE BE SUCH **POVERTY** IN THIS FAMOUSLY **RICH** AND **DEVELOPED** COUNTRY?
I ♥ NY
IT REMINDS ME OF WHAT MY CHINESE FRIENDS USED TO TELL ME ABOUT THE INJUSTICES OF THE "**AMERICAN IMPERIALIST PAPER TIGER**"—HOW IT EXPLOITS THE **POOR** FOR THE BENEFIT OF THE **RICH**.
THE MOTORCADE CROSSES THE EAST RIVER INTO MANHATTAN.

MARCH 10, 1978: *"Recently the Chinese have intensified their propaganda about the 'unprecedented happiness in Tibet today' through radio broadcasts and pictorial magazines. If the six million Tibetans in Tibet are really happy and prosperous as never before, there is no reason for us to argue otherwise. If the Tibetans are really happy, the Chinese should allow every interested foreigner to visit Tibet without restricting their movements or meetings with the Tibetan people. This would enable the visitors to really know the true conditions in Tibet."*

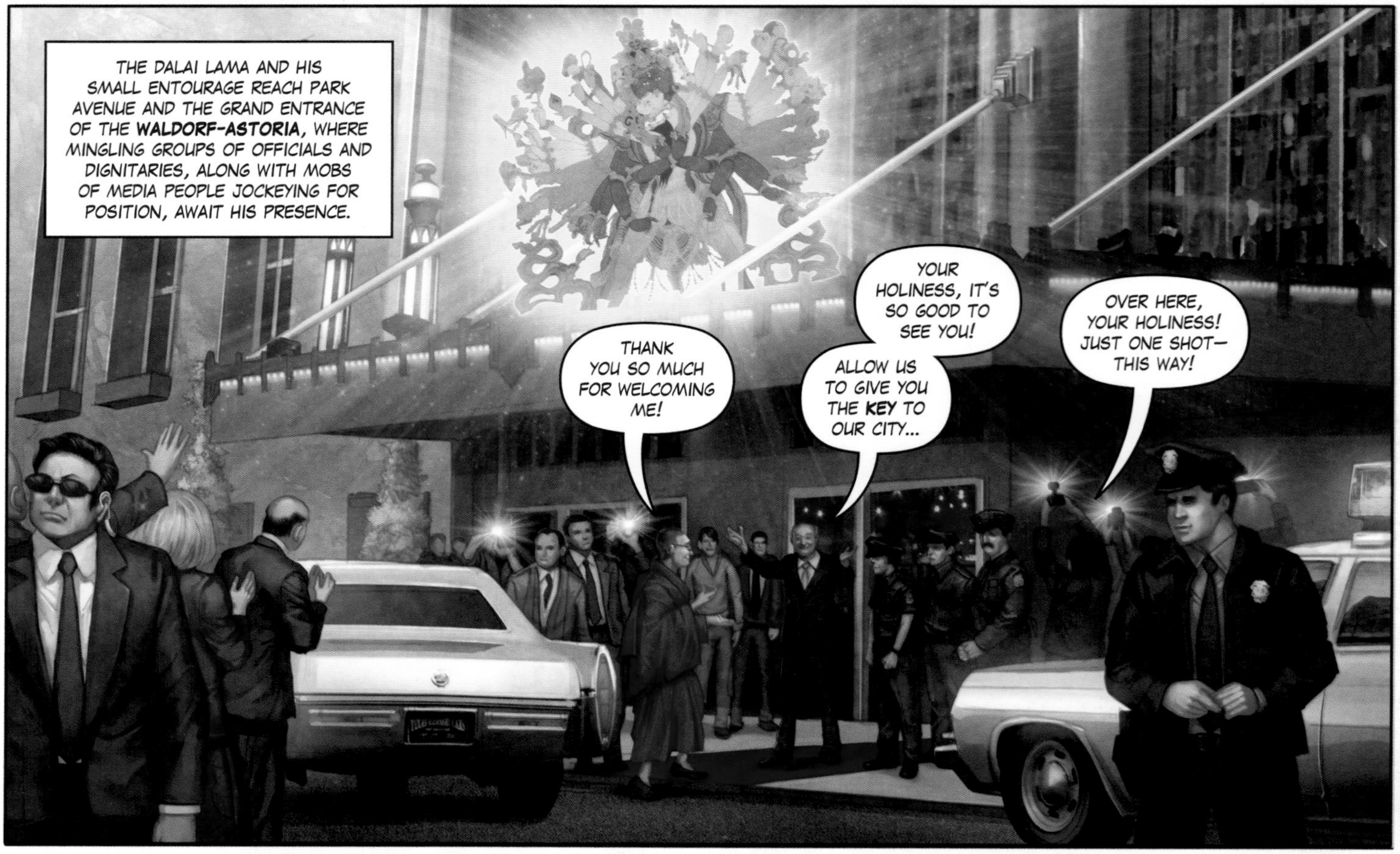

THE DALAI LAMA AND HIS SMALL ENTOURAGE REACH PARK AVENUE AND THE GRAND ENTRANCE OF THE **WALDORF-ASTORIA**, WHERE MINGLING GROUPS OF OFFICIALS AND DIGNITARIES, ALONG WITH MOBS OF MEDIA PEOPLE JOCKEYING FOR POSITION, AWAIT HIS PRESENCE.
THANK YOU SO MUCH FOR WELCOMING ME!
YOUR HOLINESS, IT'S SO GOOD TO SEE YOU!
ALLOW US TO GIVE YOU THE **KEY** TO OUR CITY...
OVER HERE, YOUR HOLINESS! JUST ONE SHOT— THIS WAY!

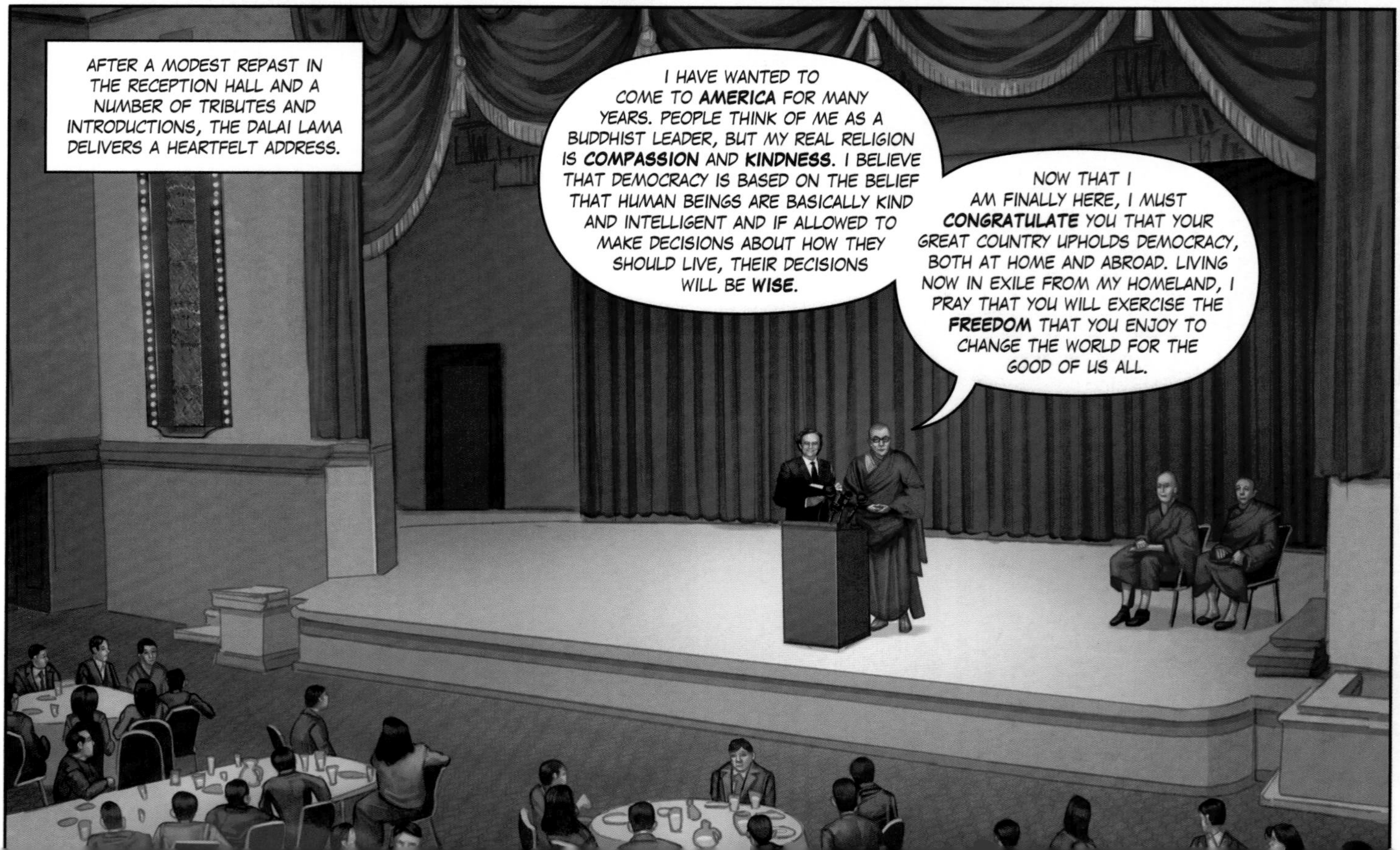

AFTER A MODEST REPAST IN THE RECEPTION HALL AND A NUMBER OF TRIBUTES AND INTRODUCTIONS, THE DALAI LAMA DELIVERS A HEARTFELT ADDRESS.
I HAVE WANTED TO COME TO **AMERICA** FOR MANY YEARS. PEOPLE THINK OF ME AS A BUDDHIST LEADER, BUT MY REAL RELIGION IS **COMPASSION** AND **KINDNESS**. I BELIEVE THAT DEMOCRACY IS BASED ON THE BELIEF THAT HUMAN BEINGS ARE BASICALLY KIND AND INTELLIGENT AND IF ALLOWED TO MAKE DECISIONS ABOUT HOW THEY SHOULD LIVE, THEIR DECISIONS WILL BE **WISE**.
NOW THAT I AM FINALLY HERE, I MUST **CONGRATULATE** YOU THAT YOUR GREAT COUNTRY UPHOLDS DEMOCRACY, BOTH AT HOME AND ABROAD. LIVING NOW IN EXILE FROM MY HOMELAND, I PRAY THAT YOU WILL EXERCISE THE **FREEDOM** THAT YOU ENJOY TO CHANGE THE WORLD FOR THE GOOD OF US ALL.

PACKING LECTURE HALLS IN MASSACHUSETTS DURING HIS 49-DAY TOUR, THE DALAI LAMA DELIVERS MAJOR ADDRESSES AT HARVARD AND AMHERST ON THE PRECIOUS NATURE OF FREEDOM. ROBERT THURMAN, NOW PROFESSOR OF INDO-TIBETAN BUDDHIST STUDIES AT AMHERST COLLEGE, GIVES THE INTRODUCTION...

I WOULD HOPE, AND I DARE SAY WE **ALL** HOPE, THAT AMERICA, THE GUARDIAN OF DEMOCRATIC IDEALS, WOULD PROTECT THE **DEVASTATED** CULTURE OF TIBET FROM FURTHER EXPLOITATION BY COMMUNIST CHINA.

THE DALAI LAMA'S GROWING ENTOURAGE ACCOMPANIES HIM TO THE **TIBETAN BUDDHIST LEARNING CENTER** IN NEW JERSEY, WHERE ITS FOUNDER, **GESHE WANGYAL**, STILL TEACHES.

REMEMBER I TOLD YOU I HAD AN INTERESTING STUDENT...

YES, HE WAS A VERY DEDICATED MONK, BUT NOT FOR **TOO LONG!**

I OFFERED BACK THE MONASTIC ROBES FOR THE ROBES OF ACADEME, BUT I STILL TRY TO SERVE YOU AND THE **DHARMA**, YOUR HOLINESS.

IN WASHINGTON, DC, WITH ANOTHER GESHE WANGYAL STUDENT, UNIVERSITY OF VIRGINIA PROFESSOR **JEFFREY HOPKINS** TRANSLATING, THE DALAI LAMA SPEAKS AT CONSTITUTION HALL ON "**SPIRITUAL DEVELOPMENT IN TODAY'S WORLD.**"

HE ALSO ADDRESSES THE CONGRESSIONAL HUMAN RIGHTS CAUCUS AT THE **CAPITOL**.

IN A VISIT TO NEARBY MONTICELLO, IN CHARLOTTESVILLE, VIRGINIA, HE TOURS THE HOME OF **THOMAS JEFFERSON**, TAKING A KEEN INTEREST IN JEFFERSON'S INVENTIVE MIND.

JEFFERSON WAS SO **INGENIOUS**—I LOVE HIS STUDY!

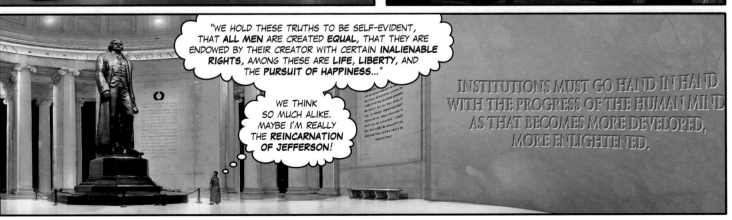

"WE HOLD THESE TRUTHS TO BE SELF-EVIDENT, THAT **ALL MEN** ARE CREATED **EQUAL**, THAT THEY ARE ENDOWED BY THEIR CREATOR WITH CERTAIN **INALIENABLE RIGHTS**, AMONG THESE ARE **LIFE, LIBERTY**, AND THE **PURSUIT OF HAPPINESS**..."

WE THINK SO MUCH ALIKE. MAYBE I'M REALLY THE **REINCARNATION OF JEFFERSON!**

INSTITUTIONS MUST GO HAND IN HAND WITH THE PROGRESS OF THE HUMAN MIND AS THAT BECOMES MORE DEVELOPED, MORE ENLIGHTENED.

MARCH 10, 1979: *"During the past 20 years, 100,000 or so Tibetan refugees have been earning their livelihood by agriculture, small business, handicrafts, etc., and they are becoming self-sufficient. Over 20,000 Tibetan youths who were provided with both traditional and modern education are joining the mainstream of modern life. Our religion and culture—considered poison by the Chinese—are not only preserved and their centers established in Tibetan settlements, but are also spreading among different peoples and gaining much interest and respect in the East and the West."*

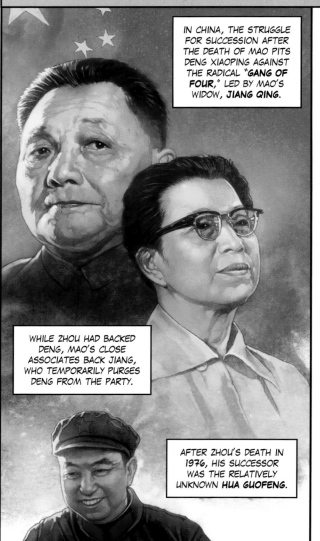

IN CHINA, THE STRUGGLE FOR SUCCESSION AFTER THE DEATH OF MAO PITS DENG XIAOPING AGAINST THE RADICAL "**GANG OF FOUR**," LED BY MAO'S WIDOW, **JIANG QING**.

WHILE ZHOU HAD BACKED DENG, MAO'S CLOSE ASSOCIATES BACK JIANG, WHO TEMPORARILY PURGES DENG FROM THE PARTY.

AFTER ZHOU'S DEATH IN 1976, HIS SUCCESSOR WAS THE RELATIVELY UNKNOWN **HUA GUOFENG**.

THROW **OUT** THE GANG OF FOUR!

HUA GAINS THE UPPER HAND AND BRINGS THE GANG OF FOUR TO TRIAL, GIVING THEM ALL LONG PRISON SENTENCES. WITH THEM GONE, THE CULTURAL REVOLUTION IS OVER. JIANG LATER COMMITS SUICIDE IN HER CELL, AND DENG IS REINSTATED AS A PARTY MEMBER IN GOOD STANDING.

IN 1977 HUA CALLS FOR A REVIVAL OF TRADITIONAL TIBETAN CUSTOMS, AND OLDER TIBETANS ARE ALLOWED FOR THE FIRST TIME IN 18 YEARS TO CIRCUMAMBULATE THE POTALA AND JOKHANG ON BUDDHA'S BIRTHDAY.

SINCE THE COLLAPSE OF THE TIBETAN GUERRILLAS, THE DALAI LAMA'S BROTHER GYALO THONDUP HAS RETREATED TO HONG KONG WITH HIS CHINESE WIFE. SUDDENLY HE IS SUMMONED TO BEIJING BY DENG. THEY MEET TO DISCUSS THE TIBETAN SITUATION.

WE MIGHT HAVE MADE **MISTAKES** IN TIBET, BUT THINGS ARE BETTER NOW. LOOKING TO THE FUTURE, ANYTHING CAN BE DISCUSSED, EXCEPT INDEPENDENCE.

IN THAT CASE, WE WOULD LIKE TO SEND **FACT-FINDING MISSIONS** TO TIBET, TO SEE FOR OURSELVES IF THINGS ARE AS IMPROVED AS YOU SAY.

FINE. INVITE THE DALAI LAMA HIMSELF TO LEAD A FACT-FINDING MISSION. WE WANT HIM TO WORK FOR ALL THE PEOPLE OF CHINA, NOT JUST FOR OUR TIBETANS.

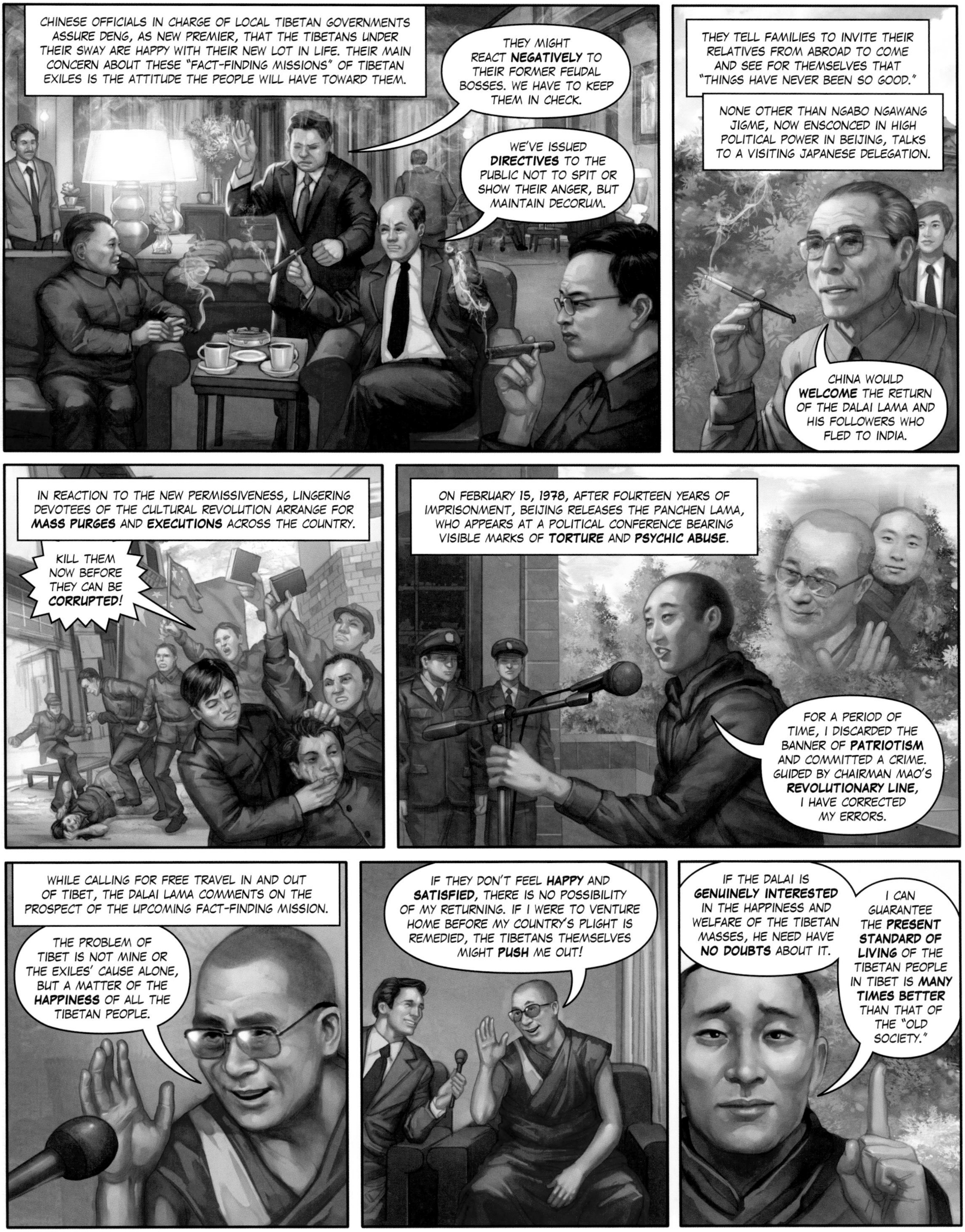
CHINESE OFFICIALS IN CHARGE OF LOCAL TIBETAN GOVERNMENTS ASSURE DENG, AS NEW PREMIER, THAT THE TIBETANS UNDER THEIR SWAY ARE HAPPY WITH THEIR NEW LOT IN LIFE. THEIR MAIN CONCERN ABOUT THESE "FACT-FINDING MISSIONS" OF TIBETAN EXILES IS THE ATTITUDE THE PEOPLE WILL HAVE TOWARD THEM.
THEY MIGHT REACT **NEGATIVELY** TO THEIR FORMER FEUDAL BOSSES. WE HAVE TO KEEP THEM IN CHECK.
WE'VE ISSUED **DIRECTIVES** TO THE PUBLIC NOT TO SPIT OR SHOW THEIR ANGER, BUT MAINTAIN DECORUM.
THEY TELL FAMILIES TO INVITE THEIR RELATIVES FROM ABROAD TO COME AND SEE FOR THEMSELVES THAT "THINGS HAVE NEVER BEEN SO GOOD."
NONE OTHER THAN NGABO NGAWANG JIGME, NOW ENSCONCED IN HIGH POLITICAL POWER IN BEIJING, TALKS TO A VISITING JAPANESE DELEGATION.
CHINA WOULD **WELCOME** THE RETURN OF THE DALAI LAMA AND HIS FOLLOWERS WHO FLED TO INDIA.
IN REACTION TO THE NEW PERMISSIVENESS, LINGERING DEVOTEES OF THE CULTURAL REVOLUTION ARRANGE FOR **MASS PURGES** AND **EXECUTIONS** ACROSS THE COUNTRY.
KILL THEM NOW BEFORE THEY CAN BE **CORRUPTED**!
ON FEBRUARY 15, 1978, AFTER FOURTEEN YEARS OF IMPRISONMENT, BEIJING RELEASES THE PANCHEN LAMA, WHO APPEARS AT A POLITICAL CONFERENCE BEARING VISIBLE MARKS OF **TORTURE** AND **PSYCHIC ABUSE**.
FOR A PERIOD OF TIME, I DISCARDED THE BANNER OF **PATRIOTISM** AND COMMITTED A CRIME. GUIDED BY CHAIRMAN MAO'S **REVOLUTIONARY LINE**, I HAVE CORRECTED MY ERRORS.
WHILE CALLING FOR FREE TRAVEL IN AND OUT OF TIBET, THE DALAI LAMA COMMENTS ON THE PROSPECT OF THE UPCOMING FACT-FINDING MISSION.
THE PROBLEM OF TIBET IS NOT MINE OR THE EXILES' CAUSE ALONE, BUT A MATTER OF THE **HAPPINESS** OF ALL THE TIBETAN PEOPLE.
IF THEY DON'T FEEL **HAPPY** AND **SATISFIED**, THERE IS NO POSSIBILITY OF MY RETURNING. IF I WERE TO VENTURE HOME BEFORE MY COUNTRY'S PLIGHT IS REMEDIED, THE TIBETANS THEMSELVES MIGHT **PUSH** ME OUT!
IF THE DALAI IS **GENUINELY INTERESTED** IN THE HAPPINESS AND WELFARE OF THE TIBETAN MASSES, HE NEED HAVE **NO DOUBTS** ABOUT IT.
I CAN GUARANTEE THE **PRESENT STANDARD OF LIVING** OF THE TIBETAN PEOPLE IN TIBET IS **MANY TIMES BETTER** THAN THAT OF THE "OLD SOCIETY."

MARCH 10, 1980: *"Twenty-one years have unfolded a shocking experience, which has no parallel in the history of Tibet. Never has there been so much systematic and extensive destruction of the religious, cultural, social and educational values of the Tibetan people. The frightening picture of abject poverty, wretched and helpless general conditions, persistent starvation and famine, had never been experienced for centuries."*

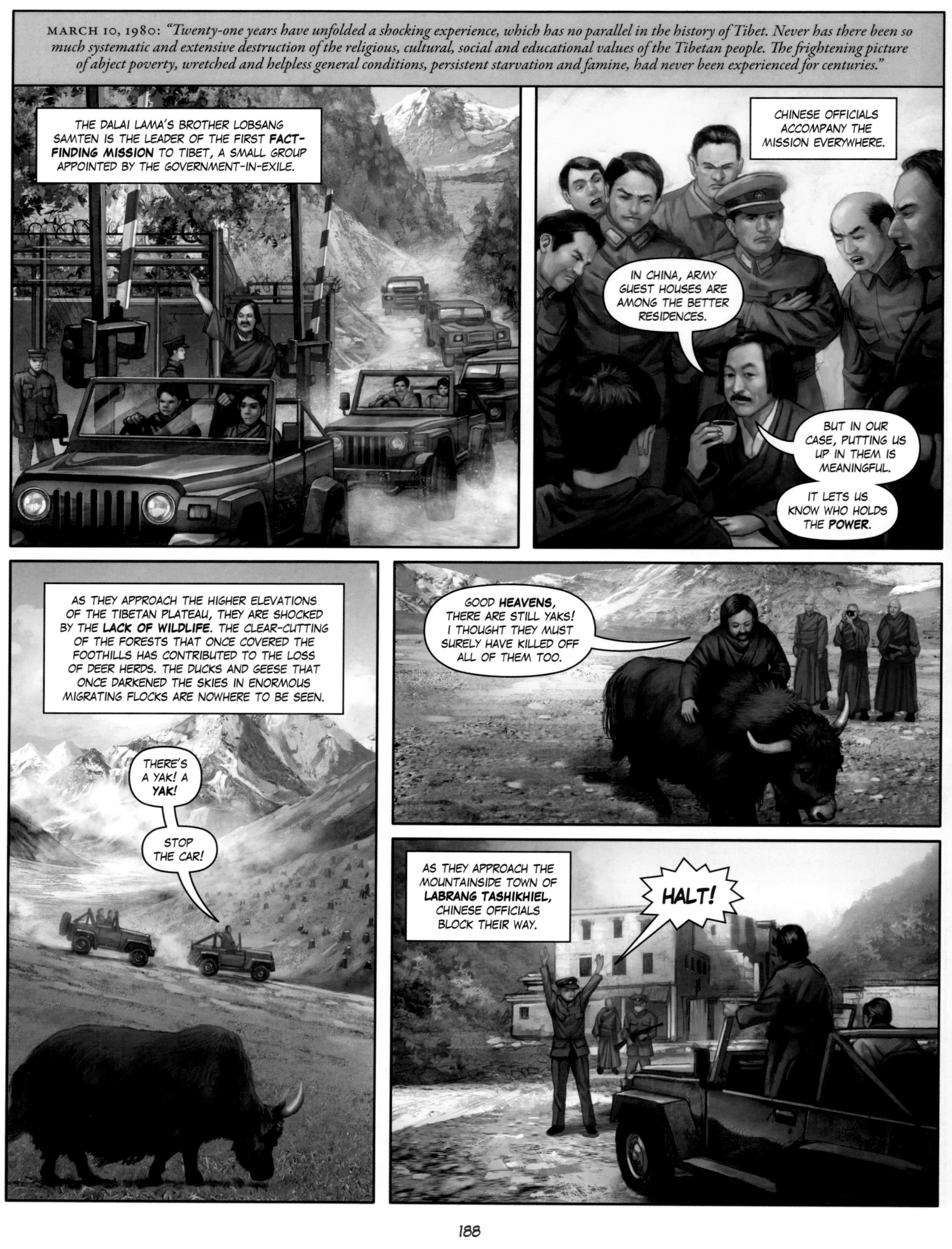
THE DALAI LAMA'S BROTHER LOBSANG SAMTEN IS THE LEADER OF THE FIRST FACT-FINDING MISSION TO TIBET, A SMALL GROUP APPOINTED BY THE GOVERNMENT-IN-EXILE.
CHINESE OFFICIALS ACCOMPANY THE MISSION EVERYWHERE.
IN CHINA, ARMY GUEST HOUSES ARE AMONG THE BETTER RESIDENCES.
BUT IN OUR CASE, PUTTING US UP IN THEM IS MEANINGFUL.
IT LETS US KNOW WHO HOLDS THE POWER.
AS THEY APPROACH THE HIGHER ELEVATIONS OF THE TIBETAN PLATEAU, THEY ARE SHOCKED BY THE LACK OF WILDLIFE. THE CLEAR-CUTTING OF THE FORESTS THAT ONCE COVERED THE FOOTHILLS HAS CONTRIBUTED TO THE LOSS OF DEER HERDS. THE DUCKS AND GEESE THAT ONCE DARKENED THE SKIES IN ENORMOUS MIGRATING FLOCKS ARE NOWHERE TO BE SEEN.
THERE'S A YAK! A YAK!
STOP THE CAR!
GOOD HEAVENS, THERE ARE STILL YAKS! I THOUGHT THEY MUST SURELY HAVE KILLED OFF ALL OF THEM TOO.
AS THEY APPROACH THE MOUNTAINSIDE TOWN OF LABRANG TASHIKHIEL, CHINESE OFFICIALS BLOCK THEIR WAY.
HALT!

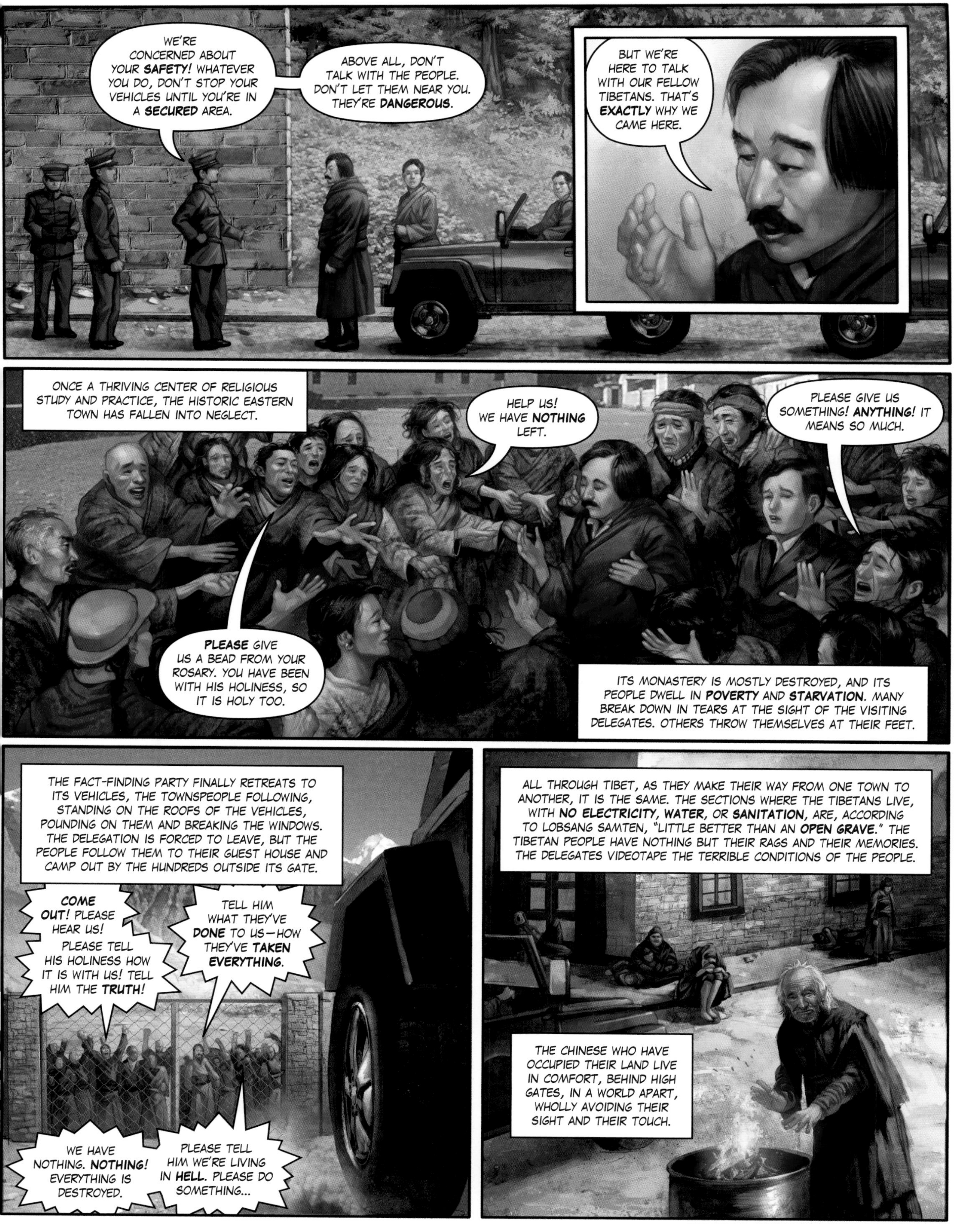
WE'RE CONCERNED ABOUT YOUR SAFETY! WHATEVER YOU DO, DON'T STOP YOUR VEHICLES UNTIL YOU'RE IN A SECURED AREA.
ABOVE ALL, DON'T TALK WITH THE PEOPLE. DON'T LET THEM NEAR YOU. THEY'RE DANGEROUS.
BUT WE'RE HERE TO TALK WITH OUR FELLOW TIBETANS. THAT'S EXACTLY WHY WE CAME HERE.
ONCE A THRIVING CENTER OF RELIGIOUS STUDY AND PRACTICE, THE HISTORIC EASTERN TOWN HAS FALLEN INTO NEGLECT.
HELP US! WE HAVE NOTHING LEFT.
PLEASE GIVE US SOMETHING! ANYTHING! IT MEANS SO MUCH.
PLEASE GIVE US A BEAD FROM YOUR ROSARY. YOU HAVE BEEN WITH HIS HOLINESS, SO IT IS HOLY TOO.
ITS MONASTERY IS MOSTLY DESTROYED, AND ITS PEOPLE DWELL IN POVERTY AND STARVATION. MANY BREAK DOWN IN TEARS AT THE SIGHT OF THE VISITING DELEGATES. OTHERS THROW THEMSELVES AT THEIR FEET.
THE FACT-FINDING PARTY FINALLY RETREATS TO ITS VEHICLES, THE TOWNSPEOPLE FOLLOWING, STANDING ON THE ROOFS OF THE VEHICLES, POUNDING ON THEM AND BREAKING THE WINDOWS. THE DELEGATION IS FORCED TO LEAVE, BUT THE PEOPLE FOLLOW THEM TO THEIR GUEST HOUSE AND CAMP OUT BY THE HUNDREDS OUTSIDE ITS GATE.
COME OUT! PLEASE HEAR US!
PLEASE TELL HIS HOLINESS HOW IT IS WITH US! TELL HIM THE TRUTH!
TELL HIM WHAT THEY'VE DONE TO US—HOW THEY'VE TAKEN EVERYTHING.
WE HAVE NOTHING. NOTHING! EVERYTHING IS DESTROYED.
PLEASE TELL HIM WE'RE LIVING IN HELL. PLEASE DO SOMETHING...
ALL THROUGH TIBET, AS THEY MAKE THEIR WAY FROM ONE TOWN TO ANOTHER, IT IS THE SAME. THE SECTIONS WHERE THE TIBETANS LIVE, WITH NO ELECTRICITY, WATER, OR SANITATION, ARE, ACCORDING TO LOBSANG SAMTEN, "LITTLE BETTER THAN AN OPEN GRAVE." THE TIBETAN PEOPLE HAVE NOTHING BUT THEIR RAGS AND THEIR MEMORIES. THE DELEGATES VIDEOTAPE THE TERRIBLE CONDITIONS OF THE PEOPLE.
THE CHINESE WHO HAVE OCCUPIED THEIR LAND LIVE IN COMFORT, BEHIND HIGH GATES, IN A WORLD APART, WHOLLY AVOIDING THEIR SIGHT AND THEIR TOUCH.

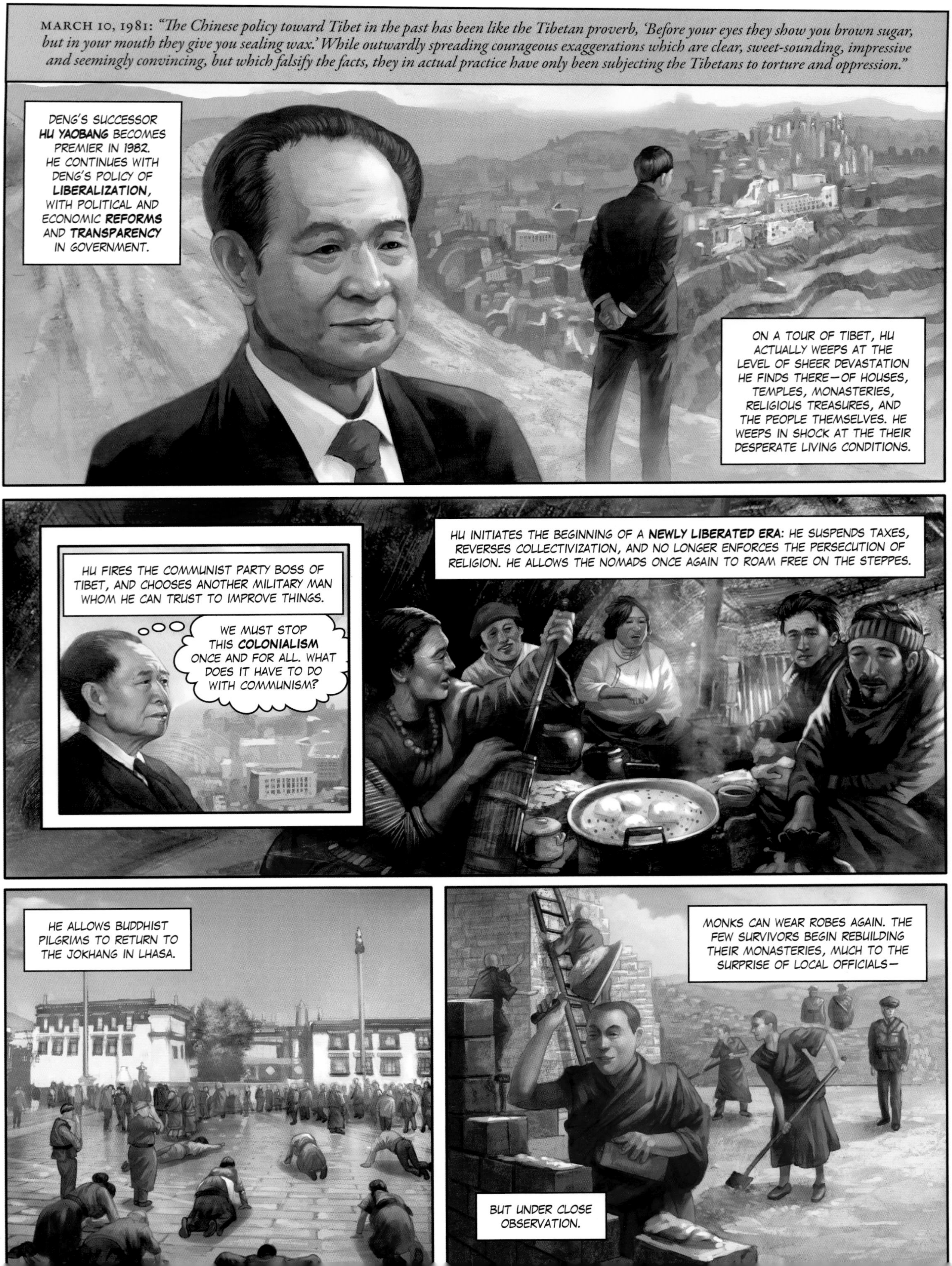
MARCH 10, 1981: "The Chinese policy toward Tibet in the past has been like the Tibetan proverb, 'Before your eyes they show you brown sugar, but in your mouth they give you sealing wax.' While outwardly spreading courageous exaggerations which are clear, sweet-sounding, impressive and seemingly convincing, but which falsify the facts, they in actual practice have only been subjecting the Tibetans to torture and oppression."
DENG'S SUCCESSOR HU YAOBANG BECOMES PREMIER IN 1982. HE CONTINUES WITH DENG'S POLICY OF LIBERALIZATION, WITH POLITICAL AND ECONOMIC REFORMS AND TRANSPARENCY IN GOVERNMENT.
ON A TOUR OF TIBET, HU ACTUALLY WEEPS AT THE LEVEL OF SHEER DEVASTATION HE FINDS THERE—OF HOUSES, TEMPLES, MONASTERIES, RELIGIOUS TREASURES, AND THE PEOPLE THEMSELVES. HE WEEPS IN SHOCK AT THE THEIR DESPERATE LIVING CONDITIONS.
HU FIRES THE COMMUNIST PARTY BOSS OF TIBET, AND CHOOSES ANOTHER MILITARY MAN WHOM HE CAN TRUST TO IMPROVE THINGS.
WE MUST STOP THIS COLONIALISM ONCE AND FOR ALL. WHAT DOES IT HAVE TO DO WITH COMMUNISM?
HU INITIATES THE BEGINNING OF A NEWLY LIBERATED ERA: HE SUSPENDS TAXES, REVERSES COLLECTIVIZATION, AND NO LONGER ENFORCES THE PERSECUTION OF RELIGION. HE ALLOWS THE NOMADS ONCE AGAIN TO ROAM FREE ON THE STEPPES.
HE ALLOWS BUDDHIST PILGRIMS TO RETURN TO THE JOKHANG IN LHASA.
MONKS CAN WEAR ROBES AGAIN. THE FEW SURVIVORS BEGIN REBUILDING THEIR MONASTERIES, MUCH TO THE SURPRISE OF LOCAL OFFICIALS—
BUT UNDER CLOSE OBSERVATION.

MARCH 10, 1982: *"The Tibetans will have to keep pace with the progressive changes that are occurring in the twentieth-century world and move towards democratic revolution. The old social system will not be resurrected. The teachings of the Buddha, as contained in the Three Baskets and three Higher Trainings, are beneficial to society, as they are based on sound reason and actual experience. These we must preserve and promote."*

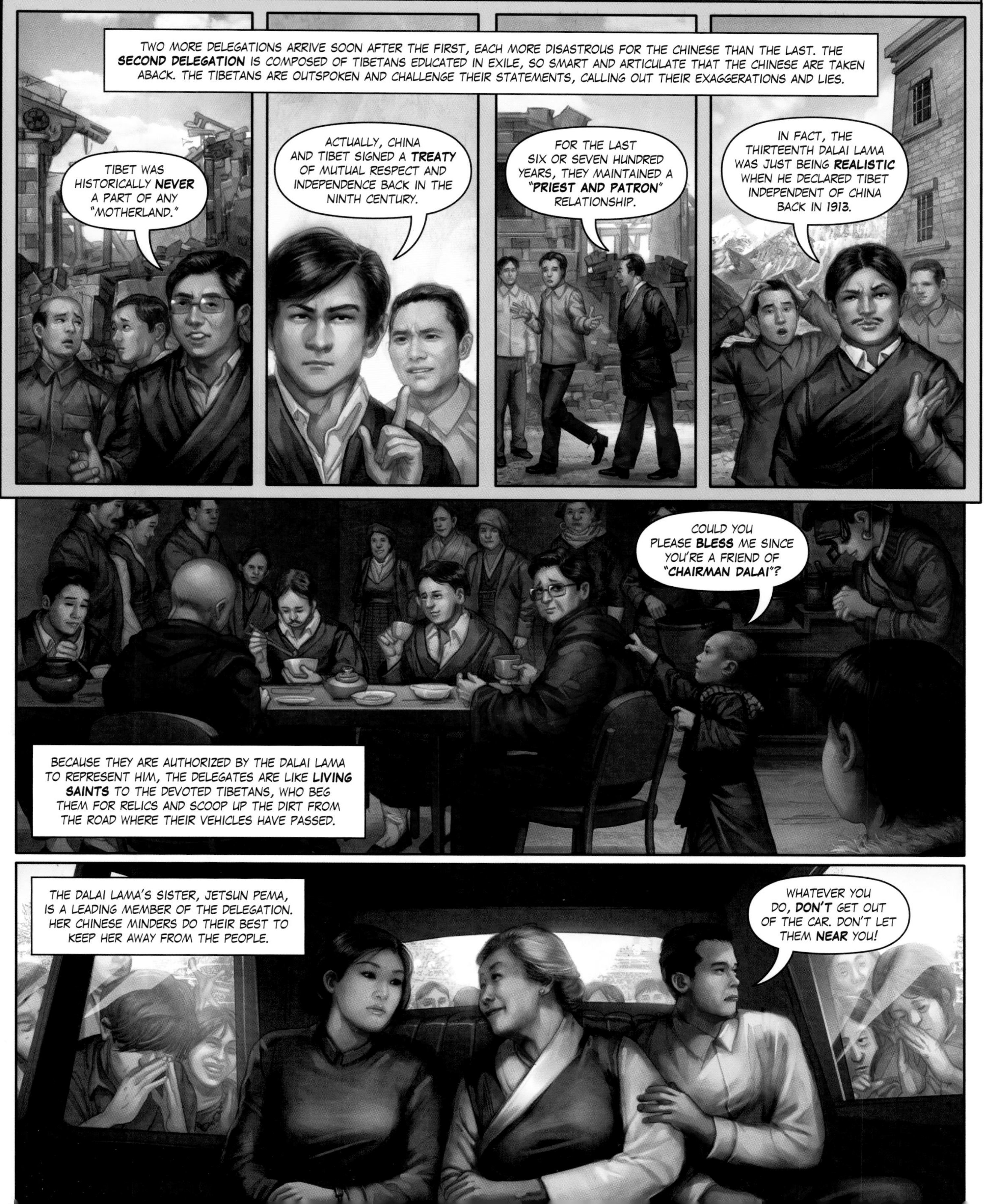

TWO MORE DELEGATIONS ARRIVE SOON AFTER THE FIRST, EACH MORE DISASTROUS FOR THE CHINESE THAN THE LAST. THE SECOND DELEGATION IS COMPOSED OF TIBETANS EDUCATED IN EXILE, SO SMART AND ARTICULATE THAT THE CHINESE ARE TAKEN ABACK. THE TIBETANS ARE OUTSPOKEN AND CHALLENGE THEIR STATEMENTS, CALLING OUT THEIR EXAGGERATIONS AND LIES.
TIBET WAS HISTORICALLY NEVER A PART OF ANY "MOTHERLAND."
ACTUALLY, CHINA AND TIBET SIGNED A TREATY OF MUTUAL RESPECT AND INDEPENDENCE BACK IN THE NINTH CENTURY.
FOR THE LAST SIX OR SEVEN HUNDRED YEARS, THEY MAINTAINED A "PRIEST AND PATRON" RELATIONSHIP.
IN FACT, THE THIRTEENTH DALAI LAMA WAS JUST BEING REALISTIC WHEN HE DECLARED TIBET INDEPENDENT OF CHINA BACK IN 1913.
COULD YOU PLEASE BLESS ME SINCE YOU'RE A FRIEND OF "CHAIRMAN DALAI"?
BECAUSE THEY ARE AUTHORIZED BY THE DALAI LAMA TO REPRESENT HIM, THE DELEGATES ARE LIKE LIVING SAINTS TO THE DEVOTED TIBETANS, WHO BEG THEM FOR RELICS AND SCOOP UP THE DIRT FROM THE ROAD WHERE THEIR VEHICLES HAVE PASSED.
THE DALAI LAMA'S SISTER, JETSUN PEMA, IS A LEADING MEMBER OF THE DELEGATION. HER CHINESE MINDERS DO THEIR BEST TO KEEP HER AWAY FROM THE PEOPLE.
WHATEVER YOU DO, DON'T GET OUT OF THE CAR. DON'T LET THEM NEAR YOU!

MARCH 10, 1983: *"The Tibetan people must have the right to preserve and enhance their cultural identity and religious freedom, determine their own destiny and manage their own affairs, and find fulfillment through their free self-expression, without interference. This is reasonable and just."*

OVER 7000 TIBETANS SURROUND THEIR JEEP AND FRANTICALLY TEAR OFF BITS OF THE ROOF CANVAS AS HOLY RELICS.

JETSUN PEMA, YOUR HOLINESS, **PLEASE** COME OUT AND BLESS US!

DON'T! LOCK THE DOORS AND ROLL UP THE WINDOWS.

IF I WANT TO **GREET** OUR PEOPLE, THAT'S THE PURPOSE. DON'T DICTATE **ORDERS** TO ME.

DON'T BE SILLY. THEY'LL **TEAR** YOU APART!

MY BROTHER SENT US TO MEET THE PEOPLE. IF YOU PERSIST IN **BLOCKING** US, I WILL RETURN TO INDIA AT ONCE.

EVERYWHERE WE GO YOU **CLAIM** YOU'VE MADE SO MUCH PROGRESS. LOOK AT THESE PEOPLE! IS **THAT** PROGRESS? WHEN DO YOU THINK THEY LAST HAD SOMETHING TO EAT? **THIS** IS WHAT YOU'VE ACHIEVED IN TWENTY YEARS?

BUT WE'VE DONE SO MUCH TO **HELP** THEM—AND YOU TOO!

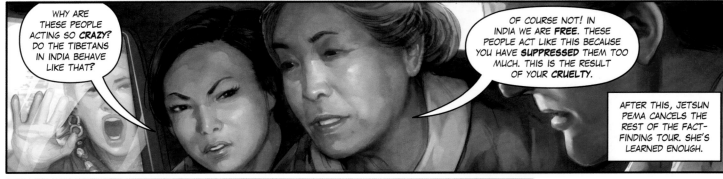

WHY ARE THESE PEOPLE ACTING SO **CRAZY**? DO THE TIBETANS IN INDIA BEHAVE LIKE THAT?

OF COURSE NOT! IN INDIA WE ARE **FREE**. THESE PEOPLE ACT LIKE THIS BECAUSE YOU HAVE **SUPPRESSED** THEM TOO MUCH. THIS IS THE RESULT OF YOUR **CRUELTY**.

AFTER THIS, JETSUN PEMA CANCELS THE REST OF THE FACT-FINDING TOUR. SHE'S LEARNED ENOUGH.

THE **THIRD DELEGATION**, MEANWHILE, HAS VISITED THE RUINS OF GANDEN MONASTERY. THE TIBETANS ARE FEVERISHLY REBUILDING A RESIDENCE FOR THE DALAI LAMA AND THE TEMPLE THAT ONCE HOUSED JEY TSONG KHAPA'S TOMB. THOUSANDS OF TIBETANS FERVENTLY CHANT THEIR HEART MANTRAS OVER AND OVER...

DENG CANCELS THE FACT-FINDING TOUR BY THE **FOURTH DELEGATION**. TO SALVAGE THE TENTATIVE PROGRESS, THE DALAI LAMA SENDS ENVOYS TO NEGOTIATE NEW TERMS FOR RECONCILIATION, BUT THE NEGOTIATIONS COME TO NOTHING.

FREEDOM AND **INDEPENDENCE** FOR TIBET!

LONG LIVE THE DALAI LAMA!

DENG ASSERTS HIS POWER AND PURGES HU YAOBANG FROM HIS POSITION AS THE LIBERALIZING CHAIRMAN OF THE PRC.

1983—THE YEAR OF THE PIG. SINCE IT IS THE DALAI LAMA'S OBSTACLE YEAR, WHATEVER **CAN** GO WRONG FOR TIBET **DOES**.

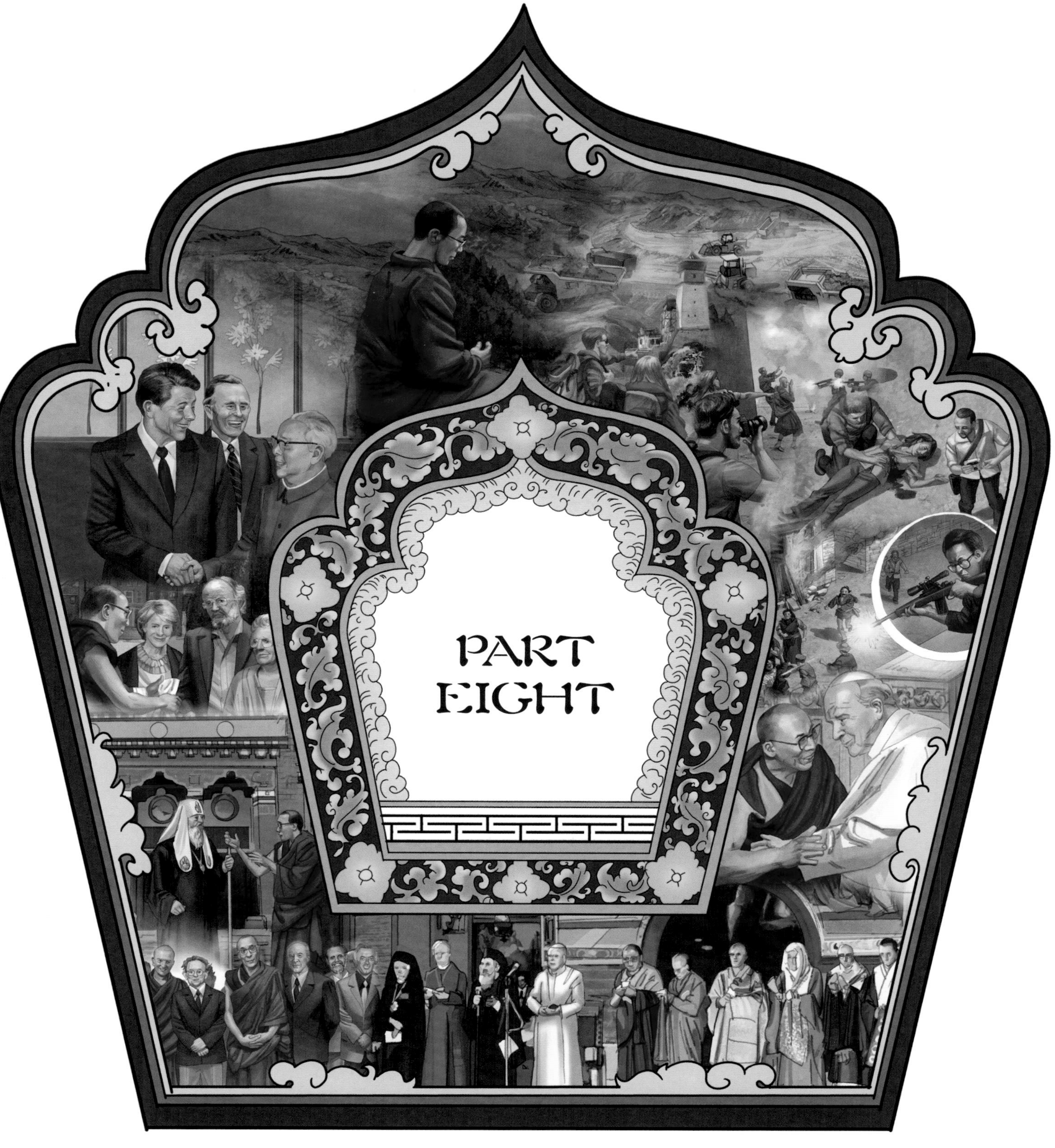

PART EIGHT

MARCH 10, 1984: *"Young Tibetans are taught the themes of our cultural heritage with the Tibetan language as the basis. They are given modern education, and today's section of young Tibetans are walking shoulder-to-shoulder with the educated youths of modern countries. As for our religion and culture, the complete teachings of the Buddha were introduced from India, and with this came the influence of an enlightened culture. Tibetans through the generations studied, practiced and preserved them. These traditions of Tibet recently underwent annihilation. However, we in exile have collected and published the scriptures and have also established centers of Buddhism where young monks can study Sutra and Tantra. . . ."*

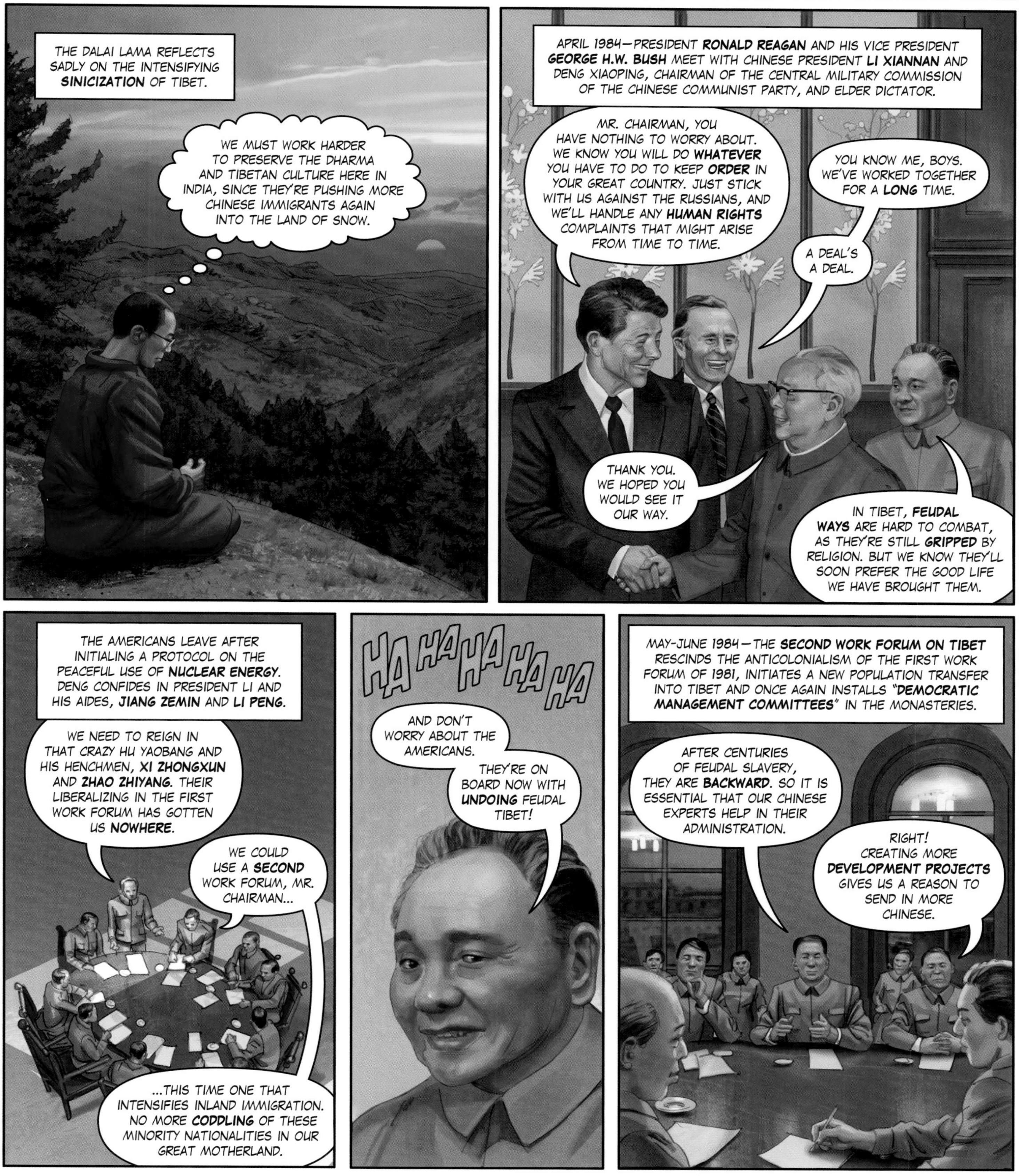
THE DALAI LAMA REFLECTS SADLY ON THE INTENSIFYING SINICIZATION OF TIBET.
WE MUST WORK HARDER TO PRESERVE THE DHARMA AND TIBETAN CULTURE HERE IN INDIA, SINCE THEY'RE PUSHING MORE CHINESE IMMIGRANTS AGAIN INTO THE LAND OF SNOW.
APRIL 1984—PRESIDENT RONALD REAGAN AND HIS VICE PRESIDENT GEORGE H.W. BUSH MEET WITH CHINESE PRESIDENT LI XIANNAN AND DENG XIAOPING, CHAIRMAN OF THE CENTRAL MILITARY COMMISSION OF THE CHINESE COMMUNIST PARTY, AND ELDER DICTATOR.
MR. CHAIRMAN, YOU HAVE NOTHING TO WORRY ABOUT. WE KNOW YOU WILL DO WHATEVER YOU HAVE TO DO TO KEEP ORDER IN YOUR GREAT COUNTRY. JUST STICK WITH US AGAINST THE RUSSIANS, AND WE'LL HANDLE ANY HUMAN RIGHTS COMPLAINTS THAT MIGHT ARISE FROM TIME TO TIME.
YOU KNOW ME, BOYS. WE'VE WORKED TOGETHER FOR A LONG TIME.
A DEAL'S A DEAL.
THANK YOU. WE HOPED YOU WOULD SEE IT OUR WAY.
IN TIBET, FEUDAL WAYS ARE HARD TO COMBAT, AS THEY'RE STILL GRIPPED BY RELIGION. BUT WE KNOW THEY'LL SOON PREFER THE GOOD LIFE WE HAVE BROUGHT THEM.
THE AMERICANS LEAVE AFTER INITIALING A PROTOCOL ON THE PEACEFUL USE OF NUCLEAR ENERGY. DENG CONFIDES IN PRESIDENT LI AND HIS AIDES, JIANG ZEMIN AND LI PENG.
WE NEED TO REIGN IN THAT CRAZY HU YAOBANG AND HIS HENCHMEN, XI ZHONGXUN AND ZHAO ZHIYANG. THEIR LIBERALIZING IN THE FIRST WORK FORUM HAS GOTTEN US NOWHERE.
WE COULD USE A SECOND WORK FORUM, MR. CHAIRMAN...
...THIS TIME ONE THAT INTENSIFIES INLAND IMMIGRATION. NO MORE CODDLING OF THESE MINORITY NATIONALITIES IN OUR GREAT MOTHERLAND.
HA HA HA HA HA HA
AND DON'T WORRY ABOUT THE AMERICANS.
THEY'RE ON BOARD NOW WITH UNDOING FEUDAL TIBET!
MAY-JUNE 1984—THE SECOND WORK FORUM ON TIBET RESCINDS THE ANTICOLONIALISM OF THE FIRST WORK FORUM OF 1981, INITIATES A NEW POPULATION TRANSFER INTO TIBET AND ONCE AGAIN INSTALLS "DEMOCRATIC MANAGEMENT COMMITTEES" IN THE MONASTERIES.
AFTER CENTURIES OF FEUDAL SLAVERY, THEY ARE BACKWARD. SO IT IS ESSENTIAL THAT OUR CHINESE EXPERTS HELP IN THEIR ADMINISTRATION.
RIGHT! CREATING MORE DEVELOPMENT PROJECTS GIVES US A REASON TO SEND IN MORE CHINESE.

MARCH 10, 1984: *"... The Tibetan written language is not used in the administration of the country, a clear indication that Tibet is in the hands of people who don't know the Tibetan language. The so-called freedom of religious worship and national autonomy is simply empty talk."*

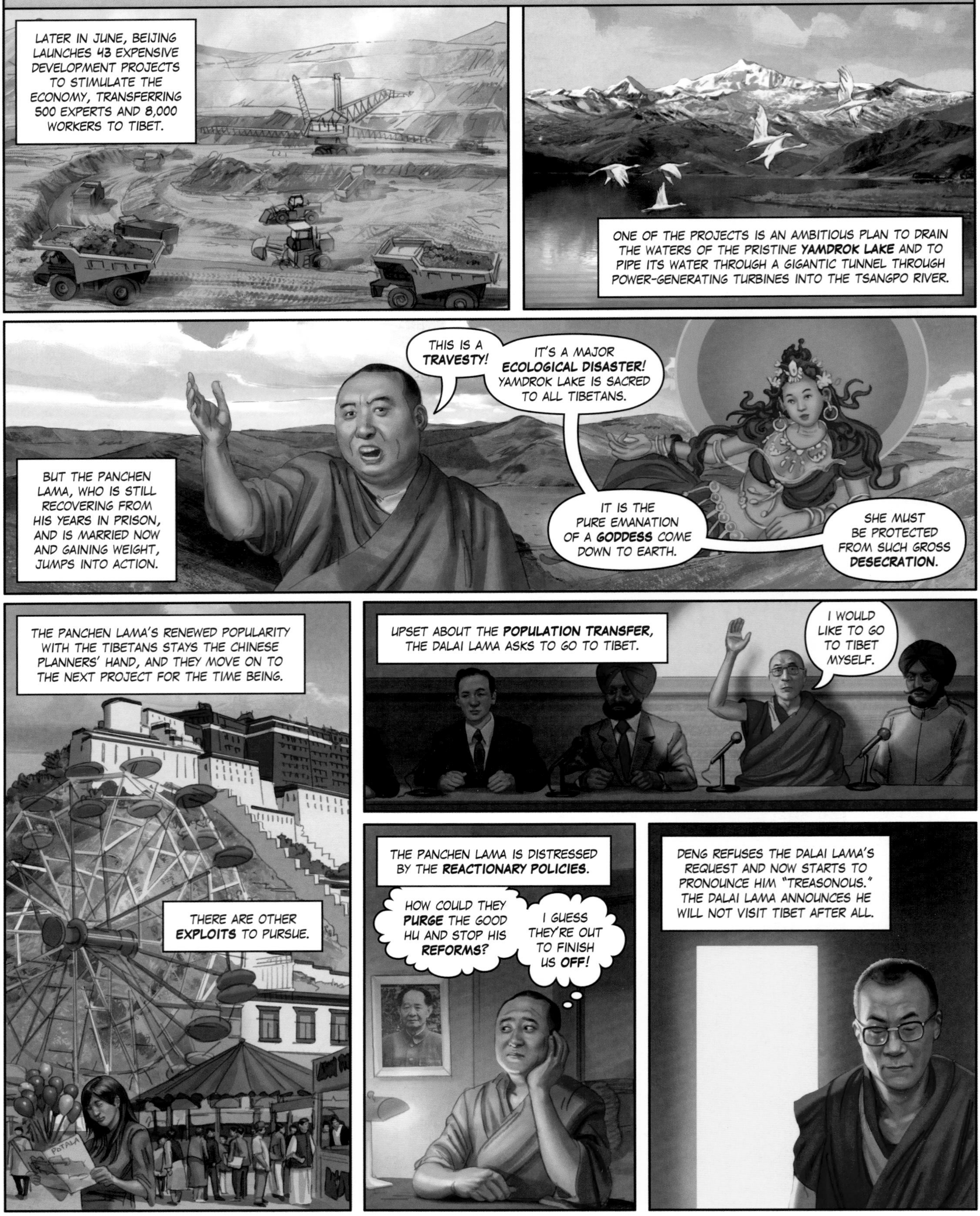

LATER IN JUNE, BEIJING LAUNCHES 43 EXPENSIVE DEVELOPMENT PROJECTS TO STIMULATE THE ECONOMY, TRANSFERRING 500 EXPERTS AND 8,000 WORKERS TO TIBET.
ONE OF THE PROJECTS IS AN AMBITIOUS PLAN TO DRAIN THE WATERS OF THE PRISTINE YAMDROK LAKE AND TO PIPE ITS WATER THROUGH A GIGANTIC TUNNEL THROUGH POWER-GENERATING TURBINES INTO THE TSANGPO RIVER.
BUT THE PANCHEN LAMA, WHO IS STILL RECOVERING FROM HIS YEARS IN PRISON, AND IS MARRIED NOW AND GAINING WEIGHT, JUMPS INTO ACTION.
THIS IS A TRAVESTY!
IT'S A MAJOR ECOLOGICAL DISASTER! YAMDROK LAKE IS SACRED TO ALL TIBETANS.
IT IS THE PURE EMANATION OF A GODDESS COME DOWN TO EARTH.
SHE MUST BE PROTECTED FROM SUCH GROSS DESECRATION.
THE PANCHEN LAMA'S RENEWED POPULARITY WITH THE TIBETANS STAYS THE CHINESE PLANNERS' HAND, AND THEY MOVE ON TO THE NEXT PROJECT FOR THE TIME BEING.
THERE ARE OTHER EXPLOITS TO PURSUE.
POTALA
UPSET ABOUT THE POPULATION TRANSFER, THE DALAI LAMA ASKS TO GO TO TIBET.
I WOULD LIKE TO GO TO TIBET MYSELF.
THE PANCHEN LAMA IS DISTRESSED BY THE REACTIONARY POLICIES.
HOW COULD THEY PURGE THE GOOD HU AND STOP HIS REFORMS?
I GUESS THEY'RE OUT TO FINISH US OFF!
DENG REFUSES THE DALAI LAMA'S REQUEST AND NOW STARTS TO PRONOUNCE HIM "TREASONOUS." THE DALAI LAMA ANNOUNCES HE WILL NOT VISIT TIBET AFTER ALL.

"I have thought deeply about science, not just its implications for the understanding of what reality is, but the still more important question of how it may influence ethics and human values. My confidence venturing into science lies in my basic belief that, as in science so in Buddhism, understanding the nature of reality is pursued by means of critical investigation." —HH the Dalai Lama, *The Universe in a Single Atom*

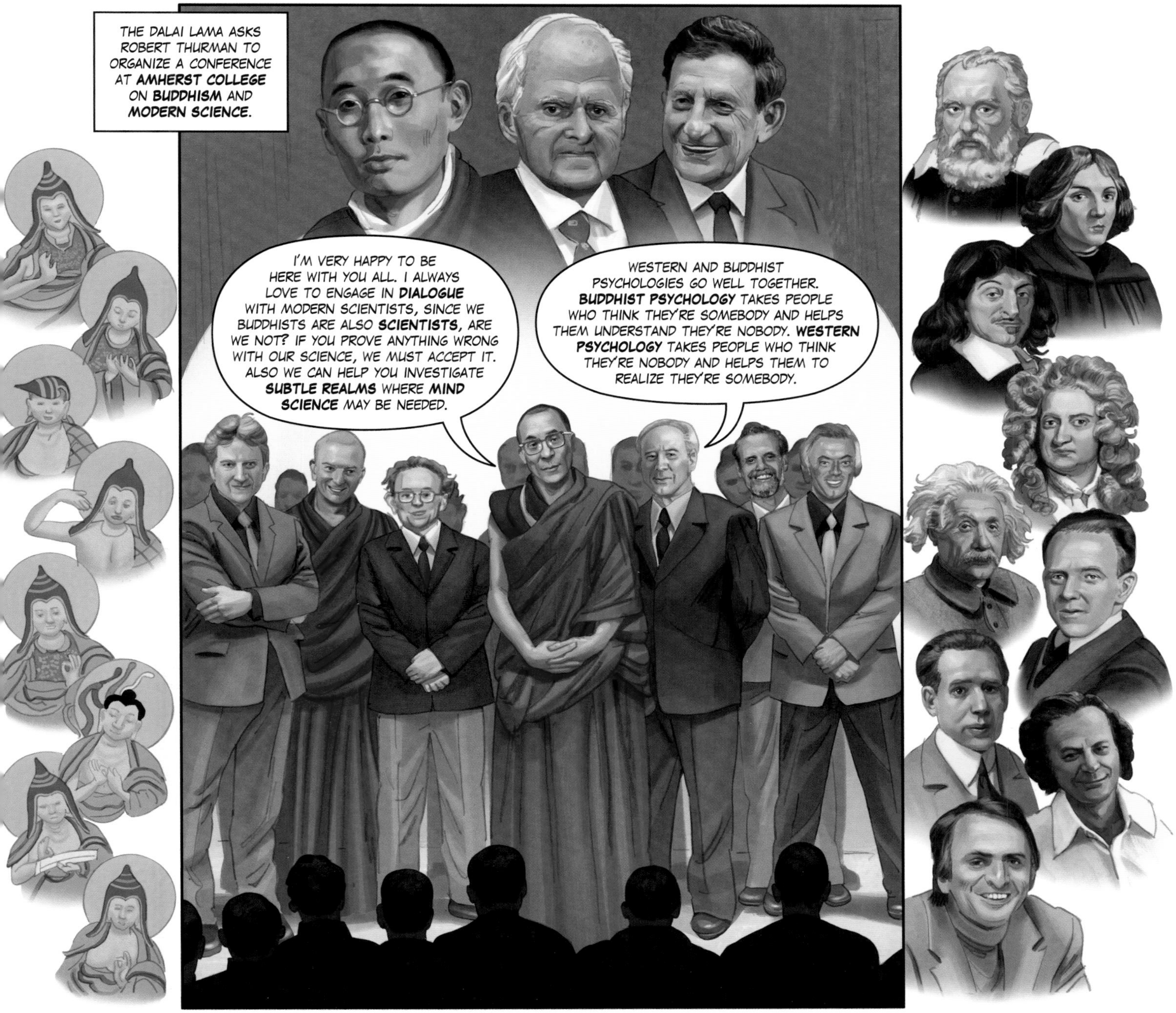
THE DALAI LAMA ASKS ROBERT THURMAN TO ORGANIZE A CONFERENCE AT AMHERST COLLEGE ON BUDDHISM AND MODERN SCIENCE.
I'M VERY HAPPY TO BE HERE WITH YOU ALL. I ALWAYS LOVE TO ENGAGE IN DIALOGUE WITH MODERN SCIENTISTS, SINCE WE BUDDHISTS ARE ALSO SCIENTISTS, ARE WE NOT? IF YOU PROVE ANYTHING WRONG WITH OUR SCIENCE, WE MUST ACCEPT IT. ALSO WE CAN HELP YOU INVESTIGATE SUBTLE REALMS WHERE MIND SCIENCE MAY BE NEEDED.
WESTERN AND BUDDHIST PSYCHOLOGIES GO WELL TOGETHER. BUDDHIST PSYCHOLOGY TAKES PEOPLE WHO THINK THEY'RE SOMEBODY AND HELPS THEM UNDERSTAND THEY'RE NOBODY. WESTERN PSYCHOLOGY TAKES PEOPLE WHO THINK THEY'RE NOBODY AND HELPS THEM TO REALIZE THEY'RE SOMEBODY.

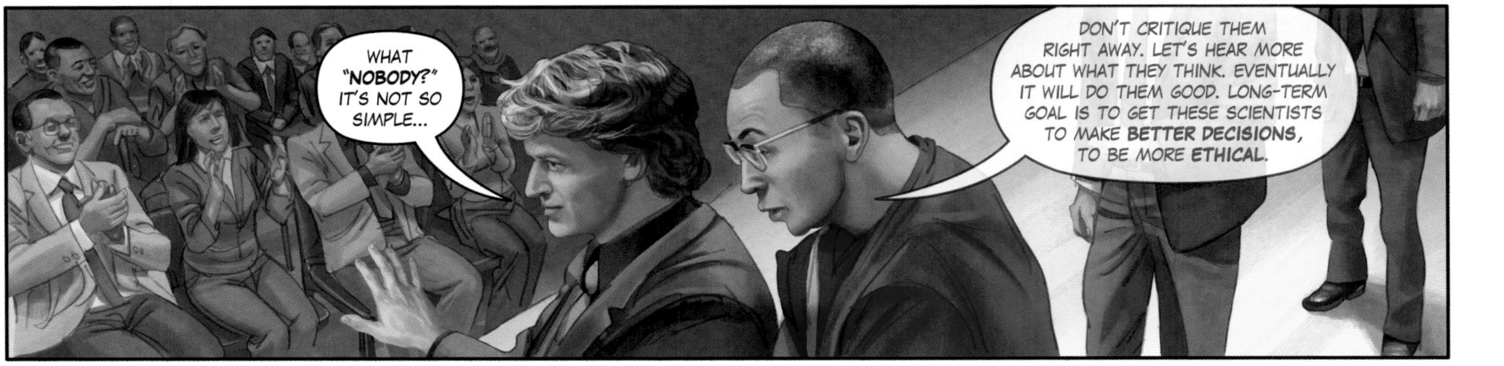
WHAT "NOBODY?" IT'S NOT SO SIMPLE...
DON'T CRITIQUE THEM RIGHT AWAY. LET'S HEAR MORE ABOUT WHAT THEY THINK. EVENTUALLY IT WILL DO THEM GOOD. LONG-TERM GOAL IS TO GET THESE SCIENTISTS TO MAKE BETTER DECISIONS, TO BE MORE ETHICAL.

MARCH 10, 1985: *"An increasing number of people throughout the world are acknowledging the fact that the Tibetan race, language, traditions, religion, culture, and political and economic systems are completely distinct and separate from those of the Chinese people, and the fact that Tibet is an independent country with a recorded history of more than a thousand years. Consequently, there is a growing number who are supporting and sympathizing with our just cause."*

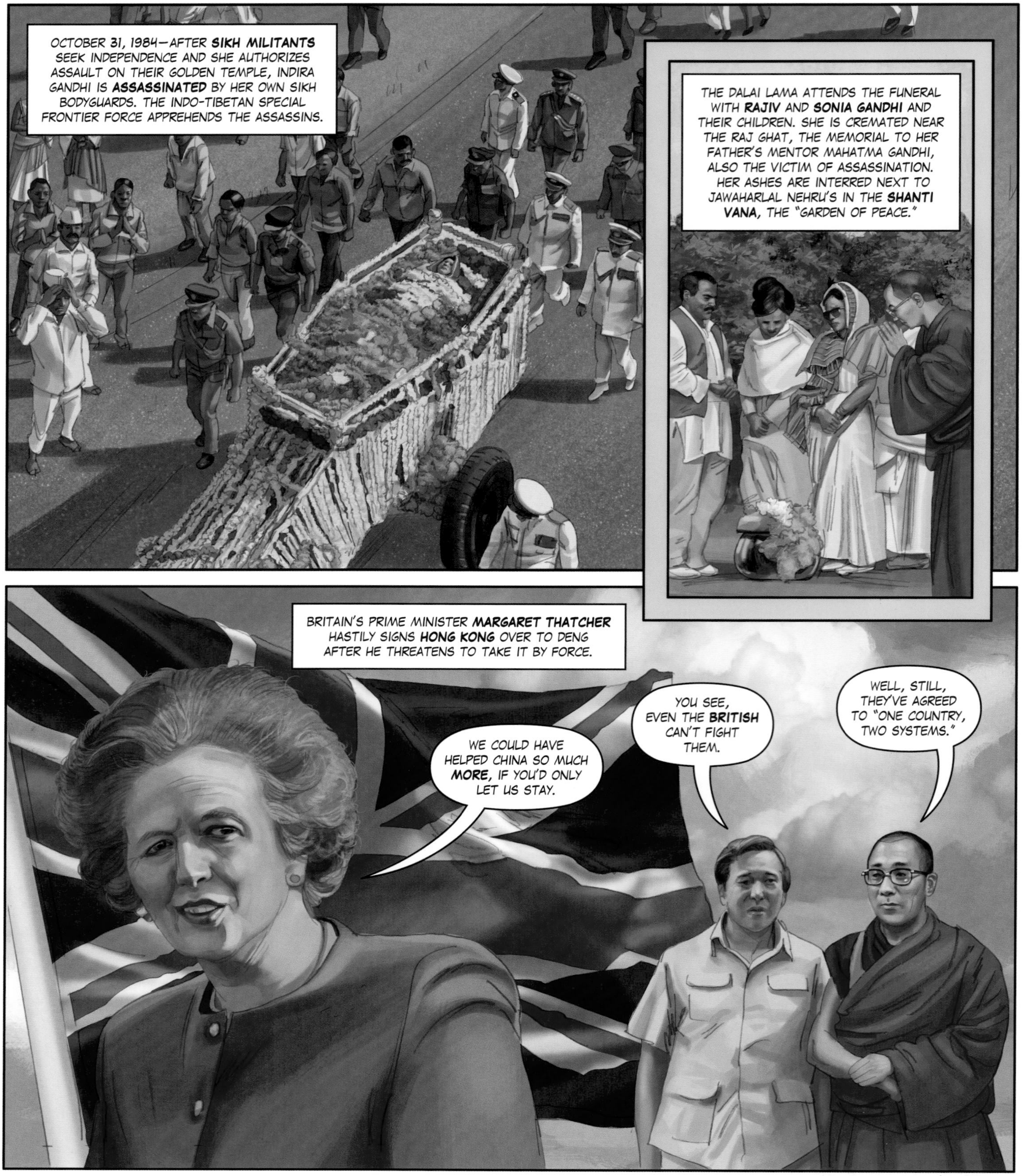
OCTOBER 31, 1984—AFTER **SIKH MILITANTS** SEEK INDEPENDENCE AND SHE AUTHORIZES ASSAULT ON THEIR GOLDEN TEMPLE, INDIRA GANDHI IS **ASSASSINATED** BY HER OWN SIKH BODYGUARDS. THE INDO-TIBETAN SPECIAL FRONTIER FORCE APPREHENDS THE ASSASSINS.
THE DALAI LAMA ATTENDS THE FUNERAL WITH **RAJIV** AND **SONIA GANDHI** AND THEIR CHILDREN. SHE IS CREMATED NEAR THE RAJ GHAT, THE MEMORIAL TO HER FATHER'S MENTOR MAHATMA GANDHI, ALSO THE VICTIM OF ASSASSINATION. HER ASHES ARE INTERRED NEXT TO JAWAHARLAL NEHRU'S IN THE **SHANTI VANA**, THE "GARDEN OF PEACE."
BRITAIN'S PRIME MINISTER **MARGARET THATCHER** HASTILY SIGNS **HONG KONG** OVER TO DENG AFTER HE THREATENS TO TAKE IT BY FORCE.
WE COULD HAVE HELPED CHINA SO MUCH **MORE**, IF YOU'D ONLY LET US STAY.
YOU SEE, EVEN THE **BRITISH** CAN'T FIGHT THEM.
WELL, STILL, THEY'VE AGREED TO "ONE COUNTRY, TWO SYSTEMS."

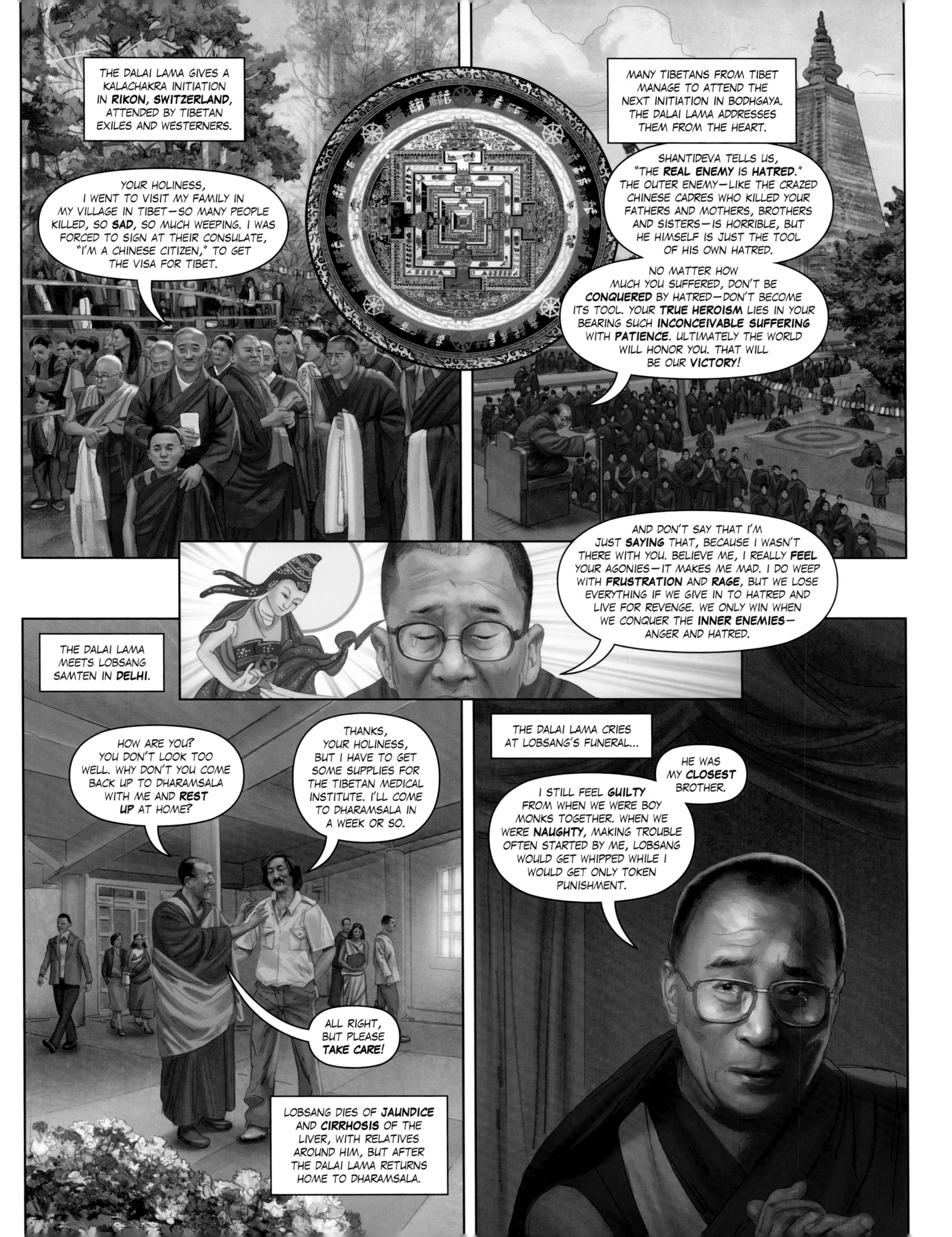

THE DALAI LAMA GIVES A KALACHAKRA INITIATION IN **RIKON, SWITZERLAND,** ATTENDED BY TIBETAN EXILES AND WESTERNERS.
YOUR HOLINESS, I WENT TO VISIT MY FAMILY IN MY VILLAGE IN TIBET—SO MANY PEOPLE KILLED, SO **SAD**, SO MUCH WEEPING. I WAS FORCED TO SIGN AT THEIR CONSULATE, "I'M A CHINESE CITIZEN," TO GET THE VISA FOR TIBET.
MANY TIBETANS FROM TIBET MANAGE TO ATTEND THE NEXT INITIATION IN BODHGAYA. THE DALAI LAMA ADDRESSES THEM FROM THE HEART.
SHANTIDEVA TELLS US, "THE **REAL ENEMY** IS **HATRED**." THE OUTER ENEMY—LIKE THE CRAZED CHINESE CADRES WHO KILLED YOUR FATHERS AND MOTHERS, BROTHERS AND SISTERS—IS HORRIBLE, BUT HE HIMSELF IS JUST THE TOOL OF HIS OWN HATRED.
NO MATTER HOW MUCH YOU SUFFERED, DON'T BE **CONQUERED** BY HATRED—DON'T BECOME ITS TOOL. YOUR **TRUE HEROISM** LIES IN YOUR BEARING SUCH **INCONCEIVABLE SUFFERING** WITH **PATIENCE**. ULTIMATELY THE WORLD WILL HONOR YOU. THAT WILL BE OUR **VICTORY**!
AND DON'T SAY THAT I'M JUST **SAYING** THAT, BECAUSE I WASN'T THERE WITH YOU. BELIEVE ME, I REALLY **FEEL** YOUR AGONIES—IT MAKES ME MAD. I DO WEEP WITH **FRUSTRATION** AND **RAGE**, BUT WE LOSE EVERYTHING IF WE GIVE IN TO HATRED AND LIVE FOR REVENGE. WE ONLY WIN WHEN WE CONQUER THE **INNER ENEMIES**—ANGER AND HATRED.
THE DALAI LAMA MEETS LOBSANG SAMTEN IN **DELHI**.
HOW ARE YOU? YOU DON'T LOOK TOO WELL. WHY DON'T YOU COME BACK UP TO DHARAMSALA WITH ME AND **REST UP** AT HOME?
THANKS, YOUR HOLINESS, BUT I HAVE TO GET SOME SUPPLIES FOR THE TIBETAN MEDICAL INSTITUTE. I'LL COME TO DHARAMSALA IN A WEEK OR SO.
ALL RIGHT, BUT PLEASE **TAKE CARE**!
LOBSANG DIES OF **JAUNDICE** AND **CIRRHOSIS** OF THE LIVER, WITH RELATIVES AROUND HIM, BUT AFTER THE DALAI LAMA RETURNS HOME TO DHARAMSALA.
THE DALAI LAMA CRIES AT LOBSANG'S FUNERAL...
HE WAS MY **CLOSEST** BROTHER.
I STILL FEEL **GUILTY** FROM WHEN WE WERE BOY MONKS TOGETHER. WHEN WE WERE **NAUGHTY**, MAKING TROUBLE OFTEN STARTED BY ME, LOBSANG WOULD GET WHIPPED WHILE I WOULD GET ONLY TOKEN PUNISHMENT.

MARCH 10, 1986: *"Under the pretext that Tibetans are not competent, large numbers of Chinese, mainly under the guise of skilled labor, are being brought into the major towns. Tibet was made the source of raw material for the economic development of China. If the present trend continues, and also if the Chinese hastily and haphazardly plan the economic development of Tibet without taking into consideration the conditions of the country and the needs of the people, there is a danger that not only economic chaos but also ecological disaster will befall Tibet."*

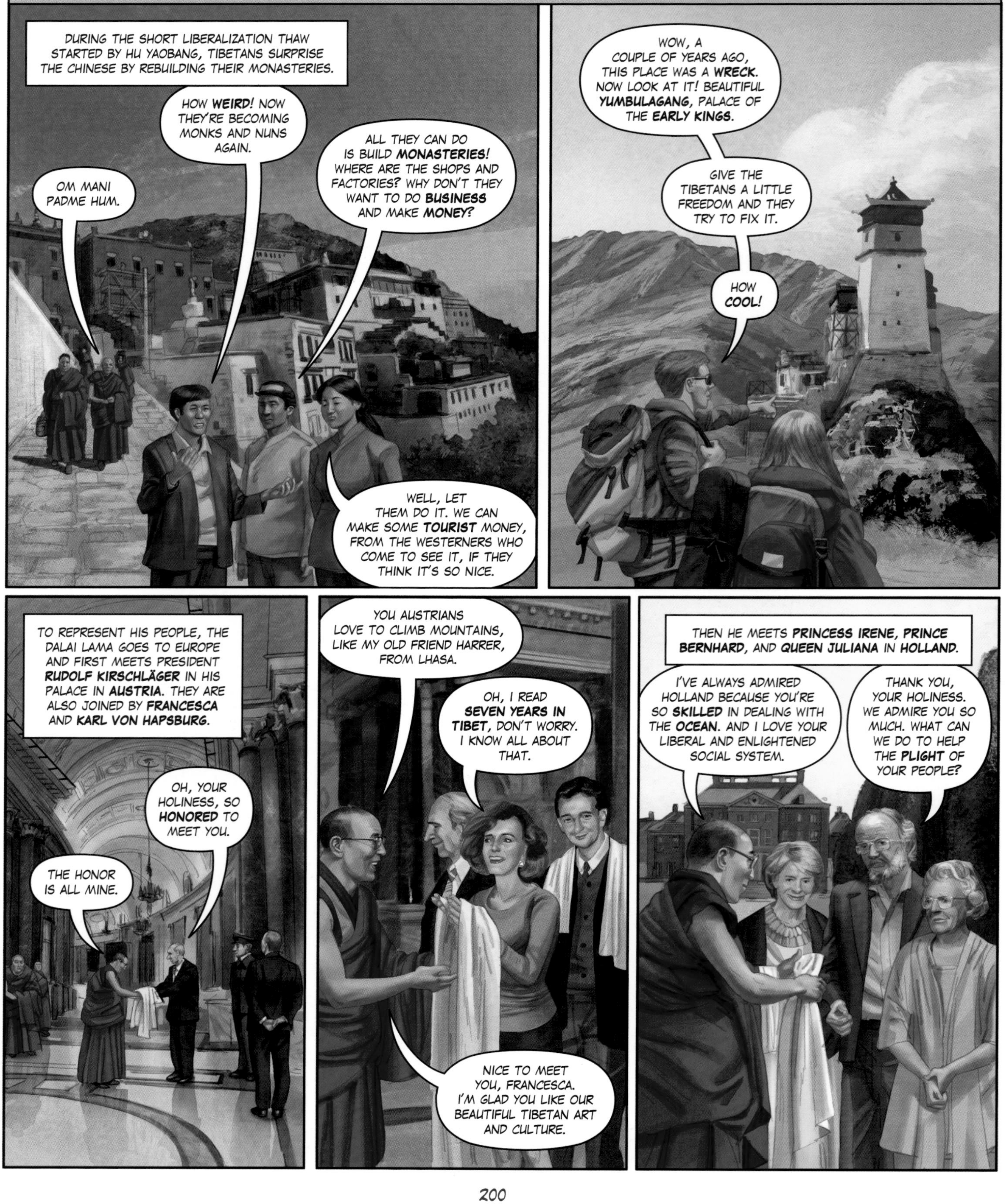
DURING THE SHORT LIBERALIZATION THAW STARTED BY HU YAOBANG, TIBETANS SURPRISE THE CHINESE BY REBUILDING THEIR MONASTERIES.
OM MANI PADME HUM.
HOW WEIRD! NOW THEY'RE BECOMING MONKS AND NUNS AGAIN.
ALL THEY CAN DO IS BUILD MONASTERIES! WHERE ARE THE SHOPS AND FACTORIES? WHY DON'T THEY WANT TO DO BUSINESS AND MAKE MONEY?
WELL, LET THEM DO IT. WE CAN MAKE SOME TOURIST MONEY, FROM THE WESTERNERS WHO COME TO SEE IT, IF THEY THINK IT'S SO NICE.
WOW, A COUPLE OF YEARS AGO, THIS PLACE WAS A WRECK. NOW LOOK AT IT! BEAUTIFUL YUMBULAGANG, PALACE OF THE EARLY KINGS.
GIVE THE TIBETANS A LITTLE FREEDOM AND THEY TRY TO FIX IT.
HOW COOL!
TO REPRESENT HIS PEOPLE, THE DALAI LAMA GOES TO EUROPE AND FIRST MEETS PRESIDENT RUDOLF KIRSCHLÄGER IN HIS PALACE IN AUSTRIA. THEY ARE ALSO JOINED BY FRANCESCA AND KARL VON HAPSBURG.
OH, YOUR HOLINESS, SO HONORED TO MEET YOU.
THE HONOR IS ALL MINE.
YOU AUSTRIANS LOVE TO CLIMB MOUNTAINS, LIKE MY OLD FRIEND HARRER, FROM LHASA.
OH, I READ SEVEN YEARS IN TIBET, DON'T WORRY. I KNOW ALL ABOUT THAT.
NICE TO MEET YOU, FRANCESCA. I'M GLAD YOU LIKE OUR BEAUTIFUL TIBETAN ART AND CULTURE.
THEN HE MEETS PRINCESS IRENE, PRINCE BERNHARD, AND QUEEN JULIANA IN HOLLAND.
I'VE ALWAYS ADMIRED HOLLAND BECAUSE YOU'RE SO SKILLED IN DEALING WITH THE OCEAN. AND I LOVE YOUR LIBERAL AND ENLIGHTENED SOCIAL SYSTEM.
THANK YOU, YOUR HOLINESS. WE ADMIRE YOU SO MUCH. WHAT CAN WE DO TO HELP THE PLIGHT OF YOUR PEOPLE?

MARCH 10, 1987: *"Our struggle is a fight for the rights that are justly upheld in today's modern times—the rights that we have inherited from our past history—and is not an act of hatred toward the Chinese. The past four decades, which witnessed the invasion and consequent occupation of Tibet by Communist China, have been the most difficult and tragic period in the long history of our country. . . ."*

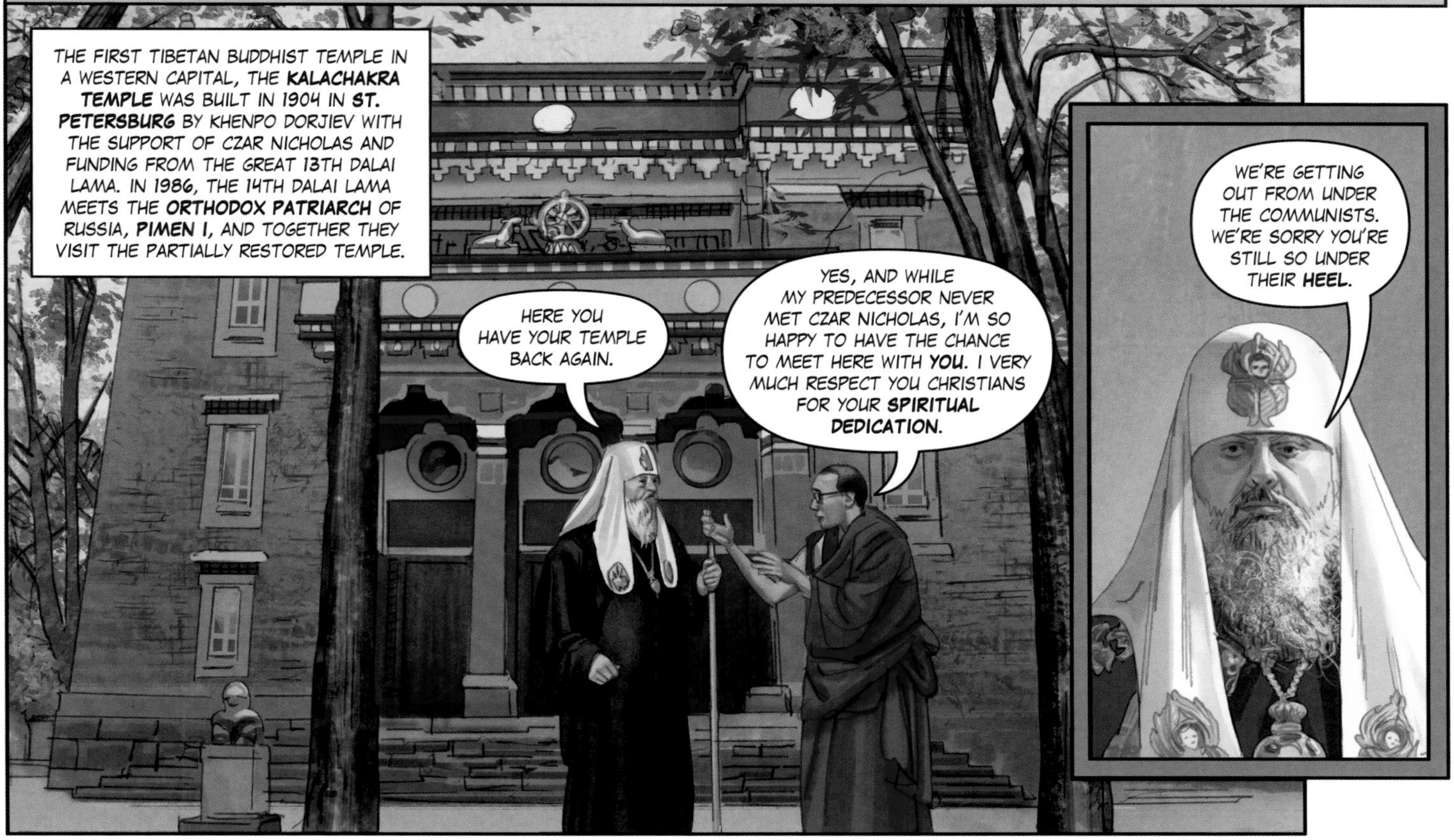
THE FIRST TIBETAN BUDDHIST TEMPLE IN A WESTERN CAPITAL, THE **KALACHAKRA TEMPLE** WAS BUILT IN 1904 IN **ST. PETERSBURG** BY KHENPO DORJIEV WITH THE SUPPORT OF CZAR NICHOLAS AND FUNDING FROM THE GREAT 13TH DALAI LAMA. IN 1986, THE 14TH DALAI LAMA MEETS THE **ORTHODOX PATRIARCH** OF RUSSIA, **PIMEN I,** AND TOGETHER THEY VISIT THE PARTIALLY RESTORED TEMPLE.
HERE YOU HAVE YOUR TEMPLE BACK AGAIN.
YES, AND WHILE MY PREDECESSOR NEVER MET CZAR NICHOLAS, I'M SO HAPPY TO HAVE THE CHANCE TO MEET HERE WITH **YOU.** I VERY MUCH RESPECT YOU CHRISTIANS FOR YOUR **SPIRITUAL DEDICATION.**
WE'RE GETTING OUT FROM UNDER THE COMMUNISTS. WE'RE SORRY YOU'RE STILL SO UNDER THEIR **HEEL.**

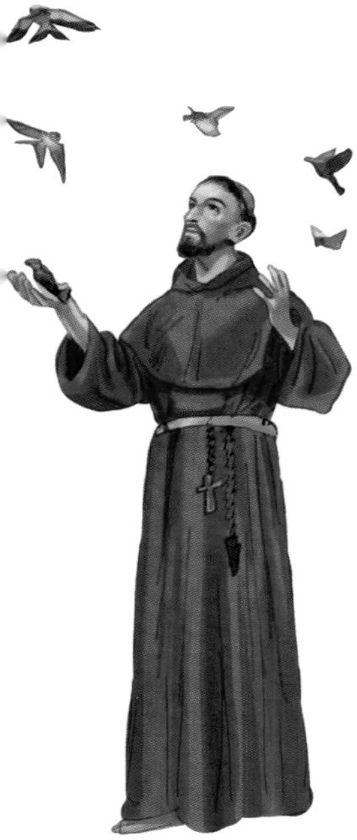

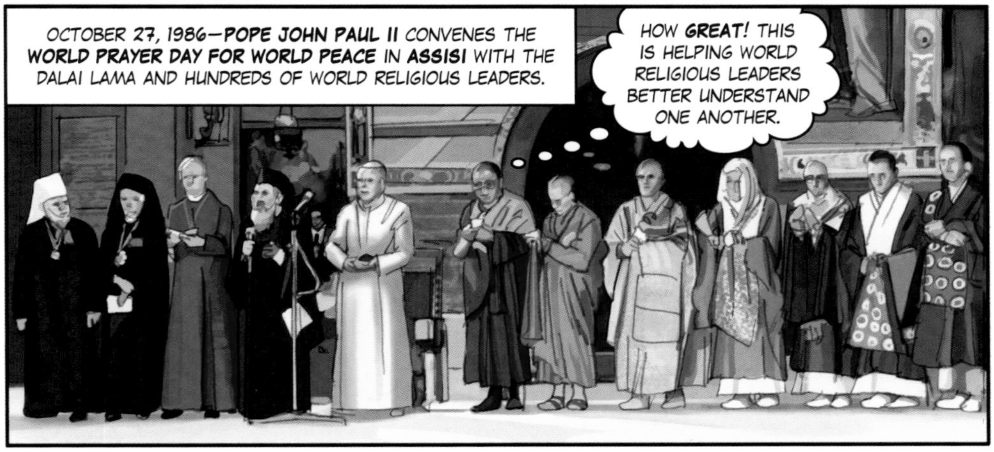
OCTOBER 27, 1986—**POPE JOHN PAUL II** CONVENES THE **WORLD PRAYER DAY FOR WORLD PEACE** IN **ASSISI** WITH THE DALAI LAMA AND HUNDREDS OF WORLD RELIGIOUS LEADERS.
HOW **GREAT!** THIS IS HELPING WORLD RELIGIOUS LEADERS BETTER UNDERSTAND ONE ANOTHER.

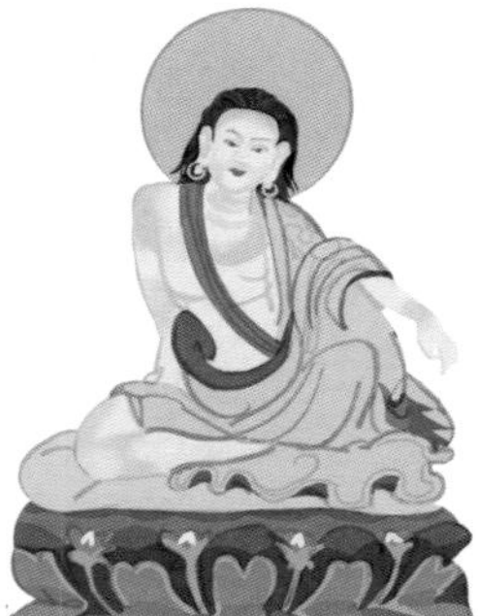

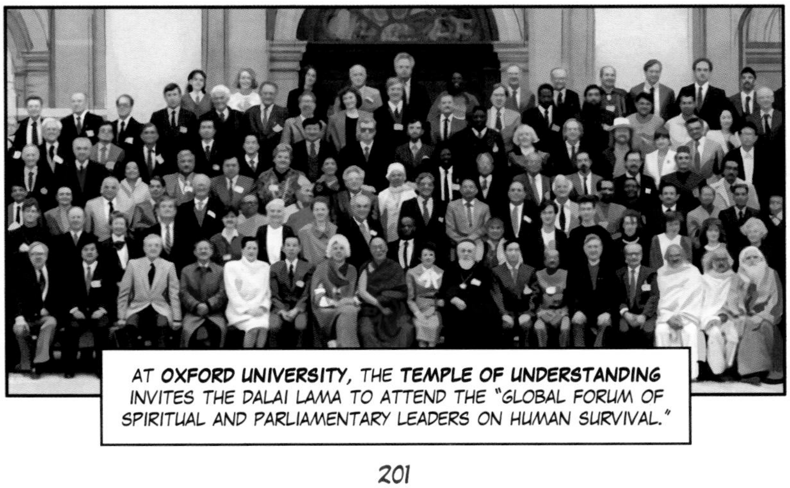
AT **OXFORD UNIVERSITY,** THE **TEMPLE OF UNDERSTANDING** INVITES THE DALAI LAMA TO ATTEND THE "GLOBAL FORUM OF SPIRITUAL AND PARLIAMENTARY LEADERS ON HUMAN SURVIVAL."

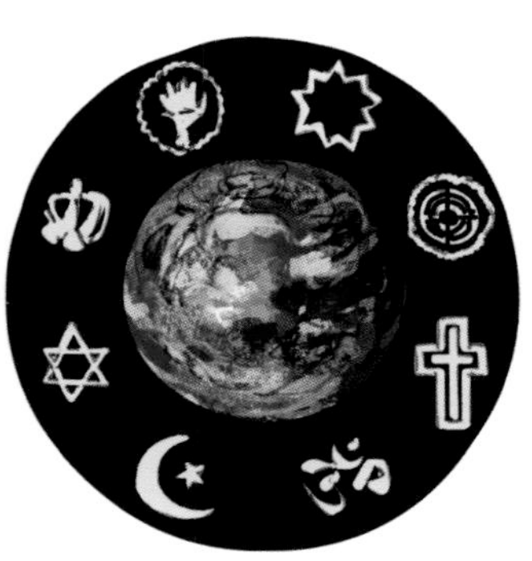

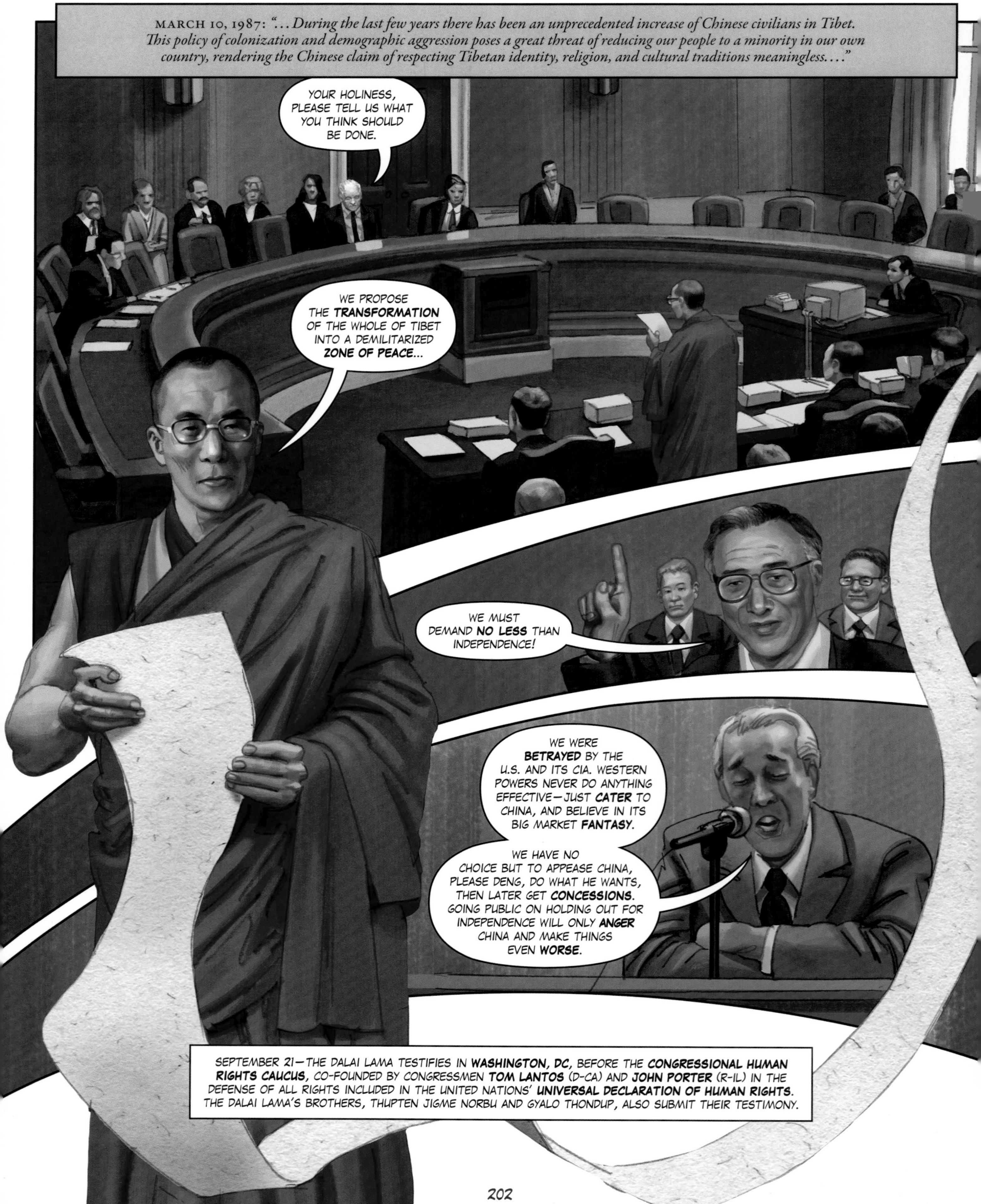
MARCH 10, 1987: "... During the last few years there has been an unprecedented increase of Chinese civilians in Tibet. This policy of colonization and demographic aggression poses a great threat of reducing our people to a minority in our own country, rendering the Chinese claim of respecting Tibetan identity, religion, and cultural traditions meaningless...."
YOUR HOLINESS, PLEASE TELL US WHAT YOU THINK SHOULD BE DONE.
WE PROPOSE THE TRANSFORMATION OF THE WHOLE OF TIBET INTO A DEMILITARIZED ZONE OF PEACE...
WE MUST DEMAND NO LESS THAN INDEPENDENCE!
WE WERE BETRAYED BY THE U.S. AND ITS CIA. WESTERN POWERS NEVER DO ANYTHING EFFECTIVE—JUST CATER TO CHINA, AND BELIEVE IN ITS BIG MARKET FANTASY.
WE HAVE NO CHOICE BUT TO APPEASE CHINA, PLEASE DENG, DO WHAT HE WANTS, THEN LATER GET CONCESSIONS. GOING PUBLIC ON HOLDING OUT FOR INDEPENDENCE WILL ONLY ANGER CHINA AND MAKE THINGS EVEN WORSE.
SEPTEMBER 21—THE DALAI LAMA TESTIFIES IN WASHINGTON, DC, BEFORE THE CONGRESSIONAL HUMAN RIGHTS CAUCUS, CO-FOUNDED BY CONGRESSMEN TOM LANTOS (D-CA) AND JOHN PORTER (R-IL) IN THE DEFENSE OF ALL RIGHTS INCLUDED IN THE UNITED NATIONS' UNIVERSAL DECLARATION OF HUMAN RIGHTS. THE DALAI LAMA'S BROTHERS, THUPTEN JIGME NORBU AND GYALO THONDUP, ALSO SUBMIT THEIR TESTIMONY.

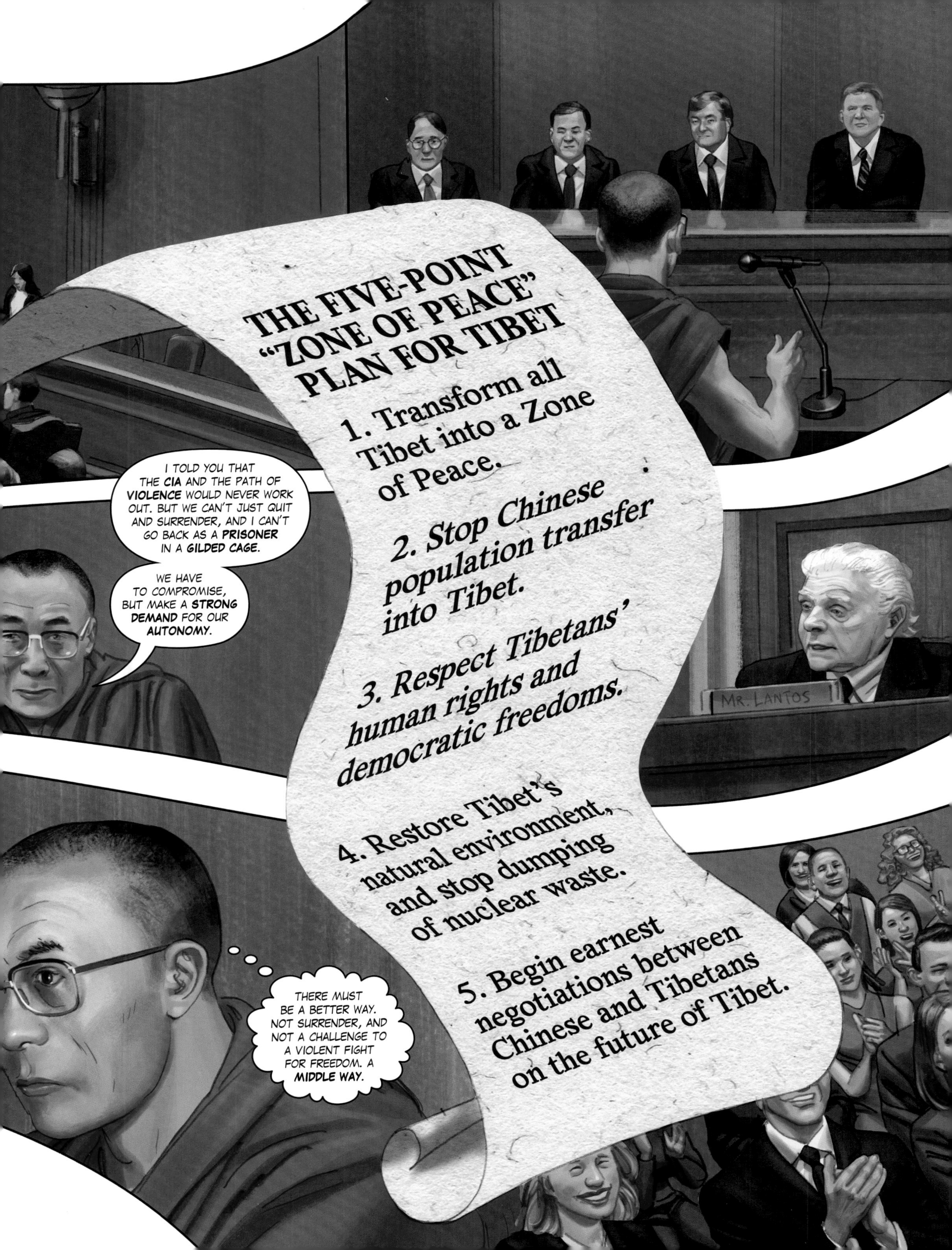
THE FIVE-POINT "ZONE OF PEACE" PLAN FOR TIBET
1. Transform all Tibet into a Zone of Peace.
2. Stop Chinese population transfer into Tibet.
3. Respect Tibetans' human rights and democratic freedoms.
4. Restore Tibet's natural environment, and stop dumping of nuclear waste.
5. Begin earnest negotiations between Chinese and Tibetans on the future of Tibet.
I TOLD YOU THAT THE CIA AND THE PATH OF VIOLENCE WOULD NEVER WORK OUT. BUT WE CAN'T JUST QUIT AND SURRENDER, AND I CAN'T GO BACK AS A PRISONER IN A GILDED CAGE.
WE HAVE TO COMPROMISE, BUT MAKE A STRONG DEMAND FOR OUR AUTONOMY.
MR. LANTOS
THERE MUST BE A BETTER WAY. NOT SURRENDER, AND NOT A CHALLENGE TO A VIOLENT FIGHT FOR FREEDOM. A MIDDLE WAY.

MARCH 10, 1987: *"... This has resulted in Chinese domination of economic and employment opportunities. Today there is greater danger than ever before to the survival of our people, our religion, culture and our country. The large-scale Chinese influx is threatening to transform Tibet into a Chinese territory. Thus, the Chinese continue the worst forms of genocide, racial discrimination and colonization in the countries under their subjugation. In any situation of human conflict, it is short-sighted to believe a lasting solution can be found through the use of force...."*

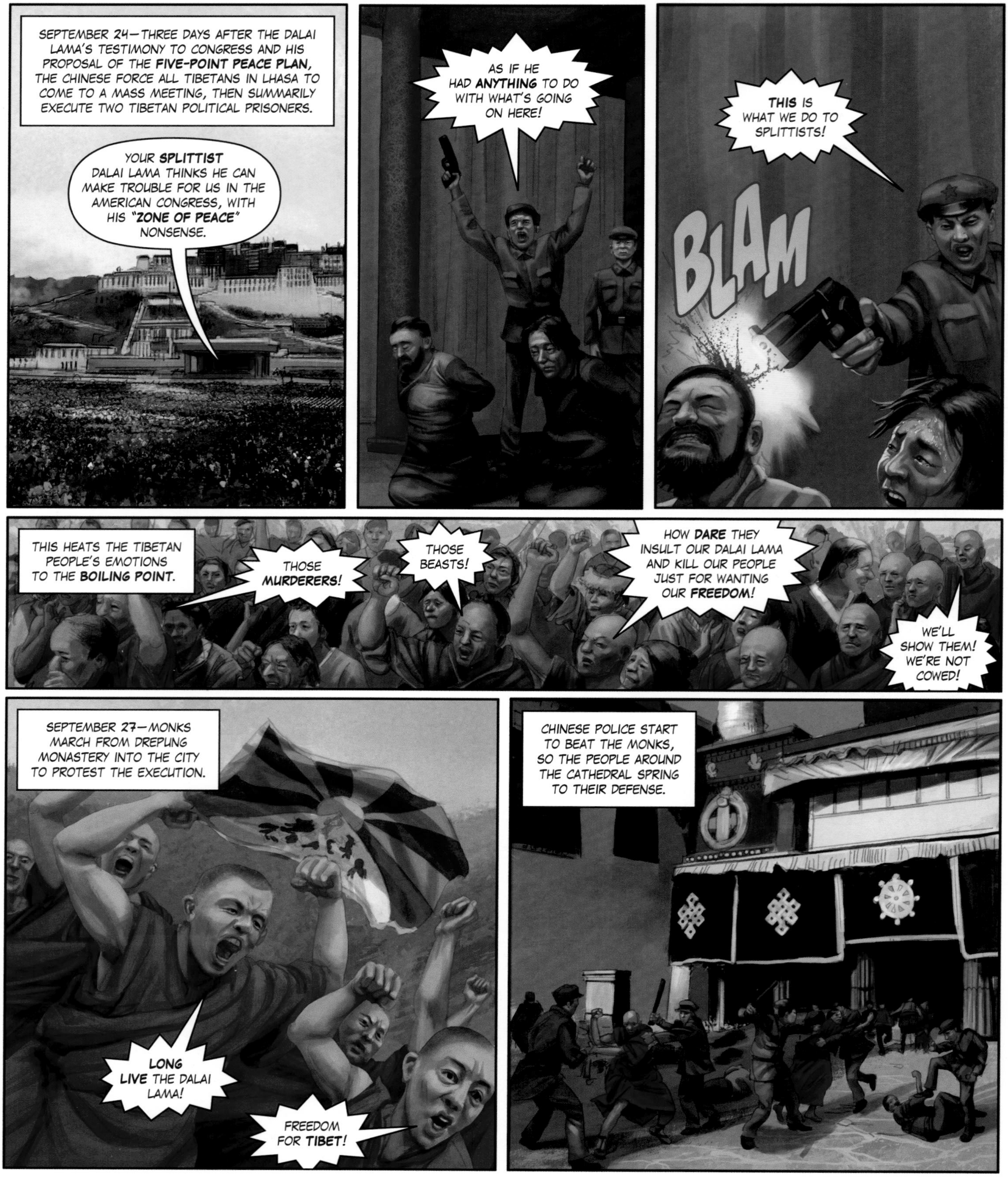
SEPTEMBER 24—THREE DAYS AFTER THE DALAI LAMA'S TESTIMONY TO CONGRESS AND HIS PROPOSAL OF THE **FIVE-POINT PEACE PLAN**, THE CHINESE FORCE ALL TIBETANS IN LHASA TO COME TO A MASS MEETING, THEN SUMMARILY EXECUTE TWO TIBETAN POLITICAL PRISONERS.
YOUR **SPLITTIST** DALAI LAMA THINKS HE CAN MAKE TROUBLE FOR US IN THE AMERICAN CONGRESS, WITH HIS **"ZONE OF PEACE"** NONSENSE.
AS IF HE HAD **ANYTHING** TO DO WITH WHAT'S GOING ON HERE!
THIS IS WHAT WE DO TO SPLITTISTS!
BLAM
THIS HEATS THE TIBETAN PEOPLE'S EMOTIONS TO THE **BOILING POINT**.
THOSE **MURDERERS!**
THOSE BEASTS!
HOW **DARE** THEY INSULT OUR DALAI LAMA AND KILL OUR PEOPLE JUST FOR WANTING OUR **FREEDOM!**
WE'LL SHOW THEM! WE'RE NOT COWED!
SEPTEMBER 27—MONKS MARCH FROM DREPUNG MONASTERY INTO THE CITY TO PROTEST THE EXECUTION.
LONG LIVE THE DALAI LAMA!
FREEDOM FOR **TIBET!**
CHINESE POLICE START TO BEAT THE MONKS, SO THE PEOPLE AROUND THE CATHEDRAL SPRING TO THEIR DEFENSE.

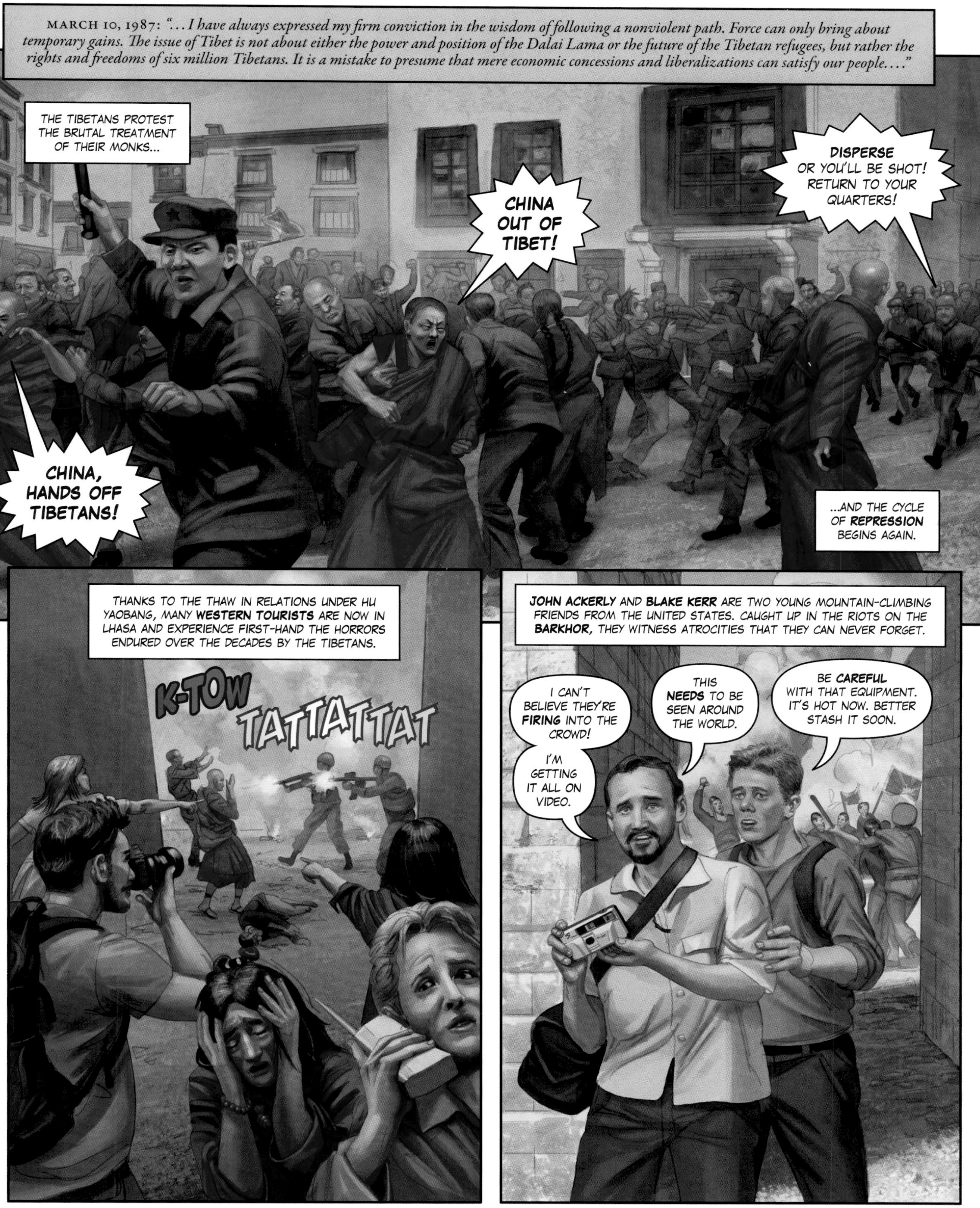
MARCH 10, 1987: "... I have always expressed my firm conviction in the wisdom of following a nonviolent path. Force can only bring about temporary gains. The issue of Tibet is not about either the power and position of the Dalai Lama or the future of the Tibetan refugees, but rather the rights and freedoms of six million Tibetans. It is a mistake to presume that mere economic concessions and liberalizations can satisfy our people. ..."
THE TIBETANS PROTEST THE BRUTAL TREATMENT OF THEIR MONKS...
CHINA OUT OF TIBET!
DISPERSE OR YOU'LL BE SHOT! RETURN TO YOUR QUARTERS!
CHINA, HANDS OFF TIBETANS!
...AND THE CYCLE OF REPRESSION BEGINS AGAIN.
THANKS TO THE THAW IN RELATIONS UNDER HU YAOBANG, MANY WESTERN TOURISTS ARE NOW IN LHASA AND EXPERIENCE FIRST-HAND THE HORRORS ENDURED OVER THE DECADES BY THE TIBETANS.
K-TOW
TATTATTAT
JOHN ACKERLY AND BLAKE KERR ARE TWO YOUNG MOUNTAIN-CLIMBING FRIENDS FROM THE UNITED STATES. CAUGHT UP IN THE RIOTS ON THE BARKHOR, THEY WITNESS ATROCITIES THAT THEY CAN NEVER FORGET.
I CAN'T BELIEVE THEY'RE FIRING INTO THE CROWD!
I'M GETTING IT ALL ON VIDEO.
THIS NEEDS TO BE SEEN AROUND THE WORLD.
BE CAREFUL WITH THAT EQUIPMENT. IT'S HOT NOW. BETTER STASH IT SOON.

MARCH 10, 1987: *"... The issue of Tibet is fundamentally political with international ramifications, and as such only a political solution can provide a meaningful answer. In the past, Tibet played an important role as a neutral buffer contributing to the stability of the region. This historical precedent provides the basis for a solution to the issue of Tibet for the benefit of all. The demilitarization of Tibet and its transformation into a zone of peace should be the first step. This will contribute in bringing peace not only to this part of Asia but also to the world at large...."*

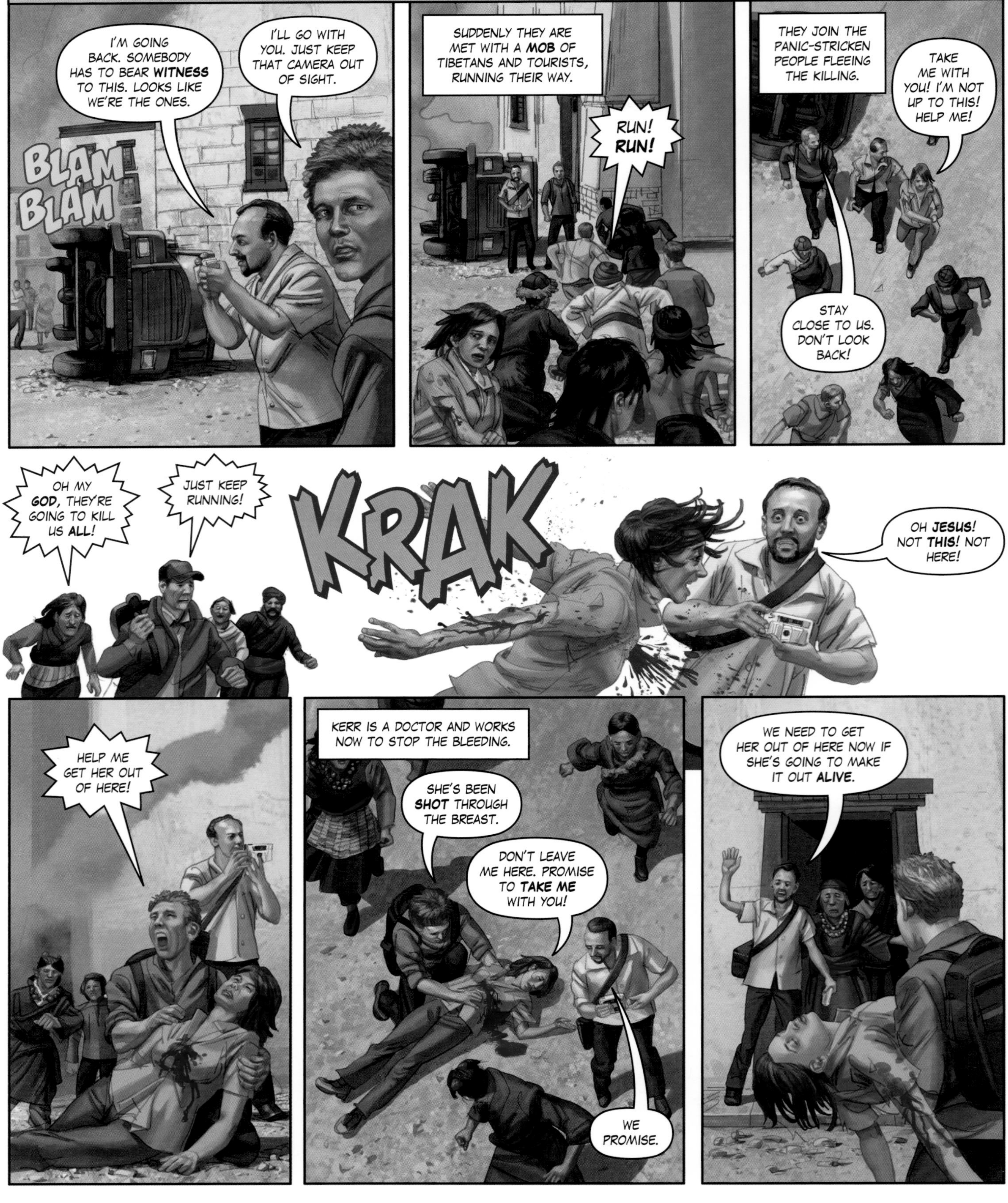

I'M GOING BACK. SOMEBODY HAS TO BEAR WITNESS TO THIS. LOOKS LIKE WE'RE THE ONES.
I'LL GO WITH YOU. JUST KEEP THAT CAMERA OUT OF SIGHT.
BLAM BLAM
SUDDENLY THEY ARE MET WITH A MOB OF TIBETANS AND TOURISTS, RUNNING THEIR WAY.
RUN! RUN!
THEY JOIN THE PANIC-STRICKEN PEOPLE FLEEING THE KILLING.
TAKE ME WITH YOU! I'M NOT UP TO THIS! HELP ME!
STAY CLOSE TO US. DON'T LOOK BACK!
OH MY GOD, THEY'RE GOING TO KILL US ALL!
JUST KEEP RUNNING!
KRAK
OH JESUS! NOT THIS! NOT HERE!
HELP ME GET HER OUT OF HERE!
KERR IS A DOCTOR AND WORKS NOW TO STOP THE BLEEDING.
SHE'S BEEN SHOT THROUGH THE BREAST.
DON'T LEAVE ME HERE. PROMISE TO TAKE ME WITH YOU!
WE PROMISE.
WE NEED TO GET HER OUT OF HERE NOW IF SHE'S GOING TO MAKE IT OUT ALIVE.

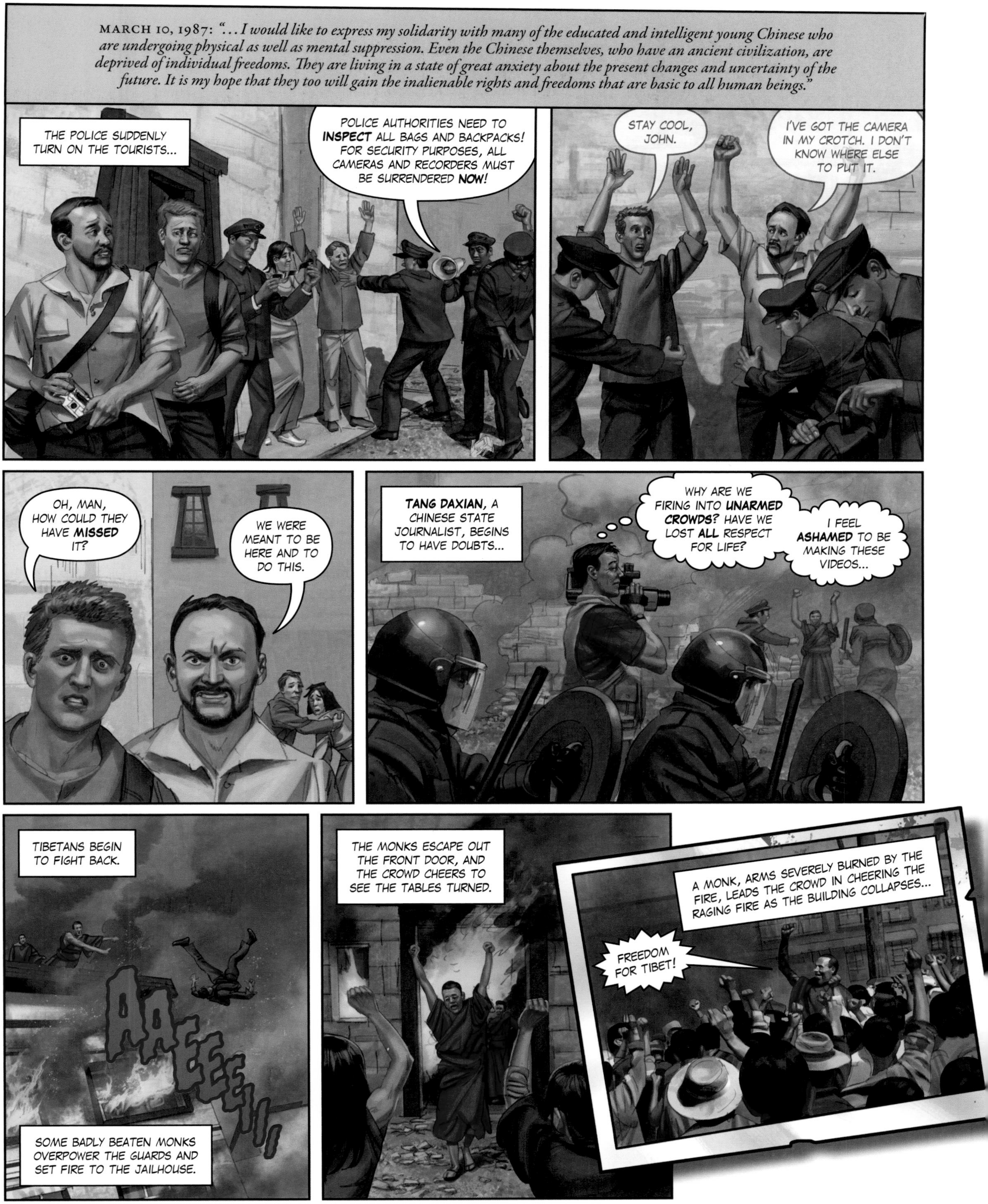
MARCH 10, 1987: "... I would like to express my solidarity with many of the educated and intelligent young Chinese who are undergoing physical as well as mental suppression. Even the Chinese themselves, who have an ancient civilization, are deprived of individual freedoms. They are living in a state of great anxiety about the present changes and uncertainty of the future. It is my hope that they too will gain the inalienable rights and freedoms that are basic to all human beings."
THE POLICE SUDDENLY TURN ON THE TOURISTS...
POLICE AUTHORITIES NEED TO **INSPECT** ALL BAGS AND BACKPACKS! FOR SECURITY PURPOSES, ALL CAMERAS AND RECORDERS MUST BE SURRENDERED **NOW!**
STAY COOL, JOHN.
I'VE GOT THE CAMERA IN MY CROTCH. I DON'T KNOW WHERE ELSE TO PUT IT.
OH, MAN, HOW COULD THEY HAVE **MISSED** IT?
WE WERE MEANT TO BE HERE AND TO DO THIS.
TANG DAXIAN, A CHINESE STATE JOURNALIST, BEGINS TO HAVE DOUBTS...
WHY ARE WE FIRING INTO **UNARMED CROWDS?** HAVE WE LOST **ALL** RESPECT FOR LIFE?
I FEEL **ASHAMED** TO BE MAKING THESE VIDEOS...
TIBETANS BEGIN TO FIGHT BACK.
AAEEE!!!
SOME BADLY BEATEN MONKS OVERPOWER THE GUARDS AND SET FIRE TO THE JAILHOUSE.
THE MONKS ESCAPE OUT THE FRONT DOOR, AND THE CROWD CHEERS TO SEE THE TABLES TURNED.
A MONK, ARMS SEVERELY BURNED BY THE FIRE, LEADS THE CROWD IN CHEERING THE RAGING FIRE AS THE BUILDING COLLAPSES...
FREEDOM FOR TIBET!

MARCH 10, 1988: *"In past months our country has been undergoing the most severe repression since the so-called Cultural Revolution. At least 32 people have died during the unrest in Lhasa, and hundreds have been arrested, beaten, and tortured. Throughout Tibet, additional security forces have been brought in, freedom of movement has now been restricted, and Chinese authorities continue to violate the people's human rights...."*

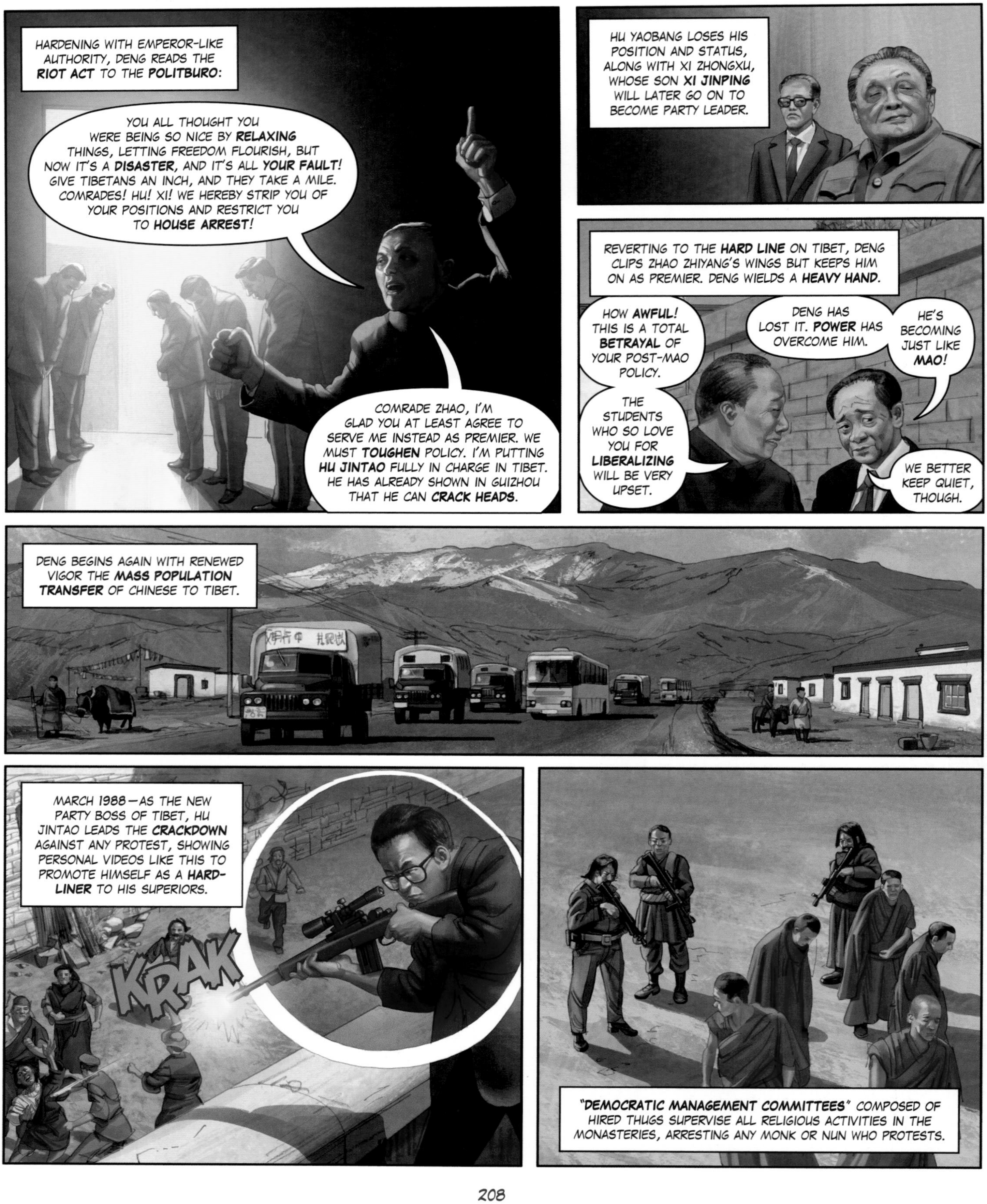
HARDENING WITH EMPEROR-LIKE AUTHORITY, DENG READS THE RIOT ACT TO THE POLITBURO:
YOU ALL THOUGHT YOU WERE BEING SO NICE BY RELAXING THINGS, LETTING FREEDOM FLOURISH, BUT NOW IT'S A DISASTER, AND IT'S ALL YOUR FAULT! GIVE TIBETANS AN INCH, AND THEY TAKE A MILE. COMRADES! HU! XI! WE HEREBY STRIP YOU OF YOUR POSITIONS AND RESTRICT YOU TO HOUSE ARREST!
COMRADE ZHAO, I'M GLAD YOU AT LEAST AGREE TO SERVE ME INSTEAD AS PREMIER. WE MUST TOUGHEN POLICY. I'M PUTTING HU JINTAO FULLY IN CHARGE IN TIBET. HE HAS ALREADY SHOWN IN GUIZHOU THAT HE CAN CRACK HEADS.
HU YAOBANG LOSES HIS POSITION AND STATUS, ALONG WITH XI ZHONGXU, WHOSE SON XI JINPING WILL LATER GO ON TO BECOME PARTY LEADER.
REVERTING TO THE HARD LINE ON TIBET, DENG CLIPS ZHAO ZHIYANG'S WINGS BUT KEEPS HIM ON AS PREMIER. DENG WIELDS A HEAVY HAND.
HOW AWFUL! THIS IS A TOTAL BETRAYAL OF YOUR POST-MAO POLICY.
DENG HAS LOST IT. POWER HAS OVERCOME HIM.
HE'S BECOMING JUST LIKE MAO!
THE STUDENTS WHO SO LOVE YOU FOR LIBERALIZING WILL BE VERY UPSET.
WE BETTER KEEP QUIET, THOUGH.
DENG BEGINS AGAIN WITH RENEWED VIGOR THE MASS POPULATION TRANSFER OF CHINESE TO TIBET.
MARCH 1988—AS THE NEW PARTY BOSS OF TIBET, HU JINTAO LEADS THE CRACKDOWN AGAINST ANY PROTEST, SHOWING PERSONAL VIDEOS LIKE THIS TO PROMOTE HIMSELF AS A HARD-LINER TO HIS SUPERIORS.
KRAK
"DEMOCRATIC MANAGEMENT COMMITTEES" COMPOSED OF HIRED THUGS SUPERVISE ALL RELIGIOUS ACTIVITIES IN THE MONASTERIES, ARRESTING ANY MONK OR NUN WHO PROTESTS.

MARCH 10, 1988: *"...We also honor the courage of our brethren in Tibet who have taken to the streets to draw attention to their suffering under Chinese colonial rule. The current unrest is unique in being witnessed by the foreign press and tourists and was widely reported. The struggle of our people is mostly nonviolent. This has made it more difficult to convince the world of the depths of our misery and the earnestness of our resolve...."*

WITH THE GROWING NEED FOR BETTER REPRESENTATION IN THE U.S., SOME OF THE DALAI LAMA'S FRIENDS—**JOEL MCCLEARY, RICHARD GERE, CHARLIE ROSE,** AND ROBERT THURMAN—MEET HIM IN WASHINGTON, DC, TO **BRAINSTORM.**

TENZIN TETHONG, THE DALAI LAMA'S REPRESENTATIVE, ALONG WITH JOEL MCCLEARY AND CONGRESSMAN TOM LANTOS, ARRANGES FOR THE DALAI LAMA TO PRESENT HIS FIVE-POINT PEACE PLAN BEFORE THE CONGRESSIONAL **HUMAN RIGHTS CAUCUS.**

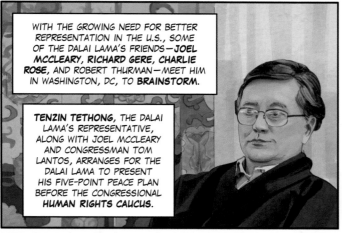

YOUR HOLINESS, WHAT CAN WE DO TO HELP?

NOW IS THE TIME TO FOUND THE **U.S. CULTURAL CENTER** I ASKED FOR IN 1979, LIKE OUR **TIBET HOUSE,** NEW DELHI. WE MUST PRESERVE OUR PRECIOUS NONVIOLENT CULTURE.

AT RICHARD'S OFFICE IN NEW YORK, PLANS ARE MADE FOR **TIBET HOUSE US...**

LET'S EDUCATE THE AMERICAN PEOPLE—CREATE A **LANDMARK EXHIBITION** OF TIBETAN ART, AND THOUSANDS OF **EVENTS** ACROSS THE U.S., MOVING ON TO EUROPE AND ASIA—1991, THE **"YEAR OF TIBET,"** OR EVEN **"DECADE OF TIBET"**...

GOOD IDEA. I CAN RAISE A LOT OF **FUNDS.**

I CAN ORGANIZE **BENEFIT CONCERTS.** MANY MUSICIANS LOVE TIBET.

I'M HONORED THAT YOU WOULD ASK ME TO CURATE A FINE ART EXHIBITION OF **TIBETAN SACRED ART.**

HIS HOLINESS WILL BE **VERY** PLEASED. CULTURE IS ALWAYS HIS **PRIORITY.**

RESPONDING TO THE TERRIBLE NEWS FROM TIBET, THE DALAI LAMA, TETHONG, AND MCCLEARY MEET WITH **MICHELLE BOHANA, JOHN AVEDON,** JOHN ACKERLY, AND BLAKE KERR. THEY PLAN FOR AN **NGO** IN DC, THE **INTERNATIONAL CAMPAIGN FOR TIBET** (ICT), TO DEFEND TIBETANS' HUMAN RIGHTS, WORK WITH THE U.S. CONGRESS AND EUROPEAN PARLIAMENTS, AND INFORM THE WORLD OF THE HUMAN ATROCITIES AND ENVIRONMENTAL DEVASTATION IN TIBET. **LODI GYARI** IS APPOINTED TO HEAD THE ORGANIZATION.

ACKERLY AND KERR, FRESH FROM THE BLOODY RIOTS IN LHASA, TELL THEIR STORY TO THE DALAI LAMA.

WE CAN'T KEEP SILENT. THIS IS **GENOCIDE.**

WE WANT TO TELL THE WORLD, THE U.N., AND CONGRESS.

IT'S JUST LIKE **NAZI GERMANY.** BUT WE'RE ONLY TWO INDIVIDUALS. WE NEED AN NGO TO GET OUR MESSAGE ACROSS...

LET'S CREATE A SUPPORT GROUP THAT WILL BE TAKEN SERIOUSLY.

THE ICT IS FOUNDED IN DC TO SERVE AS A CENTRAL FOCUS FOR THE TIBET SUPPORT GROUPS SPRINGING UP AROUND THE WORLD.

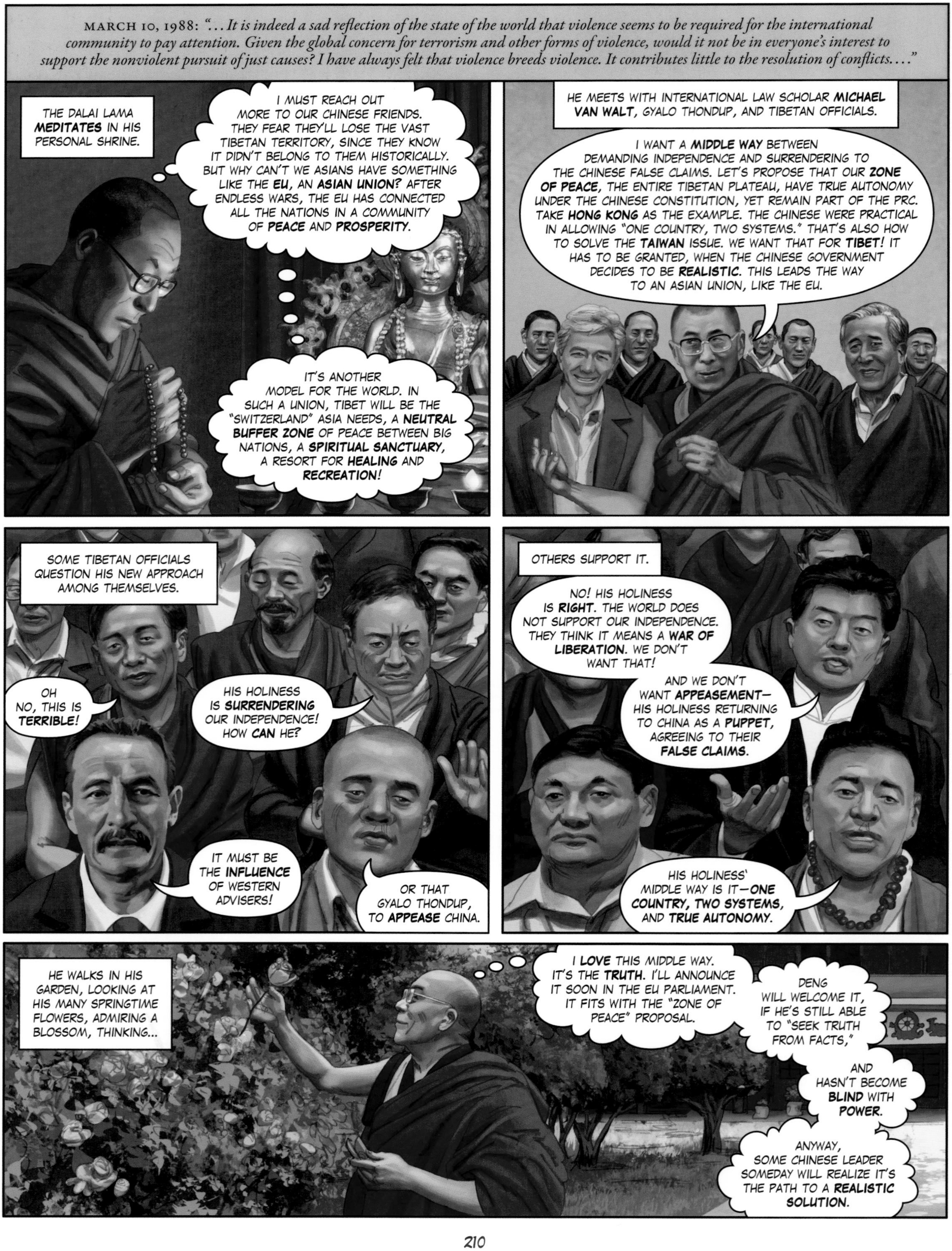
MARCH 10, 1988: "... It is indeed a sad reflection of the state of the world that violence seems to be required for the international community to pay attention. Given the global concern for terrorism and other forms of violence, would it not be in everyone's interest to support the nonviolent pursuit of just causes? I have always felt that violence breeds violence. It contributes little to the resolution of conflicts...."
THE DALAI LAMA MEDITATES IN HIS PERSONAL SHRINE.
I MUST REACH OUT MORE TO OUR CHINESE FRIENDS. THEY FEAR THEY'LL LOSE THE VAST TIBETAN TERRITORY, SINCE THEY KNOW IT DIDN'T BELONG TO THEM HISTORICALLY. BUT WHY CAN'T WE ASIANS HAVE SOMETHING LIKE THE EU, AN ASIAN UNION? AFTER ENDLESS WARS, THE EU HAS CONNECTED ALL THE NATIONS IN A COMMUNITY OF PEACE AND PROSPERITY.
IT'S ANOTHER MODEL FOR THE WORLD. IN SUCH A UNION, TIBET WILL BE THE "SWITZERLAND" ASIA NEEDS, A NEUTRAL BUFFER ZONE OF PEACE BETWEEN BIG NATIONS, A SPIRITUAL SANCTUARY, A RESORT FOR HEALING AND RECREATION!
HE MEETS WITH INTERNATIONAL LAW SCHOLAR MICHAEL VAN WALT, GYALO THONDUP, AND TIBETAN OFFICIALS.
I WANT A MIDDLE WAY BETWEEN DEMANDING INDEPENDENCE AND SURRENDERING TO THE CHINESE FALSE CLAIMS. LET'S PROPOSE THAT OUR ZONE OF PEACE, THE ENTIRE TIBETAN PLATEAU, HAVE TRUE AUTONOMY UNDER THE CHINESE CONSTITUTION, YET REMAIN PART OF THE PRC. TAKE HONG KONG AS THE EXAMPLE. THE CHINESE WERE PRACTICAL IN ALLOWING "ONE COUNTRY, TWO SYSTEMS." THAT'S ALSO HOW TO SOLVE THE TAIWAN ISSUE. WE WANT THAT FOR TIBET! IT HAS TO BE GRANTED, WHEN THE CHINESE GOVERNMENT DECIDES TO BE REALISTIC. THIS LEADS THE WAY TO AN ASIAN UNION, LIKE THE EU.
SOME TIBETAN OFFICIALS QUESTION HIS NEW APPROACH AMONG THEMSELVES.
OH NO, THIS IS TERRIBLE!
HIS HOLINESS IS SURRENDERING OUR INDEPENDENCE! HOW CAN HE?
IT MUST BE THE INFLUENCE OF WESTERN ADVISERS!
OR THAT GYALO THONDUP, TO APPEASE CHINA.
OTHERS SUPPORT IT.
NO! HIS HOLINESS IS RIGHT. THE WORLD DOES NOT SUPPORT OUR INDEPENDENCE. THEY THINK IT MEANS A WAR OF LIBERATION. WE DON'T WANT THAT!
AND WE DON'T WANT APPEASEMENT—HIS HOLINESS RETURNING TO CHINA AS A PUPPET, AGREEING TO THEIR FALSE CLAIMS.
HIS HOLINESS' MIDDLE WAY IS IT—ONE COUNTRY, TWO SYSTEMS, AND TRUE AUTONOMY.
HE WALKS IN HIS GARDEN, LOOKING AT HIS MANY SPRINGTIME FLOWERS, ADMIRING A BLOSSOM, THINKING...
I LOVE THIS MIDDLE WAY. IT'S THE TRUTH. I'LL ANNOUNCE IT SOON IN THE EU PARLIAMENT. IT FITS WITH THE "ZONE OF PEACE" PROPOSAL.
DENG WILL WELCOME IT, IF HE'S STILL ABLE TO "SEEK TRUTH FROM FACTS,"
AND HASN'T BECOME BLIND WITH POWER.
ANYWAY, SOME CHINESE LEADER SOMEDAY WILL REALIZE IT'S THE PATH TO A REALISTIC SOLUTION.

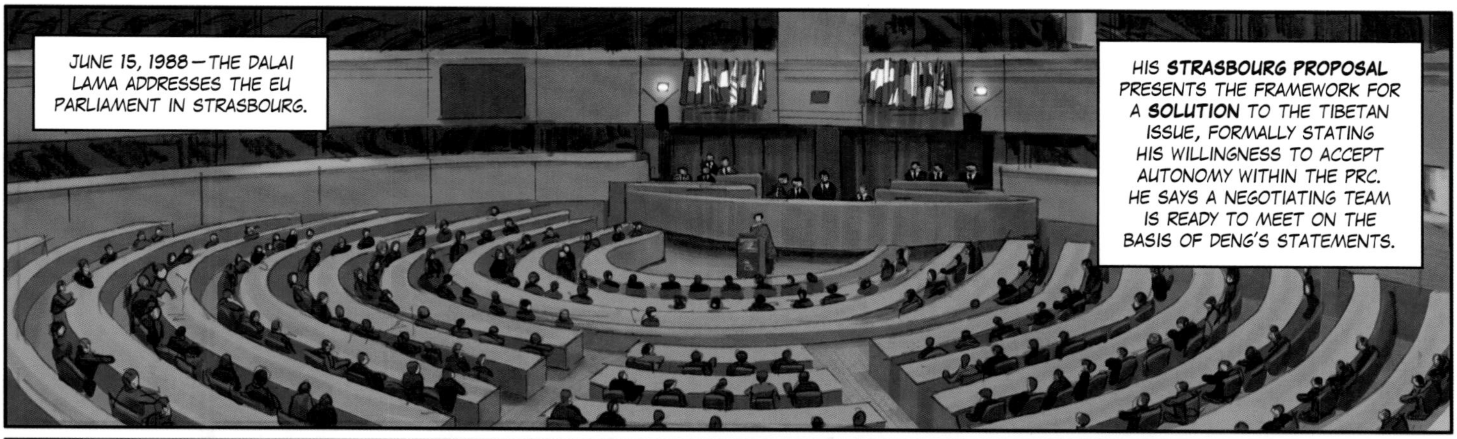
JUNE 15, 1988—THE DALAI LAMA ADDRESSES THE EU PARLIAMENT IN STRASBOURG.
HIS **STRASBOURG PROPOSAL** PRESENTS THE FRAMEWORK FOR A **SOLUTION** TO THE TIBETAN ISSUE, FORMALLY STATING HIS WILLINGNESS TO ACCEPT AUTONOMY WITHIN THE PRC. HE SAYS A NEGOTIATING TEAM IS READY TO MEET ON THE BASIS OF DENG'S STATEMENTS.

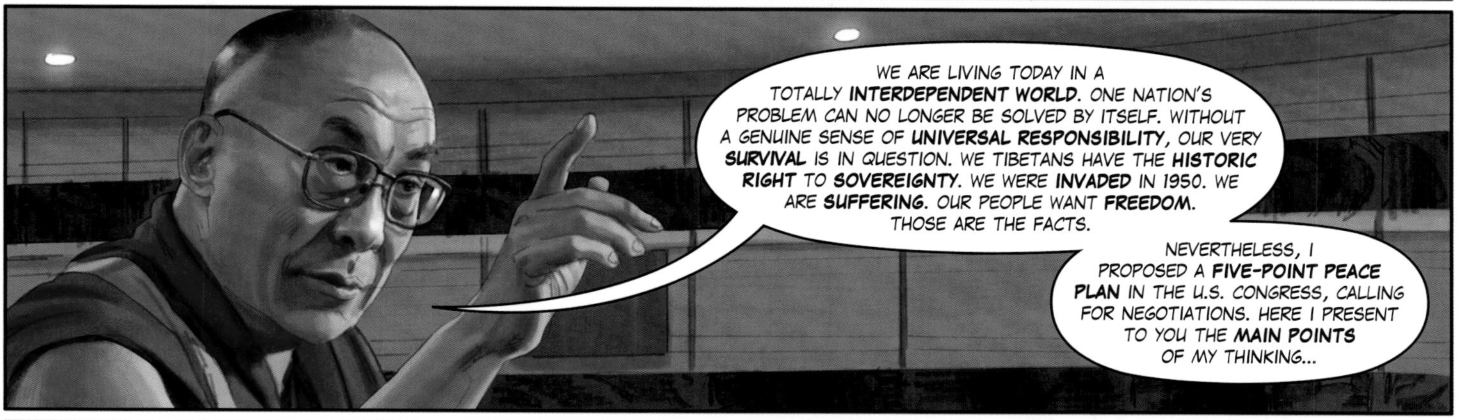
WE ARE LIVING TODAY IN A TOTALLY **INTERDEPENDENT WORLD**. ONE NATION'S PROBLEM CAN NO LONGER BE SOLVED BY ITSELF. WITHOUT A GENUINE SENSE OF **UNIVERSAL RESPONSIBILITY**, OUR VERY **SURVIVAL** IS IN QUESTION. WE TIBETANS HAVE THE **HISTORIC RIGHT** TO **SOVEREIGNTY**. WE WERE **INVADED** IN 1950. WE ARE **SUFFERING**. OUR PEOPLE WANT **FREEDOM**. THOSE ARE THE FACTS.
NEVERTHELESS, I PROPOSED A **FIVE-POINT PEACE PLAN** IN THE U.S. CONGRESS, CALLING FOR NEGOTIATIONS. HERE I PRESENT TO YOU THE **MAIN POINTS** OF MY THINKING...

The historic Strasbourg Proposal of 1988 offers five main points:

1. Reunite the three provinces of Tibet—U-Tsang, Kham, and Amdo—as a self-governing, democratic entity in association with the People's Republic of China.
2. The PRC remains responsible for Tibet's foreign policy. The Government of Tibet (GoT) maintains its own foreign affairs bureau for nonpolitical activities.
3. The GoT in Lhasa is founded on a Constitution for a democratic system, to ensure economic equality, social justice, and protection of the environment—as well as Tibetans' freedom of speech, assembly, and religion.
4. The GoT protects wildlife and regulates the use of natural resources. Nuclear weapons are prohibited, and any technologies producing hazardous waste. The goal—to transform Tibet into the planet's largest natural preserve.
5. A regional peace conference is held to make Tibet a genuine demilitarized sanctuary of peace. Until then, the PRC maintains a few military installations for defense purposes, while agreeing to cease Tibetan human-rights violations and Chinese population transfer to Tibet.

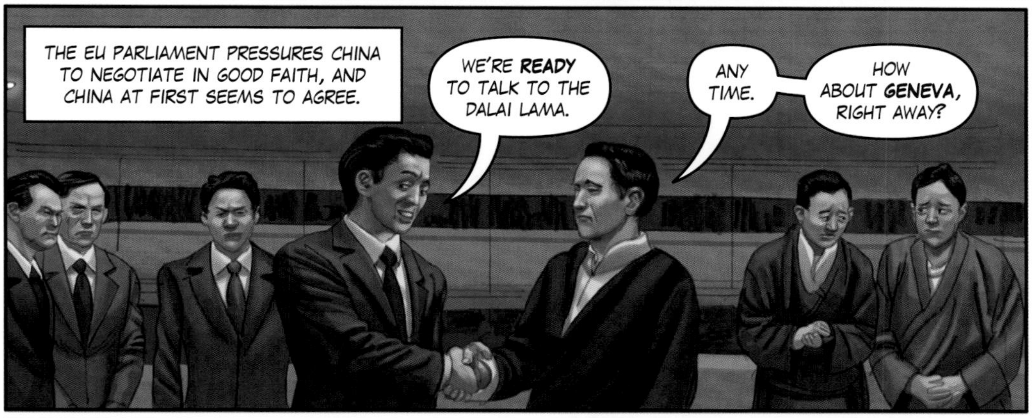
THE EU PARLIAMENT PRESSURES CHINA TO NEGOTIATE IN GOOD FAITH, AND CHINA AT FIRST SEEMS TO AGREE.
WE'RE **READY** TO TALK TO THE DALAI LAMA.
ANY TIME.
HOW ABOUT **GENEVA**, RIGHT AWAY?

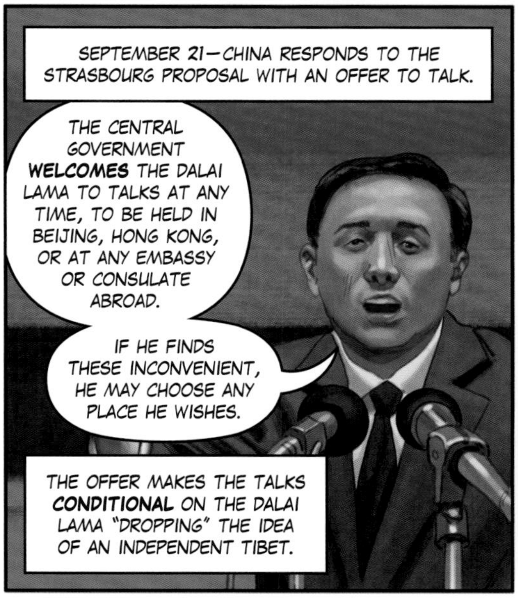
SEPTEMBER 21—CHINA RESPONDS TO THE STRASBOURG PROPOSAL WITH AN OFFER TO TALK.
THE CENTRAL GOVERNMENT **WELCOMES** THE DALAI LAMA TO TALKS AT ANY TIME, TO BE HELD IN BEIJING, HONG KONG, OR AT ANY EMBASSY OR CONSULATE ABROAD.
IF HE FINDS THESE INCONVENIENT, HE MAY CHOOSE ANY PLACE HE WISHES.
THE OFFER MAKES THE TALKS **CONDITIONAL** ON THE DALAI LAMA "DROPPING" THE IDEA OF AN INDEPENDENT TIBET.

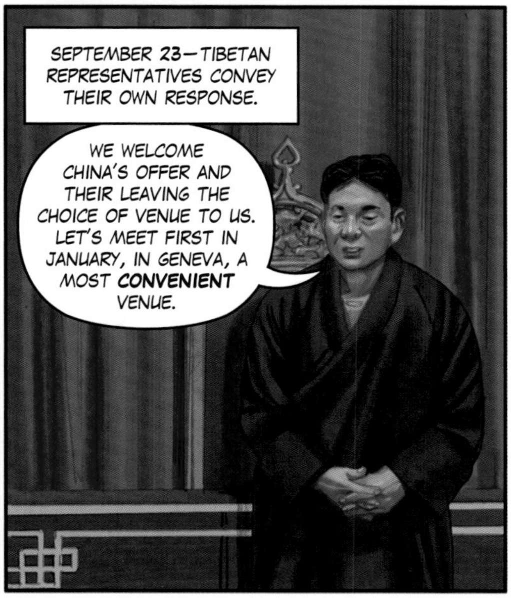
SEPTEMBER 23—TIBETAN REPRESENTATIVES CONVEY THEIR OWN RESPONSE.
WE WELCOME CHINA'S OFFER AND THEIR LEAVING THE CHOICE OF VENUE TO US. LET'S MEET FIRST IN JANUARY, IN GENEVA, A MOST **CONVENIENT** VENUE.

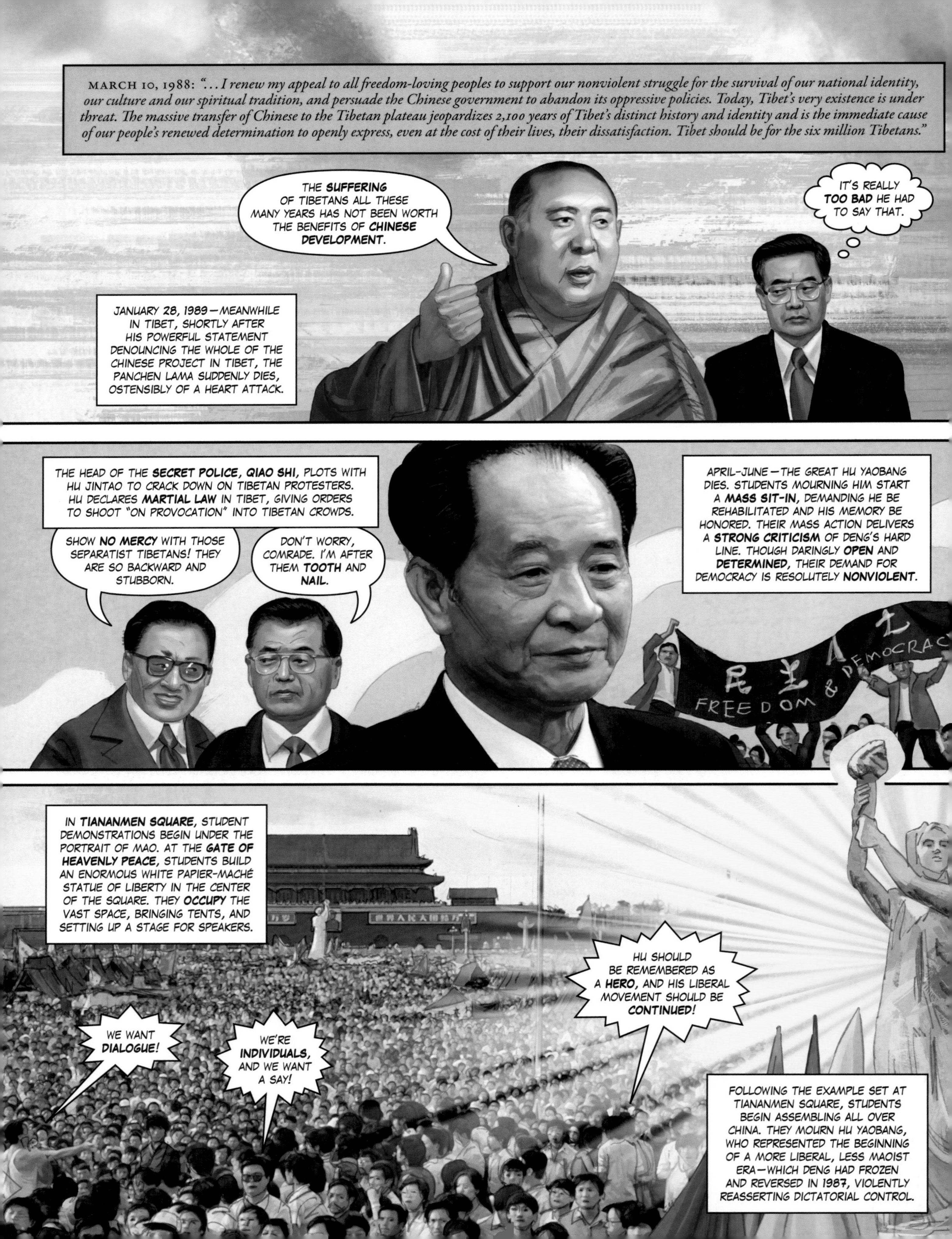

MARCH 10, 1988: "… I renew my appeal to all freedom-loving peoples to support our nonviolent struggle for the survival of our national identity, our culture and our spiritual tradition, and persuade the Chinese government to abandon its oppressive policies. Today, Tibet's very existence is under threat. The massive transfer of Chinese to the Tibetan plateau jeopardizes 2,100 years of Tibet's distinct history and identity and is the immediate cause of our people's renewed determination to openly express, even at the cost of their lives, their dissatisfaction. Tibet should be for the six million Tibetans."
THE SUFFERING OF TIBETANS ALL THESE MANY YEARS HAS NOT BEEN WORTH THE BENEFITS OF CHINESE DEVELOPMENT.
IT'S REALLY TOO BAD HE HAD TO SAY THAT.
JANUARY 28, 1989—MEANWHILE IN TIBET, SHORTLY AFTER HIS POWERFUL STATEMENT DENOUNCING THE WHOLE OF THE CHINESE PROJECT IN TIBET, THE PANCHEN LAMA SUDDENLY DIES, OSTENSIBLY OF A HEART ATTACK.
THE HEAD OF THE SECRET POLICE, QIAO SHI, PLOTS WITH HU JINTAO TO CRACK DOWN ON TIBETAN PROTESTERS. HU DECLARES MARTIAL LAW IN TIBET, GIVING ORDERS TO SHOOT "ON PROVOCATION" INTO TIBETAN CROWDS.
SHOW NO MERCY WITH THOSE SEPARATIST TIBETANS! THEY ARE SO BACKWARD AND STUBBORN.
DON'T WORRY, COMRADE. I'M AFTER THEM TOOTH AND NAIL.
APRIL–JUNE—THE GREAT HU YAOBANG DIES. STUDENTS MOURNING HIM START A MASS SIT-IN, DEMANDING HE BE REHABILITATED AND HIS MEMORY BE HONORED. THEIR MASS ACTION DELIVERS A STRONG CRITICISM OF DENG'S HARD LINE. THOUGH DARINGLY OPEN AND DETERMINED, THEIR DEMAND FOR DEMOCRACY IS RESOLUTELY NONVIOLENT.
FREEDOM &
IN TIANANMEN SQUARE, STUDENT DEMONSTRATIONS BEGIN UNDER THE PORTRAIT OF MAO. AT THE GATE OF HEAVENLY PEACE, STUDENTS BUILD AN ENORMOUS WHITE PAPIER-MACHÉ STATUE OF LIBERTY IN THE CENTER OF THE SQUARE. THEY OCCUPY THE VAST SPACE, BRINGING TENTS, AND SETTING UP A STAGE FOR SPEAKERS.
HU SHOULD BE REMEMBERED AS A HERO, AND HIS LIBERAL MOVEMENT SHOULD BE CONTINUED!
WE WANT DIALOGUE!
WE'RE INDIVIDUALS, AND WE WANT A SAY!
FOLLOWING THE EXAMPLE SET AT TIANANMEN SQUARE, STUDENTS BEGIN ASSEMBLING ALL OVER CHINA. THEY MOURN HU YAOBANG, WHO REPRESENTED THE BEGINNING OF A MORE LIBERAL, LESS MAOIST ERA—WHICH DENG HAD FROZEN AND REVERSED IN 1987, VIOLENTLY REASSERTING DICTATORIAL CONTROL.

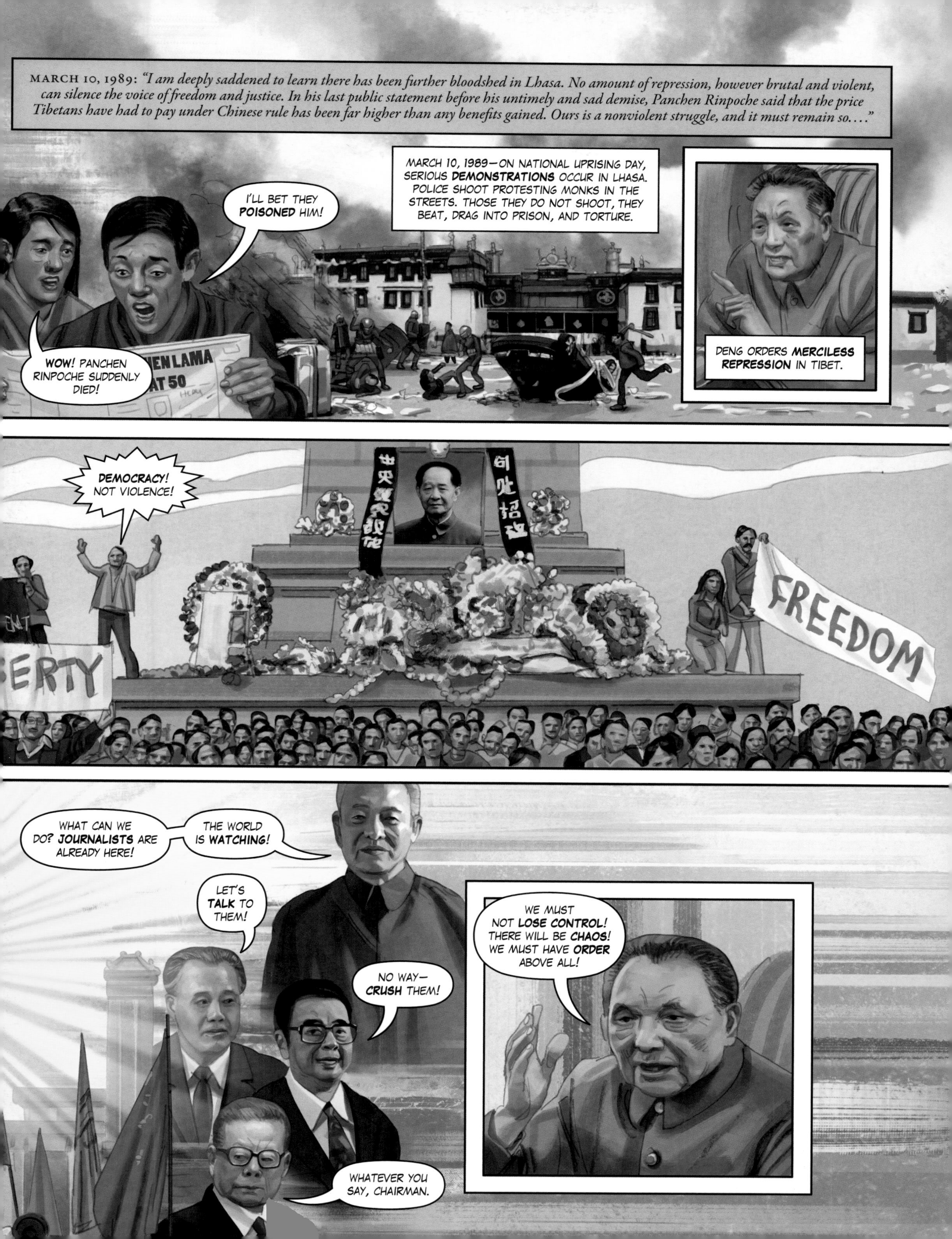
MARCH 10, 1989: "I am deeply saddened to learn there has been further bloodshed in Lhasa. No amount of repression, however brutal and violent, can silence the voice of freedom and justice. In his last public statement before his untimely and sad demise, Panchen Rinpoche said that the price Tibetans have had to pay under Chinese rule has been far higher than any benefits gained. Ours is a nonviolent struggle, and it must remain so. . . ."
WOW! PANCHEN RINPOCHE SUDDENLY DIED!
I'LL BET THEY POISONED HIM!
MARCH 10, 1989—ON NATIONAL UPRISING DAY, SERIOUS DEMONSTRATIONS OCCUR IN LHASA. POLICE SHOOT PROTESTING MONKS IN THE STREETS. THOSE THEY DO NOT SHOOT, THEY BEAT, DRAG INTO PRISON, AND TORTURE.
DENG ORDERS MERCILESS REPRESSION IN TIBET.
DEMOCRACY! NOT VIOLENCE!
FREEDOM
WHAT CAN WE DO? JOURNALISTS ARE ALREADY HERE!
THE WORLD IS WATCHING!
LET'S TALK TO THEM!
NO WAY— CRUSH THEM!
WHATEVER YOU SAY, CHAIRMAN.
WE MUST NOT LOSE CONTROL! THERE WILL BE CHAOS! WE MUST HAVE ORDER ABOVE ALL!

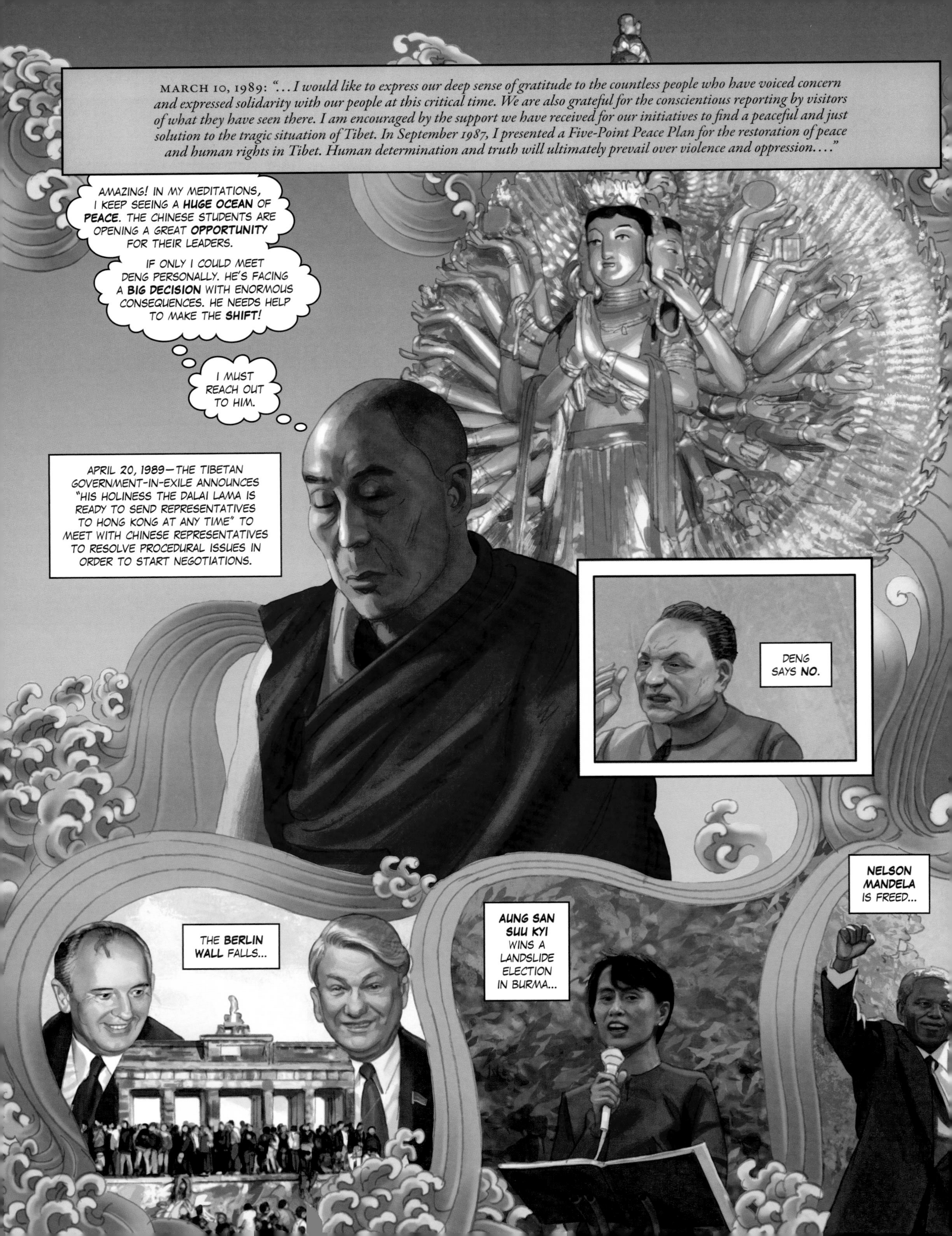
MARCH 10, 1989: "...I would like to express our deep sense of gratitude to the countless people who have voiced concern and expressed solidarity with our people at this critical time. We are also grateful for the conscientious reporting by visitors of what they have seen there. I am encouraged by the support we have received for our initiatives to find a peaceful and just solution to the tragic situation of Tibet. In September 1987, I presented a Five-Point Peace Plan for the restoration of peace and human rights in Tibet. Human determination and truth will ultimately prevail over violence and oppression...."
AMAZING! IN MY MEDITATIONS, I KEEP SEEING A **HUGE OCEAN** OF **PEACE**. THE CHINESE STUDENTS ARE OPENING A GREAT **OPPORTUNITY** FOR THEIR LEADERS.
IF ONLY I COULD MEET DENG PERSONALLY. HE'S FACING A **BIG DECISION** WITH ENORMOUS CONSEQUENCES. HE NEEDS HELP TO MAKE THE **SHIFT!**
I MUST REACH OUT TO HIM.
APRIL 20, 1989—THE TIBETAN GOVERNMENT-IN-EXILE ANNOUNCES "HIS HOLINESS THE DALAI LAMA IS READY TO SEND REPRESENTATIVES TO HONG KONG AT ANY TIME" TO MEET WITH CHINESE REPRESENTATIVES TO RESOLVE PROCEDURAL ISSUES IN ORDER TO START NEGOTIATIONS.
DENG SAYS **NO.**
THE **BERLIN WALL** FALLS...
AUNG SAN SUU KYI WINS A LANDSLIDE ELECTION IN BURMA...
NELSON MANDELA IS FREED...

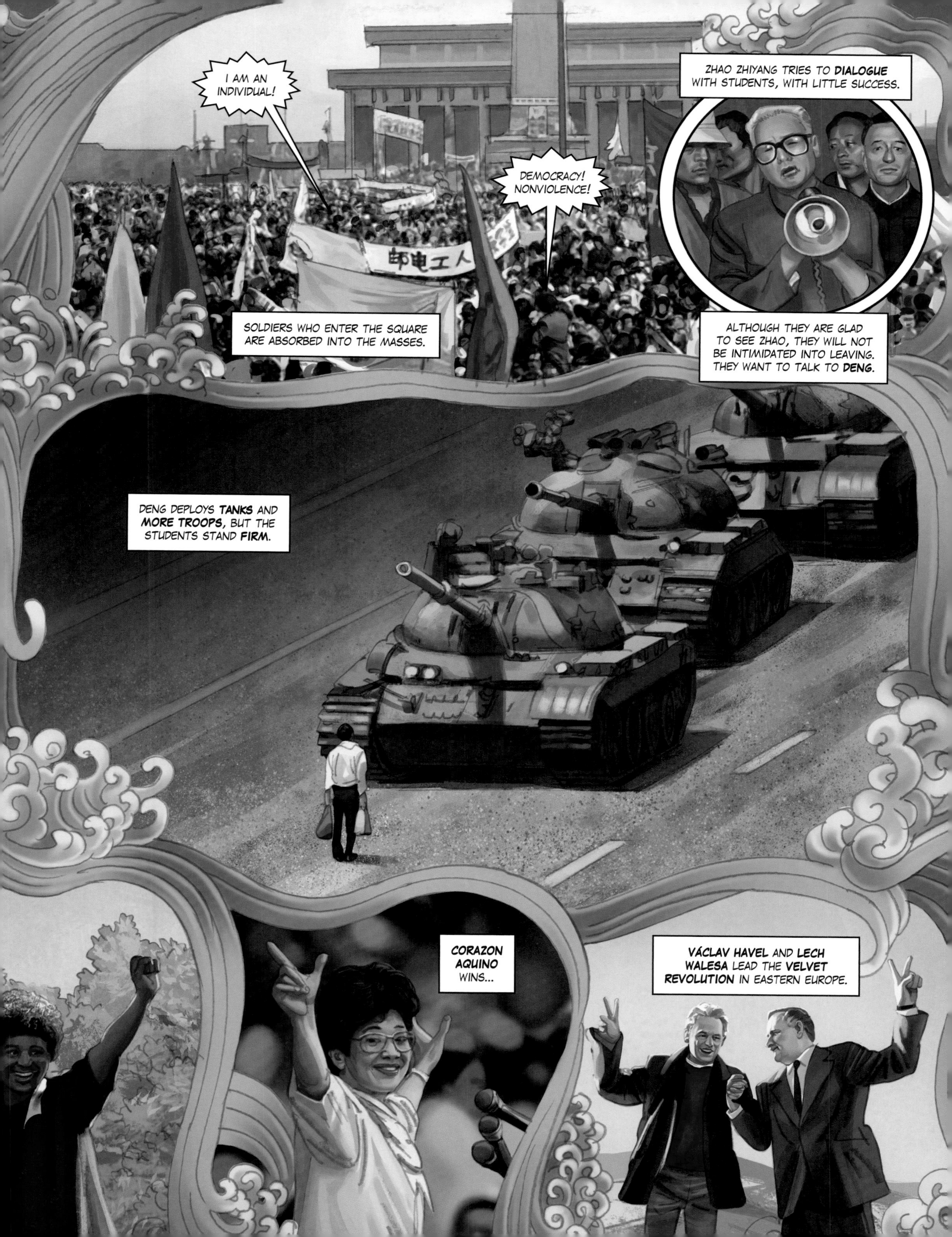
I AM AN INDIVIDUAL!
DEMOCRACY! NONVIOLENCE!
邮电工人
SOLDIERS WHO ENTER THE SQUARE ARE ABSORBED INTO THE MASSES.
ZHAO ZHIYANG TRIES TO **DIALOGUE** WITH STUDENTS, WITH LITTLE SUCCESS.
ALTHOUGH THEY ARE GLAD TO SEE ZHAO, THEY WILL NOT BE INTIMIDATED INTO LEAVING. THEY WANT TO TALK TO **DENG**.
DENG DEPLOYS **TANKS** AND **MORE TROOPS**, BUT THE STUDENTS STAND **FIRM**.
CORAZON AQUINO WINS...
VÁCLAV HAVEL AND **LECH WALESA** LEAD THE **VELVET REVOLUTION** IN EASTERN EUROPE.

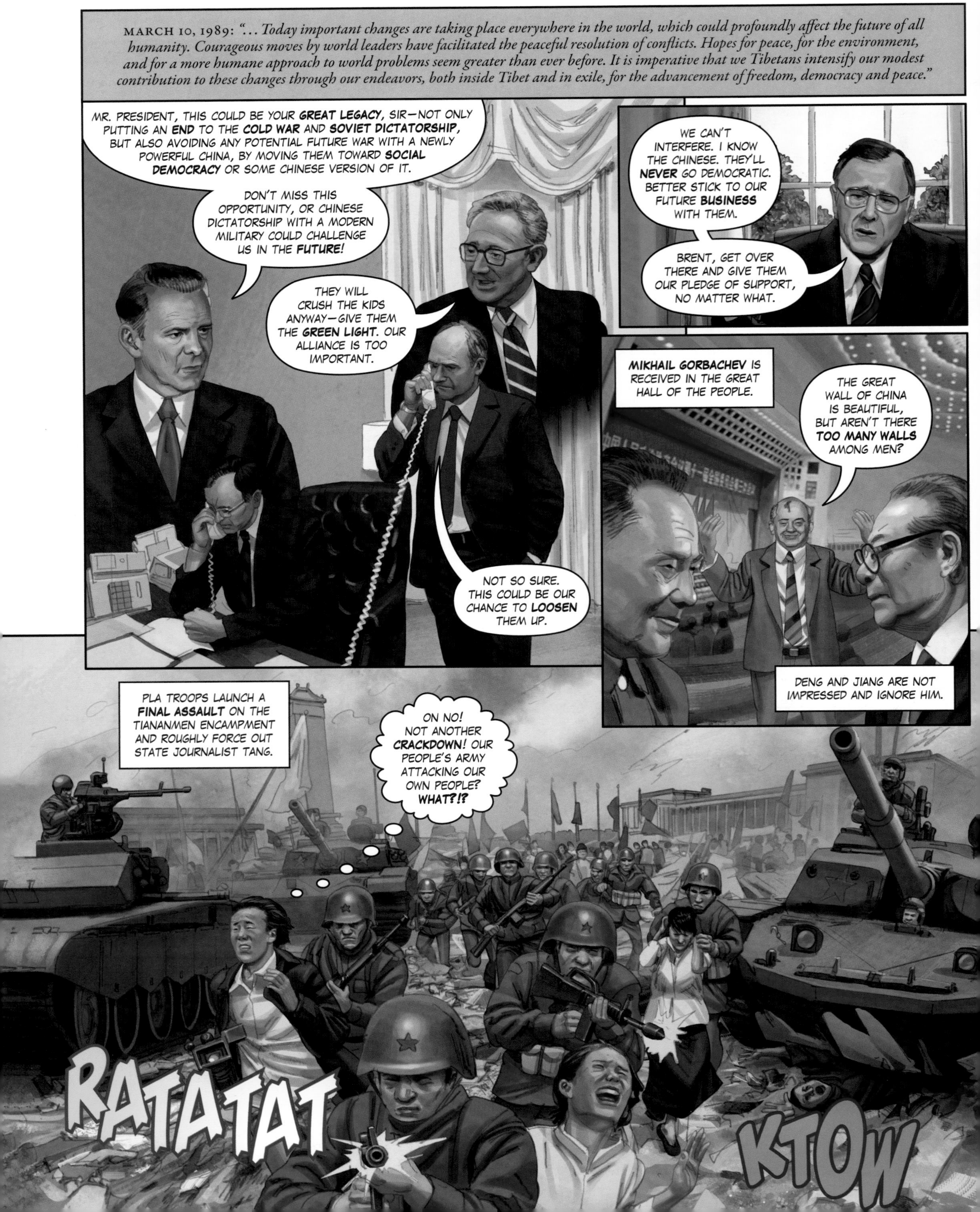
MARCH 10, 1989: "... Today important changes are taking place everywhere in the world, which could profoundly affect the future of all humanity. Courageous moves by world leaders have facilitated the peaceful resolution of conflicts. Hopes for peace, for the environment, and for a more humane approach to world problems seem greater than ever before. It is imperative that we Tibetans intensify our modest contribution to these changes through our endeavors, both inside Tibet and in exile, for the advancement of freedom, democracy and peace."
MR. PRESIDENT, THIS COULD BE YOUR GREAT LEGACY, SIR—NOT ONLY PUTTING AN END TO THE COLD WAR AND SOVIET DICTATORSHIP, BUT ALSO AVOIDING ANY POTENTIAL FUTURE WAR WITH A NEWLY POWERFUL CHINA, BY MOVING THEM TOWARD SOCIAL DEMOCRACY OR SOME CHINESE VERSION OF IT.
DON'T MISS THIS OPPORTUNITY, OR CHINESE DICTATORSHIP WITH A MODERN MILITARY COULD CHALLENGE US IN THE FUTURE!
THEY WILL CRUSH THE KIDS ANYWAY—GIVE THEM THE GREEN LIGHT. OUR ALLIANCE IS TOO IMPORTANT.
NOT SO SURE. THIS COULD BE OUR CHANCE TO LOOSEN THEM UP.
WE CAN'T INTERFERE. I KNOW THE CHINESE. THEY'LL NEVER GO DEMOCRATIC. BETTER STICK TO OUR FUTURE BUSINESS WITH THEM.
BRENT, GET OVER THERE AND GIVE THEM OUR PLEDGE OF SUPPORT, NO MATTER WHAT.
MIKHAIL GORBACHEV IS RECEIVED IN THE GREAT HALL OF THE PEOPLE.
THE GREAT WALL OF CHINA IS BEAUTIFUL, BUT AREN'T THERE TOO MANY WALLS AMONG MEN?
DENG AND JIANG ARE NOT IMPRESSED AND IGNORE HIM.
PLA TROOPS LAUNCH A FINAL ASSAULT ON THE TIANANMEN ENCAMPMENT AND ROUGHLY FORCE OUT STATE JOURNALIST TANG.
ON NO! NOT ANOTHER CRACKDOWN! OUR PEOPLE'S ARMY ATTACKING OUR OWN PEOPLE? WHAT?!?
RATATAT
KTOW

DEC. 11, 1989, Nobel Peace Prize Lecture: *"I decided to share with you some of my thoughts concerning the common problems all of us face as members of the human family. Because we all share this small planet Earth, we have to learn to live in harmony and peace with each other and with nature. That is not just a dream but a necessity. We are dependent on each other in so many ways that we can no longer live in isolated communities, and we must share the good fortune that we enjoy. I speak to you as just another human being—as a simple monk."*

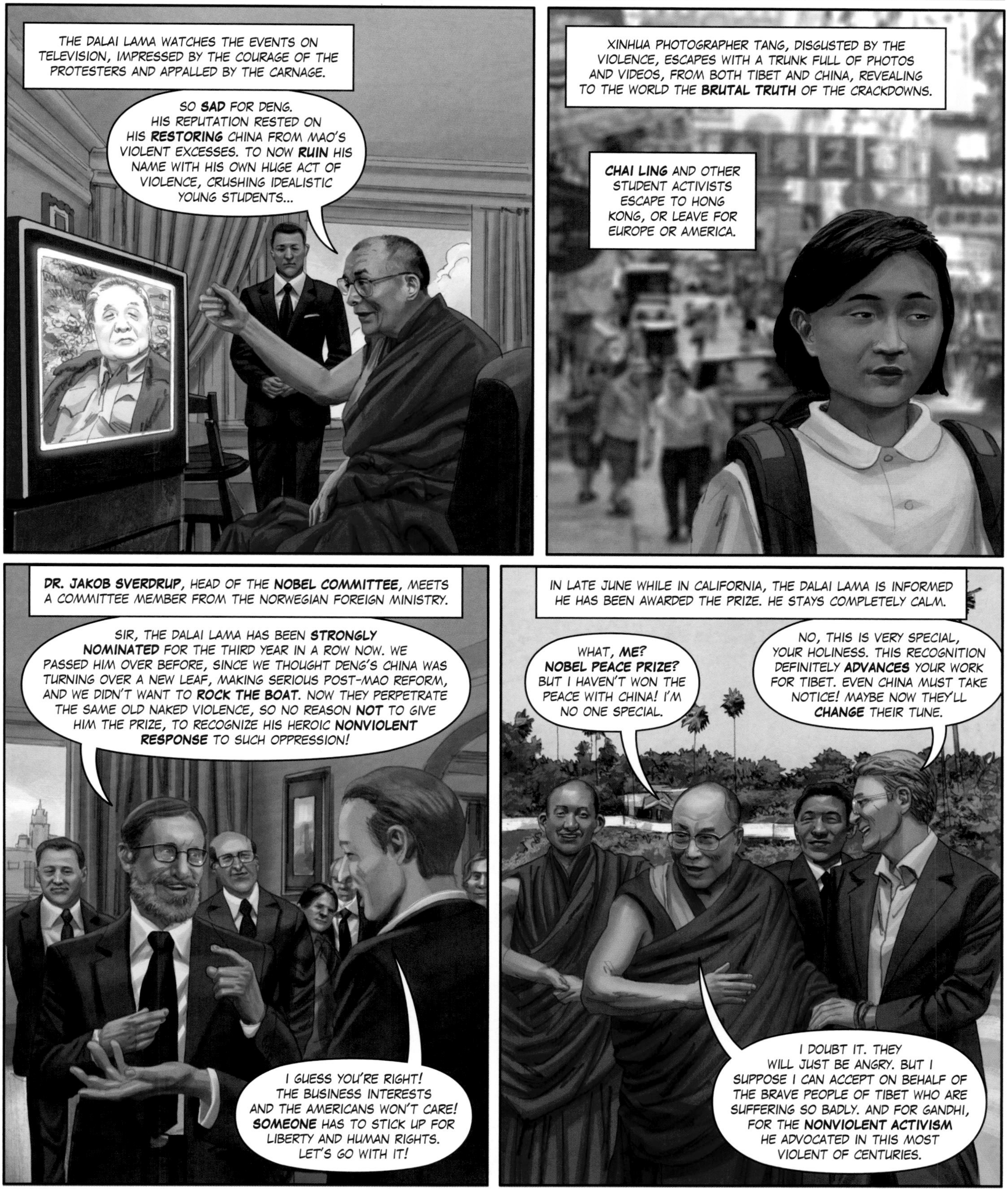
THE DALAI LAMA WATCHES THE EVENTS ON TELEVISION, IMPRESSED BY THE COURAGE OF THE PROTESTERS AND APPALLED BY THE CARNAGE.
SO SAD FOR DENG. HIS REPUTATION RESTED ON HIS RESTORING CHINA FROM MAO'S VIOLENT EXCESSES. TO NOW RUIN HIS NAME WITH HIS OWN HUGE ACT OF VIOLENCE, CRUSHING IDEALISTIC YOUNG STUDENTS...
XINHUA PHOTOGRAPHER TANG, DISGUSTED BY THE VIOLENCE, ESCAPES WITH A TRUNK FULL OF PHOTOS AND VIDEOS, FROM BOTH TIBET AND CHINA, REVEALING TO THE WORLD THE BRUTAL TRUTH OF THE CRACKDOWNS.
CHAI LING AND OTHER STUDENT ACTIVISTS ESCAPE TO HONG KONG, OR LEAVE FOR EUROPE OR AMERICA.
DR. JAKOB SVERDRUP, HEAD OF THE NOBEL COMMITTEE, MEETS A COMMITTEE MEMBER FROM THE NORWEGIAN FOREIGN MINISTRY.
SIR, THE DALAI LAMA HAS BEEN STRONGLY NOMINATED FOR THE THIRD YEAR IN A ROW NOW. WE PASSED HIM OVER BEFORE, SINCE WE THOUGHT DENG'S CHINA WAS TURNING OVER A NEW LEAF, MAKING SERIOUS POST-MAO REFORM, AND WE DIDN'T WANT TO ROCK THE BOAT. NOW THEY PERPETRATE THE SAME OLD NAKED VIOLENCE, SO NO REASON NOT TO GIVE HIM THE PRIZE, TO RECOGNIZE HIS HEROIC NONVIOLENT RESPONSE TO SUCH OPPRESSION!
I GUESS YOU'RE RIGHT! THE BUSINESS INTERESTS AND THE AMERICANS WON'T CARE! SOMEONE HAS TO STICK UP FOR LIBERTY AND HUMAN RIGHTS. LET'S GO WITH IT!
IN LATE JUNE WHILE IN CALIFORNIA, THE DALAI LAMA IS INFORMED HE HAS BEEN AWARDED THE PRIZE. HE STAYS COMPLETELY CALM.
WHAT, ME? NOBEL PEACE PRIZE? BUT I HAVEN'T WON THE PEACE WITH CHINA! I'M NO ONE SPECIAL.
NO, THIS IS VERY SPECIAL, YOUR HOLINESS. THIS RECOGNITION DEFINITELY ADVANCES YOUR WORK FOR TIBET. EVEN CHINA MUST TAKE NOTICE! MAYBE NOW THEY'LL CHANGE THEIR TUNE.
I DOUBT IT. THEY WILL JUST BE ANGRY. BUT I SUPPOSE I CAN ACCEPT ON BEHALF OF THE BRAVE PEOPLE OF TIBET WHO ARE SUFFERING SO BADLY. AND FOR GANDHI, FOR THE NONVIOLENT ACTIVISM HE ADVOCATED IN THIS MOST VIOLENT OF CENTURIES.

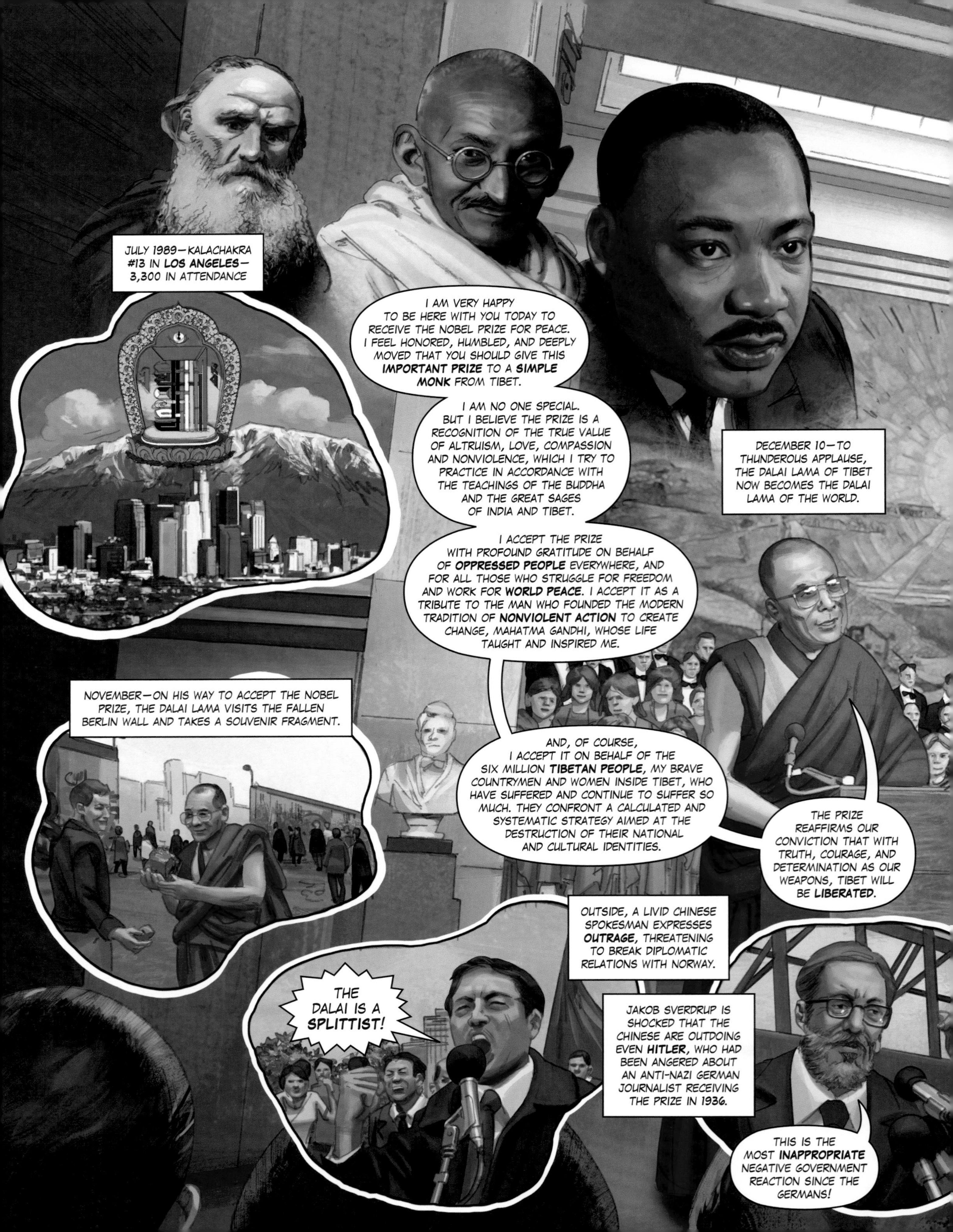

JULY 1989—KALACHAKRA #13 IN LOS ANGELES—3,300 IN ATTENDANCE
I AM VERY HAPPY TO BE HERE WITH YOU TODAY TO RECEIVE THE NOBEL PRIZE FOR PEACE. I FEEL HONORED, HUMBLED, AND DEEPLY MOVED THAT YOU SHOULD GIVE THIS IMPORTANT PRIZE TO A SIMPLE MONK FROM TIBET.
I AM NO ONE SPECIAL. BUT I BELIEVE THE PRIZE IS A RECOGNITION OF THE TRUE VALUE OF ALTRUISM, LOVE, COMPASSION AND NONVIOLENCE, WHICH I TRY TO PRACTICE IN ACCORDANCE WITH THE TEACHINGS OF THE BUDDHA AND THE GREAT SAGES OF INDIA AND TIBET.
DECEMBER 10—TO THUNDEROUS APPLAUSE, THE DALAI LAMA OF TIBET NOW BECOMES THE DALAI LAMA OF THE WORLD.
I ACCEPT THE PRIZE WITH PROFOUND GRATITUDE ON BEHALF OF OPPRESSED PEOPLE EVERYWHERE, AND FOR ALL THOSE WHO STRUGGLE FOR FREEDOM AND WORK FOR WORLD PEACE. I ACCEPT IT AS A TRIBUTE TO THE MAN WHO FOUNDED THE MODERN TRADITION OF NONVIOLENT ACTION TO CREATE CHANGE, MAHATMA GANDHI, WHOSE LIFE TAUGHT AND INSPIRED ME.
NOVEMBER—ON HIS WAY TO ACCEPT THE NOBEL PRIZE, THE DALAI LAMA VISITS THE FALLEN BERLIN WALL AND TAKES A SOUVENIR FRAGMENT.
AND, OF COURSE, I ACCEPT IT ON BEHALF OF THE SIX MILLION TIBETAN PEOPLE, MY BRAVE COUNTRYMEN AND WOMEN INSIDE TIBET, WHO HAVE SUFFERED AND CONTINUE TO SUFFER SO MUCH. THEY CONFRONT A CALCULATED AND SYSTEMATIC STRATEGY AIMED AT THE DESTRUCTION OF THEIR NATIONAL AND CULTURAL IDENTITIES.
THE PRIZE REAFFIRMS OUR CONVICTION THAT WITH TRUTH, COURAGE, AND DETERMINATION AS OUR WEAPONS, TIBET WILL BE LIBERATED.
OUTSIDE, A LIVID CHINESE SPOKESMAN EXPRESSES OUTRAGE, THREATENING TO BREAK DIPLOMATIC RELATIONS WITH NORWAY.
THE DALAI IS A SPLITTIST!
JAKOB SVERDRUP IS SHOCKED THAT THE CHINESE ARE OUTDOING EVEN HITLER, WHO HAD BEEN ANGERED ABOUT AN ANTI-NAZI GERMAN JOURNALIST RECEIVING THE PRIZE IN 1936.
THIS IS THE MOST INAPPROPRIATE NEGATIVE GOVERNMENT REACTION SINCE THE GERMANS!

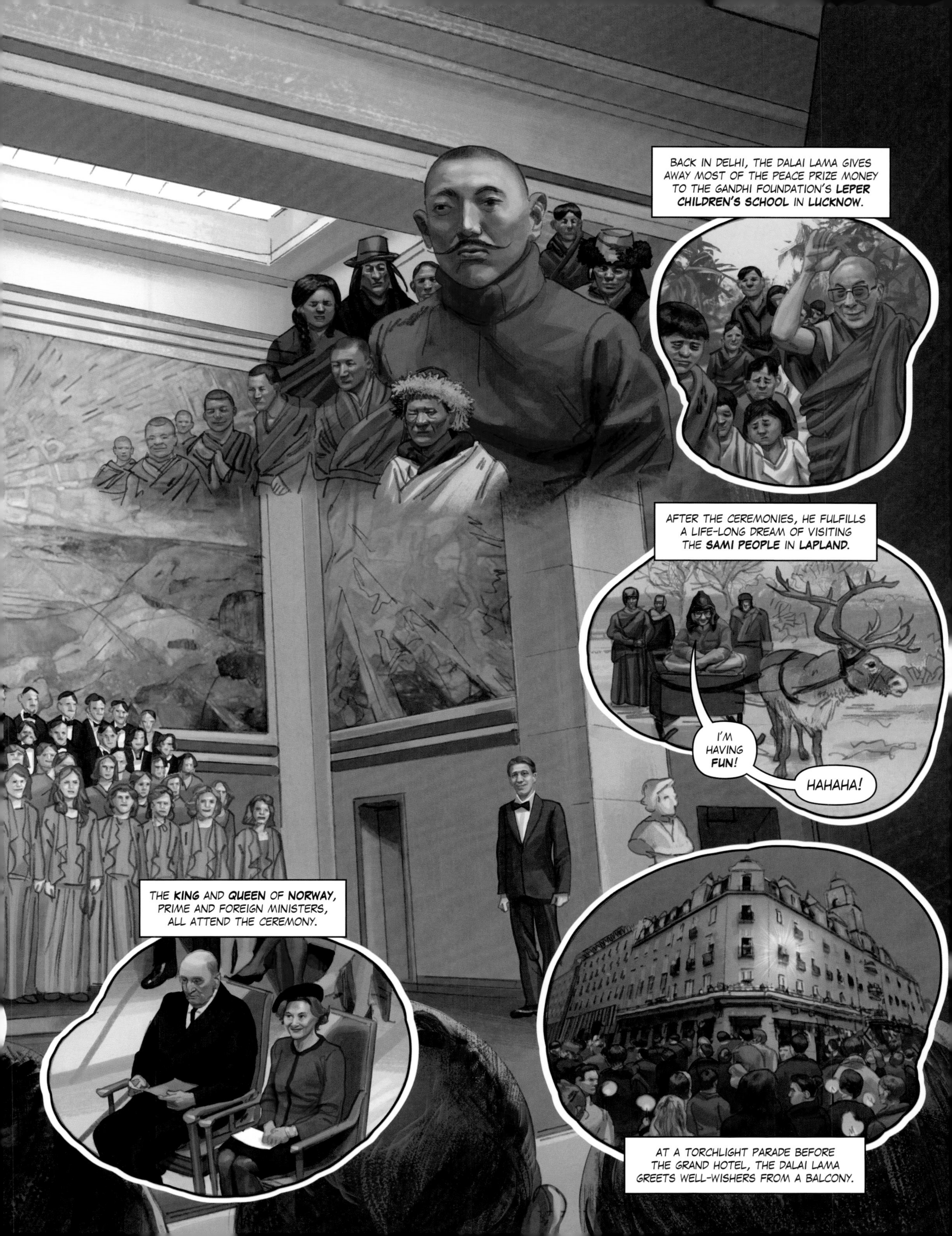
BACK IN DELHI, THE DALAI LAMA GIVES AWAY MOST OF THE PEACE PRIZE MONEY TO THE GANDHI FOUNDATION'S **LEPER CHILDREN'S SCHOOL** IN **LUCKNOW**.
AFTER THE CEREMONIES, HE FULFILLS A LIFE-LONG DREAM OF VISITING THE **SAMI PEOPLE** IN **LAPLAND**.
I'M HAVING **FUN**!
HAHAHA!
THE **KING** AND **QUEEN** OF **NORWAY**, PRIME AND FOREIGN MINISTERS, ALL ATTEND THE CEREMONY.
AT A TORCHLIGHT PARADE BEFORE THE GRAND HOTEL, THE DALAI LAMA GREETS WELL-WISHERS FROM A BALCONY.

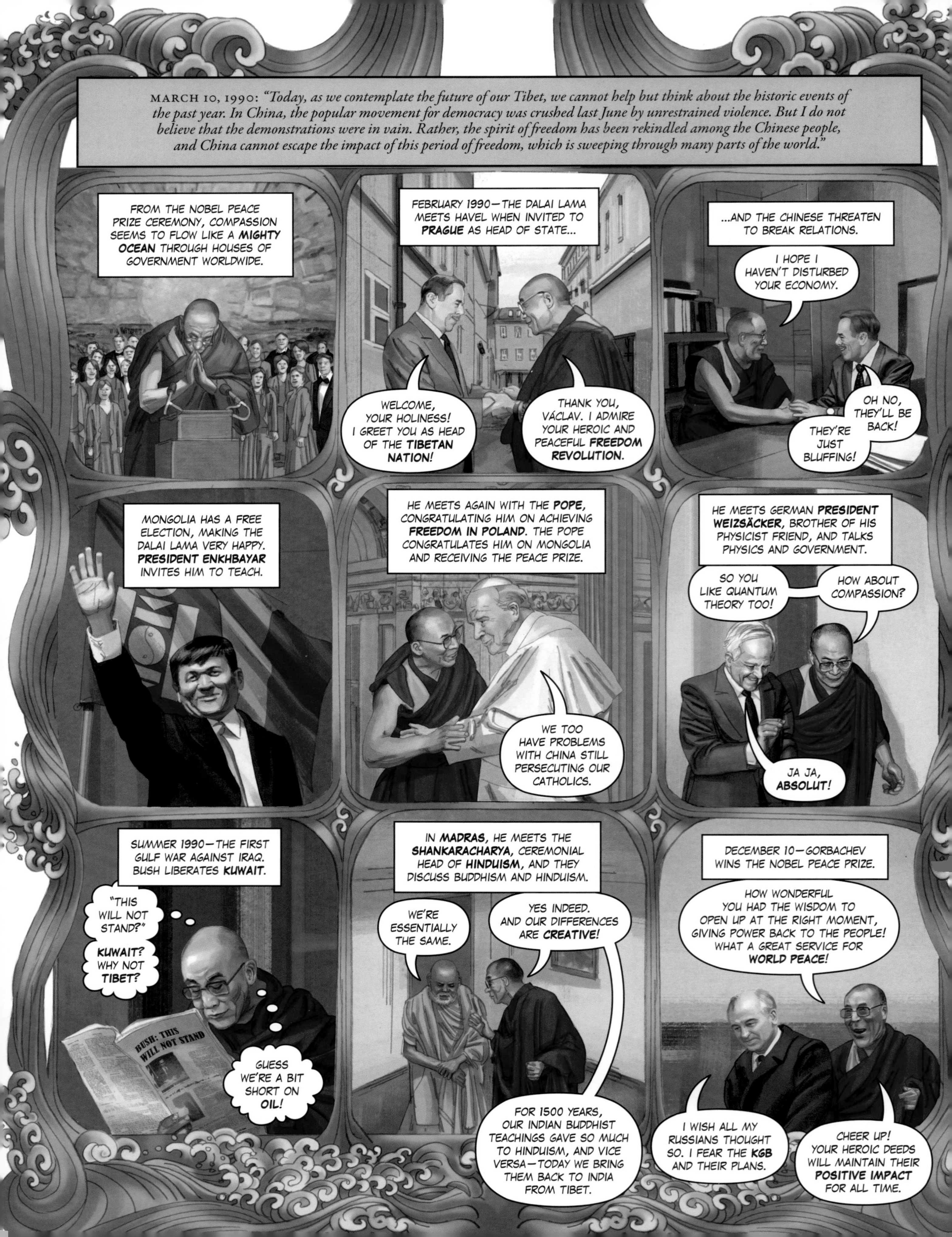
MARCH 10, 1990: "Today, as we contemplate the future of our Tibet, we cannot help but think about the historic events of the past year. In China, the popular movement for democracy was crushed last June by unrestrained violence. But I do not believe that the demonstrations were in vain. Rather, the spirit of freedom has been rekindled among the Chinese people, and China cannot escape the impact of this period of freedom, which is sweeping through many parts of the world."
FROM THE NOBEL PEACE PRIZE CEREMONY, COMPASSION SEEMS TO FLOW LIKE A MIGHTY OCEAN THROUGH HOUSES OF GOVERNMENT WORLDWIDE.
FEBRUARY 1990—THE DALAI LAMA MEETS HAVEL WHEN INVITED TO PRAGUE AS HEAD OF STATE...
WELCOME, YOUR HOLINESS! I GREET YOU AS HEAD OF THE TIBETAN NATION!
THANK YOU, VÁCLAV. I ADMIRE YOUR HEROIC AND PEACEFUL FREEDOM REVOLUTION.
...AND THE CHINESE THREATEN TO BREAK RELATIONS.
I HOPE I HAVEN'T DISTURBED YOUR ECONOMY.
OH NO, THEY'LL BE BACK!
THEY'RE JUST BLUFFING!
MONGOLIA HAS A FREE ELECTION, MAKING THE DALAI LAMA VERY HAPPY. PRESIDENT ENKHBAYAR INVITES HIM TO TEACH.
HE MEETS AGAIN WITH THE POPE, CONGRATULATING HIM ON ACHIEVING FREEDOM IN POLAND. THE POPE CONGRATULATES HIM ON MONGOLIA AND RECEIVING THE PEACE PRIZE.
WE TOO HAVE PROBLEMS WITH CHINA STILL PERSECUTING OUR CATHOLICS.
HE MEETS GERMAN PRESIDENT WEIZSÄCKER, BROTHER OF HIS PHYSICIST FRIEND, AND TALKS PHYSICS AND GOVERNMENT.
SO YOU LIKE QUANTUM THEORY TOO!
HOW ABOUT COMPASSION?
JA JA, ABSOLUT!
SUMMER 1990—THE FIRST GULF WAR AGAINST IRAQ. BUSH LIBERATES KUWAIT.
"THIS WILL NOT STAND?"
KUWAIT? WHY NOT TIBET?
BUSH: THIS WILL NOT STAND
GUESS WE'RE A BIT SHORT ON OIL!
IN MADRAS, HE MEETS THE SHANKARACHARYA, CEREMONIAL HEAD OF HINDUISM, AND THEY DISCUSS BUDDHISM AND HINDUISM.
WE'RE ESSENTIALLY THE SAME.
YES INDEED. AND OUR DIFFERENCES ARE CREATIVE!
FOR 1500 YEARS, OUR INDIAN BUDDHIST TEACHINGS GAVE SO MUCH TO HINDUISM, AND VICE VERSA—TODAY WE BRING THEM BACK TO INDIA FROM TIBET.
DECEMBER 10—GORBACHEV WINS THE NOBEL PEACE PRIZE.
HOW WONDERFUL YOU HAD THE WISDOM TO OPEN UP AT THE RIGHT MOMENT, GIVING POWER BACK TO THE PEOPLE! WHAT A GREAT SERVICE FOR WORLD PEACE!
I WISH ALL MY RUSSIANS THOUGHT SO. I FEAR THE KGB AND THEIR PLANS.
CHEER UP! YOUR HEROIC DEEDS WILL MAINTAIN THEIR POSITIVE IMPACT FOR ALL TIME.

MARCH 10, 1991: *"For stability and peace to return to Asia as a whole, a new China should join a new democratic community of states, created for the mutual benefit of all its members. Such an Asian community could include Tibet, East Turkestan, and Inner Mongolia, who seek freedom from Chinese colonialist rule, and could also include other nations interested in building an Asian community. It is therefore a matter of great pride for me that last month the Tibetan exiles went to the polls for the eleventh time to elect a new assembly."*

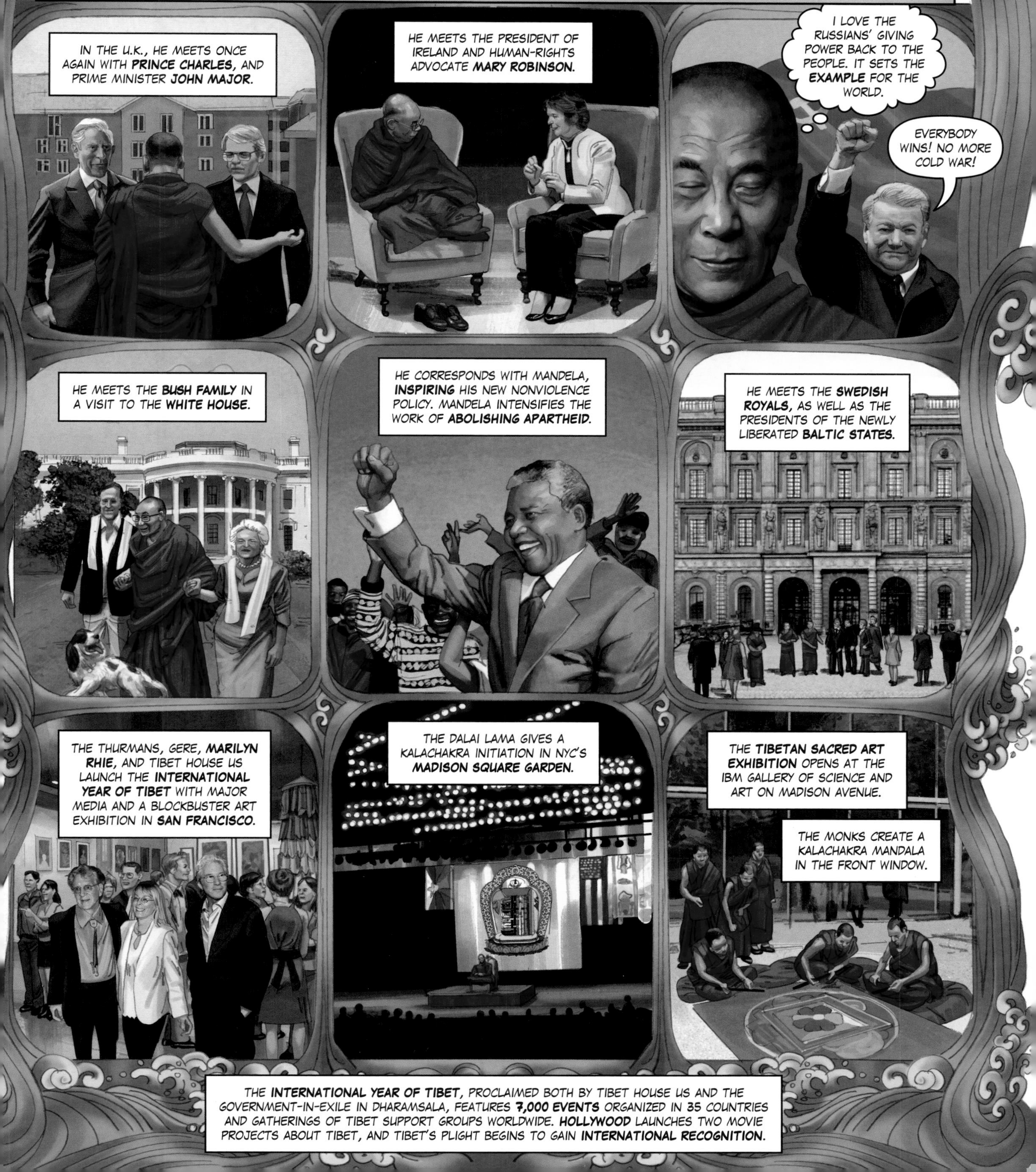
IN THE U.K., HE MEETS ONCE AGAIN WITH **PRINCE CHARLES,** AND PRIME MINISTER **JOHN MAJOR.**
HE MEETS THE PRESIDENT OF IRELAND AND HUMAN-RIGHTS ADVOCATE **MARY ROBINSON.**
I LOVE THE RUSSIANS' GIVING POWER BACK TO THE PEOPLE. IT SETS THE **EXAMPLE** FOR THE WORLD.
EVERYBODY WINS! NO MORE COLD WAR!
HE MEETS THE **BUSH FAMILY** IN A VISIT TO THE **WHITE HOUSE.**
HE CORRESPONDS WITH MANDELA, **INSPIRING** HIS NEW NONVIOLENCE POLICY. MANDELA INTENSIFIES THE WORK OF **ABOLISHING APARTHEID.**
HE MEETS THE **SWEDISH ROYALS,** AS WELL AS THE PRESIDENTS OF THE NEWLY LIBERATED **BALTIC STATES.**
THE THURMANS, GERE, **MARILYN RHIE,** AND TIBET HOUSE US LAUNCH THE **INTERNATIONAL YEAR OF TIBET** WITH MAJOR MEDIA AND A BLOCKBUSTER ART EXHIBITION IN **SAN FRANCISCO.**
THE DALAI LAMA GIVES A KALACHAKRA INITIATION IN NYC'S **MADISON SQUARE GARDEN.**
THE **TIBETAN SACRED ART EXHIBITION** OPENS AT THE IBM GALLERY OF SCIENCE AND ART ON MADISON AVENUE.
THE MONKS CREATE A KALACHAKRA MANDALA IN THE FRONT WINDOW.
THE **INTERNATIONAL YEAR OF TIBET**, PROCLAIMED BOTH BY TIBET HOUSE US AND THE GOVERNMENT-IN-EXILE IN DHARAMSALA, FEATURES **7,000 EVENTS** ORGANIZED IN 35 COUNTRIES AND GATHERINGS OF TIBET SUPPORT GROUPS WORLDWIDE. **HOLLYWOOD** LAUNCHES TWO MOVIE PROJECTS ABOUT TIBET, AND TIBET'S PLIGHT BEGINS TO GAIN **INTERNATIONAL RECOGNITION.**

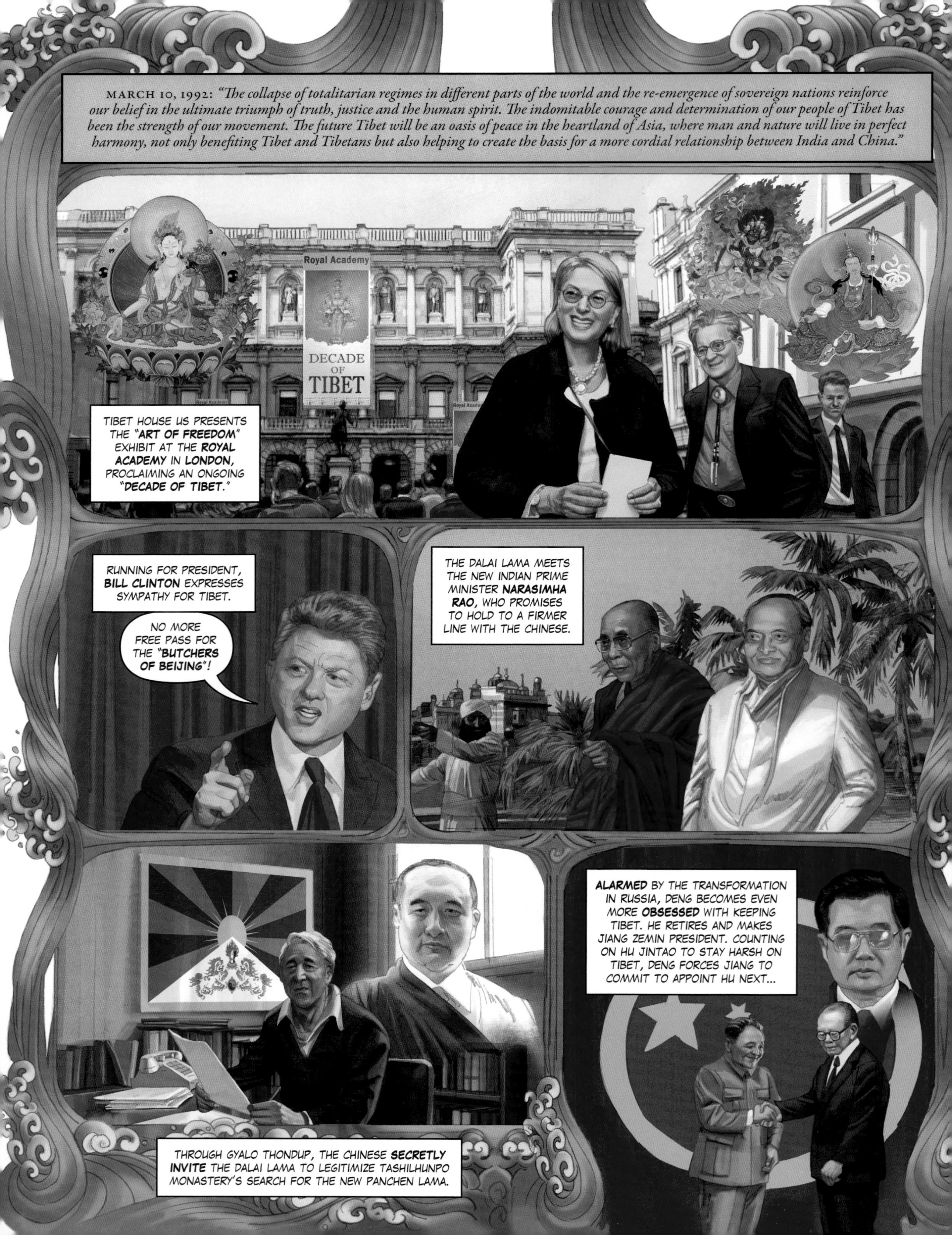
MARCH 10, 1992: "The collapse of totalitarian regimes in different parts of the world and the re-emergence of sovereign nations reinforce our belief in the ultimate triumph of truth, justice and the human spirit. The indomitable courage and determination of our people of Tibet has been the strength of our movement. The future Tibet will be an oasis of peace in the heartland of Asia, where man and nature will live in perfect harmony, not only benefiting Tibet and Tibetans but also helping to create the basis for a more cordial relationship between India and China."
Royal Academy
DECADE OF TIBET
TIBET HOUSE US PRESENTS THE "ART OF FREEDOM" EXHIBIT AT THE ROYAL ACADEMY IN LONDON, PROCLAIMING AN ONGOING "DECADE OF TIBET."
RUNNING FOR PRESIDENT, BILL CLINTON EXPRESSES SYMPATHY FOR TIBET.
NO MORE FREE PASS FOR THE "BUTCHERS OF BEIJING"!
THE DALAI LAMA MEETS THE NEW INDIAN PRIME MINISTER NARASIMHA RAO, WHO PROMISES TO HOLD TO A FIRMER LINE WITH THE CHINESE.
THROUGH GYALO THONDUP, THE CHINESE SECRETLY INVITE THE DALAI LAMA TO LEGITIMIZE TASHILHUNPO MONASTERY'S SEARCH FOR THE NEW PANCHEN LAMA.
ALARMED BY THE TRANSFORMATION IN RUSSIA, DENG BECOMES EVEN MORE OBSESSED WITH KEEPING TIBET. HE RETIRES AND MAKES JIANG ZEMIN PRESIDENT. COUNTING ON HU JINTAO TO STAY HARSH ON TIBET, DENG FORCES JIANG TO COMMIT TO APPOINT HU NEXT...

MARCH 10, 1993: *"Millions who live under the repressive yoke of communism and other forms of dictatorship are now free, and democratic aspirations are on the rise on all the continents. The Tibetan people continue to resist subjugation and colonization with courage and determination. No amount of repression and propaganda has lessened their yearning for a life of peace and dignity. I am more optimistic than ever before that freedom and peace for the Tibetan people are now within our reach."*

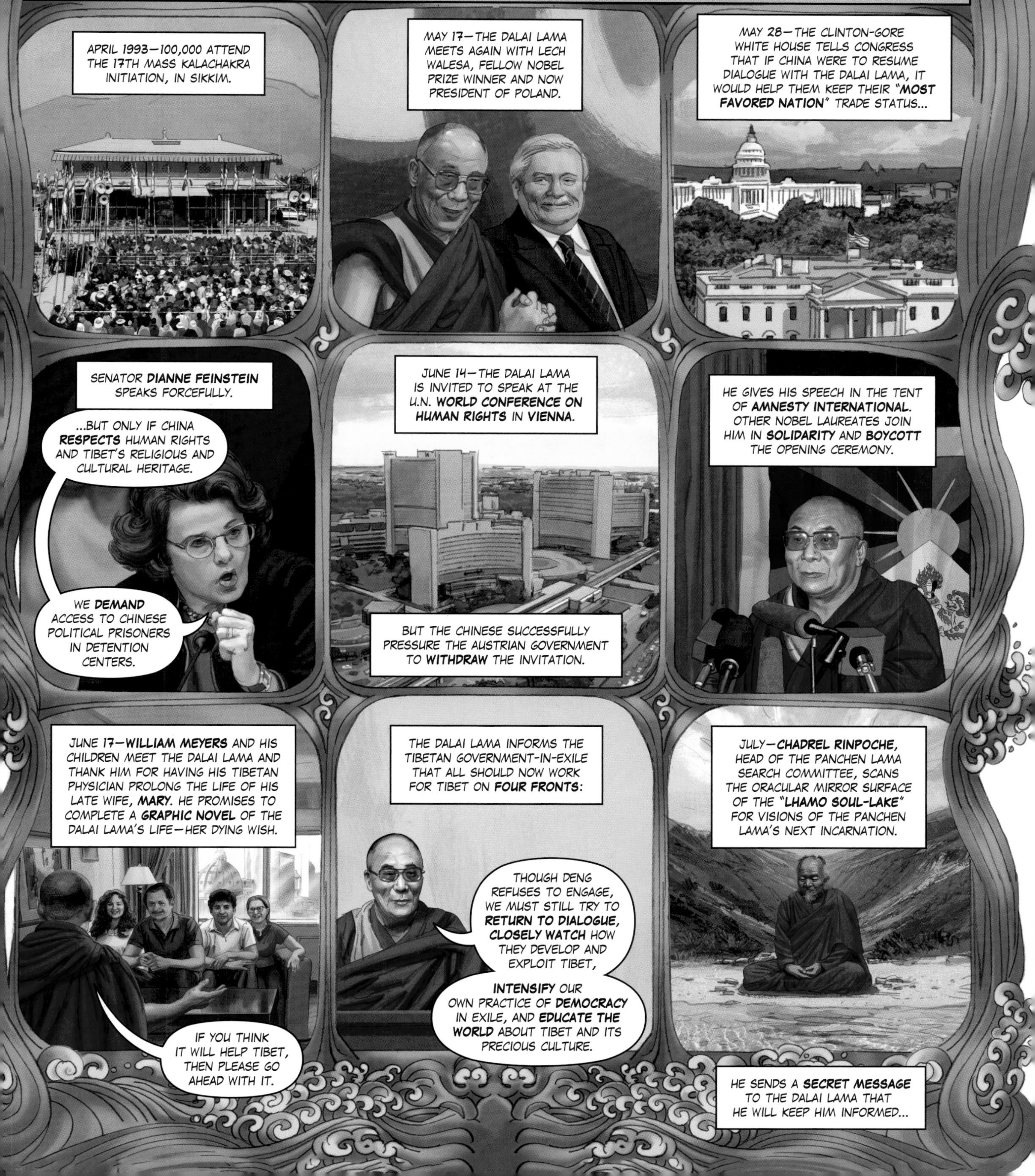

APRIL 1993—100,000 ATTEND THE 17TH MASS KALACHAKRA INITIATION, IN SIKKIM.
MAY 17—THE DALAI LAMA MEETS AGAIN WITH LECH WALESA, FELLOW NOBEL PRIZE WINNER AND NOW PRESIDENT OF POLAND.
MAY 28—THE CLINTON-GORE WHITE HOUSE TELLS CONGRESS THAT IF CHINA WERE TO RESUME DIALOGUE WITH THE DALAI LAMA, IT WOULD HELP THEM KEEP THEIR "MOST FAVORED NATION" TRADE STATUS...
SENATOR DIANNE FEINSTEIN SPEAKS FORCEFULLY.
...BUT ONLY IF CHINA RESPECTS HUMAN RIGHTS AND TIBET'S RELIGIOUS AND CULTURAL HERITAGE.
WE DEMAND ACCESS TO CHINESE POLITICAL PRISONERS IN DETENTION CENTERS.
JUNE 14—THE DALAI LAMA IS INVITED TO SPEAK AT THE U.N. WORLD CONFERENCE ON HUMAN RIGHTS IN VIENNA.
BUT THE CHINESE SUCCESSFULLY PRESSURE THE AUSTRIAN GOVERNMENT TO WITHDRAW THE INVITATION.
HE GIVES HIS SPEECH IN THE TENT OF AMNESTY INTERNATIONAL. OTHER NOBEL LAUREATES JOIN HIM IN SOLIDARITY AND BOYCOTT THE OPENING CEREMONY.
JUNE 17—WILLIAM MEYERS AND HIS CHILDREN MEET THE DALAI LAMA AND THANK HIM FOR HAVING HIS TIBETAN PHYSICIAN PROLONG THE LIFE OF HIS LATE WIFE, MARY. HE PROMISES TO COMPLETE A GRAPHIC NOVEL OF THE DALAI LAMA'S LIFE—HER DYING WISH.
IF YOU THINK IT WILL HELP TIBET, THEN PLEASE GO AHEAD WITH IT.
THE DALAI LAMA INFORMS THE TIBETAN GOVERNMENT-IN-EXILE THAT ALL SHOULD NOW WORK FOR TIBET ON FOUR FRONTS:
THOUGH DENG REFUSES TO ENGAGE, WE MUST STILL TRY TO RETURN TO DIALOGUE, CLOSELY WATCH HOW THEY DEVELOP AND EXPLOIT TIBET,
INTENSIFY OUR OWN PRACTICE OF DEMOCRACY IN EXILE, AND EDUCATE THE WORLD ABOUT TIBET AND ITS PRECIOUS CULTURE.
JULY—CHADREL RINPOCHE, HEAD OF THE PANCHEN LAMA SEARCH COMMITTEE, SCANS THE ORACULAR MIRROR SURFACE OF THE "LHAMO SOUL-LAKE" FOR VISIONS OF THE PANCHEN LAMA'S NEXT INCARNATION.
HE SENDS A SECRET MESSAGE TO THE DALAI LAMA THAT HE WILL KEEP HIM INFORMED...

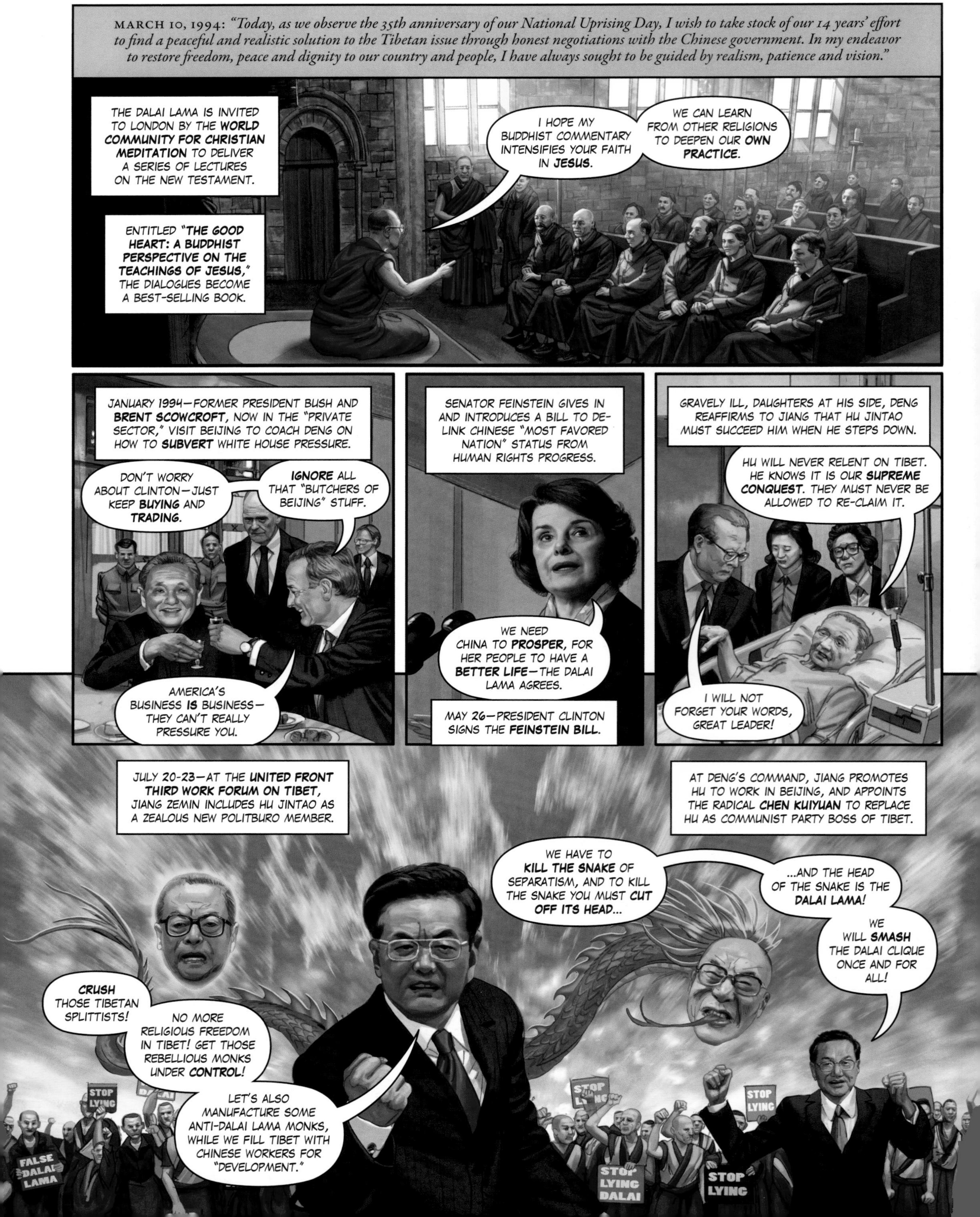
MARCH 10, 1994: "Today, as we observe the 35th anniversary of our National Uprising Day, I wish to take stock of our 14 years' effort to find a peaceful and realistic solution to the Tibetan issue through honest negotiations with the Chinese government. In my endeavor to restore freedom, peace and dignity to our country and people, I have always sought to be guided by realism, patience and vision."
THE DALAI LAMA IS INVITED TO LONDON BY THE **WORLD COMMUNITY FOR CHRISTIAN MEDITATION** TO DELIVER A SERIES OF LECTURES ON THE NEW TESTAMENT.
ENTITLED "**THE GOOD HEART: A BUDDHIST PERSPECTIVE ON THE TEACHINGS OF JESUS,**" THE DIALOGUES BECOME A BEST-SELLING BOOK.
I HOPE MY BUDDHIST COMMENTARY INTENSIFIES YOUR FAITH IN **JESUS**.
WE CAN LEARN FROM OTHER RELIGIONS TO DEEPEN OUR **OWN PRACTICE**.
JANUARY 1994—FORMER PRESIDENT BUSH AND **BRENT SCOWCROFT**, NOW IN THE "PRIVATE SECTOR," VISIT BEIJING TO COACH DENG ON HOW TO **SUBVERT** WHITE HOUSE PRESSURE.
DON'T WORRY ABOUT CLINTON—JUST KEEP **BUYING** AND **TRADING**.
IGNORE ALL THAT "BUTCHERS OF BEIJING" STUFF.
AMERICA'S BUSINESS **IS** BUSINESS—THEY CAN'T REALLY PRESSURE YOU.
SENATOR FEINSTEIN GIVES IN AND INTRODUCES A BILL TO DE-LINK CHINESE "MOST FAVORED NATION" STATUS FROM HUMAN RIGHTS PROGRESS.
WE NEED CHINA TO **PROSPER**, FOR HER PEOPLE TO HAVE A **BETTER LIFE**—THE DALAI LAMA AGREES.
MAY 26—PRESIDENT CLINTON SIGNS THE **FEINSTEIN BILL**.
GRAVELY ILL, DAUGHTERS AT HIS SIDE, DENG REAFFIRMS TO JIANG THAT HU JINTAO MUST SUCCEED HIM WHEN HE STEPS DOWN.
HU WILL NEVER RELENT ON TIBET. HE KNOWS IT IS OUR **SUPREME CONQUEST**. THEY MUST NEVER BE ALLOWED TO RE-CLAIM IT.
I WILL NOT FORGET YOUR WORDS, GREAT LEADER!
JULY 20-23—AT THE **UNITED FRONT THIRD WORK FORUM ON TIBET**, JIANG ZEMIN INCLUDES HU JINTAO AS A ZEALOUS NEW POLITBURO MEMBER.
AT DENG'S COMMAND, JIANG PROMOTES HU TO WORK IN BEIJING, AND APPOINTS THE RADICAL **CHEN KUIYUAN** TO REPLACE HU AS COMMUNIST PARTY BOSS OF TIBET.
WE HAVE TO **KILL THE SNAKE** OF SEPARATISM, AND TO KILL THE SNAKE YOU MUST **CUT OFF ITS HEAD**...
...AND THE HEAD OF THE SNAKE IS THE **DALAI LAMA!**
WE WILL **SMASH** THE DALAI CLIQUE ONCE AND FOR ALL!
CRUSH THOSE TIBETAN SPLITTISTS!
NO MORE RELIGIOUS FREEDOM IN TIBET! GET THOSE REBELLIOUS MONKS UNDER **CONTROL!**
LET'S ALSO MANUFACTURE SOME ANTI-DALAI LAMA MONKS, WHILE WE FILL TIBET WITH CHINESE WORKERS FOR "DEVELOPMENT."
STOP LYING
FALSE DALAI LAMA
STOP LYING DALAI
STOP LYING
STOP LYING

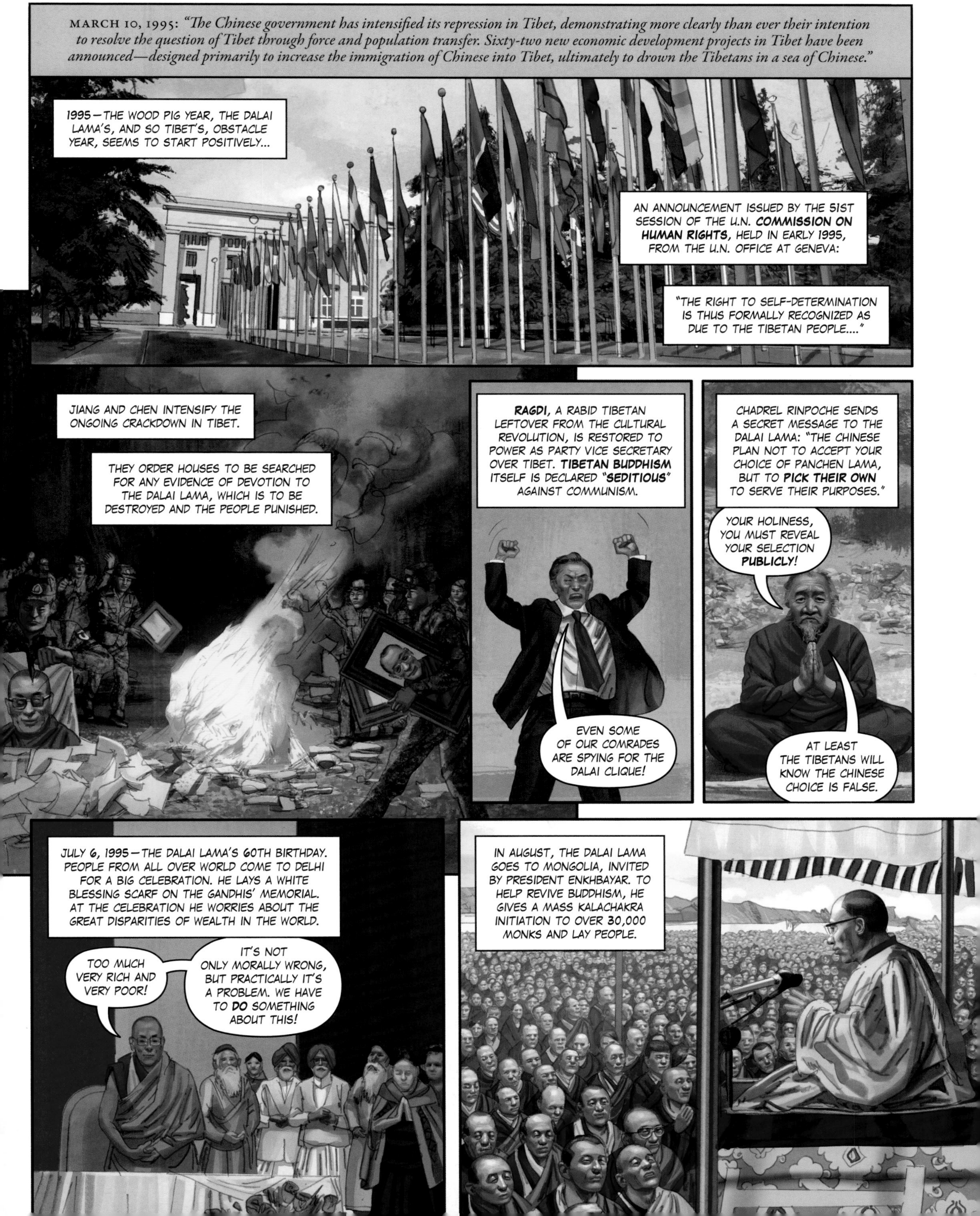
MARCH 10, 1995: "The Chinese government has intensified its repression in Tibet, demonstrating more clearly than ever their intention to resolve the question of Tibet through force and population transfer. Sixty-two new economic development projects in Tibet have been announced—designed primarily to increase the immigration of Chinese into Tibet, ultimately to drown the Tibetans in a sea of Chinese."
1995—THE WOOD PIG YEAR, THE DALAI LAMA'S, AND SO TIBET'S, OBSTACLE YEAR, SEEMS TO START POSITIVELY...
AN ANNOUNCEMENT ISSUED BY THE 51ST SESSION OF THE U.N. COMMISSION ON HUMAN RIGHTS, HELD IN EARLY 1995, FROM THE U.N. OFFICE AT GENEVA:
"THE RIGHT TO SELF-DETERMINATION IS THUS FORMALLY RECOGNIZED AS DUE TO THE TIBETAN PEOPLE...."
JIANG AND CHEN INTENSIFY THE ONGOING CRACKDOWN IN TIBET.
THEY ORDER HOUSES TO BE SEARCHED FOR ANY EVIDENCE OF DEVOTION TO THE DALAI LAMA, WHICH IS TO BE DESTROYED AND THE PEOPLE PUNISHED.
RAGDI, A RABID TIBETAN LEFTOVER FROM THE CULTURAL REVOLUTION, IS RESTORED TO POWER AS PARTY VICE SECRETARY OVER TIBET. TIBETAN BUDDHISM ITSELF IS DECLARED "SEDITIOUS" AGAINST COMMUNISM.
EVEN SOME OF OUR COMRADES ARE SPYING FOR THE DALAI CLIQUE!
CHADREL RINPOCHE SENDS A SECRET MESSAGE TO THE DALAI LAMA: "THE CHINESE PLAN NOT TO ACCEPT YOUR CHOICE OF PANCHEN LAMA, BUT TO PICK THEIR OWN TO SERVE THEIR PURPOSES."
YOUR HOLINESS, YOU MUST REVEAL YOUR SELECTION PUBLICLY!
AT LEAST THE TIBETANS WILL KNOW THE CHINESE CHOICE IS FALSE.
JULY 6, 1995—THE DALAI LAMA'S 60TH BIRTHDAY. PEOPLE FROM ALL OVER WORLD COME TO DELHI FOR A BIG CELEBRATION. HE LAYS A WHITE BLESSING SCARF ON THE GANDHIS' MEMORIAL. AT THE CELEBRATION HE WORRIES ABOUT THE GREAT DISPARITIES OF WEALTH IN THE WORLD.
TOO MUCH VERY RICH AND VERY POOR!
IT'S NOT ONLY MORALLY WRONG, BUT PRACTICALLY IT'S A PROBLEM. WE HAVE TO DO SOMETHING ABOUT THIS!
IN AUGUST, THE DALAI LAMA GOES TO MONGOLIA, INVITED BY PRESIDENT ENKHBAYAR. TO HELP REVIVE BUDDHISM, HE GIVES A MASS KALACHAKRA INITIATION TO OVER 30,000 MONKS AND LAY PEOPLE.

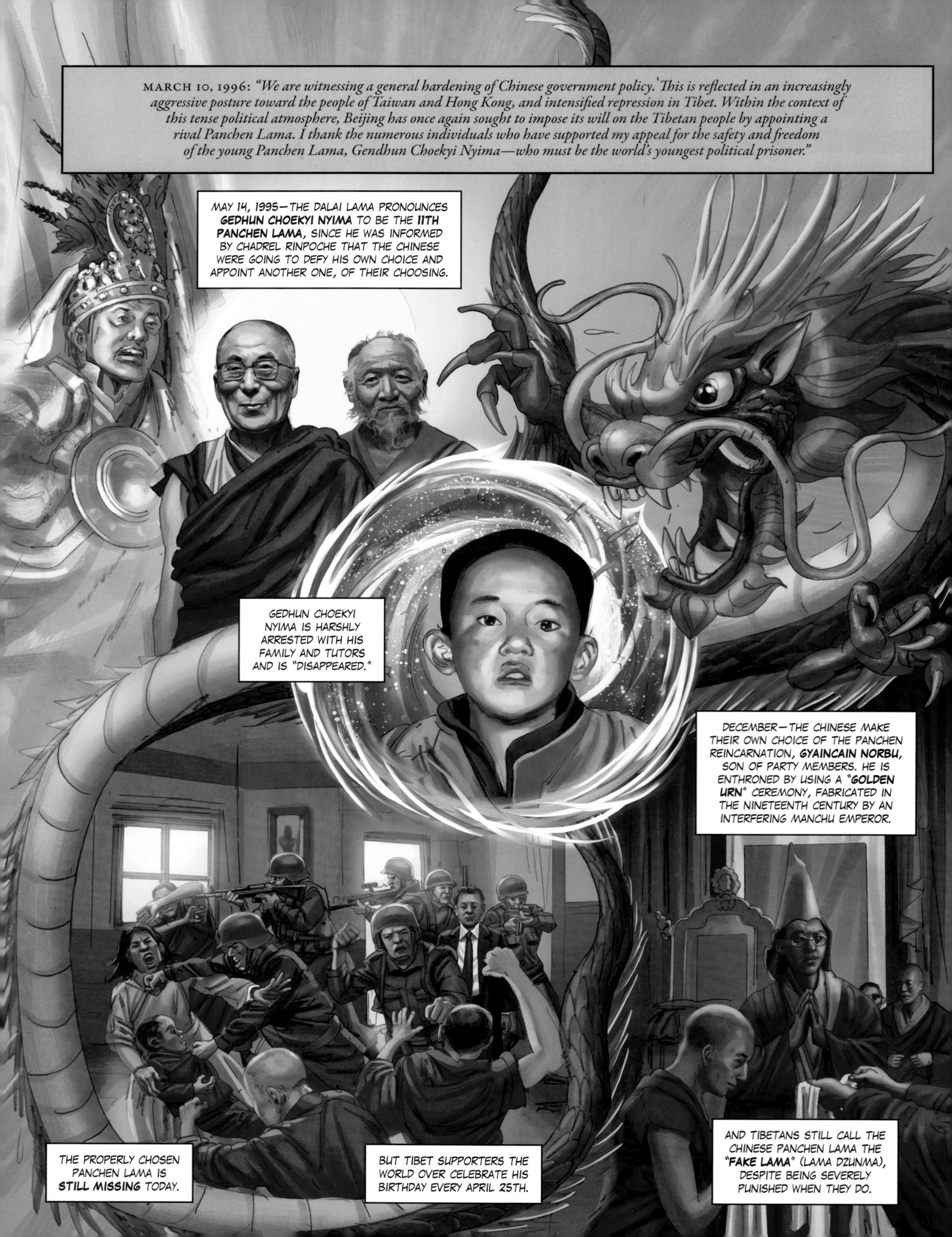
MARCH 10, 1996: "We are witnessing a general hardening of Chinese government policy. This is reflected in an increasingly aggressive posture toward the people of Taiwan and Hong Kong, and intensified repression in Tibet. Within the context of this tense political atmosphere, Beijing has once again sought to impose its will on the Tibetan people by appointing a rival Panchen Lama. I thank the numerous individuals who have supported my appeal for the safety and freedom of the young Panchen Lama, Gendhun Choekyi Nyima—who must be the world's youngest political prisoner."
MAY 14, 1995—THE DALAI LAMA PRONOUNCES GEDHUN CHOEKYI NYIMA TO BE THE 11TH PANCHEN LAMA, SINCE HE WAS INFORMED BY CHADREL RINPOCHE THAT THE CHINESE WERE GOING TO DEFY HIS OWN CHOICE AND APPOINT ANOTHER ONE, OF THEIR CHOOSING.
GEDHUN CHOEKYI NYIMA IS HARSHLY ARRESTED WITH HIS FAMILY AND TUTORS AND IS "DISAPPEARED."
DECEMBER—THE CHINESE MAKE THEIR OWN CHOICE OF THE PANCHEN REINCARNATION, GYAINCAIN NORBU, SON OF PARTY MEMBERS. HE IS ENTHRONED BY USING A "GOLDEN URN" CEREMONY, FABRICATED IN THE NINETEENTH CENTURY BY AN INTERFERING MANCHU EMPEROR.
THE PROPERLY CHOSEN PANCHEN LAMA IS STILL MISSING TODAY.
BUT TIBET SUPPORTERS THE WORLD OVER CELEBRATE HIS BIRTHDAY EVERY APRIL 25TH.
AND TIBETANS STILL CALL THE CHINESE PANCHEN LAMA THE "FAKE LAMA" (LAMA DZUNMA), DESPITE BEING SEVERELY PUNISHED WHEN THEY DO.

PART NINE

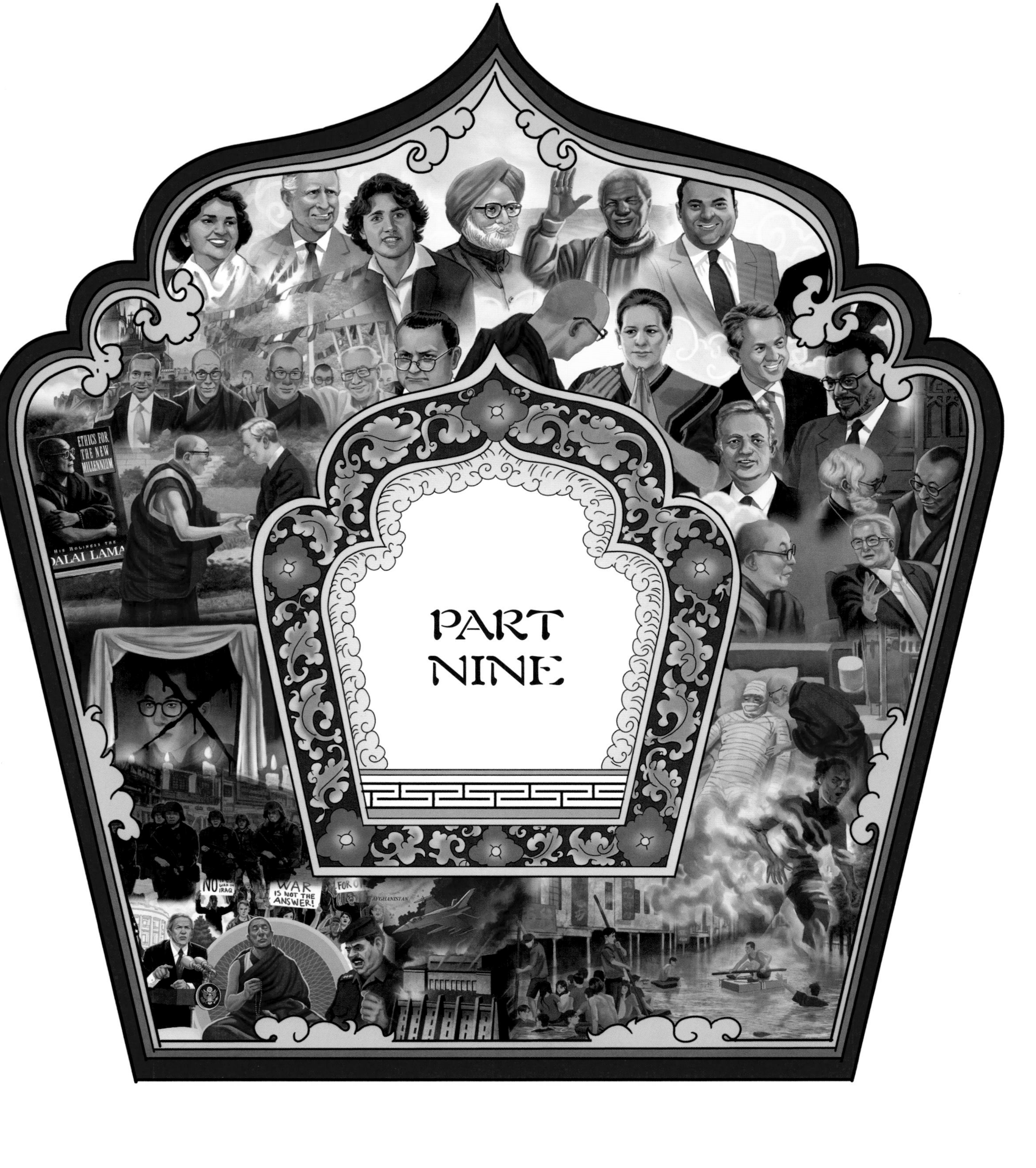
ETHICS FOR THE NEW MILLENNIUM
HIS HOLINESS THE
DALAI LAMA
WAR IS NOT THE ANSWER!
AFGHANISTAN

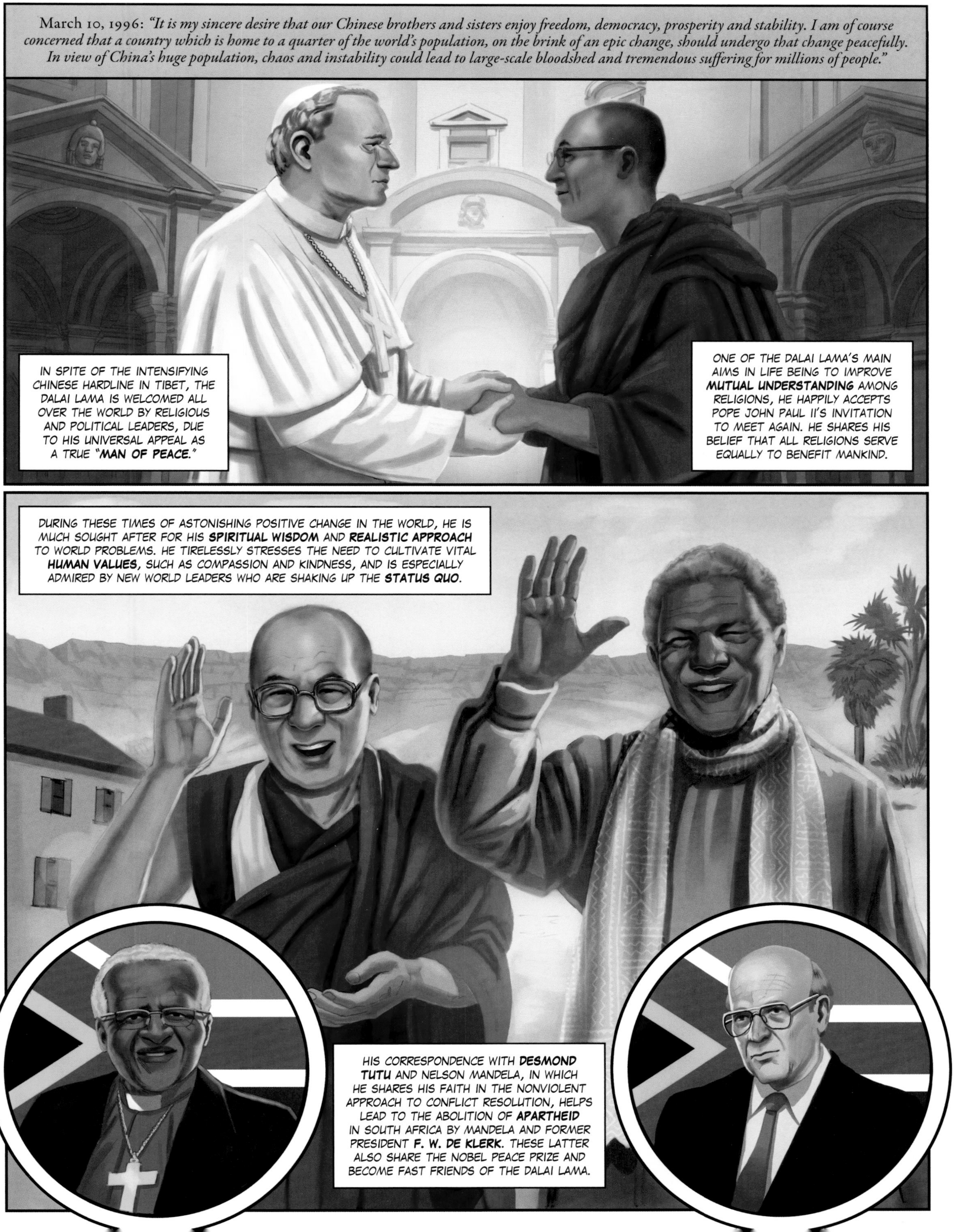
March 10, 1996: "It is my sincere desire that our Chinese brothers and sisters enjoy freedom, democracy, prosperity and stability. I am of course concerned that a country which is home to a quarter of the world's population, on the brink of an epic change, should undergo that change peacefully. In view of China's huge population, chaos and instability could lead to large-scale bloodshed and tremendous suffering for millions of people."
IN SPITE OF THE INTENSIFYING CHINESE HARDLINE IN TIBET, THE DALAI LAMA IS WELCOMED ALL OVER THE WORLD BY RELIGIOUS AND POLITICAL LEADERS, DUE TO HIS UNIVERSAL APPEAL AS A TRUE "MAN OF PEACE."
ONE OF THE DALAI LAMA'S MAIN AIMS IN LIFE BEING TO IMPROVE MUTUAL UNDERSTANDING AMONG RELIGIONS, HE HAPPILY ACCEPTS POPE JOHN PAUL II'S INVITATION TO MEET AGAIN. HE SHARES HIS BELIEF THAT ALL RELIGIONS SERVE EQUALLY TO BENEFIT MANKIND.
DURING THESE TIMES OF ASTONISHING POSITIVE CHANGE IN THE WORLD, HE IS MUCH SOUGHT AFTER FOR HIS SPIRITUAL WISDOM AND REALISTIC APPROACH TO WORLD PROBLEMS. HE TIRELESSLY STRESSES THE NEED TO CULTIVATE VITAL HUMAN VALUES, SUCH AS COMPASSION AND KINDNESS, AND IS ESPECIALLY ADMIRED BY NEW WORLD LEADERS WHO ARE SHAKING UP THE STATUS QUO.
HIS CORRESPONDENCE WITH DESMOND TUTU AND NELSON MANDELA, IN WHICH HE SHARES HIS FAITH IN THE NONVIOLENT APPROACH TO CONFLICT RESOLUTION, HELPS LEAD TO THE ABOLITION OF APARTHEID IN SOUTH AFRICA BY MANDELA AND FORMER PRESIDENT F. W. DE KLERK. THESE LATTER ALSO SHARE THE NOBEL PEACE PRIZE AND BECOME FAST FRIENDS OF THE DALAI LAMA.

MARCH 10, 1997: *"The world is becoming smaller and increasingly interdependent. Without a sense of universal responsibility, our very future is in danger. Today's problems of militarization, development, ecology, population, and the constant search for new sources of energy and raw materials require more than piecemeal actions and short-term problem-solving. Modern scientific development has helped in solving mankind's problems. However, there is the need to cultivate not only the rational mind but also other faculties of the human spirit: love, compassion and solidarity. . . ."*

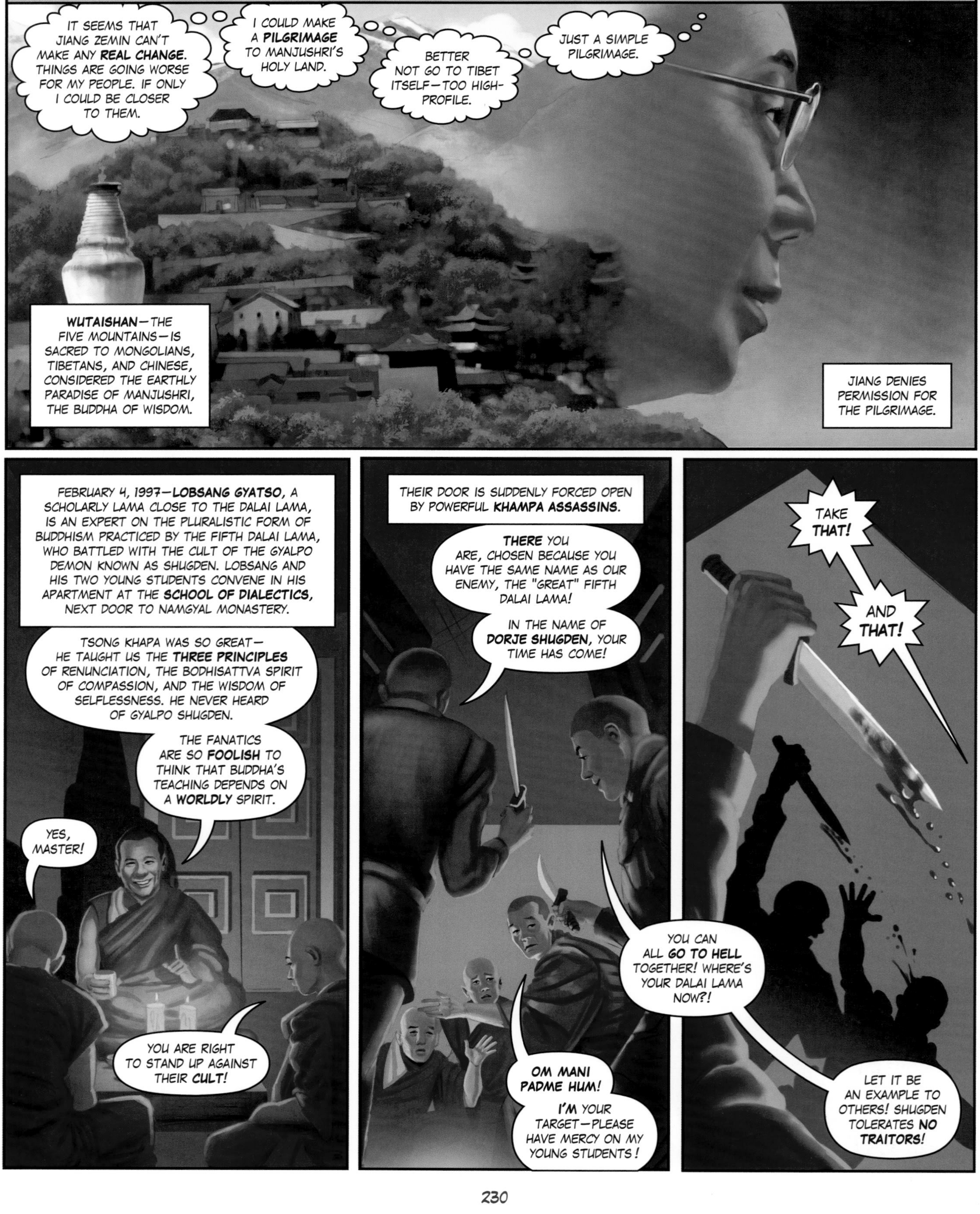

IT SEEMS THAT JIANG ZEMIN CAN'T MAKE ANY REAL CHANGE. THINGS ARE GOING WORSE FOR MY PEOPLE. IF ONLY I COULD BE CLOSER TO THEM.
I COULD MAKE A PILGRIMAGE TO MANJUSHRI'S HOLY LAND.
BETTER NOT GO TO TIBET ITSELF—TOO HIGH-PROFILE.
JUST A SIMPLE PILGRIMAGE.
WUTAISHAN—THE FIVE MOUNTAINS—IS SACRED TO MONGOLIANS, TIBETANS, AND CHINESE, CONSIDERED THE EARTHLY PARADISE OF MANJUSHRI, THE BUDDHA OF WISDOM.
JIANG DENIES PERMISSION FOR THE PILGRIMAGE.
FEBRUARY 4, 1997—LOBSANG GYATSO, A SCHOLARLY LAMA CLOSE TO THE DALAI LAMA, IS AN EXPERT ON THE PLURALISTIC FORM OF BUDDHISM PRACTICED BY THE FIFTH DALAI LAMA, WHO BATTLED WITH THE CULT OF THE GYALPO DEMON KNOWN AS SHUGDEN. LOBSANG AND HIS TWO YOUNG STUDENTS CONVENE IN HIS APARTMENT AT THE SCHOOL OF DIALECTICS, NEXT DOOR TO NAMGYAL MONASTERY.
TSONG KHAPA WAS SO GREAT—HE TAUGHT US THE THREE PRINCIPLES OF RENUNCIATION, THE BODHISATTVA SPIRIT OF COMPASSION, AND THE WISDOM OF SELFLESSNESS. HE NEVER HEARD OF GYALPO SHUGDEN.
THE FANATICS ARE SO FOOLISH TO THINK THAT BUDDHA'S TEACHING DEPENDS ON A WORLDLY SPIRIT.
YES, MASTER!
YOU ARE RIGHT TO STAND UP AGAINST THEIR CULT!
THEIR DOOR IS SUDDENLY FORCED OPEN BY POWERFUL KHAMPA ASSASSINS.
THERE YOU ARE, CHOSEN BECAUSE YOU HAVE THE SAME NAME AS OUR ENEMY, THE "GREAT" FIFTH DALAI LAMA!
IN THE NAME OF DORJE SHUGDEN, YOUR TIME HAS COME!
OM MANI PADME HUM!
I'M YOUR TARGET—PLEASE HAVE MERCY ON MY YOUNG STUDENTS!
TAKE THAT!
AND THAT!
YOU CAN ALL GO TO HELL TOGETHER! WHERE'S YOUR DALAI LAMA NOW?!
LET IT BE AN EXAMPLE TO OTHERS! SHUGDEN TOLERATES NO TRAITORS!

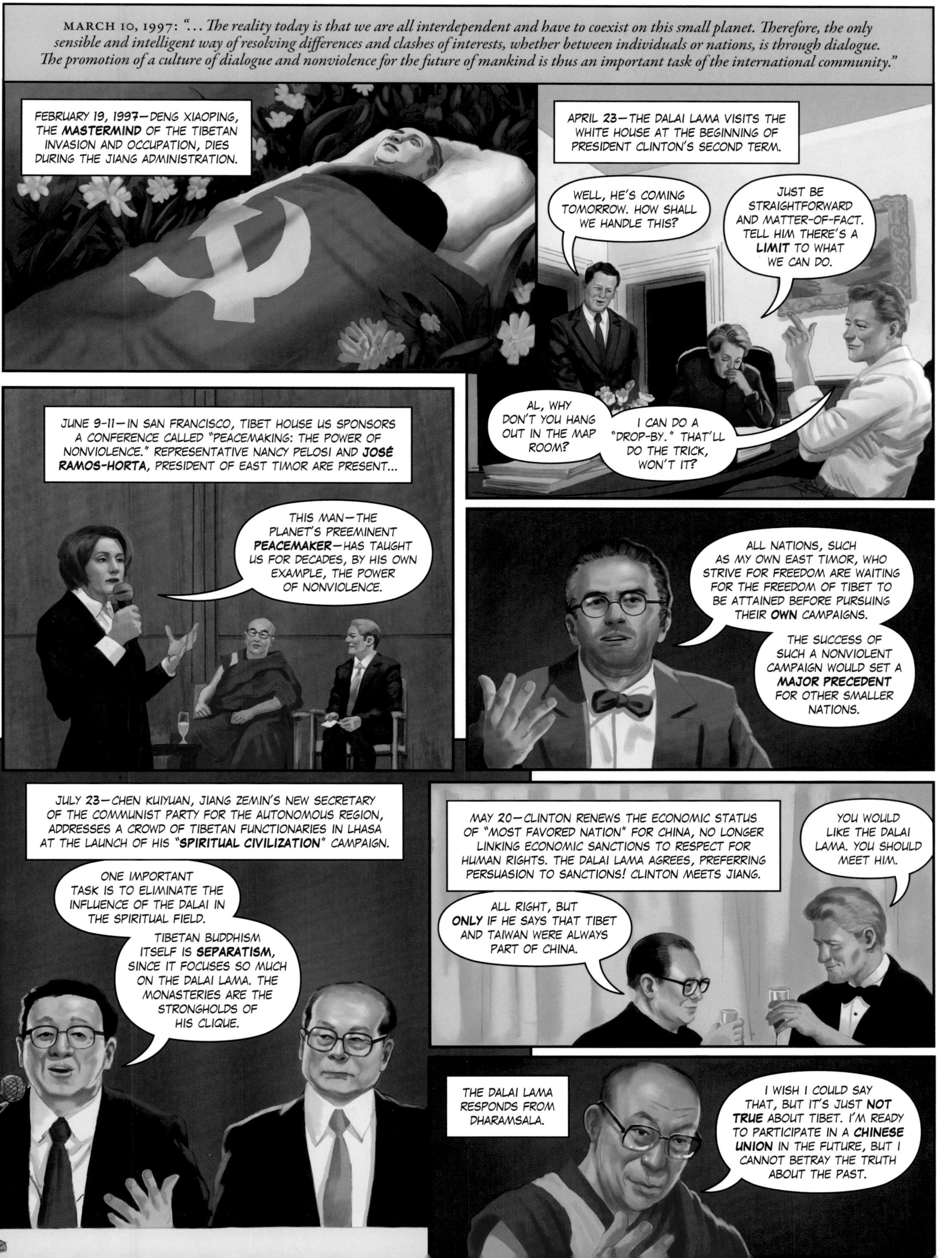
MARCH 10, 1997: "... The reality today is that we are all interdependent and have to coexist on this small planet. Therefore, the only sensible and intelligent way of resolving differences and clashes of interests, whether between individuals or nations, is through dialogue. The promotion of a culture of dialogue and nonviolence for the future of mankind is thus an important task of the international community."
FEBRUARY 19, 1997—DENG XIAOPING, THE MASTERMIND OF THE TIBETAN INVASION AND OCCUPATION, DIES DURING THE JIANG ADMINISTRATION.
APRIL 23—THE DALAI LAMA VISITS THE WHITE HOUSE AT THE BEGINNING OF PRESIDENT CLINTON'S SECOND TERM.
WELL, HE'S COMING TOMORROW. HOW SHALL WE HANDLE THIS?
JUST BE STRAIGHTFORWARD AND MATTER-OF-FACT. TELL HIM THERE'S A LIMIT TO WHAT WE CAN DO.
AL, WHY DON'T YOU HANG OUT IN THE MAP ROOM?
I CAN DO A "DROP-BY." THAT'LL DO THE TRICK, WON'T IT?
JUNE 9-11—IN SAN FRANCISCO, TIBET HOUSE US SPONSORS A CONFERENCE CALLED "PEACEMAKING: THE POWER OF NONVIOLENCE." REPRESENTATIVE NANCY PELOSI AND JOSÉ RAMOS-HORTA, PRESIDENT OF EAST TIMOR ARE PRESENT...
THIS MAN—THE PLANET'S PREEMINENT PEACEMAKER—HAS TAUGHT US FOR DECADES, BY HIS OWN EXAMPLE, THE POWER OF NONVIOLENCE.
ALL NATIONS, SUCH AS MY OWN EAST TIMOR, WHO STRIVE FOR FREEDOM ARE WAITING FOR THE FREEDOM OF TIBET TO BE ATTAINED BEFORE PURSUING THEIR OWN CAMPAIGNS.
THE SUCCESS OF SUCH A NONVIOLENT CAMPAIGN WOULD SET A MAJOR PRECEDENT FOR OTHER SMALLER NATIONS.
JULY 23—CHEN KUIYUAN, JIANG ZEMIN'S NEW SECRETARY OF THE COMMUNIST PARTY FOR THE AUTONOMOUS REGION, ADDRESSES A CROWD OF TIBETAN FUNCTIONARIES IN LHASA AT THE LAUNCH OF HIS "SPIRITUAL CIVILIZATION" CAMPAIGN.
ONE IMPORTANT TASK IS TO ELIMINATE THE INFLUENCE OF THE DALAI IN THE SPIRITUAL FIELD.
TIBETAN BUDDHISM ITSELF IS SEPARATISM, SINCE IT FOCUSES SO MUCH ON THE DALAI LAMA. THE MONASTERIES ARE THE STRONGHOLDS OF HIS CLIQUE.
MAY 20—CLINTON RENEWS THE ECONOMIC STATUS OF "MOST FAVORED NATION" FOR CHINA, NO LONGER LINKING ECONOMIC SANCTIONS TO RESPECT FOR HUMAN RIGHTS. THE DALAI LAMA AGREES, PREFERRING PERSUASION TO SANCTIONS! CLINTON MEETS JIANG.
YOU WOULD LIKE THE DALAI LAMA. YOU SHOULD MEET HIM.
ALL RIGHT, BUT ONLY IF HE SAYS THAT TIBET AND TAIWAN WERE ALWAYS PART OF CHINA.
THE DALAI LAMA RESPONDS FROM DHARAMSALA.
I WISH I COULD SAY THAT, BUT IT'S JUST NOT TRUE ABOUT TIBET. I'M READY TO PARTICIPATE IN A CHINESE UNION IN THE FUTURE, BUT I CANNOT BETRAY THE TRUTH ABOUT THE PAST.

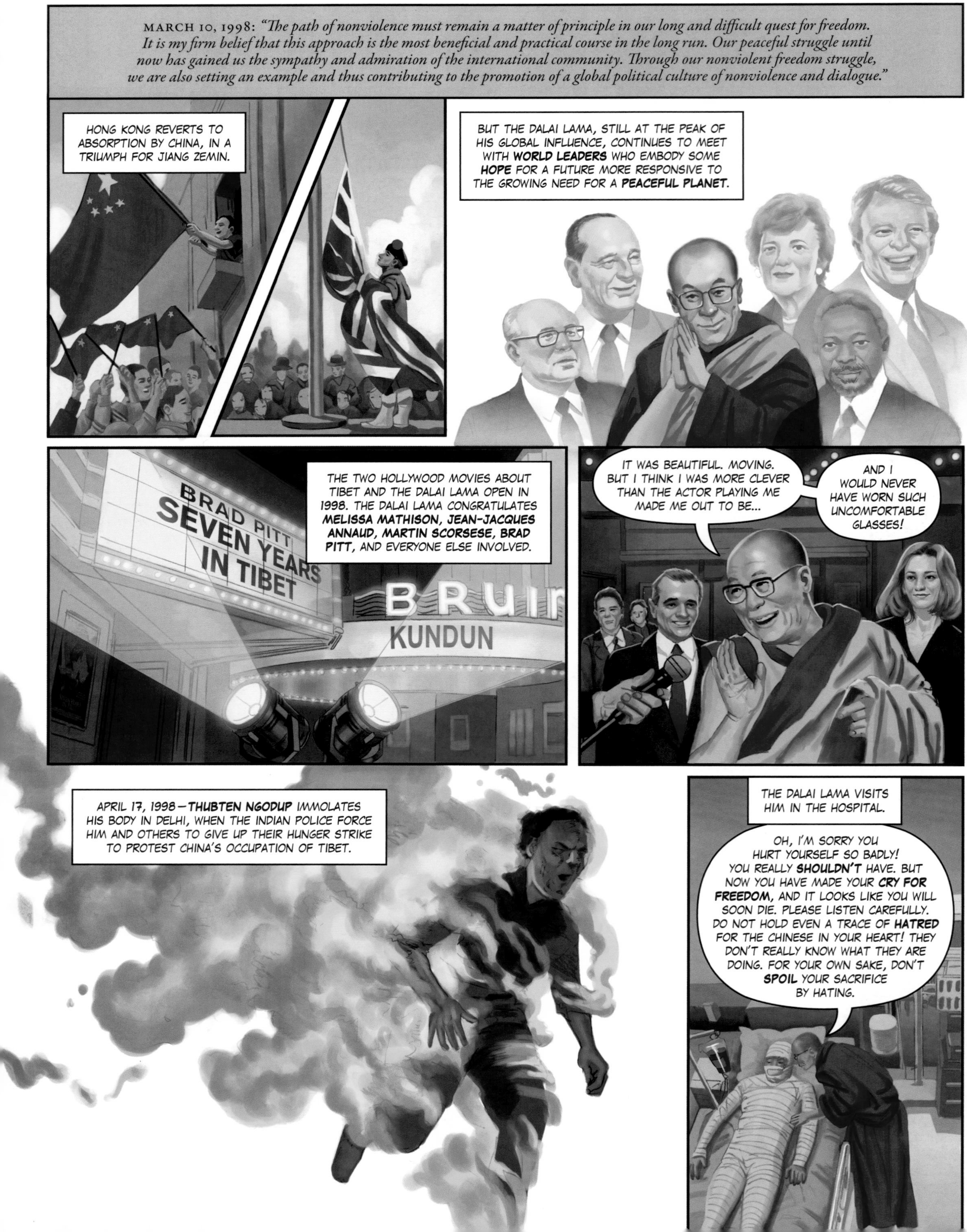
MARCH 10, 1998: "The path of nonviolence must remain a matter of principle in our long and difficult quest for freedom. It is my firm belief that this approach is the most beneficial and practical course in the long run. Our peaceful struggle until now has gained us the sympathy and admiration of the international community. Through our nonviolent freedom struggle, we are also setting an example and thus contributing to the promotion of a global political culture of nonviolence and dialogue."
HONG KONG REVERTS TO ABSORPTION BY CHINA, IN A TRIUMPH FOR JIANG ZEMIN.
BUT THE DALAI LAMA, STILL AT THE PEAK OF HIS GLOBAL INFLUENCE, CONTINUES TO MEET WITH **WORLD LEADERS** WHO EMBODY SOME **HOPE** FOR A FUTURE MORE RESPONSIVE TO THE GROWING NEED FOR A **PEACEFUL PLANET**.
BRAD PITT
SEVEN YEARS IN TIBET
THE TWO HOLLYWOOD MOVIES ABOUT TIBET AND THE DALAI LAMA OPEN IN 1998. THE DALAI LAMA CONGRATULATES **MELISSA MATHISON, JEAN-JACQUES ANNAUD, MARTIN SCORSESE, BRAD PITT**, AND EVERYONE ELSE INVOLVED.
BRUI
KUNDUN
IT WAS BEAUTIFUL. MOVING. BUT I THINK I WAS MORE CLEVER THAN THE ACTOR PLAYING ME MADE ME OUT TO BE...
AND I WOULD NEVER HAVE WORN SUCH UNCOMFORTABLE GLASSES!
APRIL 17, 1998—**THUBTEN NGODUP** IMMOLATES HIS BODY IN DELHI, WHEN THE INDIAN POLICE FORCE HIM AND OTHERS TO GIVE UP THEIR HUNGER STRIKE TO PROTEST CHINA'S OCCUPATION OF TIBET.
THE DALAI LAMA VISITS HIM IN THE HOSPITAL.
OH, I'M SORRY YOU HURT YOURSELF SO BADLY! YOU REALLY **SHOULDN'T** HAVE. BUT NOW YOU HAVE MADE YOUR **CRY FOR FREEDOM**, AND IT LOOKS LIKE YOU WILL SOON DIE. PLEASE LISTEN CAREFULLY. DO NOT HOLD EVEN A TRACE OF **HATRED** FOR THE CHINESE IN YOUR HEART! THEY DON'T REALLY KNOW WHAT THEY ARE DOING. FOR YOUR OWN SAKE, DON'T **SPOIL** YOUR SACRIFICE BY HATING.

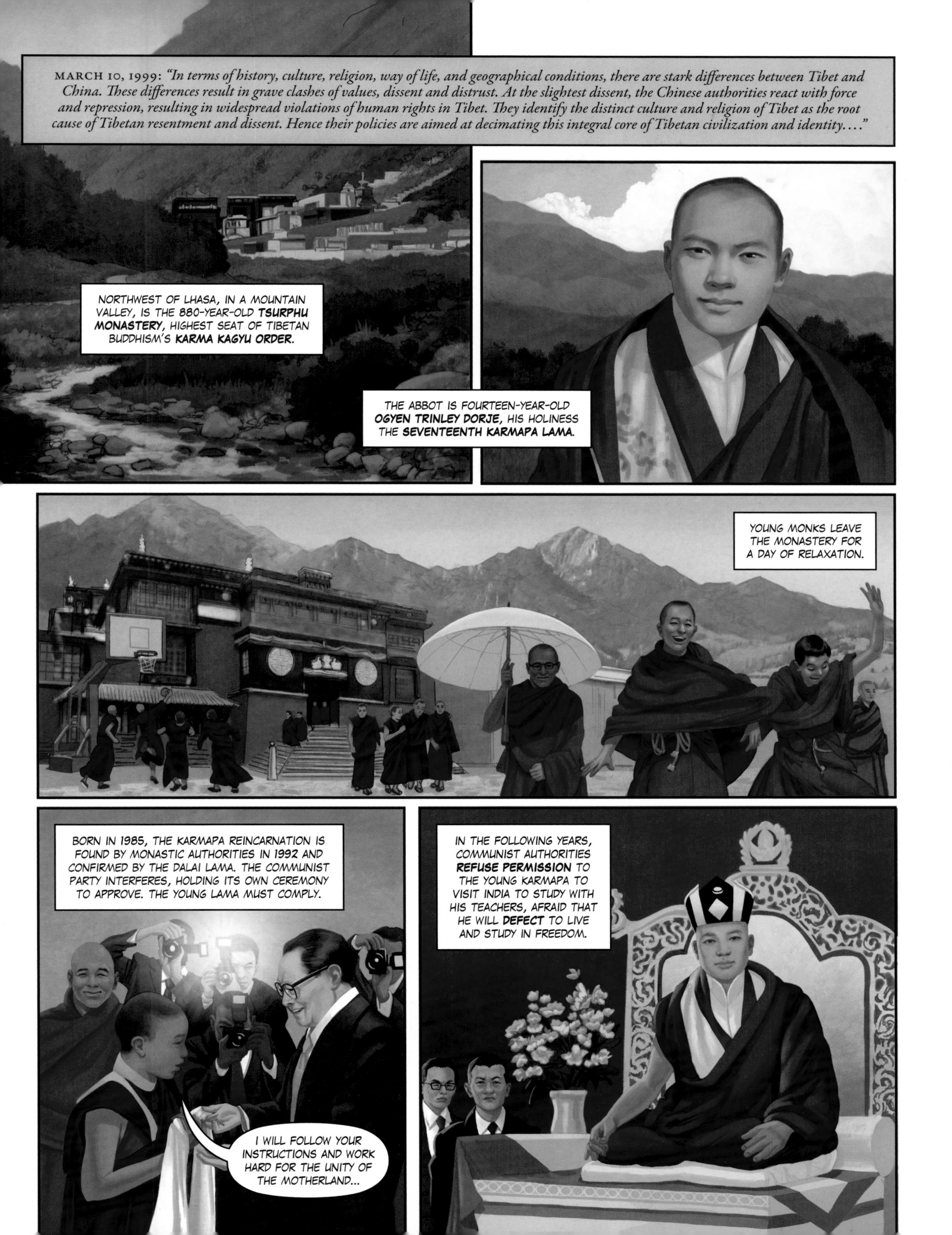
MARCH 10, 1999: "In terms of history, culture, religion, way of life, and geographical conditions, there are stark differences between Tibet and China. These differences result in grave clashes of values, dissent and distrust. At the slightest dissent, the Chinese authorities react with force and repression, resulting in widespread violations of human rights in Tibet. They identify the distinct culture and religion of Tibet as the root cause of Tibetan resentment and dissent. Hence their policies are aimed at decimating this integral core of Tibetan civilization and identity…."
NORTHWEST OF LHASA, IN A MOUNTAIN VALLEY, IS THE 880-YEAR-OLD **TSURPHU MONASTERY**, HIGHEST SEAT OF TIBETAN BUDDHISM'S **KARMA KAGYU ORDER**.
THE ABBOT IS FOURTEEN-YEAR-OLD **OGYEN TRINLEY DORJE**, HIS HOLINESS THE **SEVENTEENTH KARMAPA LAMA**.
YOUNG MONKS LEAVE THE MONASTERY FOR A DAY OF RELAXATION.
BORN IN 1985, THE KARMAPA REINCARNATION IS FOUND BY MONASTIC AUTHORITIES IN 1992 AND CONFIRMED BY THE DALAI LAMA. THE COMMUNIST PARTY INTERFERES, HOLDING ITS OWN CEREMONY TO APPROVE. THE YOUNG LAMA MUST COMPLY.
I WILL FOLLOW YOUR INSTRUCTIONS AND WORK HARD FOR THE UNITY OF THE MOTHERLAND...
IN THE FOLLOWING YEARS, COMMUNIST AUTHORITIES **REFUSE PERMISSION** TO THE YOUNG KARMAPA TO VISIT INDIA TO STUDY WITH HIS TEACHERS, AFRAID THAT HE WILL **DEFECT** TO LIVE AND STUDY IN FREEDOM.

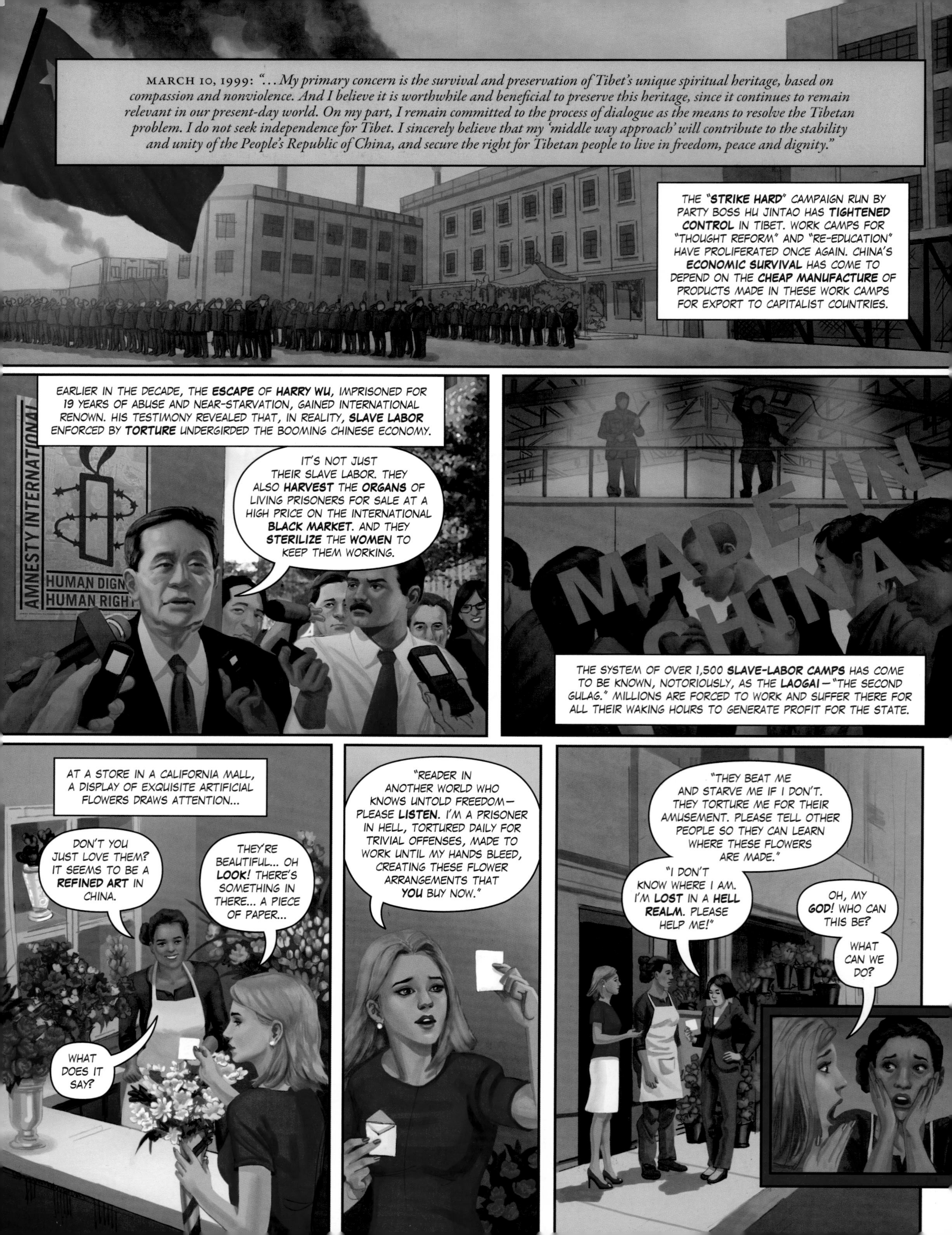
MARCH 10, 1999: "...My primary concern is the survival and preservation of Tibet's unique spiritual heritage, based on compassion and nonviolence. And I believe it is worthwhile and beneficial to preserve this heritage, since it continues to remain relevant in our present-day world. On my part, I remain committed to the process of dialogue as the means to resolve the Tibetan problem. I do not seek independence for Tibet. I sincerely believe that my 'middle way approach' will contribute to the stability and unity of the People's Republic of China, and secure the right for Tibetan people to live in freedom, peace and dignity."
THE "STRIKE HARD" CAMPAIGN RUN BY PARTY BOSS HU JINTAO HAS TIGHTENED CONTROL IN TIBET. WORK CAMPS FOR "THOUGHT REFORM" AND "RE-EDUCATION" HAVE PROLIFERATED ONCE AGAIN. CHINA'S ECONOMIC SURVIVAL HAS COME TO DEPEND ON THE CHEAP MANUFACTURE OF PRODUCTS MADE IN THESE WORK CAMPS FOR EXPORT TO CAPITALIST COUNTRIES.
EARLIER IN THE DECADE, THE ESCAPE OF HARRY WU, IMPRISONED FOR 19 YEARS OF ABUSE AND NEAR-STARVATION, GAINED INTERNATIONAL RENOWN. HIS TESTIMONY REVEALED THAT, IN REALITY, SLAVE LABOR ENFORCED BY TORTURE UNDERGIRDED THE BOOMING CHINESE ECONOMY.
AMNESTY INTERNATIONAL
HUMAN DIGN
HUMAN RIGHT
IT'S NOT JUST THEIR SLAVE LABOR. THEY ALSO HARVEST THE ORGANS OF LIVING PRISONERS FOR SALE AT A HIGH PRICE ON THE INTERNATIONAL BLACK MARKET. AND THEY STERILIZE THE WOMEN TO KEEP THEM WORKING.
MADE IN CHINA
THE SYSTEM OF OVER 1,500 SLAVE-LABOR CAMPS HAS COME TO BE KNOWN, NOTORIOUSLY, AS THE LAOGAI—"THE SECOND GULAG." MILLIONS ARE FORCED TO WORK AND SUFFER THERE FOR ALL THEIR WAKING HOURS TO GENERATE PROFIT FOR THE STATE.
AT A STORE IN A CALIFORNIA MALL, A DISPLAY OF EXQUISITE ARTIFICIAL FLOWERS DRAWS ATTENTION...
DON'T YOU JUST LOVE THEM? IT SEEMS TO BE A REFINED ART IN CHINA.
THEY'RE BEAUTIFUL... OH LOOK! THERE'S SOMETHING IN THERE... A PIECE OF PAPER...
WHAT DOES IT SAY?
"READER IN ANOTHER WORLD WHO KNOWS UNTOLD FREEDOM—PLEASE LISTEN. I'M A PRISONER IN HELL, TORTURED DAILY FOR TRIVIAL OFFENSES, MADE TO WORK UNTIL MY HANDS BLEED, CREATING THESE FLOWER ARRANGEMENTS THAT YOU BUY NOW."
"THEY BEAT ME AND STARVE ME IF I DON'T. THEY TORTURE ME FOR THEIR AMUSEMENT. PLEASE TELL OTHER PEOPLE SO THEY CAN LEARN WHERE THESE FLOWERS ARE MADE."
"I DON'T KNOW WHERE I AM. I'M LOST IN A HELL REALM. PLEASE HELP ME!"
OH, MY GOD! WHO CAN THIS BE?
WHAT CAN WE DO?

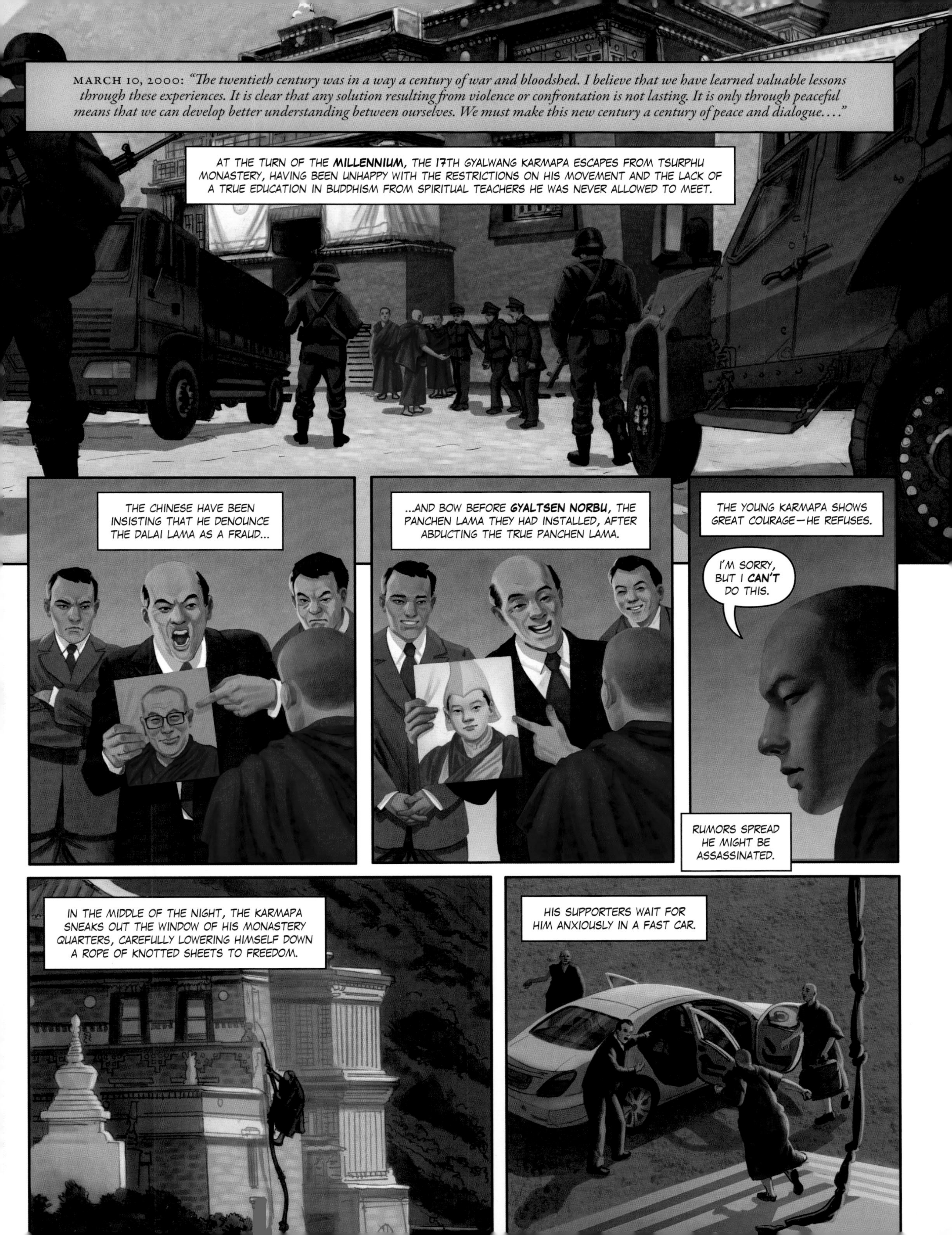
MARCH 10, 2000: "The twentieth century was in a way a century of war and bloodshed. I believe that we have learned valuable lessons through these experiences. It is clear that any solution resulting from violence or confrontation is not lasting. It is only through peaceful means that we can develop better understanding between ourselves. We must make this new century a century of peace and dialogue. . . ."
AT THE TURN OF THE MILLENNIUM, THE 17TH GYALWANG KARMAPA ESCAPES FROM TSURPHU MONASTERY, HAVING BEEN UNHAPPY WITH THE RESTRICTIONS ON HIS MOVEMENT AND THE LACK OF A TRUE EDUCATION IN BUDDHISM FROM SPIRITUAL TEACHERS HE WAS NEVER ALLOWED TO MEET.
THE CHINESE HAVE BEEN INSISTING THAT HE DENOUNCE THE DALAI LAMA AS A FRAUD...
...AND BOW BEFORE GYALTSEN NORBU, THE PANCHEN LAMA THEY HAD INSTALLED, AFTER ABDUCTING THE TRUE PANCHEN LAMA.
THE YOUNG KARMAPA SHOWS GREAT COURAGE—HE REFUSES.
I'M SORRY, BUT I CAN'T DO THIS.
RUMORS SPREAD HE MIGHT BE ASSASSINATED.
IN THE MIDDLE OF THE NIGHT, THE KARMAPA SNEAKS OUT THE WINDOW OF HIS MONASTERY QUARTERS, CAREFULLY LOWERING HIMSELF DOWN A ROPE OF KNOTTED SHEETS TO FREEDOM.
HIS SUPPORTERS WAIT FOR HIM ANXIOUSLY IN A FAST CAR.

MARCH 10, 2000: "*. . . The state of affairs of our freedom struggle is complex and multifarious, yet the spirit of resistance of our people inside Tibet continues to increase. It is also encouraging to note that worldwide support for our cause is increasing. The sad state of affairs in Tibet does nothing to alleviate the suffering of the Tibetan people or to bring stability and unity to the People's Republic of China. If China is seriously concerned about unity, she must make honest efforts to win over the hearts of Tibetans and not attempt to impose her will on them. . . .*"

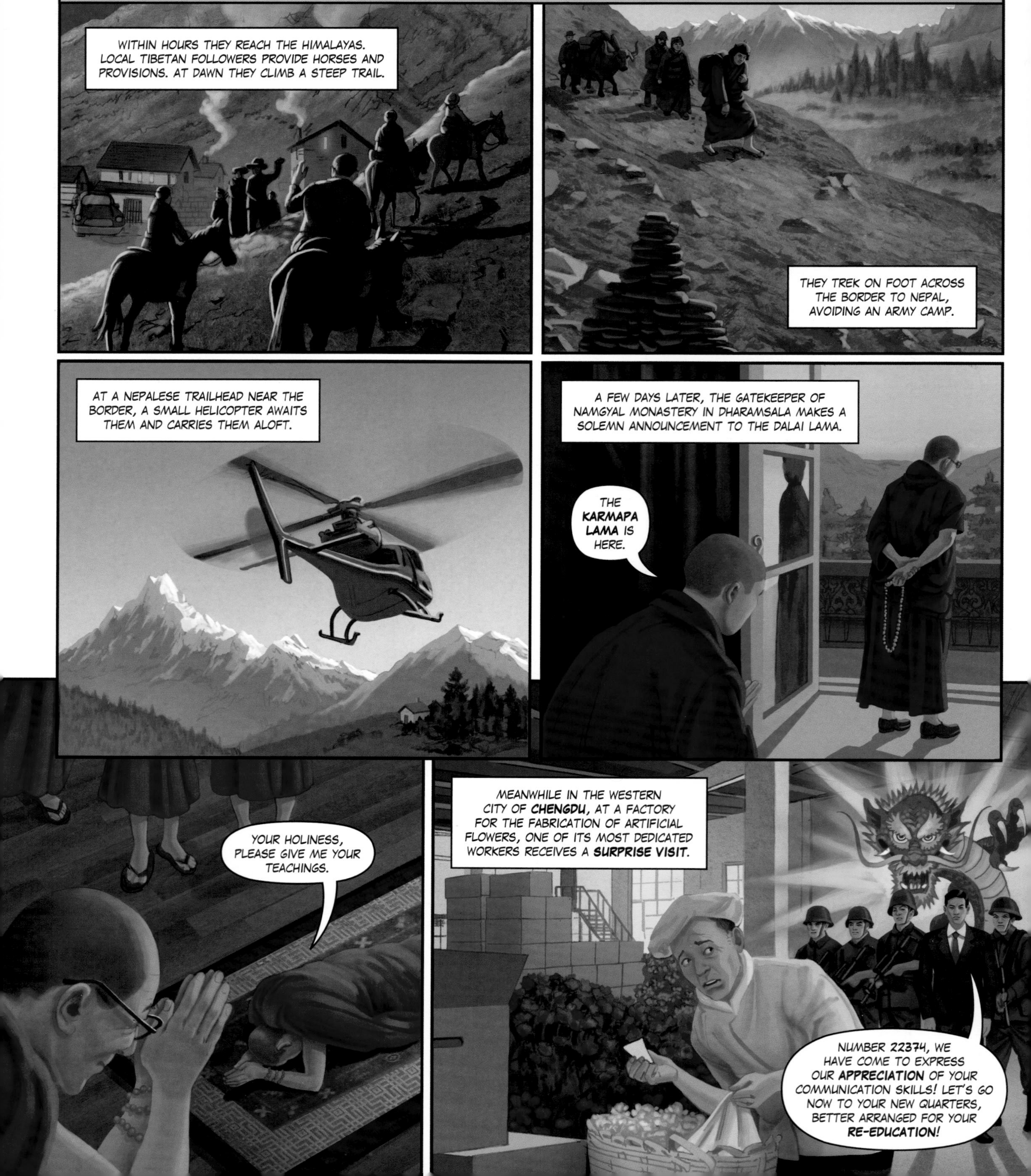
WITHIN HOURS THEY REACH THE HIMALAYAS. LOCAL TIBETAN FOLLOWERS PROVIDE HORSES AND PROVISIONS. AT DAWN THEY CLIMB A STEEP TRAIL.
THEY TREK ON FOOT ACROSS THE BORDER TO NEPAL, AVOIDING AN ARMY CAMP.
AT A NEPALESE TRAILHEAD NEAR THE BORDER, A SMALL HELICOPTER AWAITS THEM AND CARRIES THEM ALOFT.
A FEW DAYS LATER, THE GATEKEEPER OF NAMGYAL MONASTERY IN DHARAMSALA MAKES A SOLEMN ANNOUNCEMENT TO THE DALAI LAMA.
THE **KARMAPA LAMA** IS HERE.
YOUR HOLINESS, PLEASE GIVE ME YOUR TEACHINGS.
MEANWHILE IN THE WESTERN CITY OF **CHENGDU**, AT A FACTORY FOR THE FABRICATION OF ARTIFICIAL FLOWERS, ONE OF ITS MOST DEDICATED WORKERS RECEIVES A **SURPRISE VISIT**.
NUMBER 22374, WE HAVE COME TO EXPRESS OUR **APPRECIATION** OF YOUR COMMUNICATION SKILLS! LET'S GO NOW TO YOUR NEW QUARTERS, BETTER ARRANGED FOR YOUR **RE-EDUCATION**!

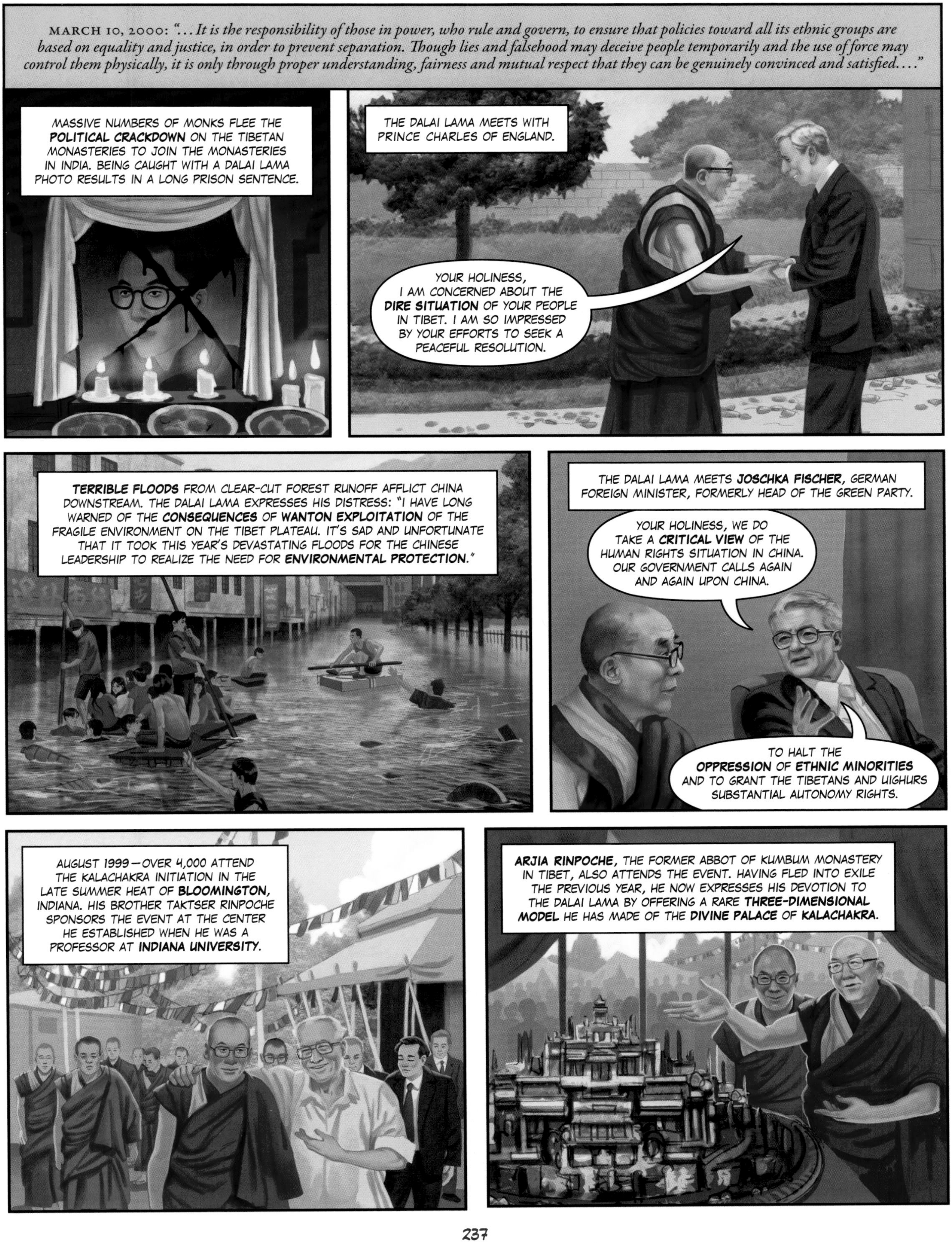
MARCH 10, 2000: "... It is the responsibility of those in power, who rule and govern, to ensure that policies toward all its ethnic groups are based on equality and justice, in order to prevent separation. Though lies and falsehood may deceive people temporarily and the use of force may control them physically, it is only through proper understanding, fairness and mutual respect that they can be genuinely convinced and satisfied...."
MASSIVE NUMBERS OF MONKS FLEE THE POLITICAL CRACKDOWN ON THE TIBETAN MONASTERIES TO JOIN THE MONASTERIES IN INDIA. BEING CAUGHT WITH A DALAI LAMA PHOTO RESULTS IN A LONG PRISON SENTENCE.
THE DALAI LAMA MEETS WITH PRINCE CHARLES OF ENGLAND.
YOUR HOLINESS, I AM CONCERNED ABOUT THE DIRE SITUATION OF YOUR PEOPLE IN TIBET. I AM SO IMPRESSED BY YOUR EFFORTS TO SEEK A PEACEFUL RESOLUTION.
TERRIBLE FLOODS FROM CLEAR-CUT FOREST RUNOFF AFFLICT CHINA DOWNSTREAM. THE DALAI LAMA EXPRESSES HIS DISTRESS: "I HAVE LONG WARNED OF THE CONSEQUENCES OF WANTON EXPLOITATION OF THE FRAGILE ENVIRONMENT ON THE TIBET PLATEAU. IT'S SAD AND UNFORTUNATE THAT IT TOOK THIS YEAR'S DEVASTATING FLOODS FOR THE CHINESE LEADERSHIP TO REALIZE THE NEED FOR ENVIRONMENTAL PROTECTION."
THE DALAI LAMA MEETS JOSCHKA FISCHER, GERMAN FOREIGN MINISTER, FORMERLY HEAD OF THE GREEN PARTY.
YOUR HOLINESS, WE DO TAKE A CRITICAL VIEW OF THE HUMAN RIGHTS SITUATION IN CHINA. OUR GOVERNMENT CALLS AGAIN AND AGAIN UPON CHINA.
TO HALT THE OPPRESSION OF ETHNIC MINORITIES AND TO GRANT THE TIBETANS AND UIGHURS SUBSTANTIAL AUTONOMY RIGHTS.
AUGUST 1999—OVER 4,000 ATTEND THE KALACHAKRA INITIATION IN THE LATE SUMMER HEAT OF BLOOMINGTON, INDIANA. HIS BROTHER TAKTSER RINPOCHE SPONSORS THE EVENT AT THE CENTER HE ESTABLISHED WHEN HE WAS A PROFESSOR AT INDIANA UNIVERSITY.
ARJIA RINPOCHE, THE FORMER ABBOT OF KUMBUM MONASTERY IN TIBET, ALSO ATTENDS THE EVENT. HAVING FLED INTO EXILE THE PREVIOUS YEAR, HE NOW EXPRESSES HIS DEVOTION TO THE DALAI LAMA BY OFFERING A RARE THREE-DIMENSIONAL MODEL HE HAS MADE OF THE DIVINE PALACE OF KALACHAKRA.

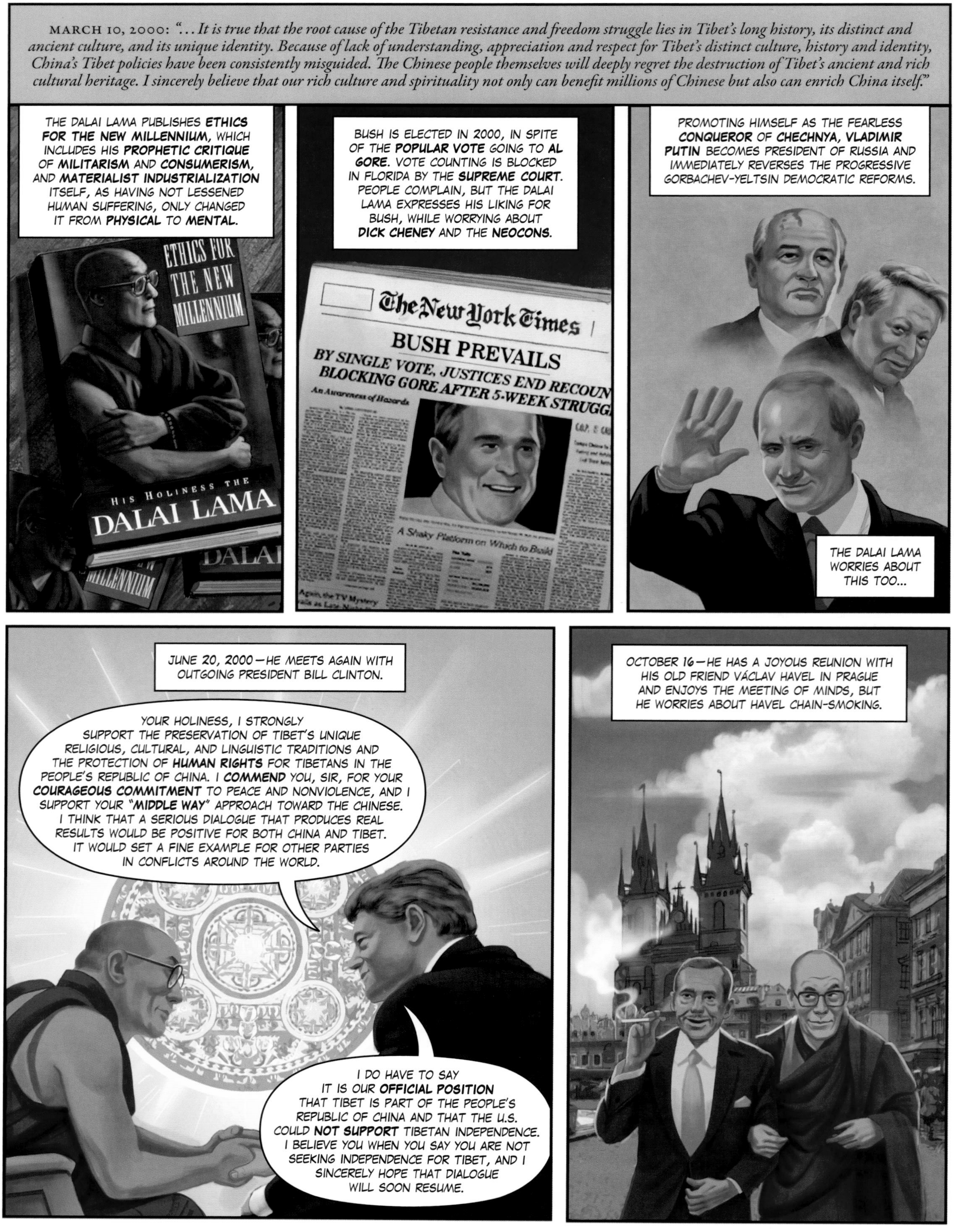
MARCH 10, 2000: "... It is true that the root cause of the Tibetan resistance and freedom struggle lies in Tibet's long history, its distinct and ancient culture, and its unique identity. Because of lack of understanding, appreciation and respect for Tibet's distinct culture, history and identity, China's Tibet policies have been consistently misguided. The Chinese people themselves will deeply regret the destruction of Tibet's ancient and rich cultural heritage. I sincerely believe that our rich culture and spirituality not only can benefit millions of Chinese but also can enrich China itself."
THE DALAI LAMA PUBLISHES **ETHICS FOR THE NEW MILLENNIUM**, WHICH INCLUDES HIS **PROPHETIC CRITIQUE** OF **MILITARISM** AND **CONSUMERISM**, AND **MATERIALIST INDUSTRIALIZATION** ITSELF, AS HAVING NOT LESSENED HUMAN SUFFERING, ONLY CHANGED IT FROM **PHYSICAL** TO **MENTAL**.
ETHICS FOR THE NEW MILLENNIUM
HIS HOLINESS THE DALAI LAMA
BUSH IS ELECTED IN 2000, IN SPITE OF THE **POPULAR VOTE** GOING TO **AL GORE**. VOTE COUNTING IS BLOCKED IN FLORIDA BY THE **SUPREME COURT**. PEOPLE COMPLAIN, BUT THE DALAI LAMA EXPRESSES HIS LIKING FOR BUSH, WHILE WORRYING ABOUT **DICK CHENEY** AND THE **NEOCONS**.
The New York Times
BUSH PREVAILS
BY SINGLE VOTE, JUSTICES END RECOUN
BLOCKING GORE AFTER 5-WEEK STRUGG
A Shaky Platform on Which to Build
PROMOTING HIMSELF AS THE FEARLESS **CONQUEROR** OF **CHECHNYA, VLADIMIR PUTIN** BECOMES PRESIDENT OF RUSSIA AND IMMEDIATELY REVERSES THE PROGRESSIVE GORBACHEV-YELTSIN DEMOCRATIC REFORMS.
THE DALAI LAMA WORRIES ABOUT THIS TOO...
JUNE 20, 2000—HE MEETS AGAIN WITH OUTGOING PRESIDENT BILL CLINTON.
YOUR HOLINESS, I STRONGLY SUPPORT THE PRESERVATION OF TIBET'S UNIQUE RELIGIOUS, CULTURAL, AND LINGUISTIC TRADITIONS AND THE PROTECTION OF **HUMAN RIGHTS** FOR TIBETANS IN THE PEOPLE'S REPUBLIC OF CHINA. I **COMMEND** YOU, SIR, FOR YOUR **COURAGEOUS COMMITMENT** TO PEACE AND NONVIOLENCE, AND I SUPPORT YOUR "**MIDDLE WAY**" APPROACH TOWARD THE CHINESE. I THINK THAT A SERIOUS DIALOGUE THAT PRODUCES REAL RESULTS WOULD BE POSITIVE FOR BOTH CHINA AND TIBET. IT WOULD SET A FINE EXAMPLE FOR OTHER PARTIES IN CONFLICTS AROUND THE WORLD.
I DO HAVE TO SAY IT IS OUR **OFFICIAL POSITION** THAT TIBET IS PART OF THE PEOPLE'S REPUBLIC OF CHINA AND THAT THE U.S. COULD **NOT SUPPORT** TIBETAN INDEPENDENCE. I BELIEVE YOU WHEN YOU SAY YOU ARE NOT SEEKING INDEPENDENCE FOR TIBET, AND I SINCERELY HOPE THAT DIALOGUE WILL SOON RESUME.
OCTOBER 16—HE HAS A JOYOUS REUNION WITH HIS OLD FRIEND VÁCLAV HAVEL IN PRAGUE AND ENJOYS THE MEETING OF MINDS, BUT HE WORRIES ABOUT HAVEL CHAIN-SMOKING.

MARCH 10, 2001: *"If the Tibetans are truly happy, the Chinese authorities should have no difficulty holding a plebiscite in Tibet. Already a number of Tibetan NGOs are advocating that. They argue that the best way to resolve this issue once and for all is to allow the Tibetans inside Tibet to choose their own destiny through a freely held referendum. They demand to let the Tibetan people speak out and decide for themselves. I have always maintained that the Tibetan people must be able to decide the future of Tibet. . . ."*

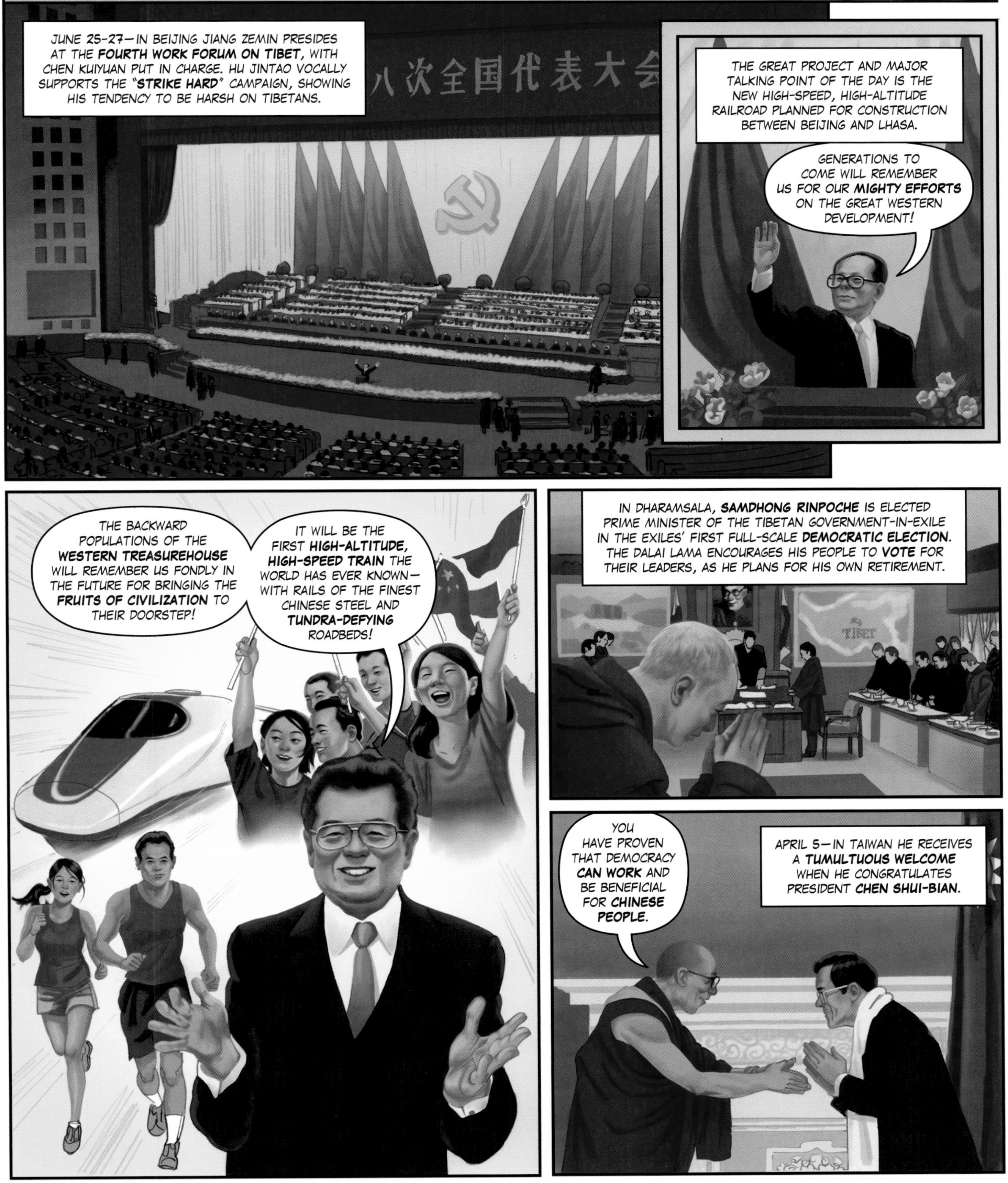
JUNE 25–27—IN BEIJING JIANG ZEMIN PRESIDES AT THE **FOURTH WORK FORUM ON TIBET,** WITH CHEN KUIYUAN PUT IN CHARGE. HU JINTAO VOCALLY SUPPORTS THE **"STRIKE HARD"** CAMPAIGN, SHOWING HIS TENDENCY TO BE HARSH ON TIBETANS.
八次全国代表大会
THE GREAT PROJECT AND MAJOR TALKING POINT OF THE DAY IS THE NEW HIGH-SPEED, HIGH-ALTITUDE RAILROAD PLANNED FOR CONSTRUCTION BETWEEN BEIJING AND LHASA.
GENERATIONS TO COME WILL REMEMBER US FOR OUR **MIGHTY EFFORTS** ON THE GREAT WESTERN DEVELOPMENT!
THE BACKWARD POPULATIONS OF THE **WESTERN TREASUREHOUSE** WILL REMEMBER US FONDLY IN THE FUTURE FOR BRINGING THE **FRUITS OF CIVILIZATION** TO THEIR DOORSTEP!
IT WILL BE THE FIRST **HIGH-ALTITUDE, HIGH-SPEED TRAIN** THE WORLD HAS EVER KNOWN—WITH RAILS OF THE FINEST CHINESE STEEL AND **TUNDRA-DEFYING** ROADBEDS!
IN DHARAMSALA, **SAMDHONG RINPOCHE** IS ELECTED PRIME MINISTER OF THE TIBETAN GOVERNMENT-IN-EXILE IN THE EXILES' FIRST FULL-SCALE **DEMOCRATIC ELECTION.** THE DALAI LAMA ENCOURAGES HIS PEOPLE TO **VOTE** FOR THEIR LEADERS, AS HE PLANS FOR HIS OWN RETIREMENT.
TIBET
APRIL 5—IN TAIWAN HE RECEIVES A **TUMULTUOUS WELCOME** WHEN HE CONGRATULATES PRESIDENT **CHEN SHUI-BIAN.**
YOU HAVE PROVEN THAT DEMOCRACY **CAN WORK** AND BE BENEFICIAL FOR **CHINESE PEOPLE.**

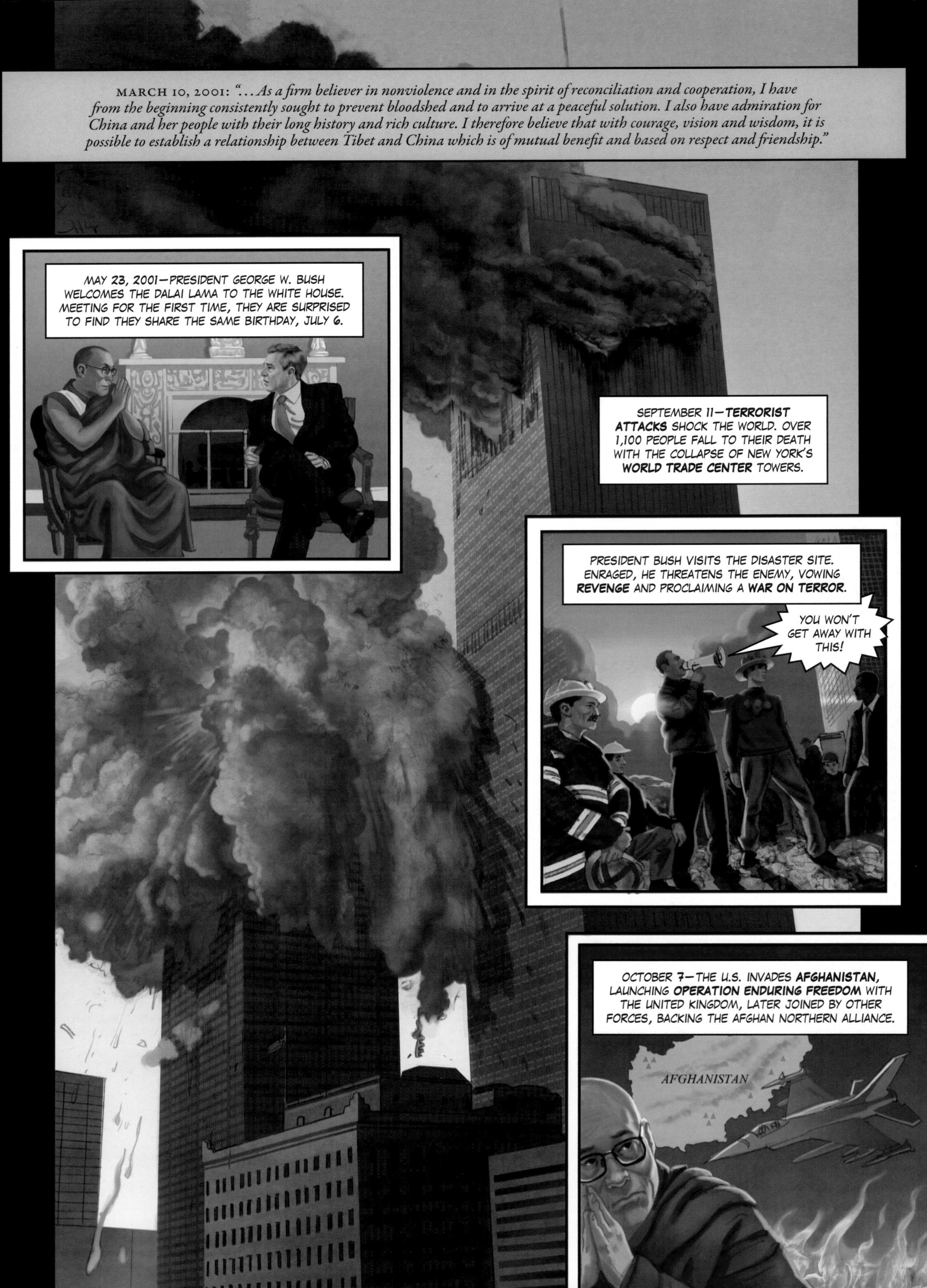
MARCH 10, 2001: "...As a firm believer in nonviolence and in the spirit of reconciliation and cooperation, I have from the beginning consistently sought to prevent bloodshed and to arrive at a peaceful solution. I also have admiration for China and her people with their long history and rich culture. I therefore believe that with courage, vision and wisdom, it is possible to establish a relationship between Tibet and China which is of mutual benefit and based on respect and friendship."
MAY 23, 2001—PRESIDENT GEORGE W. BUSH WELCOMES THE DALAI LAMA TO THE WHITE HOUSE. MEETING FOR THE FIRST TIME, THEY ARE SURPRISED TO FIND THEY SHARE THE SAME BIRTHDAY, JULY 6.
SEPTEMBER 11—TERRORIST ATTACKS SHOCK THE WORLD. OVER 1,100 PEOPLE FALL TO THEIR DEATH WITH THE COLLAPSE OF NEW YORK'S WORLD TRADE CENTER TOWERS.
PRESIDENT BUSH VISITS THE DISASTER SITE. ENRAGED, HE THREATENS THE ENEMY, VOWING REVENGE AND PROCLAIMING A WAR ON TERROR.
YOU WON'T GET AWAY WITH THIS!
OCTOBER 7—THE U.S. INVADES AFGHANISTAN, LAUNCHING OPERATION ENDURING FREEDOM WITH THE UNITED KINGDOM, LATER JOINED BY OTHER FORCES, BACKING THE AFGHAN NORTHERN ALLIANCE.
AFGHANISTAN

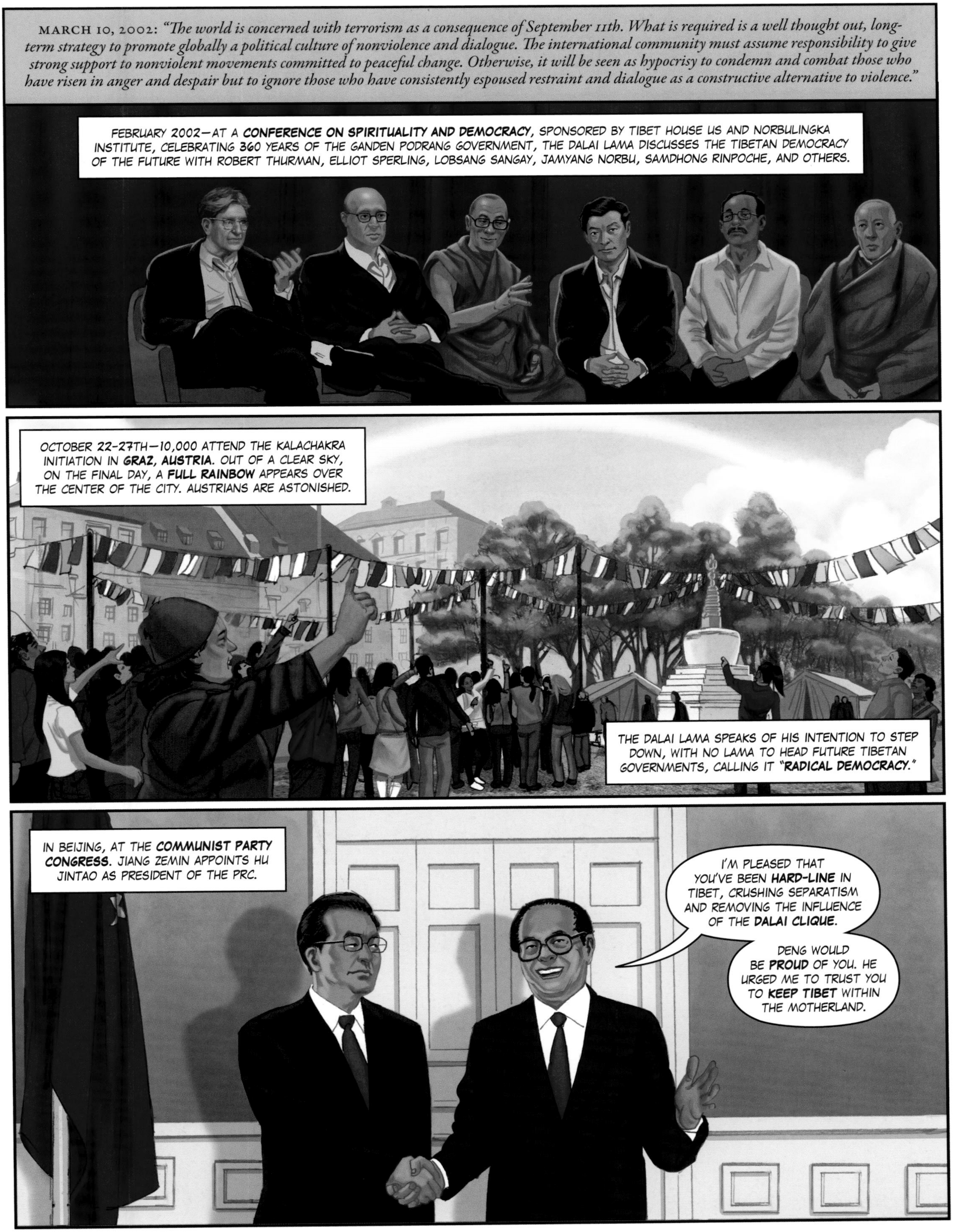
MARCH 10, 2002: "The world is concerned with terrorism as a consequence of September 11th. What is required is a well thought out, long-term strategy to promote globally a political culture of nonviolence and dialogue. The international community must assume responsibility to give strong support to nonviolent movements committed to peaceful change. Otherwise, it will be seen as hypocrisy to condemn and combat those who have risen in anger and despair but to ignore those who have consistently espoused restraint and dialogue as a constructive alternative to violence."
FEBRUARY 2002—AT A CONFERENCE ON SPIRITUALITY AND DEMOCRACY, SPONSORED BY TIBET HOUSE US AND NORBULINGKA INSTITUTE, CELEBRATING 360 YEARS OF THE GANDEN PODRANG GOVERNMENT, THE DALAI LAMA DISCUSSES THE TIBETAN DEMOCRACY OF THE FUTURE WITH ROBERT THURMAN, ELLIOT SPERLING, LOBSANG SANGAY, JAMYANG NORBU, SAMDHONG RINPOCHE, AND OTHERS.
OCTOBER 22-27TH—10,000 ATTEND THE KALACHAKRA INITIATION IN GRAZ, AUSTRIA. OUT OF A CLEAR SKY, ON THE FINAL DAY, A FULL RAINBOW APPEARS OVER THE CENTER OF THE CITY. AUSTRIANS ARE ASTONISHED.
THE DALAI LAMA SPEAKS OF HIS INTENTION TO STEP DOWN, WITH NO LAMA TO HEAD FUTURE TIBETAN GOVERNMENTS, CALLING IT "RADICAL DEMOCRACY."
IN BEIJING, AT THE COMMUNIST PARTY CONGRESS. JIANG ZEMIN APPOINTS HU JINTAO AS PRESIDENT OF THE PRC.
I'M PLEASED THAT YOU'VE BEEN HARD-LINE IN TIBET, CRUSHING SEPARATISM AND REMOVING THE INFLUENCE OF THE DALAI CLIQUE.
DENG WOULD BE PROUD OF YOU. HE URGED ME TO TRUST YOU TO KEEP TIBET WITHIN THE MOTHERLAND.

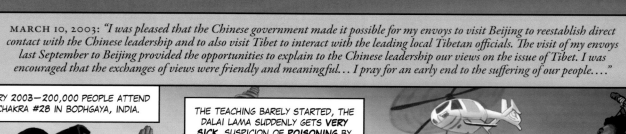

MARCH 10, 2003: *"I was pleased that the Chinese government made it possible for my envoys to visit Beijing to reestablish direct contact with the Chinese leadership and to also visit Tibet to interact with the leading local Tibetan officials. The visit of my envoys last September to Beijing provided the opportunities to explain to the Chinese leadership our views on the issue of Tibet. I was encouraged that the exchanges of views were friendly and meaningful... I pray for an early end to the suffering of our people...."*

JANUARY 2003—200,000 PEOPLE ATTEND KALACHAKRA #28 IN BODHGAYA, INDIA.

THE TEACHING BARELY STARTED, THE DALAI LAMA SUDDENLY GETS **VERY SICK.** SUSPICION OF **POISONING** BY THE CHINESE IS WIDELY RUMORED.

DRASTICALLY DEHYDRATED, HE HAS TO BE AIRLIFTED TO MUMBAI FOR SPECIAL TREATMENT. WITH THE SUDDEN LOSS OF 55 LBS, HE SEEMS TO BE **NEAR DEATH.** BUT THE DANGEROUS MOMENT PASSES.

FEBRUARY 15—AROUND THE WORLD 36 MILLION PEOPLE PROTEST THE IMPENDING **WAR ON IRAQ.**

NO TO U.S. WAR ON IRAQ

WAR IS NOT THE ANSWER!

THE DALAI LAMA OFFERS TO GO TO IRAQ TO TRY TO PREVENT WAR IF BISHOP TUTU AND OTHER LAUREATES WOULD JOIN HIM.

WHAT GOOD WILL IT DO TO **DESTROY** IRAQ? SADDAM MAY NOT BE NICE, BUT WHY NOT AT LEAST **TRY** TO TALK TO HIM?

MARCH—JUST BEFORE THE IRAQ INVASION, THE DALAI LAMA WRITES A LETTER TO BUSH, QUESTIONING THE EFFECTIVENESS OF VIOLENCE.

I personally believe we need to think seriously whether a violent action is the right thing to do in the long run. I believe violence will only increase the cycle of violence. But how do we deal with hatred and anger, which are often the root causes. This is a very difficult question. I am sure that you will make the right decision.

With my prayers and good wishes

The Dalai Lama

HIS SECRETARIES TRY TO PREVENT HIS USE OF THE WORD "VIOLENCE" TO DESCRIBE THE ANTICIPATED MILITARY INVASION BY U.S. FORCES, BUT HE REINSERTS IT ANYWAY.

IT'LL BE OK. I DON'T THINK THEY'LL PUT ME IN PRISON.

MARCH 10, 2003: *"... The only sensible and intelligent way of resolving differences, whether between individuals, peoples or nations, is through a political culture of nonviolence and dialogue. Since our struggle is based on truth, justice and nonviolence, and is not directed against China, we have been fortunate to receive increasing worldwide sympathy and support, including from among the Chinese."*

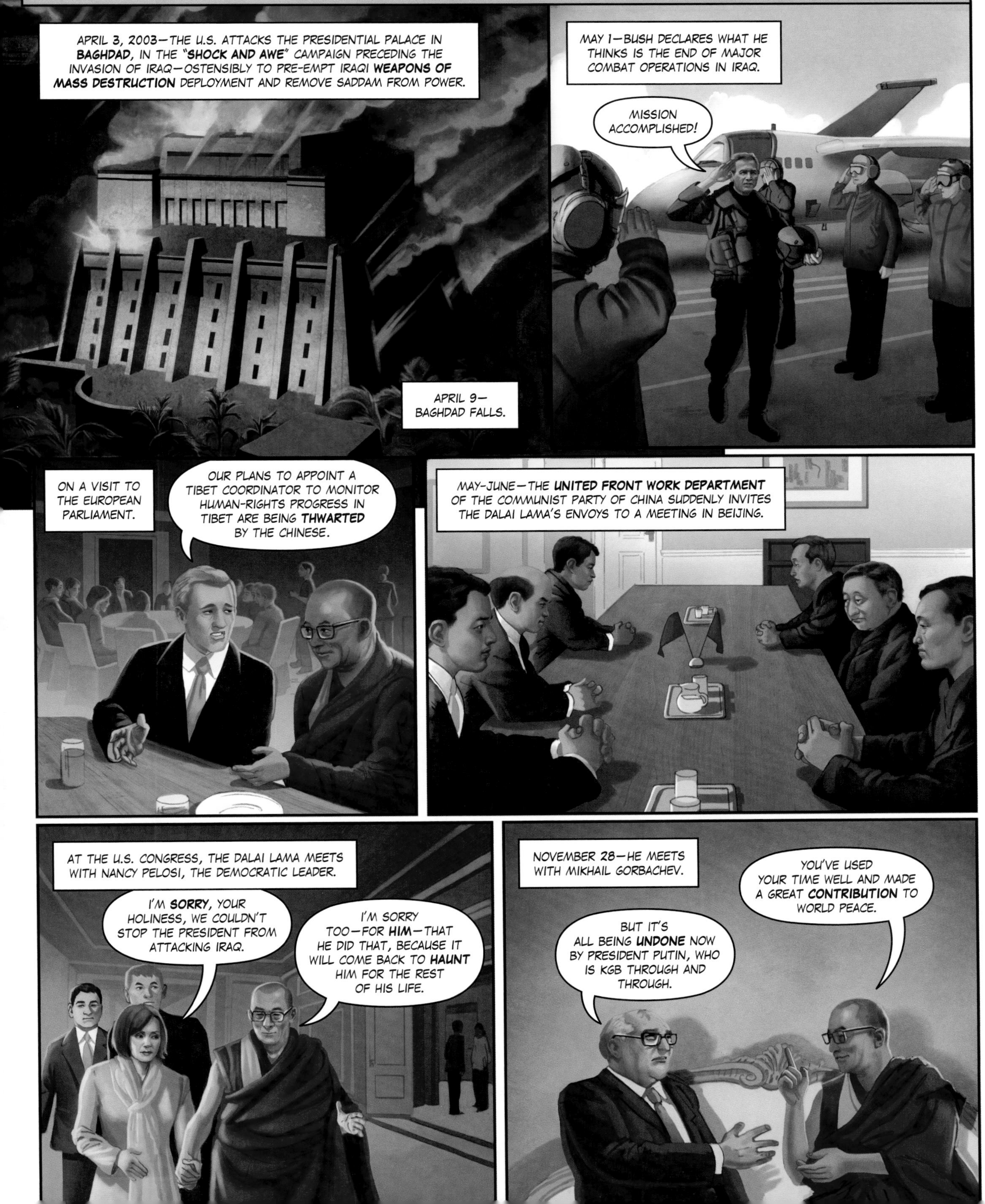

APRIL 3, 2003—THE U.S. ATTACKS THE PRESIDENTIAL PALACE IN BAGHDAD, IN THE "SHOCK AND AWE" CAMPAIGN PRECEDING THE INVASION OF IRAQ—OSTENSIBLY TO PRE-EMPT IRAQI WEAPONS OF MASS DESTRUCTION DEPLOYMENT AND REMOVE SADDAM FROM POWER.
APRIL 9— BAGHDAD FALLS.
MAY 1—BUSH DECLARES WHAT HE THINKS IS THE END OF MAJOR COMBAT OPERATIONS IN IRAQ.
MISSION ACCOMPLISHED!
ON A VISIT TO THE EUROPEAN PARLIAMENT.
OUR PLANS TO APPOINT A TIBET COORDINATOR TO MONITOR HUMAN-RIGHTS PROGRESS IN TIBET ARE BEING THWARTED BY THE CHINESE.
MAY-JUNE—THE UNITED FRONT WORK DEPARTMENT OF THE COMMUNIST PARTY OF CHINA SUDDENLY INVITES THE DALAI LAMA'S ENVOYS TO A MEETING IN BEIJING.
AT THE U.S. CONGRESS, THE DALAI LAMA MEETS WITH NANCY PELOSI, THE DEMOCRATIC LEADER.
I'M SORRY, YOUR HOLINESS, WE COULDN'T STOP THE PRESIDENT FROM ATTACKING IRAQ.
I'M SORRY TOO—FOR HIM—THAT HE DID THAT, BECAUSE IT WILL COME BACK TO HAUNT HIM FOR THE REST OF HIS LIFE.
NOVEMBER 28—HE MEETS WITH MIKHAIL GORBACHEV.
YOU'VE USED YOUR TIME WELL AND MADE A GREAT CONTRIBUTION TO WORLD PEACE.
BUT IT'S ALL BEING UNDONE NOW BY PRESIDENT PUTIN, WHO IS KGB THROUGH AND THROUGH.

MARCH 10, 2004: *"This year marks 50 years since my visit to mainland China in 1954 to meet with the then Chinese leaders, especially Mao Zedong. My hope is that this year may see a significant breakthrough. As in 1954, so today, I leave no stone unturned in seeking a mutually beneficial solution that will both address Chinese concerns and achieve for the Tibetan people a life of freedom, peace and dignity."*

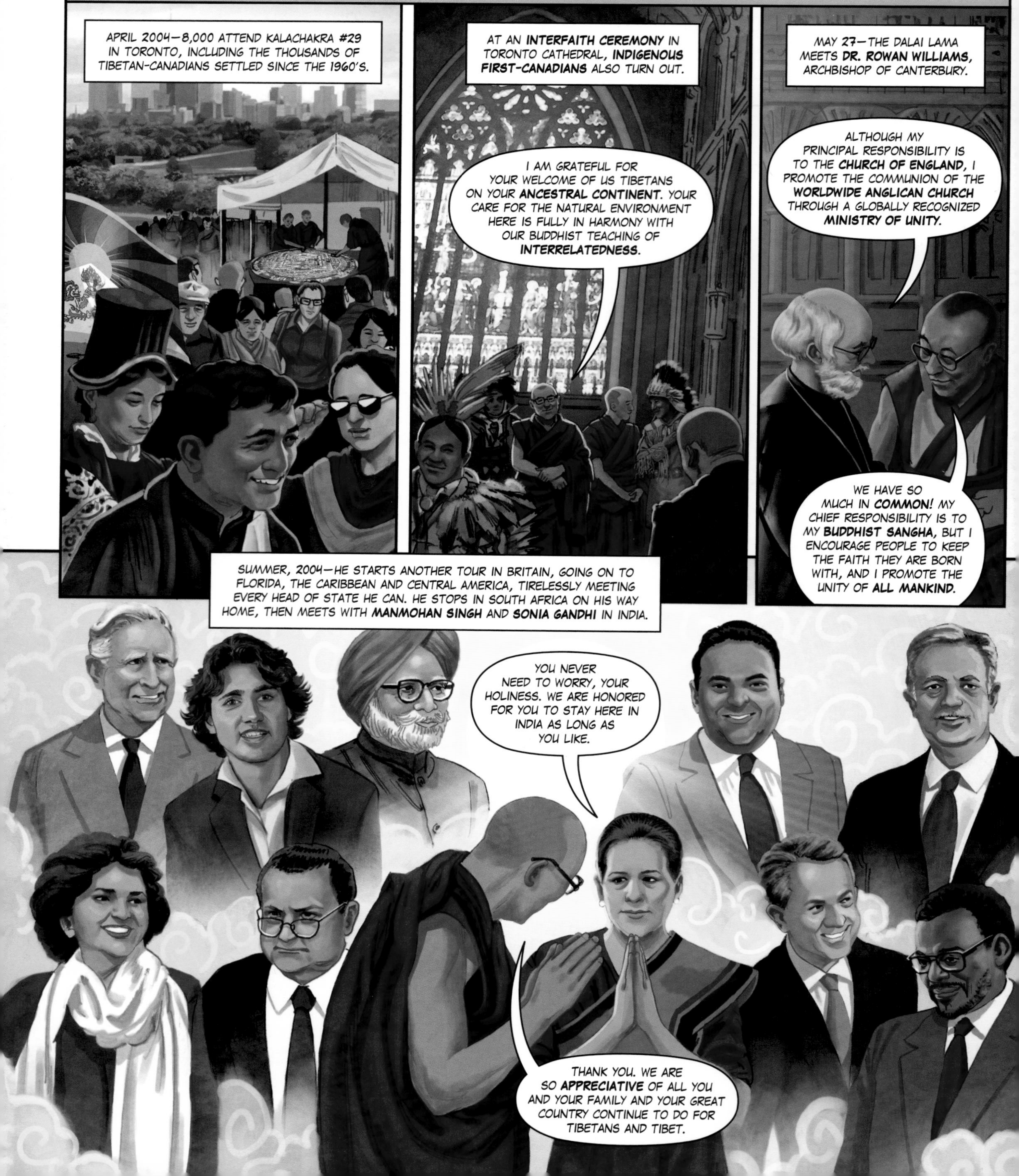
APRIL 2004—8,000 ATTEND KALACHAKRA #29 IN TORONTO, INCLUDING THE THOUSANDS OF TIBETAN-CANADIANS SETTLED SINCE THE 1960'S.
AT AN **INTERFAITH CEREMONY** IN TORONTO CATHEDRAL, **INDIGENOUS FIRST-CANADIANS** ALSO TURN OUT.
I AM GRATEFUL FOR YOUR WELCOME OF US TIBETANS ON YOUR **ANCESTRAL CONTINENT**. YOUR CARE FOR THE NATURAL ENVIRONMENT HERE IS FULLY IN HARMONY WITH OUR BUDDHIST TEACHING OF **INTERRELATEDNESS**.
MAY 27—THE DALAI LAMA MEETS **DR. ROWAN WILLIAMS**, ARCHBISHOP OF CANTERBURY.
ALTHOUGH MY PRINCIPAL RESPONSIBILITY IS TO THE **CHURCH OF ENGLAND**, I PROMOTE THE COMMUNION OF THE **WORLDWIDE ANGLICAN CHURCH** THROUGH A GLOBALLY RECOGNIZED **MINISTRY OF UNITY**.
WE HAVE SO MUCH IN **COMMON**! MY CHIEF RESPONSIBILITY IS TO MY **BUDDHIST SANGHA**, BUT I ENCOURAGE PEOPLE TO KEEP THE FAITH THEY ARE BORN WITH, AND I PROMOTE THE UNITY OF **ALL MANKIND**.
SUMMER, 2004—HE STARTS ANOTHER TOUR IN BRITAIN, GOING ON TO FLORIDA, THE CARIBBEAN AND CENTRAL AMERICA, TIRELESSLY MEETING EVERY HEAD OF STATE HE CAN. HE STOPS IN SOUTH AFRICA ON HIS WAY HOME, THEN MEETS WITH **MANMOHAN SINGH** AND **SONIA GANDHI** IN INDIA.
YOU NEVER NEED TO WORRY, YOUR HOLINESS. WE ARE HONORED FOR YOU TO STAY HERE IN INDIA AS LONG AS YOU LIKE.
THANK YOU. WE ARE SO **APPRECIATIVE** OF ALL YOU AND YOUR FAMILY AND YOUR GREAT COUNTRY CONTINUE TO DO FOR TIBETANS AND TIBET.

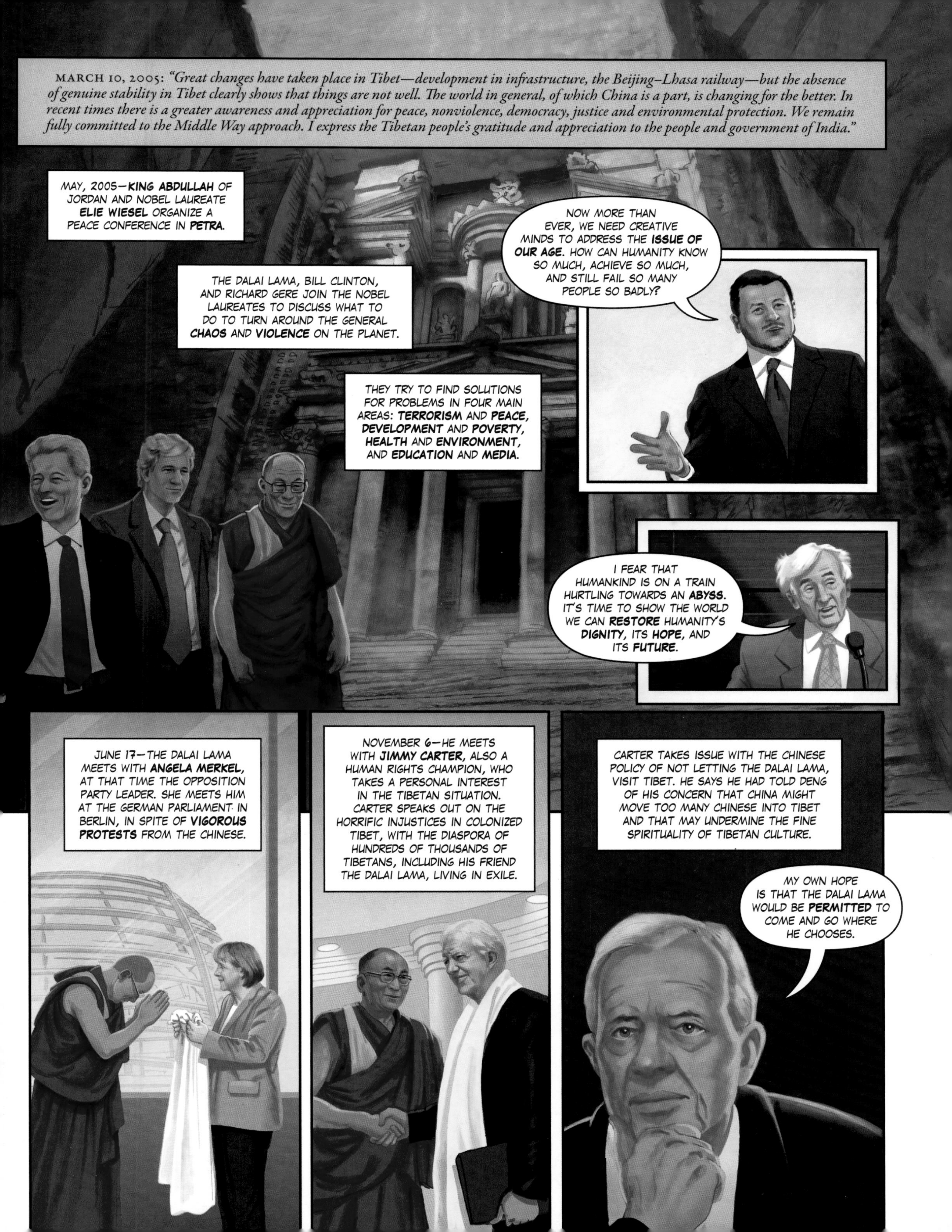
MARCH 10, 2005: "Great changes have taken place in Tibet—development in infrastructure, the Beijing–Lhasa railway—but the absence of genuine stability in Tibet clearly shows that things are not well. The world in general, of which China is a part, is changing for the better. In recent times there is a greater awareness and appreciation for peace, nonviolence, democracy, justice and environmental protection. We remain fully committed to the Middle Way approach. I express the Tibetan people's gratitude and appreciation to the people and government of India."
MAY, 2005—KING ABDULLAH OF JORDAN AND NOBEL LAUREATE ELIE WIESEL ORGANIZE A PEACE CONFERENCE IN PETRA.
THE DALAI LAMA, BILL CLINTON, AND RICHARD GERE JOIN THE NOBEL LAUREATES TO DISCUSS WHAT TO DO TO TURN AROUND THE GENERAL CHAOS AND VIOLENCE ON THE PLANET.
NOW MORE THAN EVER, WE NEED CREATIVE MINDS TO ADDRESS THE ISSUE OF OUR AGE. HOW CAN HUMANITY KNOW SO MUCH, ACHIEVE SO MUCH, AND STILL FAIL SO MANY PEOPLE SO BADLY?
THEY TRY TO FIND SOLUTIONS FOR PROBLEMS IN FOUR MAIN AREAS: TERRORISM AND PEACE, DEVELOPMENT AND POVERTY, HEALTH AND ENVIRONMENT, AND EDUCATION AND MEDIA.
I FEAR THAT HUMANKIND IS ON A TRAIN HURTLING TOWARDS AN ABYSS. IT'S TIME TO SHOW THE WORLD WE CAN RESTORE HUMANITY'S DIGNITY, ITS HOPE, AND ITS FUTURE.
JUNE 17—THE DALAI LAMA MEETS WITH ANGELA MERKEL, AT THAT TIME THE OPPOSITION PARTY LEADER. SHE MEETS HIM AT THE GERMAN PARLIAMENT IN BERLIN, IN SPITE OF VIGOROUS PROTESTS FROM THE CHINESE.
NOVEMBER 6—HE MEETS WITH JIMMY CARTER, ALSO A HUMAN RIGHTS CHAMPION, WHO TAKES A PERSONAL INTEREST IN THE TIBETAN SITUATION. CARTER SPEAKS OUT ON THE HORRIFIC INJUSTICES IN COLONIZED TIBET, WITH THE DIASPORA OF HUNDREDS OF THOUSANDS OF TIBETANS, INCLUDING HIS FRIEND THE DALAI LAMA, LIVING IN EXILE.
CARTER TAKES ISSUE WITH THE CHINESE POLICY OF NOT LETTING THE DALAI LAMA, VISIT TIBET. HE SAYS HE HAD TOLD DENG OF HIS CONCERN THAT CHINA MIGHT MOVE TOO MANY CHINESE INTO TIBET AND THAT MAY UNDERMINE THE FINE SPIRITUALITY OF TIBETAN CULTURE.
MY OWN HOPE IS THAT THE DALAI LAMA WOULD BE PERMITTED TO COME AND GO WHERE HE CHOOSES.

MARCH 10, 2006: *"In the fifth round of talks held in January 2006, my envoys reiterated my wish to visit China on a pilgrimage. I have only one demand: self-rule and genuine autonomy for all Tibetans—the Tibetan nationality in its entirety. The fundamental issue that must be addressed is that in tandem with political power and economic development, China must also follow the modern trend in terms of developing a more open society, a free press, and policy transparency. This, as every sensible person can see, is the foundation of genuine peace, harmony and stability."*

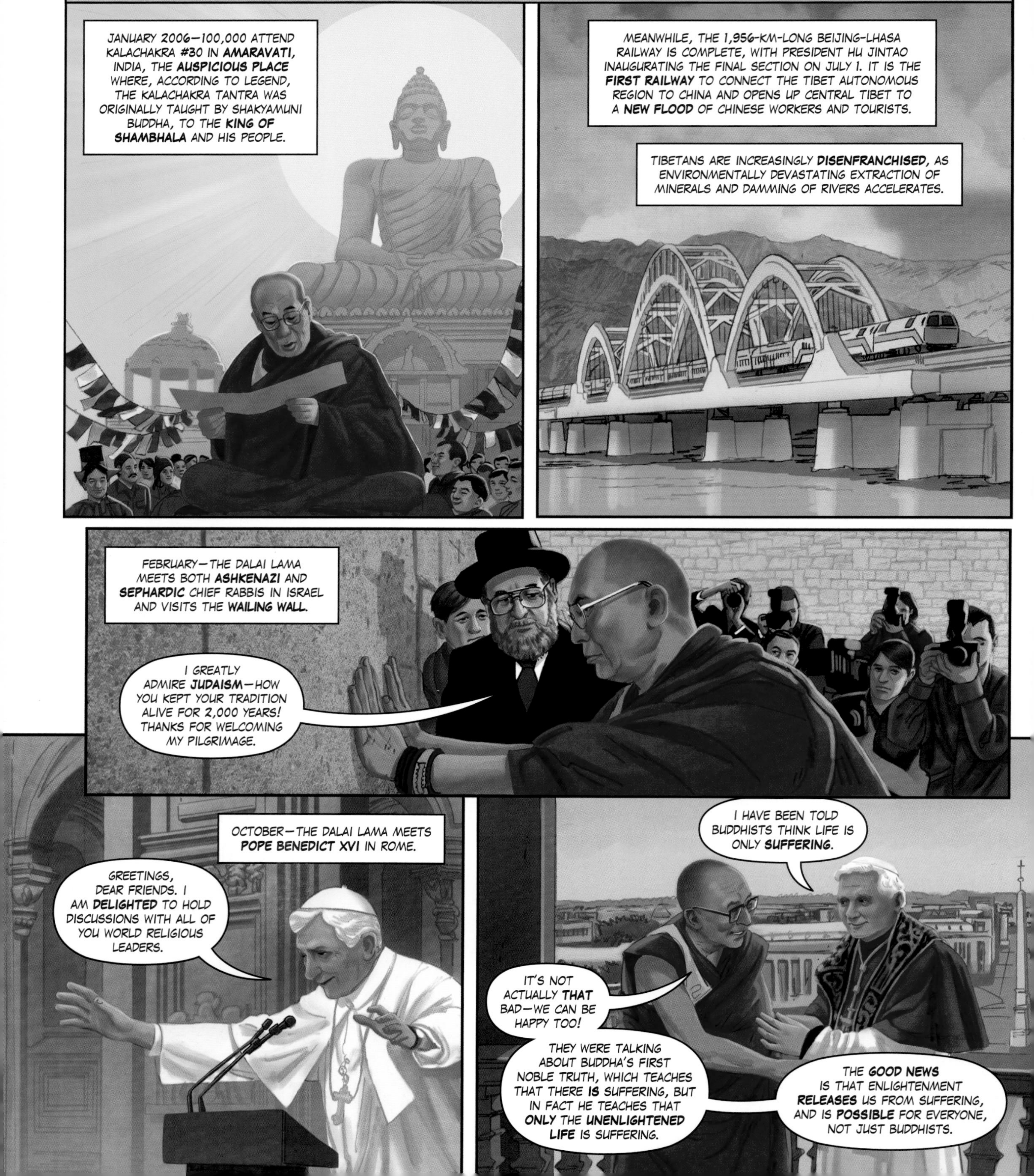
JANUARY 2006—100,000 ATTEND KALACHAKRA #30 IN AMARAVATI, INDIA, THE AUSPICIOUS PLACE WHERE, ACCORDING TO LEGEND, THE KALACHAKRA TANTRA WAS ORIGINALLY TAUGHT BY SHAKYAMUNI BUDDHA, TO THE KING OF SHAMBHALA AND HIS PEOPLE.
MEANWHILE, THE 1,956-KM-LONG BEIJING-LHASA RAILWAY IS COMPLETE, WITH PRESIDENT HU JINTAO INAUGURATING THE FINAL SECTION ON JULY 1. IT IS THE FIRST RAILWAY TO CONNECT THE TIBET AUTONOMOUS REGION TO CHINA AND OPENS UP CENTRAL TIBET TO A NEW FLOOD OF CHINESE WORKERS AND TOURISTS.
TIBETANS ARE INCREASINGLY DISENFRANCHISED, AS ENVIRONMENTALLY DEVASTATING EXTRACTION OF MINERALS AND DAMMING OF RIVERS ACCELERATES.
FEBRUARY—THE DALAI LAMA MEETS BOTH ASHKENAZI AND SEPHARDIC CHIEF RABBIS IN ISRAEL AND VISITS THE WAILING WALL.
I GREATLY ADMIRE JUDAISM—HOW YOU KEPT YOUR TRADITION ALIVE FOR 2,000 YEARS! THANKS FOR WELCOMING MY PILGRIMAGE.
OCTOBER—THE DALAI LAMA MEETS POPE BENEDICT XVI IN ROME.
GREETINGS, DEAR FRIENDS. I AM DELIGHTED TO HOLD DISCUSSIONS WITH ALL OF YOU WORLD RELIGIOUS LEADERS.
I HAVE BEEN TOLD BUDDHISTS THINK LIFE IS ONLY SUFFERING.
IT'S NOT ACTUALLY THAT BAD—WE CAN BE HAPPY TOO!
THEY WERE TALKING ABOUT BUDDHA'S FIRST NOBLE TRUTH, WHICH TEACHES THAT THERE IS SUFFERING, BUT IN FACT HE TEACHES THAT ONLY THE UNENLIGHTENED LIFE IS SUFFERING.
THE GOOD NEWS IS THAT ENLIGHTENMENT RELEASES US FROM SUFFERING, AND IS POSSIBLE FOR EVERYONE, NOT JUST BUDDHISTS.

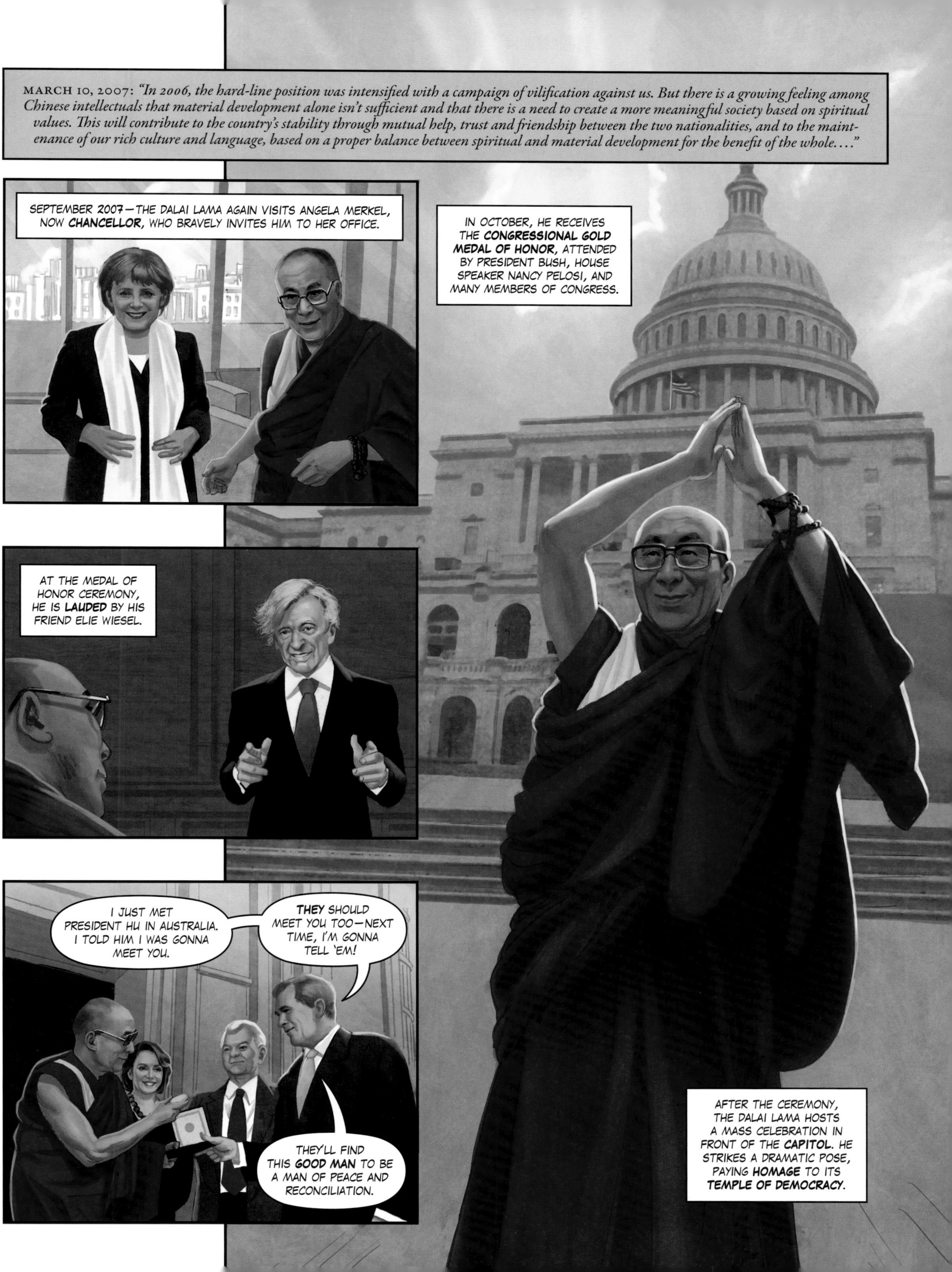
MARCH 10, 2007: "In 2006, the hard-line position was intensified with a campaign of vilification against us. But there is a growing feeling among Chinese intellectuals that material development alone isn't sufficient and that there is a need to create a more meaningful society based on spiritual values. This will contribute to the country's stability through mutual help, trust and friendship between the two nationalities, and to the maintenance of our rich culture and language, based on a proper balance between spiritual and material development for the benefit of the whole...."
SEPTEMBER 2007—THE DALAI LAMA AGAIN VISITS ANGELA MERKEL, NOW CHANCELLOR, WHO BRAVELY INVITES HIM TO HER OFFICE.
IN OCTOBER, HE RECEIVES THE CONGRESSIONAL GOLD MEDAL OF HONOR, ATTENDED BY PRESIDENT BUSH, HOUSE SPEAKER NANCY PELOSI, AND MANY MEMBERS OF CONGRESS.
AT THE MEDAL OF HONOR CEREMONY, HE IS LAUDED BY HIS FRIEND ELIE WIESEL.
I JUST MET PRESIDENT HU IN AUSTRALIA. I TOLD HIM I WAS GONNA MEET YOU.
THEY SHOULD MEET YOU TOO—NEXT TIME, I'M GONNA TELL 'EM!
THEY'LL FIND THIS GOOD MAN TO BE A MAN OF PEACE AND RECONCILIATION.
AFTER THE CEREMONY, THE DALAI LAMA HOSTS A MASS CELEBRATION IN FRONT OF THE CAPITOL. HE STRIKES A DRAMATIC POSE, PAYING HOMAGE TO ITS TEMPLE OF DEMOCRACY.

MARCH 10, 2007: *"... Tibet has seen a further increase in Chinese population transfer, deterioration of its environment, misuse and pollution of its water, and exploitation of its natural resources, all causing huge devastation to the land and all those who inhabit it. Our demand for a single administration of the Tibetan nationality is sincere, just and transparent. It is clear to the world that we have no hidden agenda."*

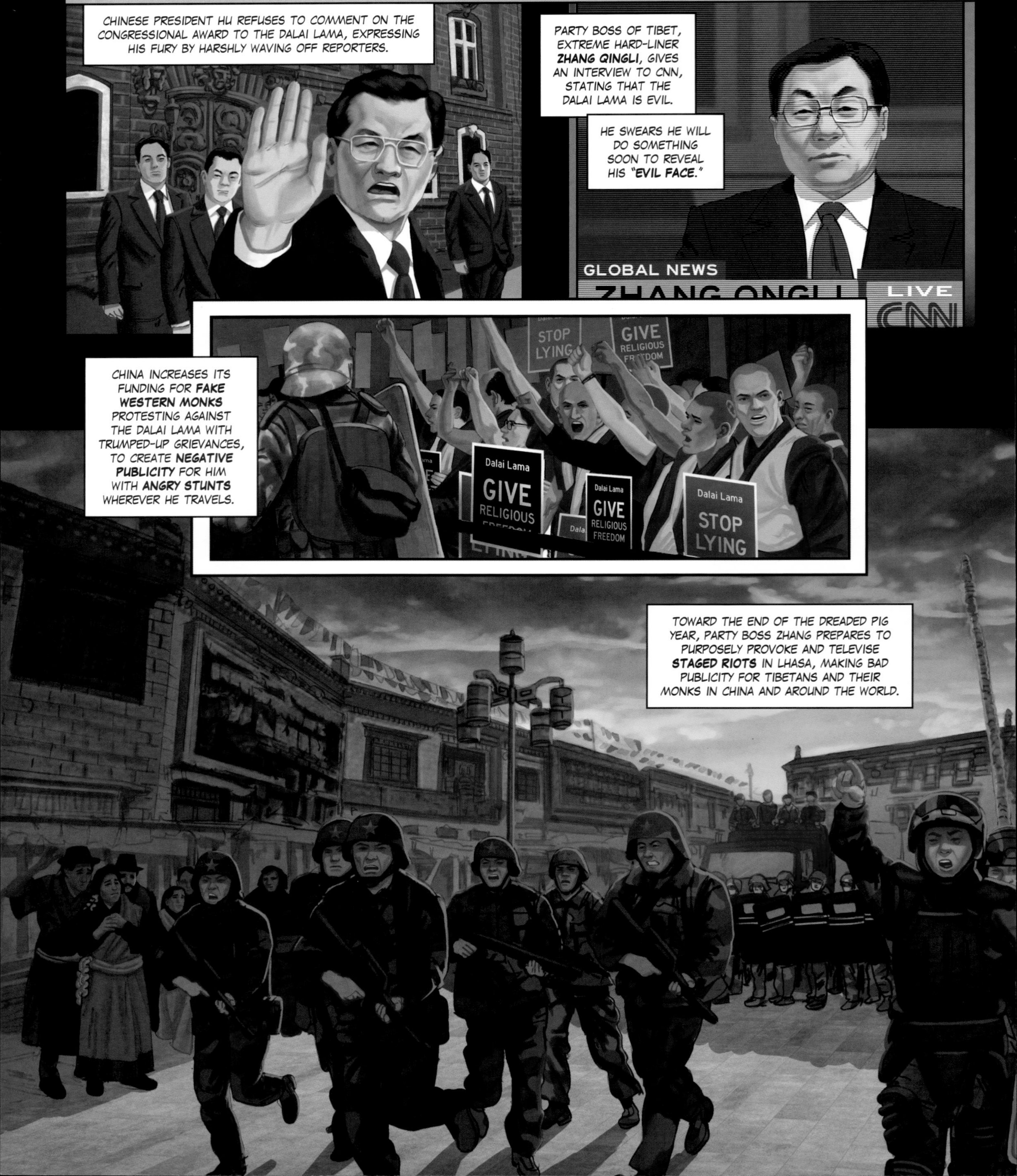

CHINESE PRESIDENT HU REFUSES TO COMMENT ON THE CONGRESSIONAL AWARD TO THE DALAI LAMA, EXPRESSING HIS FURY BY HARSHLY WAVING OFF REPORTERS.
PARTY BOSS OF TIBET, EXTREME HARD-LINER ZHANG QINGLI, GIVES AN INTERVIEW TO CNN, STATING THAT THE DALAI LAMA IS EVIL.
HE SWEARS HE WILL DO SOMETHING SOON TO REVEAL HIS "EVIL FACE."
GLOBAL NEWS
LIVE
CNN
CHINA INCREASES ITS FUNDING FOR FAKE WESTERN MONKS PROTESTING AGAINST THE DALAI LAMA WITH TRUMPED-UP GRIEVANCES, TO CREATE NEGATIVE PUBLICITY FOR HIM WITH ANGRY STUNTS WHEREVER HE TRAVELS.
STOP LYING
GIVE RELIGIOUS FREEDOM
Dalai Lama GIVE RELIGIOUS
Dalai Lama GIVE RELIGIOUS FREEDOM
Dalai Lama STOP LYING
TOWARD THE END OF THE DREADED PIG YEAR, PARTY BOSS ZHANG PREPARES TO PURPOSELY PROVOKE AND TELEVISE STAGED RIOTS IN LHASA, MAKING BAD PUBLICITY FOR TIBETANS AND THEIR MONKS IN CHINA AND AROUND THE WORLD.

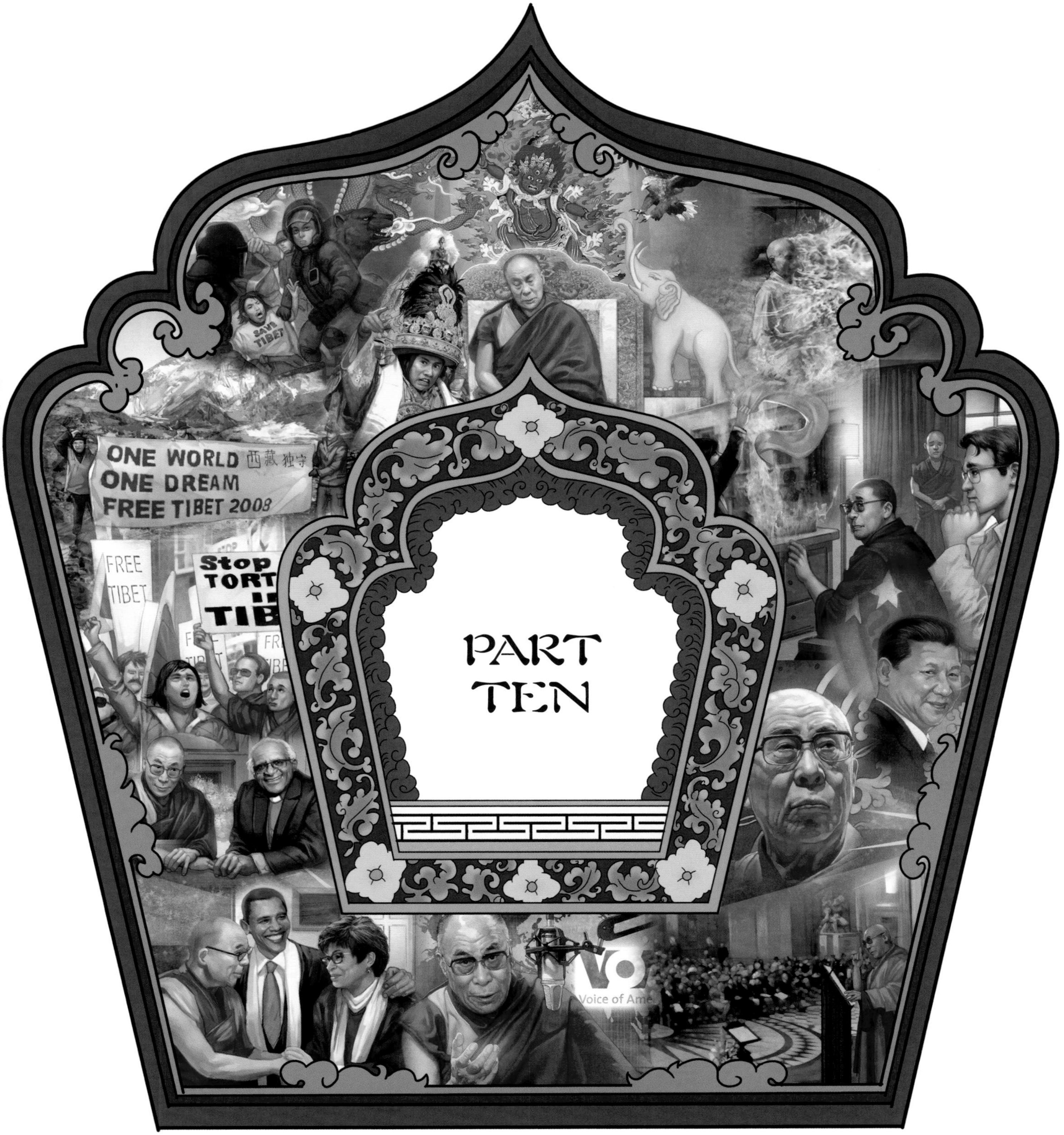
SAVE TIBET
ONE WORLD
ONE DREAM
FREE TIBET 2008
FREE TIBET

PART TEN

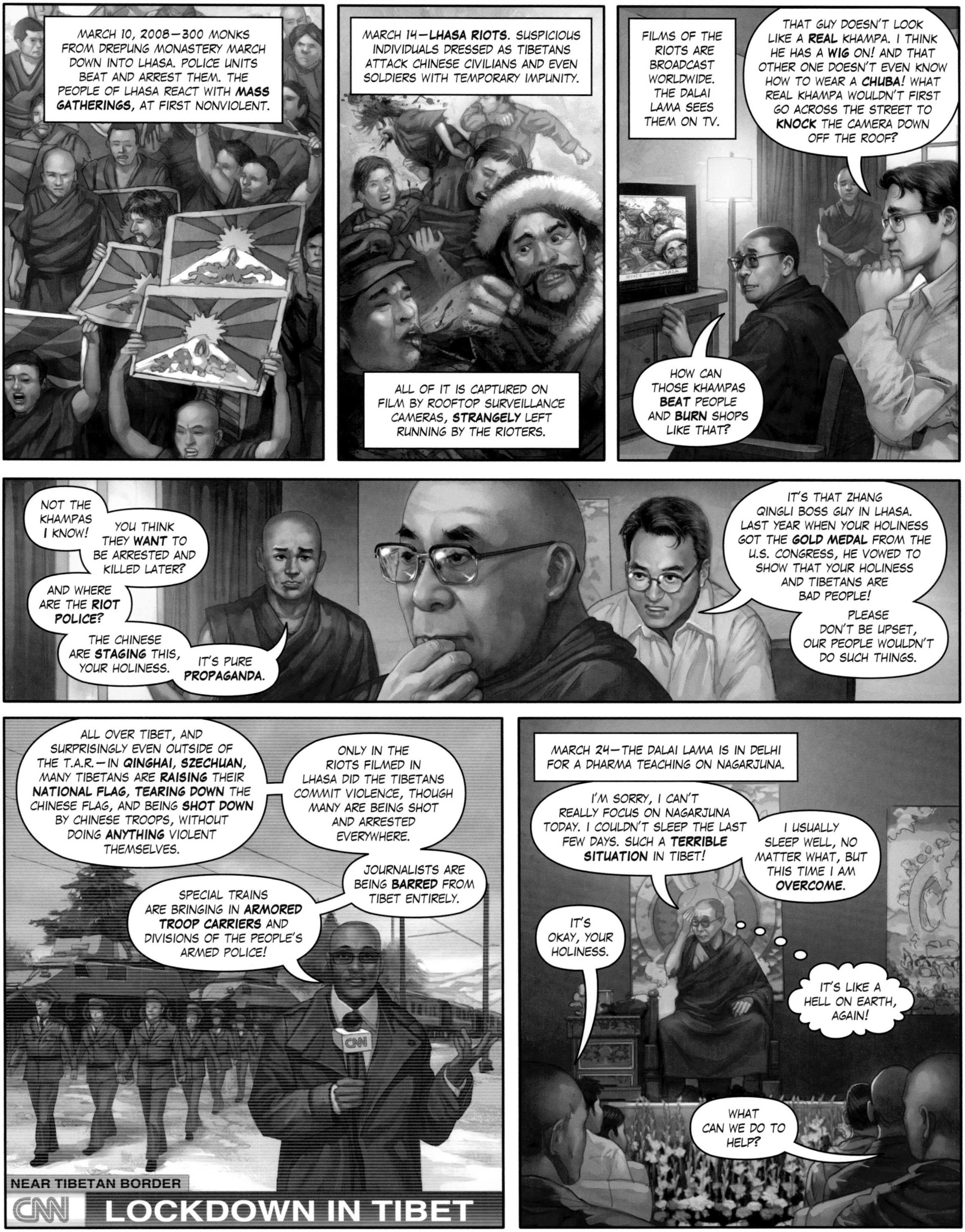
MARCH 10, 2008—300 MONKS FROM DREPUNG MONASTERY MARCH DOWN INTO LHASA. POLICE UNITS BEAT AND ARREST THEM. THE PEOPLE OF LHASA REACT WITH MASS GATHERINGS, AT FIRST NONVIOLENT.
MARCH 14—LHASA RIOTS. SUSPICIOUS INDIVIDUALS DRESSED AS TIBETANS ATTACK CHINESE CIVILIANS AND EVEN SOLDIERS WITH TEMPORARY IMPUNITY.
ALL OF IT IS CAPTURED ON FILM BY ROOFTOP SURVEILLANCE CAMERAS, STRANGELY LEFT RUNNING BY THE RIOTERS.
FILMS OF THE RIOTS ARE BROADCAST WORLDWIDE. THE DALAI LAMA SEES THEM ON TV.
HOW CAN THOSE KHAMPAS BEAT PEOPLE AND BURN SHOPS LIKE THAT?
THAT GUY DOESN'T LOOK LIKE A REAL KHAMPA. I THINK HE HAS A WIG ON! AND THAT OTHER ONE DOESN'T EVEN KNOW HOW TO WEAR A CHUBA! WHAT REAL KHAMPA WOULDN'T FIRST GO ACROSS THE STREET TO KNOCK THE CAMERA DOWN OFF THE ROOF?
NOT THE KHAMPAS I KNOW!
YOU THINK THEY WANT TO BE ARRESTED AND KILLED LATER?
AND WHERE ARE THE RIOT POLICE?
THE CHINESE ARE STAGING THIS, YOUR HOLINESS.
IT'S PURE PROPAGANDA.
IT'S THAT ZHANG QINGLI BOSS GUY IN LHASA. LAST YEAR WHEN YOUR HOLINESS GOT THE GOLD MEDAL FROM THE U.S. CONGRESS, HE VOWED TO SHOW THAT YOUR HOLINESS AND TIBETANS ARE BAD PEOPLE!
PLEASE DON'T BE UPSET, OUR PEOPLE WOULDN'T DO SUCH THINGS.
ALL OVER TIBET, AND SURPRISINGLY EVEN OUTSIDE OF THE T.A.R.—IN QINGHAI, SZECHUAN, MANY TIBETANS ARE RAISING THEIR NATIONAL FLAG, TEARING DOWN THE CHINESE FLAG, AND BEING SHOT DOWN BY CHINESE TROOPS, WITHOUT DOING ANYTHING VIOLENT THEMSELVES.
ONLY IN THE RIOTS FILMED IN LHASA DID THE TIBETANS COMMIT VIOLENCE, THOUGH MANY ARE BEING SHOT AND ARRESTED EVERYWHERE.
JOURNALISTS ARE BEING BARRED FROM TIBET ENTIRELY.
SPECIAL TRAINS ARE BRINGING IN ARMORED TROOP CARRIERS AND DIVISIONS OF THE PEOPLE'S ARMED POLICE!
CNN
NEAR TIBETAN BORDER
CNN LOCKDOWN IN TIBET
MARCH 24—THE DALAI LAMA IS IN DELHI FOR A DHARMA TEACHING ON NAGARJUNA.
I'M SORRY, I CAN'T REALLY FOCUS ON NAGARJUNA TODAY. I COULDN'T SLEEP THE LAST FEW DAYS. SUCH A TERRIBLE SITUATION IN TIBET!
I USUALLY SLEEP WELL, NO MATTER WHAT, BUT THIS TIME I AM OVERCOME.
IT'S OKAY, YOUR HOLINESS.
IT'S LIKE A HELL ON EARTH, AGAIN!
WHAT CAN WE DO TO HELP?

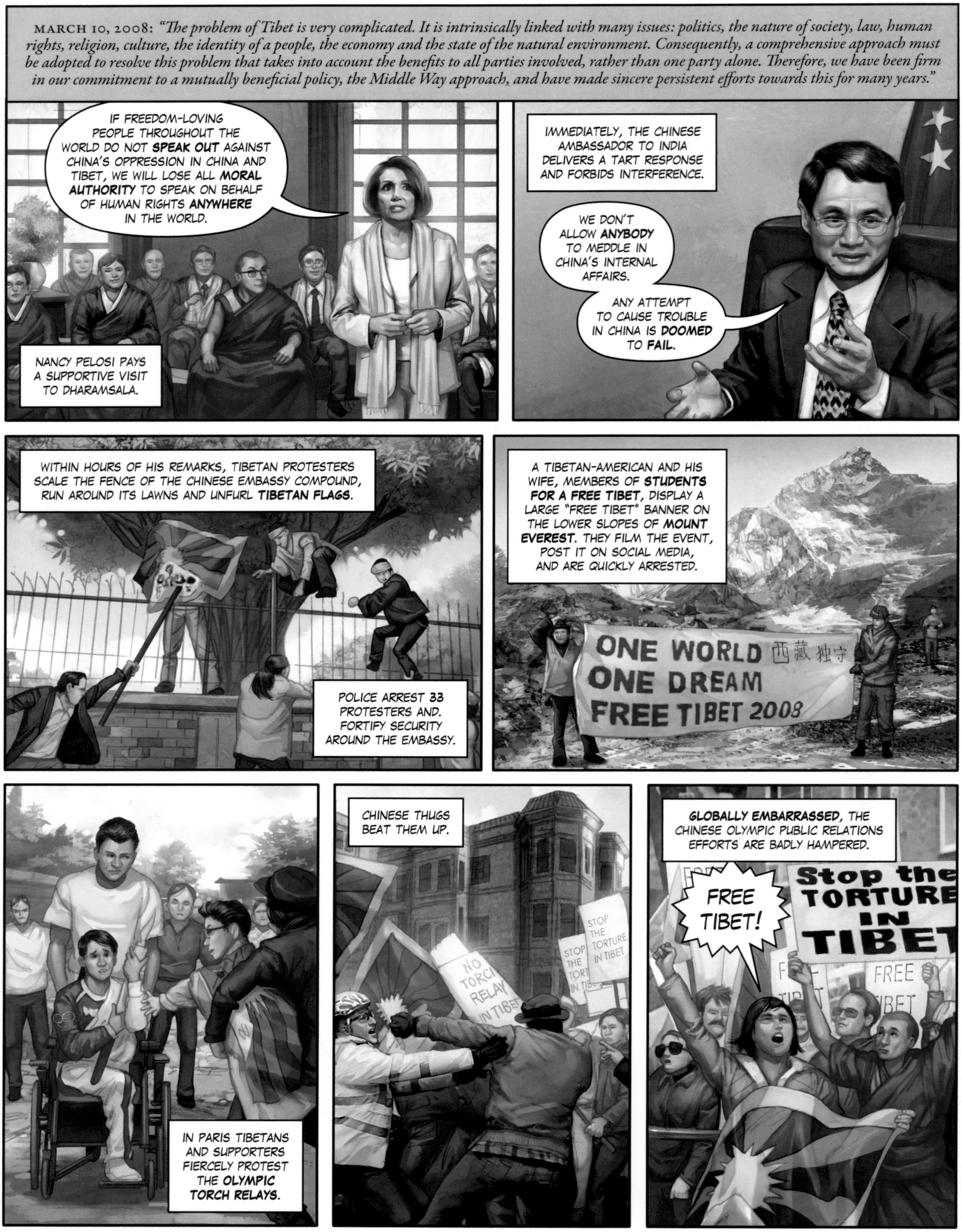
MARCH 10, 2008: *"The problem of Tibet is very complicated. It is intrinsically linked with many issues: politics, the nature of society, law, human rights, religion, culture, the identity of a people, the economy and the state of the natural environment. Consequently, a comprehensive approach must be adopted to resolve this problem that takes into account the benefits to all parties involved, rather than one party alone. Therefore, we have been firm in our commitment to a mutually beneficial policy, the Middle Way approach, and have made sincere persistent efforts towards this for many years."*
IF FREEDOM-LOVING PEOPLE THROUGHOUT THE WORLD DO NOT **SPEAK OUT** AGAINST CHINA'S OPPRESSION IN CHINA AND TIBET, WE WILL LOSE ALL **MORAL AUTHORITY** TO SPEAK ON BEHALF OF HUMAN RIGHTS **ANYWHERE** IN THE WORLD.
NANCY PELOSI PAYS A SUPPORTIVE VISIT TO DHARAMSALA.
IMMEDIATELY, THE CHINESE AMBASSADOR TO INDIA DELIVERS A TART RESPONSE AND FORBIDS INTERFERENCE.
WE DON'T ALLOW **ANYBODY** TO MEDDLE IN CHINA'S INTERNAL AFFAIRS.
ANY ATTEMPT TO CAUSE TROUBLE IN CHINA IS **DOOMED** TO **FAIL**.
WITHIN HOURS OF HIS REMARKS, TIBETAN PROTESTERS SCALE THE FENCE OF THE CHINESE EMBASSY COMPOUND, RUN AROUND ITS LAWNS AND UNFURL **TIBETAN FLAGS**.
POLICE ARREST **33** PROTESTERS AND. FORTIFY SECURITY AROUND THE EMBASSY.
A TIBETAN-AMERICAN AND HIS WIFE, MEMBERS OF **STUDENTS FOR A FREE TIBET**, DISPLAY A LARGE "FREE TIBET" BANNER ON THE LOWER SLOPES OF **MOUNT EVEREST**. THEY FILM THE EVENT, POST IT ON SOCIAL MEDIA, AND ARE QUICKLY ARRESTED.
ONE WORLD 西藏独守
ONE DREAM
FREE TIBET 2008
IN PARIS TIBETANS AND SUPPORTERS FIERCELY PROTEST THE **OLYMPIC TORCH RELAYS**.
CHINESE THUGS BEAT THEM UP.
NO TORCH RELAY IN TIBET
STOP THE TORTURE IN TIBET
STOP THE TORTURE IN TIBET
GLOBALLY EMBARRASSED, THE CHINESE OLYMPIC PUBLIC RELATIONS EFFORTS ARE BADLY HAMPERED.
FREE TIBET!
Stop the TORTURE IN TIBET
FREE TIBET
FREE TIBET

MARCH 10, 2009: *"We pay tribute and offer our prayers for all those who died, were tortured and suffered tremendous hardships. Having occupied Tibet, the Chinese Communist government carried out a series of repressive and violent campaigns that have included 'democratic' reform, class struggle, communes, the Cultural Revolution, the imposition of martial law, and more recently the patriotic reeducation and the 'strike hard' campaigns. These thrust Tibetans into such depths of suffering and hardship that they literally experienced hell on earth...."*

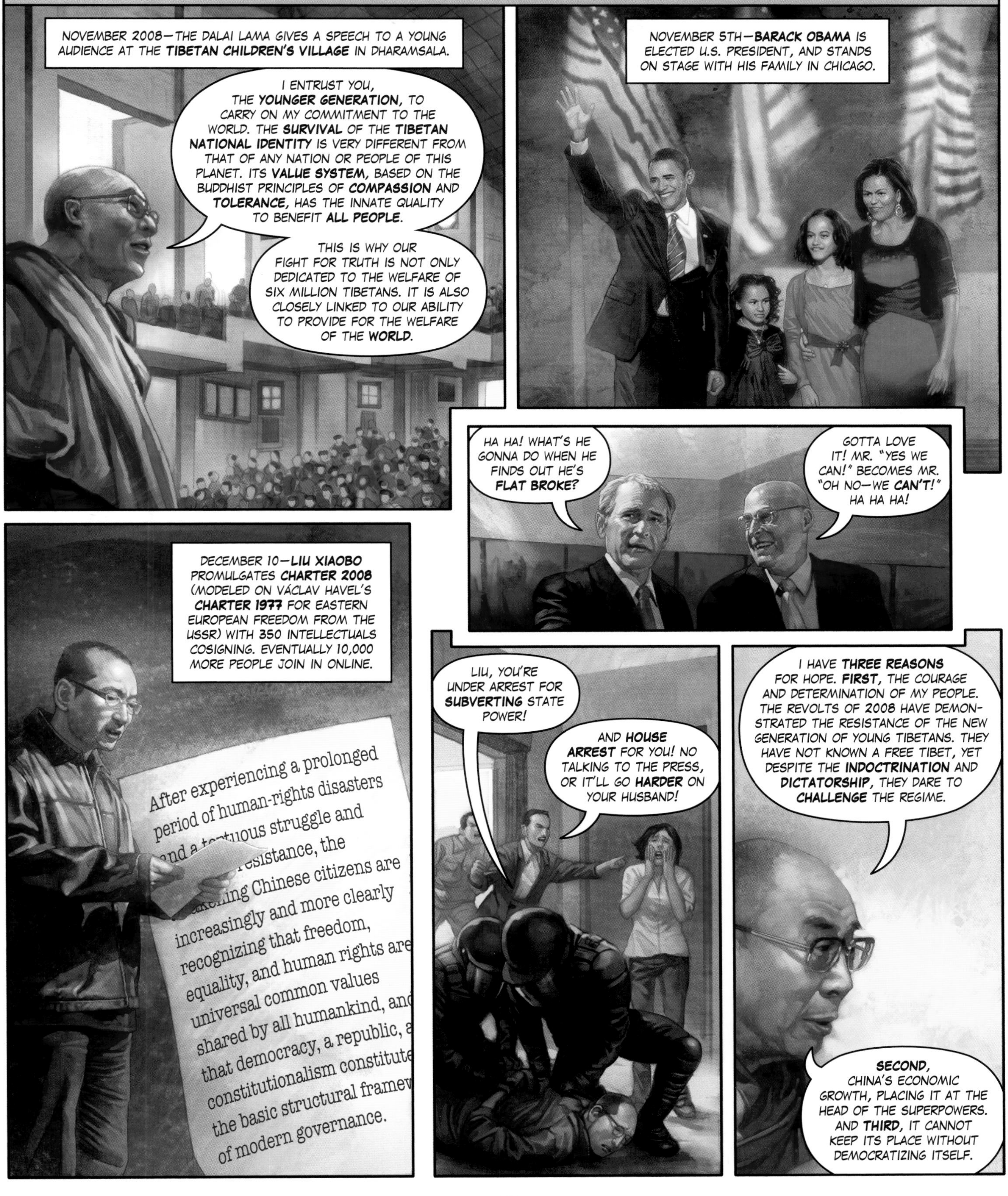
NOVEMBER 2008—THE DALAI LAMA GIVES A SPEECH TO A YOUNG AUDIENCE AT THE TIBETAN CHILDREN'S VILLAGE IN DHARAMSALA.
I ENTRUST YOU, THE YOUNGER GENERATION, TO CARRY ON MY COMMITMENT TO THE WORLD. THE SURVIVAL OF THE TIBETAN NATIONAL IDENTITY IS VERY DIFFERENT FROM THAT OF ANY NATION OR PEOPLE OF THIS PLANET. ITS VALUE SYSTEM, BASED ON THE BUDDHIST PRINCIPLES OF COMPASSION AND TOLERANCE, HAS THE INNATE QUALITY TO BENEFIT ALL PEOPLE.
THIS IS WHY OUR FIGHT FOR TRUTH IS NOT ONLY DEDICATED TO THE WELFARE OF SIX MILLION TIBETANS. IT IS ALSO CLOSELY LINKED TO OUR ABILITY TO PROVIDE FOR THE WELFARE OF THE WORLD.
NOVEMBER 5TH—BARACK OBAMA IS ELECTED U.S. PRESIDENT, AND STANDS ON STAGE WITH HIS FAMILY IN CHICAGO.
HA HA! WHAT'S HE GONNA DO WHEN HE FINDS OUT HE'S FLAT BROKE?
GOTTA LOVE IT! MR. "YES WE CAN!" BECOMES MR. "OH NO—WE CAN'T!" HA HA HA!
DECEMBER 10—LIU XIAOBO PROMULGATES CHARTER 2008 (MODELED ON VÁCLAV HAVEL'S CHARTER 1977 FOR EASTERN EUROPEAN FREEDOM FROM THE USSR) WITH 350 INTELLECTUALS COSIGNING. EVENTUALLY 10,000 MORE PEOPLE JOIN IN ONLINE.
After experiencing a prolonged
period of human-rights disasters
and a tortuous struggle and
resistance, the
Chinese citizens are
increasingly and more clearly
recognizing that freedom,
equality, and human rights are
universal common values
shared by all humankind, and
that democracy, a republic, a
constitutionalism constitute
the basic structural framew
of modern governance.
LIU, YOU'RE UNDER ARREST FOR SUBVERTING STATE POWER!
AND HOUSE ARREST FOR YOU! NO TALKING TO THE PRESS, OR IT'LL GO HARDER ON YOUR HUSBAND!
I HAVE THREE REASONS FOR HOPE. FIRST, THE COURAGE AND DETERMINATION OF MY PEOPLE. THE REVOLTS OF 2008 HAVE DEMON-STRATED THE RESISTANCE OF THE NEW GENERATION OF YOUNG TIBETANS. THEY HAVE NOT KNOWN A FREE TIBET, YET DESPITE THE INDOCTRINATION AND DICTATORSHIP, THEY DARE TO CHALLENGE THE REGIME.
SECOND, CHINA'S ECONOMIC GROWTH, PLACING IT AT THE HEAD OF THE SUPERPOWERS. AND THIRD, IT CANNOT KEEP ITS PLACE WITHOUT DEMOCRATIZING ITSELF.

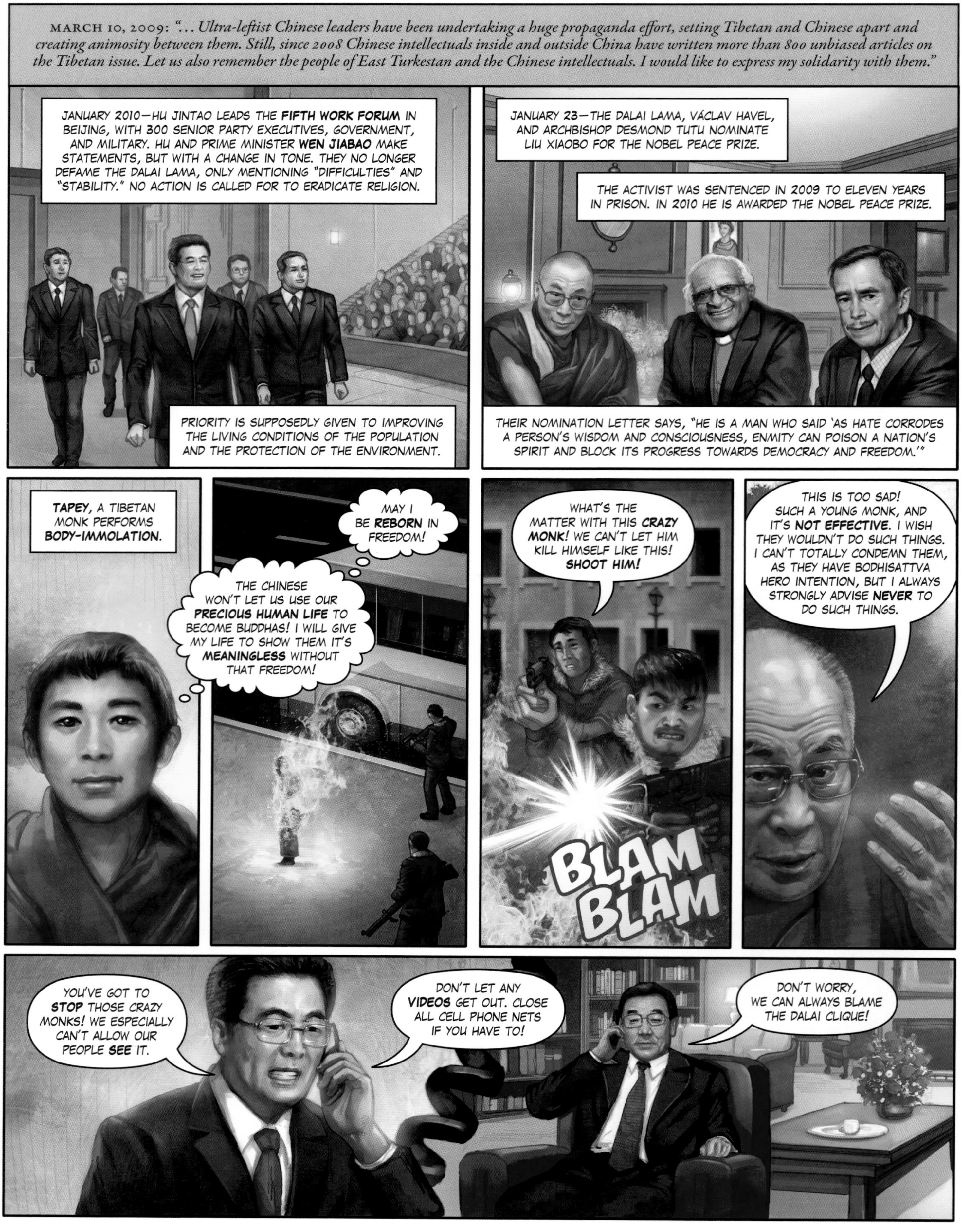
MARCH 10, 2009: "... Ultra-leftist Chinese leaders have been undertaking a huge propaganda effort, setting Tibetan and Chinese apart and creating animosity between them. Still, since 2008 Chinese intellectuals inside and outside China have written more than 800 unbiased articles on the Tibetan issue. Let us also remember the people of East Turkestan and the Chinese intellectuals. I would like to express my solidarity with them."
JANUARY 2010—HU JINTAO LEADS THE FIFTH WORK FORUM IN BEIJING, WITH 300 SENIOR PARTY EXECUTIVES, GOVERNMENT, AND MILITARY. HU AND PRIME MINISTER WEN JIABAO MAKE STATEMENTS, BUT WITH A CHANGE IN TONE. THEY NO LONGER DEFAME THE DALAI LAMA, ONLY MENTIONING "DIFFICULTIES" AND "STABILITY." NO ACTION IS CALLED FOR TO ERADICATE RELIGION.
PRIORITY IS SUPPOSEDLY GIVEN TO IMPROVING THE LIVING CONDITIONS OF THE POPULATION AND THE PROTECTION OF THE ENVIRONMENT.
JANUARY 23—THE DALAI LAMA, VÁCLAV HAVEL, AND ARCHBISHOP DESMOND TUTU NOMINATE LIU XIAOBO FOR THE NOBEL PEACE PRIZE.
THE ACTIVIST WAS SENTENCED IN 2009 TO ELEVEN YEARS IN PRISON. IN 2010 HE IS AWARDED THE NOBEL PEACE PRIZE.
THEIR NOMINATION LETTER SAYS, "HE IS A MAN WHO SAID 'AS HATE CORRODES A PERSON'S WISDOM AND CONSCIOUSNESS, ENMITY CAN POISON A NATION'S SPIRIT AND BLOCK ITS PROGRESS TOWARDS DEMOCRACY AND FREEDOM.'"
TAPEY, A TIBETAN MONK PERFORMS BODY-IMMOLATION.
MAY I BE REBORN IN FREEDOM!
THE CHINESE WON'T LET US USE OUR PRECIOUS HUMAN LIFE TO BECOME BUDDHAS! I WILL GIVE MY LIFE TO SHOW THEM IT'S MEANINGLESS WITHOUT THAT FREEDOM!
WHAT'S THE MATTER WITH THIS CRAZY MONK! WE CAN'T LET HIM KILL HIMSELF LIKE THIS! SHOOT HIM!
BLAM BLAM
THIS IS TOO SAD! SUCH A YOUNG MONK, AND IT'S NOT EFFECTIVE. I WISH THEY WOULDN'T DO SUCH THINGS. I CAN'T TOTALLY CONDEMN THEM, AS THEY HAVE BODHISATTVA HERO INTENTION, BUT I ALWAYS STRONGLY ADVISE NEVER TO DO SUCH THINGS.
YOU'VE GOT TO STOP THOSE CRAZY MONKS! WE ESPECIALLY CAN'T ALLOW OUR PEOPLE SEE IT.
DON'T LET ANY VIDEOS GET OUT. CLOSE ALL CELL PHONE NETS IF YOU HAVE TO!
DON'T WORRY, WE CAN ALWAYS BLAME THE DALAI CLIQUE!

MARCH 10, 2010: *"There will be a time when truth will prevail. Therefore, it is important that everyone not give up. The PRC's new decision* [to treat the plateau as a whole] *accords with our wish for a single administration for all Tibetan areas. We must be vigilant that progress does not damage our precious culture and language, and the natural environment of the Tibetan plateau, which is linked to the well-being of the whole of Asia."*

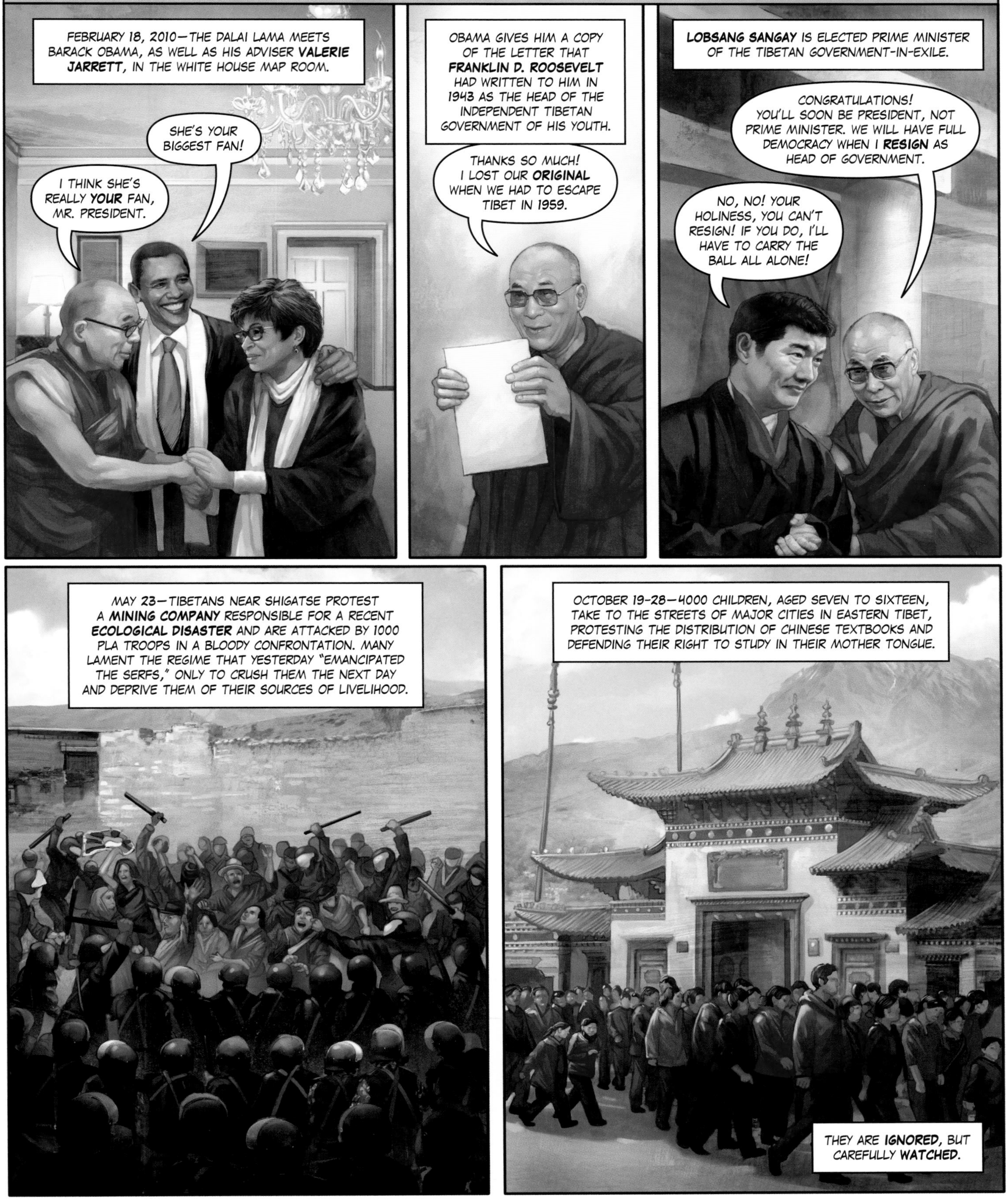

FEBRUARY 18, 2010—THE DALAI LAMA MEETS BARACK OBAMA, AS WELL AS HIS ADVISER VALERIE JARRETT, IN THE WHITE HOUSE MAP ROOM.
SHE'S YOUR BIGGEST FAN!
I THINK SHE'S REALLY YOUR FAN, MR. PRESIDENT.
OBAMA GIVES HIM A COPY OF THE LETTER THAT FRANKLIN D. ROOSEVELT HAD WRITTEN TO HIM IN 1943 AS THE HEAD OF THE INDEPENDENT TIBETAN GOVERNMENT OF HIS YOUTH.
THANKS SO MUCH! I LOST OUR ORIGINAL WHEN WE HAD TO ESCAPE TIBET IN 1959.
LOBSANG SANGAY IS ELECTED PRIME MINISTER OF THE TIBETAN GOVERNMENT-IN-EXILE.
CONGRATULATIONS! YOU'LL SOON BE PRESIDENT, NOT PRIME MINISTER. WE WILL HAVE FULL DEMOCRACY WHEN I RESIGN AS HEAD OF GOVERNMENT.
NO, NO! YOUR HOLINESS, YOU CAN'T RESIGN! IF YOU DO, I'LL HAVE TO CARRY THE BALL ALL ALONE!
MAY 23—TIBETANS NEAR SHIGATSE PROTEST A MINING COMPANY RESPONSIBLE FOR A RECENT ECOLOGICAL DISASTER AND ARE ATTACKED BY 1000 PLA TROOPS IN A BLOODY CONFRONTATION. MANY LAMENT THE REGIME THAT YESTERDAY "EMANCIPATED THE SERFS," ONLY TO CRUSH THEM THE NEXT DAY AND DEPRIVE THEM OF THEIR SOURCES OF LIVELIHOOD.
OCTOBER 19–28—4000 CHILDREN, AGED SEVEN TO SIXTEEN, TAKE TO THE STREETS OF MAJOR CITIES IN EASTERN TIBET, PROTESTING THE DISTRIBUTION OF CHINESE TEXTBOOKS AND DEFENDING THEIR RIGHT TO STUDY IN THEIR MOTHER TONGUE.
THEY ARE IGNORED, BUT CAREFULLY WATCHED.

I MUST SET AN **EXAMPLE** OF GIVING UP POWER, RESIGNING POLITICAL LEADERSHIP. I WANT TO SHOW THAT POWER IS **NOT** THE BE-ALL AND END-ALL.
I MUST NOW RESIGN AS **POLITICAL HEAD** OF THE GOVERNMENT-IN-EXILE, ENDING THE GANDEN PALACE GOVERNMENT CREATED BY THE GREAT FIFTH DALAI LAMA. WE HAVE WRITTEN INTO OUR **CONSTITUTION** THAT WE WILL HAVE A NEW, AUTONOMOUS, DEMOCRATIC, ALL-TIBETAN LOCAL GOVERNMENT. THERE WILL BE NO DALAI LAMA HEAD—THE PRESIDENT WILL BE **ELECTED** BY THE **PEOPLE**.
PLEASE DON'T RESIGN, YOUR HOLINESS! WE STILL **NEED** YOU!

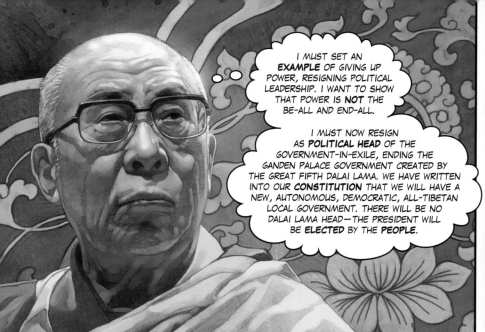

MARCH 10, 2011: "Today marks the 52nd anniversary of the Tibetan people's peaceful uprising of 1959 against Communist China's repression in the Tibetan capital of Lhasa, and the third anniversary of the nonviolent demonstrations that took place across Tibet in 2008. On this occasion, I would like to pay tribute to and pray for those brave men and women who sacrificed their lives for the just cause of Tibet. I express my solidarity with those who continue to suffer repression and pray for the well-being of all sentient beings.

"For more than sixty years, Tibetans, despite being deprived of freedom and living in fear and insecurity, have been able to maintain their unique Tibetan identity and cultural values. More consequentially, successive new generations, who have no experience of free Tibet, have courageously taken responsibility in advancing the cause of Tibet. This is admirable, for they exemplify the strength of Tibetan resilience.

"This Earth belongs to humanity, and the People's Republic of China (the PRC) belongs to its 1.3 billion citizens, who have the right to know the truth about the state of affairs in their country and the world at large. If citizens are fully informed, they have the ability to distinguish right from wrong. Censorship and the restriction of information violate basic human decency. For instance, China's leaders consider the communist ideology and its policies to be correct. If this were so, these policies should be made public with confidence and open to scrutiny. China, with the world's largest population, is an emerging world power, and I admire the economic development it has made. It also has huge potential to contribute to human progress and world peace. But to do that, China must earn the international community's respect and trust. In order to earn such respect, China's leaders must develop greater transparency, their actions corresponding to their words. To ensure this, freedom of expression and freedom of the press are essential. Similarly, transparency in governance can help check corruption. In recent years, China has seen an increasing number of intellectuals calling for political reform and greater openness. Premier Wen Jiabao has also expressed support for these concerns. These are significant indications, and I welcome them.

"The PRC is a country comprising many nationalities, enriched by a diversity of languages and cultures. Protection of the language and culture of each nationality is a policy of the PRC, which is clearly spelled out in its constitution. Tibetan is the only language to preserve the entire range of the Buddha's teachings, including the texts on logic and theories of knowledge (epistemology), which we inherited from India's Nalanda University. This is a system of knowledge governed by reason and logic that has the potential to contribute to the peace and happiness of all beings. Therefore, the policy of undermining such a culture, instead of protecting and developing it, will in the long run amount to the destruction of humanity's common heritage.

"The Chinese government frequently states that stability and development in Tibet is the foundation for its long-term well-being. However, the authorities still station large numbers of troops all across Tibet, increasing restrictions on the Tibetan people. Tibetans live in constant fear and anxiety. More recently, many Tibetan intellectuals, public figures and environmentalists have been punished for articulating the Tibetan people's basic aspirations. They have been imprisoned allegedly for "subverting state power" when actually they have been giving voice to the Tibetan identity and cultural heritage. Such repressive measures undermine unity and stability. Likewise, in China, lawyers defending people's rights, independent writers and human rights activists have been arrested. I strongly urge the Chinese leaders to review these developments and release these prisoners of conscience forthwith.

"The Chinese government claims there is no problem in Tibet other than the personal privileges and status of the Dalai Lama. The reality is that the ongoing oppression of the Tibetan people has provoked widespread, deep resentment against current official policies. People from all walks of life frequently express their discontentment. That there is a problem in Tibet is reflected in the Chinese authorities' failure to trust Tibetans or win their loyalty. Instead, the Tibetan people live under constant suspicion and surveillance. Chinese and foreign visitors to Tibet corroborate this grim reality.

"Therefore, just as we were able to send fact-finding delegations to Tibet in the late 1970s and early 1980s from among Tibetans in exile, we propose similar visits again. At the same time, we would encourage the sending of representatives of independent international bodies, including parliamentarians. If they were to find that Tibetans in Tibet are happy, we would readily accept it.

DON'T WORRY, I WILL HELP YOU AS **ADVISER**. WE MUST LIVE BY OUR PRINCIPLES. IT IS CRITICAL FOR OUR **MISSION** THAT WE SHOW HOW **REAL POWER** IS NOT JUST CLINGING TO OFFICE.
I DON'T WANT TO BE A **HYPOCRITE** AND TALK ABOUT DEMOCRACY WHILE HOLDING ON TO POWER. IT'S ESPECIALLY GOOD TO LEAVE WHILE STILL QUITE **POPULAR**!

The spirit of realism that prevailed under Mao's leadership in the early 1950s led China to sign the 17-point agreement with Tibet. A similar spirit of realism prevailed once more during Hu Yaobang's time in the early 1980s. If there had been a continuation of such realism, the Tibetan issue, as well as several other problems, could easily have been solved. Unfortunately, conservative views derailed these policies. The result is that after more than six decades, the problem has become more intractable.

"The Tibetan Plateau is the source of the major rivers of Asia. Because it has the largest concentration of glaciers apart from the two Poles, it is considered to be the Third Pole. Environmental degradation in Tibet will have a detrimental impact on large parts of Asia, particularly on China and the Indian subcontinent. Both the central and local governments, as well as the Chinese public, should be aware of the degradation of the Tibetan environment and develop sustainable measures to safeguard it. I appeal to China to take into account the survival of people affected by what happens environmentally on the Tibetan Plateau.

"In our efforts to solve the issue of Tibet, we have consistently pursued the mutually beneficial Middle Way Approach, which seeks genuine autonomy for the Tibetan people within the PRC. In our talks with officials of the Chinese government's United Front Work Department, we have clearly explained in detail the Tibetan people's hopes and aspirations. The lack of any positive response to our reasonable proposals makes us wonder whether these were fully and accurately conveyed to the higher authorities.

"Since ancient times, Tibetan and Chinese peoples have lived as neighbors. It would be a mistake if our unresolved differences were to affect this age-old friendship. Special efforts are being made to promote good relations between Tibetans and Chinese living abroad, and I am happy that this has contributed to better understanding and friendship between us. Tibetans inside Tibet should also cultivate good relations with our Chinese brothers and sisters.

In recent weeks we have witnessed remarkable nonviolent struggles for freedom and democracy in various parts of North Africa and elsewhere. I am a firm believer in nonviolence and people power, and these events have shown once again that determined nonviolent action can indeed bring about positive change. We must all hope that these inspiring changes lead to genuine freedom, happiness and prosperity for the peoples in these countries.

"One of the aspirations I have cherished since childhood is the reform of Tibet's political and social structure, and in the few years when I held effective power in Tibet, I managed to make some fundamental changes. Although I was unable to take this further in Tibet, I have made every effort to do so since we came into exile. Today, within the framework of the Charter for Tibetans in Exile, the Kalon Tripa, the political leadership and the people's representatives are directly elected by the people. We have been able to implement democracy in exile that is in keeping with the standards of an open society.

"As early as the 1960s, I have repeatedly stressed that Tibetans need a leader, elected freely by the Tibetan people, to whom I can devolve power. Now, we have clearly reached the time to put this into effect. During the forthcoming eleventh session of the fourteenth Tibetan Parliament in Exile, which begins on the 14th of March, I will formally propose that the necessary amendments be made to the Charter for Tibetans in Exile, reflecting my decision to devolve my formal authority to the elected leader.

"Since I made my intention clear, I have received repeated and earnest requests from both within Tibet and outside, to continue to provide political leadership. My desire to devolve authority has nothing to do with a wish to shirk responsibility. It is to benefit Tibetans in the long run. It is not because I feel disheartened. Tibetans have placed such faith and trust in me that as one among them I am committed to playing my part in the just cause of Tibet. I trust that gradually people will come to understand my intention, will support my decision and accordingly let it take effect.

"I would like to take this opportunity to remember the kindness of the leaders of various nations that cherish justice, members of parliaments, intellectuals and Tibet support groups, who have been steadfast in their support for the Tibetan people. In particular, we will always remember the kindness and consistent support of the people and Government of India and State Governments for generously helping Tibetans preserve and promote their religion and culture and ensuring the welfare of Tibetans in exile. To all of them I offer my heartfelt gratitude."

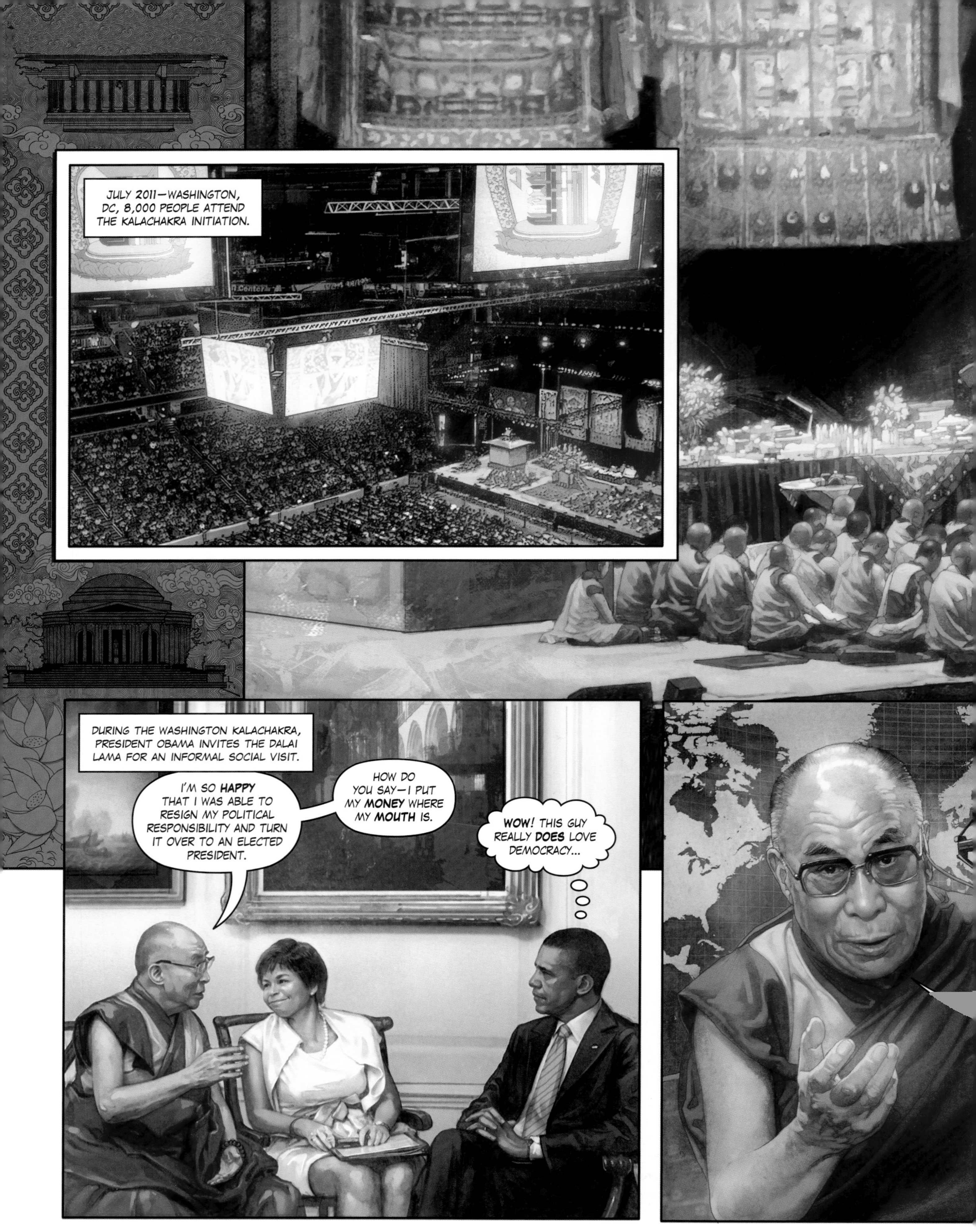

JULY 2011—WASHINGTON, DC, 8,000 PEOPLE ATTEND THE KALACHAKRA INITIATION.
DURING THE WASHINGTON KALACHAKRA, PRESIDENT OBAMA INVITES THE DALAI LAMA FOR AN INFORMAL SOCIAL VISIT.
I'M SO HAPPY THAT I WAS ABLE TO RESIGN MY POLITICAL RESPONSIBILITY AND TURN IT OVER TO AN ELECTED PRESIDENT.
HOW DO YOU SAY—I PUT MY MONEY WHERE MY MOUTH IS.
WOW! THIS GUY REALLY DOES LOVE DEMOCRACY...

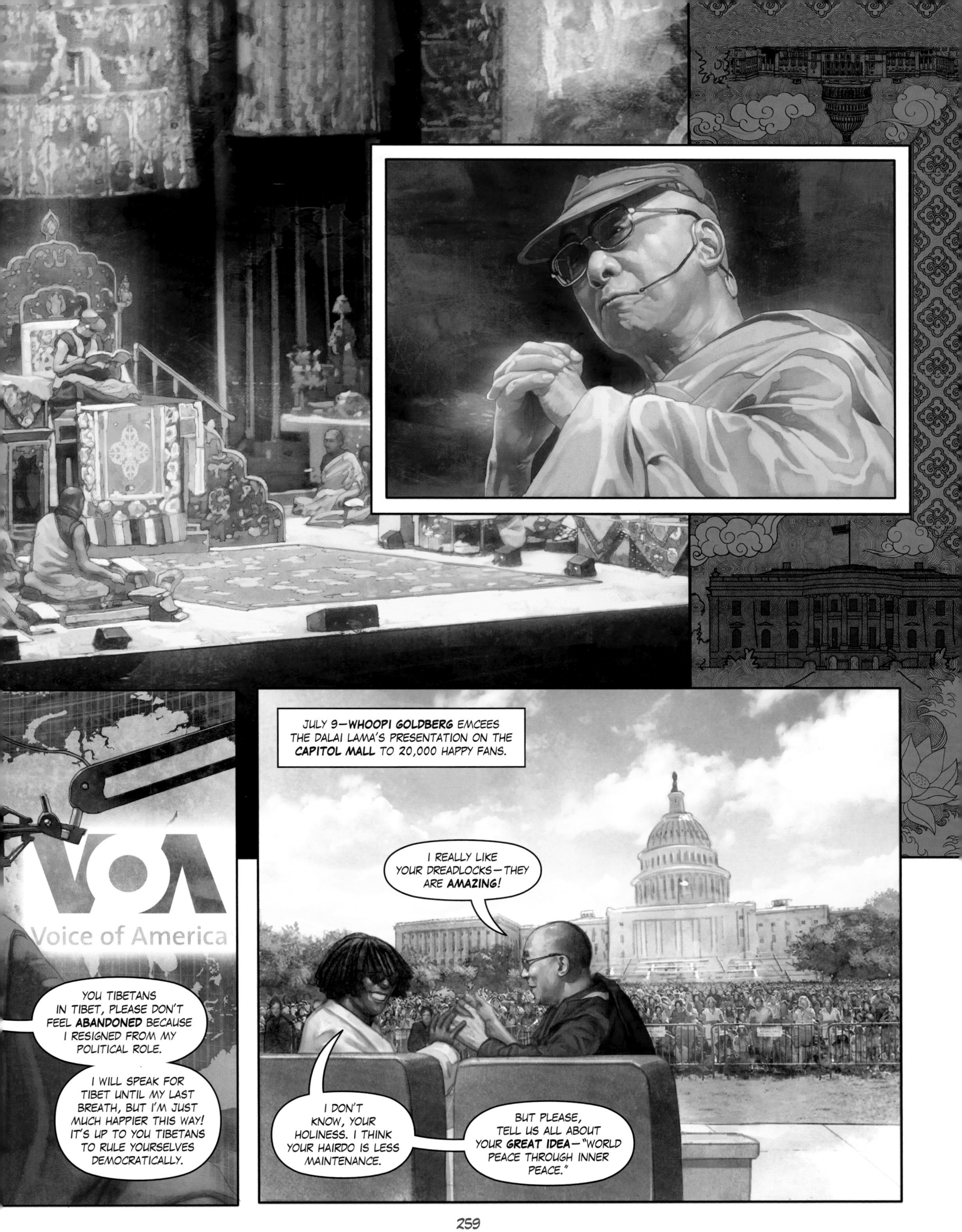
Voice of America
YOU TIBETANS IN TIBET, PLEASE DON'T FEEL ABANDONED BECAUSE I RESIGNED FROM MY POLITICAL ROLE.
I WILL SPEAK FOR TIBET UNTIL MY LAST BREATH, BUT I'M JUST MUCH HAPPIER THIS WAY! IT'S UP TO YOU TIBETANS TO RULE YOURSELVES DEMOCRATICALLY.
JULY 9—WHOOPI GOLDBERG EMCEES THE DALAI LAMA'S PRESENTATION ON THE CAPITOL MALL TO 20,000 HAPPY FANS.
I REALLY LIKE YOUR DREADLOCKS—THEY ARE AMAZING!
I DON'T KNOW, YOUR HOLINESS. I THINK YOUR HAIRDO IS LESS MAINTENANCE.
BUT PLEASE, TELL US ALL ABOUT YOUR GREAT IDEA—"WORLD PEACE THROUGH INNER PEACE."

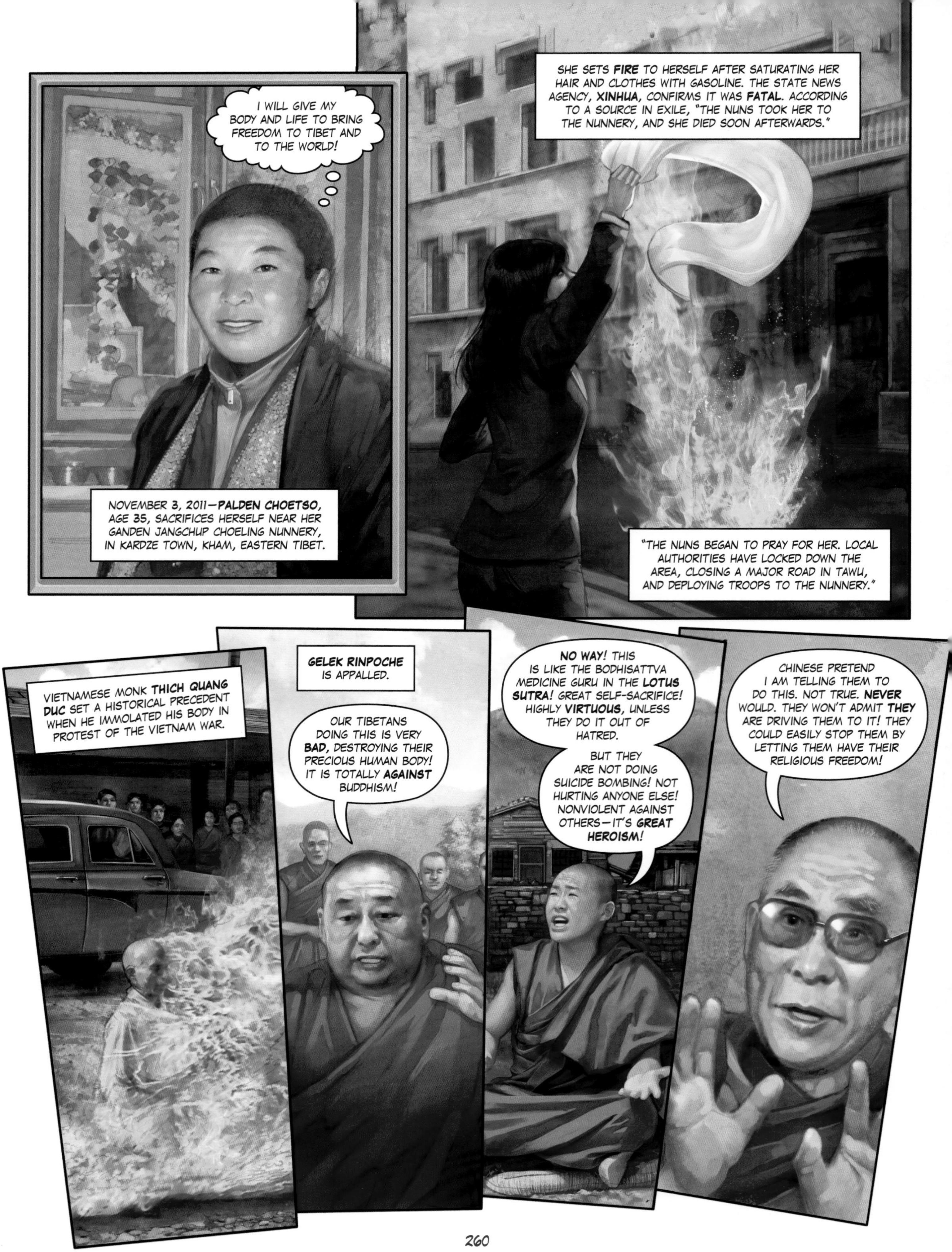
I WILL GIVE MY BODY AND LIFE TO BRING FREEDOM TO TIBET AND TO THE WORLD!
NOVEMBER 3, 2011—PALDEN CHOETSO, AGE 35, SACRIFICES HERSELF NEAR HER GANDEN JANGCHUP CHOELING NUNNERY, IN KARDZE TOWN, KHAM, EASTERN TIBET.
SHE SETS FIRE TO HERSELF AFTER SATURATING HER HAIR AND CLOTHES WITH GASOLINE. THE STATE NEWS AGENCY, XINHUA, CONFIRMS IT WAS FATAL. ACCORDING TO A SOURCE IN EXILE, "THE NUNS TOOK HER TO THE NUNNERY, AND SHE DIED SOON AFTERWARDS."
"THE NUNS BEGAN TO PRAY FOR HER. LOCAL AUTHORITIES HAVE LOCKED DOWN THE AREA, CLOSING A MAJOR ROAD IN TAWU, AND DEPLOYING TROOPS TO THE NUNNERY."
VIETNAMESE MONK THICH QUANG DUC SET A HISTORICAL PRECEDENT WHEN HE IMMOLATED HIS BODY IN PROTEST OF THE VIETNAM WAR.
GELEK RINPOCHE IS APPALLED.
OUR TIBETANS DOING THIS IS VERY BAD, DESTROYING THEIR PRECIOUS HUMAN BODY! IT IS TOTALLY AGAINST BUDDHISM!
NO WAY! THIS IS LIKE THE BODHISATTVA MEDICINE GURU IN THE LOTUS SUTRA! GREAT SELF-SACRIFICE! HIGHLY VIRTUOUS, UNLESS THEY DO IT OUT OF HATRED.
BUT THEY ARE NOT DOING SUICIDE BOMBING! NOT HURTING ANYONE ELSE! NONVIOLENT AGAINST OTHERS—IT'S GREAT HEROISM!
CHINESE PRETEND I AM TELLING THEM TO DO THIS. NOT TRUE. NEVER WOULD. THEY WON'T ADMIT THEY ARE DRIVING THEM TO IT! THEY COULD EASILY STOP THEM BY LETTING THEM HAVE THEIR RELIGIOUS FREEDOM!

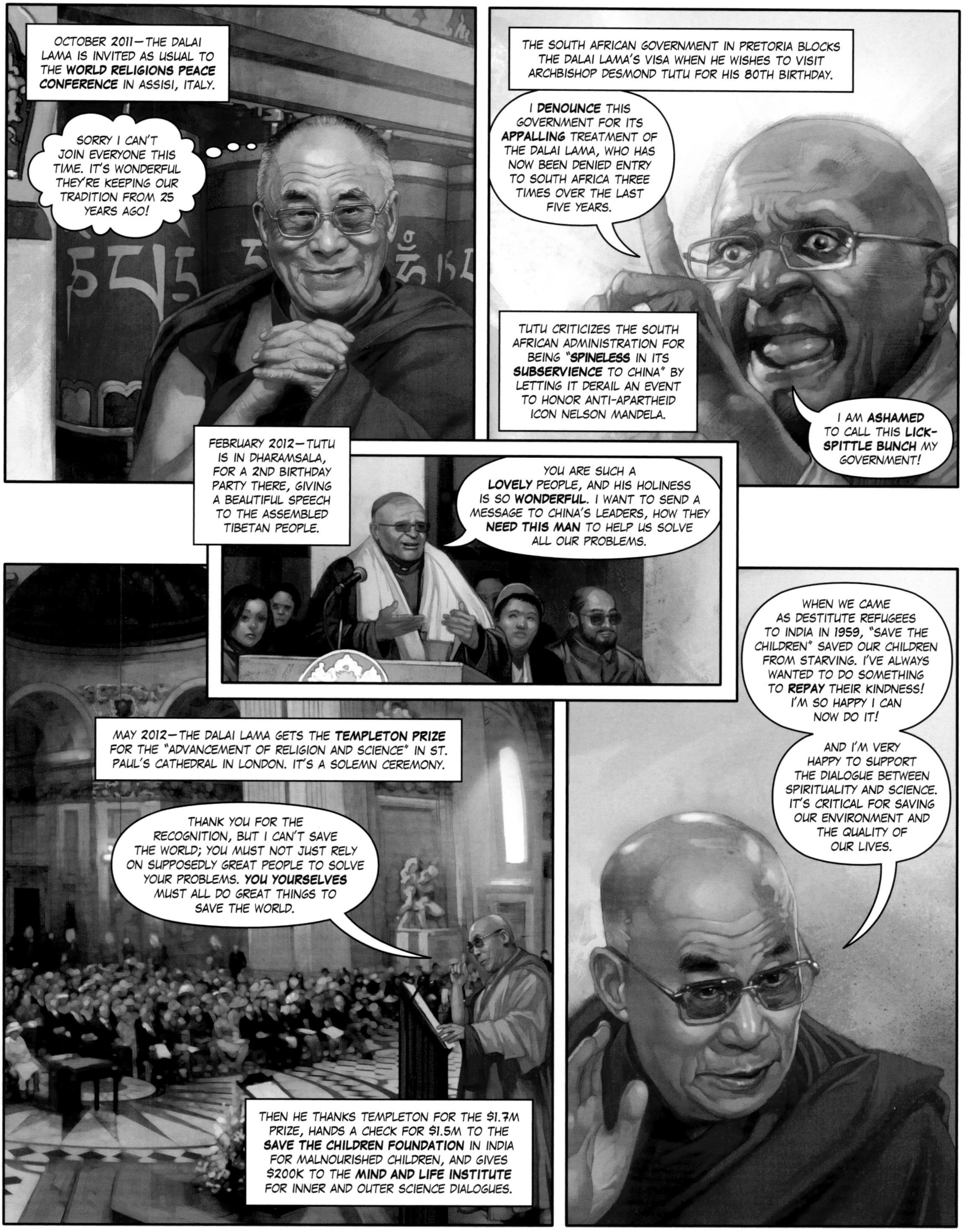
OCTOBER 2011—THE DALAI LAMA IS INVITED AS USUAL TO THE WORLD RELIGIONS PEACE CONFERENCE IN ASSISI, ITALY.
SORRY I CAN'T JOIN EVERYONE THIS TIME. IT'S WONDERFUL THEY'RE KEEPING OUR TRADITION FROM 25 YEARS AGO!
THE SOUTH AFRICAN GOVERNMENT IN PRETORIA BLOCKS THE DALAI LAMA'S VISA WHEN HE WISHES TO VISIT ARCHBISHOP DESMOND TUTU FOR HIS 80TH BIRTHDAY.
I DENOUNCE THIS GOVERNMENT FOR ITS APPALLING TREATMENT OF THE DALAI LAMA, WHO HAS NOW BEEN DENIED ENTRY TO SOUTH AFRICA THREE TIMES OVER THE LAST FIVE YEARS.
TUTU CRITICIZES THE SOUTH AFRICAN ADMINISTRATION FOR BEING "SPINELESS IN ITS SUBSERVIENCE TO CHINA" BY LETTING IT DERAIL AN EVENT TO HONOR ANTI-APARTHEID ICON NELSON MANDELA.
I AM ASHAMED TO CALL THIS LICK-SPITTLE BUNCH MY GOVERNMENT!
FEBRUARY 2012—TUTU IS IN DHARAMSALA, FOR A 2ND BIRTHDAY PARTY THERE, GIVING A BEAUTIFUL SPEECH TO THE ASSEMBLED TIBETAN PEOPLE.
YOU ARE SUCH A LOVELY PEOPLE, AND HIS HOLINESS IS SO WONDERFUL. I WANT TO SEND A MESSAGE TO CHINA'S LEADERS, HOW THEY NEED THIS MAN TO HELP US SOLVE ALL OUR PROBLEMS.
MAY 2012—THE DALAI LAMA GETS THE TEMPLETON PRIZE FOR THE "ADVANCEMENT OF RELIGION AND SCIENCE" IN ST. PAUL'S CATHEDRAL IN LONDON. IT'S A SOLEMN CEREMONY.
THANK YOU FOR THE RECOGNITION, BUT I CAN'T SAVE THE WORLD; YOU MUST NOT JUST RELY ON SUPPOSEDLY GREAT PEOPLE TO SOLVE YOUR PROBLEMS. YOU YOURSELVES MUST ALL DO GREAT THINGS TO SAVE THE WORLD.
THEN HE THANKS TEMPLETON FOR THE $1.7M PRIZE, HANDS A CHECK FOR $1.5M TO THE SAVE THE CHILDREN FOUNDATION IN INDIA FOR MALNOURISHED CHILDREN, AND GIVES $200K TO THE MIND AND LIFE INSTITUTE FOR INNER AND OUTER SCIENCE DIALOGUES.
WHEN WE CAME AS DESTITUTE REFUGEES TO INDIA IN 1959, "SAVE THE CHILDREN" SAVED OUR CHILDREN FROM STARVING. I'VE ALWAYS WANTED TO DO SOMETHING TO REPAY THEIR KINDNESS! I'M SO HAPPY I CAN NOW DO IT!
AND I'M VERY HAPPY TO SUPPORT THE DIALOGUE BETWEEN SPIRITUALITY AND SCIENCE. IT'S CRITICAL FOR SAVING OUR ENVIRONMENT AND THE QUALITY OF OUR LIVES.

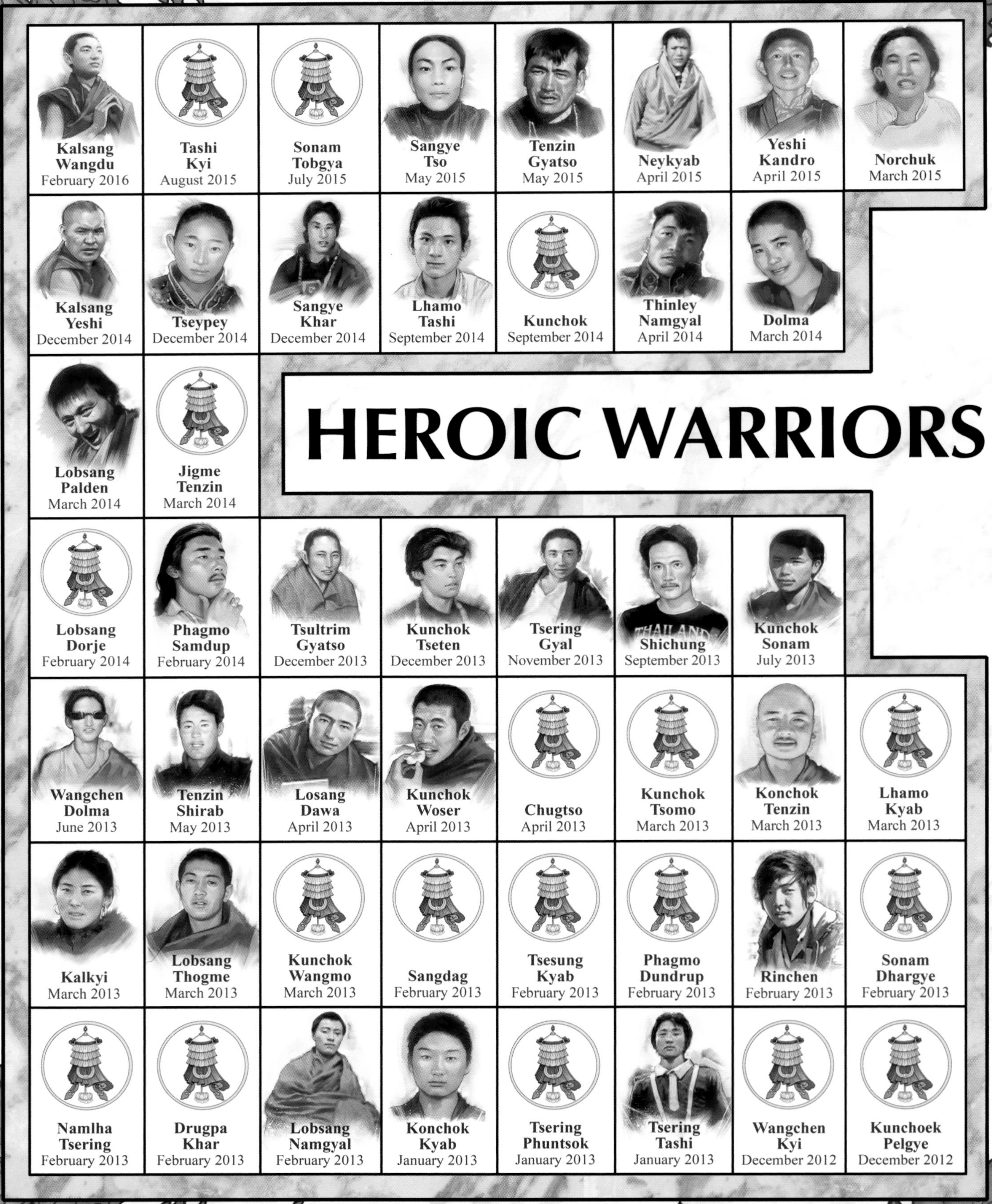
HEROIC WARRIORS
Kalsang Wangdu February 2016
Tashi Kyi August 2015
Sonam Tobgya July 2015
Sangye Tso May 2015
Tenzin Gyatso May 2015
Neykyab April 2015
Yeshi Kandro April 2015
Norchuk March 2015
Kalsang Yeshi December 2014
Tseypey December 2014
Sangye Khar December 2014
Lhamo Tashi September 2014
Kunchok September 2014
Thinley Namgyal April 2014
Dolma March 2014
Lobsang Palden March 2014
Jigme Tenzin March 2014
Lobsang Dorje February 2014
Phagmo Samdup February 2014
Tsultrim Gyatso December 2013
Kunchok Tseten December 2013
Tsering Gyal November 2013
THAILAND
Shichung September 2013
Kunchok Sonam July 2013
Wangchen Dolma June 2013
Tenzin Shirab May 2013
Losang Dawa April 2013
Kunchok Woser April 2013
Chugtso April 2013
Kunchok Tsomo March 2013
Konchok Tenzin March 2013
Lhamo Kyab March 2013
Kalkyi March 2013
Lobsang Thogme March 2013
Kunchok Wangmo March 2013
Sangdag February 2013
Tsesung Kyab February 2013
Phagmo Dundrup February 2013
Rinchen February 2013
Sonam Dhargye February 2013
Namlha Tsering February 2013
Drugpa Khar February 2013
Lobsang Namgyal February 2013
Konchok Kyab January 2013
Tsering Phuntsok January 2013
Tsering Tashi January 2013
Wangchen Kyi December 2012
Kunchoek Pelgye December 2012

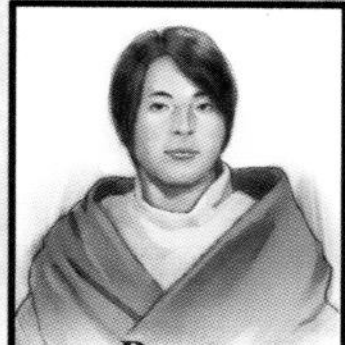
Pema Dorjee
December 2012

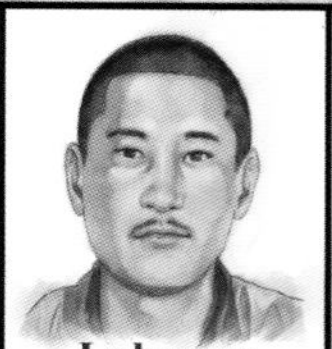
Lobsang Geleg
December 2012

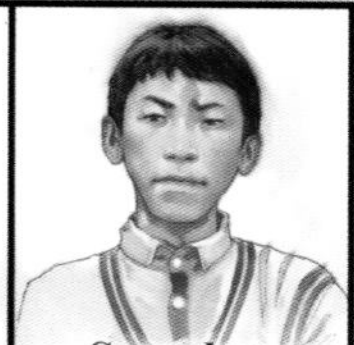
Sungdue Kyab
December 2012

Kunchok Kyab
November 2012

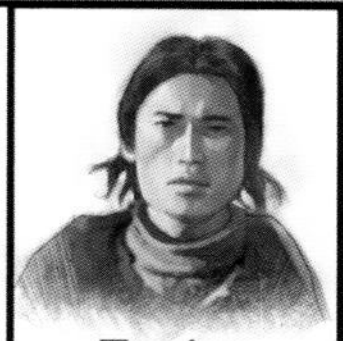
Tsering Namgyal
November 2012

Wande Khar
November 2012

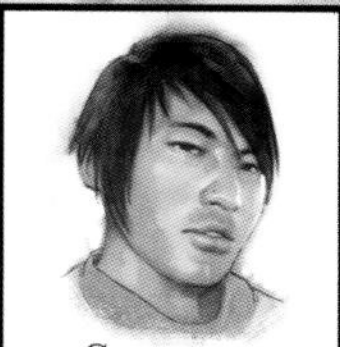
Sanggye Tashi
November 2012

Kalsang Kyab
November 2012

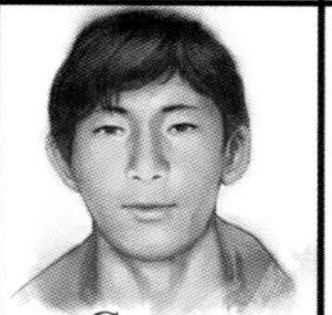
Gonpo Tsering
November 2012

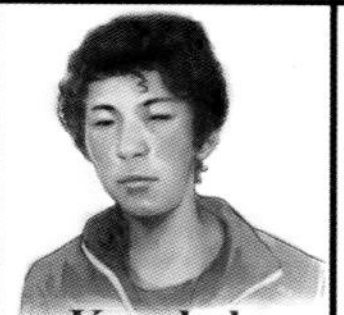
Kunchok Tsering
November 2012

Wangyal
November 2012

Sangay Dolma
November 2012

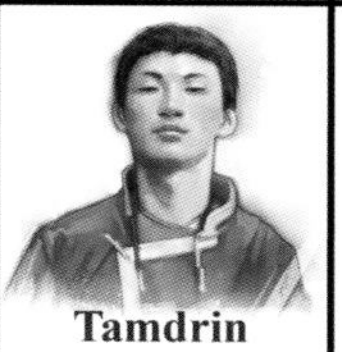
Tamdrin Kyab
November 2012

Tamdrin Dorjee
November 2012

Lubhum Gyal
November 2012

OF NONVIOLENCE

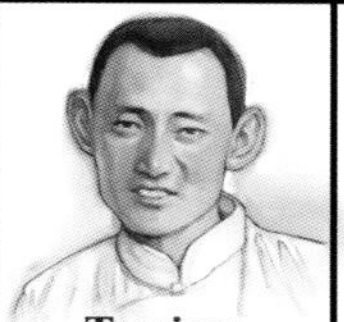
Tsering Dundrup
November 2012

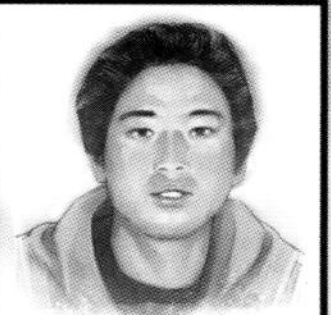
Wangchen Norbu
November 2012

Sangdag Tsering
November 2012

Chagmo Kyi
November 2012

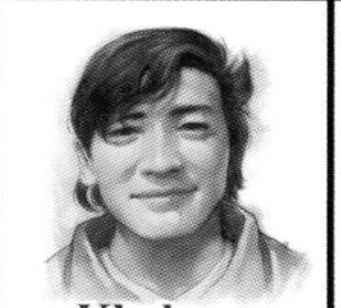
Khabum Gyal
November 2102

Tenzin Dolma
November 2012

Nyangchag Bum
November 2012

Nyangkar Tashi
November 2012

Gonpo Tsering
November 2012

Jinpa Gyatso
November 2012

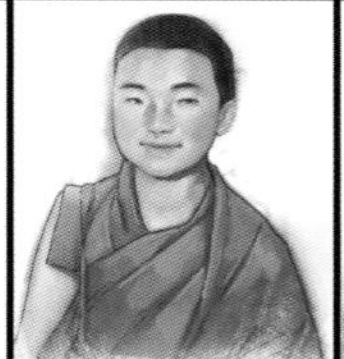
Dorjee
November 2012

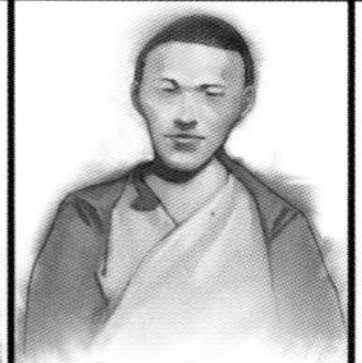
Samdrup
November 2012

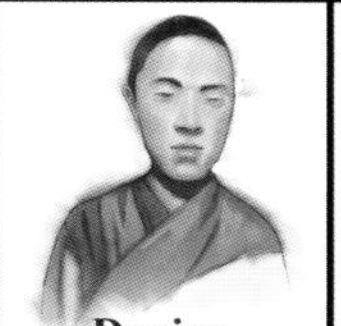
Dorjee Kyab
November 2012

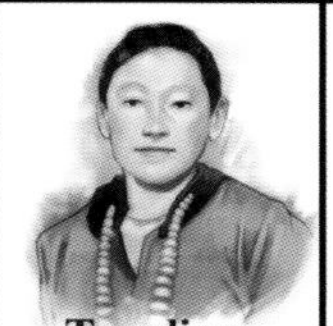
Tamding Tso
November 2012

Tsegyal
November 2012

Dorje Lhundrup
November 2012

Tsewang Kyab
October 2012

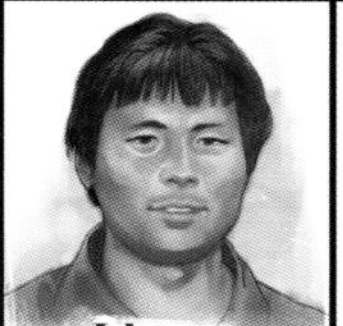
Lhamo Tseten
October 2012

Tsepo
October 2012

Tenzin
October 2012

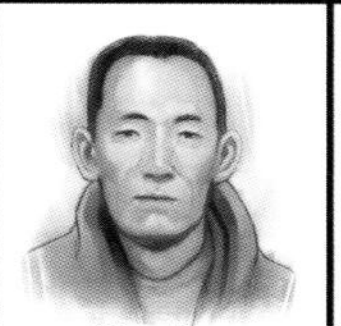
Dorje Rinchen
October 2012

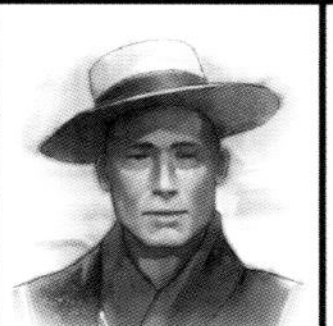
Dhondup
October 2012

Lhamo Kyab
October 2012

Tamdin Dorje
October 2012

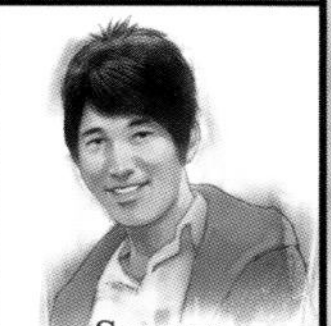
Sangay Gyatso
October 2012

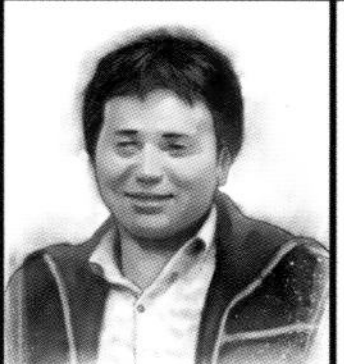
Gudrub
October 2012

Yangdang
September 2012

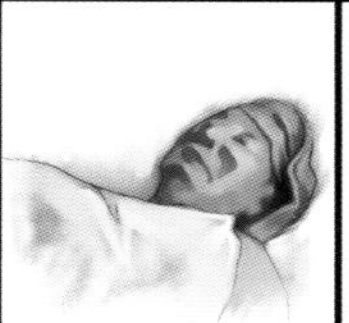
Passang Lhamo
September 2012

Lobsang Damchoe
August 2012

Lobsang Kelsang
August 2012

Lungtok
August 2012

Tashi
August 2012

Chopa
August 2012

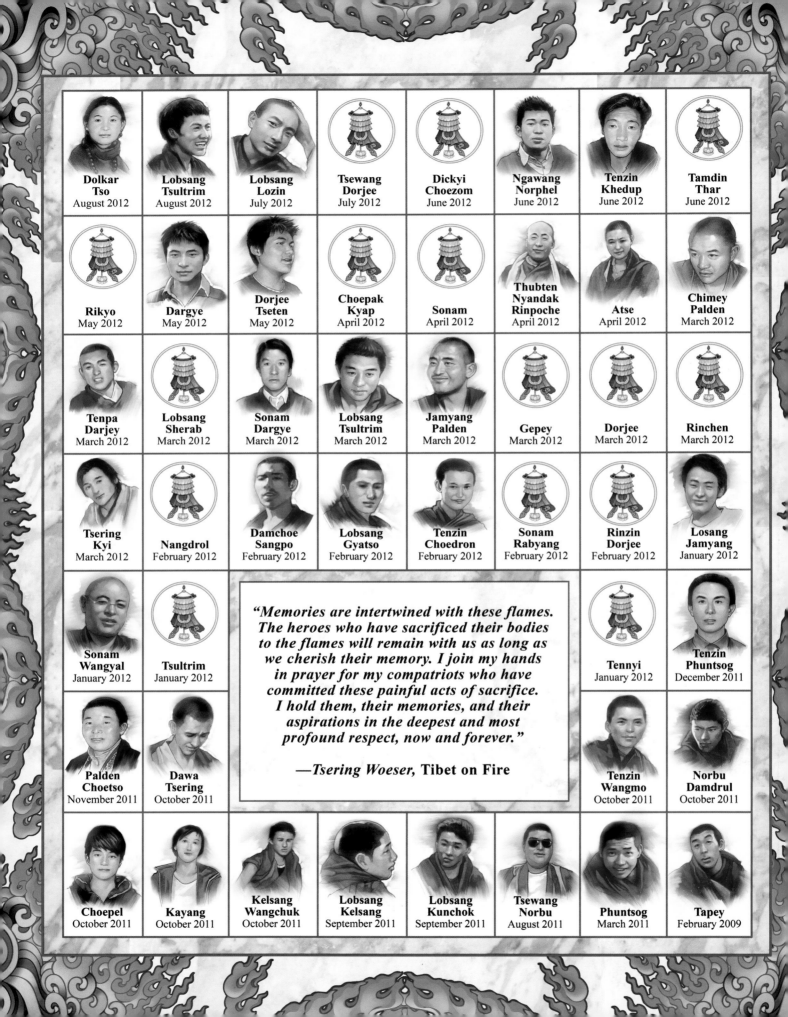

Dolkar Tso
August 2012

Lobsang Tsultrim
August 2012

Lobsang Lozin
July 2012

Tsewang Dorjee
July 2012

Dickyi Choezom
June 2012

Ngawang Norphel
June 2012

Tenzin Khedup
June 2012

Tamdin Thar
June 2012

Rikyo
May 2012

Dargye
May 2012

Dorjee Tseten
May 2012

Choepak Kyap
April 2012

Sonam
April 2012

Thubten Nyandak Rinpoche
April 2012

Atse
April 2012

Chimey Palden
March 2012

Tenpa Darjey
March 2012

Lobsang Sherab
March 2012

Sonam Dargye
March 2012

Lobsang Tsultrim
March 2012

Jamyang Palden
March 2012

Gepey
March 2012

Dorjee
March 2012

Rinchen
March 2012

Tsering Kyi
March 2012

Nangdrol
February 2012

Damchoe Sangpo
February 2012

Lobsang Gyatso
February 2012

Tenzin Choedron
February 2012

Sonam Rabyang
February 2012

Rinzin Dorjee
February 2012

Losang Jamyang
January 2012

Sonam Wangyal
January 2012

Tsultrim
January 2012

"Memories are intertwined with these flames. The heroes who have sacrificed their bodies to the flames will remain with us as long as we cherish their memory. I join my hands in prayer for my compatriots who have committed these painful acts of sacrifice. I hold them, their memories, and their aspirations in the deepest and most profound respect, now and forever."

—Tsering Woeser, **Tibet on Fire**

Tennyi
January 2012

Tenzin Phuntsog
December 2011

Palden Choetso
November 2011

Dawa Tsering
October 2011

Tenzin Wangmo
October 2011

Norbu Damdrul
October 2011

Choepel
October 2011

Kayang
October 2011

Kelsang Wangchuk
October 2011

Lobsang Kelsang
September 2011

Lobsang Kunchok
September 2011

Tsewang Norbu
August 2011

Phuntsog
March 2011

Tapey
February 2009

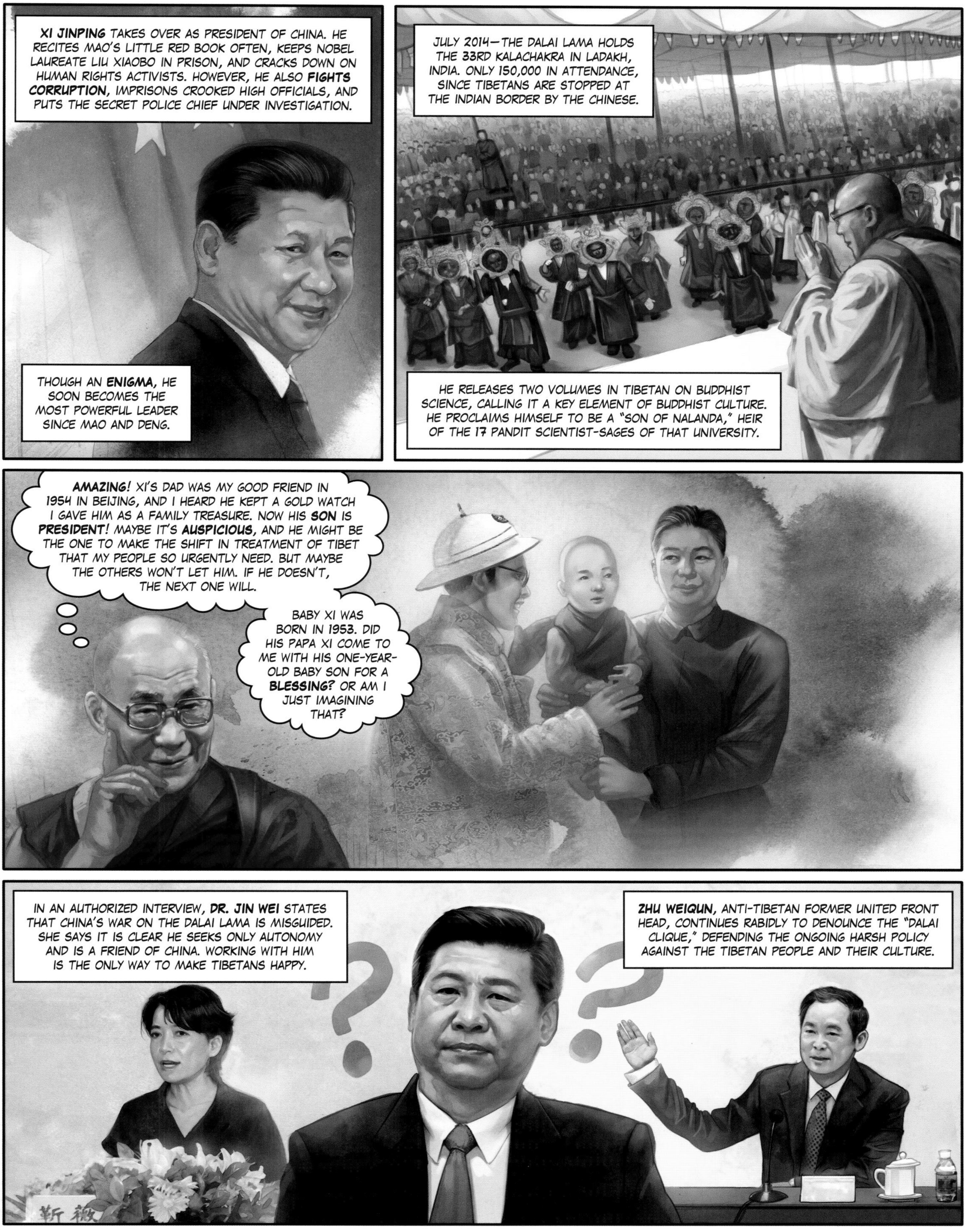
XI JINPING TAKES OVER AS PRESIDENT OF CHINA. HE RECITES MAO'S LITTLE RED BOOK OFTEN, KEEPS NOBEL LAUREATE LIU XIAOBO IN PRISON, AND CRACKS DOWN ON HUMAN RIGHTS ACTIVISTS. HOWEVER, HE ALSO FIGHTS CORRUPTION, IMPRISONS CROOKED HIGH OFFICIALS, AND PUTS THE SECRET POLICE CHIEF UNDER INVESTIGATION.
THOUGH AN ENIGMA, HE SOON BECOMES THE MOST POWERFUL LEADER SINCE MAO AND DENG.
JULY 2014—THE DALAI LAMA HOLDS THE 33RD KALACHAKRA IN LADAKH, INDIA. ONLY 150,000 IN ATTENDANCE, SINCE TIBETANS ARE STOPPED AT THE INDIAN BORDER BY THE CHINESE.
HE RELEASES TWO VOLUMES IN TIBETAN ON BUDDHIST SCIENCE, CALLING IT A KEY ELEMENT OF BUDDHIST CULTURE. HE PROCLAIMS HIMSELF TO BE A "SON OF NALANDA," HEIR OF THE 17 PANDIT SCIENTIST-SAGES OF THAT UNIVERSITY.
AMAZING! XI'S DAD WAS MY GOOD FRIEND IN 1954 IN BEIJING, AND I HEARD HE KEPT A GOLD WATCH I GAVE HIM AS A FAMILY TREASURE. NOW HIS SON IS PRESIDENT! MAYBE IT'S AUSPICIOUS, AND HE MIGHT BE THE ONE TO MAKE THE SHIFT IN TREATMENT OF TIBET THAT MY PEOPLE SO URGENTLY NEED. BUT MAYBE THE OTHERS WON'T LET HIM. IF HE DOESN'T, THE NEXT ONE WILL.
BABY XI WAS BORN IN 1953. DID HIS PAPA XI COME TO ME WITH HIS ONE-YEAR-OLD BABY SON FOR A BLESSING? OR AM I JUST IMAGINING THAT?
IN AN AUTHORIZED INTERVIEW, DR. JIN WEI STATES THAT CHINA'S WAR ON THE DALAI LAMA IS MISGUIDED. SHE SAYS IT IS CLEAR HE SEEKS ONLY AUTONOMY AND IS A FRIEND OF CHINA. WORKING WITH HIM IS THE ONLY WAY TO MAKE TIBETANS HAPPY.
ZHU WEIQUN, ANTI-TIBETAN FORMER UNITED FRONT HEAD, CONTINUES RABIDLY TO DENOUNCE THE "DALAI CLIQUE," DEFENDING THE ONGOING HARSH POLICY AGAINST THE TIBETAN PEOPLE AND THEIR CULTURE.

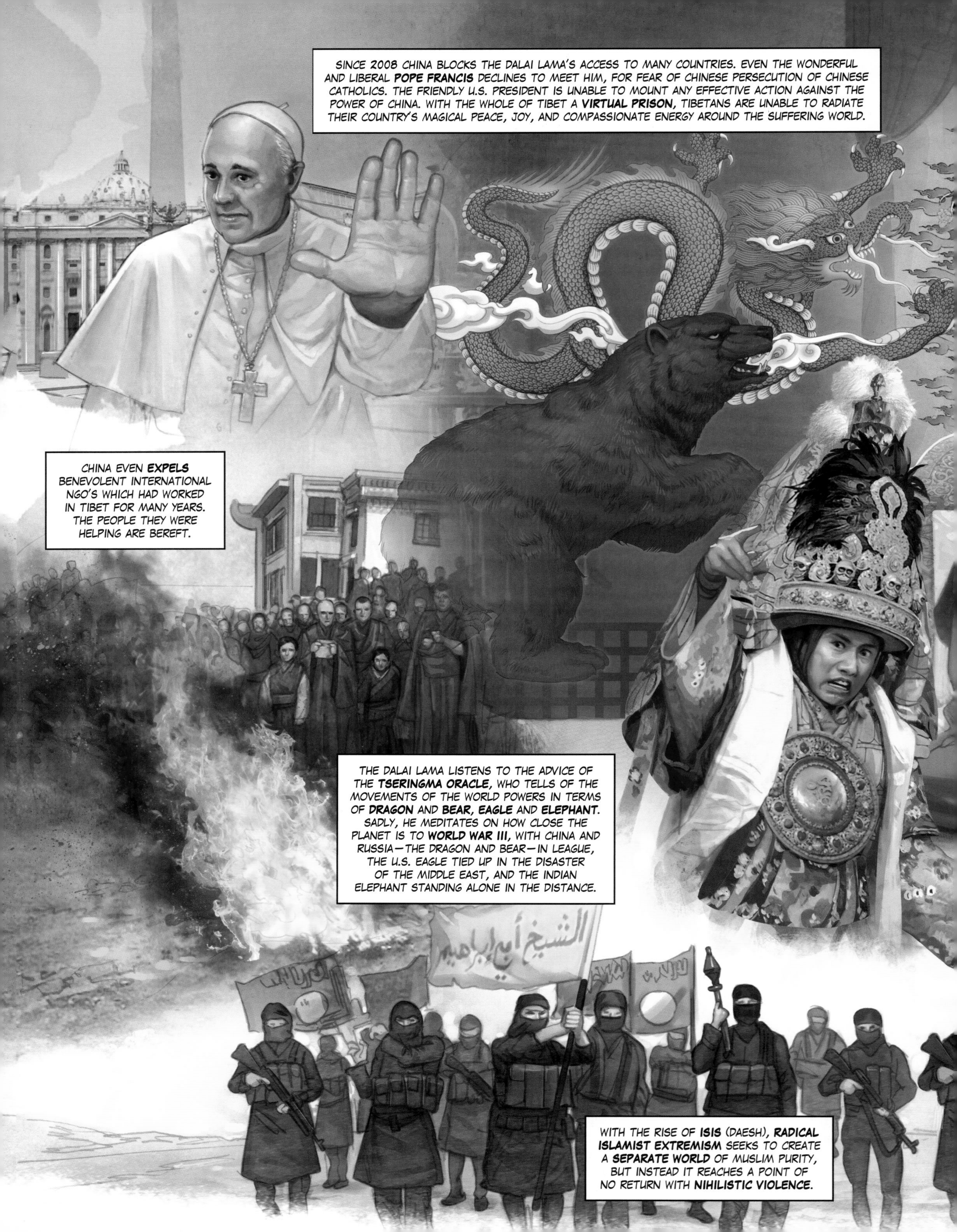
SINCE 2008 CHINA BLOCKS THE DALAI LAMA'S ACCESS TO MANY COUNTRIES. EVEN THE WONDERFUL AND LIBERAL **POPE FRANCIS** DECLINES TO MEET HIM, FOR FEAR OF CHINESE PERSECUTION OF CHINESE CATHOLICS. THE FRIENDLY U.S. PRESIDENT IS UNABLE TO MOUNT ANY EFFECTIVE ACTION AGAINST THE POWER OF CHINA. WITH THE WHOLE OF TIBET A **VIRTUAL PRISON,** TIBETANS ARE UNABLE TO RADIATE THEIR COUNTRY'S MAGICAL PEACE, JOY, AND COMPASSIONATE ENERGY AROUND THE SUFFERING WORLD.
CHINA EVEN **EXPELS** BENEVOLENT INTERNATIONAL NGO'S WHICH HAD WORKED IN TIBET FOR MANY YEARS. THE PEOPLE THEY WERE HELPING ARE BEREFT.
THE DALAI LAMA LISTENS TO THE ADVICE OF THE **TSERINGMA ORACLE,** WHO TELLS OF THE MOVEMENTS OF THE WORLD POWERS IN TERMS OF **DRAGON** AND **BEAR, EAGLE** AND **ELEPHANT**. SADLY, HE MEDITATES ON HOW CLOSE THE PLANET IS TO **WORLD WAR III,** WITH CHINA AND RUSSIA—THE DRAGON AND BEAR—IN LEAGUE, THE U.S. EAGLE TIED UP IN THE DISASTER OF THE MIDDLE EAST, AND THE INDIAN ELEPHANT STANDING ALONE IN THE DISTANCE.
WITH THE RISE OF **ISIS** (DAESH), **RADICAL ISLAMIST EXTREMISM** SEEKS TO CREATE A **SEPARATE WORLD** OF MUSLIM PURITY, BUT INSTEAD IT REACHES A POINT OF NO RETURN WITH **NIHILISTIC VIOLENCE**.

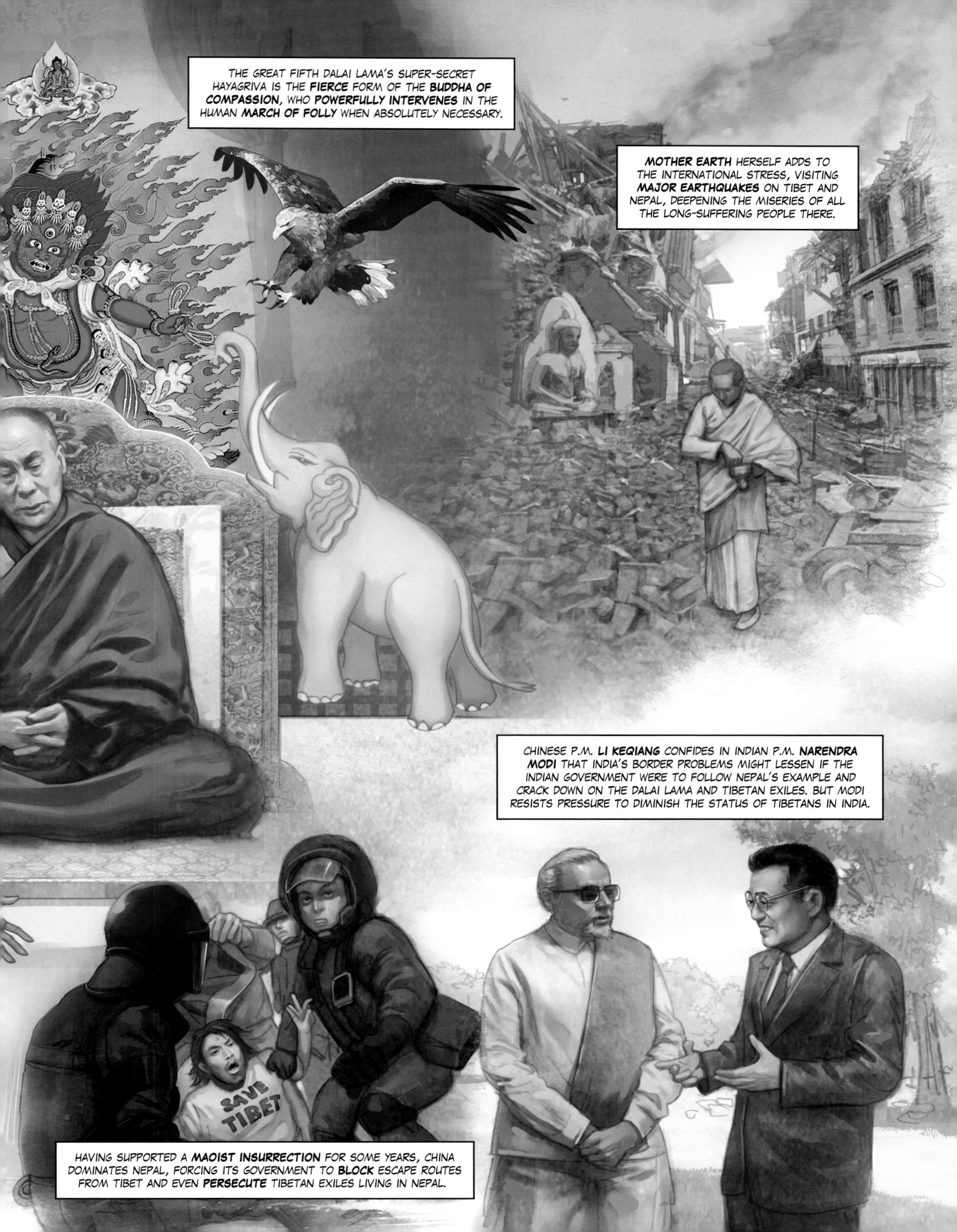
THE GREAT FIFTH DALAI LAMA'S SUPER-SECRET HAYAGRIVA IS THE FIERCE FORM OF THE BUDDHA OF COMPASSION, WHO POWERFULLY INTERVENES IN THE HUMAN MARCH OF FOLLY WHEN ABSOLUTELY NECESSARY.
MOTHER EARTH HERSELF ADDS TO THE INTERNATIONAL STRESS, VISITING MAJOR EARTHQUAKES ON TIBET AND NEPAL, DEEPENING THE MISERIES OF ALL THE LONG-SUFFERING PEOPLE THERE.
CHINESE P.M. LI KEQIANG CONFIDES IN INDIAN P.M. NARENDRA MODI THAT INDIA'S BORDER PROBLEMS MIGHT LESSEN IF THE INDIAN GOVERNMENT WERE TO FOLLOW NEPAL'S EXAMPLE AND CRACK DOWN ON THE DALAI LAMA AND TIBETAN EXILES. BUT MODI RESISTS PRESSURE TO DIMINISH THE STATUS OF TIBETANS IN INDIA.
SAVE TIBET
HAVING SUPPORTED A MAOIST INSURRECTION FOR SOME YEARS, CHINA DOMINATES NEPAL, FORCING ITS GOVERNMENT TO BLOCK ESCAPE ROUTES FROM TIBET AND EVEN PERSECUTE TIBETAN EXILES LIVING IN NEPAL.

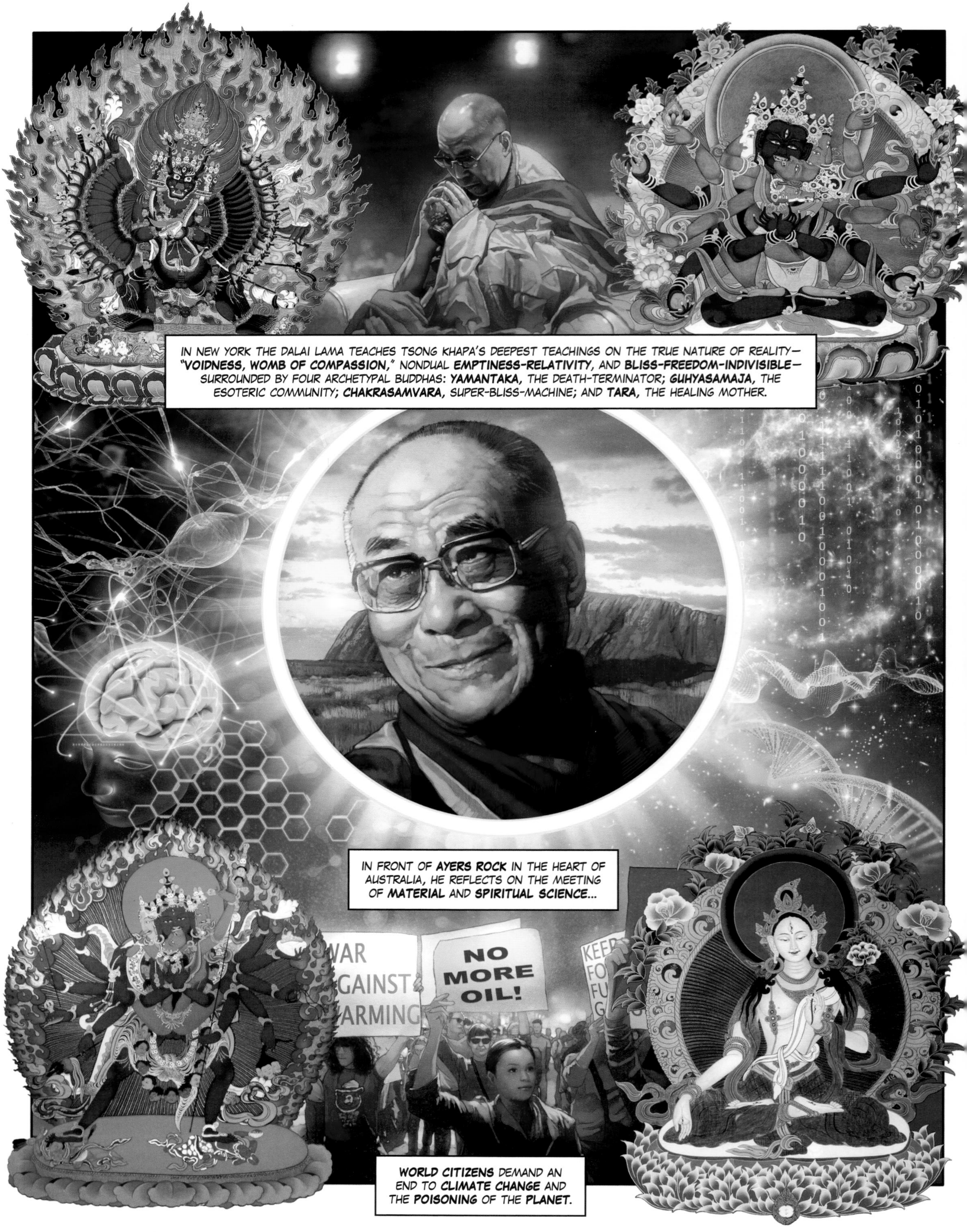
IN NEW YORK THE DALAI LAMA TEACHES TSONG KHAPA'S DEEPEST TEACHINGS ON THE TRUE NATURE OF REALITY—**"VOIDNESS, WOMB OF COMPASSION,"** NONDUAL **EMPTINESS-RELATIVITY**, AND **BLISS-FREEDOM-INDIVISIBLE**—SURROUNDED BY FOUR ARCHETYPAL BUDDHAS: **YAMANTAKA**, THE DEATH-TERMINATOR; **GUHYASAMAJA**, THE ESOTERIC COMMUNITY; **CHAKRASAMVARA**, SUPER-BLISS-MACHINE; AND **TARA**, THE HEALING MOTHER.
IN FRONT OF **AYERS ROCK** IN THE HEART OF AUSTRALIA, HE REFLECTS ON THE MEETING OF **MATERIAL** AND **SPIRITUAL SCIENCE**...
NO MORE OIL!
WORLD CITIZENS DEMAND AN END TO **CLIMATE CHANGE** AND THE **POISONING** OF THE **PLANET**.

EPILOGUE

Dalai Lama at Home

His Holiness the Dalai Lama's
favorite prayer,
from Shantideva . . .

For as long as space endures
For as long as living beings remain,
Until then may I too remain
To dispel the misery of the world.

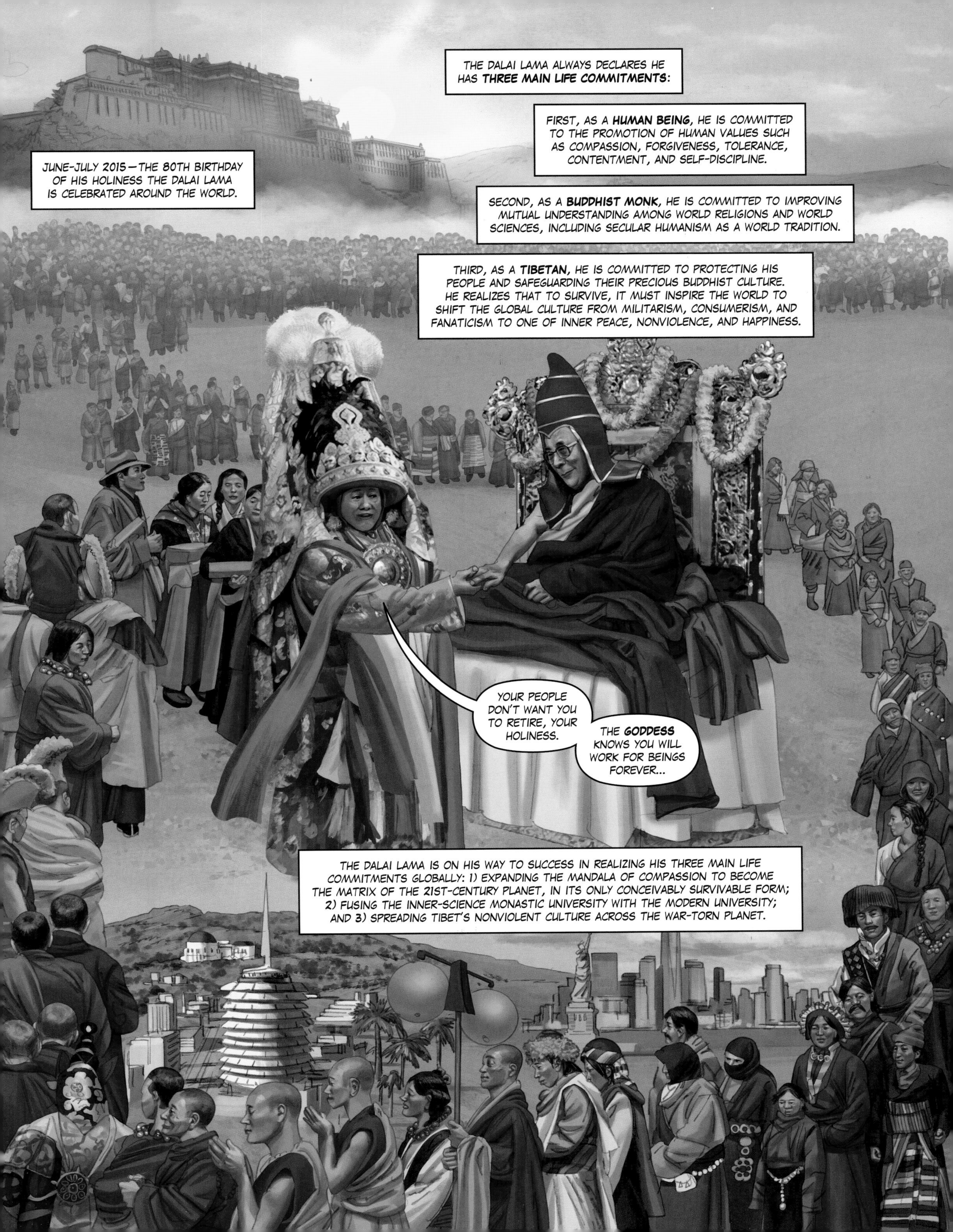
JUNE-JULY 2015—THE 80TH BIRTHDAY OF HIS HOLINESS THE DALAI LAMA IS CELEBRATED AROUND THE WORLD.
THE DALAI LAMA ALWAYS DECLARES HE HAS **THREE MAIN LIFE COMMITMENTS**:
FIRST, AS A **HUMAN BEING**, HE IS COMMITTED TO THE PROMOTION OF HUMAN VALUES SUCH AS COMPASSION, FORGIVENESS, TOLERANCE, CONTENTMENT, AND SELF-DISCIPLINE.
SECOND, AS A **BUDDHIST MONK**, HE IS COMMITTED TO IMPROVING MUTUAL UNDERSTANDING AMONG WORLD RELIGIONS AND WORLD SCIENCES, INCLUDING SECULAR HUMANISM AS A WORLD TRADITION.
THIRD, AS A **TIBETAN**, HE IS COMMITTED TO PROTECTING HIS PEOPLE AND SAFEGUARDING THEIR PRECIOUS BUDDHIST CULTURE. HE REALIZES THAT TO SURVIVE, IT MUST INSPIRE THE WORLD TO SHIFT THE GLOBAL CULTURE FROM MILITARISM, CONSUMERISM, AND FANATICISM TO ONE OF INNER PEACE, NONVIOLENCE, AND HAPPINESS.
YOUR PEOPLE DON'T WANT YOU TO RETIRE, YOUR HOLINESS.
THE **GODDESS** KNOWS YOU WILL WORK FOR BEINGS FOREVER...
THE DALAI LAMA IS ON HIS WAY TO SUCCESS IN REALIZING HIS THREE MAIN LIFE COMMITMENTS GLOBALLY: 1) EXPANDING THE MANDALA OF COMPASSION TO BECOME THE MATRIX OF THE 21ST-CENTURY PLANET, IN ITS ONLY CONCEIVABLY SURVIVABLE FORM; 2) FUSING THE INNER-SCIENCE MONASTIC UNIVERSITY WITH THE MODERN UNIVERSITY; AND 3) SPREADING TIBET'S NONVIOLENT CULTURE ACROSS THE WAR-TORN PLANET.

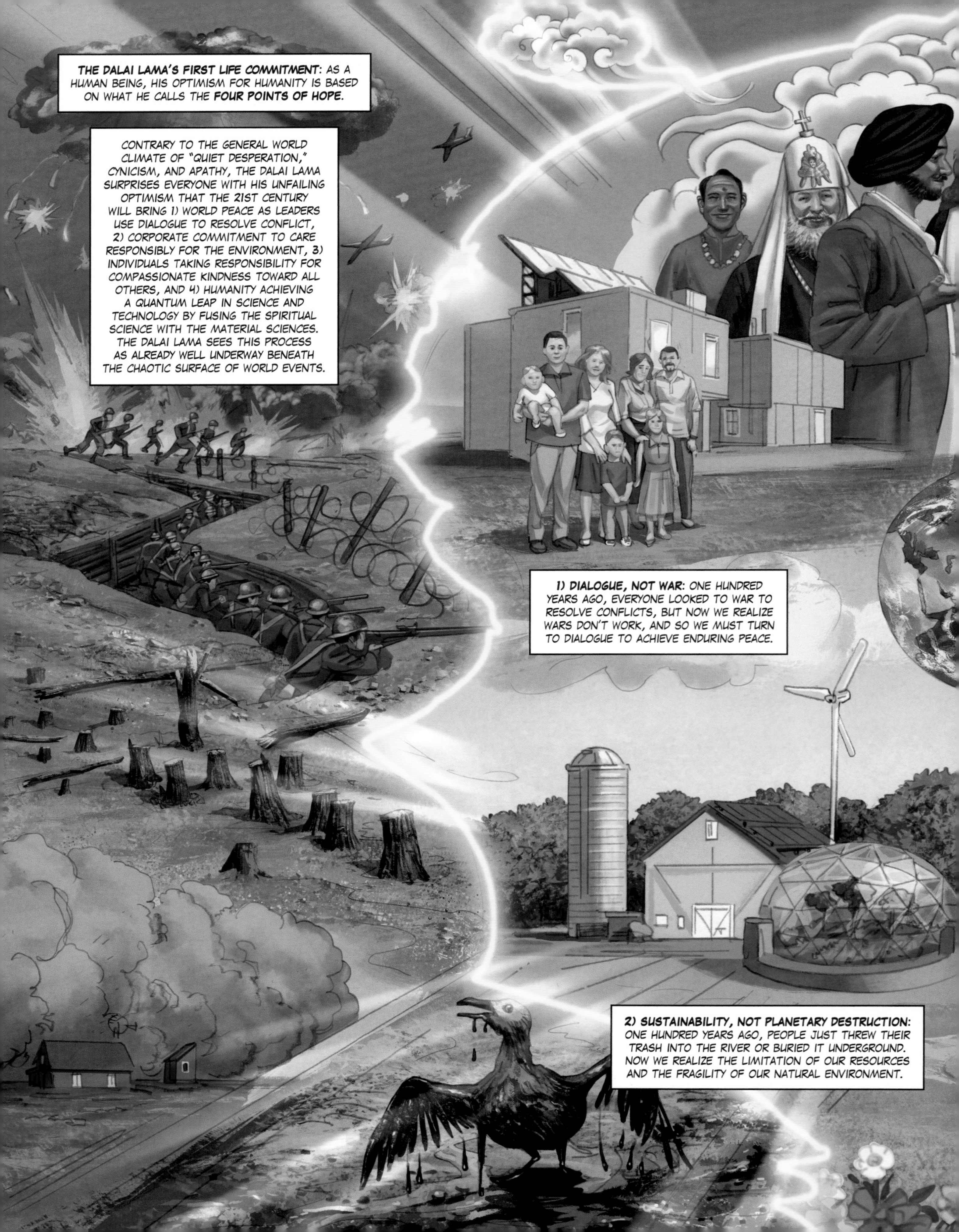
THE DALAI LAMA'S FIRST LIFE COMMITMENT: AS A HUMAN BEING, HIS OPTIMISM FOR HUMANITY IS BASED ON WHAT HE CALLS THE FOUR POINTS OF HOPE.
CONTRARY TO THE GENERAL WORLD CLIMATE OF "QUIET DESPERATION," CYNICISM, AND APATHY, THE DALAI LAMA SURPRISES EVERYONE WITH HIS UNFAILING OPTIMISM THAT THE 21ST CENTURY WILL BRING 1) WORLD PEACE AS LEADERS USE DIALOGUE TO RESOLVE CONFLICT, 2) CORPORATE COMMITMENT TO CARE RESPONSIBLY FOR THE ENVIRONMENT, 3) INDIVIDUALS TAKING RESPONSIBILITY FOR COMPASSIONATE KINDNESS TOWARD ALL OTHERS, AND 4) HUMANITY ACHIEVING A QUANTUM LEAP IN SCIENCE AND TECHNOLOGY BY FUSING THE SPIRITUAL SCIENCE WITH THE MATERIAL SCIENCES. THE DALAI LAMA SEES THIS PROCESS AS ALREADY WELL UNDERWAY BENEATH THE CHAOTIC SURFACE OF WORLD EVENTS.
1) DIALOGUE, NOT WAR: ONE HUNDRED YEARS AGO, EVERYONE LOOKED TO WAR TO RESOLVE CONFLICTS, BUT NOW WE REALIZE WARS DON'T WORK, AND SO WE MUST TURN TO DIALOGUE TO ACHIEVE ENDURING PEACE.
2) SUSTAINABILITY, NOT PLANETARY DESTRUCTION: ONE HUNDRED YEARS AGO, PEOPLE JUST THREW THEIR TRASH INTO THE RIVER OR BURIED IT UNDERGROUND. NOW WE REALIZE THE LIMITATION OF OUR RESOURCES AND THE FRAGILITY OF OUR NATURAL ENVIRONMENT.

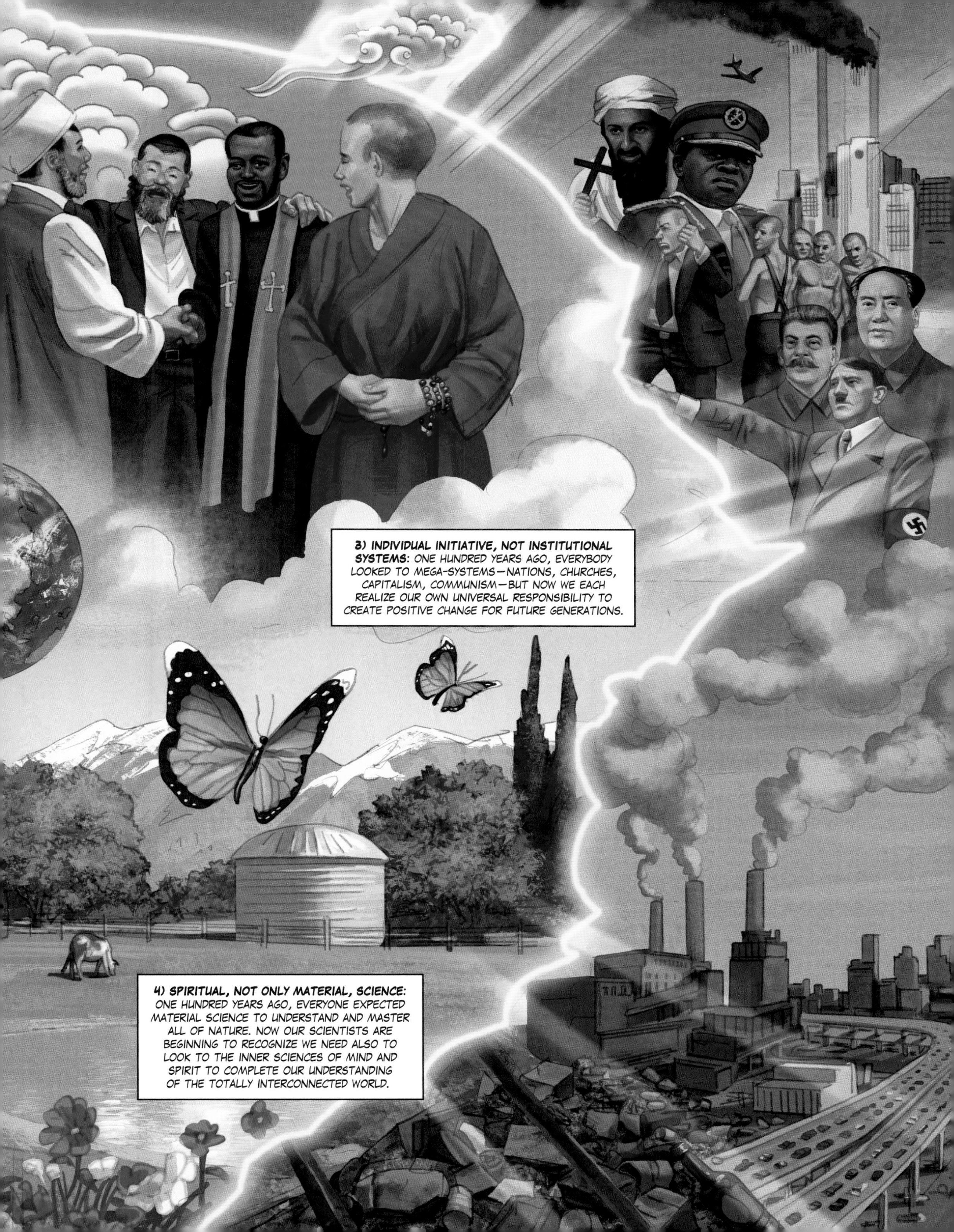
3) INDIVIDUAL INITIATIVE, NOT INSTITUTIONAL SYSTEMS: ONE HUNDRED YEARS AGO, EVERYBODY LOOKED TO MEGA-SYSTEMS—NATIONS, CHURCHES, CAPITALISM, COMMUNISM—BUT NOW WE EACH REALIZE OUR OWN UNIVERSAL RESPONSIBILITY TO CREATE POSITIVE CHANGE FOR FUTURE GENERATIONS.
4) SPIRITUAL, NOT ONLY MATERIAL, SCIENCE: ONE HUNDRED YEARS AGO, EVERYONE EXPECTED MATERIAL SCIENCE TO UNDERSTAND AND MASTER ALL OF NATURE. NOW OUR SCIENTISTS ARE BEGINNING TO RECOGNIZE WE NEED ALSO TO LOOK TO THE INNER SCIENCES OF MIND AND SPIRIT TO COMPLETE OUR UNDERSTANDING OF THE TOTALLY INTERCONNECTED WORLD.

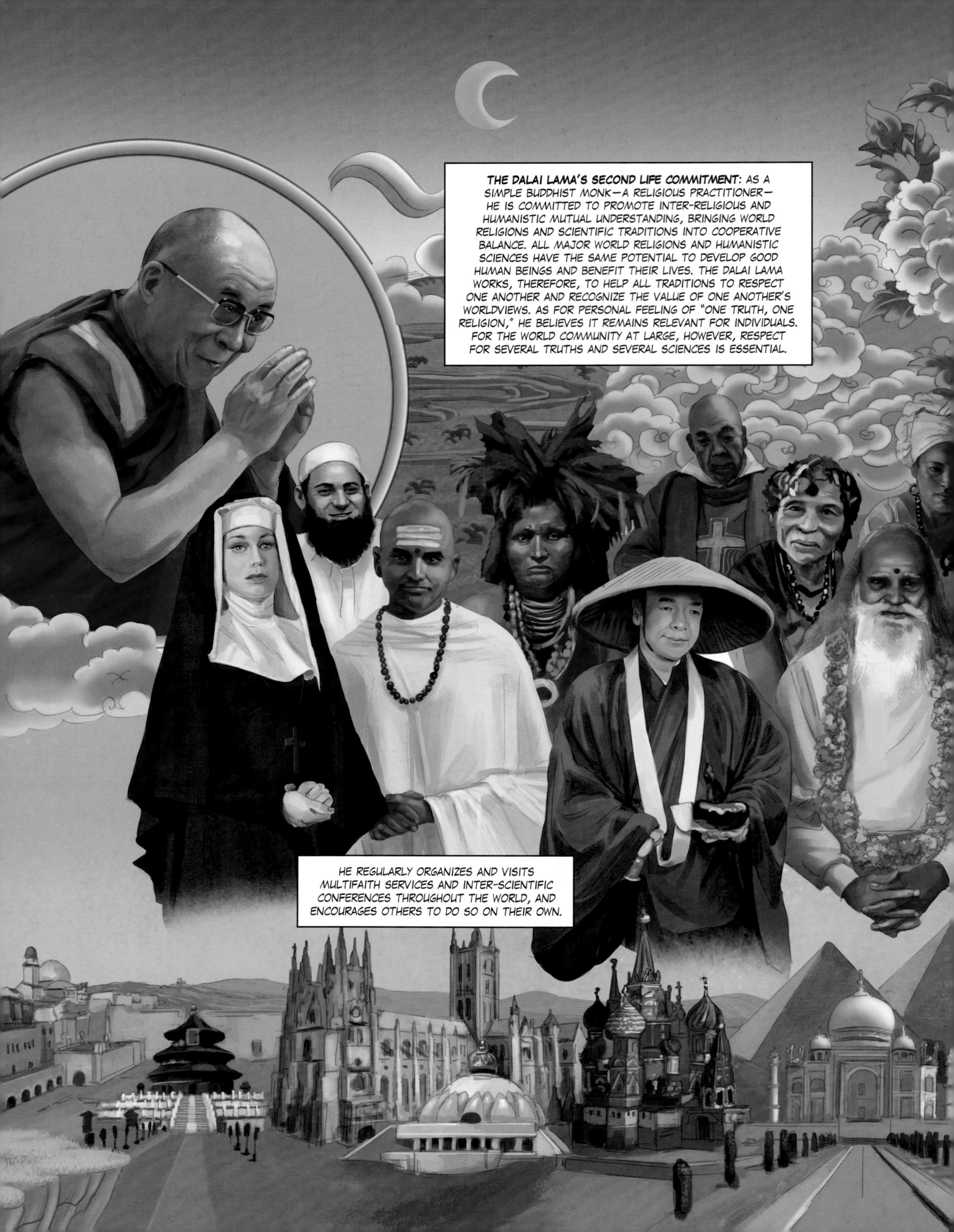
THE DALAI LAMA'S SECOND LIFE COMMITMENT: AS A SIMPLE BUDDHIST MONK—A RELIGIOUS PRACTITIONER—HE IS COMMITTED TO PROMOTE INTER-RELIGIOUS AND HUMANISTIC MUTUAL UNDERSTANDING, BRINGING WORLD RELIGIONS AND SCIENTIFIC TRADITIONS INTO COOPERATIVE BALANCE. ALL MAJOR WORLD RELIGIONS AND HUMANISTIC SCIENCES HAVE THE SAME POTENTIAL TO DEVELOP GOOD HUMAN BEINGS AND BENEFIT THEIR LIVES. THE DALAI LAMA WORKS, THEREFORE, TO HELP ALL TRADITIONS TO RESPECT ONE ANOTHER AND RECOGNIZE THE VALUE OF ONE ANOTHER'S WORLDVIEWS. AS FOR PERSONAL FEELING OF "ONE TRUTH, ONE RELIGION," HE BELIEVES IT REMAINS RELEVANT FOR INDIVIDUALS. FOR THE WORLD COMMUNITY AT LARGE, HOWEVER, RESPECT FOR SEVERAL TRUTHS AND SEVERAL SCIENCES IS ESSENTIAL.
HE REGULARLY ORGANIZES AND VISITS MULTIFAITH SERVICES AND INTER-SCIENTIFIC CONFERENCES THROUGHOUT THE WORLD, AND ENCOURAGES OTHERS TO DO SO ON THEIR OWN.

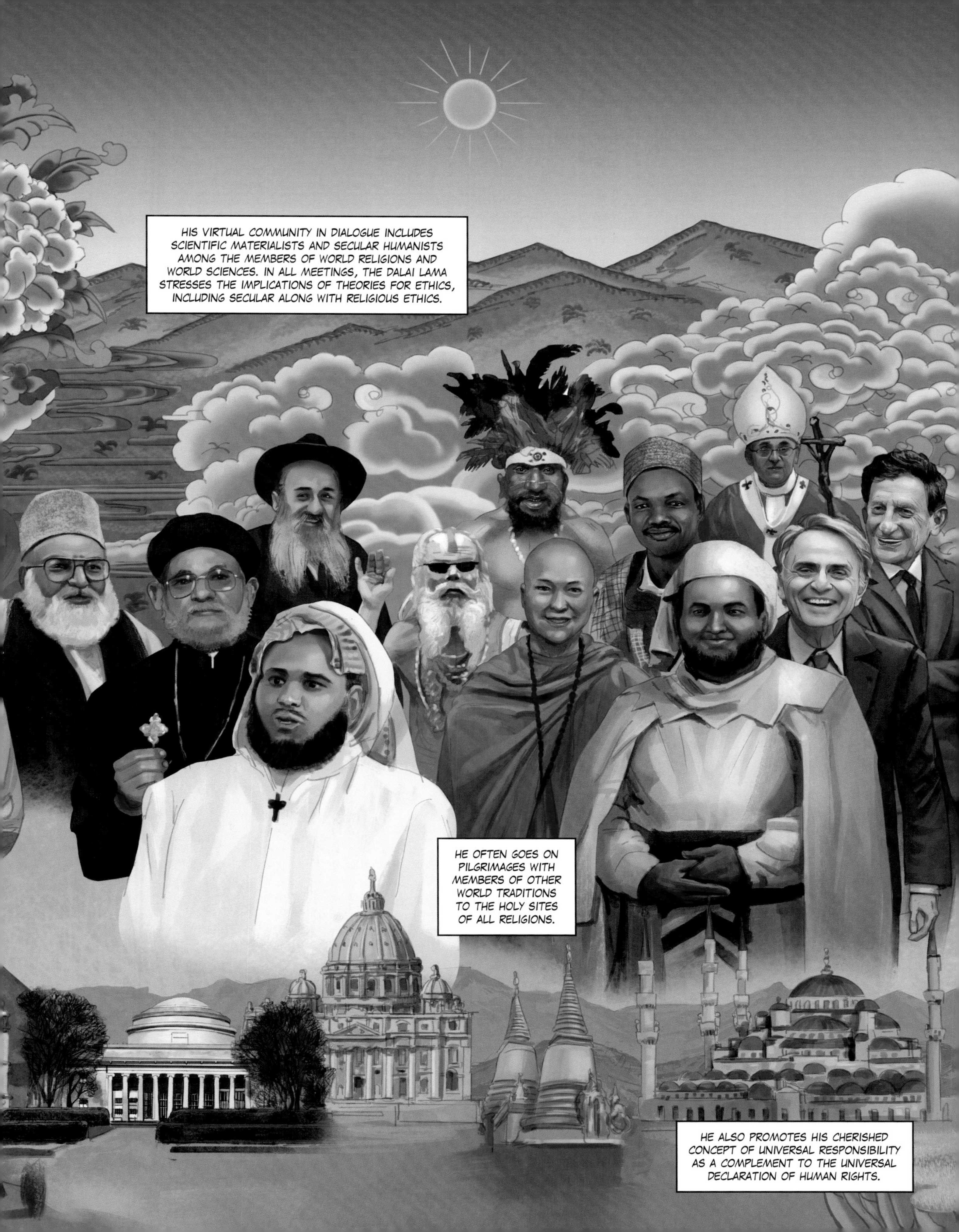
HIS VIRTUAL COMMUNITY IN DIALOGUE INCLUDES SCIENTIFIC MATERIALISTS AND SECULAR HUMANISTS AMONG THE MEMBERS OF WORLD RELIGIONS AND WORLD SCIENCES. IN ALL MEETINGS, THE DALAI LAMA STRESSES THE IMPLICATIONS OF THEORIES FOR ETHICS, INCLUDING SECULAR ALONG WITH RELIGIOUS ETHICS.
HE OFTEN GOES ON PILGRIMAGES WITH MEMBERS OF OTHER WORLD TRADITIONS TO THE HOLY SITES OF ALL RELIGIONS.
HE ALSO PROMOTES HIS CHERISHED CONCEPT OF UNIVERSAL RESPONSIBILITY AS A COMPLEMENT TO THE UNIVERSAL DECLARATION OF HUMAN RIGHTS.

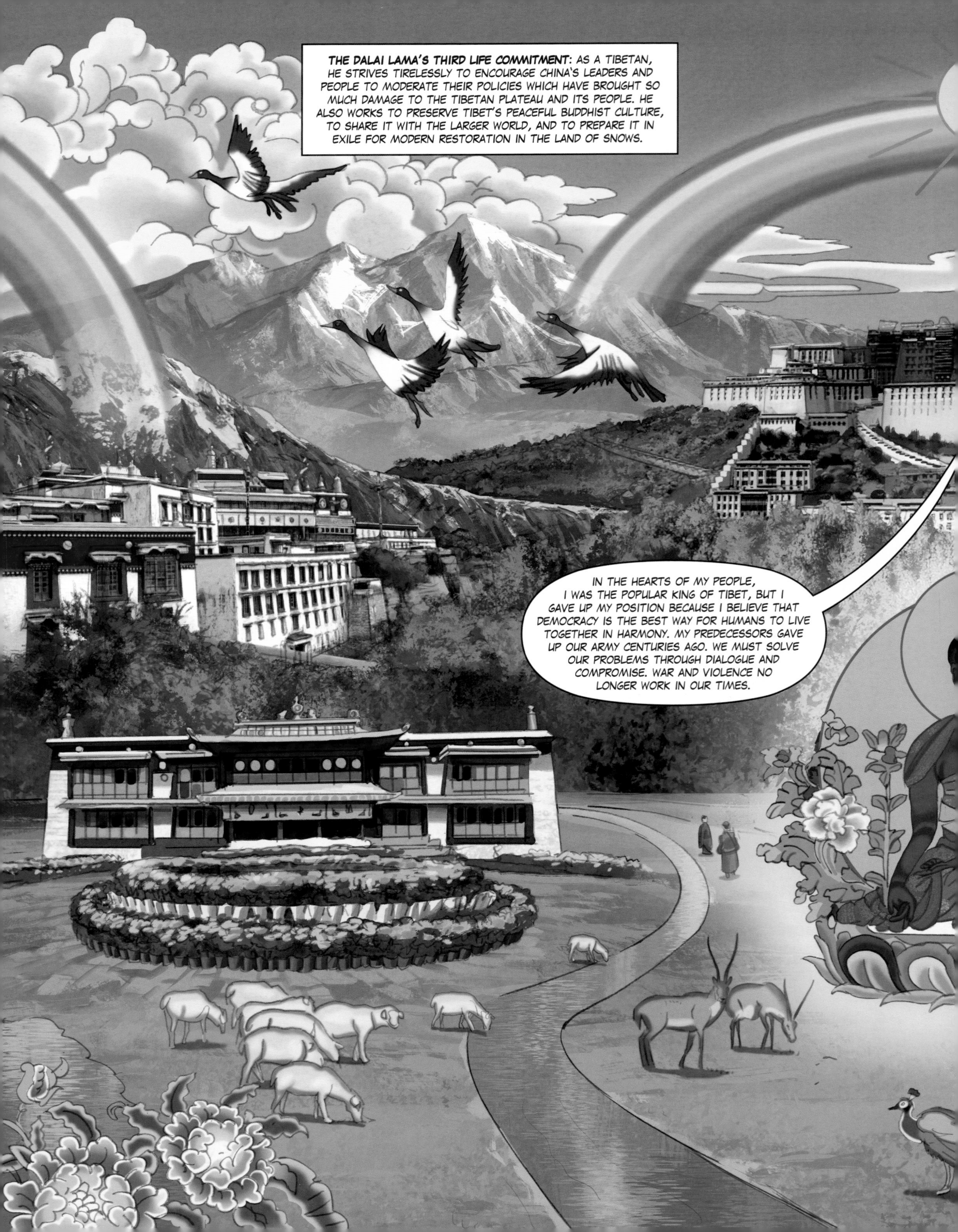
THE DALAI LAMA'S THIRD LIFE COMMITMENT: AS A TIBETAN, HE STRIVES TIRELESSLY TO ENCOURAGE CHINA'S LEADERS AND PEOPLE TO MODERATE THEIR POLICIES WHICH HAVE BROUGHT SO MUCH DAMAGE TO THE TIBETAN PLATEAU AND ITS PEOPLE. HE ALSO WORKS TO PRESERVE TIBET'S PEACEFUL BUDDHIST CULTURE, TO SHARE IT WITH THE LARGER WORLD, AND TO PREPARE IT IN EXILE FOR MODERN RESTORATION IN THE LAND OF SNOWS.
IN THE HEARTS OF MY PEOPLE, I WAS THE POPULAR KING OF TIBET, BUT I GAVE UP MY POSITION BECAUSE I BELIEVE THAT DEMOCRACY IS THE BEST WAY FOR HUMANS TO LIVE TOGETHER IN HARMONY. MY PREDECESSORS GAVE UP OUR ARMY CENTURIES AGO. WE MUST SOLVE OUR PROBLEMS THROUGH DIALOGUE AND COMPROMISE. WAR AND VIOLENCE NO LONGER WORK IN OUR TIMES.

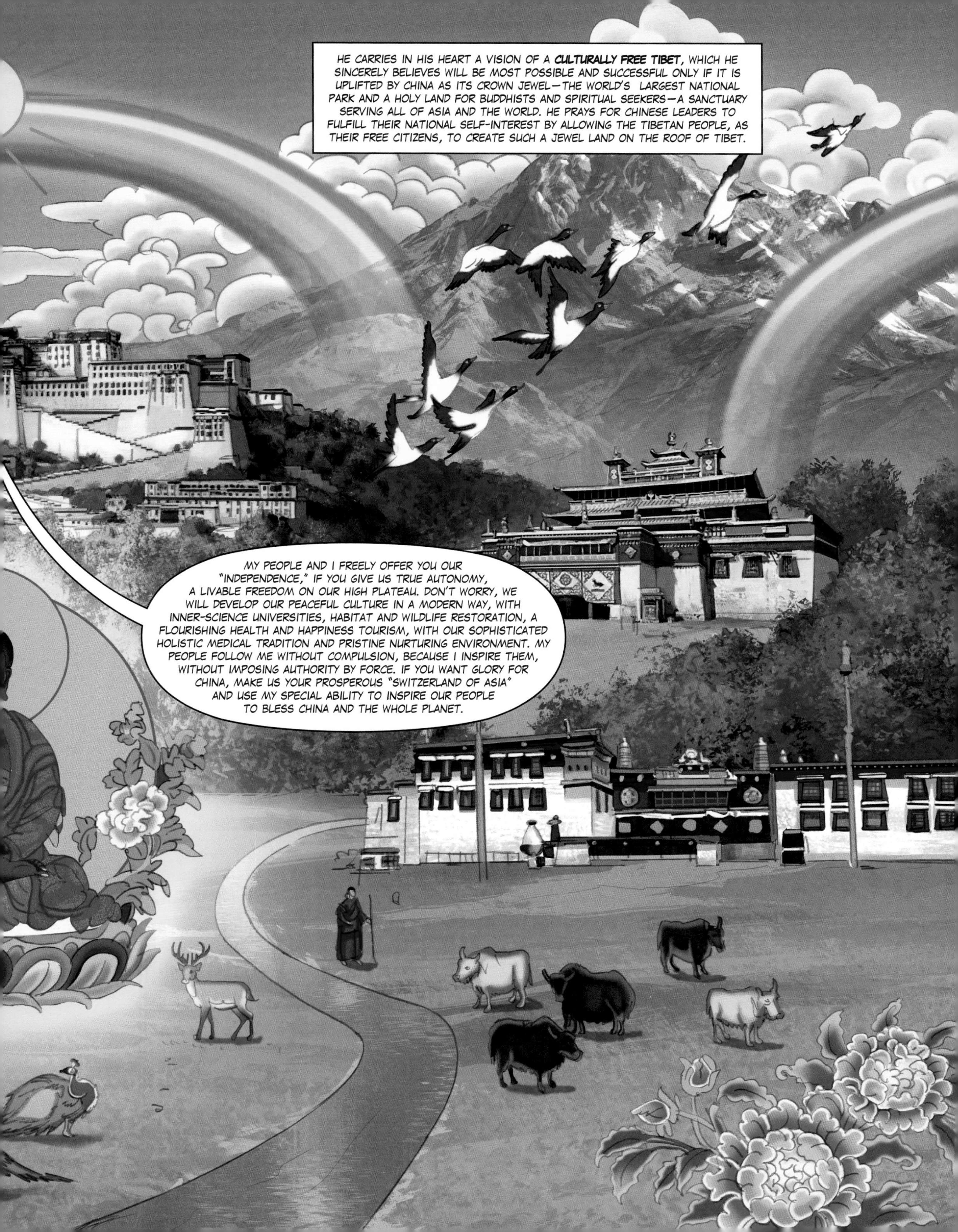
HE CARRIES IN HIS HEART A VISION OF A **CULTURALLY FREE TIBET**, WHICH HE SINCERELY BELIEVES WILL BE MOST POSSIBLE AND SUCCESSFUL ONLY IF IT IS UPLIFTED BY CHINA AS ITS CROWN JEWEL—THE WORLD'S LARGEST NATIONAL PARK AND A HOLY LAND FOR BUDDHISTS AND SPIRITUAL SEEKERS—A SANCTUARY SERVING ALL OF ASIA AND THE WORLD. HE PRAYS FOR CHINESE LEADERS TO FULFILL THEIR NATIONAL SELF-INTEREST BY ALLOWING THE TIBETAN PEOPLE, AS THEIR FREE CITIZENS, TO CREATE SUCH A JEWEL LAND ON THE ROOF OF TIBET.
MY PEOPLE AND I FREELY OFFER YOU OUR "INDEPENDENCE," IF YOU GIVE US TRUE AUTONOMY, A LIVABLE FREEDOM ON OUR HIGH PLATEAU. DON'T WORRY, WE WILL DEVELOP OUR PEACEFUL CULTURE IN A MODERN WAY, WITH INNER-SCIENCE UNIVERSITIES, HABITAT AND WILDLIFE RESTORATION, A FLOURISHING HEALTH AND HAPPINESS TOURISM, WITH OUR SOPHISTICATED HOLISTIC MEDICAL TRADITION AND PRISTINE NURTURING ENVIRONMENT. MY PEOPLE FOLLOW ME WITHOUT COMPULSION, BECAUSE I INSPIRE THEM, WITHOUT IMPOSING AUTHORITY BY FORCE. IF YOU WANT GLORY FOR CHINA, MAKE US YOUR PROSPEROUS "SWITZERLAND OF ASIA" AND USE MY SPECIAL ABILITY TO INSPIRE OUR PEOPLE TO BLESS CHINA AND THE WHOLE PLANET.

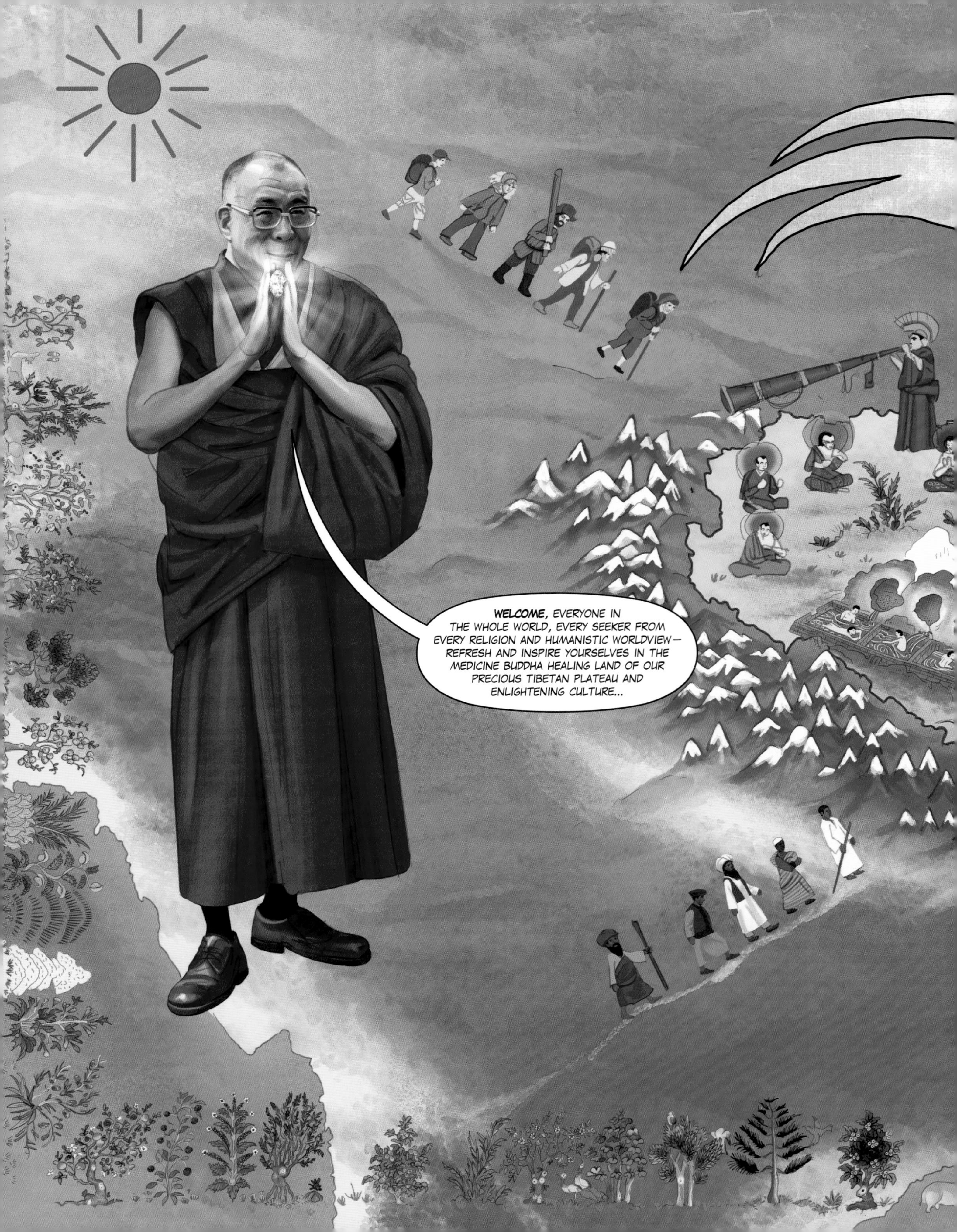
WELCOME, EVERYONE IN THE WHOLE WORLD, EVERY SEEKER FROM EVERY RELIGION AND HUMANISTIC WORLDVIEW—REFRESH AND INSPIRE YOURSELVES IN THE MEDICINE BUDDHA HEALING LAND OF OUR PRECIOUS TIBETAN PLATEAU AND ENLIGHTENING CULTURE...

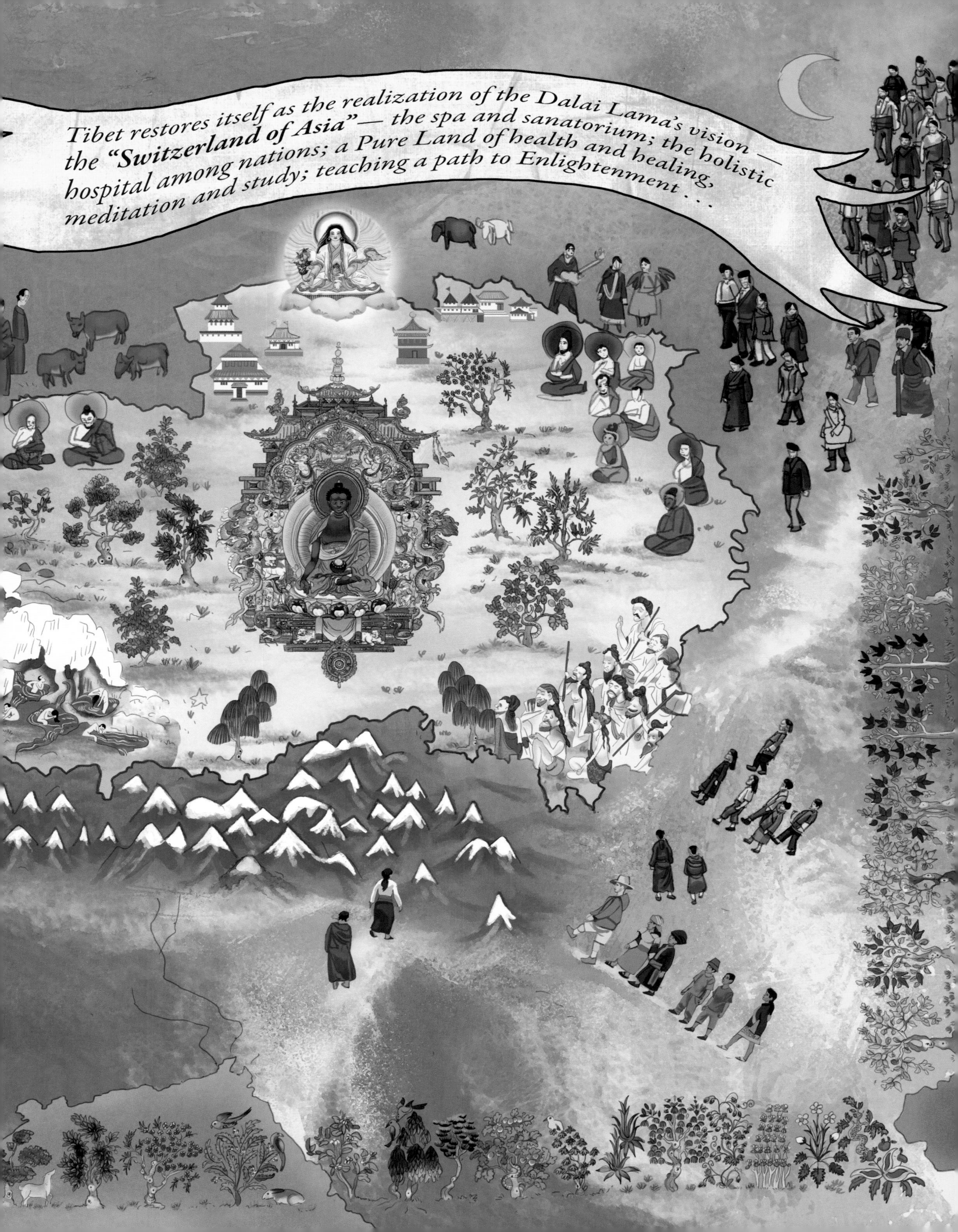
Tibet restores itself as the realization of the Dalai Lama's vision —
the "Switzerland of Asia"— the spa and sanatorium; the holistic
hospital among nations; a Pure Land of health and healing,
meditation and study; teaching a path to Enlightenment . . .

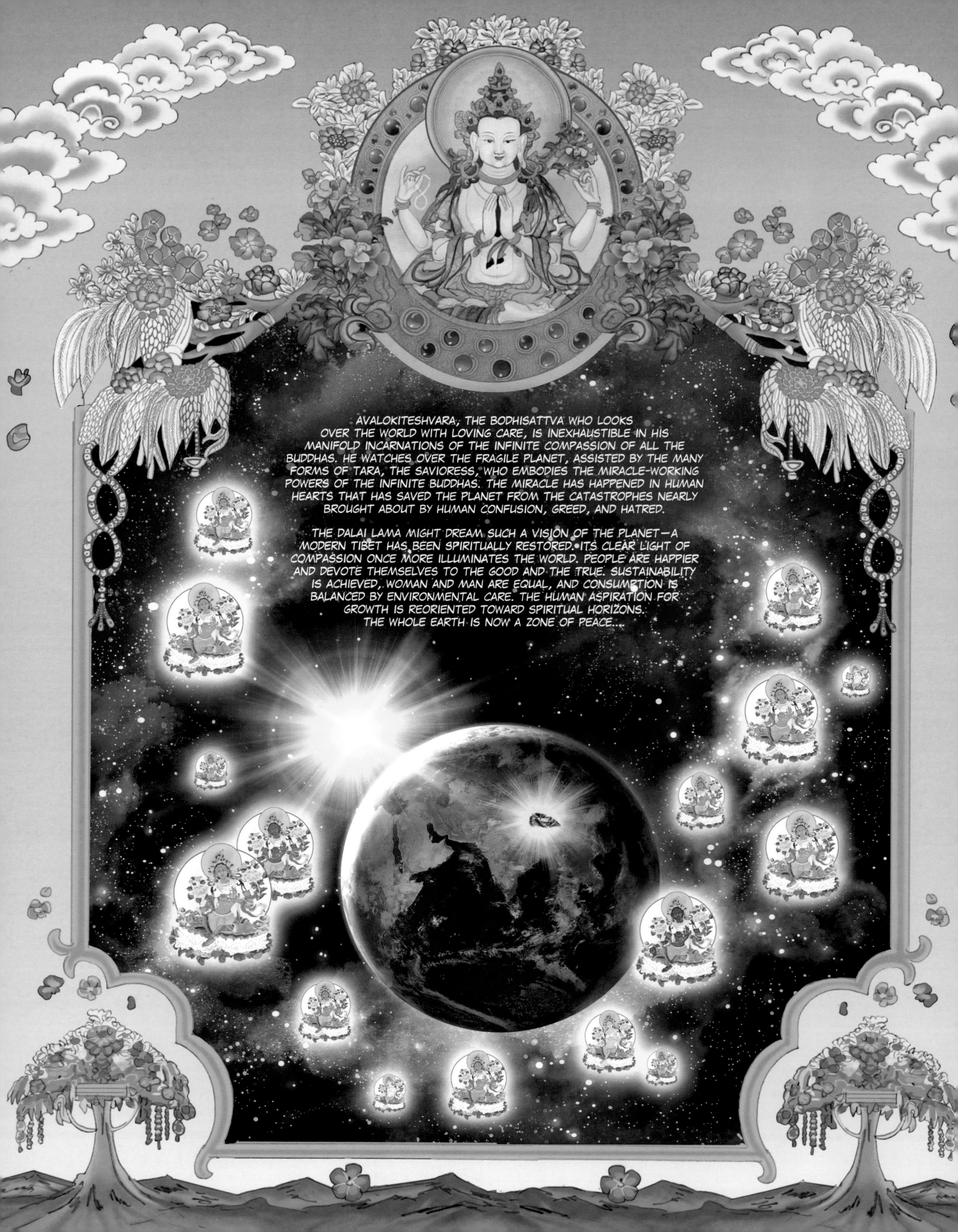
AVALOKITESHVARA, THE BODHISATTVA WHO LOOKS OVER THE WORLD WITH LOVING CARE, IS INEXHAUSTIBLE IN HIS MANIFOLD INCARNATIONS OF THE INFINITE COMPASSION OF ALL THE BUDDHAS. HE WATCHES OVER THE FRAGILE PLANET, ASSISTED BY THE MANY FORMS OF TARA, THE SAVIORESS, WHO EMBODIES THE MIRACLE-WORKING POWERS OF THE INFINITE BUDDHAS. THE MIRACLE HAS HAPPENED IN HUMAN HEARTS THAT HAS SAVED THE PLANET FROM THE CATASTROPHES NEARLY BROUGHT ABOUT BY HUMAN CONFUSION, GREED, AND HATRED.
THE DALAI LAMA MIGHT DREAM SUCH A VISION OF THE PLANET—A MODERN TIBET HAS BEEN SPIRITUALLY RESTORED. ITS CLEAR LIGHT OF COMPASSION ONCE MORE ILLUMINATES THE WORLD. PEOPLE ARE HAPPIER AND DEVOTE THEMSELVES TO THE GOOD AND THE TRUE. SUSTAINABILITY IS ACHIEVED, WOMAN AND MAN ARE EQUAL, AND CONSUMPTION IS BALANCED BY ENVIRONMENTAL CARE. THE HUMAN ASPIRATION FOR GROWTH IS REORIENTED TOWARD SPIRITUAL HORIZONS. THE WHOLE EARTH IS NOW A ZONE OF PEACE...

THE COVER PAINTING

Dalai Lama is a portrait of the Tibetan religious leader
and representative of the bodhisattvic ideal of wisdom
and compassion. He is shown in a prayerful blessing
posture, which is his common greeting. He describes
himself as a simple monk, but his followers know him
also as the worldly incarnation of the Buddha of ac-
tive compassion, *Avalokiteshvara*, who is shown trans-
lucently behind the monk. The prayer to this Buddha
is also the national mantra of Tibet, *Om Mani Padme
Hum*, and it is repeated in the background as a manifes-
tation of the skylike nature of mind. The Dalai Lama's
magnificent residence in Tibet, the Potala, is also seen.
For over six decades the Chinese military has occupied
Tibet, destroyed monasteries, and committed atrocities against the Tibetan people. Nevertheless, the Dalai
Lama, who lives in exile from his homeland, remains
one of the world's foremost proponents of nonviolence
and peaceful resolution.

—Alex Grey

ACKNOWLEDGMENTS

THIS BOOK in itself is my acknowledgment of the inspiring life work of His Holiness the Dalai Lama in serving the world as a true Man of Peace. I especially wish to acknowledge his extraordinary compassion and kindness to my wife Mary in 1991, when he helped her find complementary medical help from his personal physician Tenzin Choedak to prolong her life, and eventually sent to her bedside the Venerable Lobsang Samten as his personal emissary to help her deal with her impending death.

I dedicate the merit of my work on this book to Mary, and I thank her for her initial impulse to create, out of her gratitude, such a graphic biography of His Holiness's life—which she began with me but was unable to finish.

I would like to offer heartfelt thanks to Bob Thurman for picking up this project, which was stalled for over a decade, and adopting it as central to the mission of Tibet House US. As one of the foremost teachers of Indo-Tibetan Buddhism in the West, Bob had already been for years my mentor in all things Buddhistic. His generous enterprise of joining me as coauthor and filling in especially the 56 years of His Holiness's life after reaching freedom in exile at the age of 24 was essential to completion of the project. Stepping in from his extremely busy life work to join forces with me as volunteer coauthor, Bob elaborated events of Tibetan history and the life of His Holiness that I was still not aware of, and with his wife Nena, eventually raised all the funding to engage a professional team of artists to see the project through as envisioned.

I owe major long-term gratitude to visionary artist Alex Grey for recognizing the project immediately, in 1994, as something the world needs, volunteering at first to do all the art, ultimately donating the amazing oil portrait reproduced here that brings vividly to mind the Dalai Lama's bodhisattvic goal of rejoining his people in freedom and friendship with China—and the world.

I would like to thank Tibetan artist Rabkar Wangchuk for starting off as a volunteer on some initial sections, and for setting a clear and pure example of the authentic Tibetan aesthetic.

I thank Michael Burbank for joining me also as a volunteer with his knowledge of comic-lettering design and graphic-novel script-writing—ultimately for his boundless energy in serving as coauthor with Bob and me.

Many thanks to Steve Buccellato, his Legendhaus Studio and Mad Science Media, for recognizing this project as a major contribution to the medium and skillfully assembling a team of artists perfect for the project, including the highly skilled penciller Donald Hudson and the brilliant colorists Kinsun Loh, Andrey Pervukhin, and Miranda Meeks, and for working tirelessly with Bob, Michael, and me in the huge task of graphically and dramatically capturing the historical sweep and spiritual essence of the story.

Thanks to Justin Stone-Diaz for running the crowd-funding campaign for this book. And thanks also to Lorna Solis and Marie Javins for having referred me to Steve Buccellato, whom they suspected might be just the person of multifaceted skills we were looking for. (He was.)

I can't express enough appreciation to Milenda Lee, my friend and colleague from Columbia University Press, for bringing her full consultative expertise to bear on our production process, finding us the reliable four-color printer we needed, and designing a cover that perfectly suits the portrait of His Holiness, in its portrayal of the victory of his vision of peace and happiness.

The gratitude I owe my devoted friend Leslie Kriesel for her many years of editorial assistance, on this project and many others, can hardly go without acknowledging.

Most of all, I owe a deep obeisance to *meine geliebte Frau, Marion Gehlker,* who has put up with my seemingly endless sessions at the computer, to the sad neglect of our yoga practice and German-language lessons, while always in support of this my heart project.

—William Meyers

Special thanks . . .

First I want to thank His Holiness the Dalai Lama himself for giving true hope, inspiration, and guidance to me and to so many others on this planet. Words simply fail to encompass how deep my gratitude runs for his awesome being, for the infinite depth of his wisdom and the vastness of his great compassion for all beings. Without His Holiness's oceanic presence, I fear I would be lost at sea.

I want to give very special thanks to Tenzin Bob Thurman for introducing me to India and Tibet, to Tibetan Buddhism, and to the Dalai Lama, inspiring my life's direction with his infectious enthusiasm and undaunted efforts to educate others in countless ways. Over the years he has gone from being, first, my academic teacher, then, my volunteer coworker and fearless President at Tibet House US and its Menla Mountain Retreat, and, finally, my personal hero and dear friend.

No mention of Bob here would be sufficient without highlighting the central role his wife and cocreator Nena Thurman has played in my life. A friend once told me when I was first getting to know the Thurmans, that while we may bow to Bob, we actually look to Nena. Indeed, over the past fifteen years, Nena has patiently, lovingly, and powerfully served as my tireless teacher and generous benefactor at Menla, as my close spiritual friend in life, and as a dynamic role model as I grow into my leadership role as Director of Menla. It is an honor to know and work with her in our efforts to preserve Tibetan culture, share the magic of Menla's hidden mountain treasures, and help introduce the ancient Tibetan Buddhist medical and spiritual tradition into our American culture.

I am very grateful to William Meyers for sharing his vision for this book with me, inviting me to help him re-animate the project after many years of incubation, and for his and Bob's letting me patiently and painstakingly learn the art of lettering "on the job" over the past six years as volunteer coordinator and later coauthor of this book.

I thank master artist Rabkar Wangchuk for working with Nena and me at Menla's Mahasukha Spa to develop its Tibetan "Shangri-la" aesthetic and for volunteering to give us an idea of what a graphic novel set in Tibet might look like in the beginning stages. His current artwork in general is a perfect blend of traditional Tibetan and modern visionary styles.

I am extremely grateful to Steve Buccellato and his team for creating such amazing art for *Man of Peace.* Not only has Steve taken the project coordination to an impeccable professional level, but he also has bestowed upon me a free and excellent education in the under-appreciated art of lettering.

I cannot thank enough my dear wife, Chisti Rabia Dryden, for patiently, selflessly sharing me with this project. I couldn't have done my small but demanding part without her loving support, encouragement, and nourishing presence. She is my partner in all things, and her gifts to me are immeasurable, beyond my ability to express adequately.

I also want to thank my family for their love and for their support of my passions for Tibet, Buddhism, and visionary art, and for instilling in me their own sterling sense of character and integrity. From them I learned the value of a good education.

Finally, I want to thank you, the reader, for sharing our inspiration by reading this book. It is my hope that the example of this Man of Peace opens a door for you and leads the way for us all to create sustainable and fruitful lives together for many generations to come.

May you, too, be a Man or Woman of Peace.

—Michael G. Burbank

ACKNOWLEDGMENTS

Inspiration . . .

I am honored that William Meyers invited me to be part of the *Man of Peace* project with such respected colleagues. It was his inspiration that led me to paint the portrait in 1995. My wife Allyson and I first saw the Dalai Lama speak at Harvard University in 1979 and then took a five-day course in 1981 at Harvard with His Holiness on Shantideva's *Guide to the Bodhisattva Way*.

Throughout the decades we have studied with the Dalai Lama, and our whole family received the Kalachakra Initiation at Madison Square Garden in 1991. Finally in 2005, I got to meet His Holiness face to face and share my art, giving him a copy of the portrait. He was so gracious and loving—he is like everyone's long-lost best friend, reminding us of what is most important, bringing love, wisdom and healing to the world.

—*Alex Grey*

Thanks and Salutation . . .

Most of all, I thank from the bottom of my heart His Holiness the Dalai Lama, whom I have known for over fifty years, as a really good friend, an inspiring teacher, and now my root Vajra Master in Tibetan Buddhism. Looking closely at the crises he has faced in his life, I have come to appreciate His Holiness even more. As ever, I thank my beloved wife and partner Nena, volunteer Tibet House US and Menla coworker, who keeps the Dalai Lama's advice present to me in all times of stress and peace, and without whom I can't get anything done at all.

I am thankful to the late Dr. Mary Meyers for getting us all started on this project, to William Meyers and his children for keeping it going and working with us strenuously as a volunteer to complete it, to Michael Burbank for lettering, coauthoring, and taking on the herculean task of pulling the final product together on the page, and to Steve Buccellato and his skilled and devoted team of artists who did such a beautiful job. My thanks to Tom Yarnall and to the staff of Tibet House US. I especially thank our beloved friend and THUS Honorary Board Director, Ms. Lavinia Currier, and her Sacharuna Foundation, for a generous and timely gift that enabled the work to reach completion after years of slow progress with volunteers, and the many generous donors who made it possible to realize the project.

I hope those who read this novel, young and old, will learn the amazing story of his deeds, will find the same kind of friendship we have enjoyed with His Holiness the Fourteenth Dalai Lama of Tibet, and will be inspired by his indefatigable optimism about the fate of our common Mother Earth. As she did for Shakyamuni Buddha, may she, as Mother Prithivi (our Persephone, our Gaia), rise to witness the truth of what His Holiness exemplifies, and may all be blessed by his tireless work, and his wish for peace and intelligent kindness be realized soon!

In case any reader who has come to feel close to the Dalai Lama from following his adventures and being aware of the crisis in which he continues to stand and persevere wishes to express that closeness by calling upon him as a spiritual friend, I wish to close by sharing his personal mantra:

OM ĀH GURU VAJRADHARA MAÑJUSHRĪ VĀGINDRA SUMATI SHASANADHARA SAMUDRA SHRĪBHADRA SARVASIDDHI HŪM PHAT

which is his name in Sanskrit, and means "OM Vajradhara, Mañjushrī, God of Speech, Oceanic Upholder of the Teaching of the Loving Minded One, Glorious Goodness—[may] all [His] wishes be accomplished! From the depth of my heart, make it so!"

—*Robert A. F. Thurman*

285

SELECTED BIBLIOGRAPHIES

Further Reading

Dalai Lama, H. H. *The World of Tibetan Buddhism: An Overview of Its Philosophy and Practice.* Boston: Wisdom, 1995.

———. *The Good Heart: A Buddhist Perspective on the Teachings of Jesus.* Boston: Wisdom, 1996.

——— (with Howard Cutler). *The Art of Happiness: A Handbook for Living.* New York: Penguin Putnam, 1998.

———. *Ethics for the New Millennium.* New York: Penguin Random House, 2001.

———. *The Universe in a Single Atom: The Convergence of Science and Spirituality.* New York: Doubleday, 2005.

———. *Beyond Religion: Ethics for a Whole World.* New York. Houghton Mifflin, 2011.

———. *Toward a True Kinship of Faiths: How the World's Religions Can Come Together.* New York: Penguin Random House, 2011.

——— (with Sofia Stril-Rever). *My Appeal to the World.* New York: Tibet House US, 2015.

——— (with Sofia Stril-Rever). *New Reality: Peace and Universal Responsibility, According to the Dalai Lama.* Paris: Les Arènes, 2016.

Dalai Lama, Desmond Tutu, and Douglas Carlton Abrams. *The Book of Joy: Lasting Happiness in a Changing World.* New York: Penguin Random House, 2016.

Hillman, Ben, and Gray Tuttle, eds. *Ethnic Conflict and Protest in Tibet and Xinjiang: Unrest in China's West.* New York: Columbia University Press, 2016.

Li, Jianglin. *Tibet in Agony: Lhasa 1959.* Trans. Susan Wolf. Cambridge, Mass.: Harvard University Press, 2016.

Luisi, Pier Luigi with the assistance of Zara Houshmand. *Mind and Life: Discussions with the Dalai Lama on the Nature of Reality.* New York: Columbia University Press, 2008.

Powers, John. *The Buddha Party: How the People's Republic of China Works to Define and Control Tibetan Buddhism.* New York: Oxford University Press, 2016.

Shakya, Tsering. *The Dragon in the Land of Snows: A History of Modern Tibet Since 1947.* New York: Columbia University Press, 1999.

Shantideva. *A Guide to the Bodhisattva's Way of Life.* Library of Tibetan Works and Archives, Dharamsala, India, 1979.

Thurman, Robert A. F. *Essential Tibetan Buddhism.* San Francisco: HarperCollinsSanFrancisco, 1995.

———. *Inner Revolution: Life, Liberty, and the Pursuit of Real Happiness.* New York: Penguin Putnam, 1998.

————. (with Tad Wise). *Circling the Sacred Mountain: A Spiritual Journey Through the Himalayas*. New York: Bantam, 1999.

————. *Infinite Life: Awakening to Bliss Within*. New York: Riverhead, 2004.

————. *The Jewel Tree of Tibet: The Enlightenment Engine of Tibetan Buddhism*. New York: Atria, 2006.

————. *Why the Dalai Lama Matters: His Act of Truth as the Solution for China, Tibet, and the World*. New York and Portland: Atria/Beyond Words, 2008.

————. and Marylin Rhie. *Wisdom and Compassion: The Sacred Art of Tibet*. New York: Abrams, 1991.

Tuttle, Gray. *Tibetan Buddhists in the Making of Modern China*. New York: Columbia University Press, 2005.

Tuttle, Gray, and Kurtis R. Schaeffer, eds. *The Tibetan History Reader*. New York: Columbia University Press, 2013.

Woeser, Tsering. *Tibet on Fire: Self-Immolations Against Chinese Rule*. London: Verso, 2016.

Woeser, Tsering, and Wang Lixiong. *Voices from Tibet: Selected Essays and Reportage*. Ed. and trans. Violet S. Law. Hong Kong: Hong Kong University Press, 2014.

www.dalailama.com—Official Website of H. H. the Dalai Lama

Sources for This Book

Andrugtsang, Gompo Tashi. *Four Rivers–Six Ranges: A True Account of Khampa Resistance to Chinese in Tibet*. Information Office of His Holiness the Dalai Lama, Dharamsala, India, 1973.

Arjia Rinpoche. *Surviving the Dragon: A Tibetan Lama's Account of 40 Years of Chinese Rule*. New York: Rodale, 2010.

Avedon, John. *In Exile from the Land of Snows*. New York: HarperCollins, 1984.

Bell, Sir Charles. *Tibet Past and Present*. 1924; reprint, London: Oxford University Press, 1968.

————. *The People of Tibet*. 1928; reprint, London: Oxford University Press, 1968.

————. *The Religion of Tibet*. 1931; reprint, London: Oxford University Press, 1968.

————. *Portrait of the Dalai Lama*. London: Collins, 1946.

Bryant, Barry. *Wheel of Time: The Tibetan Sand Mandala*. New York: HarperCollins, 1992.

Bultrini, Raimondo. *The Dalai Lama and the King Demon: Tracking a Triple Murder Mystery Through the Mists of Time*. New York: Tibet House US, 2014.

Craig, Mary. *Kundun: A Biography of the Family of the Dalai Lama*. New York: Counterpoint, 1997.

Dalai Lama, H. H. *My Land and My People: Memoirs of the Dalai Lama of Tibet*. New York: Potala, 1983.

————. *Freedom in Exile: The Autobiography of the Dalai Lama*. New York: HarperCollins, 1990.

————. *The World of Tibetan Buddhism: An Overview of Its Philosophy and Practice*. Boston: Wisdom, 1995.

————. *The Good Heart: A Buddhist Perspective on the Teachings of Jesus*. Boston: Wisdom, 1996.

————. (with Howard Cutler). *The Art of Happiness: A Handbook for Living*. New York: Penguin Putnam, 1998.

————. *Ethics for the New Millennium*. New York: Penguin Random House, 2001.

————. *The Universe in a Single Atom: The Convergence of Science and Spirituality*. New York: Doubleday, 2005.

————. *Beyond Religion: Ethics for a Whole World*. New York: Houghton Mifflin, 2011.

————. *Toward a True Kinship of Faiths: How the World's Religions Can Come Together*. New York: Penguin Random House, 2011.

————. (with Sofia Stril-Rever). *My Appeal to the World*. New York: Tibet House, 2015.

Dunham, Mikhel. *Buddha's Warriors*. New York: Tarcher/Penguin, 2004.

Gibb, Christopher. *The Dalai Lama* (People Who Have Helped the World series). Milwaukee: Gareth Stevens Children's Books, 1990.

Harrer, Heinrich. *Seven Years in Tibet*. New York: Tarcher/St. Martin's, 1953.

————. *Lost Lhasa*. New York: Abrams, 1992.

International Commission of Jurists. *The Question of Tibet and the Rule of Law*. Geneva, 1959.

————. *Tibet and the Chinese People's Republic*. Geneva, 1960.

Isserman, Maurice. *World War II*. New York: Facts On File, 1991.

Khétsun, Tubten. *Memories of Life in Lhasa Under Chinese Rule*. Trans. Matthew Akester. New York: Columbia University Press, 2008.

Luisi, Pier Luigi with the assistance of Zara Houshmand. *Mind and Life: Discussions with the Dalai Lama on the Nature of Reality.* New York: Columbia University Press, 2008.

"Miraculous Escape of the Dalai Lama." *Life* Magazine, May 4, 1959.

Mullin, Glenn H. *The Fourteen Dalai Lamas: A Sacred Legacy of Reincarnation.* Santa Fe: Clear Light, 2001.

Norbu, Dawa. *Red Star over Tibet.* London: Collins, 1974.

Norbu, Jamyang. *Horseman in the Snow.* Information Office of His Holiness the Dalai Lama, Dharamsala, India, 1979.

Norbu, Thubten Jigme, and Heinrich Harrer. *Tibet Is My Country.* New York: Dutton, 1961.

Norbu, Thubten Jigme, and Colin M. Turnbull. *Tibet.* New York: Simon and Schuster, 1968.

Perkins, Jane. *Tibet in Exile.* San Francisco: Chronicle, 1991.

Richardson, H. E. *Tibet and Its History.* London: Oxford University Press, 1962.

Schaeffer, Kurtis R., Matthew T. Kapstein, and Gray Tuttle, eds. *Sources of Tibetan Tradition.* New York: Columbia University Press, 2013.

Schwieger, Peter. *The Dalai Lama and the Emperor of China: A Political History of the Tibetan Institution of Reincarnation.* New York: Columbia University Press, 2015.

Shakya, Tsering. *The Dragon in the Land of Snows: A History of Modern Tibet Since 1947.* New York: Columbia University Press, 1999.

Shantideva. *A Guide to the Bodhisattva's Way of Life.* Library of Tibetan Works and Archives, Dharamsala, India, 1979.

Snellgrove, David, and Hugh Richardson. *A Cultural History of Tibet.* 1968; reprint, Boulder, Colo.: Prajna Press, 1980.

Thomas, Lowell Jr. *Out of This World.* New York: Greystone Press, 1950.

Thurman, Robert A. F. *Why the Dalai Lama Matters: His Act of Truth as the Solution for China, Tibet, and the World.* New York: Atria/Beyond Words, 2008.

Tibet in the United Nations. Bureau of His Holiness the Dalai Lama, New Delhi, 1961.

Tibet: The Sacred Realm. New York: Philadelphia Museum of Art/Aperture, 1983.

Tuttle, Gray. *Tibetan Buddhists in the Making of Modern China.* New York: Columbia University Press, 2005.

Van Walts Van Praag, M. C. *Tibet and the Right to Self-Determination.* Information Office of His Holiness the Dalai Lama, Dharamsala, India, 1979.

Wangdu, Sonam. *The Discovery of the Fourteenth Dalai Lama.* Bangkok: Khett Thai Publications, 1975.

Woeser, Tsering. *Tibet on Fire: Self-Immolations Against Chinese Rule.* London: Verso, 2016.